The Sound of Hope

The Sound of Hope

Music as Solace, Resistance and Salvation During the Holocaust and World War II

Kellie D. Brown

McFarland & Company, Inc., Publishers
Jefferson, North Carolina

LIBRARY OF CONGRESS CATALOGUING-IN-PUBLICATION DATA

Names: Brown, Kellie D., author.
Title: The sound of hope : music as solace, resistance and salvation during the Holocaust and World War II / Kellie D. Brown.
Description: Jefferson, North Carolina : McFarland & Company, Inc., Publishers, 2020. | Includes bibliographical references and index.
Identifiers: LCCN 2020017547 | ISBN 9781476670560 (paperback ; acid free paper) ∞
ISBN 9781476639949 (ebook)
Subjects: LCSH: Jewish musicians—Europe—Biography. | Musicians—Europe—Biography. | Holocaust victims—Europe—Biography. | Jews—Europe—Music—History and criticism. | Concentration camp inmates as musicians—Europe. | World War, 1939-1945—Concentration camps—Europe. | Concentration camp inmates—Europe—Biography.
Classification: LCC ML3776 .B76 2020 | DDC 780.89/924—dc23
LC record available at https://lccn.loc.gov/2020017547

BRITISH LIBRARY CATALOGUING DATA ARE AVAILABLE

ISBN (print) 978-1-4766-7056-0
ISBN (ebook) 978-1-4766-3994-9

© 2020 Kellie D. Brown. All rights reserved

No part of this book may be reproduced or transmitted in any form or by any means, electronic or mechanical, including photocopying or recording, or by any information storage and retrieval system, without permission in writing from the publisher.

Front cover artwork © Art Brown

Printed in the United States of America

*McFarland & Company, Inc., Publishers
Box 611, Jefferson, North Carolina 28640
www.mcfarlandpub.com*

Dedicated to those who continued
to play and sing music, refusing to allow
their oppressors to silence the gift and the power.

Only guard yourself and guard your soul carefully, lest you forget the things your eyes saw, and lest these things depart your heart all the days of your life. And you shall make them known to your children, and to your children's children.

—Deuteronomy 4:9 (inscription behind the eternal flame in the Hall of Remembrance at the United States Holocaust Memorial Museum)

Table of Contents

Acknowledgments	ix
Preface	1
Introduction: The Power of Music	5
1. The Rise of the Third Reich and Its Cultural Agenda	9
2. Alma Rosé and the Women's Orchestra at Auschwitz-Birkenau	21
3. Dr. Herbert Zipper: From Dachau to the World	61
4. Alice Herz-Sommer and the Music in Terezín	79
5. Władysław Szpilman and the Warsaw Ghetto	121
6. Olivier Messiaen: A Composer Confronts the End of Time	157
7. Dmitri Shostakovich and the Musical Redemption of Leningrad	185
8. The Vocal Orchestra: Female POWs on Sumatra	227
Epilogue: Out of the Ashes—The Israel Philharmonic and Violins of Hope	277
Chapter Notes	295
Bibliography	301
Index	305

Acknowledgments

I am deeply grateful to my dear friends Anne Elliott, Wanda Kerns, Debbie Beebe, Alicia Garst, Kayla Walker Edin, and Anne Sorrell, who read drafts of my chapters and gave me their feedback and encouragement along the way. I also wish to thank all of those who helped in the onerous process of acquiring photo permissions and digital images, including Mary Jackson at Milligan University, Avshi Weinstein with Violins of Hope, Ray Heigemeir at Stanford University, the staff at the Yad Vashem archives, Jean Hung and Brian McMillan at the University of Western Ontario, the staff at the Israel Philharmonic Orchestra archives, Martina Šiknerová at the Terezín Memorial, Jan Kaplon at The Auschwitz-Birkenau State Museum, the staff at the Herbert Zipper Archive at Crossroads School for Arts & Sciences, and Reinhard Piechocki.

I extend my heartfelt thanks to Madelyn van Rijckevorsel and Sonia Beker, family members of survivors, who have assisted me with their stories, photos, and encouragement.

Words are not adequate to express my appreciation to Melissa Nipper, who has served as my editor and spirit guide on this journey. This project would not have made it to fruition without your wise counsel and the expert strokes of your pen.

I would be remiss if I did not mention a few of the teachers who influenced me in such profound ways. To the late Patsy Denny and the late Nellie McNeil, you helped me fall in love with books and with writing. I have tried to live up to your incredibly high standards in the researching and writing of this book. Your absence from my life has certainly created a void. And to Frau Professor Dr. Jane Chew, I want you to know that your enthusiasm for the German language and your charismatic lecture style enchanted me from the first day that I walked into your classroom at Furman University. What we did in that class planted a seed that has grown into this book. Finally, to Jane Hicks, who has intersected my life in so many ways, from teacher to poet to fellow pilgrim, thank you for teaching me that sometimes it is hard to get words "to lie down on the page," but that in the end, they will.

To my husband Art Brown, who has been my rock and sounding board not only for this project but for our many years together, I thank you for lending your incredible talents to illustrate and design the cover for this book and for being my loyal companion through the ups and downs of life. Your astute observations and sense of humor have made my days so much richer.

Finally, to my son Jordan, I thank you for helping me in more ways than you can ever know toward completing this project. Your kindness and love have sustained me through many times when it all seemed too hard. I love you.

Preface

Over the years, I have given countless presentations throughout the United States on music during the Holocaust and World War II, and almost without fail, I get asked the same two questions—"How did you get interested in this topic?" and "How can you stand to spend so much time immersed in such a painful and barbaric moment in history?" I have formulated some succinct responses to these inquiries, but the more complete answers remain complex and multi-layered. On the surface, my introduction to this subject matter appears to be just one of those serendipitous moments that took the form of a casual stroll in the early 1990s through a used bookstore in Johnson City, Tennessee, looking for something entertaining and inexpensive to read. I love the way my senses become so involved in the act of book browsing, all the sights, smells, and textures make the experience take on a ritual-like quality. That day, my hand did its familiar slide across the spines as my eyes quickly took in the titles, then the slight pause, before pulling a book off the shelf for a closer examination. *Vienna Prelude* by Bodie Thoene had been published in 1989. The Austrian setting certainly appealed to me, but more than anything, it was the cover image that reeled me in, as is so often the case during my bookstore rambles—under the title stood a hauntingly beautiful woman playing the violin, with swastika-adorned flags draped in the background.

Most days, I do not believe in coincidences, and I certainly do not consider that my hand finding that particular book was just a random happening. Instead, it formed the next step on a journey that I had been preparing to embark on for my whole life—from all of the years of music lessons starting at age five, to the countless hours spent with my violin in a practice room or rehearsal hall, and then my discovery of and fascination with the German language during college. All the while, my deeply held Christian faith and the relationship of my music to that faith created the fertile ground needed for what would become my life's work to take root.

Vienna Prelude introduced me to the particular atrocities that Jewish musicians suffered at the hands of the Nazi regime and to the plight of their non-Jewish friends and colleagues who were forced to choose sides, often at the risk of their own safety. That work of historical fiction served as the launching point, and from there, I sought out scholarly research about music and musicians during the Holocaust. Published in 2000, Richard Newman and Karen Kirtley's book *Alma Rosé: Vienna to Auschwitz* made the seminal connection for me between years of studying music history in fin de siècle Vienna, where celebrated composers such as Gustav Mahler and Richard Strauss worked, and the eventual ripping apart of that society by anti-Semitic rhetoric and Nazi barbarity. That Mahler's niece, Alma Rosé, had been sent to Auschwitz, despite her family's international renown, came as a shocking realization to me. Through her story,

I learned about the Women's Orchestra at Auschwitz-Birkenau and the prevalence of orchestras in many of the Nazi concentration camps as products of forced music labor initiatives.

The more I discovered about music during the Holocaust, the more I realized that music's role remained a scarcely known aspect, despite how thoroughly explored and documented the subject of the Holocaust had been by researchers. This intrigued me, as did the pursuit of obscure sources from around the world that could provide the next piece of the puzzle. Each book I found led to the names of other Jewish musicians whose music appeared inseparably woven into the stories of their suffering. I came to know remarkable people—Anita Lasker-Wallfisch, Herbert Zipper, Alice Herz-Sommer, Władysław Szpilman, and so many more. But while a single book or memoir might have been devoted to one of these individuals, I discovered that the connection between their stories that resounded through the power of music had been neglected in the scholarly literature. As a result, this book represents an attempt to unite the historical, political, cultural, and sociological contexts of the camps, ghettos, and other war-torn locations with the music and musicians that forged indelible links with these places. In addition to providing this more comprehensive narrative that demonstrates music's capacity for solace, empowerment, and spiritual resistance, my research also seeks to explore the complicated issues of artistic censorship and manipulation.

Each chapter in this book focuses on a key person and place, and often the story unfolds in some of the most notorious settings of Nazi horrors—Auschwitz, Dachau, Terezín, and the Warsaw Ghetto. But also during the research process, I began to identify musical connections with other lives and locations during World War II that were not specifically associated with the Jewish people. This expanded the scope of my book to include two internationally renowned composers, Olivier Messiaen and Dmitri Shostakovich, whose music figured prominently in the struggles of the time. Having been drafted into the French Army, Messiaen was later captured by the Germans. He spent part of the war in the POW camp Stalag VIII A, where he brought music to his fellow prisoners and wrote his most well-known work, *Quartet for the End of Time*. Shostakovich found himself trapped in Leningrad, the city of his birth, as the Germans laid siege to it. Undeterred by the bleak situation, Shostakovich began to compose his "Leningrad" Symphony, a piece which would play an important role in the miraculous turning of the tide for these beleaguered people. Finally, I did not want to neglect music's presence in the Pacific war theater and so have correlated the musical narratives from Eastern and Western Europe with those in the Philippines through the Jewish refugee and conductor Herbert Zipper and with those on the island of Sumatra, where female POWs held by the Japanese created life-sustaining music through a vocal orchestra.

The research materials used to reconstruct the stories of these people and places include a wide sampling of the scholarly literature on the subject, as well as essential primary sources such as diaries, letters, memoirs, compositions, and art pieces. For every person mentioned in this book, there were many who could not be named because of space considerations. I also believe that there are other compelling narratives left to discover. During my more than 20 years of research, I have become increasingly grateful for the people whose lives I have described in these chapters. They have taught me that music holds the power to uplift the human spirit and to triumph over oppression, even amid incredible tragedy and suffering. I hope that their testimony can serve as a reminder for our world of what hatred and prejudice can lead to and of how vital the arts remain in understanding the human condition and in spreading peace and goodness on a global scale. Finally, I pray that I have brought honor to their memories as I have undertaken the holy calling of bearing witness to these stories and lifting back the folds of darkness to reveal moments of light and beauty, to discover where grace abounds.

Introduction: The Power of Music

Laughter, song, and dance create emotional and spiritual connection; they remind us of the one thing that truly matters when we are searching for comfort, celebration, inspiration, or healing: We are not alone.
—Brené Brown, *The Gifts of Imperfection*, 118

The belief in music's incomparable ability to touch and resonate with the human spirit traces back to ancient civilization through storytelling and philosophical musings. In the Old Testament, David, a young boy and future king of the Israelites, played the harp to soothe the troubled moods of King Saul. The Greeks devoted much time to studying and writing about music, from Pythagoras' discoveries of acoustical properties to Plato's views on the importance of music in the education and development of quality citizens and leaders. Greek philosophers clung devoutly to the conviction that music intertwined with human *ethos* or emotion, and therefore could powerfully affect a person's character.

In more recent years many of the great writers and minds of the 19th and 20th centuries have also ruminated on the profound and impactful nature of music. According to Victor Hugo, the celebrated French poet and novelist, "Music expresses that which cannot be said, and on which it is impossible to be silent."[1] For English author Aldous Huxley, music ranked second only to silence—"After silence that which comes nearest to expressing the inexpressible is music."[2] Even the often cranky philosopher Friedrich Nietzsche wrote reverently about this art form saying, "Music unites all qualities: it can exalt us, divert us, cheer us up, or break the hardest of hearts…"[3] But in *Musicophilia: Tales of Music and the Brain*, the revered neurologist Dr. Oliver Sacks, with both his extensive knowledge of brain physiology and his astute observations of that which transcends scientific explanation, captured perhaps the most candid yet elusive description. "Music, uniquely among the arts, is both completely abstract and profoundly emotional. It has no power to represent anything particular or external, but it has a unique power to express inner states or feelings."[4]

While the evidence of music's impact on the human condition renders little doubt, identifying the source or nature of this power remains the more salient and mysterious inquiry. At the most fundamental level, music's influence seems related to its fleeting temporal quality, as it only exists in a given moment and not truly in a permanent physical form. Unlike a painting where the object on display does not merely represent the potential for a work of art but is the tangible creation, musical works on paper in their notated form provide only the instructions or blueprint for the creation of music. But regardless of its ephemeral nature, music seems ever present across geographical and cultural boundaries whenever emotions such as joy or despair need a voice. Music succeeds where words fail.

Regrettably though, the reverence and gravitas upheld for so long by philosophers, writers, and musicians have been degraded in recent decades by some who regard music as merely a form of entertainment or as an ambient soundtrack for life's activities. Music, however, far surpasses the classification as entertainment or sonic distraction because it represents a valuable means of communication that most likely stems back to the very nascency of speech. But as music can be a tool for communication and enhanced emotional expression, it can also be enlisted as a medium for manipulation when paired with a given ideology or narrative. The subjective nature of music allows it to be molded to serve a variety of situations and masters, including those of the oppressor and the oppressed. While this manipulation can be benign as in product commercials, it can also foster more serious ramifications when employed as political or religious propaganda. As the Greeks suspected, music can influence human behavior in powerful ways, and through its persuasive quality can be a device for promoting ideologies and encouraging collective thought and action by a group of people. Music assumes intentionality when strategically partnered with certain messages in order to enhance or even create unspoken components to the narrative.

In addition to its role in communication, music contributes to cultural identity, most significantly by establishing borders between groups of people. Music can enhance the communal cohesion of a group, but it can also be used to inflict harm as an instrument of isolation and censorship. Concerning the latter, state governments and religious institutions represent the two primary censors of cultural artifacts. The artistic creations of a people relate powerfully to the group's identity, and therefore when condemned, banned, or even celebrated, have a profound influence on corporate ideologies and behavior. While acts of music censorship in Europe can be traced back as far as the early years of the Common Era, this control was exercised predominately to protect citizens from obscene or lewd songs or as a means for the early Christian Church to distance itself from music used in the polytheistic worship of the Romans. But nothing in the historical record comes close to the malicious and crushing censorship in the 20th century by Joseph Stalin and his Communist regime or Adolf Hitler's Third Reich.

The Nazi leadership recognized and harnessed the power of music with exacting aptitude and malevolence. Joseph Goebbels, the high ranking Reich Minister of Propaganda, believed music to be the mightiest of the arts because of its effect on the human heart and emotions, sentiments that had been expressed influentially in Germany by the 19th century philosopher Arthur Schopenhauer. Music, in fact, became so important throughout Germany during the 1930s and 40s that musicologist Lily Hirsch describes it as a "musical currency,"[5] a currency the Nazis wielded as propaganda and that Holocaust victims clung to for solace, distraction, and spiritual resistance. For the National Socialist Party, controlling and censoring such a potent force remained paramount. While conceptually the term censorship conjures a negative connotation as in an authority figure or group depriving another of access, in certain circumstances as mentioned earlier, it has also been defined as an attempt to insulate a population from negative expressions such as hate speech. But for an oppressive regime such as Nazi Germany, their dogged insistence that censorship offered protection to their citizens from damaging influences actually played a key role in their meticulous and ruthless campaign to purify the culture that they felt had been so wrongfully polluted by Jews and modernists.

Despite the Third Reich's reliance on the arts in transmitting its creed of hate and intolerance, music actually kept a remnant of democracy alive in the hearts of the afflicted people as they chose to make music to express their sorrow, fear, or uncertainty, as well as to mount psychological resistance. Many stubbornly clung to music, wherever and however they could, to preserve their culture, even as the Nazis formally and systematically stripped it away through dismissals from orchestras and teaching posts. Remarkable instances can be seen where the message of defiance inherent in the music of the oppressed failed to even register with their Nazi captors, who instead reveled in the enjoyment of it in a bizarre naïveté. The guards themselves often found an ironic comfort in their victims' music as a panacea for the stresses of war and the loneliness of separation from family. But for the Jews and other persecuted peoples, songs of resistance could be secretly transmitted orally or scribbled down on scraps of paper as a way to share and document these indescribable circumstances as well as to cope and sustain morale. The creation of art, the performance of music, all part of the imaginative mind, withstood Nazi attempts to silence it. Artistic expression triumphed as well under other oppressive regimes and in other locations, including Japanese internment camps in the Pacific. By embracing acts of creativity, the oppressed discovered that they could transcend their circumstances, whether they found themselves in a hiding place, or a ghetto, or a concentration camp.

1

The Rise of the Third Reich and Its Cultural Agenda

The first step in liquidating a people is to erase its memory. Destroy its books, its culture, its history. Then have somebody write new books, manufacture a new culture, invent a new history. Before long the nation will begin to forget what it is and what it was. The world around it will forget even faster.
—Milan Kundera, *The Book of Laughter and Forgetting*, 218

For Germanic people living in the 19th and early 20th centuries, nothing felt quite as beloved and treasured as their musical heritage. Important German composers could be traced all the way back to the Middle Ages with the progressive abbess Hildegard of Bingen. But the era from the Baroque through the Romantic period, where Bach, Mozart, Beethoven, and Wagner reigned supreme, evoked a special sense of pride. Nevertheless, during the 19th century in particular, some voiced concerns that this magnificent art form was being tarnished by the influences of Jewish musicians, teachers, and composers. German composer Richard Wagner harbored an extreme hatred for the Jews and saw them as a threat to the culture of Germany and to its very destiny. He shamelessly advocated for the removal of all Jewish traces from the arts and culture of Germany. Wagner had been greatly influenced by French writer Arthur de Gobineau, who in 1855 had published *Essai sur l'inégalité des races humaines* (An Essay on the Inequality of the Human Races). In this work, Gobineau pronounced white Europeans as superior to other races and coined the term "degenerate" to describe inferior or impure races. In his own essay, *Das Judenthum in der Musik* (Jewishness in Music), Wagner argued that those of Jewish descent would never be capable of comprehending the culture of Western Europe since it was based on Christianity, and as a result, could not contribute positively to it. In an eerie foreshadowing, Wagner even proffered the need for a "great solution"[1] to the Jewish problem in his 1881 publication, *Erkenne dich selbst* (Know Thyself).

Wagner's writings not only served to articulate his views on how Jews had corrupted German culture, but generated a following of like-minded individuals who absorbed this ideology not only through his words but also from his music. Wagner's racial diatribe pervaded his operas, or what he preferred to call "music dramas." Many of his operas, such as *Lohengrin* and *Der Ring des Nibelungen*, featured superheroes, representative of the Aryan race, who ultimately triumphed over other races and even supernatural forces. Wagner's final opera, *Parsifal* (1882), has been considered by some to be the most dangerous music ever written, as it was explicitly used at the time to fan the flames of anti–Semitism and then later to justify the Nazi agenda. An analytical treatise on *Parsifal* from 1913 was one of the 80 books that Hitler carried with him into the bunker, where he would eventually take his own life.[2]

But in actuality, Wagner's grudge against the Jews and his anti-Semitic writings may have been more of a retaliation than a truly held belief. Many of Wagner's contemporaries, Jewish composers such as Giacomo Meyerbeer and Jacques Offenbach, enjoyed great success with their operas in Paris, while Wagner struggled there. He blamed his failures on the fact that so many of the conductors were Jewish, and as a result, the Jews were determining musical programming and thus influencing audience tastes. Some scholars have even suggested that Israel's renouncement of Wagner's music after the war had more to do with how the Nazis had made use of it, than any inherent anti-Semitism in the music.

For the Nazi Party, Wagner's music and his unapologetic anti-Semitism certainly became an effective tool to wield in support of eradicating all evidence of Jewish art and culture—first through censorship and later through ethnic cleansing. Wagner's association with the Nazi paradigm reverberated so vehemently that it indeed led to a nearly 60-year moratorium on his music in Israel. In 2000, conductor and Holocaust survivor Mendi Rodan controversially programmed Wagner's *Siegfried Idyll* on a concert near Tel Aviv. This move incited protests among many of the residents and led an 83-year-old Holocaust survivor to petition for a restraining order from the courts. The Israeli Supreme Court denied the request, however, and the concert continued as scheduled.

Despite the anti-Semitic sentiments and rhetoric that surfaced periodically in the 19th century, people of Jewish ancestry had made considerable advances into German society by the early 20th century. Interestingly, what constituted being "German" at that time allowed for a much broader definition and geographic fluidity than what the term denotes today. It would only be after 1945 and the defeat of the Third Reich that the word German evolved to mean someone from Germany. In fact, that label had referred to people of diverse regional and cultural backgrounds, including Slavs and Hungarians, who were scattered over a wide swath of Europe. Many of the individuals championed as great contributors to German culture in the 19th century came from regions outside of Germany's modern-day borders, including Gustav Mahler from Bohemia, now known as the Czech Republic, and Sigmund Freud from present-day Russia.

After the Napoleonic Wars, the German-speaking principalities had begun to push for unification in order to better defend themselves in the future, especially from the French. This resulted in the creation of two states: the Austria-Hungary dual monarchy in 1867 headed by the Austrian Emperor and the German Reich in 1871 with the Prussian King as its leader. Although Jews had been granted civil rights in the 18th century, these liberties had not insulated them from public opinion that still viewed them mostly as a foreign presence. Only when the two German-speaking states materialized did Jews truly realize freedom, both socially and politically, in the form of constitutional provisions. Europe, and particularly these two regions, boasted such cultural and ethnic diversity at the time that the gesture actually conjured a fleeting spirit of universal brotherhood and acceptance. After living among them for 2,000 years, the Jews finally received the invitation they desired to join fully into the culture and society. As a result, they became zealous in forging new identities and fervently nationalistic, with many shedding their Jewishness in order to acclimate more completely. But predictably, not everyone viewed this transformation as positive. The contingent of anti-Semites found the Jews' exuberant assimilation offensive, a perceived injustice that would continue to fester into a catastrophic outcome.

The arts in particular had provided a compelling vehicle for the Jewish entrance into German society, and when attacked by anti-Semitic voices, Jews relied on their contributions to and enrichment of German culture as a defense and justification. But unfortunately for these Jews, Germany's 200 years of musical supremacy, roughly from Bach through Wagner, appeared to be coming to an end in the early 20th century, and many blamed the Jewish influence, particularly their atonal, modernist tendencies. No one suffered the effects of this sentiment more acutely than Gustav Mahler, who despite having converted from Judaism to Catholicism in an attempt to protect and bolster his career, felt completely isolated in Vienna, a city he saw as unapologetically hostile and mean-spirited toward Jews. His unease indeed proved prescient as the Viennese musical establishment eventually forced him out of his position as conductor of the Vienna State Opera, disregarding his remarkable prowess at conducting opera and his internationally renowned status. Mahler himself would not live to witness the chilling rise of the Nazi Party, dying in 1911 at age 50, but the approaching storm would impact his surviving daughter, Anna Justine, an accomplished sculptor forced to flee her Nazi-occupied homeland along with many other well-regarded artists.

While the new territorial arrangements established in 1867 and 1871 proved advantageous in numerous ways, the establishment of a definite border around Germany, however, left the country needing to defend itself on all sides and ultimately led to a feeling of paranoia and a readiness for a fight that by 1914 escalated into the Great War. World War I delivered devastating military and civilian casualties all around, a total of 17 million dead and 20 million injured, making it one of the deadliest conflicts in history. Especially hard hit were European countries, with France, Germany, and Russia each losing almost two million men. Austria's death toll soared over one million, and Britain's hovered at almost one million. The Spanish influenza in 1918 compounded the cataclysm, wiping out 3 percent of the world's population.

Although anti–Semitism certainly existed prior to World War I, the economic disasters following the German defeat and the arduous reparations and austerity they faced set the scene for a virulent rise in anti–Jewish feelings and scapegoating. The German loss resulted in the formation of a parliamentary democracy known as the Weimar Republic. The 1919 armistice treaty mandated that Germany and Austria not only accept full responsibility for the war, but also make reparations, which further debilitated their struggling economies. Since Germany had not even been invited to the negotiations, many of its veterans and nationalists regarded the terms of the treaty as unfair and the overall proceedings as a crushing humiliation. They refused to affirm those provisions that saddled them with all of the blame, insisting instead that the war ended in a stalemate with no clear winner or loser. Many Germans also clung bitterly to the opinion that they could have won the war if not for the ineptitude of their politicians. In the end, Austria suffered the most, including loss of vital agricultural land to Hungary and one of its ports to Italy. The few natural resources remaining kept most of the population in extreme poverty and left a growing number of Austrians longing to be united with Germany.

In addition to the economic and political woes of a defeated Germany, the country experienced a loss of cultural status as well. As the preeminence of German Romanticism waned, Paris donned the prestigious mantle as capital of the musical and artistic world that had once belonged to Vienna and Berlin. This reversal did not sit well with the Germans, who vowed to reestablish and reassert their cultural dominance. For some, the main obstacle to achieving this goal stemmed from the Jews, who continued to make tremendous strides into German society. By 1925, 16 percent of Germany's physicians came from Jewish descent, as did 25 percent of its lawyers, even though the total number of Jewish inhabitants constituted less than 1 percent of the entire population. Many felt that the Jews had also become disproportionally represented in cultural and artistic activities, comprising 7 percent of Germany's writers and visual artists and 3 percent of its professional musicians. This increase in status and influence contributed markedly to a rise in anti–Semitism.

Amid all of these post-war difficulties and discontent, the U.S. stock market crash in 1929 and the resulting depression negatively impacted much of the Western world. The arts in Germany and Austria suffered an especially hard hit, with orchestras, theaters, and opera houses scrambling for financial solvency in response to declining ticket sales and due to the diverting of government funding away from the arts and toward welfare relief for its citizens. Consequently, thousands of musicians faced unemployment by 1931. Even the renowned Berlin Philharmonic faced a severe crisis with its government support reduced by half, forcing it to merge with the Berlin Symphony Orchestra as a means of survival. With the daily hardships underscored by percolating human tensions and tempers, the stage appeared set for a disastrous aftershock.

And so, during this volatile time, a brooding and frustrated young man named Adolf Hitler entered the scene. Hitler's aspirations as an artist had been irreparably quashed by a failed entrance exam to the Vienna Academy of Fine Arts in 1904. Following World War I, he turned his anger and energy into an obsessive diatribe about how unfairly the German people had been treated, both by their own leaders and by the international community. Hitler's bigotry guided him in cultivating and disseminating an ideology that ultimately blamed all of his country's hardships on the Jews. With anti–Semitic feelings already stirring, his words resonated among the many who still regarded Jewish people as outsiders and resented their perceived encroachment into German society.

Hitler joined the German Workers' Party, later renamed the National Socialist Party (Nazi Party), in 1919 at age 30, and with his charisma, he quickly ascended the ranks of leadership. His caustic rhetoric, which conflated anti–Semitism with resentment from the war, made his public speeches and rallies popular, drawing impressive crowds. Although the Party was banned for a time because of its fearmongering rhetoric and its unsuccessful attempt to overthrow the government, the German economic collapse provided a fertile ground for Hitler to rebuild and reconfigure the struggling organization. He took advantage of people's anger and frustration to peddle his scapegoat conspiracy theories and boldly promised that he could restore the Fatherland to its former pre-war glory. In his 1925 manifesto *Mein Kampf* (My Struggle), Hitler stated right from the opening paragraph that Germany and Austria must unite and together create an unstoppable alliance.

As his Party's ideas gained traction and their Parliamentary votes increased, Hitler ran for President in 1932, but lost to General von Hindenburg. Advisors lobbied Hindenburg the following year to appoint Hitler as Chancellor, hoping to capitalize on his growing popularity. Hindenburg reluctantly acquiesced, and Adolf Hitler became Chancellor of the Parliament on January 30, 1933. Right away, Hitler shrewdly expanded the authority of his office, even granting himself emergency powers. This allowed him to sanction anti–Jewish laws and abolish freedom of the press. Then with the untimely death of President Hindenburg of cancer in August 1934, Hitler assumed complete control by prohibiting further elections, eliminating the Office of the President, and declaring himself the Führer (leader) of the people. The Weimar Republic disappeared, and the Third Reich, with Hitler at the helm as Reich Chancellor, was born.

Germany's new Führer worked swiftly to create a highly structured bureaucracy that put loyal supporters in leadership roles, and he established the Gestapo secret police and the SS (*Schutzstaffel*) to enforce the policies he planned to enact in support of the Party's ideologies. The Nazi creed centered around a core belief that people of Aryan descent were racially superior and that the restoration of German supremacy could only be accomplished by promoting Aryan culture and genetics, while limiting or even eliminating those deemed inferior, including Jews, Roma (Gypsies), Slavs, the mentally and physically handicapped, and homosexuals. Their blindingly relentless quest for racial purity extended to animals as well. Through people such as Lutz Heck, the director of the Berlin Zoo, the Nazis developed a fascination with breeding and trying to resurrect extinct species. They especially hoped to revive the aurochsen, an Ice Age bull that had been worshiped in the ancient cultures of Egypt and Crete and that featured prominently in Greek mythology as a symbol of power. The Nazi eugenics program for animals embraced the same fundamental aim as with humans—the removal of the feeble and the inferior from the gene pool. Konrad Lorenz, a Nobel-awarded scientist much respected by the Nazis, began to use Gobineau's term "degenerate" to classify types of people and to brand physical ugliness as a form of cancer. He callously assigned values to individuals, either a "full" value or an "inferior" value, and supported purging anyone of a certain race or with a disability. This type of warfare waged at the cellular level would lead French biophysicist Pierre Lecomte du Noüy to conclude in his 1944 publication, *La dignité humaine* (Human Dignity), that "Germany's crime is the greatest crime the world has ever known, because it is not on the scale of History: *it is on the scale of evolution.*"[3]

Implementing the new Nazi racial protocols would constitute a massive undertaking, since over nine million Jews lived in Europe and most of those in countries that the Third Reich would occupy or influence. Undaunted by the numbers, the Nazi Party was eager to realize its utopian dream of a superior master race by separating out the desirables and then purging the degenerate and imperfect. One of the crucial components in the success of this Nazi objective involved an elaborate propaganda campaign for children and adults that would turn the German people against the "undesirables." Another equally essential stage of the plan would be achieved through legal means.

On April 7, 1933, Hitler enacted a law called the Restoration of the Professional Civil Service, which mandated that persons of Jewish descent be removed from all public positions. This included firefighters and educators, along with those who worked in museums, opera companies, and orchestras. This edict became one of Hitler's landmark initiatives to cleanse what he viewed as Jewish pollution and provided the cornerstone for the Legislative Solution, a strategy through which the Nazi government thought it could satisfactorily deal with the Jewish problem by disentangling them from German society. In conjunction with this fundamental piece of legislation, officials targeted Jews through a myriad of other punitive laws and restrictions, such as freezing bank accounts and confiscating personal property, along with enforcing nightly curfews and branding them with yellow stars.

In 1935, the Nazis introduced the infamous Nuremberg Race Laws. One of these, the Citizenship Law, stated that only those who could prove through records and stringent formulas that they possessed pure German blood qualified for citizenship. Those who could not were unceremoniously stripped of their citizenship and therefore all of their political and civil rights. The Law for the Defense of German Blood and Honor rendered marriage and sexual relations illegal between Jews and Germans. In addition to the punitive damage these laws would inflict, the Nazis hoped that they would intimidate Jews into fleeing to other countries.

In dealing with the substantial Jewish populations that resided in its controlled territories, the Reich government faced the challenge of segregating them not only economically, but also physically. The Nazis had not needed to invent the concept of the ghetto, only pilfer inspiration from the long and complicated history of anti–Semitism. The Venetians actually developed the first ghettos in 1516 as a response to fear over the expanding Jewish population in their city. As the Venetians cloistered and cordoned off the Jews, the idea spread to other European cities. The early Catholic Church also participated zealously in isolating Jews to preclude them from contaminating converts to Christianity. But eventually, the pendulum of favor swung in the other direction. Jews gained greater acceptance into European society, and by the dawn of the 20th century, mandatory confinement evolved into concentrated living communities labeled as quarters. With the arrival of the 1930s, the dilemma of the Jewish question emerged yet again. High-ranking Nazi officials wrestled with the reinstitution of an absolute and compulsory ghetto, but no acceptable solution on German soil could be ascertained because it seemed that any ghetto would still require that the Jews interact with the German economy in some way through buying and selling. In the end, the Nazi regime brutally imposed forced segregation on the Jews in countries such as Poland and Czechoslovakia because, as much as they despised their own Jews, the Nazis reserved their most virulent revulsion for the Jews of Eastern Europe. Through the availability of inexpensive barbed wire, a technology invented in the 1860s, a *cordon sanitaire* procedure corralled Eastern European Jewry into overcrowded ghettos with strict rules, rampant disease, and relentless shortages of food and other necessities. Jewish-German writer and political philosopher Hannah Arendt denounced this tactic with piercing clarity. "Terror can rule absolutely only over men who are isolated against each other.... Therefore, one of the primary concerns of all tyrannical government is to bring this isolation about ... isolated men are powerless by definition."[4]

The German government also ordered the construction of a variety of transit and labor camps for Jews and other targets of racial, ethnic, or political persecution that they wanted purged from society. Included on the Nazi "hit list" were those aligned with Communist or Socialist ideologies and Jehovah's Witnesses, whose religious belief system did not permit them to salute flags, vote in elections, or participate in nationalistic celebrations. But the primary focus always remained on the Jews, and when mere segregation failed to satisfy, the leadership conceived of a "Final Solution" (*Endlösung*) to eradicate the Jews once and for all. Chiefly envisioned by Heinrich Himmler, this Final Solution materialized in the form of extermination camps to which prisoners were transported via railroad in cattle cars. The journey often lasted four or more days, during which time the individuals suffered under appalling conditions of overcrowding, deprivation of food and water, and intolerable temperatures. Upon arrival, those still alive endured a selection process in which officials separated out many of the children, along with the elderly and impaired, and conveyed them directly to the gas chambers. The remaining prisoners underwent a terrifying and humiliating intake procedure that included having their heads shaved and their arms tattooed with a number, followed by a period of quarantine. Meanwhile, the guards greedily confiscated all luggage and personal belongings.

In addition to the death camps, the Nazi leadership engineered mobile killing units, known as *Einsatzgruppen,* to carry out mass-murder operations against Jews, Roma, and many others. More than one million Jewish men, women, and children were murdered by these units. The German government also initiated a euthanasia program that eventually slaughtered at least 200,000 physically and mentally disabled people. By the end of the war in 1945, the Nazi killing machine, with its unprecedented degree of cruelty and efficiency, had brought about a catastrophic genocide that defied belief—two out of every three European Jews had been exterminated.

In conjunction with legislative policies and forced relocations, the censorship of all art forms emerged as another strategy aimed at racial and cultural purification. Reich officials sought to eliminate any influences they felt contaminated Aryan culture and identity. From the beginning, music became inseparably entwined with Nazi racial policies and politics, and the control of it and the other arts grew extensive and intrusive. In 1933, the German fondness for bureaucracy and organization led to the creation of seven departments under the larger umbrella of the *Reichskulturekammer* (Reich Chamber of Culture). Headed by the propaganda minister Joseph Goebbels, these offices were tasked with regulating the various art forms. The *Reichsmusikkammer* (Reich Music Chamber) supervised all musical activities and dictated through its exclusive membership roster which musicians in the Third Reich could continue to work. Since by law, membership qualifications excluded Jews and others deemed unreliable and unsuitable, such as Roma, Socialists, and nonwhites, the government swiftly silenced those it no longer wished to hear.

In light of the new Nazi regulations, both Jewish and non–Jewish musicians had to navigate an evolving system of rules, including Richard Strauss, the highly celebrated German composer and conductor. Although Strauss participated in and composed music for some propaganda events early on, he seemed to do so without much personal investment in the Nazi cause or ideology. In fact, Strauss' primary interest myopically and naively focused on the promotion of "serious" music, and to that end, he considered the race of the composer or performer irrelevant. The Nazis hoped that Strauss would become an ardent supporter and that his stature in the musical world would then lend credence to their artistic agenda. They appointed him as the first president of the Reich Music Chamber in 1934, with fellow conductor Wilhelm Furtwängler as his deputy. Strauss initially cooperated, but then appeared to waver. Strauss' misgivings, along with his collaborations with the Jewish librettist Stefan Zweig, resulted in his firing in 1935. Fortunately, worldwide fame insulated Strauss from any serious reprisals, but his influence with the government indeed waned. When officials detained his wife's grandmother, Paula Neumann, and sent her to Terezín in 1942, Strauss traveled in a car right up to the gates of the camp where he announced his name and demanded to see her. But apparently, his credentials no longer held sway. The guards turned Strauss away, and he eventually just faded out of the public eye.

Despite Strauss' somewhat voluntary withdrawal from the active musical life of Vienna, he did continue to compose on what would in hindsight appear an unnervingly morbid synchronicity with Nazi atrocities and world events. In early 1941, he began work on a new chamber opera titled *Capriccio*, which he finished on August 3, coinciding with a particularly gruesome killing day by the Nazis—in Chernovtsy, Romania, 682 Jews murdered; in Jelgava, Latvia, 15,000, and untold numbers in Ukraine. When the opera premiered in Munich on October 28, 1942, it unwittingly correlated with the first convoy of Jews shipped from the Czech camp Terezín to Auschwitz in Poland, where 90 percent of them went directly to the gas chamber. Later, Strauss would finish *Metamorphosen*, a funereal work for strings, on April 12, 1945, the day of Franklin Delano Roosevelt's death and just a few weeks before Hitler's suicide on April 30.

Unlike his colleague Richard Strauss, Herbert von Karajan eagerly joined the Nazi Party to obtain more favorable and prestigious conducting positions and became adept at playing both sides. He enthusiastically served the Nazis, but then just as zealously denounced them after the war. In fact, Karajan cooperated so keenly and sycophantically with the committee working on the denazification process that eventually the knowledge of his past as a Nazi collaborator seemed of little consequence. After a brief three-year ban from the podium, which lifted in 1948, Karajan emerged as one of Europe's most popular conductors and the permanent director of the Berlin Philharmonic in 1958. Many regard him as the 20th century's most successful conductor, having been worth over $200 million upon his death in 1989. Karajan's reincarnation as a Phoenix rising from the ashes became yet another troubling, but certainly not rare, footnote in the story of the Holocaust. Countless individuals seemed to have gotten by relatively unscathed despite their egregious Nazi collusion.

While non–Jewish musicians such as Strauss and Karajan experienced little or no personal repercussions starting in 1933, the same could not be said for their Jewish colleagues. The law enacted in April 1933 that prohibited Jews from involvement in the public sector also included the music professions of teaching, conducting, and performing. Franz Schreker, a respected composer and conductor serving as director of the Music Academy in Berlin, lost his job and had his music banned. The resulting stress led to a fatal stroke in March 1934 at age 56, rendering him the Nazis' first well-known Jewish musical victim. Regardless of their fame or success before Hitler, Jewish musicians were now much sought-after targets. Nazi harassment even extended to those of the highest profile, such as conductor Bruno Walter. After locking him out of his concert hall, officials explained that the concert could only proceed with an Aryan replacement on the podium. Realizing that his career and also his safety were in jeopardy, Walter fled to the United States, where he joined many other famous musicians forced to escape the Nazi scourge, including Victor Borge, Lukas Foss, Gregor Piatigorsky, Erich Korngold, Kurt Weill, Otto Klemperer, and George Szell.

Even Arnold Schoenberg, the internationally renowned Viennese-Jewish composer, abandoned Germany for the United States, where he eventually accepted a teaching post at UCLA. The Nazis regarded Schoenberg as particularly abhorrent because he offended them on two fronts—his atonal, expressionist music and his Jewish ancestry. In the early years of the 20th century, Schoenberg's musical goal had been to break down the barriers between consonance and dissonance, and thereby simplify the complex harmonic structure of the previous century so that melodic development could predominate. His resulting mathematical composition system, known as dodecaphonic or 12-tone, while an intriguing concept, ultimately failed because only those who understood its complexity could appreciate it, while the average listener remained merely baffled.

Like Gustav Mahler, Arnold Schoenberg had realized, even as a young man, that the stigma of his Jewishness was likely to stymie his career. So in 1892 at age 18, he renounced Judaism and converted to Protestantism, a compromise that he relied on for almost 30 years. Then in 1921, Schoenberg traveled to the lakeside resort Mattsee for a vacation with his family. Upon arrival, an official notified them that the area was for Aryans only and would not allow them entrance. This solitary encounter left him with the undeniable realization that no matter how he viewed himself or what label he attached to himself, that he would always be a Jew. Schoenberg made no immediate declarations, but on July 24, 1933, the same year that he fled Germany, Schoenberg rededicated himself to Judaism in a synagogue ceremony in Paris. So as a result of Nazi persecution, Schoenberg actually became more in touch with his Jewish heritage than ever before, and some of his most profound works, such as *A Survivor from Warsaw* (1947), would rise from this rediscovery.

As Jewish musicians, actors, and artists faced mass unemployment starting in 1933, Kurt Baumann, a young man working as a production assistant in several of Berlin's opera houses, began plans for an organization he called the *Kulturbund Deutscher Juden* (Culture League of German Jews), later renamed the *Jüdischer Kulturbund* (Jewish Culture League). The Culture League would consist of eight departments that represented the various art forms, not unlike the Reich Chamber of Culture created by the Nazi regime. Baumann calculated that one-third of Germany's Jewish residents, about 175,000, lived in Berlin and that such a large population could support a Jewish cultural group, both as artists and patrons. Berlin had established itself as the artistic center after German unification in 1871 and housed a melting pot of cultures, languages, and traditions. Such a cosmopolitan city offered a vast array of artistic experiences as well as cultivated a breeding ground for innovative ideas. Almost equally important for Baumann's initiative was the fact that Berlin lived in the international spotlight, and the Third Reich realized that it needed to tread lighter there with their anti–Semitic campaigns than in other cities less likely to attract much attention.

Baumann partnered with Dr. Kurt Singer, a well-known conductor, to help bring the organization to fruition. In May 1933, Singer persuaded Nazi official Hans Hinkel to allow this paradoxical affiliation between the Jews and the German government to proceed, conceding that strict guidelines and oversight would prevail. Nazi regulations for the new Culture League specified that all participants, both artists and audience members, must be Jewish and that each audience member must pay a monthly subscription fee, precluding the sale of tickets for individual events. The musicians could not perform works by German or Austrian composers, such as Bach, Beethoven, or Mozart, and the repertoire for any performance had to be approved no later than one month before by Hinkel.

Despite the arduous stipulations, the Culture League allowed the disenfranchised Jewish population to use music and the other arts as not only a means of economic survival, but as a way to maintain some ability to maneuver through the politics of the 1930s. While the League supported out-of-work artists and provided Jewish communities with cultural activities, it also served the Nazi propaganda machine as a shield to blunt international criticism and to convince the outside world of the Reich's humane treatment of its Jewish contingency. The League benefited the Nazi government in an even more insidious way, as well, by pacifying the Jews while the Third Reich slowly and methodically formed an invisible ghetto around them.

By 1934, Berlin's Culture League roster soared to 20,000 members, demonstrating that this endeavor had been greatly needed. Consequently, the popularity of this League inspired other cities, such as Frankfurt, Hamburg, and Cologne, to start their own. In time, 46 Culture Leagues operated throughout Germany, with a collective membership of over 70,000 by 1936. But sadly, the tremendous success of the program was short-lived. The Leagues began closing down in 1937 because emigration, impoverishment, incarceration, and death had decimated their member rosters. The Nazi government dissolved the last of the Jewish Culture Leagues in 1941. With the benefit of hindsight, some scholars have concluded that the presence of this organization may have furthered the Nazi agenda and cost more Jewish lives than anyone could have realized at the time. As historian Alan Steinweis has offered, "By providing Jewish artists and audiences with an outlet for creative expression, the Kulturbund rendered Jewish existence in National Socialist Germany somewhat less desperate than it otherwise might have been, thereby lulling German Jews into a tragically false sense of security about the future."[5]

Meanwhile, as Jewish musicians grappled with tough restrictions and diminishing options, non–Jewish artists hoped to garner more government support and patronage. Many believed that the Nazi purging of "foreign influences" would result in more opportunities for them, which it frequently did if they were willing to make some moral concessions. German musicians often found themselves straddling a fence between wanting to concede enough to improve their status and avoid reprisals, but not so far as to align completely with the Nazi agenda and methodology. For survival, most composers did have to compromise their own musical and political ideas for those of the Führer. These included Schoenberg's protégés, Alban Berg and Anton Webern. While both received heavy criticism for their degenerate modernism, they were Aryan and so did not face the threat of annihilation that their teacher did. Without explicitly embracing the beliefs of the National Socialist Party, Berg played along to further his career and keep himself in good standing. Webern, who had actually been sympathetic with Socialist causes, quickly engineered an about-face and emerged as an unabashedly enthusiastic supporter of the Nazi Party. But neither lived long enough to face any post-war scrutiny or repercussions. Berg died suddenly from septicemia in December 1935. Oddly, and perhaps even ironically, Webern became an unintended casualty of the war. On September 15, 1945, the 61-year-old composer stepped outside of his daughter's home near Salzburg to smoke a cigar after curfew and was fatally shot by an American soldier.

The temptation to support the Nazi regime for the sake of one's career was not limited to just artists of German descent. Finland's chief composer, Jean Sibelius, gave in to it as well. Having maintained a justifiably hostile relationship with the Soviet Union, Finland eventually made friendly with the Nazi government. As a result, the Reich championed Sibelius' music, and he returned the favor by sending his best wishes to the German troops. But while many kowtowed to Hitler and his lackeys, others, such as conductors Szymon Pullman, Marian Neuteich, and Adam Furmanski, lost their lives at the hands of the Nazis.

In addition to securing artistic alliances and enforcing cultural censorship, another hallmark of the Nazi strategic plan involved commandeering the arts for propaganda. Music had certainly been employed for such purposes in the past, but no group had ever utilized it so effectively and comprehensively as the Third Reich. Music, both in its concrete form and as an analogy, seemed to lend itself to the dark and sinister designs of the Nazis. In his 1944 poem "Death Fugue," Holocaust survivor Paul Celan wrote about a Nazi guard who forced prisoners to dig their own graves, comparing the scene to a conductor urging the violin section to "bow more darkly."[6] Music historian Alex Ross simply concedes that music's inherently malleable nature allowed it to be used at will by Nazi Germany. Speaking of music, Ross concludes, "It is always in the world, neither guilty nor innocent, subject to the ever-changing human landscape in which it moves."[7]

So however the philosophical or metaphorical underpinnings of music may have contributed to its accessibility, German art music did develop into an integral and inseparable component of Nazi politics and activities. But in contrast to the openly aggressive and self-aggrandizing way that Stalin had seized control of his country's music, Hitler employed a more subtle and manipulative approach, even demanding in 1935 that no musical works be written in honor of him or specifically for Nazi Party use. Instead, he remained ardently committed to the musical repertoire of the great German masters and felt that nothing could be newly composed that would eclipse those works. But his declaration did not mean that this revered music would not play a role in the Reich's agenda and propaganda, quite the opposite. The music and musicians of Germany would provide the soundtrack for the glorious triumphs of the Führer and the Fatherland.

Cultivating the country's sense of pride in its robust musical heritage proved an effective means for the Third Reich to fuel and exploit the populist nationalism that surged during the 1930s. Nazi leaders freely appropriated great icons of German culture to undergird their dogma and objectives and felt no aversion even toward reinventing people's lives or ideological perspectives in order to make them more fully compatible with the Party line. The most notable example involved Wolfgang Amadeus Mozart. Viewing himself as a citizen of the world, Mozart had expressed almost no nationalistic sentiments in his letters or music. Instead, the Austrian composer had subscribed to a more libertarian view of government. Much about Mozart's life should have disqualified him with the Nazis, especially his zealous involvement in the Freemasons, not to mention his close friendship and collaboration with Jewish librettist Lorenzo Da Ponte. But even though Mozart's philosophical and political perspectives glaringly misaligned with Nazi principles, Party officials decided to commandeer his treasured status to support their claims of racial and cultural superiority. To this end, they organized an elaborate revisionist campaign to transform him into a German nationalistic hero, starting with celebrations throughout the Third Reich on the 150th anniversary of his death. And so, quite effortlessly, Mozart joined the roster of Nazi-approved composers, standing alongside Beethoven, Brahms, Bruckner, Schumann, and of course, Wagner.

In addition to stipulating what musical styles and composers represented the noble ideals of the German people, the Nazi censorship campaign vehemently crusaded against music deemed *Entartete Musik* (Degenerate Music). Highly restrictive policies banned all compositions written by Jews, Jewish sympathizers, and political opponents, in addition to atonal and expressionist compositions. Jazz fell under a similar prohibition because so many of its performers were Jewish or black. Kurt Weill, a composer who had enjoyed tremendous popularity in the 1920s Berlin cabaret scene, now found his music forbidden on two counts—his Jewish ancestry and his incorporation of jazz idioms into German musical theater, as in his *The Three Penny Opera*. As Jewish musicians and composers vanished from the stage, recordings of their performances lapsed silent on the radio and disappeared from store shelves. In response to this complex and unprecedented level of musical censorship, musicologists in Frankfurt published *Lexikon der Juden in der Musik* (Lexicon of Jews in Music), a reference book from which anyone who sold music or programmed concerts could view the names of every blacklisted Jew, and thereby ensure their compliance with the absolute boycott of Jewish musical product.

As seen by the anti–Jewish reference book, the implementation of such rigid controls on art and music required multi-pronged strategies for disseminating that information. Inspired by a 1937 exhibit of degenerate art in Munich, Hans Severus Ziegler organized an exhibition of degenerate music in Düsseldorf during May 1938 as part of the *Reichmusiktage* (Reich Music Days). The Düsseldorf exhibit featured portraits of the scorned composers, including Schoenberg and Stravinsky, accompanied by recordings of their music, which played on gramophones positioned throughout the space. But unlike the well-attended *Entartete Kunst* (Degenerate Art) display the previous year, the music exposition received only a tepid response. The whole process of curating the event had caused considerable friction among the organizers as they vied over what works and composers should be included. Atonal works were seen by some, including Ziegler, as a Jewish product via Schoenberg, but others disagreed, citing that Richard Strauss had insisted that atonal works were still an acceptable part of Germany's art music when he served as president of the Reich Music Chamber. In the end, achieving any kind of consistent policy regarding the exhibit's content provided futile, as illustrated by the fact that Strauss himself had written some starkly atonal music in his opera *Salome,* yet his name and work had been excluded. So, it appeared that Nazi policies offered some flexibility if the individual in question possessed the "right" racial pedigree.

Hungarian composer and ethnomusicologist Béla Bartók probably experienced the most interesting relationship with the Third Reich's degenerate list. Bartók felt deeply troubled by Hungary's slide toward Fascism and by what he saw happening in Germany and Italy. So after the Nazis seized power, Bartók forbade all performances and broadcasts of his music in the Third Reich and Fascist Italy, a decision that rendered him financially destitute since most of his royalties stemmed from performances in Germany. Subsequently, when Goebbels compiled the official list of *Entartete Musik* in 1938, Bartók actually requested that he be added to the list. Such bold stances certainly garnered risks, and Bartók eventually fled to the United States in 1940, where he could be protected from any Nazi retaliations. But in the end, despite their aggressive and obsessive attempts to control music through regulations, the National Socialists opted for the most effective form of censorship—genocide.

The damage to German music by Nazi policy, censorship, and propaganda resulted in the unmooring of a once vibrant culture. As Hitler began the process of removing Jews and their contributions from the musical sphere of Germany, it became the equivalent of amputating a limb, cutting off something fundamental. The incalculable loss of Jewish musicians created an immediate and lasting hardship, and their departure signaled the forfeiture of tradition and connection. As Jewish musicians disappeared physically from the stage, the music of Jewish composers, such as Felix Mendelssohn, faded from concert programs, thus achieving the total exclusion of Jewish influences in music, even down to the sonic level. According to Alex Ross, even the broad concept of music as an art form experienced a profound loss—its "moral authority."[8] After the war, the Allies would attempt to rebrand the tainted German music, even drawing attention to the fact that the familiar four-note motive of Beethoven's *Fifth Symphony* was the same as the Morse code for "V or Victory." But despite the various post-war efforts, the harm inflicted on the reputation of the great German composers and masterpieces would persist for some time.

2

Alma Rosé and the Women's Orchestra at Auschwitz-Birkenau

If we don't play well, we'll go to the gas.
—Alma Rosé quoted in Richard Newman and
Karen Kirtley, Alma Rosé: Vienna to Auschwitz, 254

During Medieval times, the flourishing trade in Vienna acted as a beacon, drawing Jews who had long been scattered from the Jewish diaspora toward its fruitful possibilities. But as the Jewish community expanded in the city, the non–Jewish population grew to despise them for their seemingly odd customs. This distrust and animosity led to a pogrom against the Jews in 1421, and those who refused to convert to Christianity were either expelled from the city or executed. This retaliation would represent only the first of many times in which Vienna would seek to rid itself of its Jewish residents, to become *Judenfrei* (free of Jews). During the ensuing years, Jews cautiously returned to Vienna, and by the mid–17th century, a ghetto known as Leopoldstadt housed approximately 500 Jewish families. But as a result of their mounting successes, Jewish inhabitants again came under attack, this time by Leopold I in 1670, who banished them. Soon, however, the Viennese experienced unexpected economic repercussions from the ouster of this dynamic constituency, so Jewish families once again established a presence in Vienna, although their relationship with the endemic populace remained tenuous.

By the 19th century, when other Western governments had embraced their Jewish residents as bona fide citizens, Austria still penalized them with restrictions stubbornly entrenched from the Middle Ages. In 1849, Emperor Franz Joseph I finally granted full citizenship to Vienna's Jews. With the introduction of this political security, the Jewish population exploded from 6,000 in 1860 to 147,000 a mere 40 years later. This floodgate of immigrants included people from Galicia, Moravia, Spain, and Budapest, to name a few, and by 1913, resulted in more than half of Vienna's population not being native born. Moving out of ghettos, Jews melded into the cultural life of the city, infusing it with the freshness of their customs, talents, and perspective, while concurrently brimming with great admiration and reverence for German culture. Many even resolved to be *überwienerisch*, "more Viennese than the Viennese,"[1] and to integrate so absolutely that their Jewishness faded into invisibility. The vibrant musical life of Vienna offered one of the most accessible avenues of assimilation for the Jews, and by the early 20th century, individuals of Jewish descent accounted for one-third of the Vienna Conservatory's violin and piano students. But still, the life of the Jews in Vienna remained persistently ambiguous, as they were simultaneously insiders and outsiders, accepted and rejected.

Despite the ambivalence that the city showed toward its Jewish populace, Vienna offered such a storied history and such magnificent opportunities that it seemed worth the societal negotiations. Unlike other great cities, such as Athens and Florence, that had enjoyed one limited era of unsurpassed brilliance, Vienna actually spawned two Golden Ages. The first arose during the late 18th and early 19th centuries when Haydn, Mozart, and Beethoven, later known collectively as the First Viennese School, plied their craft. The Vienna of Mozart's day managed to cultivate not just a single individual of exceptional talent, but an entire "musical ecosystem."[2] It fostered a habitat conducive to generating genius levels of musical innovation, which explains why all three composers flocked to this location that was not their birthplace. Vienna's second Golden Age materialized roughly 100 years later at the dawn of the 20th century, incubating genius not just in the arts with Arnold Schoenberg's Second Viennese School, but in literature, science, psychology, architecture, and a myriad of other disciplines, and through brilliant minds such as Sigmund Freud and Adolf Loos.

Vienna's final Golden Age, however, failed to fade away gradually as customarily happens with brightly burning times and places. Instead, it halted with a jolting shock in Sarajevo on June 28, 1914, when a young Serbian man, Gavrilo Princip, assassinated Archduke Franz Ferdinand, the Austrian emperor's nephew and heir to the throne. The resulting world war, both in casualties and punitive post-war reparations, devastated Austria, leaving it politically and fiscally crippled. Severed from its larger, pre-war empire, Austria now labored under a small, independent government. But while the capital managed to retain its status as a grand and vital city, housing one-third of the entire population of Austria, Vienna also became the first European city to feel the devastating effects of the U.S. stock market crash in October 1929, and the subsequent Depression. By 1933, Vienna's staggering unemployment rate left two-thirds of its residents without work. Yet, despite the collapse of the Hapsburg Empire in 1918 and the mounting difficulties of the post-war era, Vienna persisted as the artistic and intellectual nexus it had been in previous centuries. Soon, however, the ascendency of Adolf Hitler and his brutal regime would tragically undermine the very fabric of this enlightened city, causing a spiritual and moral tectonic shift.

Karl Lueger, the mayor of Vienna, had achieved tremendous popularity since his election in 1897. An ardent anti–Semite, Lueger helped found the Christian Social Party, a group that championed a populist message and would later evolve into the National Socialist (Nazi) Party. Some newspapers of the time promoted his Party's views and published articles railing against the contaminating presence of Jews in high-ranking positions and in the arts. In 1922, Jewish writer Hugo Bettauer released the controversial and best-selling novel, *Die Stadt Ohne Juden* (The City Without Jews). Its story described a satirical vision of the future in which unchecked anti–Semitism in Vienna led to the vitriolic expulsion of the Jews, as in centuries past. In 1924, Austrian filmmakers released an acclaimed silent movie based on the book, which then drifted into obscurity and was thought lost forever until a copy surfaced at a Paris flea market in 2015. Bettauer could not have realized the chillingly prophetic nature of his book or that he would ironically become the first Jew to die at the hands of the Nazis, gunned down in 1925 by Party member Otto Rothstock. Rothstock only served 20 months in a mental institution for Bettauer's murder and emerged as a celebrated hero to Vienna's anti–Semites.

After Hitler's rise to power in 1933, anti–Semitic sentiments amplified in Austria, as citizens continued to suffer escalating economic hardships. Five years later, on February 12, 1938, Kurt Von Schuschnigg, Chancellor of Austria, met secretly with Hitler, who pressured him into agreeing to the unification of Germany and Austria, known as the Anschluss. Schuschnigg addressed the Austrian nation via radio on Friday, March 11, 1938, and announced that the country would join the Third Reich. The following day, Nazi troops marched into Vienna. Considering the exploits of the Huns and the Turks, this 1938 incursion was certainly not the first time that Vienna had been overtaken by barbarians.

At the time of the Anschluss, Vienna's Jewish residents numbered approximately 200,000 or about one-sixth of the city's total population. They formed a heterogeneous group, despite their shared ancestry, splitting philosophically between assimilationists, orthodox observers, and zealous Zionists. But regardless of their political or religious leanings at the time, Vienna's Jewish citizenry overwhelmingly viewed themselves primarily as Viennese, leaving them utterly bewildered as the Nazis immediately stripped them of their citizenship and all rights pertaining to it. Austria's Jews were also thrown out of their places of business and fired from long-held positions. As a macabre soundtrack to these unspeakable travesties, a great frenzy arose in the streets as anti–Semitic Viennese cheered and shouted their support. Indeed, some of the most fervent and violent anti–Jewish behavior witnessed in Europe during this time occurred in Austria.

Within the musical circles of Vienna during the year of the Anschluss, none was more well-known or celebrated than the Mahler-Rosé family. Born Arnold Josef Rosenblum on October 24, 1863, in present-day Romania, Arnold moved at the age of four with his family to Vienna because his parents believed that he and his brother Eduard showed musical promise. Indeed, the foresight of his parents gleaned stellar results as Arnold became one of the most famous violinists of the late 19th and early 20th century. He performed his debut as a professional violinist in 1879 at age 16 and was subsequently appointed, at the staggeringly young age of 17, as concertmaster of the Vienna Philharmonic and Vienna Opera Orchestra, posts that he would occupy for over 50 years. In 1882, he adopted the stage name Arnold Rosé and founded the Rosé String Quartet, which included his brother Eduard on the cello. Eduard also assumed the new surname, but only played with the quartet for one year. Arnold, on the other hand, would lead this string quartet for six decades and witness its rise as one of Europe's finest chamber ensembles. The Rosé String Quartet premiered many works by renowned composers, including Johannes Brahms and Arnold Schoenberg. Brahms actually performed at the piano with the group between 1880 and 1895 for several of his own compositions, such as the *Piano Trio in B Major, Op. 8*. The Rosé Quartet championed the music of Schoenberg and performed the premiere of his *Verklärte Nacht* (Transfigured Night) in 1902. Unfortunately, the piece's modern tonality was greeted with such disdain by the audience that fistfights erupted, causing authorities to cancel a second performance scheduled in 1904 for fear of unrest. In addition to his fame as a performer, Arnold's legacy would be that of an expert teacher, joining the faculty of the Vienna Conservatory in 1893. The musical world considered him an authority on the interpretation of Bach and particularly Beethoven, and he produced well-regarded editions of the violin sonatas of Bach and Beethoven, as well as Beethoven's Opus 18 string quartets.

As the Rosé brothers ascended the hallowed ranks of Vienna's artistic establishment, they became acquainted with the city's most famous and arguably controversial musical figure—composer and conductor Gustav Mahler. By the time the Vienna Opera appointed Mahler as its conductor in 1897, he and Arnold had known each other for several years and could enjoy a comfortable rapport as conductor and concertmaster. One day, Mahler invited Arnold home for lunch where he met Mahler's sister Justine, who had dedicated herself to caring for her chronically disorganized brother by managing his household and maintaining his professional calendar. Although immediately drawn to each other, Arnold and Justine courted for five years before marrying, hoping to keep their relationship secret from her brother, who remained so utterly reliant on her. Fortunately for the couple, Gustav Mahler met the love of his life in November 1901, the young socialite and budding composer Alma Schindler, 19 years his junior. With someone else now able to assume the care of her brother, Justine consented to marriage. In fact, both couples wed in March 1902, the Mahlers on March 9 and the Rosés on March 10.

Arnold and Justine Rosé welcomed their first child on December 11, 1902, a son they called Alfred, followed four years later by a daughter on November 3, 1906, named Alma after her aunt and godmother Alma Mahler. Alma's birth year coincided serendipitously with the 150th anniversary of Mozart's birth, labeled the "Mozart Year," which featured performances of his music, especially operas, throughout Vienna. Justine had endured a difficult pregnancy, forcing Arnold to cancel some performing engagements so he could help with the rambunctious 3-year-old Alfred. Gustav Mahler received the news of his niece's arrival at the opera house where he was conducting that evening alongside his protégé Bruno Walter, a close family friend that Alma would know as Uncle Bruno. Gustav and Alma Mahler especially rejoiced that this child had been born on the same day as their first daughter Maria Anna, who had turned four that very day. In honor of the cousins' shared birthday, Alfred and Justine gave her the middle name Maria.

Alma Maria Rosé was baptized a Protestant, as her brother Alfred had been. Arnold and Justine did not identify with their Jewish ancestry, merely considered themselves Viennese, and had officially declared themselves Christians a decade earlier to avoid any anti–Semitic prejudices. Gustav Mahler had converted to Catholicism back in 1897. Quite irate at the apparent necessity of this, his sister Justine, nevertheless, had not wanted her brother to endure it alone, so she converted as well. The decision proved worthwhile, because a few months later, any misgivings about Mahler becoming conductor of the Vienna Opera seemed to fade. Arnold Rosé had converted to Protestantism for his career as well, a prevailing trend among his Jewish orchestra colleagues. The citizens of Vienna, for whom opera ranked of utmost importance, treated the Mahler-Rosé family as musical royals, and some claim that only the Emperor and the mayor of Vienna garnered more respect. Arnold, in particular, received so many honors that when he traveled to the opera house to perform, a resplendent court carriage adorned with the royal crest transported him. One of Alma's earliest memories of her father recalled him climbing into that carriage dressed in his formal attire, complete with a cape.

In 1910, the Rosé family moved to Pyrkergasse 23, where they resided on the first two floors. The upstairs accessed bedrooms by a sweeping spiral staircase, and the lower level housed the kitchen and dining room, in addition to the famous music room where esteemed visitors would make music, including piano duets played by Gustav Mahler and Bruno Walter. Alma, affectionately known as Almschi, led a privileged life as her family hobnobbed with the elite of Vienna. Regular visitors to her home represented a veritable "Who's Who" of the musical world, including Arturo Toscanini, Alban Berg, Richard Strauss, and Anton Webern. Alma's brother Alfred assumed the family business at an early age. He initially studied the violin with his father, but their lessons descended so frequently into explosive disagreements that Alfred switched to the piano. He developed into an accomplished pianist and aspired to a career as a composer and conductor like his Uncle Gustav. But tragically, Alfred's time with his uncle would be cut short.

Gustav Mahler died at age 50 on May 18, 1911, from heart failure. Mahler's death devastated the family, particularly Justine, who never fully recovered and mourned him for the rest of her life. Unlike her brother, Alma adored the violin and her father's instruction. She started playing at age five and received a lesson from him every morning that he was in town. Alma idolized her father and missed him greatly when he traveled for orchestral and quartet performances. An English governess provided the other educational opportunities for Alma and Arnold in their early years, allowing them to become fluent in English. As children, they actually spoke English better than German, which created difficulties since their father did not speak English. Alma also studied piano and became quite proficient, although she never lost sight of her main goal of becoming the kind of violinist that would make her father proud. Similarly, Arnold wanted her to follow in his footsteps so desperately that he forbade her to play any sports or games that might injure her hands. By age 12, Alma practiced the violin six hours a day and entered the Vienna Conservatory, where she studied with the famed Czech violinist and teacher Otakar Ševčík.

When World War I erupted, the Rosé family seemed less affected than the average Viennese household, and their pantry remained better stocked than most, even though they did have to stand in line to buy bread and other necessities. Despite shortages of food and coal, music persisted in the life of Vienna and for the Rosés, who continued to excel musically despite the dreadful conflict. A couple of years after the war, Arnold confided in Kurt Adler, a young aspiring conductor, that he thought that Alma would one day be a gifted conductor. In his long and illustrious career as a concertmaster, Arnold had sat under many of the world's greatest conductors, and his prediction seemed to be a genuine observation and not just a father's bias. He could not know at that time how his prophecy would manifest in such a profound and macabre way.

Alma made her solo debut in Vienna at age 20 on December 16, 1926, playing the Beethoven *Romance in F Major*, the Tchaikovsky *Concerto for Violin in D Major*, and the Bach *Concerto for Two Violins* with her father. For this premiere concert, Alma's father conducted the chamber orchestra that accompanied her, with violinist and composer Adolf Busch assuming the podium for the Bach. The family's reputation assured the attendance of a large audience, including musical celebrities such as Richard Strauss. This performance exerted tremendous pressure on Alma since she not only represented the next generation of the acclaimed Mahler-Rosé family, but intensely feared not measuring up to her father's expectations. Unfortunately, the reviews from the recital ran a bit tepid as they compared her playing to that of her seasoned father, a trend that would be a lifelong burden for Alma. But regardless, this performance ensured that Bach's *Double Violin Concerto* would remain a special piece for father and daughter, who eventually recorded it. Today, it is the only extant recording of Alma Rosé.

The following year, Alma met 27-year-old Czech violinist Váša Příhoda, a much celebrated performer in Central Europe, whom some people hailed as a present-day Paganini. A spark ignited immediately between the two. Arnold voiced a strong opinion in favor of the match, as he admired the violinist's sparkling technique, but Justine expressed considerable caution as to whether Váša constituted the right match for her daughter. Meanwhile, Alma continued to perform and finally started to elicit more favorable reviews, although she still contended with the albatross of her family's musical pedigree. She had her first of many performance in Poland in 1929, the year she and Váša announced their engagement. They married on September 16, 1930. Alma was 24 years old, and Váša 30.

While Alma's career only gradually made headway, Váša's soared, providing him a considerable income, which he spent on extravagant purchases, such as the construction of a lavish villa near Prague and an impressive fleet of vehicles. In addition to his quick fingers, he became known for his fast driving, often seen behind the wheel of a huge white Mercedes-Benz touring car. Váša's parents and his brother lived at the villa with the newlyweds, and his mother cooked and managed the household, skills that Alma did not possess nor aspire to learn. Although their life together had begun as a whirlwind romance, not unlike those of Hollywood movie stars, it faltered as Váša was often away on concert tours. Alma traveled with him when she could and sometimes performed with Váša, but as time went on, Alma repeatedly found herself alone and depressed, while contending with rumors about Váša's dalliances with other women. After just two years of marriage, Alma felt frustrated and jealous over her husband's successes, while she struggled for recognition despite her talents and family connections. This, along with concern about her mother's failing health due to diabetes and a heart condition, caused Alma to return to Vienna when Váša toured. Neighbors never failed to notice when she visited because of her flashy red Aero convertible, another placating gift from Váša.

Alma Rosé, 1931 publicity photograph (Gustav Mahler-Alfred Rosé Collection, Music Library, Western University, London, Canada).

Determined to improve her current situation, Alma launched a plan in 1932 to found a woman's orchestra she would name *Die Wiener Walzermädeln* (The Vienna Waltzing Girls). Although an all-female ensemble that performed light classics was not a novelty in Vienna, Alma envisioned something more elevated, a chamber orchestra that would embody the highest of musical standards and discipline. She also determined that her group would tour throughout Europe and not be limited just to performances in Vienna. After hosting auditions, which her father helped judge, Alma's orchestra consisted of several singers, two harpists, a pianist, and assorted string players, all outfitted with exquisite blue and white gowns. Her brother Alfred assisted by writing some arrangements for the group, and Alma called on Professor Michal Karin to create much of their repertoire. In 1933, The Vienna Waltzing Girls played their first performance in Vienna to great acclaim. As the ensemble prepared to embark on a European tour, Alma excelled at selecting repertoire that would please their respective audiences, featuring music by

Henryk Wieniawski when in Poland and Antonin Dvořák in Czechoslovakia, in addition to their standard selections by Fritz Kreisler and Johann Strauss, as well as Pablo de Sarasate's violin show piece *Zigeunerweisen*. Alma always played at least one solo on each program and that, combined with the overall success of the orchestra, bolstered her career. But despite favorable reviews, Alma continued to be a demanding director, insisting on perfection and unwilling to accept any compromises. She required all of the music to be performed from memory, a daunting task as more and more pieces accumulated for their international tours. Her accomplishments with this ensemble proved particularly noteworthy because of the way the professional music world restricted women at that time. According to Ingeborg Tonneyck-Müller, a former member of the group, "Alma was a tremendous rarity. Women simply did not do what Alma was doing in those days."[3]

Despite the economic distress in Austria and the troubling politics in Germany during the early 1930s, the Rosé family maintained a busy performance schedule. Alma's orchestra arranged its first out-of-town concert for March 1933 in Munich. Regrettably, the Rosés seemed to have little awareness or grasp of the dangerous winds that blew around them and thus failed to take heed. They naively believed that their status, and even music itself, would shield them from any impending maelstrom. Consequently, Alma continued with her orchestra's scheduled performance in Germany, even after Hitler assumed power as Chancellor on January 30, fueling anti–Semitic tensions. But just a few hours before the start time, officials cancelled the concert, inflicting a terrible blow to her financially. Without payment from the performance, she and the other women were stranded without sufficient funds to get home. Frantic, Alma contacted Váša, who paid for their return to Vienna.

In addition to interfering with Alma's Munich concert, the year of 1933 heralded numerous changes for the Rosé family. One of these involved plastic surgery on Alma's nose. Scholars disagree on the reason Alma elected to have this procedure. Some feel that she chose this purely for cosmetic concerns since friends recall that her musical perfectionism extended to criticalness of her appearance. Others posit that the motivation behind the surgery was to render her facial structure less Jewish. Regardless, finally alarmed by mounting anti–Semitism, Alma was baptized a Catholic that same year in the tradition of her mother and uncle. Her brother Alfred also converted to Catholicism in preparation for his marriage to fellow Viennese Maria Schmutzer. Alfred's musical career had flourished, earning him quite a reputation as a pianist, accompanist, composer, and especially as the conducting protégé of Richard Strauss at the Vienna Opera. Alfred had even been given the prestigious honor of conducting Vienna's premiere of Igor Stravinsky's ballet *Pulcinella*. But now with anti–Jewish sentiments on the rise, Alfred scrambled to contact influential friends of his family, such as conductor Sir Adrian Boult in England, to see if any opportunities existed outside of Austria. Meanwhile, despite the setback in Munich, Alma's orchestra continued with many successful concerts. They were especially popular in Poland, performing in Warsaw in 1934 and then in Krakow in 1935, a location only 45 minutes away from a significantly less friendly destination for Alma in eight years.

In 1935, the Nazi government enacted the Nuremberg Race Laws, legislation designed to codify what constituted being Jewish, as well as to forbid marriage between Jews and non–Jews, and to invalidate any prior mixed race marriages. These laws forced Alma to accept that the Nazi government considered her a Jew, a reality that would profoundly influence her in the not too distant future. That same year, her marriage, which had been on shaky ground for quite some time, dissolved irreparably. Váša wanted a divorce, but Alma resisted. Despite their bitter quarrels, she was still madly in love with him. Alma did realize, however, that he regarded her more as his friend than a wife, since he refused to give her the children she longed to have. Váša filed for divorce in March 1935, promising Alma that if she would grant him a divorce that they would remain close and continue their relationship. Convinced of his intentions toward her, she conceded. But Váša did not honor his promise, leaving Alma inconsolable. Some have speculated that Váša ended his marriage to Alma because she was a Jewess, since the timing of the divorce coincided with the introduction of the race laws. Even though these laws had not yet been instituted in Czechoslovakia where he and Alma lived, Váša toured all over the world and appeared frequently in Germany. But others dispute any connection to Alma's ancestry, citing that Váša married a lawyer of Jewish descent two years later and remained married to her throughout World War II. Regardless, Váša continued to perform extensively throughout the Reich, facing severe criticism after the war for colluding with the Nazis. His home country of Czechoslovakia charged him a fine and banned him from playing there. In 1956, he finally received a dispensation to perform again in his birthplace, but Vienna would remain his home. He taught at the Vienna State Academy during the last decade of his life until his death on July 26, 1960, at age 59.

With Alma bitterly unhappy, it seemed that music, especially chamber music with her father and brother, became one of the only activities capable of reigniting her characteristic spark. But despite this personal setback, Alma's determination, strength, and unwavering moral conscience would never leave her. So, during the years of 1936–37, Alma used her influence to assist friends and acquaintances who faced Nazi harassment and persecution, including a German-Jewish concert manager she helped escape to Holland. Meanwhile, the late 1930s heaped more hardships on the Rosé family. Throughout 1937 and the early months of 1938, both Alma and her father had to curtail some of their performances because of Justine's failing health. But one bright spot for Alma was that she had fallen in love again, this time with Heinrich (Heini) Salzer, an engineer whose family owned a paper and publishing empire. Heini doted on Alma, giving her the kind of attention that had been missing from her marriage, and the fact that he knew nothing about music seemed all the more perfect to Alma.

On the evening of March 11, 1938, the Vienna Opera performed Tchaikovsky's lyric opera *Eugene Onegin*. During the first half, audience members could hear noise emanating from the streets. When they ventured outside at intermission to ascertain the source of the disturbance, they encountered rowdy demonstrators and terrifying images of swastikas. Many decided to go straight home and not return to the opera house. That night would be Arnold Rosé's last performance in the orchestra pit. After the opera concluded, he endured a harrowing journey home on the tram, as voices shouted "*Heil Hitler*" in the streets, and thugs assaulted unfortunate Jews. The next day, March 12, 1938, German troops marched into Austria without resistance, finalizing the unification with the Third Reich.

Without delay, the oppressive laws against people of Jewish heritage took effect in Austria. Music teachers and performers lost their jobs and livelihoods, including people of great renown. Arnold, Alfred, and Alma, all found themselves forbidden to perform in public, and Alfred's compositions were banned as well. After 57 years of devoted service to the Vienna Philharmonic and the Vienna Opera Orchestra, 75-year-old Arnold Rosé was dismissed, along with all of the Jewish members. Officials also stripped him of his faculty post at the Vienna Conservatory. The once celebrated interpreter of the works of Beethoven was now prohibited from even playing any of Beethoven's music. Cruelly divested of his life's work, Arnold sank into complete despair. The triumphant era of Vienna's Mahler-Rosé family had ended.

To manage the Third Reich's removal of the Jewish pestilence, the Nazi government placed Adolf Eichmann, a high-ranking Nazi official from Austria, in charge of "encouraging" Jewish emigration. The Nazis hoped that intense discrimination and calculated violence toward the Jews would incentivize them to leave. To this end, Eichmann created the *Zentralstelle für jüdische Auswanderung* (Central Office for Jewish Emigration), an administrative agency that would be the sole issuer of exit permits. During the first six months after the Anschluss, Eichmann's agency processed the departure of around 45,000 Austrian Jews. Meanwhile, his organization secretly registered all of the Jews living in Germany and Austria, and then later used these rosters to round up individuals for deportation to ghettos and concentration camps. Indeed, through his office, Eichmann facilitated the entire bureaucratic machine that enabled the Nazis to commit genocide on such an unprecedented level. After the war, Eichmann fled to Argentina to avoid prosecution, but the Israeli Security Service eventually apprehended him in 1960. After being found guilty of heinous war crimes at a trial in Jerusalem, Adolf Eichmann was hanged on June 1, 1962.

Stunned and appalled by the events in Vienna following the Anschluss, many musicians around the world boycotted performances there, including famed conductor Arturo Toscanini, who cancelled his conducting engagement at the prestigious Salzburg Festival. Others followed suit, and the festival organizers scrambled to fill the mounting vacancies. But while this solidarity certainly provided some comfort, none of these gestures changed anything about the daily struggles for the Rosé family. Fortunately for Alma, the fact that she retained a Czech passport from her marriage did benefit her during this time because it caused Austria's Nazi government to label her a foreign Jew, which meant that she was not subject to impending arrest. Nevertheless, Alma still needed to exercise great caution in avoiding any forbidden areas or activities, including marriage to Heini. Alma could have actually left Austria immediately via her Czech papers, but her mother and father desperately needed her, so she stayed to care for both. As a young Jewish man, Alfred faced imminent risk of apprehension and indeed heard rumors that his name had been placed on an arrest list. So, he desperately renewed his efforts to secure sponsorship and a position outside of the Third Reich.

Alma's mother deteriorated rapidly in the summer of 1938, and because of their total loss of income, the once prosperous Rosé family had to rely on friends to pay for Justine's medicine and medical care. On August 22, 1938, Justine Mahler Rosé died at age 69. Now, without his beloved wife and his music, Arnold felt particularly isolated in Vienna. Many of his close friends had fled, and others he had thought were his friends, such as Richard Strauss, no longer visited. During the dark days after her divorce and throughout her mother's illness, Alma clung to the philosophical writings of the Roman statesman Seneca. Following the funeral, she handed a copy of his essays to her brother Alfred, in which she inscribed, "May this book help you as much as you have helped us live through this our worst time, I am, in the truest sense, your sister."[4] Whether this gift meant much to Alfred at the time remains unknown, but its presence on his bedside table at the time of his death in 1975 testifies to the unbreakable bond he shared with the giver.

Having finally received commitments of sponsorship from friends in Holland and the United States, Alfred and his wife Maria departed Vienna on September 28, 1938. That same day would become known as "Black Wednesday," because of Hitler's campaign to reacquire the Sudetenland, a territory ceded from Austria to Czechoslovakia as part of The Treaty of Versailles at the end of World War I. With three million Germans still living in the region, Hitler demanded the complete surrender of the land to Germany by September 28, otherwise he would launch an armed invasion. Hitler pledged to world leaders that he would not attempt to acquire any additional Czech land after the annexation of the Sudetenland, and as a result, they capitulated to him. Not surprisingly, within just a few weeks, Hitler began drafting plans to procure all of Czechoslovakia; and if Hitler controlled Czechoslovakia, then it would no longer harbor a safe haven for Alma Rosé.

Aware of the Rosé family's desperate financial straits, their good friend in England, violinist Carl Flesch, created a relief fund, and many people who greatly admired Arnold Rosé contributed, including former U.S. First Lady Elizabeth Sprague Coolidge. Alma briefly left Vienna on October 29, 1938, to meet with acquaintances in several countries in hopes of garnering the necessary sponsorship for her father to exit Vienna with her and Heini. In addition to visiting with Carl Flesch, she met with Sir Adrian Boult to propose the resurrection of the Rosé String Quartet in London, with herself playing second violin and Friedrich Buxbaum, who had already fled Vienna for England, on cello. Meanwhile, Bruno Walter pulled strings with his connections to expedite the paperwork needed for the Rosé family to enter England. The assistance fund that Flesch had started now contained £300, which would be sufficient to pay the necessary fees. Alma arrived home in the early hours of Christmas morning and excitedly shared the details of her successful trip with her father. Again, it appeared that Alma's strength and determination had made the impossible possible. But still, they continued to jump through relentless bureaucratic hoops in Vienna during the first few months of 1939. The pressure for a speedy departure weighed on them, especially since government officials had ordered Alma and her father to vacate their home on Pyrkergasse by the beginning of March so it could be turned over to an Aryan family.

By this time, Alfred and Maria had arrived in the United States, where he sought to establish himself in the musical world by placing ads that cited his pedigree as the nephew of Gustav Mahler. In just a few months, they relayed the wonderful news that Alfred was teaching and that some of his compositions were being performed. But back in Vienna, Alma worked so feverishly to navigate the immigration labyrinth that she fell quite ill in February with a throat infection and nervous exhaustion. Fortunately, the new intended residents of the Rosé home extended unexpected generosity, agreeing to delay their occupancy until the Rosé family could sort out its affairs. On March 15, 1939, Hitler finally succeeded in appropriating all of Czechoslovakia for the Third Reich, and with it, rendered Alma's Czech passport virtually useless. Rather than risk losing their window of opportunity, Alma and Heini fled Vienna for London that same day. Since her father's passport had been delayed, she arranged for him to stay with friends in Vienna while this last necessary piece processed. Alma felt especially relieved that she had been able to leave Vienna with both of their precious violins and with the gold watch that Emperor Franz Josef had given her father. Less than two months later, on May 1, Arnold joined them in England. Before departing Vienna, Arnold visited his wife's grave one more time, and as he stared at the headstone designed with room for his name too, he fervently hoped that he was not parting from his beloved homeland forever.

Alma and her father amused themselves in their early days in London by playing music together, but unable to find work, Heini grew increasingly restless. At the end of June, one of his friends and a friend of his father's arrived unannounced in London and admonished Heini to return to Vienna, citing the inevitability of war with England. They emphasized that in London he would be labeled an "enemy" and sent to an internment camp. Convinced, Heini cowardly snuck away without telling Alma. After learning of his abandonment, Alma became inconsolable. Heini continued to write her, professing his love and his belief that they would be reunited after the war. She never saw him again.

At age 32, Alma now assumed the sole responsibility of caring for her aging father, as well as learning to cook and manage a household. Fortunately, as she had intended, the Rosé String Quartet reconstituted, and those paid performances helped their precarious financial situation somewhat. Alma had also planned to start a women's orchestra in London, but could not get her British work permit expanded to allow for anything beyond the quartet. Once money became tight again, their friend Bruno Walter encouraged Arnold to sell "Mysa," the 1718 Stradivari violin he had been given in 1913 as an expression of gratitude for his contributions to the musical life of Vienna. But Alma asserted her strong will, adamant that they would never part with that violin, and instead began to explore performance options in Holland, a country she hoped would remain neutral in the event of a war, as it had in World War I.

Meanwhile, the Third Reich's aggressive campaign to usurp as much European territory as possible continued unabated throughout 1939. On September 1, Germany invaded Poland, and as sworn allies of Poland, France and Britain declared war on September 3. The Nazi agenda had now given rise to another world war. By the end of September, Poland succumbed to the complete control of the Third Reich, an extremely difficult outcome for the proud Poles and an especially frightening reality for its large Jewish population. Gerda Weissmann Klein, who had been a young Jewish girl living in Poland at the time, described the terrible transformation. "I realized that we were outsiders, strangers in our own home, at the mercy of those who until then had been our friends. Although I was only fifteen I had a strong feeling, more instinct than reason, that our lives were no longer our own, but lay in the hands of a deadly enemy."[5]

Setting aside fears of Nazi advancement on Holland, Alma decided on November 6 to accept the two-month contract she had been offered to perform at the Grand Hotel Central in The Hague, but requested permission from the British government to be gone for up to five months. Arnold supported her decision and secured a substitute for Alma in his quartet for their impending engagements. But as time went on, he grew anxious and implored her to come home because of the unpredictable nature of the Nazi leadership. Alma, however, was experiencing so many musical successes in Holland, including solo performing opportunities, that she delayed her return.

In April 1940, Hitler attacked the next targets on his list—Norway and Denmark. Although it seemed inevitable that the Low Countries of Belgium, Holland, and Luxembourg would soon follow, Alma overstayed her permitted time in Holland, which had expired on May 2. Friends pleaded with her to leave for England, but again she refused to relinquish her newfound musical life. The Germans invaded a few days later on May 10 and easily conquered the Low Countries. Alma had made a devastating miscalculation and was trapped with no way to return to her father. The Nazi scourge seemed to know no limits, as most of the European continent, about a hundred million people, now languished irretrievably in their possession.

With the capitulation of the Low Countries, Nazi policies became the law of the land in Holland as they had in other occupied territories, forcing Jews to register. Understandably, Alma felt frantic, especially from her inability to contact her father directly or to send him money. She at least found some solace in the fact that she had secretly carried the provenance papers for her father's Stradivari violin with her to Holland, for fear that he would sell it while she was gone. Alma's life in Holland no longer showered her with the musical opportunities that had retained her there injudiciously. Sometimes she could still get work as a violinist and sometimes not. Alma would have been completely without income if it had not been for "house concerts," private performances in homes that had emerged as a way for musicians and patrons to circumvent Nazi restrictions in Holland and throughout the Third Reich. She wrote anxious letters to her brother and other acquaintances trying to secure sponsorship in the United States. Alfred worked diligently on both Alma and their father's behalf, but without a job contract with an orchestra or for a teaching position, they would not be granted entry. Forced to relocate frequently, Alma always managed to find someone willing to take her in, although the conditions could be less than ideal at times. In one home, she slept on a bench in the dining room, and another place was so cold that she developed chilblains on her hands and pain from arthritis. But continuing to receive passionate letters of devotion from Heini buoyed her spirits, until abruptly, his letters stopped. After an extended period of silence, he wrote one more time on December 20, 1940, to inform her of his recent nuptials.

Despite her difficulties and moments of despair and anxiety, Alma consistently impressed those she encountered with her commanding presence and formidable will. She enjoyed a brief respite from worry when two affidavits from the United States arrived at the U.S. consulate in Rotterdam on June 11, 1941. These documents constituted part of the essential paperwork needed for immigration to the U.S. But unfortunately, they reached her too late, as heightened tensions between the U.S. and Germany caused each to shut down their respective government offices a few days later, which halted any further application processing. By August, Alma urgently grasped at other possible solutions, including relocation to Cuba, but the continuously shifting political winds made finding any resolution nearly impossible. After the Japanese bombing at Pearl Harbor on December 7, 1941, and the subsequent entry of the U.S. in the war, Alma could no longer exchange lengthy letters with Alfred, which had been such a vital lifeline for her. They continued to relay some messages back and forth through the Red Cross, but these were limited to 25 words. Regardless of the circumstances, though, Alma's beauty and sensuous demeanor had never left her lacking for suitors, and she found herself again in a relationship and in love. Her latest paramour was Leonard Jongkees, a physician six years younger, who played the cello and had been performing chamber music with her since the summer of 1941.

As the Nazi plan shifted toward the "Final Solution" in the early days of 1942, life for Jews in the Third Reich worsened exponentially. In Holland, the walls were swiftly closing in as the SS began to utilize the Dutch camp Westerbork as a transit camp for Jews slated for death camps in the East, instead of its intended purpose as a German refugee camp. One Jewish family living in Amsterdam, the Franks, had fled to the Netherlands as a safe haven from Germany in 1933 after the rise of Hitler. The Nazi presence in Holland now forced the Frank family into hiding on July 9, 1942. Their youngest daughter, 13-year-old Anne, kept a diary of those two years spent secreted away, before their betrayal and deportation to Auschwitz on September 6, 1944. Nazi officials later transferred Anne, along with her mother and sister, to Bergen-Belsen concentration camp in October 1944, where they all three died in the early months of 1945. Only her father Otto survived the camps. After the war, he recovered her diary that still lay in their "secret annex." *The Diary of a Young Girl* would become one of the most important and moving testaments to the horrors of the Holocaust. In her journal entry on April 4, 1944, a few months before their arrest, Anne had presciently written, "I want to go on living even after my death!"[6]

At the start of 1942, the only recourse remaining for Alma seemed to be marriage to a non–Jew, which might provide a modicum of protection. Even though her lover Leonard met the necessary requirements, Alma stubbornly refused for their relationship to become a pawn forced by political circumstances, so she and friends sought another match. They finally settled on 34-year-old Constant (Connie) August van Leeuwen Boomkamp, a perfect candidate since he was known to wander aimlessly as a spoiled, wealthy vagabond, and to have absolutely no interest in women. Their marriage took place on March 4, 1942, after which, she and Connie unceremoniously went their separate ways, assuming no actual marital responsibilities.

In June of that year, Adolf Eichmann announced deportation plans for 40,000 Jews from Holland to labor camps, although in actuality, the gas chambers were the intended destination for many. People whom Alma knew started disappearing, and she remained uncertain as to whether they had been deported, managed to escape, or had burrowed down into hiding. Alma's turn for arrest came on August 2 when officials stormed into the home she shared with friends and took her to a former theater in Amsterdam named the Hollandse Schouwburg, where thousands of people awaited deportation to the East. Fortunately, Alma could still rely on her dear friend, the lawyer Marie Anne Tellegen, whose connections and assistance in contacting Alma's "husband" Connie managed to secure her release later that same evening. The whole incident left Alma shaken to the core. It would also be the only time that her recent marriage would save her. The Nazis had discovered the trend of sham marriages, and by September 1942, only mixed marriages where children had been produced or the Jewish partner submitted to voluntary sterilization afforded them any protection.

Alma's continued survival, as did that of so many other Jews in Holland, depended daily on kind-hearted and courageous Dutch people, who put their own lives at risk to save individuals from Nazi atrocities. One of the most well-known of these families was the Ten Booms, watchmakers by trade who resided in Haarlem, about 20 miles from Amsterdam. One of their daughters, Corrie Ten Boom, had actually become Holland's first female-licensed watchmaker in 1924 at age 32. In 1942, she became affiliated with the underground Dutch Resistance, and the family constructed a hiding place in their home. For two years, she and her family hid and saved an estimated 800 people. Arrested on February 28, 1944, Corrie and her sister Betsie ended up in Ravensbrück concentration camp in September 1944. The only family member to survive the war, Corrie published a powerful memoir in 1971 at age 79, which detailed her time in the Resistance and in the camps, aptly called *The Hiding Place*.[7]

In November 1942, sensing that her days were numbered, Alma drafted a will instructing that her possessions not go to her husband, but to her friend Marie Anne Tellegen, who would also assume responsibility for funeral arrangements. When Alma received the order from the Gestapo to report to Westerbork, she ignored the urgings of her friends and Leonard to go into hiding and instead decided that an escape attempt to Switzerland remained her only viable option. Alma entrusted her treasured 1757 Guadagnini violin, which her father had purchased in 1924, with Leonard for safe keeping, and all of her other possessions to Marie. In the early morning hours of December 14, Alma Rosé quietly disappeared through an underground network destined to convey her through Belgium and France to the Swiss border.

After several harrowing days of clandestine meetings and covert destinations, Alma was apprehended by Gestapo agents on December 19, 1942, in Dijon, France, already aboard the train bound for Switzerland—a mere 90 minutes from freedom. She had most likely been betrayed by the man she had just paid for her false papers. Authorities transferred Alma to Drancy internment camp on January 12, 1943, where some estimated 76,000 Jews would wait during the war for deportation to concentration camps, most destined for Auschwitz. Horribly overcrowded, Drancy was a miserable place with little food and much disease. At least, Alma could send letters to her friends in Holland, and she hoped that their influence, particularly Marie Tellegen's, would facilitate her release. She especially needed her marriage documents that she had left behind in Utretcht, where she had lived for the past year and a half with her dear friends Paul and Marye Staercke. Ever resourceful, Marie arranged for an acquaintance traveling to Paris to smuggle Alma's papers ingeniously wrapped in sandwiches in her lunch bag. But despite numerous interventions, none succeeded, and pressure from high-ranking Nazi officials to increase the number of transports to Auschwitz sealed Alma's fate, particularly when Adolf Eichmann placed an ambitious and ruthless Austrian, SS Captain Alois Brunner, in charge of meeting these quotas. Seven months after her arrest in Dijon, Alma climbed into a cattle car along with a thousand other Jewish prisoners at 9 a.m. on Sunday, July 18, 1943. At age 36, Alma Rosé, a Viennese violinist of the highest pedigree, headed toward Auschwitz. Fewer than 60 of those on board would survive to witness the end of the war.

The German word *Gleichschaltung*, which simply means "coordination," became the all-inclusive term used to reference the envisioning and constructing of approximately 5,000 concentration camps in Third Reich territories. The *Konzentrationslager* (concentration camp) or simply *KZ* represented one of the most critical components in the Nazi strategy to contain and dispose of those that Hitler deemed *Untermenschen* (subhumans). The Reich constructed six concentration camps in Poland. Built in 1940, Auschwitz stood as the largest and most notorious of the Nazi death camps. Even the phrase "being shipped East" was considered synonymous with being sent there. About 30 miles southwest of Krakow, the town of Osweicim, Poland, supported a population of around 12,000 in 1939, including 5,000 Jews. The Germans renamed the town Auschwitz that year, following Poland's defeat. Heinrich Himmler, the Nazi architect of the Jewish extermination plan, selected this town because of its choice geographic location. This area's natural resources would provide an excellent place for German citizens to live, as soon as the Poles and Jews disappeared. The Nazi government also regarded it as an ideal spot for industry. The I.G. Farben Company began constructing a plant there in 1941, with labor provided by camp prisoners.

As a grandiose Nazi initiative, Auschwitz evolved into a giant, organic complex of subcamps. The main camp, known later as Auschwitz I, functioned at first as a labor camp for Polish political prisoners, receiving its inaugural transport of detainees in June 1940. These same Polish prisoners were tasked with the job of constructing the main gate and fashioning the wrought-iron slogan that would perch on the top—*Arbeit Macht Frei* (Work Sets You Free). This mocking statement would serve to greet new arrivals, for whom no amount of labor would free them from Auschwitz's death grip. As with many of the Nazi trappings, this phrase had not been of their own creation. It had been borrowed from the title of a novel by a 19th century German librarian, minister, and linguist named Lorenz Diefenbach. In his novel, the protagonist, a man who has made his livelihood via cheating, rehabilitates himself through honest work. The Nazis especially enjoyed such a hateful twisting of this sentiment. Under the direction of master blacksmith Jan Liwacz, the Auschwitz prisoners ordered to place those infamous words on the gate decided to voice their resistance by inverting the letter B.[8] The camp command never noticed the upside down B, and under the auspices of that cynical motto, guards subjected inmates to brutal conditions, torture, and execution. Auschwitz would be forever remembered as a well-crafted accomplice to mass genocide.

In October 1941, construction began on a second satellite camp, known as Birkenau or sometimes Auschwitz II, situated a little less than two miles from the main camp. Much larger than Auschwitz I, Birkenau was capable of housing three times the number of prisoners through an elaborate system of subcamps that segregated men, women, Roma, and other categories of inmates. Charged with the primary mission of extermination, Birkenau contained numerous gas chambers and crematoria. It actually housed four out of the five total crematoria at Auschwitz, which burned continuously, with the capacity to incinerate at least 5,000 corpses per day. A special prisoner label detail, the *Sonderkommando*, was forced to carry out some of the most dehumanizing work in the camp—the disposal of corpses through the cremation protocol. Nazi officials added Monowitz, a third auxiliary camp, in 1942 to house labor for the I.G. Buna, also known as I.G. Farben, chemical plant.

The usual transportation for prisoners to Auschwitz involved overcrowded cattle cars, where the only food or drink available was whatever the deportees had managed to bring themselves. The SS inhumanely packed these cars to such an extent that people had to take turns lying down, with only a bucket in the corner to relieve themselves. They might languish for days in these conditions with no respite. Once the train pulled up to the camp platform, guards ordered everyone out of the cattle cars and into lines separated by male and female. SS doctors then began the process known as "selection," a standard sorting procedure used at death camps. After giving each person a cursory glance, doctors ordered some to head toward the right. These had been selected as strong enough to work. Others, particularly the old, very young, or infirm, they motioned to the left, often separating them from their family members who had been sent in the opposite direction. These unfortunate souls climbed into awaiting trucks emblazoned with the Red Cross symbol, an especially heinous Nazi trick to disguise the conveyance that would take its passengers straight to the gas chambers. The charade continued as guards convinced the condemned that they were being taken to showers, admonishing them to remember where they left their clothes and luggage for retrieval after bathing. But no water spewed from the shower heads, only the deadly nerve gas Zyklon B, which caused lung paralysis, suffocating its victims in three to 15 minutes. The Reich then took possession of their belongings and even extracted the gold from the teeth of the corpses.

Unaware of what had befallen their fellow passengers, those who had "passed" the initial selection now endured a barbarous initiation ritual performed by Auschwitz prisoners. Stripped naked with their heads newly shaved, the recent arrivals faced the final dehumanizing blow to their dignity, having an identification number tattooed in blue ink on their left arm. In the early years of Auschwitz, prisoners were issued striped uniforms, but by the end of the war, depleted supplies left some prisoners to wear whatever ill-fitting, mismatched clothes could be obtained from the stockpile, which were then painted with a large white × on the back so that escapees could be easily recognized. After processing, guards ordered the inmates to barracks in the overcrowded Quarantine Blocks, where as many as six shared one wooden bunk. Disease ran rampant there, in addition to deprivation of every kind. Some never survived beyond this initial stop. Those who did learned to fear the additional selections that constituted a daily part of life at Auschwitz, a Nazi tool to alleviate overcrowding, combat disease, and basically rid the camp population of anyone no longer useful.

Auschwitz functioned as its own microcosm, with a defined hierarchy not only of guards and officials, but also among the inmates. For every housing barrack, referred to as a block, camp guards appointed a fellow prisoner as block leader, the *Blockova*. These leaders became quite powerful within the prison population because they possessed the authority to punish or report the other prisoners in their block and especially since they controlled the daily distribution of the food rations, from which they frequently stole an extra share for themselves. Other choice duty assignments existed in Auschwitz, such as working in the camp hospital or the storehouse, and any prisoner assigned to one of these also ranked higher in the pecking order.

Most camps maintained a well-stocked storehouse filled with all kinds of items that had been stolen from the arriving prisoners, including musical instruments, shoes, eye glasses, and jewelry. At Auschwitz, this warehouse bore the nickname "Canada," somehow related to that country's status as a wealthy nation. Prisoners covertly acquired the supplies they needed from Canada by a bartering process known as "organizing." Bread represented the most valuable currency, and with enough bread to trade, almost anything could be obtained. According to Auschwitz survivor Zippy Spitzer, "You could laugh about death, our constant companion, but you could not joke about food, our greatest need."[9]

For the average prisoner without special status, the mortality rate figured especially high in Auschwitz, where brutal conditions could result in debilitating exhaustion and starvation in as little as a few weeks. Guards commanded the prisoners to line up in the early morning in rows of five for *Appell* (roll call) and then marched them to their work details. Completely drained, with some carrying their ill or even dead comrades, prisoners marched back into camp at evening to be counted again. The guards might also torture their captives with a surprise roll call in the middle of the night, forcing them to stand at attention in the elements for hours, all with the awareness that they would be sent to the gas chamber if they moved or appeared too weak to work the next day. But frequently, inmates did collapse during *Appell*, unable either mentally or physically to endure any longer.

Those in the shocking final stage of physical and mental exhaustion became known as *Muselmänner* (living skeletons). Crazed by hunger and thirst, these inmates appeared to have little recognition that they were still alive. Instead, they remained briefly suspended in time as their bodies and souls negotiated that last transition from the living to the dead. The deceased in Auschwitz then made yet one more conversion—from blood and bone to ash. With multiple crematoria incinerating corpses around-the-clock, the most overwhelming and unforgettable image of Auschwitz became the air, always thick with black smoke and greasy ashes that rained down, accompanied by the sickening smell of charred flesh that filled the nostrils. The whole of Auschwitz, a deranged human terrarium teeming with depraved treatment and regulated by unrepentant misanthropes, even became too much for the SS to handle at times. Heinz Thilo, a well-known SS doctor who conducted selections, christened the place, *anus mundi* (anus of the world), a descriptive phrase that would be forever linked with Auschwitz.[10]

After five years of unspeakable horrors, Auschwitz would finally be liberated by Soviet troops on January 27, 1945. The total number of people shipped there remains unknown because most were gassed upon arrival and therefore not entered into the written records. According to the tattoo numbers, the camp officially registered 404,222. Rudolf Höss, who had served as the Commandant of Auschwitz, claimed after the war that 2.5 million were murdered there, but scholars estimate that death count at closer to 1.6 million. In the end, only about 65,000 prisoners, or less than one percent, actually survived Auschwitz.

It was into this unspeakably wicked place that Alma Rosé, a member of one of Vienna's most prestigious families, arrived on July 20, 1943, after three miserable days spent crammed in a cattle car. Out of the one thousand prisoners with her, the SS ordered at least half to the left and immediate death, including 126 children. Having been sorted to the right, Alma marched toward Auschwitz I, where she suffered the usual induction, her arm now declaring her #50381. She was not, however, sent to the Quarantine Blocks. Instead, officials slated her for Block 10, the experimental medicine block, made infamous because Dr. Josef Mengele, later known as the "Angel of Death," and many other doctors performed horrific pseudo-medical experiments there. Gynecological issues held particular interest, and doctors frequently applied radiation to the ovaries of prisoners to predict its effectiveness as a mass sterilization protocol. Dr. Mengele's primary research focused on twin studies, and he acquired any sets of identical twins that entered Auschwitz. The camp's Block 10 revealed one of the many maniacal paradoxes surrounding the Nazi mentality. Known as great lovers of animals and champions of conservation, the Nazis censured a biologist for not giving worms enough anesthesia during an experiment. At the same time, they applauded the SS doctors for their sadistic research on human beings, which included crude surgeries without any anesthesia.

Many prisoners who had medical training, both nurses and doctors, were assigned to work in Block 10. Again, as in countless times in the past, Alma's reputation came to her rescue. One of the prisoner-nurses at Block 10, a young Dutch woman named Ima van Esso, recognized her. Alma had actually been to her family's home many times to play music with Ima's mother, a singer, and to accompany Ima herself on the flute. Straight away, Alma asked Ima for a violin. Believing that her life would end soon, she wanted the solace of her music. Divorce notwithstanding, Alma justified her request by emphasizing her status as the wife of Váša Příhoda, who was more revered and well known there in Eastern Europe than her own family. The block leader, a Jewish prisoner from Hungary named Magda Hellinger, sent a message to the Birkenau main office where Helen "Zippy" Spitzer, an ever resourceful prisoner, notified camp officials of Alma's presence and requested a violin. Zippy indeed worked her magic, and a very fine violin was delivered to Alma. At 6 p.m. after the SS left the block, Alma played, the beauty of her music filling Block 10 and uplifting those present. Alma continued the nightly concerts, while the prisoner-workers shielded her during the day from becoming the subject of any medical procedures or experiments. Along with the Polish actress Mila Potasinski, Alma organized evening cabarets that the women who were well enough participated in with great joy and abandon. Eventually, Alma's violin playing brought her to the attention of Maria Mandel, the *Lagerfuhrerin* or head of the Birkenau women's camp. Mandel had formed a fledgling women's orchestra there and believed that someone as talented and pedigreed as Alma Rosé could elevate it into an impressive ensemble. For Alma, Mandel's interest brought the realization that this place of horror possessed an orchestra, a co-existence that she struggled to reconcile.

But in fact, a wide range of musical activities occurred in the ghettos and the camps, some formally organized as orchestras and choirs, but others more unstructured. The use of music, particularly singing, among people facing adversity spanned a long and documented history. For the captives, music and other cultural activities helped them maintain a sense, however fleeting, of normalcy and familiarity, which they would sustain until the point that their circumstances became so dire from disease, starvation, or other forms of deprivation that these endeavors could no longer continue.

The level of suffering during the Holocaust created a need for music to an unprecedented degree. Spontaneous music-making in the form of singing happened frequently in the cattle cars as deportees tried to comfort one another and distract themselves from their own fear and hunger. Once in the camps, some remarked that by singing or humming a tune, they could preserve a piece of their identity. They might retain very little that represented their former selves and be known solely by a number tattooed on their arm, but they could have a signature tune, a *leitmotif*, that their oppressors could not steal. To that end, *Lager-lieder* (concentration camp songs) developed as a new genre. These songs circulated among the inmates and spread throughout the entire camp system as prisoners relocated. For those composing or performing music, particularly songs, they could attach a varied narrative, from espousing their own religious or political beliefs to condemning their Nazi oppressors. But often, the refrains were just meant to provide affirmation and encouragement; and the more conditions deteriorated, the more they desperately clung to any message of hope.

But although the use of music as spiritual resistance and empowerment in the Holocaust remains widely documented, historian Shirli Gilbert cautions that music's presence and function in the camps and ghettos cannot always be viewed that simply or reductively.[11] For one reason, the camp environment did not allow for unmitigated solidarity among inmates. Because of the vast variation in the status and hierarchy of prisoners based on ethnic and political backgrounds, among many other factors, music could not always be available for all. The more voluntary acts of music tended to occur among the "privileged" inmates, and musical opportunities were rarely experienced homogeneously in any given situation. All involved were human and therefore subject to rapid change and contradiction in response to their attempts to understand and cope with the situations they faced. Music, as an art form, was also not inviolable nor immune to contamination and corruption by both sides. While it might be easier to polarize camp happenings to black and white and to label people as either demons or heroes, the captors and captives involved were often more complicated and nuanced than that, neither wholly saints nor sadists, victims nor defilers. Dr. Primo Levi, a Jewish-Italian chemist sent to Auschwitz in February 1944 at age 25, penned numerous memoirs and novels that chronicled his experiences in the camp before tragically committing suicide in 1987. In *The Drowned and the Saved,* he posited that there existed a gray zone, an area of moral ambiguity, in which it was not possible to divide people into only good or evil. He clearly described the moral collapse that he had witnessed among fellow prisoners and then soberly admonished that similarly horrendous deeds could happen again because of the fickle and sieve-like nature of human memory.[12]

For Shirli Gilbert, the attempt to counteract criticism about any perceived passivity on the part of the Jews also colors the way that music and other forms of spiritual resistance have been described.[13] Although there were certainly examples of armed uprisings, often the defiant struggle manifested through music, theater, and other artistic media. For those who survived the war, the stories of these activities provided tangible evidence that something had yielded from their suffering—that it had not been in vain. Frequently, the lack of actual physical resistance resulted from the Nazis' carefully orchestrated plans of deception and misinformation that left victims rarely knowing what was happening to them or how to parse rumor from fact. That their circumstances felt so unbelievable contributed as well. By the time they finally realized the true nature of their plight, it was often too late to intervene. In her memoir, *All But My Life*, survivor Gerda Weissmann Klein testified to this reality.

> Why did we walk like meek sheep to the slaughterhouse? Why did we not fight back? What had we to lose? Nothing but our lives. Why did we not run away and hide? We might have had a chance to survive. Why did we walk deliberately and obediently into their clutches? I know why. Because we had

faith in humanity. Because we did not really think that human beings were capable of committing such crimes.[14]

But while music did provide solace and even survival in some cases for those imprisoned in concentration camps, their captors employed music as a means of degradation, deception, and manipulation that compounded the suffering. The Nazis fully realized the power of music and how it could be siphoned to accomplish their purposes, which in some cases just meant humiliation or torment. In the camps, for example, prisoners were forced to sing about how happy they felt and how wonderful the food tasted. Anyone who did not sing with convincing enthusiasm received a severe punishment. At times, the guards even ordered inmates to sing on their way to the gas chambers. Music proved an especially effective means of manipulation, and the Nazi command often used it to lull new camp arrivals into a false complacency, thereby reducing the threat of resistance. In the Belzec death camp, however, the orchestra was forced to taunt arriving captives by performing the popular German song, "Everything Passes, Everything Goes By."

But sometimes the musical exploitation by Reich guards and soldiers stemmed from more practical motivations. Music performed by prisoners or played over loudspeakers was frequently used to mask the sounds of Nazi violence. In September 1941 at the massacre of Babi Yar in Ukraine, *Einsatzgruppen* (Nazi mobile killing units) slaughtered 34,000 Jews in just two days, while loudspeakers blasted music to cover the screams and gunfire. In the camps, officials appropriated music as the accompaniment to forced activities, such as marching to and from work details, and formed ensembles, especially bands and orchestras, to accomplish this task. They had no trouble "recruiting" musicians for these ensembles due to such vast pools of prisoners and to the realization among the inmates that special skills made them particularly valuable to their captors, subsequently providing a possible path to survival. In the end, their music certainly pointed to "…a bitter irony that the Austro-German music tradition held in such high esteem by the third generation of emancipated, assimilated Jews was last heard wafting across the tundra and barbed wire of Eastern Europe's death camps, played by desperate inmates, most of whom would not survive."[15]

Of the various musical happenings in the camps, the morning and evening marching music accounted for the most consistent utilization of music, becoming ritualistic. The Nazis reveled in sadistic pleasure as their favorite tunes created a soundtrack to humiliation and obedience when the prisoners marched in and out of the camps twice a day. This counterpoint left a vividly morbid impression on Primo Levi, which stayed with him for the rest of his life.

> The tunes are few, a dozen, the same ones every day, morning and evening: marches and popular songs dear to every German. They lie engraven on our minds and will be the last thing in Lager [Camp] that we shall forget: they are the voice of the Lager, the perceptible expression of its geometrical madness, of the resolution of others to annihilate us first as men in order to kill us more slowly afterwards….
> When this music plays we know that our comrades, out in the fog, are marching like automatons; their souls are dead and the music drives them, like the wind drives dead leaves, and takes the place of their wills. There is no longer any will: every beat of the drum becomes a step, a reflected contraction of exhausted muscles.[16]

As a companion to their abusive intents, the Nazis also relied on music personally as a means to uphold and cling to what they highly valued in German culture. In yet another paradox, these German oppressors retained an enduring love for music and a desire to surround themselves with it, while simultaneously utilizing it in diabolically cruel ways.

In fact, Himmler actually instructed his officers to use music to help soothe and maintain the mental health of the soldiers under their command who had to carry out such "difficult tasks." The unfathomable contradiction of remorseless murder coupled with musical pleasure appears through the story of Shony Alex Braun, a violin prodigy from Romania, who was arrested at age 13 and sent to Auschwitz. After being transferred to Dachau and on the verge of starvation and hopelessness, Shony recalled that one day an SS officer entered his barracks with a violin and said that he would give food to whoever could play it to his satisfaction. In addition to Shony, two others volunteered. The first man played Bach quite well, but the officer beat him to death anyway. The second, now too frightened to play, was executed on the spot. Having no other choice but to play, Shony chose the beloved *Blue Danube Waltz*, and even though it had been a year since he last played, his music pleased the officer. After that, Shony regularly entertained the SS in exchange for food, and these extra rations helped him to survive the war.

The psychopathic acts of Dr. Mengele, in particular, demonstrate a pathological enmeshment between violence and music. In charge of the selection process for new arrivals at Auschwitz, Mengele often chose as many as 90 percent to be sent directly to the gas chambers. Survivors remember that he often whistled favorite classical tunes by Mozart and other composers as he so nonchalantly condemned these people to death. An avid lover and consumer of art music and opera, Mengele, like so many of his compatriots, could juxtapose music with their insidious behaviors, creating a conundrum that may never be fully deciphered. Somehow, pleasurable and sentimental feelings toward music could be compartmentalized from the hatred and violence exhibited toward fellow human beings. The ability to exert complete control over another, with all boundaries of humanity and decency removed, allowed an animalistic and instinctual side capable of gross atrocities to surface.

Of all of the musical connections associated with the Final Solution, the implementation of compulsory music labor in the concentration camps of the Third Reich, particularly the *Lagerkapelle* (camp orchestra/band), has probably generated the most research and speculation. Orchestras and other music ensembles existed in almost all of the large concentration camps. For example, Belzec had a six-member ensemble often forced to play next to the gas chambers to accompany corpse removal, as well as to entertain the SS. Treblinka, second only to Auschwitz in the number of murders, housed an orchestra, two choirs, and a jazz band, all directed by a prisoner named Arthur Gold, who had been a well-known musician in Warsaw. Because so many accomplished musicians were sent to the camps, these inmate orchestras often played quite well. But for music historian Gabriele Knapp, the term "orchestra" fails to capture the disturbing reality of music making as forced labor, and she has suggested that a more apt term for the group would be "Music Command."[17] Regardless of the nomenclature, these prisoner ensembles became an integral part of daily camp life, with their primary role being to play music for the work details. Even though many of the inmates could barely walk, the Nazis insisted that they march completely in step as they went to and from the camp, and so to that end, music set the cadence. This process sometimes took up to two and a half hours, during which the orchestra played continuously without a break.

The camp guards sometimes forced ensembles to perform popular songs about life and happiness, which did nothing to cheer the captives, but merely reminded them of how much they had lost. Some prisoners despised and even spat at orchestra members, whom they perceived as having it "good" in the camp or as colluding with their captors. Trapped in this netherworld between their fellow inmates and the camp command, with music as an instrument of conscription, the ensemble members waged a terrible battle with their very souls. According to Helena Dunicz Niwińska, one of the Birkenau violinists, "There was something infernal about the music we played. We quickly began to realize this, and we therefore went through moral dilemmas and spiritual conflicts about whether we should play or not."[18]

When the orchestras had to play for the dying in the infirmary, their music did not always comfort; instead, some screamed to be left alone to die in peace. Many of the survivors of the camp orchestras recounted that it took all of their strength to make themselves play music that facilitated the Nazi killing apparatus. Yet at the same time, they lacked an alternative to following orders, just like the rest of the camp population. Helena certainly experienced the weight of this reality. "The feeling of total impotence against violence and injustice that overwhelmed each prisoner brought paralysis in both physical and mental terms. Any attempt to appeal to justice or the law was simply out of the question."[19]

Indeed, feelings of guilt and complicity weighed heavily on many, even occasionally leading to suicide. Leon Bloorman, who had taught violin at the Jewish Conservatory of Music in Rotterdam, Holland, was forced one day to play "Le Marseillaise," the French national anthem, while the guards hanged a French prisoner. Afterwards, he could not come to terms with this debasement to himself personally and to his life's work. A few nights later, he committed suicide by charging the electric fence. When the orchestra assembled the next morning for rehearsal, they found the violinist's dead body tied to his orchestra chair, a cruel taunt from the guards. After the war, the orchestra survivors dealt with these disturbing experiences in different ways. Some continued to make music, even becoming well-known performers, while others totally abandoned music, not being able to continue an activity they associated with such grief and violence. Ultimately, the circumstances of their particular ordeal left them somewhat isolated from other survivor-artists as they struggled with the reality that their captors had forced music to emerge as the only art form to have collaborated in the genocide of the Jews.[20]

But despite the relatively small remnant that Holocaust musicians comprised after the war, their numbers in specific camps and ghettos could be significant. Of all the camps, Auschwitz certainly made the largest and most intentional use of orchestral music, and therefore impacted the lives of over a thousand musicians during its years of operation. In its main camp, Nazi officials assembled a men's orchestra in 1941 after the arrest and deportation of an entire Polish radio orchestra. At first, the SS forbade Jews from being members, but then later allowed them to join. In spite of a high turnover rate due to exhaustion, disease, starvation, execution, and suicide, this orchestra eventually expanded to 120 musicians, with more than 800 different players cycling through over its four-year existence. Being in this orchestra provided some substantial advantages, but it did not preclude a member from being deported or executed. One violinist was selected for the gas chamber right in the middle of rehearsal. The SS guards insisted, however, that he finish playing the piece they were practicing, then hauled him off to his death.

Birkenau or Auschwitz II also housed a men's orchestra. The presence of a camp orchestra was considered prestigious and therefore advantageous for the careers of the SS leadership, so commanders became eager to establish them. During August 1942, Camp Commander Johann Schwarzhuber decided to form an orchestra in Birkenau modeled after the one in the main camp, except for permitting Jewish membership right from the start. The Birkenau Men's Orchestra eventually came under the musical leadership

Men's Orchestra at Auschwitz (Yad Vashem Photo Archive, Jerusalem. 1137/237).

of a Polish Jew from Warsaw named Szymon Laks. An accomplished pianist, violinist, and composer, Laks was highly educated, having studied math at Vilnius University and music at both conservatories in Warsaw and Paris. He spoke fluent Polish, Russian, French, English, and German. Moving to Vienna in 1926, he had accompanied silent films on the piano to earn a living before relocating to Paris where he worked as a composer. Nazi officials arrested Laks there in 1941 and deported him to Auschwitz in July 1942, where he would remain incarcerated for two and a half years. His arm indicated a new identity of #49543, and his clothing bore the Star of David with one yellow triangle, the Jewish denotation, and one pink triangle that branded him a homosexual. After 20 days in a harsh work detail, Laks was deteriorating quickly. But then, he experienced a stroke of luck when one of the block leaders asked if anyone spoke Polish and played bridge. During the bridge game with three block elders, Laks mentioned his pre-war career as a composer and violinist, which resulted in his transfer to the men's orchestra. About this astonishing turn of events, where an impromptu bridge game led to membership in the orchestra, Laks acknowledged it as "the first miracle in a long series of miracles that kept me alive and ultimately restored my freedom."[21]

Jan Zaborski conducted the Birkenau Men's Orchestra at that time and handed Laks a violin to play for the audition. Laks chose the Mendelssohn *Violin Concerto*, although Mendelssohn was a Jewish composer and therefore forbidden. Fortunately, the guards did not recognize the piece, saving Laks from certain death. After being transferred to Block 15, which housed the orchestra, Laks' days consisted of playing violin and working in the fields. Eventually, Zaborski promoted him to the position of chief music copyist, which meant that he worked in Block 15 the whole time composing musical arrangements. Camp officials pressured the orchestra relentlessly, always wanting to hear new repertoire. This demand made Laks' job difficult, especially with the scarcity of printed music. Some pieces he arranged from available piano sheet music, but many strictly from memory. Laks also composed original works, often in the style of German marches.

Ambitious by nature, Laks focused on advancing his role in the orchestra as a means of self-preservation. When Maestro Zaborski died in November 1942, a mediocre musician named Kopka, whom Laks referred to as his nemesis, lobbied to take over as the conductor. Laks then countered with a "dirty trick,"[22] for which he felt no remorse. He deliberately made his musical arrangements so difficult that Kopka did not have the ability to rehearse them or lead any performances. Eventually, Kopka made a derogatory statement about Polish music, and Lagerfuhrer Schwarzhuber not only stripped him of his title as *Kapellmeister*, but dismissed him totally from the orchestra. Szymon Laks assumed the position of conductor.

As the orchestra received increasing pressure to expand their repertoire, Laks petitioned for work release time to add more rehearsals and succeeded in getting two three-hour reprieves per week for the group. He also convinced officials that the orchestra should not perform outside during inclement weather because it damaged the instruments and that the players should be given light work details so their hands would be spared. While Laks used music and his position in the orchestra as a means of survival, he also continued to strive for musical quality and to cleave stubbornly to the belief that music remained an elevated expression of humanity.

Later, as part of the evacuation of Auschwitz, the SS deported Laks to Kaufering, a subcamp of Dachau, in November 1944, where American soldiers liberated him on May 3, 1945. After the war, Laks returned to Paris and to his work as a composer, through which he promoted Polish nationalism. He first wrote an account of his time in Birkenau in 1948, but had trouble getting it published. His story was finally released in Polish in 1979, and the English translation in 1989, six years after his death in Paris on December 11, 1983. Laks echoed in his memoir what other survivors had related about hierarchies among the camp population based on ethnicity, nationality, and indispensability. According to Laks, another significant factor in rank as a prisoner depended on the number tattooed on the arm. The lower the number, the longer the prisoner had survived in Auschwitz, affording him or her an extra measure of respect. But ultimately, he classified the prisoners into just two categories—the paupers and the VIPs. Szymon Laks had definitely evolved into a VIP because of the orchestra and his unique skill set, and therefore acquired privileges that helped him survive for two and a half years.

In his memoir, Laks fittingly referred to his time playing music in the horrors of Auschwitz as "music in a distorting mirror"[23] and challenged the assumption that music always served as solace to the prisoners. He recounted a heart-wrenching story of when the guards ordered him and a few other musicians to play Christmas carols at the infirmary in the women's camp on Christmas Eve. By the time they started the second carol, some of the sick began to sob and then scream to be left alone. "Clear out! Let us croak in peace!"[24] The musicians left right away. Indeed, throughout his testimony, Laks refused to mollify his own opinions and experiences as a forced music laborer.

> There are many publications that claim, not without a certain emphasis, that music kept up the spirits of the emaciated prisoners and gave them the strength to survive. Others assert that music had a directly opposite effect, that it demoralized the poor wretches and contributed instead to their earlier demise. I personally share the latter opinion.[25]

Laks certainly recognized the absurdity of music in such a place. He wrote of it creating a fundamental contradiction, as "music—that most sublime expression of the human spirit—also became entangled in the hellish enterprise of the extermination of millions of people."[26] In response to the paradox of the Nazi emotional reaction to music despite their inhumane treatment of prisoners, Laks offered no satisfactory answer. "Could people who love music to this extent, people who can cry when they hear it, be at the same time capable of committing so many atrocities on the rest of humanity? There are realities in which one cannot believe. And yet…"[27]

Alma Rosé glanced for the first time into Szymon Laks' "distorting mirror" when she came to the attention of SS Lagerfuhrerin Maria Mandel and was subsequently transferred from the Medical Block in Auschwitz's main camp to the Music Block in Birkenau. Mandel had established the Auschwitz-Birkenau Women's Orchestra in April 1943 to advance her career, as well as to serve her love for music. The venture did provide her with the sought-after prestige, since her orchestra at Birkenau became the only *Frauenlagerkapelle* (female camp band) in the entire camp system. As with many of the SS, Mandel proved to be a woman of great contradictions. Replete with an imposing presence, she could be deeply moved by music, while simultaneously taking sadistic pleasure in the pain and death of others.

In forming her orchestra, Mandel enlisted the assistance of the prisoner-workers in the Birkenau main office to look through camp records and identify musicians among the female prison population, especially Polish women because of the strong tradition of music education in the schools of Eastern Europe. Particularly helpful in this process was Zippy Spitzer, who would later procure a violin for Alma and eventually join the orchestra herself as a mandolinist. In the early days, Mandel only allowed non–Jews to participate, but soon after permitted Jewish members and established the Music Block, a unique place where Jews and Aryans lived together.

The orchestra's first conductor was a 40-year-old Polish prisoner named Zofia Czajkowska. There exists a discrepancy among accounts as to whether she had been a music teacher. Some have claimed that she had little to no musical knowledge, but that assertion seems unlikely. Surely, the astute Mandel would not have appointed her to that important position without her having demonstrated some musical skills. But speculation even exists that since the pronunciation of Zofia's surname Czajkowska so resembled that of composer Peter Ilyich Tchaikovsky, that Mandel might have wrongly perceived a connection. Regardless, all seem to agree that Zofia Czajkowska proved an unexceptional musician, which limited the progress of the orchestra.

Mandel's orchestra began in April 1943 with just six musicians—one Ukrainian and five Poles. Then in May, when Jewish prisoners gained admittance, it grew to 20 members. The only true requirement for acceptance into the ensemble seemed to be basic skills on an instrument. But in reality, many could barely play or could not play at all and took jobs as *Notenschreiberinnen* (music copyists). Instruments were obtained from the huge storehouse in the main Auschwitz camp with help from the men's orchestra there, who also supplied them with some piano sheet music. Even though the Nazis employed a group of German musicologists, known collectively as *Sonderstab Musik,* to confiscate valuable musical instruments and manuscripts from Jewish owners in the similar way that art work was being plundered, plenty of good quality instruments still made it to the camps and into the hands of prisoner ensembles. But far from a traditional orchestra, Mandel's group consisted mostly of folk musicians and featured an odd assortment of instruments, including guitars, accordions, violins, recorders, and mandolins, which aurally lent it a unique timbre and visually created a curious vignette. The unconventional instrumentation coupled with limited skills allowed for only a simple repertoire, and so the fledgling women's orchestra played folk songs and German marches to accompany the prisoner details as they paraded to and from work.

After discovering Alma Rosé, Maria Mandel replaced Zofia Czajkowska with her as conductor, which immediately increased the orchestra's chances of success and survival. Although obviously not pleased with the demotion, Zofia became the block leader, still a privileged position. She almost certainly realized that Alma's elevation of the ensemble would benefit them all. Fundamentally, this group functioned as any other *Kommando* (work detail) in the camp, and the head of that group, its Kapo, operated as a vital liaison to the camp leadership. As the new Kapo of the Music Block, Alma was expected to create an outstanding orchestra from this rag-tag assembly of predominately amateur musicians. The dearth of professional musicians available for this orchestra, as compared to the various men's orchestras, reflected the minimal presence of women in European professional orchestras at that time.

Through discipline and uncompromisingly high standards, Alma began to transform the orchestra, which she viewed as essential to their survival. Rather than produce excellent music in a purely abstract sense, her primary aim became to use music to save lives. This approach stood in stark contrast to that of her male counterpart Szymon Laks, whose goal centered solely on making quality music, and to that end, he begrudgingly had "the gloomy obligation of carefully observing the physical and mental health of my less hardy colleagues"[28] so that they would not die and leave him short-handed in the orchestra. When most of the Czech subcamp, some 4,000 people, were murdered in one day, including their orchestra, Laks merely celebrated his good fortune of inheriting their instruments and music stands. "Not only would it enrich the sound of our orchestra, but it would give me the opportunity of forming a string quartet."[29]

Laks recognized the great disparity between his viewpoint and Alma's when he pronounced that, "She had snatched more than one of them from the jaws of death."[30] Alma did indeed frequently assume the role as savior. One day, a French violinist named Violette Jacquet requested a second audition with Alma, having been rejected previously when she auditioned for Zofia. A truly terrible violin player, Violette burst into tears at the thought of being turned away from the orchestra again. Compassionately, Alma relented and accepted her. This was the first time that Alma saved her life. Later, having been quite ill with typhus, Violette lagged behind as the orchestra walked to its post at the gate. An SS guard stopped Alma and said that this musician, referring to Violette, appeared too weak to continue in the orchestra, but Alma insisted that she was an essential member, saying, "This is one of my best violinists."[31] The SS not only allowed her to remain in the orchestra, but allotted Violette three months of extra rations to facilitate her recovery. Later, Violette gratefully acknowledged that she was far from a good violinist and that Alma had lied to protect her. Remarkably, survivors note that, under Alma's tenure, not a single member of the orchestra was killed, although a few did succumb to disease. The orchestra permitted most to persist against all odds through the end of the war. One orchestra survivor, percussionist Hilde Grünbaum Zimche, remembered Alma instructing them that they would "Survive together or die together. There was no halfway road."[32]

In addition to saving lives, Alma did desire to mold this ensemble into a proper orchestra with the highest standards possible. Alma switched some of the extremely poor musicians to copying music or doing other tasks in the Music Block. Because of the extreme deficiencies in most of the players, Alma had to drill the music note by note, but fortunately she was an excellent teacher with clear and creative methods for explaining the music. At times, she even became swept up in a great zeal for her work that seemed out of place in such ominous surroundings. The Auschwitz-Birkenau Women's Orchestra expanded to 42 players by October 1943, including singers who benefited from Alma's ingenious arrangements of operatic selections and popular songs. Two-thirds of the members were now Jews from a variety of countries, such as France, Russia, Czechoslovakia, and the Netherlands. Alma constantly sought out new musicians, and the frequent arrival of transports provided her with endless recruitment opportunities. But she had to maintain a careful balance between Jews and non–Jews, after a frightening encounter with an SS official who accused her of favoring Jews and insisted that she accept a Polish violinist whom she had initially rejected. The desperate scramble of inmates hoping to join the orchestra could be a burden for Alma. When she announced auditions for an accordion player in August 1943, 150 claimed to play. Alma regretted that in the end, she could only accept one.

Performing had always been an escape for Alma, but never without discipline. Even now, she demanded excellence in her own playing and her orchestra's, as though they sat inside a chandeliered concert hall and not outside in a concentration camp where the air suffocated them with greasy smoke. She also maintained meticulous standards concerning their appearance and the tidiness of the Music Block. Alma's intense striving for musical perfection caused her to be extremely strict. She often doled out punishments for bad playing that took the form of manual chores, such as scrubbing the floor. While one orchestra member claimed after the war that Alma physically assaulted members with slaps or baton hits, the other survivors vehemently deny this. Alma's experience in the professional orchestral world of that time had been one where the conductor engendered the utmost respect and managed the ensemble with an authoritarian approach, her uncle Gustav Mahler being a quintessential example of this type of leader. Alma's explosions of temper indeed became well known to the orchestra players and even to others around Auschwitz, but most of the orchestra survivors understood this behavior, at least in hindsight, as Alma dealt with intense stress and frustration every day. But most importantly for these women, regardless of a moment of overwhelming exasperation, Alma never wavered in her dedication to saving them, and she never ejected anyone from the group, which would have been a death sentence. Alma certainly found herself in a formidable role—the leader and mentor for the women in her orchestra, while also a prisoner herself, a fellow companion in their suffering.

As with Szymon Laks, camp officials pressured Alma and her orchestra for more and more new music. The SS did provide some sheet music for the group in the form of piano reductions, but they had to be orchestrated for this motley crew and copied by hand into parts. With music paper unavailable, Zippy, through her camp office connections, secured paper and pencils, and the music staves were then drawn by hand. Alma composed the arrangements, and others copied the parts. She often worked all night on these arrangements and seemed at times to vacillate from mania to depression. When manic, Alma rarely slept, which took a toll on her body, and her hair noticeably grayed. Through this massive effort, the orchestra's repertoire expanded to over 200 pieces, which included marches by Schubert and Strauss; opera and operetta melodies by Puccini, Rossini, Verdi, and von Suppé; classical works by Schumann, Brahms, and Mozart; and popular German songs of the day.

Except for playing outside in the mornings and evenings, all of the quotidian work, including rehearsing and accumulating repertoire, happened in the orchestra barracks. On the exterior, the Music Block looked like all of the other rudimental housing structures, built merely for function with no thought to comfort. But inside, it afforded some "luxuries" not available in other blocks. These musician-prisoners had clean bedding, including blankets and sheets on the standard three-level bunk beds, and if forced to share a bunk, it was only two and not the typical four or five to a bed. The interior separated into a large room for rehearsals, complete with cabinets for storing their instruments, and a living area with beds. Alma and Zofia had small private rooms. The orchestra women even had use of a latrine right outside the Music Block.

Alma worked miracles as she imposed her unyielding will on the camp leadership to garner special privileges for her charges, all under the guise of improving the musical product. Guards supplied a wooden floor for the rehearsal room and a stove for warmth, as Alma had insisted that the maintenance of the instruments required it. Alma requested a piano, which the SS provided, making it easier for her to arrange new repertoire, in addition to its benefit for rehearsals and performances. Alma also contended that the long roll calls outside with the other prisoners wasted valuable rehearsal time, so her players were counted separately inside. By most accounts, those in the Music Block received double food rations, although some dispute this claim saying they ate the same as the other prisoners. Regardless, the foul-tasting food lacked substantial nutritional value, and the orchestra members suffered daily from hunger. But despite the certain leniencies afforded her, Alma faced daunting musical challenges, including how exceedingly difficult it was to find women who played all the instruments needed, especially the double bass. Never deterred, Alma persuaded the camp commandant to allow a double bass player from the men's orchestra to come over and teach one of her girls. As a result, authorities regularly dispatched Heinz Lewin to the women's Music Block for several months to give lessons to Yvette Assael, a 15-year-old Jewish girl from Greece who played the accordion.

Although these special accommodations did render existence in the camp a bit more tolerable, they certainly did not fashion an easy or comfortable life for the residents of the Music Block. The orchestra members rose one hour before dawn, earlier than most other prisoners. Some had the responsibility of carrying music stands and chairs out to where they would play for the morning march. Then, they lined up for *Appell* so the orchestra could be counted. After a hot drink that was a poor substitute for real coffee and whatever rations had been saved from the day before, orchestra members marched in rows of five, with Alma walking ahead of them, to their performance area at the main gate. After all of the prisoners had marched from the camp, the musicians hauled the music stands and chairs back to the Music Block for rehearsals, until repeating this whole process in the evening. Unlike the men in the other Auschwitz orchestras, the camp leadership did not require the female orchestra members to do additional hard labor. Comprised of mostly amateur musicians, Alma's orchestra had to practice at least eight hours a day, six days a week. The members were young as well, ranging from 14 to mid–30s, with an average age of 19. Their lack of proficiency coupled with such inexperience necessitated the grueling amount of rehearsal time, which taxed them both physically and mentally, especially those who had not been serious music students or professional performers before the war. Fainting during rehearsals from complete exhaustion occurred frequently.

In addition to the rigorous rehearsal demands, the SS required frequent weekly concerts, as well as impromptu performances at any time day or night. Part of the orchestra's regular responsibilities included Sunday afternoon concerts for the SS and certain select prisoners and performances for any official functions in the camp where high-ranking

Party members would be present. For special performances, the players donned blue pleated skirts, white blouses, and matching head scarfs. While these outfits were far from the attire of Alma's Waltzing Girls, they exuded a somewhat impressive, albeit incongruent, image within the confines of Auschwitz and certainly testified to Alma's dogged insistence on high standards.

The orchestra performed concerts as often as twice a week for the patients in the women's camp hospital, known as the *Revier*. Although some reports indicate that guards forced this orchestra to play near the camp entrance as transports arrived or as prisoners were led to the gas chambers, orchestra survivors dispute this. But due to the sheer number of hours that they played on any given day and their close proximity to the railroad tracks, music habitually wafted through the air and could often be heard by those who arrived, which explains post-war accounts where prisoners exiting cattle cars described being greeted by music. The visual vantage point of the Music Block also meant that they tragically witnessed the lines forming that ushered the unsuspecting to be gassed and were powerless to do anything but continue playing. Saddled with such an onerous work load coupled with mental and spiritual distress, the women of the orchestra orbited the camp world in a perpetually exhausted state, strained from the knowledge that so much hinged on the acceptability of their latest performance.

Among the noted diversity within the Auschwitz-Birkenau Women's Orchestra, three members especially distinguished themselves with their musical gifts and then later for their survivor memoirs. Polish violinist Helena Dunicz Niwińska had been enamored with Alma Rosé since childhood when Alma performed a concert in Helena's hometown of Lwów in 1930 on her first tour of Poland. Alma's playing and beauty had completely mesmerized the young Helena. At age 10, Helena had begun studying the violin at the insistence of her father, who was a great lover of music, although not a musician himself. She demonstrated excellent aptitude for music and studied both violin and music theory at the Polish Musical Society Conservatory. Then on September 17, 1939, the Soviets annexed the part of Poland where she lived, and her family fell under an oppressive occupation, living in constant fear of the secret police for almost two years.

On the morning of June 30, 1941, Helena saw unusually clad troops advancing down her street. The Nonaggression Pact between the Germans and Soviets, which had allowed the two countries to carve up Eastern Europe, had fallen through as Hitler turned on Stalin. For Helena, that meant that a new German occupation would now replace the Soviet one. By this time, Helena's father had died, and her brothers had left Lwów. Helena and her mother suffered from severe hunger, with no fuel to keep warm in the winter time. In the early morning hours of January 19, 1943, the Gestapo pounded on their door. Her mother's inquiry as to the reason for their arrest was met with a slap across the face. After the war, Helena learned that, unbeknownst to her or her mother, some of the lodgers they had taken in worked for the Lwów Underground, which had indirectly indicted them as collaborators. Following harsh interrogations, they languished in prison for nine months, subjected to inhumane treatment and deplorable living conditions. Then, on September 30, 1943, Helena and her mother were escorted with a large group of other prisoners to a train where they boarded cattle cars, so overcrowded that they had to stand for the entire 72-hour journey to Auschwitz. A fellow prisoner processed the 28-year-old Helena as she had her head shaved and received the tattoo brand of #64118. In the course of that procedure, Helena commented that she played the violin, and as a result, Helena inexplicably found herself standing before Alma Rosé, the remarkable violinist whose once striking black hair was growing back mixed with gray. The Music Block would save Helena's life.

Singer and pianist Fania Fénelon would become the most infamous member of the Women's Orchestra due to her publication of a fiercely contested account of the orchestra after the war. Born Fany Goldstein in Paris on September 2, 1908, to a Catholic mother and Jewish father, she would later claim her birth year as 1918. Unfortunately, discrepancies appear frequently in her accounts, and many scholars have concluded that she was prone to fabricating dates and information in her desire to appear younger and more exceptional than she was. A talented pianist and soprano, Fany studied music at the Paris Conservatory from 1922 to 1925. Despite her boasts of winning the *premiere prix* (first prize) in piano there, records indicate that she neither received a diploma nor any awards. Adopting the stage name Fania Fénelon, she embarked on a career as a professional performer, especially popular in Parisian cabarets. According to her memoir, Fania joined the French Resistance in 1940 after becoming so disgusted with Hitler that she vowed to dedicate her life to destroying the Nazi scourge. The Resistance benefited from adding her to their ranks since she spoke fluent Russian, French, English, and German, plus her musical activities provided excellent cover and access. Fania performed frequently in cabarets attended by Nazi officials, stealthily photographing their documents when they became too drunk to notice. Although the complete veracity of her claims about working in the Resistance also remains in question, the Gestapo did arrest Fania in 1943 and sent her to a detention center in Drancy, the same place that had held Alma Rosé. After nine months in Drancy, Nazi officials deported Fania to Auschwitz on January 23, 1944. Her transport from Drancy contained 1,153 Jews, and of those, 1,113 were selected upon arrival to be gassed immediately. Fania Fénelon would be one of only 40, who even entered the camp.

After the typical camp initiation, where she became #74862 and spent time in the appalling Quarantine Blocks, Fania experienced a miracle. A French musician in the orchestra recognized her and informed Alma, who then sent for her. Fania described her introduction to the orchestra in such vivid details that it has become one of the most compelling and retold stories of the Women's Orchestra. A Polish prisoner entered Fania's barrack, hollering "Madame Butterfly," because it was an aria from this Puccini opera that the girl who recognized Fania remembered her singing. Escorted to the music barrack, Fania encountered an unfathomable sight—women, and their instruments, and a Bechstein grand piano, all overseen by a most unique leader. Alma instructed her to play and sing something from *Madame Butterfly*. Fania hesitantly touched the piano keys, momentarily overcome by the contrast of the white ivories with her filthy hands. Placing her bare feet on the piano pedals, she played and sang Puccini's famous aria, "Un bel di." The next words uttered to her in French by Alma, "I'll have you in the orchestra,"[33] were an invitation to life. As the only truly accomplished musician besides Alma, Fania became an important member of the orchestra as a singer and arranger. Quite a bit older than the majority of the other girls, Fania assumed a sense of elevated status since most of her fellow musicians lacked talent and experience. In fact, Maria Mandel showed particular favor toward Fania and frequently asked for her to sing, the first time at a 3 a.m. command performance of that aria from *Madame Butterfly*.

But unlike Szymon Laks and Alma Rosé, Fania refused to rely on her music as personal solace and distraction, instead denouncing it as contaminated and violated in this atmosphere. During a command performance for three SS, Fania described the disgust she felt.

> For me, singing was a free act, and I was not free; it was above all a way of giving pleasure, giving love, and I felt a frantic desire to see those three SS men stuck like pigs, right here, at my feet. Standing in front of those men with their buttocks spread out over their chairs, with that parody of an orchestra behind me, I felt as though I were living through one of those nightmares in which you want to cry out and can't.[34]

Fania also wrote bitterly about how being in the orchestra caused the other prisoners to hate her, a troubling reality for all the women in the orchestra. As they played for the prisoners to march to and from work, sometimes the women would yell at them, shouting "traitors." Fania despaired at the "farcical nature of this orchestra, conducted by this elegant woman, these comfortably dressed girls sitting on chairs playing to these virtual skeletons, shadows showing us faces which were faces no longer."[35] Similar to Szymon Laks' Christmas Eve experience, Fania recounted performing a concert in the infirmary for women selected to be gassed the next day and how the music caused the women to shriek, adding further to their suffering and to the orchestra's own feelings of guilt and collusion. Fania did not spare Alma Rosé from her indicting exposé, painting a derogatory picture of Alma as unrepentantly cruel and as unwilling to appeal to the SS for more food because she felt that they played too horribly to deserve extra rations. These accusations against Alma, however, fail to ring true based on the compelling evidence of Alma's sacrifice on behalf of the women under her charge, in addition to the contradictory testimony of other orchestra survivors.

A contrast to Fania Fénelon in so many ways, including age and experience, Anita Lasker became one of the youngest members of the Auschwitz-Birkenau Women's Orchestra. Anita was born on July 17, 1925, to an educated and extremely close-knit, middle-class family in Breslau, Germany. Considered well-off, the Lasker family employed two maids and lived in a spacious flat, but prided themselves on frugality. Anita's father, Dr. Alfons Lasker, was a prominent lawyer and good singer. He loved languages and urged his children to learn multiple languages including French. Her mother Edith also brought considerable talents to the family as a violinist and seamstress. Anita's parents visited the synagogue on high holidays, but gave little thought to their Jewishness the rest of the time. Chamber music sounded frequently in their home from Anita and her two older sisters. Marianne played the piano, and Renate the violin; so with Anita on the cello, the sisters constituted a fine string trio.

As a child in 1933, Anita intuited a vague sense of something amiss, but her young age prohibited her from fully grasping it. Later, while attending a private school, Anita experienced her first personal encounter with anti–Semitism when, as she used a sponge to clean the blackboard, a fellow student shouted, "Don't let the Jew have the sponge."[36] After the Nazi rise to power lent de facto permission to once veiled anti–Jewish sentiment, Anita sometimes endured remarks from people on the street, snidely pronouncing her a "dirty Jew."[37] More than anything, these comments left her extremely confused because she did not consider herself a Jew.

But as people of Jewish descent, the Laskers became subject to the numerous discriminatory laws in the early 1930s that restricted where they could go and what they could do. Although they knew people who were leaving the country, Anita's family could not figure out a way to procure the necessary exit papers or how Dr. Lasker could work in another country since his legal training and credentials would not be applicable outside of Germany. As their precarious situation deteriorated even further, Anita's father desperately appealed to friends and acquaintances throughout Europe, but due to prohibitive costs or quotas, nothing could be arranged for their escape.

In 1938, Anita's parents sent her to Berlin to study cello with Jewish cellist Leo Rostal, since no one in their smaller town of Breslau would risk teaching a Jewish child. She had just turned 13 years old. But after a mere six months, Anita's parents made her return home because they worried that it had become too tenuous a time for the family to be separated. Her teacher must have also grown unable to withstand the dangerous *zeitgeist*, since shortly after Anita's departure, Leo Rostal immigrated to the United States, becoming a member of the NBC Symphony. But regardless, Anita longed to go back to Berlin and secure another cello teacher. A precocious teenager with a fierce passion for music, Anita bravely walked alone into the Gestapo headquarters and requested permission to travel to Berlin. They rudely ejected her from the building. Soon after, the Lasker family received notice from the Gestapo to vacate their flat by November 15, forcing them to move in with Mrs. Lasker's sister.

Without access to a cello instructor, Anita continued her musical studies in harmony and theory. In 1941, government officials assigned her and her sister Renate to work in a paper factory, where they became involved with forging papers and smuggling information for the Resistance. Marianne, the oldest sister and a zealous Zionist, had been the only member of the immediate family to escape Germany. To the bewilderment of her parents, Marianne had completed a carpentry apprenticeship and moved to England before the war as part of her unconventional plan to help build Palestine. The declaration of war left her stuck in England where she used her skills, especially in roof thatching, to earn a living. Eventually, Marianne did make it to Palestine.

As part of the Nazis' accelerated campaign to oust Jews, Anita's parents were deported on April 9, 1942. She received only one letter from them and then a final postcard on which her father had simply written Psalm 121:1, "I will lift up mine eyes unto the hills from whence cometh my help." Anita never saw them again. Later, in her own darkest days, Anita often thought of this verse her father had scribbled on a postcard and somehow managed to mail. On September 7, 1942, the government ordered Anita and Renate to an orphanage since their parents, aunt and uncle, and grandmother had all been deported. Through their work with the Resistance, they decided to forge papers for themselves and try to escape to Paris. But the Gestapo had been aware of their clandestine activities and subsequently arrested them at the train station on September 16. They waited in a Breslau prison for a trial that did not transpire until June 5, 1943. After both were found guilty, officials deported Anita to Auschwitz. She was 17 years old.

The humiliating induction process upon arrival severely traumatized Anita. She endured being stripped naked and tattooed with #69388, but the loss of her hair cried out as an unbearable injustice, causing her to feel no longer like an individual person, but an anonymous figure, indistinguishable from the others shuffling around the camp. During the intake procedures, the prisoners asked her questions as they worked about the outside world and eventually about what she did before the war. Later, she would frequently ponder why she had said that she played the cello, which seemed so irrelevant in such a place. But after her declaration, the response came, "That is fantastic....you will be saved."[38] Anita was told to wait, and after a while, an elegant woman dressed in a camel-hair coat entered the room and began to question her about her musical background, while Anita stood naked, clutching a toothbrush. The woman introduced herself as Alma Rosé and expressed her delight at finding a cellist since she had no low instruments to play the bass lines. She informed Anita that after her mandatory time in the Quarantine Block that she would be sent to her for an official audition. When Anita eventually entered the Music Block, she was handed a cello.

Since it had been almost two years since she had last held an instrument, she requested a minute to warm up and then attempted to play some of the slow movement from the Boccherini *Cello Concerto*. The orchestra now had a cellist, and she had become one of "the girls in the band."[39] That was the first time the cello saved her. Later, Anita was spared from a selection while ill in the camp hospital because one of the SS guards recognized her value as the orchestra's only cello player.

After a couple of weeks in the orchestra, Anita learned that her sister Renate had arrived at Auschwitz. Despite the joy of their unexpected reunion, Renate deteriorated rapidly from being stuck in the squalid Quarantine Block for an extended period. Anita realized the precarious nature of her sister's health and summoned the undaunted courage that had enabled her to march into Gestapo headquarters four years earlier. Anita brazenly approached Lagerfuhrerin Maria Mandel in hopes that Mandel's fondness for the orchestra would allow Anita to garner a favor. She asked that her sister be allowed to be a *Läuferin* (camp messenger), a privileged job that involved running errands throughout the camp and provided better food rations. Anita's risky ploy worked. The orchestra not only saved her life, but Renate's as well.

For inmates such as Anita or Fania who spoke multiple languages, navigating Auschwitz and the diverse dynamics within the orchestra proved easier. Interpersonal discord in the Music Block almost always stemmed from a communication breakdown, the language barrier that one survivor referred to as "a veritable tower of Babel,"[40] which easily led to misunderstandings among fellow prisoners. Those who did not speak German faced overwhelming obstacles since all camp orders were naturally issued in this language, including Alma's musical directives. The orchestra's mixture of ethnicities and political ideologies, plus the intermingling of Jews and non–Jews, indeed produced some conflict, especially considering the historically fierce animosity of Poles toward Jews.

In Auschwitz, Jewish prisoners endured even greater injustices than others, including being denied the privilege of receiving parcels from their family. Understandably, it grieved and infuriated them to watch fellow musicians unwrap packages filled with food and other necessities, knowing that it would never be an option for them. Concerning the problems between the Polish and Jewish prisoners, Helena insisted, however, that "its foundation was not anti–Semitism; rather, it was the brutal strength of hunger that, in the German camp, defeated the ideal of universal solidarity, humanity, and empathy."[41] Anita vehemently rejected Fania's account, which depicted the members as engaged in a perpetual and mean-spirited struggle, insisting instead that they created a close-knit and supportive community and that she developed dear friendships that lasted long past the war. In addressing Fania's memoir as a whole, Anita declared, "It is a pity that Fania created such a misleading impression about the camp orchestra…. For reasons best known to herself, she indulged in the most preposterous distortions of the truth about practically everyone…"[42]

Of the many internal and external enemies of the inmates at Auschwitz, typhus became one of the most feared because of the widespread devastation such a contagious pathogen could render in the cesspool of a concentration camp. Anita contracted typhus and had to spend time in the infirmary. When she returned to the orchestra, she still felt extremely weak and could not play very well. Apparently lacking any sympathy for Anita, Alma punished her for her poor playing by making her scrub the floors. Although furious with Alma at the time, after the war Anita emphasized, "I now have nothing less than the greatest admiration for Alma's attitude."[43] Through Alma's relentless discipline and drive, she actually succeeded in distracting the women from their dire circumstances and from the daily threat of the gas chambers, so that the thing to be feared was playing a wrong note. Alma's perfectionism in the midst of musical rubbish constituted a way to keep herself and her charges sane. Not generous with compliments, Alma's highest form of praise, according to Anita, would be to say, "This would have been good enough to be heard by my father."[44]

Alma frequently spoke of her father, who was incredibly important to her, and longed to be reunited with him and to follow in his footsteps as a great performer of chamber music. She tried to maintain a positive outlook about the future, even pondering how she could take this orchestra on a concert tour as she had her Waltzing Girls. Although it seemed unrealistic to hope of getting out of Auschwitz alive, Anita asserted in her memoir that human instinct kept a person striving to survive and that Alma Rosé was the "supreme example of this instinct for survival."[45] But understandably, Alma sometimes sank into despair. During one of these low moments when she believed she would not live through the war, Alma entreated that if any of them survived, to please go tell her father about the orchestra.

On April 2, 1944, the orchestra performed an afternoon concert outside of the *Revier*, as was their custom on Sundays. But unlike all the others, this performance would assume great significance over the next two days, searing its details in the minds of many of the players. Even almost 70 years later, Helena vividly remembered the start of the concert, the moment that Alma stepped up onto the conductor's podium. The amount of death and atrocities at Auschwitz had markedly increased in recent weeks, causing a profound depression to descend on them and their conductor.

> It was a beautiful sunny day. I can remember how we were all ready to play, and only waiting for Alma. I can still see her as she walks onto the conductor's rostrum situated right up against the wall of the block. We wait for a sign from her, but she stands motionless for a moment with her arms outspread and then turns her head slightly so that she is facing the sun. She looks as if she is drinking in its springtime rays, but there is a look of deep melancholy on her face.[46]

Later that evening, Alma attended a birthday party for Frau Else Schmidt, a fellow prisoner who had become the powerful Kapo in charge of the clothing storehouse and laundry, with whom Alma had developed a cautious friendship. Upon returning to the Music Block, Alma complained of feeling sick with a terrible headache, plus dizziness and vomiting. As with so many instances involving the orchestra, there are discrepancies among accounts of the exact order of events and people involved the night Alma took ill. It appears that some of the orchestra members sent for Maria Mandel, who arrived accompanied by a Jewish prisoner and medical student who worked in the *Revier* named Manca Švalbová, but known as Dr. Mancy. She and Alma had become quite close friends. Dr. Mancy confirms in her memoir that someone came and got her in the early morning of April 3, saying that Alma was quite sick. She arrived at the Music Block, noting that Alma presented with a high fever, headache, and vomiting. When questioned about what she had eaten the day before, Alma admitted that she had drunk some vodka. Drinking any alcohol in the camp posed a substantial threat because most of it was methylated and could cause alcohol poisoning. Dr. Mancy scolded Alma for her carelessness, although others who knew Alma and Frau Schmidt insisted that the women were much too savvy about the camp and had survived it too long to be so reckless.

Alma was transported on a stretcher to the *Revier* where Dr. Mancy and other doctors scrambled to find a diagnosis. They pumped her stomach, but Alma's condition continued to deteriorate with bouts of unconsciousness and convulsions, as well as the appearance of strange blue spots on her skin. The medical staff considered numerous theories, including meningitis, typhus, and alcohol poisoning, but none seemed to account completely for the symptoms. Rumors began to circulate wildly through the camp in response to Alma's absence at the podium for the morning march. Speculation focused on Frau Schmidt, who was also missing from her post and with whom Alma had spent several hours before becoming ill. It seems, however, that the *Revier* housed Frau Schmidt as well, with comparable symptoms, and that other guests from the party felt unwell. The camp medical team raced to save Alma's life, going to extraordinary and unfathomable lengths for a Jewish prisoner. On April 4, they even summoned Dr. Mengele, although he did not normally tend patients in the *Revier*. He ordered a spinal tap, which came back negative for meningitis. Other laboratory tests similarly failed to reveal a diagnosis.

Alma Rosé died at 4 a.m. on April 5, 1944, with her friend Dr. Mancy at her side. The Music Block leader, Zofia Czajkowska, delivered the shocking news to the orchestra members. Alma's devastating loss fueled rampant speculation. Some continued to point an accusing finger at Frau Schmidt for deliberately poisoning Alma due to personal jealousies. But, the prevalent theory held by scholars today, after years of extensive research, indicates botulism, a dangerous form of food poisoning that attacks the central nervous system and presents consistently with Alma's symptoms. Both Alma and Frau Schmidt ate tinned meat at the birthday party, but according to witnesses, Frau Schmidt only ate a small amount, while Alma consumed a much larger serving. Frau Schmidt fully recovered and lived to see the liberation of the camps. She was sitting in a Prague restaurant not long after the war when a fellow survivor recognized her and delivered a deft punch to her face, payback for abuses she had suffered at the hands of a cruel Kapo.

When trying to provide a summative description of Alma, Anita recounted, "Alma was herself a very fine violinist, but her most notable quality was her powerful personality. She commanded absolute respect from us, and to all appearances from the SS as well."[47] Alma's unique station at Auschwitz can be seen in the unprecedented way the SS handled her death. They laid her body out in state, clothed in a dress, on a white cloth in the *Revier* and permitted the orchestra members to file past the improvised catafalque and pay their respects. The SS seemed visibly upset by Alma's death as well, but inevitably her body joined hundreds of others that day in the Birkenau crematoria. Now that Alma's once commanding baton hung on the wall of the Music Block, tied with a black crepe ribbon, the orchestra members felt not only distraught at her death, but insecure about their future. Alma's persuasive influence with the SS had been unparalleled. Her ability to liaise with the camp command to secure extra food rations and better conditions had offered a sense of protection and security for the women in her charge. They now feared that loss as well, including the possible dissolution of the orchestra and their transport to the gas chambers.

Alma indeed proved irreplaceable. After her death, the orchestra's pianist, a Russian who had been an officer in the Soviet Army named Sonia Winogradowa, assumed the role of director, but with her mediocre musical talents, the orchestra members did not respect her. As a result, the orchestra devolved into entropy, and the repertoire scaled back to the marches and easy folk songs of the group's early days. Sunday concerts were cancelled, and the orchestra played only for morning and evening work details. The vital SS interest in the orchestra waned, and by the summer of 1944, the group had limited rehearsals and had been assigned supplemental work details, such as knitting.

As the Allies neared Auschwitz, SS officials scrambled to conceal what had happened there by destroying the crematoria and burning 29 of the 35 overflowing storerooms. Within the six that remained, the Soviet troops who liberated the camp on January 27, 1945, found seven tons of human hair, innumerable pairs of eyeglasses and shoes, and a million coats.

Most of the 65,000 prisoners housed at Auschwitz had been relocated to other camps by mid–January through what became known as death marches due to the staggering mortality rate. Only 7,000 prisoners remained in the camp when the Soviets arrived. The Jewish members of the Women's Orchestra had been transferred via cattle car in late October 1944 to another camp, Bergen-Belsen, and the non–Jewish members moved to the main camp at Auschwitz. All of the instruments, music, and music stands lay abandoned in the Music Block. For the orchestra members leaving Auschwitz, their departure by the main gate seemed miraculous, as they had assumed that they would die there. Mercifully, they had no way of knowing that their intended destination would be more horrendous than the place they exited.

Bergen-Belsen's first set of barracks was built in 1935 to house workers who replaced deported peasants. The German government also planned to conduct military exercises and store weapons there, but escalations in the war rendered it more essential as a concentration camp. After the fall of France in 1940, Belsen held French and Belgian POWs, who provided the necessary labor to enlarge the camp further. The following year, Germany betrayed her Russian allies, and as a result, large transports of Russian prisoners, around 14,000 total, arrived at Belsen. The Russian prisoners faced particularly deplorable conditions, raging disease, and overcrowding, which left them to sleep in the open air. As many as 300 inmates died per day, leaving Belsen practically deserted by 1942. Its purpose transitioned yet again starting in 1943, with part of it functioning as a military hospital, while the rest served as a residential camp, housing privileged Jews identified as foreign nationals whom the Germans thought they might barter in a prisoner exchange.

The train ride from Auschwitz to Bergen-Belsen in freezing temperatures lasted four miserable days. The orchestra members distracted themselves by singing pieces from their repertoire, each member knowing her own part by heart. Upon arrival at Belsen, they encountered a facility stretched way beyond its capacity. The guards handed these new arrivals a blanket and ordered them to a large tent where they were expected to lie on the frozen ground, their accommodations more bivouac than residential camp. Not long after, a terrible storm collapsed the tent and left the former orchestra members, with their insufficient clothing and malnourished bodies, completely exposed to the elements. They experienced a bit of reprieve when the guards eventually relocated them to a storage facility full of shoes. Although crowded, it did provide shelter. Hopefully, they did not know that the Russian POWs housed there had most likely been executed to allow them this space. As the SS emptied camps, thousands more marched toward Belsen. But unlike Auschwitz, there was no organization at Belsen and no procedures for dealing with the dead. Food and water became scarcer and scarcer, causing mounds of corpses to pile up throughout the camp. According to Anita, "Auschwitz was a place where people were *murdered*. In Belsen they *perished*."[48]

Typhus proved as formidable an enemy in Belsen as it had been at Auschwitz. For those who had contracted it in other camps and survived, they blessedly remained immune, but for the others, it ravaged relentlessly. Camp conditions steadily deteriorated, leaving prisoners without food for several days at a time and forcing some men in the camp to resort to cannibalism. Tragically, so much of the suffering could have been avoided. They learned after the war that the Red Cross had delivered substantial amounts of blankets and tinned food, including meats, biscuits, and Ovaltine. But somehow these provisions sat undetected and were never distributed until after the liberation, when the Allied soldiers used them to rehabilitate those still alive.

Fania Fénelon was one of the orchestra members who did survive to see the liberation of Belsen, but just barely. Near death from starvation, exposure, and typhus, Fania weighed only 65 pounds when the British army arrived on April 15, 1945. After learning who she was, a British soldier thrust a microphone at her and begged her to sing for airing on the BBC. Miraculously, she managed to sing both the French and British national anthems. A month later, Fania was performing again, this time in Paris as part of a troupe entertaining U.S. soldiers, but her health continued to be fragile, making it difficult to reestablish a professional career. She moved to East Germany and taught in East Berlin at a high school for musically gifted students. After retirement, she moved back home to Paris in 1972.

Almost 30 years after the war, Fania penned her famous and controversial memoir about the Auschwitz-Birkenau Women's Orchestra, published in French in 1976 as *Sursis pour l'Orchestre* and then in English as *Playing for Time*. It was later translated into numerous languages and distributed to millions around the world. In 1979, Arthur Miller, the renowned American playwright, adapted her story as a TV movie for CBS, airing on September 30, 1980. Three years later, Fania Fénelon died of cancer on December 17, 1983, at age 75.

Fania emerged as the most well-known member of the Women's Orchestra through her successful memoir, and her account, as the first record, became the fundamental source of knowledge and scholarship on the group. But many find this unfortunate because of its blatant unreliability, given the repeated contradictions Fania made during her lifetime and the failure of other members to corroborate much of her story. According to Arie Olewski, the son of the orchestra survivor Rachela Zelmanowicz Olewski, "I have learned the lesson that he who is first to write his memories, can rewrite history. After he does, others have to react and deny it from a worst position."[49] *Playing for Time* has been voraciously challenged by other survivors, including Anita Lasker-Wallfisch and Helena Dunicz Niwińska. Musicologist Susan Eischeid sought to shed light on the accusations of exaggerations and falsehoods through her 2016 study, published as *The Truth about Fania Fénelon and the Women's Orchestra of Auschwitz-Birkenau*. But in the end, it should never be forgotten or discounted that Fania Fénelon suffered greatly in the concentration camps, and along with the other survivors, spent the rest of her life combating painful memories and reconciling tragic losses.

Anita Lasker also survived to tell of her experiences in the camps and to build a life after the war. Her account of their time in Bergen-Belsen provided insightful commentary on that final part of the orchestra's journey and on the protracted nature of Anita's personal struggle to reestablish herself as an individual. During the evacuation of the orchestra from Auschwitz, Anita could not bear to be separated from her sister, so Renate just filed in with them. Thankfully, no one stopped her, although in hindsight, Anita could not figure out why the SS did not just gas them, instead of dragging prisoners to another location.

Life became so intractable at Belsen that Anita no longer even dared to hope for the future, especially when she noticed the presence of fewer and fewer SS, indicating that they had basically been abandoned. On Sunday, April 15, 1945, at around 5 p.m., Anita heard the rumble of trucks and someone shouting that a British tank had arrived, but she refused to believe at first. By that time, she had not had any food for days and was quite sick with a fever, hardly able to stand. At age 19, she felt more like 90. A harrowing sight greeted their liberators, approximately 50,000 corpse-like prisoners and about 10,000 dead bodies. Those still alive were barely alive, decimated by dehydration and starvation, with many suffering from typhus. Their rescuers had descended into an abyss of unbearable stench and heartbreaking misery.

Not surprisingly, these soldiers did not have training to deal with the condition of the people they liberated, and many died from being given too much food after such a long period of deprivation. The British army confronted a monumental task of securing medical treatment and accommodations, in addition to registering names and information to help families locate their loved ones. A van with transmitting equipment made rounds through the camp, recording messages from survivors to be broadcast over the BBC. Anita recorded a message, and miraculously her sister Marianne's neighbor heard it and let her know the fabulous news that Anita and Renate were both alive.

On May 21, soldiers with flamethrowers burned down the last of the barracks along with a picture of Hitler and a swastika attached to it. The remaining survivors were transferred about two miles down the road to a military facility. The 12,000 stricken with typhus had to be placed in a quarantined area, and the English Red Cross was brought in to care for them. The Lasker sisters both worked as interpreters, while they attempted to secure papers and permission to immigrate to England where Marianne still lived. They had no interest in returning to Germany, especially their home town of Breslau, which the Russians now controlled. The magnitude of the devastation that the Nazis had inflicted on so many people confounded efforts to accommodate displaced persons, especially German Jews, a new "species." After the Holocaust, many survivors had to take shelter in displaced persons camps (DP camps) overseen by Allied powers. The last DP camp did not close until 12 years later in 1957.

Three members of the Women's Orchestra in Auschwitz-Birkenau at the Bergen-Belsen Displaced Persons Camp, May 1945. From the right: Hilde (Grünbaum) Zimche, Anita Lasker-Wallfisch and "little" Helen (Yad Vashem Artifacts Collection / Courtesy Hilde Zimche, Kibbuts Netzer Sereni, Israel).

As time dragged on, it became harder for Anita to tolerate the camp, even though conditions were relatively good, and she had been given her heart's desire—a cello. Anita had expressed a strong conviction that she would not accept an instrument that had been taken from another person by the Nazis. Fortunately on June 17, a British military friend of hers named Captain Powell discovered an abandoned cello on top of a cupboard and gifted it to her. She began diligently working to rehabilitate her stiff fingers, a challenging proposition not just because of the lack of practice, but also due to malnutrition and other abuses her body had withstood. She began to perform some around the camp as a soloist and in chamber ensembles with other musicians she met, including Giuseppe Selmi, who had been the principal cellist of the Radio Rome Orchestra before the war. The only problem with her cello was that the strings were quite old and frayed. She had to play gingerly while she endured the interminable wait for a parcel of strings and rosin from her sister Marianne. At one point, her A string broke, and Anita was forced to play with just three strings. She finally received her supplies from England along with some music she requested, including the Bach Cello Suites. On July 27, 1945, Anita attended a wonderful concert performed by renowned violinist Yehudi Menuhin for the survivors of Belsen. He played a variety of repertoire, including the Mendelssohn *Violin Concerto* and Beethoven's *Kreutzer Sonata*. Especially impressed with his accompanist, Anita later discovered that it was none other than Benjamin Britten.

In September 1945, British military officials summoned Anita to give testimony at the Lüneberg Trial, also known as the Belsen Trial, where 45 former SS guards and Kapos from Auschwitz and Bergen-Belsen faced war crime charges. She found it extremely difficult not only to look into the eyes of the evil people who had so mistreated her and her fellow prisoners, but to reconcile that they were afforded a defense counsel and the presumption of "innocent until proven guilty." Shortly after the completion of that 54-day trial, in November 1945, the British government passed a bill allowing displaced persons to enter England if they met the two criteria of being under the age of 21 and having a relative in England, but no relatives in any other country. While a hopeful development for the Lasker sisters, it also presented a couple of problems, namely that Renate had already turned 21 and that they had an uncle, well-known chess master Edward Lasker, living in the United States. They rectified the first inconvenience by paying a small bribe in cigarettes to get new documents with revised birth dates, a relatively easy accomplishment since they had no official papers or birth certificates. Their real challenge involved getting transportation to Brussels, which housed the closest British Passport Control Office where they could apply to emigrate. Fortunately, another one of their British military friends, Captain Hans Alexander, heard about their plight and offered to let them ride with him the next day, December 27, on his trip to Brussels.

Anita and Renate soon discovered that getting to Brussels did not guarantee success because officials did indeed deny their application since they had an uncle living in the United States. They spent the next few months filing appeals, finally touching English soil on March 18, 1946, 11 months after their liberation. Unfortunately, by the time they arrived, their sister Marianne had already left for Palestine. Regretfully, Anita would only see her two times, once when Marianne came for a brief visit to London and then another time when Anita traveled to Israel. Marianne tragically died in 1952 giving birth to her second child.

Once in England, Anita began studying with renowned cellist and teacher William Pleeth at the Guildhall School of Music. Pleeth would develop quite a reputation later as the teacher of internationally acclaimed cellist Jacqueline du Pré. Anita joined the larger community of musical émigrés in London and eventually embarked on a professional career, including as one of the founding members of the English Chamber Orchestra. She married pianist Peter Wallfisch in 1952, and their son Raphael would continue the family business as a professional cellist. In 2000, Anita published an important memoir of her life in the camps titled *Inherit the Truth*. Today, her grandson Benjamin Wallfisch is a composer, especially known for his film scores. Along with Hans Zimmer and Pharrell Williams, he earned a Golden Globe award for best original score in 2017 for *Hidden Figures*. At age 94 at the time of this writing, Anita Lasker-Wallfisch remains one of the most vocal of the Holocaust survivors and still confronts daily what happened to her over 70 years ago. For Anita, it is still hard to speak about the unspeakable things.

> I feel humiliated on behalf of the millions of the dead, and I also feel guilty. It's the age-old guilt of survivors who wonder why they should be in a position to talk at all.[50] … The millions who were murdered rely on those survivors to bear witness to their existence. To some extent that helps to expiate the guilt many of us feel at having survived.[51]

Anita realizes after so many years that the memory of being in a concentration camp will never leave you. "When you have seen and gone through what we have, those experiences become an integral part of you, and they inevitably colour your whole make-up."[52] Auschwitz survivor Elie Wiesel noted a similar reality in his memoir *Night*. "Never shall I forget that night, the first night in camp, that turned my life into one long night."[53]

Throughout her "long night" in Auschwitz, Alma Rosé led "that valiant band for whom music meant life,"[54] but was tragically unable to save herself. The devastating news of her passing shocked her family, friends, and the music world. Immediately after the war, with information so unreliable, false accounts and rumors of Alma's cause of death circulated wildly from suicide by poison to suicide by hanging herself in the Music Block. Her father Arnold Rosé had continued to practice and perform while he waited for news from Alma. Finally, with the liberation of Holland in May 1945, her brother Alfred contacted Alma's friends Marye and Paul Staercke. Marye wrote to Alfred with what particulars she knew about Alma's life and death in the camp and alluded to a capsule of poison she knew Alma had obtained and the possibility that she had committed suicide. Marye urged Alfred to spare his father the more horrendous details. Alfred Rosé also received a letter from Alma's friend Marie Tellegen in August 1945, informing him that she had Alma's violin and other belongings and that she would send these items to him.

In 1947, Alma's 1757 Guadagnini violin was sold to Felix Eyle, a former violin student of her father's. Eyle became the concertmaster of the Metropolitan Opera Orchestra in New York shortly after the purchase and played the remarkably beautiful instrument in that pit until his retirement in 1970. Given the indelible impact of the Mahler-Rosé family on the opera culture of Vienna, it certainly seemed a fitting home for Alma's beloved violin.

Alfred broke the news to his father in a letter and began secretly to make arrangements to bring his ailing and grief-stricken father to the United States. After hearing of Alma's death, Arnold lost his desire to play music and sold his beloved Stradivari. He received an offer in 1946 to be reinstated as concertmaster of the Vienna Philharmonic, but declined. Miraculously, Anita Lasker was able to honor Alma's wish that her father be told about her camp orchestra. When she arrived in London, Anita visited Arnold and told him the unbelievable story of Alma's orchestra and about her heroism and the lives she had saved, including her own. Arnold never made it to the United States, but died in his sleep on August 25, 1946, of heart failure at age 82. He was cremated and his ashes buried temporarily in England, then moved five years later to rest in the grave with his beloved wife Justine at Grinzinger Friedhof Cemetery in Vienna, near that of Gustav Mahler. Alma Rosé's name also appears on the grave stone, although her body had joined that indicting chorus of ashes at Auschwitz.

Alfred felt such anger and bitterness over his sister's death that he had a falling out with long-time family friend Bruno Walter for conducting the Vienna Philharmonic on a U.S. tour. Alfred could not forgive what had been taken from his sister, and his father, and himself. He and his wife Maria left the United States in 1948 and moved to Ontario, Canada, where he taught music at the University of Western Ontario until his retirement in 1973. Despite his personal tragedy, he never lost his belief in the power of music and emerged as a pioneer in the fledgling field of music therapy, establishing treatment programs at Westminster Hospital in 1952 and then later in 1956 at the London Ontario Psychiatric Hospital. The Rosé home in Canada adopted the nickname "Little Vienna" because of all of the Old World memorabilia on display. Included in the items from their past was a photograph of Alma playing the violin that Alfred had placed in his study, a daily reminder of her immeasurable loss.

One day in the 1970s while Alfred and Maria browsed a market, a fellow shopper heard his name and asked if he was related to Alma Rosé, the violinist from Auschwitz. He replied that she was his sister. Remarkably, this woman had been a prisoner in Auschwitz and remembered Alma and the music that she and the orchestra had produced. It had brought her comfort. She said, "Your sister saved the lives of many."[55] Alfred had struggled for 30 years over the death of Alma, unable to accept it. On his deathbed in 1975 at age 73, he remembered the words of the woman in the market, and they offered him a sense of solace. He repeated the four words, "she saved many lives,"[56] near the end, a final benediction for a beloved sister.

3

Dr. Herbert Zipper: From Dachau to the World

Where they have burned books, they will end in burning human beings.
—Heinrich Heine in his 1821 play *Almansor*

A suburb of Munich, the city of Dachau perches on a hill about 12 miles to the northwest. Dating back to the Middle Ages, this historic Bavarian town housed many members of Germany's noble and ruling families over the centuries. Dachau later acquired considerable renown as a destination for artists, so that by the late 19th century, its name figured into the great German cultural achievements of the time. But with the onset of World War I, the military installed a large ammunition factory there, alongside its flourishing artists' colony. The factory's presence was short-lived, however, and its closing after the war left thousands without work. Then, as Germany again plunged toward another global conflict in the 1930s, the remnants of the plant's infrastructure made Dachau the ideal location for a concentration camp.

Under the direction of Heinrich Himmler, the *Reichsführer* (Reich Leader) in charge of the Nazis' elite and notorious SS corps, the city of Dachau became the site of the first of the large Nazi concentration camps in Germany. With his level of power surpassed only by Adolf Hitler himself, Himmler proved a sinister architect of destruction. The Dachau camp opened on March 22, 1933, and although designed to house 5,000 prisoners, it quickly exceeded that, with roughly 9,000 by the summer of 1933. Dachau emerged as a model for other camps and as a training center for the SS, in addition to a vital labor camp for war productions. The first inmates incarcerated there were political prisoners—Communists and Socialists whose clothing bore red triangles. In time, Dachau confined a diverse group of people that the Nazis opposed, including Jews, of course, but also homosexuals with their pink triangles and Jehovah's Witnesses. Its front gates held the same disturbing inscription that those at Auschwitz would later display—*Arbeit Macht Frei* (Work Sets You Free). By the war's end, this entrance would bear witness to over 200,000 prisoners and a death toll near 30,000. Although not originally intended as an extermination camp, Dachau certainly caused much death and utilized an on-site crematorium to dispose of those it murdered.

The prisoners at Dachau endured crushing humiliations and a myriad of deprivations—food, sleep, privacy, hygiene, to name a few. Guards inflicted barbaric punishments for even minor infractions, such as tying the inmates' hands behind their backs and then suspending them from their hands, leaving many to suffer irreparable damage to their arms. Other forms of psychological intimidation and torture became "games" for the SS. One of their favorites involved forcing the prisoners to remove their caps on command—on off, on off—at an increasingly frantic pace; and if the motions failed to occur with precise synchronization, the guards doled out penalties. All the while, as the captives in Dachau endured these atrocities each day, they did so to the accompaniment of music blaring over the camp's loudspeakers.

Dachau's elaborate system of loudspeakers became operational just a few months after the opening of the camp and would serve as a prototype for similar installments in future camps. For Nazi Germany, the fundamental goal of this particular type of camp centered on "re-education." Using "good" German music to reinforce nationalistic principles and indoctrinate Nazi ideologies represented a deliberate and integral part of that campaign, and in time would brand Dachau as the camp with the most intentional incorporation of music into daily operations. In fact, the camp command exploited music to create a perpetual soundtrack. Marches and patriotic German songs often blasted over the loudspeakers at night and during meal times, disturbing what little peace the prisoners had. Music also covered the screams of inmates during torture sessions and played as a sadistic underscoring for the relentless atrocities of the SS, paradoxically able to motivate and simultaneously disengage them from their actions. Such a toxic sonic environment was certainly antithetical to Dr. Herbert Zipper, one of Vienna's most gifted musicians. Yet, on May 31, 1938, roughly five years after the camp's founding, Herbert Zipper exited a cattle car after a harrowing and humiliating train journey. This would become the most defining moment in his life, what his friend and biographer Paul Cummins referred to as "B.D. and A.D.—Before Dachau and After Dachau."[1]

Born in Vienna on April 24, 1904, Herbert Zipper belonged to a well-off middle class family who, like so many Jews living in Vienna at that time, were not religious and did not participate in Jewish customs, but identified themselves by only one label—Viennese. His father Emil Zipper, born in 1875 as the youngest of 11 children, had grown up in Vienna, where he later studied engineering and made a living as an inventor and entrepreneur. He married the young and beautiful Regina "Rosie" Westreich in 1901. They had three sons: Walter (1902), Herbert (1904), and Otto (1914), and a daughter named Hedy in 1907.

Herbert Zipper loved reading from an early age and expertly memorized poetry. His father, a serious reader of literature and philosophy as well as an opera aficionado, instilled these loves in his young son. Zipper also inherited his father's sense of humor, and this, along with his remarkable memory, would serve him well in the darker times of his life. In addition, Zipper received instruction early on from his governess Emma Kaspar, who had been educated in a Catholic convent before being employed by the Zipper family in 1909. She became a major influence through stimulating a love and appreciation for literature and the visual arts. Vienna's iconic musical heritage encouraged music lessons for children as an integral part of life in the city, and the Zipper home was no exception. Herbert and Hedy both studied piano, while Walter studied the piano and cello. Only Otto, the last of the Zipper siblings and the one whose childhood coincided with the dismal post–World War I years, did not receive any music lessons.

Herbert Zipper began piano lessons at age 5 and moved through a series of teachers in just a few years. His extraordinary musical talent, apparent from that young age, soon developed into an ardent devotion, prompting him to practice several hours a day by age 10. Besides piano studies, his other early music education was acquired mostly autodidactically. He devoured books on music history and played chamber music with others as often as he could. He sight-read voraciously. His nascent musical training also encompassed the wonderful concerts and operas that took place in his city. He attended operas by Wagner and fell in love with the music of Mozart, Schubert, and Beethoven. He witnessed live performances by some of the world's greatest musicians, including cellist Pablo Casals and pianist Sergei Rachmaninoff.

In Zipper's formative years, the eclectic instruction at home via his governess and parents proved to be as or more important than what he received in public school. At school he was often bored and academically at a level well above his peers. Vienna, with its rich artistic and intellectual activities, also served as a great educator, as well as a profound reminder in its buildings and statuaries of the elevated culture that had produced so many great minds and talents. Zipper shared this remarkable heritage with the city's other gifted young people, including his Viennese contemporary Alma Rosé. Born within two years of each other, Zipper and Alma would both make an indelible mark on the music world, although her membership in the Mahler-Rosé family undoubtedly provided her with a much more impressive pedigree than his. But while these two burgeoning musicians did move within the oddly intimate musical circles of Vienna, whether they ever met remains unknown.

Meanwhile, Zipper grew up feeling quite secure in his family and his city. Although both of his parents had observed Jewish religious customs as part of their upbringing, they did not raise their children in the faith. Neither Zipper nor his siblings attended synagogue or celebrated any Jewish holidays. This absence of the divine in his life would be a permanent state for Zipper, even during the darkest of times. Having heartily embraced scientific inquiry and rationalism, he trusted instead in his own reasoning abilities and moral compass, much as his agnostic and humanistic father did. This objective detachment served as an effective coping mechanism for Zipper, and he would rely on it for the rest of his life as a means of retreating into himself when faced with difficult circumstances.

Alongside his reverence for scientific principles, Zipper also embodied a tenderhearted soul, which imbued his own artistic sensitivities and guided his dealings with those around him. He longed for unity among all and felt especially drawn to those whose life work involved building and creating. One of the early influences on this way of thinking came from a poet named Thorn, whom young Zipper met in 1914. Thorn spoke eloquently on the horrors of war and about his belief that war's only true purpose was to make a certain group of people rich and powerful, such as gun manufacturers, all at the expense of the lives of innocent young men. Meanwhile, Zipper's maternal grandfather Emanuel Westreich, who espoused similar views, came to live with them that same year. These seminal ideas planted important seeds that would eventually grow into Zipper's more mature political philosophy.

The Zippers fared better than many during World War I. But the Vienna of 1918, although spared from bombings, remained a dreary place with food scarcities and rampant inflation, in addition to the Spanish influenza, which afflicted the masses indiscriminately. The Viennese people, however, were hearty and motivated to rebuild and achieve, particularly through the arts and intellectual inquiry. Zipper graduated from high school in 1921 and began to study music with Felix Rosenthal, a composer, music theorist, and pianist. Later, Zipper enrolled at the State Academy of Music and the Performing Arts, where he participated in a rigorous program from 1923 to 1928 and had opportunities there to learn from guest lecturers of great renown, such as Maurice Ravel and Richard Strauss. It was during this time that he began a serious study of conducting and assembled an orchestra of fellow students at his parents' home every Thursday night to read through the great symphonic literature. These evenings certainly provided mutual benefit, as the orchestra members learned to play the repertoire, while Zipper mastered how to conduct it.

While at the Academy, Zipper also realized the importance of discipline in the study and performance of music, which he adopted as a lifelong creed and practice. In addition to his musical growth, the 19-year-old Zipper expanded his connection to the visual arts through a chance meeting in 1923 with the great Expressionist Viennese artist Oskar Kokoschka. While Zipper stood admiring some of Kokoschka's drawings in the window of a bookstore, the artist approached him. Kokoschka then graciously invited him to visit his studio, which he did frequently. In fact, Zipper continued to correspond with Kokoschka until the artist's death in 1980, and their talks and friendship profoundly impacted his philosophy about the nature of art.

A few years later in 1927, Zipper attended a party where he met an exceptional young woman. Although only 14 years old, Trudl Dubsky was already a professional dancer with the Bodenwieser Company and a gifted artist who seemed to never be without paper and a pencil or paint brush. Certainly mature beyond her years, Trudl lived independently and supported herself financially. Later, at only 17, she would become a teacher at the State Academy of Music and the Performing Arts, where Zipper had attended. So despite the almost 10-year age difference, Zipper fell in love with her on the spot. That night launched the beginning of a lifelong romance that would eventually culminate in marriage, after a lengthy and somewhat unorthodox courtship. Although they professed their love for each other right away, both were fiercely dedicated to their art and refused to compromise one for the other. Trudl's career, in particular, progressed at an impressive rate for such a young woman and pulled her away from Zipper to London, where he visited as often as he could. She taught there at the Bedford College for Women and, along with Jeanette Rutherston, founded the Rutherston-Dubsky Dance School. Trudl's exceptional talents as a dancer and choreographer made her in demand by some of the biggest names in London, including Sir Thomas Beecham, and her artistic skills allowed her to design costumes and sets as well.

Meanwhile, Zipper's career proceeded at a more modest pace. He acquired his first professional conducting post in 1929 with the Vienna Madrigal Society. This group of 20 singers often gave casual performances in homes instead of concert halls, which served as a catalyst for Zipper's future zealousness for bringing music to all people, not just the elite and wealthy. In 1932, he accepted a more substantial position as the director of the state chorus, Staedtische Musikverein, in Düsseldorf, as well as a teaching post at the conservatory there. A large city in western Germany, Düsseldorf functioned as a vital industrial center and also supported a vibrant arts community. Everywhere Zipper went in Düsseldorf, he seemed to come into contact with influential people. One of the most memorable encounters occurred when he met Dr. Albert Schweitzer, the famed physician and theologian who would win the Nobel Peace Prize in 1952. Schweitzer had also distinguished himself as an organist and exhibited a great interest in art and literature, as well as music. Schweitzer happened to be a longtime friend of the General Music Director of Düsseldorf, Hans Weisbach, who had taken the young Herbert Zipper under his wings as a sort of protégé. Zipper often spent time with Weisbach and his wife in their home, where he not only dined with Schweitzer, but with a whole cadre of internationally renowned composers, including Paul Hindemith, Darius Milhaud, Kurt Weill, William Walton, and Igor Stravinsky.

But some of the joy surrounding his musical successes became somewhat tempered as Zipper grew increasingly fearful of the rhetoric of Adolf Hitler, a dangerous man whose hateful message apparently appealed to large numbers of people and whose charisma and sway held command at massive rallies. Indeed, Zipper's uneasiness proved justified when on January 30, 1933, those threats and demands, with their inherent anti–Semitism, suddenly became national policy. As a result, Herbert Zipper's life quickly descended into anxiety and uncertainty. It only took two weeks for his friends in Düsseldorf to shun him, most surprisingly the Weisbachs, who sent him a note asking that he not come to their house anymore. Zipper also received a warning from a member of his chorus that some of the singers were out to get him, so he resigned as conductor and retreated to Holland for a few days until he deemed it safe to return. He fled a second time in February for a week after another warning, then again came home to Düsseldorf. The love for his students, along with his generous spirit, kept Zipper hopeful that this hateful time would soon pass.

Then during the month of May, Zipper witnessed a book burning in Düsseldorf, which devastated him as a lifelong lover of books and knowledge. The implementation of the Nazi agenda involved not only traditional weapons and military strategy, but also required a war on ideas, a battle waged in the mind. The book burnings, known as *Feuersprüche* (Fire Incantations), and the state sponsored library purges began in 1933 and, by the end of the war, would result in the estimated destruction of over 100 million books and manuscripts throughout Nazi-occupied Europe. Dr. Joseph Goebbels, a top Nazi official, oversaw this particular campaign. Goebbels' official title of Reich Minister of Public Enlightenment and Propaganda gave him control over anything that fell broadly under the artistic realm, including literature, radio, music, art, and film. Hitler had entrusted Goebbels with the task of shaping culture and ideas through these powerful tools so that Germany's young children and adults would be led down the "proper" path.

Goebbels organized squads, the *Brenn-Kommandos*, to burn books at synagogues and libraries. Books sanctioned for burning, also known as "sentenced to death,"[2] included those by Jewish authors, along with any others thought to contain ideas incompatible with Nazi beliefs and causes, such as socialism, pacifism, and equality. Some of the condemned works came from internationally renowned figures, including Sigmund Freud, Albert Einstein, and Bertolt Brecht. Rather than have the destruction take place in private, Goebbels turned the burnings into major events, which drew enthusiastic crowds. As at Hitler's rallies, those in attendance galvanized into a heinous fervor, cheering as they tossed books into the flames. Some of the larger book burnings were even broadcast live on the radio and shown later as short films in movie theaters. That one man, Adolf Hitler, could incite such an eager and violent following in just a few months certainly stood as an omen of things to come, while the chilling and prophetic words of German poet Heinrich Heine's 1821 play *Almansor* hovered unspoken in the air—"Where they have burned books, they will end in burning human beings."

Despite the growing hostilities toward the Jews in Düsseldorf, Zipper remained devoted to his students and hesitated to leave permanently, but finally in June 1933, he surrendered to the unrelenting storm and departed for Vienna. Zipper had actually been offered the position of conductor for the Leipzig Radio Orchestra, a post that would have been a considerable step forward on his career path, but he was unable to accept the job because of Hitler's anti–Jewish policies. Trudl also came home to Vienna from England in the summer of 1933 for lung treatments. She had fallen ill in February with tuberculosis, putting her career on hold. With her mother terminally ill from cancer, Trudl decided to remain in Vienna to care for her and subsequently resumed her former position with the Bodenwieser Company.

When Zipper boarded the train for Vienna, he was not the only musician or artist fleeing Germany. At every stop, more climbed aboard trying to reach the safety they thought Austria and Czechoslovakia harbored. Although Zipper knew many of them, the nature of the journey allowed for only a strained and uneasy reunion. He and the other exiles crowded into Vienna with their creative talents and their stories of the atrocities happening outside of Austria. But Austria was certainly experiencing its own problems with Fascism. The Chancellor of Austria, Engelbert Dollfuss, had been moving the country away from democracy since taking office in May 1932, which deeply polarized those on the Right and the Left. In February 1934, these tensions boiled over into a three-day civil war between the Socialists and the Right Wing Christian Socials, which claimed hundreds of lives. Not surprisingly, the Socialists lost. Although Zipper embraced the Socialist philosophy and cause, he did not participate in the fighting because of his commitment to pacifism, but did support them through food supplies. Zipper would eventually evolve into a more aggressive political activist, but for now, he approached the conflict merely from a philosophical position and harnessed his energies into his career.

Now that he was living in Vienna again, Zipper refused to wait for good fortune to come to him. Instead, he established a lifelong pattern of making his own opportunities. So, since there were no available conducting positions, he formed his own orchestra to conduct—the Vienna Konzert Orchestra. Zipper proved quite adept at garnering financial support for his new ensemble, and this, along with his musical and organizational talents, made this venture a reality. But regretfully, the Vienna Konzert Orchestra's success was short lived. It disbanded in the summer of 1934 after the Nazis assassinated Chancellor Dollfuss. Collateral damage from that political maneuver meant that the park where the orchestra performed closed and the sold-out season tickets had to be refunded. The fledgling organization could not absorb the staggering financial loss. Now, without work in a city oversaturated with musicians, Zipper made contact with friends in Russia, which resulted in a four-month stint of guest conducting from September–December 1935.

After returning to Vienna from Russia, Zipper focused on writing music for radio and for political cabarets in the underground theater movement, the only venue for this type of drama since the major theaters suffered under strict censorship. Many of the resulting productions were satires that did little to disguise their ridicule and hatred for Hitler and his henchmen. Political theater became an important source for income for Zipper. But aware that his work with the leftist dramas could damage the professional career that he aspired to, he used the pseudonym Walter Drix for his cabaret work. Through these projects, he became acquainted with Jura Soyfer. Like Zipper, Soyfer was of Jewish descent, born on December 8, 1912, in Kharkow, present-day Ukraine. His father had prospered in the Russian steel business, and the family had lived well. But after the Revolution, the Soyfers fled Russia and eventually settled in Vienna. Jura Soyfer became active in politics and joined a Socialist group. But when they failed to act as aggressively as he deemed necessary, Soyfer left them for the Communist Party. Because of his Jewish ancestry, political leanings, and anti-Fascist cabarets, Soyfer understood that it was only a matter of time before government officials incarcerated him, which they did in November 1937 for a three-month period.

Meanwhile, Zipper and his fiancé Trudl enjoyed the extended time that they could spend together by living in the same city. Then in September 1937, Trudl received an offer for a one-year appointment to establish a dance department in Manila at the University of the Philippines. Although Manila might have seemed an exotic and alien destination, the Jewish diaspora had spread its people throughout the globe from Siberia to Ethiopia, including the Philippines. A small community of Jews had assimilated rather easily into the Filipino culture, especially in Manila where they set up businesses and banks that benefited all of the residents. This population enlarged significantly starting in the 1930s with a great influx of German Jews fleeing Hitler and Russian Jews escaping Stalin. The Philippine

Islands seemed a safe asylum at the time and an irresistible job opportunity for Trudl, although it separated her from Zipper once again.

Five months later on March 12, 1938, Hitler annexed Austria, unleashing all of the prejudice and violence that had been smoldering against the Jews, including in Zipper's beloved Vienna. The Zipper family was certainly not immune to this hatred. On Sunday, March 13, when Zipper ventured to the radio station to collect payment for his latest composition, he was forcibly thrown into the streets. The dire situation rendered Zipper so depressed and disillusioned that he stopped composing for several months, as he mourned the loss of everything he loved about the city of his birth and feared what the future held for his friends and family.

An unusually astute young man, 34-year-old Herbert Zipper divined the impending doom more than many, but his efforts to urge his family to leave failed. The Zippers stalled as they tried to figure out how to sort through their possessions and how to complete the necessary paperwork. The Jews of Vienna, like so many across Europe, neglected to acknowledge the extent of the danger, despite the overwhelming evidence from Hitler's speeches and the torrid history of anti–Semitism in Europe. Some had been wise enough to escape early, while others relied on their years of acceptance into society without the label or stigma of being Jews. That the Jewish community had played such a vital role in establishing the current Golden Age of Vienna also contributed to their denial. The list of internationally renowned Jewish artists and intellectuals of the era presented a staggering list of Who's Who—Sigmund Freud, Martin Buber, Arnold Schoenberg, and Otto Klemperer, to name only a few. As historian George E. Berkley so aptly concluded, the reality of how passionately, and ultimately tragically, that the Jews loved the city of Vienna, more so than in other cities, "produced what is undoubtedly the most unrequited love affair in urban history."[3]

The salvation of the Zipper family would ultimately be the result of an ordinary, but fortuitous business trip Emil Zipper made to England right before the Anschluss. Being outside of Austria allowed him to travel unhindered to Paris where he initiated paperwork to evacuate his family. But the lugubrious bureaucratic process just failed to move swiftly enough. On May 27, 1938, the Gestapo entered the Zipper home and arrested Herbert Zipper, along with his two brothers Otto and Walter. They transported them to a police station with 20 others to fill out paperwork and then on to a former public school, now commandeered as a detention center. In what would be the first of many acts of bravery, Herbert Zipper insisted that his brother Otto be released because of a chronic lung condition, and his persuasive nature miraculously convinced the Nazi officials to let Otto go. Zipper's intercession had spared Otto from Dachau, a place where his fragile health would have meant almost certain death. Confined in the wretched detention center, the two remaining brothers' fates became intertwined with more than 500 other detainees, whose lives had been cruelly interrupted and left devoid of any information or food.

After two interminable days, the guards assembled a group, including Zipper and his brother, for departure to the train station. Even the preparations for the journey exposed the viciousness of the Nazi mindset, as the SS forcibly and brutally crammed prisoners into third-class passenger cars. Zipper suffered several broken ribs from the butt of a rifle and had one eye swollen shut, but he was luckier than some whom the guards shot and killed on the spot. Once their train pulled into Munich, Nazi guards transferred them to cattle cars, overloaded beyond capacity. It was late morning on May 31 when Zipper finally arrived at Dachau. Despite days without food, he then had to stand perfectly still in the check-in line. With his last name being Zipper, this took until sundown.

Many years after that fateful train ride to Dachau, Herbert Zipper would confide in his friend and biographer Paul Cummins about the transformation that he experienced during that journey. Zipper had always exhibited a resilient spirit, a logical mind, and a steadfast conscience. So, in that cattle car, he resolved that he would not live in fear or permit the Nazis to observe any weakness in him. He also rededicated himself to the practice of generosity. Zipper instinctively realized that controlling his thoughts, feelings, and actions would be critical to enduring the camps, and that the disposition of order and restraint, so highly valued in the Viennese society of his childhood, would serve him well in this regard. Despite how many choices his captors would strip from him, he could still be master of his own mind and attitude.

Zipper's intense interest in people and their behaviors provided a much needed distraction for him at Dachau. His analytical observations of others allowed him to disconnect from the dire circumstances and focus instead on how his fellow prisoners responded to the hardships and atrocities. Based on the commitments he had made to himself on the train, he took particular note of those who evolved into better and more generous people, and then those whose humanity dissolved into selfishness and brutality. Zipper discerned no correlation between these eventualities and levels of education or socio-economic class, but simply concluded that trying times brought to the surface the true state of each person's heart and spirit.

With Zipper's commitment to help others came a growing realization of how essential the arts would be in strengthening and ennobling the human spirit to rise above these circumstances. Even from the earliest of hours in the camp, he clung to his belief in music's power to uplift the soul and fortify human resolve. On his arrival in Dachau, the SS commanded him to sing, and so Zipper belted out Beethoven's "Ode to Joy" as a way of expressing solidarity with his fellow prisoners. He also relied on his sense of humor, especially when the Nazi requirements and activities in the camp were at their most absurd. Instead of rail against them or fall into bitterness, he would just laugh. Still, even the wise and resilient Herbert Zipper could plummet into despair at times. One such moment happened in August 1938, just a couple of months after his arrival, when Heinrich Himmler himself paid a visit to Dachau. To impress this high-ranking Nazi official, the guards ordered the prisoners to haul an entire rock quarry from one side of the camp to the other. After finally finishing this back-breaking work, they were then forced to move it back to its original location. But despite all of the humiliations and inhumane treatment, the inmates at Dachau were fortunate in one regard. The Nazis had not yet reconstituted their focus toward extermination, which meant that the hope of survival and a life after the camps remained.

Zipper had only been in the camp two or three days when one night, after the evening meal of watery soup and a crust of bread, he and another prisoner began reciting poetry, specifically lines from Goethe's *Faust*. Zipper's excellent education and phenomenal memory served him well in this task, and he found that those around him were starving for this kind of beauty amid such ugliness. Even those with almost no education realized that these words had lifted their spirits and helped them momentarily transcend their wretched situation. So, the evening poetry recitations continued and gave the men something to look forward to during the hard labor of the day. This experience, and those that would follow, challenged Zipper to rethink his philosophical stance that the arts primarily existed as a tool to promote high-minded ideals or to enact political change. Instead, he now understood that art actually made life worth living and that it could sustain a person's spirit and will, even as their body weakened.

At Dachau, Zipper's first job was digging ditches, but doing this 12 hours a day caused his muscles to rip and affected his shoulders to such an extent that he could not raise his arms. Fearing that the guards would execute him if he could not continue shoveling, he welcomed the fortuitous reassignment of hauling cement as a human pack-horse. Although back-breaking work, this task did not require lifting his arms and afforded him the opportunity to talk to other prisoners. Once Zipper started lugging supplies around the camp, he got to know people and within a few weeks had met many musicians, including a couple of accomplished string players. More importantly, he became acquainted with some instrument makers who had been assigned to the woodworking shop. He convinced them to construct a few instruments and even persuaded a sympathetic guard to procure violin strings. Rather than conclude that the effort required to create music in such a bleak setting was simply too great, Zipper knew that offering music to his fellow prisoners felt not only natural, but necessary. So after locating a couple of instruments around the camp in addition to the newly made ones, Zipper once again founded his own orchestra, although this ensemble of 14 prisoners had little in common with his earlier groups. His composition skills proved indispensable as Zipper needed to compose original music for this motley crew and create arrangements of popular classical works. The ensemble rehearsed in secret on Sundays in an unused latrine. This location also served as the venue for short, 15-minute concerts that they repeatedly gave over a period of three hours to a rotating audience of 20 or 30 prisoners at a time. Not meant as merely entertainment or distraction, these performances proved popular and worth the risk because they returned some dignity to those who had been stripped of so much.

Then in late June, Jura Soyfer, Zipper's acquaintance from his underground cabaret days, arrived in Dachau. Soyfer had tried to escape Vienna on skis to Switzerland, but was arrested en route. He and Zipper reconnected, becoming closer friends than they had ever been in Vienna. They often engaged in deep discussions about their need to use words and music to cope with their circumstances. One afternoon in September while the two men walked back to their barracks, the phrase written above the entrance gate, *Arbeit Macht Frei* (Work Sets You Free), prompted Zipper to propose that it should form the basis of a song. He suggested that Soyfer write a poem that would parody the motto. Within just a few days, Soyfer had completed the words, and in less than a week, Zipper had set them to a march-like tune. Their new piece, *Dachau Song* (Dachau Lied), featured multiple stanzas of burning satire about life in the camp, punctuated with a repeating refrain that mockingly extolled Dachau's captives to work hard since "work leads to freedom alone!"[4] As soon as they finished the song, the two comrades began to teach the words and music by ear to their musician friends in the camp. The song spread like wildfire through Dachau, empowering the prisoners with a sense of rebellion against their Nazi captors. *Dachau Song* eventually made its way to other concentration camps and then to other countries, spanning from Holland to Mexico. It not only survived in its oral form, but appeared in a 1953 anthology of concentration camp protest songs published in East Germany.

That same month, September 1938, the Nazi command at Dachau transferred Herbert Zipper, his brother Walter, and Jura Soyfer to Buchenwald. At the time of its construction in 1937, Buchenwald was the largest of the German concentration camps. Its main camp sat on a hill in eastern Germany near the city of Weimar and was eventually expanded to include 85 subcamps throughout the region. Buchenwald witnessed a similar cycle of inmates as Dachau—first political prisoners, and then other groups the Nazis opposed, such as Jews, Roma, and homosexuals. After the war began, the camp also housed POWs, especially Soviet and Polish soldiers. Its prisoners, like those at Dachau, provided critical war labor. As the U.S. troops approached in 1945, the Nazi guards abandoned the main camp, and the captives freed themselves. Some of the prisoners at the subcamps, however, were murdered by their guards before they fled. In the end, almost 240,000 inmates passed in and out of Buchenwald, including 20,000 Jews. Although its total population had ranked similarly with that of Dachau, Buchenwald's death tolls were almost doubled at around 56,000.

When Zipper arrived at Buchenwald, he immediately discovered that the administration of this camp differed greatly from that of Dachau. Where Dachau had been uncompromisingly organized and precise, Buchenwald marched to a messy and chaotic cadence, with many of those in charge perpetually drunk. The camp even lacked running water until January 1939, which severely limited the fluid intake for Zipper and his fellow prisoners, as well as left them no way to bathe or brush their teeth for months. One of the additional challenges of working at Buchenwald involved its hilly geography, which forced prisoners to climb up and down all day in clay dirt that sucked at their shoes and made every maneuver exhausting.

For his work assignment, Zipper joined a group of 24 prisoners, almost all university graduates, who were responsible for the disgusting and dangerous job of emptying the latrines, which had to be done with five gallon buckets that they lowered into the latrine pits and then hauled down the hill. Although large and deep, the four pits proved insufficient to accommodate Buchenwald's thousands of prisoners and needed to be completely drained every day. Because the latrines had no seats and nothing to hold on to or lean against, sometimes people fell into the pits or were even pushed by the guards as sick entertainment. Many died at the bottom of these pits because no one would help them. In an act of tremendous bravery and generosity, Zipper rescued a man once, even though it left him also covered in excrement with no effective way to get clean.

Due to the dreadful circumstances at Buchenwald, Zipper found no opportunities to organize musicians or performances as he had in Dachau, although Soyfer did become involved in some underground cabarets. Zipper was still imprisoned at Buchenwald when *Kristallnacht* (Night of Broken Glass) took place on November 9, 1938. In response to the fatal shooting of German official Ernst vom Rath in Paris by a young Polish Jew named Herschel Grynszpan, the Nazis conducted their first major pogrom, a 24-hour rampage throughout Germany that targeted synagogues, Jewish homes, and Jewish businesses, which were all well labeled with the mandatory Star of David. The violence led to the burning of over 200 synagogues and the looting of approximately 10,000 Jewish shops. The damage from just the broken glass was estimated at five million marks or over one million in U.S. dollars.

Nazi officials also arrested about 30,000 Jews that night, and Zipper noted the arrival of 244 of them at his camp. As an additional retaliation for vom Rath's assassination, guards at Buchenwald slashed food rations for the Jewish inmates by half, resulting in a marked increase of deaths from starvation. Life in the camp further declined as typhoid ravaged the inmate population. Zipper also had to clean the separate typhoid latrine, and although many with that job succumbed to the disease themselves, he was mercifully spared. In fact, Zipper and his friend Soyfer regularly volunteered for whatever grim duty needed to be done, which often involved corpse removal, because they wanted to witness the atrocities first hand in order to provide a full and unblinking account after the war. So as a result, Zipper observed unspeakable acts of brutality and subjugation at Buchenwald, and it weighed heavily on him that one human being could inflict such cruelty on another for the sake of an ideology.

One of the only encouragements for Zipper during this time was being allowed to write his family every other week, although no mention has been made about whether he also corresponded with Trudl in the Philippines. His family had all escaped to Paris, and Zipper used a clever coding system so that his letters would pass inspection. Even in the late 1930s, Jews with means, like the Zipper family, could still obtain visas and immigrate to other countries; and prisoners such as Zipper, who had been designated as in "protective custody," could be released if their families could garner an emigration visa for them. But by 1941, emigration would become impossible as Nazi hatred for the Jews found no balm except unfettered annihilation. Deportation alone had ceased to satisfy since they still viewed those with Jewish ancestry as a threat and pestilence, regardless of where they lived. October 1941 saw the last group of Jewish refugees allowed to leave Vienna.

Finally, after almost a year of captivity, remarkable news arrived in February 1939 that Zipper's father had secured Uruguay visas for him and his brother and that they would soon be released. The excitement, however, became somewhat overshadowed by the declining health of Jura Soyfer, who had contracted typhoid from handling the contaminated corpses and, with no real medical treatment available, was unlikely to survive. Zipper sorely regretted this for two reasons: one being, obviously, the loss of such a true friend and the other, the forfeiture of a gifted writer who would have been able to capture the experiences in the camps with such skill and undaunted conviction. Tragically, Jura Soyfer died on February 16, 1939, at age 26, only a few weeks before his own scheduled release date.

Four days later, on February 20, 1939, Herbert and Walter Zipper's freedom day arrived. After administering a perfunctory medical exam, camp officials returned the clothes they had been wearing when arrested. So, adorned in bloody clothes from his assault nine months earlier, Herbert Zipper walked outside the camp gates with his brother to await buses that would transport them to the train station in Weimar. The first leg of the trip sent them to Leipzig, a city where J.S. Bach had been such a prominent musician. Then from Leipzig, another train carried them to Vienna on February 21, where they found temporary lodging while undergoing the arduous process of negotiating with Reich officials to obtain a passport with their Uruguay visas. Finally on March 16, the Zipper brothers boarded a train for Paris that transported them to a joyful reunion with their parents and other siblings. Not surprisingly, Zipper's family noticed an unmistakable change in him. His demeanor exuded a new depth and intensity that underscored the seriousness of purpose that had always been part of his temperament. For Zipper, of all of the injustices he had endured in the concentration camps, the most difficult and heartbreaking had been the loss of time, the stealing of his life and career. For a man so driven and passionate, this theft had been almost unbearable. But nevertheless, he made the conscious choice that he would use the horrific experiences of the camps to reinvent himself as a citizen of the world.

After arriving in Paris, Zipper sent a telegram to Trudl to let her know he was safe. Her one-year appointment in the Philippines had turned into a permanent position, and she had also created a dance department at the Academy of Music in Manila and founded a dance company named Ballet Moderne. Their 12-year love affair continued undiminished, despite the fact that so much of it had been spent apart. Never idle, Zipper reunited with colleagues in Paris who had also fled and actually received a commission right away to write music for an opera. He eventually met with Jura Soyfer's girlfriend, Helly Andis, and shared the details about their time in the camps. During this visit, he wrote down Soyfer's text to *Dachau Song* for her. Zipper also created a copy of both the words and melody for Hans Wiegel, a former colleague in the underground theater, and asked Wiegel to make another to send to Eric Simon, one of Zipper's musician friends from Vienna. Simon had managed to escape to the United States, and Zipper wanted to get a copy of the song to another continent.

Less than three months after his release from Buchenwald, Zipper received a job offer on May 3 via telegram from the Philippines to replace the late Austrian-born Dr. Alexander Lippay as the conductor of the Manila Symphony and director of the Academy of Music. This presented the perfect opportunity for Zipper professionally and personally. He would have invigorating and steady employment, and he would be reunited with the love of his life. Trudl had made sure that Zipper's talents were well known in Manila and to Trinidad Legarda, the influential president of the Manila Symphony Society, who subsequently extended the offer to him. Leaving his family so soon constituted Zipper's only regret, but he was not the only sibling to abandon Paris. His sister Hedy and her husband immigrated to the United States later that year, and Walter departed for England. None of them could have foreseen the Nazi invasion of France on May 10, 1940, and the ensuing occupation of Paris a month later that trapped their parents and brother Otto.

Herbert Zipper in Paris, 1939 (Herbert Zipper Archive at Crossroads School for Arts & Sciences).

Zipper left Paris on May 27, 1939, first via train to Milan, then by boat to Manila, arriving on June 23. After a busy first day in Manila of receptions, ceremonies, and some much needed time with Trudl, Zipper started work the very next day with a rehearsal of the Manila Symphony in preparation of their upcoming performance of Tchaikovsky's *Symphony No. 6*, the "Pathétique," as a memorial to their recently deceased conductor. But this rehearsal caused quite a shock for Maestro Zipper, who had eagerly accepted the job without much information and apparently without any prior warning from Trudl, who seemed to have shrewdly failed to mention some crucial details. Zipper discovered that many of the orchestra members had little experience playing their instruments, especially the wind and brass players, who used to be supplied to the symphony from the constabulary band. But a new law now prohibited that, so music students and other non-orchestral musicians had recently been recruited to learn these instruments. The Manila Symphony functioned as an undeniably odd contingent of skilled and unskilled musicians.

Fortunately, as a highly capable teacher, Zipper possessed the patience and determination to make this orchestra succeed. He began working immediately with the new musicians, and the inchoate orchestra progressed quickly and performed several concerts that same year. He also founded a symphony chorus so that they and the orchestra could perform masterworks such as Mozart's *Requiem*, which they did. Frank Ephraim, a Jewish child who had fled from Berlin to Manila with his family, fondly remembered Herbert Zipper's presence in the musical happenings of the city. In his memoir *Escape to Manila*,[5] Ephraim shared his recollections of sitting in the concert hall as the Manila Symphony rehearsed Beethoven's *Ninth Symphony* under the baton of Maestro Zipper and with his mother singing in the choir. He recalled that Zipper had decided that the "Ode to Joy" would be sung in English and not the original German because of the atrocities that had been committed in the name of German nationalism. But regardless of his busy schedule, Zipper finally found time to focus on his personal life during his early months in Manila. After so many years of waiting, Herbert Zipper married Trudl Dubsky on October 1, 1939, in an elaborate and well-attended ceremony at the Arch-Bishop's palace.

Following the conclusion of his first successful concert season with the Manila Symphony Orchestra, Zipper again called upon his talents for fundraising and persuasion. He indeed succeeded in securing the MSO an extended summer concert season in the mountain retreat city of Baguio. In addition to its beauty, this location provided a welcome relief from the oppressive tropical heat of Manila, which along with being uncomfortable also created serious hygiene problems and disease, especially for the refugees who were not accustomed to it. But despite his professional and personal triumphs, Zipper could not ignore the mounting threat from Japan that loomed over the Pacific region. The Japanese had been amassing an impressive Navy, and there seemed little doubt that they intended to launch an offensive. He also grew increasingly worried about his parents and Otto, who were still trapped in Nazi-occupied Paris. In this regard, he turned to his friend Francis Sayre, who served as the High Commissioner of the Philippines, a position that named him the proxy for the President of the United States over this U.S. territory. The political maneuverings could prove tricky at times because the United States had occupied the Philippines since 1898 when it was ceded along with Puerto Rico and Guam as a condition of the Treaty of Paris that had ended the Spanish-American War. Nevertheless, Sayre used his influence to secure visas for Zipper's family to the United States, where they reunited with Hedy and remained for the rest of their lives.

On December 7, 1941, Zipper's fears were confirmed with the Japanese attack on Pearl Harbor, an incident that ushered in dire consequences for the Philippines. For whatever reason, General Douglas MacArthur, the commander of the Allied forces in the Pacific, delayed his response for nine hours. This hesitation afforded the Japanese, with their exceptional war resources and intricate spy network, time to destroy almost all of the United States Air Force planes in the Far East. Japan's devastating blow certainly shared an eerie similarity with how Hitler had taken advantage of a bewildered Stalin earlier that summer and preemptively wiped out the majority of Russia's planes in the first few hours of Operation Barbarossa.

When Zipper heard the news about Pearl Harbor, he knew that at any moment the Japanese bombs would start falling around them in the Philippines, which they did, and without any resistance from the U.S. Air Force. Manila, the densely populated capital, was left defenseless as the U.S. retreated from its losses. Zipper must have marveled at the prescient timing of the Manila Symphony Orchestra and Chorus's performance of Mozart's *Requiem* just two days before this attack at a concert to commemorate the 150th anniversary of the composer's death. Now, as a result of the Japanese onslaught, the Academy of Music and the University of the Philippines closed, and the orchestra disbanded so as not to become a propaganda tool for the Japanese. But always with an eye toward the future, Zipper decided that the instruments and music library should be secured, so his wealthy and influential friend Benito Legarda offered one of his unused distilleries as an ideal hiding place.

The Japanese army officially seized control of Manila on January 1, 1942. That same month, they arrested Herbert Zipper because of his friendships with high-ranking U.S. officials, such as Sayre, and for his outspokenness against the Axis powers. Ironically, Zipper found himself imprisoned at the university's music conservatory, which had been converted to a jail. On February 1, the Japanese began a four-week-long interrogation to extract information they erroneously assumed Zipper possessed due to his American ties. Fortunately, they only questioned him and did not resort to physical abuse or torture. After receiving no helpful intelligence, the Japanese formulated another use for Zipper. By convincing him to reestablish the orchestra and program a series of concerts, they hoped to garner favor and acquiescence from the people of Manila. So, if he would agree to this condition, his captors promised to release him. But after leaving the jail, Zipper engaged in a clever cat and mouse game with the Japanese, in which he stalled by concocting all kinds of excuses concerning lost instruments and unavailable players. Despite their pressure, Zipper continued to be evasive. In fact, the only work that he and Trudl did during this time was to give private lessons, usually bartered for food.

As the war dragged on, food became scarcer, and after the flooding from a typhoon in November 1943, conditions deteriorated further, causing many citizens to die of starvation. Not content to sit around helplessly, Zipper joined the underground resistance operation, through which he supplied information to the U.S. forces via an illegal radio. He continued to aid the U.S. efforts until the end of the war, while resolutely keeping his actions secret from Trudl, so as not to endanger her. Just as his time in the two concentration camps had changed him, Zipper's work in Manila brought about further transformation, particularly his active participation in the resistance, which fueled an ongoing departure from the privileged and intellectual lifestyle of his birthplace and childhood. "The seeds were set for his second life as a community worker. He had lost Europe but had gained a more global humanity."[6]

Finally on September 23, 1944, Filipino residents received cause for hope with the arrival of U.S. planes that delivered a crushing blow to Japanese ships and planes. The difficult battle to liberate Manila commenced in earnest on February 3, 1945, taking MacArthur's troops 30 days to accomplish. But with this victory came catastrophic destruction to buildings and the entire infrastructure of the city, as the Japanese did not give up easily. Japan's army also committed unspeakable atrocities against the people of Manila, murdering approximately 100,000 during the final battle, which constituted 10 percent of the estimated one million civilian casualties in the Philippines during the war in the Pacific. The grim aftermath left survivors stranded amid the rubble of a demolished city and surrounded by decomposing corpses.

The 30-day siege of Manila had also taken a harrowing toll on the Zippers, who narrowly skirted death on an almost daily basis. They had moved frantically from place to place to avoid bombings and had scrounged for bits of food and water, all while carrying what few possessions remained and their dachshund Niddy. Fortunately, Zipper and Trudl both possessed keen instincts and a sheer relentlessness that navigated them and many others safely through such a daunting and perilous time. Somehow, despite the circumstances, Trudl had also managed to use her artistic abilities to capture the city of Manila under the occupation of the Japanese in watercolors that communicated more than words ever could. These illustrations would finally be published in a collection, *Manila 1944–45 As Trudl Saw It*, in 1994, almost 20 years after her death.

The fighting died down by March 1, and even though the Zippers had lost almost all of their belongings, Herbert Zipper resolved to offer music to the devastated city. After three years of not stepping onto the podium, he believed more than ever in the power of music to provide solace and catalyze healing. So, he began making plans to reorganize the Manila Symphony Orchestra and boldly wrote a letter to General MacArthur, which requested his help and explained why music was vital for the city at this time. He hand delivered it to MacArthur's headquarters at 2 p.m., and at 5 p.m., two high-ranking officers arrived at Zipper's home to see what was needed. He provided them with a list of musical supplies that would have to be sent by air from San Francisco, and as further evidence of his charismatic and persuasive flair, the request received immediate approval, signed by MacArthur himself. The package arrived in less than a week, despite the ongoing war.

Materials in hand, Zipper assembled the symphony board and presented his plan. After facing some initial resistance, he convinced them of the necessity for a concert. He then undertook the almost impossible task of locating musicians, as so many had left Manila, or been killed, or appeared too weak from malnutrition to play. Especially tragic was the loss of the orchestra's concertmaster, Ernesto Vallejo, who had been burned alive with a large group of people that the Japanese had locked in a church before setting fire to it.

The U.S. Army continued to assist Zipper and responded with food and clothes for the orchestra members he located. With the aid of the board members, Zipper arranged for the Santa Cruz Cathedral, at least what was left of it, to serve as the concert venue and started rehearsals in early April. The concert, slated for May 9, 1945, caused tremendous excitement, and in spite of the destitute conditions, all 2,400 tickets for the event sold out the same morning they went on sale. Now, Zipper's most pressing problem involved not enough chairs for the audience. With only 200 in his possession, he scoured the city for thousands more. Zipper eventually struck a deal with an elderly Chinese man, who agreed to travel throughout Manila rounding up seating for a rental fee of 35 cents per chair.

But all of the effort to stage this performance would be worth it, as this emotional concert would be one that Maestro Zipper and the audience never forgot. The beleaguered citizens of Manila filed into the audience seats, joining with numerous dignitaries, U.S. Army officials, and Jean MacArthur, the wife of General MacArthur. Illuminated by U.S. Army searchlights, Zipper led the Manila Symphony Orchestra in Beethoven's *Eroica Symphony*, a work he had vowed to perform when the Nazis were crushed, and in Dvořák's *New World Symphony*, as a salute to the United States who had helped defeat the Nazis and liberate the Philippines. Trinidad Legarda gave a moving speech at intermission that reiterated the need for music in these perilous times, since it alone was able to transcend words and communicate feelings too deep and profound to be expressed in any other way. In an event filled with such significance for those in attendance, perhaps the most meaningful moment occurred in the second movement of the Beethoven, the funeral march, as the distant sounds of the war could still be heard, and the juxtaposition of this music and the artillery magnified the symbolism of the evening.

The U.S. Army, which had been so instrumental in assisting Zipper, asked him to repeat the concert for the soldiers, which he did. Then, having witnessed for themselves the transformational nature of music, army officials requested that he present a concert every day, which again he did for the next 45 weeks through February 1946. These performances took place at a rented movie theater called The Rex, with the repertoire changing every two weeks. The daily rehearsals and concerts sustained Zipper, the musicians, and the people of Manila from 1945 to 1946 and endowed a musical legacy that would have a profound impact for many years.

But despite their successes in the Philippines, Herbert and Trudl Zipper felt ready to move on and find a permanent home country in which to establish citizenship. On February 12, 1946, the Zippers boarded a ship for a 31-day voyage to the United States, arriving on March 14 in the San Francisco Bay. Zipper had accepted a new position as liaison between the United States and the newly formed Committee for the Cultural Rehabilitation of the Philippines. After a heartfelt reunion with his parents, Hedy, and Otto, Zipper headed to the East Coast to start his work. But he soon learned that the government of the Philippines, through changes in leadership, had decided to put this project on hold. Fortunately, Zipper never seemed to be without stimulating opportunities for very long and was invited to revive a defunct orchestra in Brooklyn, New York. And so, his life's work of resurrection and creation would continue and flourish in his new country, where he and Trudl became citizens in 1951. During the intervening years, Zipper made periodic trips back to Manila to conduct concerts with the Manila Symphony and to champion arts education. Part of his heart would always be with the Filipino people.

Word of Herbert and Trudl Zipper's talents and passion spread throughout their newly adopted country. She would teach, choreograph, and establish dance departments and dance companies wherever they lived. He would work as an educator and conductor in New York and Chicago, before finally settling in Los Angeles in 1972 to teach at the University of Southern California. Although a bit late, the Zippers became part of the large group of Jewish émigrés that resided in Southern California. The rise of Hollywood and the subsequent need for composers and musicians for the film industry had coincided, in an almost macabre symbiosis, with the mass exodus from Europe affected by Hitler's reign of terror. This juxtaposition steered many to where this budding industry offered work, as well as asylum, and the more the prominent names flocked to this area, the more it became a draw and destination for others. Most, including Arnold Schoenberg and Erich Korngold, would choose to remain there for the rest of their lives.

Once in California, Zipper initiated, as he had in other cities, a targeted effort to reach the youngest of children through establishing arts education programs for preschool and elementary aged children, which ranged from instruction in the schools to educational concerts that the students could attend. Sadly on July 3, 1976, after only a few years in California, Zipper lost Trudl, the woman who had been his love and life's companion for almost 50 years, after a prolonged and agonizing battle with cancer. But Zipper refused to allow his grief or age to limit him. In 1981, he traveled to China and embraced yet another country where he could spread his love of music and work tirelessly to bring joy to children and adults through music. Then on September 23, 1988, Zipper conducted the 50th anniversary performance of his *Dachau Song* for the Autumn Festival in Graz, Austria, with a male chorus and a new orchestration that he had composed. In a way, this event signified a closure of his life's story, as his days as a young intellectual in Vienna and then the horrors of the Holocaust and World War II circled back to this piece of music as a culminating celebration of life and freedom.

On October 1, 1995, the United States Holocaust Memorial Museum in Washington, D.C, honored the 91-year-old Herbert Zipper for his contributions during and after the war. At the ceremony, in another remarkable expression of symmetry, Frank Ephraim, the young boy who had listened to Zipper's orchestra rehearsals in Manila, was in attendance as a museum volunteer and finally got to officially make the acquaintance of Maestro Zipper after

Herbert Zipper conducting the 50th anniversary performance of "Dachau Lied" at the Autumn Festival in Graz, Austria, on September 23, 1988 (Herbert Zipper Archive at Crossroads School for Arts & Sciences).

so many years. Never one to quit, Zipper remained active, conducting children's concerts and assisting with arts education programs in Los Angeles until just a few months before his death from lung cancer on April 21, 1997, at age 92.

The life of Dr. Herbert Zipper has been described by many honorifics—remarkable, unforgettable, and aspirational. His impact encompassed not just the ways that he reverentially harnessed music to empower, to provide solace, and to heal the battered human spirit, but also the sheer breadth of his days from 19th century *fin de siècle* Vienna through the entire 20th century, with its wars and unprecedented rate of change. Zipper's life represented an incredible odyssey, from concentration camps, to Manila, to the United States, and finally to China. Although born into privilege and endowed with extraordinary musical gifts, Zipper did not always have an easy journey, but a necessary one. As a result of his difficult and often harrowing experiences, Herbert Zipper became convinced that "his life's mission was to spread the gift of classical music to those who might not otherwise experience it."[7] The various facets of Zipper's life as musician, conductor, prisoner, arts advocate, and educator stood as a testament to his talents, passion, and love of humankind. As Paul Cummins so aptly concluded, Herbert Zipper's true calling was as a "builder." All over the world he built musical and educational opportunities, regardless of the circumstances. "Whatever the practical obstacles, he [has] found ways to overcome and to 'only connect' people with each other, with ideas, with the Arts, with their better selves."[8]

4

Alice Herz-Sommer and the Music in Terezín

Music was life. We did not, could not, would not give up.
—Alice Herz-Sommer quoted in Caroline Stoessinger,
A Century of Wisdom, 108

The 300-member audience waited with eager anticipation for the music to begin. Finally, one of Czechoslovakia's most celebrated pianists, Alice Herz-Sommer, took her seat at the piano after acknowledging the enthusiastic applause and making quick eye contact with her 6-year-old son Rafi on the front row. The first notes to fill the room were Bach's, as they were every day during Alice's rigorous practice regimen. For Alice, the music of Johann Sebastian Bach felt the most spiritual, the most capable of communication with a higher power. She held a particular connection with Bach's *Partita in B flat Major*, which she had chosen as the opening work on the evening's program, followed by music of Chopin and Beethoven, all pouring forth from her agile fingers and from the wells of passion in her heart. For those listening, this music, in this moment, provided a portal to another time and place, transporting them away from their dire circumstances. For unlike so many of the concerts that Alice had played on the finest pianos and in exquisite concert halls, this one took place on a beat-up instrument in a small, dilapidated auditorium in a place that functioned as both a ghetto and a concentration camp, a place called Terezín.

Alice Herz had been born in Prague on November 26, 1903. Her father Friedrich Herz ran a successful business manufacturing precision scales and became one of the first people in Prague to own a car. Her mother Sofie was a talented pianist, as well as a highly intelligent and well-read woman who hobnobbed with the artistic aristocracy of the day, including Gustav Mahler, Thomas Mann, Rainer Maria Rilke, and Franz Kafka. Her marriage to Friedrich had been arranged in the Ashkenazi tradition by a *schadchen* (marriage broker), but despite her efforts, Sofie never grew to love him. She remained unhappy throughout their almost 50-year marriage. Blessed with both intellectual prowess and artistic sensibilities, Sofie felt that she had married beneath her and had thus been sentenced to spend life joined to a man, almost twice her age, with whom she could not converse. But even though her feelings for Friedrich ran less than warm, Sofie embraced her role as a mother. Alice had four siblings: two older brothers named Georg and Paul, a sister Irma who was 12 years her senior, and a twin named Marianne, but known affectionately as Mizzi.

Music flourished as a vital aspect of life in Prague, and Alice grew up frequenting concerts by many of the world's greatest performers. She especially loved sitting in the beautiful theater where Mozart had premiered his opera *Don Giovanni* and relished in the knowledge that Prague had been a favorite city of the renowned composer. Alice experienced an unspeakable thrill whenever she touched Mozart's piano that still sat in the house where he and his wife had lived during the production of the opera. In addition to the many grand musical events that took place throughout the city, informal house concerts, often hosted by amateur musicians, constituted a popular pastime throughout Eastern Europe and in the Herz home. Frequently, composers attended these concerts and offered the first hearing of their latest work.

In the running of the household, Alice's mother was strict and even harsh at times. Sofie had dedicated herself to embracing German high culture and distancing herself and the children from the Judaism of her childhood and her Yiddish mother tongue. She insisted on German as the acceptable language in the Herz home, although her bilingual children spoke Czech with their friends. But Sofie's efforts did not completely eliminate the scourge of anti–Semitism aimed toward her children, as they encountered racial slurs sometimes on the playground. The Herz home frequently reverberated with caustic arguments between Alice's parents, especially over the subject of money. Friedrich exercised complete control of the family's finances and remained unrepentantly stingy his entire life, forcing his wife to beg him for money for even the basics such as groceries. During the difficult moments, Alice retreated to her grandmother, Fanny Schulz, who lived with them. She was an intelligent and interesting woman, with whom Alice loved spending time and listening to the stories of her mother's childhood. The Schulz family had lived in the town of Iglau, just a few streets from the Mahler family. Alice especially enjoyed hearing how her mother had gotten to know Gustav during their youth and had watched him develop his prodigious musical talents.

Alice eagerly began her piano study in 1910 at age 7, having been inspired by her mother's love of the instrument and by an unforgettable meeting in Vienna when she was 4 years old. Her mother had taken her via train to Vienna to hear Gustav Mahler conduct his *Second Symphony* on November 24, 1907. Sometime after the concert, quite possibly at the train station the next morning, Alice's mother spoke briefly with the composer, and little Alice shyly exchanged a few words with him as well. This momentary encounter left an indelible impression on the young child.

Alice's older sister Irma served as her first piano teacher. A highly motivated pupil, Alice practiced with dedication on her grandmother's piano, easily memorizing all of her pieces and working up to four hours a day. Then the following year, as a child of 8, she met Franz Kafka for the first time. Kafka became a frequent visitor to the Herz residence and an honorary family member known to Alice as Uncle Franz. He often ate meals at their home and joined them for Jewish holidays such as Passover, the only occasions when the Herz family proffered any acknowledgment of their Jewish ancestry. When the weather allowed, Kafka took the twins Alice and Mizzi for strolls and picnics in the resplendent countryside. The Herz family, and especially Alice, maintained a close relationship with Kafka until his tragically young death from tuberculosis on June 3, 1924, at age 40.

Throughout their formative years, the Herz children continued to embrace their mother's devotion to music. Alice's older brother Paul studied the violin, and he and Alice played duets. By the time Alice turned 10 and Paul 13, they played together almost every day and performed frequently for family and friends. They were especially celebrated for their interpretation of Schumann's *Träumerei*. Through their music, Paul and Alice developed a special bond that would later prove vital in the darker times of their lives. By 1915, Alice had made such progress on the piano that Irma took her to audition for her own beloved teacher, Václav Štěphán, who at only 25 years of age had already distinguished himself as a pianist and musicologist. Alice played a Beethoven sonata for him, and he agreed to take her on as his pupil. Alice adored him right away as a teacher and fellow music lover. She also was captivated by his mysterious air, no doubt compounded by the black eye patch he wore, having lost an eye fighting at the beginning of the Great War.

At first, the Herz children had appeared mostly unaffected by the start of World War I. Their father's successful factory enabled them for a time to keep their pantries well stocked. But as the years wore on, they too joined the long bread lines with the other citizens of Prague. Alice's father had invested heavily in war loans, and at the end of the war, all of that money was lost. The subsequent creation of Czechoslovakia also negatively impacted the Herz family. With the new government came a surge of nationalism among the native Czechs, which fueled animosity toward German-speakers and Jews. This included an onslaught against German culture that threatened to uproot some of Prague's cherished artistic institutions and communities.

The much revered Prague Conservatory became a state institution with an ardent Czech nationalistic ethos that often alienated German students. As a result, separate schools for the arts emerged to serve the German population, including the German Academy of Music in Prague, which was headed by Alexander Zemlinsky, a former student of Johannes Brahms. Once the new Academy opened, Alice eagerly scheduled an audition and practiced eight or more hours a day in preparation. Her impressive playing earned her a much coveted spot. For Alice, the more difficult hurdle was convincing her father to pay the expensive tuition. But in the end, she and her mother prevailed. At the Academy, Alice's exceptionally warm and engaging spirit drew people to her, and Zemlinsky himself became a lifelong friend. In an almost reverent communion, her music study there remained only one generation removed from some of the greatest masters. Her piano teacher, Conrad Ansorge, had been a student of Franz Liszt, and many of the other faculty members had studied or been friends with Chopin and Brahms. After several years of dedicated work with Ansorge, Alice made her professional debut in 1924 as a soloist, playing Chopin's *Piano Concerto in E minor* with the Czech Philharmonic.

Even though Alice poured almost all of her time and energy into the piano throughout the 1920s, she still made time for her friends, especially Trude Hutter. Trude and Alice had met as young girls and bonded playing piano duets. In 1925, Trude introduced Alice to Leopold Sommer, a successful businessman and fine violinist, while hosting a summer evening house concert in which Alice performed. Alice and Leopold felt a strong connection right away, and that night marked the beginning of their prolonged, but deeply satisfying, courtship. During these years, Alice cared for her declining father who suffered from heart problems. Her mother was also unwell because of chronic blood clots in her legs. But through everything, including her father's passing in 1930, Leopold remained by her side. Alice and Leopold finally married the next year in 1931, and their only child, a son named Raphael, was born on June 21, 1937.[1]

Alice's musical aspirations continued to blossom in the 1930s, as she solidified a reputation for flawless technique and moving interpretations. But the ascendency of the Third Reich in Germany and its ravenous hunger to claim more land for its empire, while simultaneously ridding those lands of what it called the Jewish pestilence, gravely concerned the Jews in Czechoslovakia. A substantial number of Jewish artists and intellectuals had fled to Prague from Germany and Austria as the Nazis assumed power, joining the already prominent Jewish population there. Alice came to know many of them through their shared interest in music. With Prague as an important cultural center that already housed ethnic Germans, these Jewish refugees felt at home. But their comfort would be short-lived.

Following the German annexation of Austria in March 1938, Alice's sisters Mizzi and Irma had begun preparations to relocate their families to Palestine, and they encouraged Alice to do the same. But as the caregiver for their elderly, widowed mother, who was not well enough to travel, Alice chose to remain in Prague, trusting as so many errantly did that their status as influential and assimilated Jews would protect them. In a selfless gesture, Alice and her mother actually provided much of the funds Mizzi and Irma needed for the exorbitant immigration fees, which in today's economy would be the equivalent of approximately $100,000 per person. But despite almost a year of meticulous planning, Alice's sisters and their families barely escaped. They departed on March 14, 1939, on what would become the last train allowed out of Prague before the German invasion of Czechoslovakia.

German reparations following their World War I defeat had mandated the dissolution of the Austro-Hungarian Empire. As a result, an area known as the Sudetenland, which bordered Germany and contained over 3 million native German speakers, became part of Czechoslovakia. Throughout the 1920s and 30s, even though these Germans occupied only about 23 percent of the population of this region, animosity between them and the Czechs intensified. One of Adolf Hitler's populist platforms emphasized the unfair demands inflicted on Germany by the Treaty of Versailles. Hitler was particularly incensed by the Fatherland's loss of territory to Czechoslovakia and vowed to reacquire it. After threatening an armed invasion to retake the Sudetenland, the Third Reich succeeded in obtaining permission from world leaders to annex that land in October 1938, through a deal known as the Munich Agreement. The leaders of France and Britain had reluctantly acquiesced to the demand in return for Hitler's promise that if given the Sudetenland, he would make no further incursions into the rest of Czechoslovakia. It seemed an acceptable price to foster peace and curtail further Nazi expansion, even though citizens of Czechoslovakia would lose important border defenses and some of their main industrial areas. But in the end, the acquisition of the Sudetenland became merely the penultimate maneuver in the Nazis' Czech campaign. Hitler reneged on his commitment and invaded the remainder of Czechoslovakia a few months later in March 1939, declaring the areas of Moravia and Bohemia, which included the city of Prague, as a protectorate of Nazi Germany.

Approximately 120,000 Jews lived in this newly conquered region. Czech President Edvard Beneš, who had served as the president of the Republic since 1935, resigned and fled to England, along with trainloads of Czech children traveling to safety with name tags hung around their necks. Emil Hácha succeeded Beneš and willingly adopted the misanthropic policies of the Third Reich, especially the initiatives targeting Jewish residents. This meant that the Nazis' institutionalized racial discrimination would go into effect in Czechoslovakia, from wearing the yellow Star of David on clothing to turning in radios. Over the next few years, the barrage of regulations and prohibitions grew increasingly onerous and absurd, including a moratorium on going to movies and using cameras, typewriters, or telephones.

Government officials heavily restricted musical activities as well. The works of composers banned by the Nazis vanished from Czech radio and concert halls, along with any works that promoted Slavic nationalism. Some Jewish musicians adopted pseudonyms in an attempt to earn a living or have their compositions performed and published. But this proved to be too great a risk. Instead, many relied on clandestine house concerts; although

4. Alice Herz-Sommer and the Music in Terezín

with an 8 p.m. Jewish curfew, sometimes audiences and performers were forced to stay overnight, a sacrifice they willingly made. The people of Eastern Europe did not consider music as merely an entertainment or a pleasant pastime, but as "a way of life, an integral part, as important as basic human needs such as food and drink."[2]

On March 16, 1939, one day after German soldiers had occupied her city, Alice Herz-Sommer trudged through the snowy streets into the center of Prague, Wenceslaus Square, to witness this atrocity for herself. She soberingly watched crowds of German-speaking Czechs cheering the arrival of the Germans and then recoiled in horror as Adolf Hitler himself rode down the street with his arm triumphantly outstretched in the Nazi salute. This surreal scene caused both great confusion and a sense of ostracism for Alice. As a German-speaking Jewish Czech, she now felt like an outsider. Not only did she not fit in with the new German occupiers, but she no longer seemed at home with native Czechs. Alice had lived her life with little thought of her Jewishness, but now it appeared to be the only identity that mattered.

Rafi Sommer standing in front of a sign forbidding Jews in 1940 (Courtesy Reinhard Piechocki).

Life for Alice and her family grew increasingly difficult with the onslaught of restrictions on Jews. Her son Rafi could no longer attend the Czech nursery school nor play in his favorite park. Jewish ration cards severely limited what food items could be purchased, with eggs, meat, cheese, jam, and many other staples forbidden. Often, only bread and potatoes filled their shopping bags. But the ever-resilient and resourceful Sommer family persevered. Alice continued teaching piano lessons, and as one of the most sought-after piano teachers in Prague, she even retained some of her non–Jewish students, who risked studying with her for a time after it became illegal. Alice also participated in the secret house concerts, where on March 3, 1940, she performed the premiere of Viktor Ullmann's *Second Piano Sonata*, a work that would remain a lifelong favorite of Alice's.

After the occupation of Prague, Nazi families began moving into the apartments in Alice's building. Four-year-old Rafi struck up an unlikely friendship with a 5-year-old boy named Johann Hermann who lived on the floor above them. They played together in the hallways, but never in each other's apartments. Johann's father worked at the Gestapo headquarters, but despite the unorthodox circumstances, Mr. and Mrs. Hermann developed a fondness for Alice's playing as they listened to her hours of practicing. Sometimes, Mrs. Hermann could even be seen reading to both boys in the stairway.

Then, in 1941, Leopold lost his job at a chemical company, again due to racial restrictions. Fearing this eventuality, he had visited Brussels back in 1939 with a friend who wanted him to partner in a business that would supply vending machines of cigarettes and candy for train stations. Leopold hoped that by establishing a successful business in Belgium that he could move his family to safety, and so persuaded his wary mother-in-law Sofie Herz to provide the required financial investment. But sadly, the venture failed, and Leopold returned home to Prague with the difficult news, especially the admission that he had lost all of his mother-in-law's investment. He eventually secured a job working for the Jewish Council in Prague, even though it entailed helping the Gestapo to compile lists of his fellow citizens for deportation. For a time, his position kept him and his family off the deportation lists, but with Prague emptying of all of its Jews, the Sommer family would ultimately be forced to leave as well.

In early 1942, Alice's mother received her notice of deportation to Terezín, a ghetto the Nazis had created for the Czech Jews. Although still a woman of considerable dignity, Sofie Herz was also a frail 72 year old, who had been living in a Jewish retirement home and suffering from a chronic thrombosis in her leg. She appeared more despondent and weak each time Alice visited, and now the government expected Sofie Herz to relocate away from her family and caregivers. As Alice tearfully watched her mother walk into the deportation center with a rucksack on her back, Alice knew that she would never see her again. Rumors had already begun to circulate in Prague about the horrible conditions in Terezín and the staggering levels of disease, deprivation, and death.

Inconsolable after her mother's departure, Alice could not sleep, eat, or play the piano, but instead walked throughout the city for hours at a time. Then one day, as she wandered in a daze down a Prague street, she heard a voice inside her say, "Practise the *24 Etudes*, they will save you."[3] Although not a religious person, Alice was deeply spiritual and took heed of this inner voice, throwing herself wholeheartedly into the process of learning the études of Chopin, some of the most difficult works in all of the piano repertoire. She spent the next year practicing and memorizing these works, whose prescient arrival in Alice's life would indeed serve her well in the coming years. But for now, ironically, her music also posed a threat. Starting in December 1941, regulations forced Jewish citizens to relinquish all of their musical instruments to the Third Reich. The Nazis confiscated Alice's cherished Förster grand piano, but they had not known about her small piccolo piano, which at risk of death, she defiantly hid from them. Now, she used it to immerse herself daily in practice. The Sunday afternoon chamber music gatherings that the Sommer family continued to host in their apartment were also illegal and dangerous for all who attended. Regardless, they drew a loyal and enthusiastic following of some of Prague's most talented Jewish performers and composers, including Viktor Ullmann, a former protégé of Arnold Schoenberg. Then in July 1943, the Sommer family—Alice, Leopold, and 6-year-old Rafi, received the long-dreaded notification that they must vacate their home and deport to Terezín.

Both native Czechs, Alice and her husband certainly knew the long history of the place they were headed to and also a little about what it had become in the hands of the Nazis. In 1780, the emperor of the Austro-Hungarian Empire, Emperor Joseph II, decided to build a garrison town about 30 kilometers outside of Prague that would include a fortress near where the Labe and Ohře Rivers came together to protect his lands from an invasion by German hordes. He named the town Theresienstadt (Theresa's Town) after his mother Empress Maria Theresa. But in Czech, it was known as Terezín. Surrounded by impressive ramparts, Terezín could house approximately 6,000 inhabitants in its 14 large barracks and 200 two-story houses, all resting securely inside a wall and surrounded by a moat. The designers had constructed the town on a square street grid that spanned about two-thirds of a mile with the only entrance or egress points being two heavily fortified gates. Across on the opposite river bank, they also built a second fortress, the "Little Fortress," which the Emperor intended as the actual military stronghold with storage rooms and ground fortifications. But it never served this purpose and instead developed into an unforgivably cruel prison. Many years after its construction, the Little Fortress received what would be its most infamous prisoner, Gavrilo Princip, whose assassination of the Archduke Franz Ferdinand in Sarajevo on June 28, 1914, precipitated the start of World War I. Before the war even ended, Princip succumbed to the harsh conditions there, dying at age 23 on April 28, 1918, of tuberculosis.

With the occupation of Czechoslovakia in 1939, Terezín fell under the complete control of the Third Reich. In September 1941, the Nazi command replaced Konstantin von Neurath, whom they had put in charge as the Protector in 1939, with SS Obergruppenfüher Reinhard Heydrich, later nicknamed, "The Hangman." The following month, Heydrich arranged several meetings with key Nazi figures, including Adolf Eichmann, to formulate a strategy for dealing with the Jews of Czechoslovakia. They decided to convert the fortress town of Terezín into a ghetto with a self-governing Jewish administration called the Council of Elders, but ultimately overseen by Hauptsturmführer Dr. Siegfried Seidls. But although the Germans referred to it as a ghetto, Terezín would exist simultaneously as a ghetto and a concentration camp, with both terms used interchangeably by those imprisoned there and later by Holocaust scholars. After meticulous planning sessions, the Reich felt confident in the viability of their proposal, especially since it had already successfully employed this type of governance system in other Eastern European ghettos. But, of course, what the newly appointed Jewish Elders did not know was that Heydrich's plan also dictated the eventual transport of all of the Jews from Terezín to Auschwitz or other extermination camps in Eastern Europe. Then, Germans would resettle the land as part of the Reich's *Lebensraum* (living space) campaign to allot more room to the Aryan race. But in the meantime, with Auschwitz always functioning beyond capacity, the Nazis felt that having a temporary transit camp would greatly assist in the logistical coordination of their "Final Solution."

Impatient to create this Jewish ghetto, the Nazis issued a mandatory evacuation order to the residents of Terezín in November 1941. The first transport of Jews arrived that same month on November 24, 1941, at the train station of Bohušovice, located about three kilometers from Terezín. Until workers built train tracks all the way to Terezín in 1943, new arrivals had to walk, weighed down by their belongings, the entire three kilometers. This inaugural group, called the *Aufbaukommando* (building detail), consisted of 342 young men charged with readying the ghetto for future transports. Many of them had actually volunteered under what later proved to be false promises from the Nazis. When they entered the ghetto and faced sleeping on the floor in unfurnished rooms with no pillows or bedding, these men realized belatedly that they had become the first prisoners of a new concentration camp. More transports arrived soon after—1,000 people from Prague on November 30 and 1,000 from Brno on December 2. Another *Aufbaukommando* team of 1,000 workers, engineers, technical staff, and physicians came on December 4. The two *Aufbaukommando* groups, delineated simply as *AK1* and *AK2*, did assume a somewhat privileged position at Terezín, with officials eventually providing them with better housing and living conditions. These *AK* units had also been assured of their exemption from deportations to the death camps, a Nazi promise they should not have trusted.

The Council of Elders assembled by the Nazi government to manage Terezín consisted of prestigious members of the Jewish Czech community, under the leadership of Jakob Edelstein. Edelstein had supported the construction of the ghetto because he thought it a better option than the risk of having the Jews of Czechoslovakia shipped to German concentration camps. Edelstein and his staff arrived on the December 4 transport with *AK2* and began to set up the Jewish governance of the "town." But the Elders soon realized the true nature of the place and of themselves as marionettes in a macabre puppet show. Edelstein had believed that the Czech ghetto would allow his people to remain safe in their homeland and that he would be their interlocutor with the Nazi regime. Terribly mistaken, of course, Edelstein eventually faced the patently impossible task of deciding which names of his fellow Terezín residents would go on the list for deportation to Auschwitz.

For most new arrivals at Terezín, the first difficult reality to face entailed separation—husbands from their wives, and often mothers from their children. The women resided in numerous barracks, including Dresdner and Hamburger. These impressive structures featured large outdoor courtyards and had, at one time, housed the Austrian infantry. For the men, barracks such as Sudeten, which had originally been built only as storage facilities, were crudely converted to living spaces. Similarly, many of the children lived in former school buildings reconfigured as children's homes. At first, Nazi officials prohibited family members from visiting each other, and determined prisoners had to take great risk and employ considerable ingenuity to see loved ones. But eventually, the camp commandant instituted visitation hours in the women's barracks.

While most of Terezín's barracks functioned primarily as housing, the Magdeburger barrack also contained the bureaucratic center of the camp. It held the offices of the seven members of the Council of Elders, in addition to those of the Nazi administration. The Elders enjoyed special living quarters in this building, privileged accommodations that provided each with one or two private rooms, a stark contrast to the men in the Sudeten barrack, where hundreds were crammed into storerooms filled with three-tiered bunks and saturated with unrelenting noise and an overwhelming stench. As in other camps, the sequestered population in Terezín constituted its own de facto state, with strict governance from Nazi headquarters in Berlin via the Gestapo office in Prague over every aspect of life from food consumption, to toilet use, to what language could be spoken. Administrated with quintessential Teutonic efficiency and order, offices staffed by prisoners also resided in Magdeburger to attend to and officiate the quotidian necessities and designated priorities, including water works, street cleaning, and agriculture. Officials assigned prisoners with special skills to the appropriate job details, such as carpenters in the lumber yard and professional bakers in the bakery.

A group of artists worked in the *Zeichenstube* (Graphics Office), where the Terezín leadership tasked them with generating detailed reports, complete with statistics and charts, to send to Berlin. Similar to corporate annual reports, these documents outlined and accounted for the functions of the camp, including statistics on coal deliveries, hospital bed counts, and water usage. But these artists also became embroiled in an infamous scandal, referred to later as the "Painters Affair." Not content with merely executing their official duties, this group secretly illustrated in paintings and sketches the true reality of the ghetto, an activity undertaken at great personal risk because, if the Nazi command discovered these unofficial "reports," they would most likely be shipped immediately to Auschwitz. The artists also found extra work painting and sketching portraits of people in exchange for food or other items, but were always careful not to sign their pieces. They traded frequently with a man named František Strass, who had been a wealthy and influential businessman before the war, and who still maintained some friends among the gendarme that guarded the ghetto. Unbeknownst to the artists, Strass added his own captions to their art work and arranged for some pieces to be smuggled out of the camp, eventually arriving in Switzerland and appearing in a Swiss newspaper. When word inevitably reached Berlin in the summer of 1944, Nazi officials descended on the artists at Terezín and, after prolonged interrogations, threw them and their families into the Little Fortress. In this hellish prison with its subterranean dungeons, they endured torture, hard labor, and deprivations of every kind, rendering survival extremely unlikely.

Not long after the ghetto opened, frequent transports left the barracks filled beyond capacity, with more than 58,000 inmates living in a fortress town designed to hold a maximum of 6,000. While the Jewish Elders enjoyed somewhat better living arrangements, everyone else endured wretched conditions, poor hygiene, and shortages of food, medicine, and most necessities. They constantly battled hunger, disease, dysentery, and infestations of bed bugs and lice, all of which led to unbelievably high mortality rates, with as many of 150 perishing per day. But in one of the many perplexing Nazi paradoxes, the Reich command at Terezín remained so obsessed with germs and cleanliness that they assigned prisoners to "toilet guard" in the latrines to ensure that fellow prisoners washed their hands, while at the same time, denying them the use of toilet paper. In the end, Terezín cycled through 139,654 prisoners during its years of operation from 1941 to 1945. A total of 33,419 died in Terezín, and another 96,934 were deported to other ghettos or camps. In the end, only about 20,000 of those who entered the gates of Terezín survived the war.

One of the most tragic facets of the Terezín ghetto involved the large number of children imprisoned there, roughly 15,000 children under the age of 15 between 1941 and 1945. With an unfathomably dismal survival rate, only about 100 of these children lived to see the end of the war and liberation. Children proved especially vulnerable in the concentration camps unless they somehow possessed the strength and maturity to work and make themselves useful to the camp officials. For the children, in addition to their own suffering from starvation and deprivations of all kinds, they watched their parents and loved ones arrested and/or killed, cruelly stealing their innocence at a time when they should have still possessed a safe and idealized view of the world. Instead, violence and death surrounded them, and they witnessed firsthand the inhumanity that people could inflict on one another. For those who managed to survive the war, the difficulty of returning to society often overwhelmed them, as powerfully described by writer Anne Lamott.

> I think often of the weeks after the end of WWII, in the refugee camps for orphans and dislocated kids. Of course the children couldn't sleep! But the grown-ups discovered that after you fed them, if you gave them each a piece of bread just to hold, they would drift off. It was holding bread. There was more to eat if they were still hungry. This was bread to hold, to remind them and connect them to the great truth—that morning would come, that there were grown-ups who cared and were watching over them, that there would be more food when they awoke.[4]

Indeed, throughout the Holocaust, parents placed the hope of their family's and their culture's survival on the children. According to survivor Dasha Lewin, who had been a young girl in Terezín, "…we were told by the elders that anything could prevail and people with strong beliefs and good causes will always survive and for us it was much stronger than just the children doing something for their mother—it was for us the hope that we could survive."[5] But in reality, the Third Reich murdered over 1.5 million children through gas chambers, disease, starvation, or other unspeakable acts. Those lost included one million Jewish children, in addition to Roma and Slavic children, and German children with mental or physical defects.

> In children the nation is eternal. Destroy them, and in a few decades the nation—or we may substitute the race—will be reduced to a few paragraphs in a history book, and culture will be attested through a few museum collections … the Jewish children became unwilling pawns in the inconspicuous, undeclared warfare between the leaders of the Czech Jewish community and their Nazi oppressors.[6]

The Third Reich did, in fact, heavily document the Jewish culture, including collecting memorabilia for displays that they believed would be all that remained of these people.

While Terezín in numerous ways appeared to be a typical Nazi concentration camp, in actuality it evolved into the most unique in the camp system, a "showpiece" or "model camp" designed for the famous and wealthy of the Jewish artistic and intellectual communities. Indeed, the Third Reich imprisoned in Terezín many of the well-regarded scholars, philosophers, artists, musicians, and writers arrested throughout Nazi-occupied Central Europe, who in turn brought their talents and creative enterprises to the ghetto. In addition to the artists and intellectuals, the Nazis slated another special population for deportation to Terezín, a group of influential Jews in Germany who had been decorated officers during World War I. The Reich leadership feared that it would elicit too much attention to send these well-known people to extermination camps, so instead they launched an elaborate but fictitious campaign inviting them to relocate to what the government advertised as *Bad Theresien* (Spa Terezín), a spa town with luxurious hotels overlooking the water. The Nazi ruse went so far as to require the intended prisoners to pay for their own travel expenses and to offer them the option to upgrade their accommodations with either a water front or mountain range view, for an extra price, of course. All of which just added further to the Third Reich's coffers. Nazi officials even instructed these German Jews to bring as many of their valuables as they wanted, and many were naïve enough to accept this offer, traveling with furs, gowns, top hats, and jewelry, only to find it all a cruel hoax. Upon arrival, these prisoners traded in their finery for work clothes and their thoughts of relaxing beside the water for hard labor. But regardless of the reality within the heavily guarded fortress of Terezín, Hitler continued to tout to the world that he had created a place of protection for the Jewish elite and intelligentsia. According to survivor Thomas Mandl, Terezín, however, had become the "devil's test-tube."[7]

From its earliest days, Terezín indeed housed a most unusual conglomeration of people. Ghetto residents formed a polyglot community where prisoners segregated themselves by nationality, with Czechs living separately from German or Austrian-born Jews. As in other camps, a social hierarchy among the prisoners developed almost immediately. Members of the Council of Elders and those who had volunteered as part of *AK1* and *AK2* made up the top tier. Next were prisoners with specialized skills in construction, medicine, engineering, and other necessary areas. The children and the elderly, most of whom would perish from disease or starvation, occupied the third level. Then finally, the average prisoner for whom Terezín constituted only a brief stay before transport to Auschwitz. But in the end, all were marked for death. As a common Nazi tactic, the captives remained unaware of their impending fate, and even as transports to Auschwitz began, they lacked reliable information, only privy to occasional rumors about what happened there.

But of all of the groups, it became the immensely gifted artistic population that the Nazis had consolidated into one ghetto that shaped Terezín's sui generis climate. The creative activity undertaken there, particularly in music, distinguished Terezín from other camps and produced a remarkable amount of musical accomplishments, both in composition and in performances, which eventually encompassed recitals, chamber music, choral concerts, and large-scale operatic productions. Many of the deportees had smuggled instruments in with them, even though Nazi regulations only allowed for necessities totaling no more than 110 pounds. One cellist had been so determined to keep his instrument that he disassembled it into multiple parts, which he hid among his clothing then reassembled with glue once inside the ghetto. Chamber music proved especially accessible right from the early days as it could be covertly rehearsed in the living quarters with small numbers of musicians and instruments. But as with most of the nascent musical endeavors at Terezín, the availability of sheet music posed a problem even though some printed music lay hidden in the luggage of arriving prisoners. Later performers acquisitioned a few works through the Council of Elders, and other resourceful prisoners who worked jobs that required them to leave the ghetto occasionally established contact with people who could help them acquire specific titles.

Despite the various obstacles and the unlikely location, the first documented musical program took place within a few weeks of the ghetto's opening on December 6, 1941, as a variety show that featured instrumental performances, recitations, and even magic tricks. Later that month, on December 17, 1941, a well-known opera singer, alto Hedda Grab-Kernmayr, arrived at Terezín, and her energy and zeal for music prompted the Jewish Council to ask her to organize secret cultural and educational events, including recitals, lectures, and readings, which she eagerly agreed to do. Soon, however, the Nazis discovered these clandestine performances, but, instead of enforcing the ban or punishing those involved, the Third Reich made a calculated decision to officially sanction the use of leisure time in Terezín for artistic and cultural activities, establishing the *Freizeitgestaltung* (Free Time Organization) or *FZG*. Their initial reasoning for this allowance rested on that premise that if the prisoners remained busy, then they would cause the camp administrators less problems. But soon the Nazi leadership wielded it as an opportunistic propaganda tool. Ironically, the Nazis fashioned a façade for the world by encouraging artistic creation, which the doomed but ingenious prisoners then used as a weapon of spiritual resistance against their captors. The creative work uplifted the prisoners and helped them stay sane amid such dire circumstances, an eventuality to which the Nazis seemed completely oblivious. As a result, Terezín actually became the most culturally free location in any of the Reich-occupied territories. A cauldron of creativity, Terezín featured cabarets, concerts, and theatrical presentations that, more than mere entertainment, represented resistance through art, with an insider knowledge and commentary lost on their persecutors. The ultimate paradox of Terezín rested in the fact that its wretched conditions generated fertile soil for creativity, which in turn cultivated a sense of hope and distraction, what survivor Zdenka Ehrlich-Fantlová described as "dancing under the gallows."[8]

Hedda Grab-Kernmayr's first official arts program under the new Nazi-sanctioned protocol took place at 3:00 in the afternoon in the women's barracks on March 21, 1942, and featured dance, readings, and various art songs that she performed herself. The enthusiastic response precipitated a need for multiple performances in both the women's and men's barracks so everyone interested could enjoy it. Hedda continued in her role as performer and organizer her entire time imprisoned at Terezín. She became one of the fortunate few who survived to see the liberation, although her experiences forever sullied her love for music. After immigrating to the United States, she ceased to have any involvement in music.

But despite the success of Hedda's first program, the latitude in regard to artistic endeavors could not be taken for granted because the Nazis leveraged its revocation as a punitive threat and did in fact ban these activities several times as retaliation for various camp infractions, including escape attempts. Consequently, while there seemed to be more liberties for the prisoners inside the ghetto than outside its walls where Nazi policies so vehemently restricted Jewish actions and movements, the appearance of freedom in any true sense, whether concerning daily life or cultural activities, constituted a mirage. Survivor Mirko Tuma, who spent over three years in Terezín, indicted this camp's ethos as a grotesque invention of the Nazis that evoked the epitome of suffering.

> Mentally and spiritually, of course, Terezín was the worst hell of the German hells because delusions and hope and macabre pretensions were nourished there. In other camps, the Nazis wanted the prisoners to manifest their Dantean suffering by screaming in infernal pain and terror, while in Theresienstadt the prisoners were required to smile as if they were in a photographer's studio.[9]

The creation of the *Freizeitgestaltung* launched, in typical Nazi fashion, a complex bureaucratic structure with numerous departments and sub-departments, including theater, cabaret, lectures, chess, sports, and a myriad of other leisure-time activities. Officials subdivided musical pursuits into three categories: instrumental, vocal, and popular music. Those who worked in the music department received permission to raid storehouses in Prague, which contained printed music and instruments confiscated from Jewish residents. Eventually, musicians in Terezín formed four orchestras and a jazz ensemble, in addition to choirs and chamber groups. Performance opportunities grew to include instrumental and vocal recitals, orchestral concerts, operas, theatrical presentations, cabarets, and jazz performances. The staggering scope of serious musical pursuits can be measured by the existence of even highly specialized undertakings such as a Collegium Musicum that focused on Medieval and Renaissance music and a group that championed contemporary works named *Studio für Neue Musik* (Studio for New Music).

The Nazi command also installed a café-like setting where those lucky enough to procure tickets could sit at a table and listen to performances by various instrumental ensembles, although without the luxury of a coffee or spirit beverage. One of the most popular groups to perform there was the Ghetto Swingers, a jazz combo founded by amateur trumpet player Erich Vogel. The group also included Heinz Jakob "Coco" Schumann, a jazz guitarist who had been a popular feature in Berlin's underground swing music scene. One of the first Germans to play the electric guitar, Schumann would survive the war and go on to become an internationally recognized jazz musician until his death in 2018. All of this, from Terezín's café to the frequent performances by the Ghetto Swingers, contributed to another baffling Nazi paradox, as the Reich had banned jazz in the 1930s after declaring it "degenerate" due to its predominance of African American and Jewish musicians.

A variety of musical performances and compositions indeed thrived in Terezín because of the large numbers of talented musicians present, including many of the most notable Czech composers, conductors, and performers. For those artists and intellectuals who contributed significantly to the *FZG,* the Nazi command considered that their work and exempted them from any manual labor. This allowed composers time to write and performers time to practice and perfect their craft. Some of the famous composer prisoners included Viktor Ullmann, Hans Krása, Pavel Haas, and Gideon Klein. That these composers wrote works at Terezín that represent almost the only notated music to survive from the concentration camps remains of considerable significance. Although much of their music was lost, fortunately, Viktor Ullmann documented many of the concerts and recitals through written concert reviews, which coupled with extant printed programs, have enabled researchers to determine the extent of the repertoire performed, both previously written and newly composed. The musical offerings at Terezín became so renowned that even high ranking government officials would visit to attend them. Adolph Eichmann would sometimes come to the camp for business, and then enjoy the various musical events while there. As the Nazi official in charge of the entire transportation component of the Final Solution, Eichmann alone decided the logistics of transporting the Jews to their deaths, including those whose music entertained him. The infamous Dr. Josef Mengele, known as "The Angel of Death" for his horrific medical experiments on prisoners in Auschwitz, even made trips to Terezín for the sole purpose of attending operas, cabarets, and concerts.

Two of the earliest composers to arrive at Terezín were Gideon Klein and Pavel Haas. Born in Moravia in 1919, Klein moved to Prague at age 11 to study piano and the liberal arts. He later enrolled at the Prague Conservatory in 1938 and graduated in only one year, regarded by many as one of the brightest and most promising composers and pianists of his generation. But after the Nazi invasion of Czechoslovakia, the subsequent enactment of the Nuremberg Laws banned him from performing or from his music even being heard. For a while Klein tried to circumvent the injunction by adopting the pseudonym Karel Vranek, but soon deemed it too dangerous. He still participated in secret house concerts, performing the Brahms' *Piano Concerto in B-flat Major* at a large villa with a second piano used as accompaniment instead of an orchestra. Nazi officials deported Klein to Terezín in December 1941 and assigned him to a hard labor job building barracks. Fortunately, his musical reputation and abilities eventually allowed him to swap artistic creation for manual labor. At first Klein focused his energy on composition since Terezín lacked a piano at that time, but later he also participated actively as a solo pianist and accompanist.

Klein's compositions while imprisoned at Terezín exhibited a musical style influenced by the renowned Czech composer Leoš Janáček and by the atonal experiments of Arnold Schoenberg. Some of these pieces included a short work for women's choir called *Bachuri, Le'an Tisa* (My Boy, Where Are You Going?), which he wrote in December 1942, with Hebrew lyrics that highlighted the uncertainty of the future felt by the young people in Terezín. In addition to many other pieces for choir, Klein wrote piano and chamber music, including *Fugue for a String Quartet* (1943) and *Sonata for Piano and String Trio* (1944). He also completed a song cycle of four songs for alto and piano called *Die Pest* (The Plague), based on the poetry of fellow prisoner Peter Kien. Unfortunately, these songs failed to survive the war. Klein died at the tragically young age of 25 on January 25, 1945, in Fürstengrube, a subcamp 19 miles outside of Auschwitz. Although he had been composing since age 15, his only extant works hail from his time in Terezín.

Also born in Moravia, Pavel Haas studied composition with Leoš Janáček at the State Conservatory in Brno. He soon developed a reputation as a talented composer, with a special interest in folk songs and music for theater. Later his enthusiasm grew to composing for film, probably due to the influence of his younger brother Hugo, an actor who fled to Hollywood after the Nazi invasion. But despite his considerable ability, Haas produced few completed works because of his tendency to start projects but never finish them. His attraction to folk songs included a strong affinity for the old Czech chorale to St. Wenceslaus, the tune of which had been set by other celebrated Czech composers in works such as Josef Suk's *Meditation on the Ancient Czech Chorale* and Bedřich Smetana's symphonic poem *Blaník*. But according to Terezín scholar Joža Karas, the most interesting aspect of Haas' fascination with the St. Wenceslaus chorale and his incorporation of the tune into his *Suite for Oboe and Piano* from 1939 became the almost ironic realization that a Jewish composer could discover solace in a Christian hymn with words that implore, "Let us not perish, us and our descendants, Saint Wenceslaus!"[10]

Hopefully, this fervent prayer for salvation remained ever present with Haas as he entered Terezín on one of the earliest transports in 1941. Already suffering from poor health coupled with debilitating bouts of depression, Haas struggled to survive in the deplorable ghetto conditions, and at first, refused to participate in the musical life of Terezín. But due to persistent encouragement from fellow musician Gideon Klein, Haas eventually began to compose, although sadly all of his compositions from this time were lost except for three. A work for men's chorus titled *Al S'fod* (Do Not Mourn) that he completed in November 1942 represents his most significant of the surviving pieces. The text instilled hope by entreating the listeners to not give up but to continue striving for Palestine, for Haas considered the imprisonment of his fellow Jews at Terezín as just another exile in the history of his people. "Do not lament, do not cry, when things are bad, do not lose heart, but work, work!"[11] Another of Haas' extant compositions from Terezín was his *Study for Strings,* which he wrote for the camp's string orchestra in 1943. He had begun sketches on a large-scale work as a memorial to all of the victims of the Nazi scourge called *Requiem for Soloists, Chorus, and Orchestra*, but did not get far into the piece before his transport to Auschwitz in October 1944, where the SS sent him immediately to the gas chamber.

Two other prominent musicians who would have a major impact on the musical life of Terezín, Karel Berman and Raphael Schächter, also arrived during that first year of operation in 1941. Born in Bohemia in 1919, Karel Berman studied voice at the Prague Conservatory starting in 1938, but had to drop out in 1940 as a result of the Nazi occupation. Much in demand to sing at house concerts during this time, Berman frequently performed art songs by Brahms and Schubert, as well as music by the Czech composers Smetana and Dvořák. The Reich deported him to Terezín in 1941 at age 22 and initially assigned him the odious job of carrying corpses to the incinerator in the crematorium, but thankfully, as with some of his peers, Berman's musical talents as a composer and conductor allowed him to move from that work to organizing and producing concerts. He also founded and conducted a girls' chorus. In addition to his many performances during his detainment,

Berman contributed some noteworthy compositions. His compositional output included a piano suite titled *Terezín* and a cycle of four songs for bass voice and piano called *Poupata* (The Rosebuds).

While in Terezín, Berman bunked with probably the most inspiring of the musical figures in the camp, Jewish composer, pianist, and conductor Raphael Schächter, who also arrived in 1941. When ordered to pack for his deportation, Schächter grabbed single copies of the vocal scores to great choral works because he could not imagine being separated from his beloved choral music. In his early days at Terezín, Schächter organized and participated in informal singing, but eventually expanded his pursuits to include the assembling of an all-male choir, and then a women's choir. Joining them together naturally formed a mixed choir and with the subsequent arrival of the talented pianist Gideon Klein to accompany the vocal ensembles, Schächter's choral aspirations seemed poised for success.

Musicians in the camp actually competed to work with Schächter because of his reputation as a consummate artist. In early 1942, Schächter collaborated with Karel Švenk, a Czech actor and director, to organize cabarets. Švenk had been known before the war for his keen and savvy ability to address political and social topics through theater, skills which he put to use in Terezín by employing satirical humor to illuminate the absurdities of their daily lives in a way that helped people laugh at them. Together, Švenk and Schächter wrote "Terezín March," a catchy melody with a text that enumerated the myriad of cruelties they faced, while also encouraging hope for the future. It became the anthem of resistance for the prisoners of Terezín. After the Nazi concession toward artistic activities, Schächter appropriated a room in the basement of one of the barracks for a rehearsal space. When he decided to perform some of the choruses from Smetana's *The Bartered Bride,* a most cherished opera in the hearts of Czech music lovers, singer Hedda Grab-Kernmayr helped by loaning him her pitch pipe since they did not have a keyboard instrument at the time. Soon after, Schächter acquired a dilapidated harmonium (small reed organ) from an old and forgotten church in Terezín and a partially broken accordion to use for accompaniment.

The presence of accomplished singers capable of performing the opera solos, such as Karel Berman, emboldened Schächter to attempt a complete concert version (music without the staging) of *The Bartered Bride,* but having proper accompaniment would be paramount. Fortunately, someone discovered a broken-down Bechstein grand piano with no legs outside of Terezín and smuggled it in during the night. Although it had to be propped up on crates in the gymnasium hall and required frequent tuning, this piano served a great need for the camp's musical community. Later in 1943, Nazi officials appointed Dr. Paul Eppstein as the new head of the Council of Elders, and he managed to have his grand piano from Berlin shipped to Terezín. Other pianos eventually made their way into the camp as well from Prague.

The premiere of *The Bartered Bride* took place on November 28, 1942, with Schächter conducting from the piano. The opera received tremendous acclaim, which fostered over 35 repeat performances. Following this achievement, Schächter staged another Smetana opera, *The Kiss,* again in a concert version. It premiered on July 2, 1943, and spawned 14 encore performances. Relentlessly driven, Schächter tackled two Mozart operas next: *The Marriage of Figaro* and *The Magic Flute,* both performed many times. Schächter only conducted one opera in a fully staged version with string orchestra and continuo accompaniment, Giovanni Battista Pergolesi's *La Serva Padrona*. For this, he relied on assistance from colleagues in the camp to create sets and tend to other theatrical needs. Inspired by Schächter, other conductors in Terezín also mounted operatic productions, some staged with piano/harmonium accompaniment or even orchestra accompaniment and others in concert versions, including Verdi's *Rigoletto* (1943), Puccini's *Tosca* (1943), and Bizet's *Carmen* (1944). Only a production of Johann Strauss' *Die Fledermaus* met any resistance, as some prisoners deemed the performance of a light German operetta grossly inappropriate in their current situation.

The accomplished musicians who had arrived on the early transports of 1941 had laid the foundation for a rich musical life in the ghetto, and in 1942, the trains to Terezín supplied additional talented musicians, including Paul Kling, Karel Ančerl, and Viktor Ullmann. Born in 1928 in Czechoslovakia, Paul Kling was such a remarkable child prodigy that the Vienna Philharmonic invited him at age 7 to perform the Mozart *Violin Concerto in A Major* with them. By the 1939 German invasion, Kling's repertoire already included 52 violin concerti, but his Jewish ancestry made continuing his musical studies or performing no longer possible. After Nazi authorities confiscated his violin, Kling missed music so much that he would sometimes risk his life by borrowing a violin to practice in secret. He even gave some clandestine performances before his deportation to Terezín in 1942 at age 14. With the unique circumstances of this transit camp, Kling's prodigious talents now ironically transformed him from a Nazi target to an asset, with camp officials encouraging and even commanding him to play the violin. Unlike so many of the musicians of Terezín, Kling survived the war. He performed for several years in Japan before moving to Kentucky where he became concertmaster of the Louisville Orchestra and taught violin at the University of Louisville. Kling later relocated to Canada where he taught at the University of Victoria, British Columbia, until retirement. He died on January 2, 2005, at age 76.

During an interview in 1994, writer Joshua Jacobson had asked Kling how a person could make music in such a hellish environment. Kling responded that he observed three types of musicians at Terezín: 1. The Naïve, who remained oblivious and unable to acknowledge their dire circumstances, so they continued to practice the same as they had before the war; 2. The Optimist, who thought that the war surely could not last much longer, so they needed to be ready to resume their careers; and 3. The Pessimist, who felt that they would die any day and should make music, as it might be their last time. So regardless of the mindset, music persisted in Terezín.[12]

Karel Ančerl studied conducting and composition at the Prague Conservatory, graduating in 1929. During the 1930s, he developed a favorable reputation for his work in the Munich Opera House. He also conducted the orchestra for the Liberated Theatre and at the State Radio where he worked as a sound engineer before being sent to Terezín in 1942. Although camp officials did not allow him to be a full-time musician in Terezín, assigning him instead to kitchen duty, Ančerl still managed impressive musical activities in his free time. Once the Nazis officially sanctioned the organization of artistic activities, Ančerl formed a large string orchestra (16 first violins, 12 seconds, 8 violas, 6 cellos, and 1 double bass) from the significant number of string players available. Unlike chamber music, an orchestra could not have been operated clandestinely, and he needed help from officials to secure instruments, mainly cellos and double basses, from outside of Terezín. All members of Ančerl's orchestra were male, typical of the professional orchestra world at that time, except oddly for a female double bass player. Many of the string orchestra's players had held prestigious positions with orchestras all over Europe. Some of the orchestra's repertoire included Mozart's *Eine Kleine Nachtmusik*, Handel's *Concerto Grosso in F Major*, and Dvořák's *Serenade for Strings* in addition to *Study for Strings* written by Pavel Haas especially for that ensemble. Due to the presence of numerous conductors in the camp, at least four other orchestras also existed in the ghetto. Many of the same musicians played in multiple groups, most notably the famed Czech violinist Karel Frölich who served as the concertmaster in all of them. The string orchestra continued to perform concerts in Terezín until Ančerl and most of the players boarded the train for Auschwitz in October 1944. Miraculously, Karel Ančerl survived the war and returned as the conductor of the Czechoslovak Radio Orchestra in Prague, then later became director of the Czech Philharmonic in 1950. Relocating to Canada, he conducted the Toronto Symphony from 1969 until his death in 1973.

Much about the childhood and family of Viktor Ullmann remains unknown except that he was born in Teschen, a town near the Moravian-Polish border in 1898, and that his father served as a high-ranking Austrian army officer of noble birth. Ullmann received his general education in Vienna and also embarked on a variety of musical studies there, including piano and conducting, before becoming a theory and composition student of Arnold Schoenberg. After World War I, Ullmann moved to Prague and began working at the New German Theater, a job that Schoenberg helped him secure since Schoenberg's brother-in-law, Alexander Zemlinsky, directed the opera there. Ullmann mostly served as a vocal coach, but did receive an opportunity to conduct as a substitute for Zemlinsky in a performance of Mozart's *Bastien and Bastienne*. As Zemlinsky grew better acquainted with Ullmann's considerable talents, he gave him more conducting responsibilities, which included operas by Smetana and various operettas. Ullmann also composed some incidental music for plays staged at the theater. In 1929, Ullmann left to pursue musical opportunities in Vienna and Zurich, but apparently missing Prague, he returned in May 1930, and taught lessons, presented lectures, and worked as a music critic. During this time, he also organized private musical gatherings where new works were heard and discussed. Several of his own compositions premiered in this type of house concert at the home of Professor Konrad Wallerstein, who had taught at the German Academy of Music in Prague. These private soirees represented one of the few performance opportunities for Jewish musicians since the German occupation.

By the start of World War II, Ullmann's personal life had produced two failed marriages and several children. He and his third wife Elisabeth attempted to leave Czechoslovakia after the Nazi invasion, but failed. When they arrived in Terezín on September 8, 1942, Ullmann's two former wives and his sons were already there, creating an awkward living situation in such confining quarters. Felicia and Johannes, Ullmann's oldest children with his second wife, however, had been two of the chosen few sent to England as part of a children's humanitarian transport. But it remains difficult to conclude whether this, in the end, represented a better option than remaining with their family and going to Terezín. So utterly traumatized by the separation, these two children, although surviving the war, spent the rest of their lives in an asylum.

Overall, Ullmann probably made the most significant contribution of any single individual to the musical life of Terezín. He composed 20 works (16 completed, 4 unfinished) while there, including songs, choral pieces, chamber music, and an opera. Those two years in Terezín actually represented the most prolific season of his life, as he seemed spurred on by a sense of dwindling time, as if watching sand fall through an hourglass. In addition to finishing a string quartet, three piano sonatas, and multiple song cycles, he composed music for the opera *Der Kaiser von Atlantis* (The Emperor of Atlantis). The libretto had been written in Terezín by poet Peter Kien, who because of the scarcity of paper, had been forced to scribble part of the text on the back of Auschwitz deportation lists.

Der Kaiser von Atlantis' plot about an egomaniacal dictator and the futility of a war of attrition presented a dangerous, but powerful indictment of Hitler and his war machine. It featured roles for five singers with accompaniment by a 13-piece chamber orchestra, which called for some unconventional instruments such as banjo and saxophone, not to mention a harpsichord that had been acquired somehow for the Pergolesi opera Schächter had produced. The music incorporated jazz elements reminiscent of Kurt Weill's work, along with a distortion of the Nazi anthem, "Deutschland Über Alles," and concluded with the great reformation chorale of Martin Luther, "Ein' feste Burg ist unser Gott" (A Mighty Fortress Is Our God). Tragically, the work went into rehearsal, but its premiere in the fall of 1944 never happened because Terezín officials deported Ullmann, along with his wife Elisabeth and most involved in the production, to Auschwitz in October 1944. His former wife Annie and their youngest son Max traveled to Auschwitz a week later, where they joined the fate of the other Ullmanns in the gas chamber.

In addition to his important compositions, Ullmann wrote 27 detailed reviews of performances in Terezín, which survived the war and have provided considerable information that would have been lost about pieces, composers, and performers. For the composers who lost their lives during the war, it was rare that much, if any, of their works remained extant, but remarkably all of Ullmann's did, due to his fortuitous decision not to carry them with him on the transport to the East as he had planned. He decided instead, at the eleventh hour, to entrust them to his friend Emil Utitz, who had been a psychology professor prior to his internment at Terezín. Ullmann instructed Utitz to pass the music along to their mutual friend, poet and musicologist Dr. H.G. Adler, after the war in the event that Ullmann did not survive. Adler and Utitz both lived to see the liberation of Terezín, and Utitz did hand over Ullmann's camp oeuvre to him. Adler then immigrated to England, and because no one else knew that he had the works, they were feared lost for many years until their rediscovery among Adler's possessions. Ullmann had believed music to be as essential to him as breathing. Even in a horrific place like Terezín, he insisted on having music in his life every day. Before departing to his death in Auschwitz, Ullmann had explained, "It must be emphasized that Terezín has served to enhance, not impede, my musical activities..."[13]

So due to the visionary leadership and stubborn tenacity of the musicians who had arrived during its first year, Terezín featured a vibrant and vital musical culture by July 1943 when Alice Herz-Sommer received the news of her impending deportation to the ghetto, along with her husband Leopold and 6-year-old son Rafi. More fortunate than most of Prague's Jews, the Sommers had been spared deportation until the last transport because of Leopold's job. Regardless, Alice now proceeded with making the necessary preparations. Luggage could be shipped ahead of time, but Leopold knew that the Nazis would most likely confiscate any belongings that arrived in advance. So instead, they focused their energies on what could be packed in rucksacks. Nazi regulations permitted each person to carry one on their person as long as it did not exceed a certain weight limit. The Sommer family filled theirs with necessities such as blankets, clothes, eating utensils, gloves, and ear muffs. They also included enough food for several days. Alice received word from Otto Zucker, a Jewish leader in Terezín who had overseen the Free Time Organization since March 1943, that she could give a piano recital shortly after arriving. In preparation, Alice practiced feverishly to the point of exhaustion, wanting to cram as many pieces into her head as she could during her last few days. In between practice sessions, friends and neighbors stopped by the apartment to say their farewells. Alice freely gave away unwanted possessions and entrusted her cherished items to a few people for safekeeping. But others callously roamed the apartment, helping themselves to whatever items they wanted, and onlookers saw people walking away with lamps, paintings, rugs, and basically anything not nailed down. The night before the scheduled departure, the German family upstairs quietly made their way to the Sommer apartment after most people in the building had fallen asleep. Mrs. Hermann presented them with a freshly baked apple cake for their journey, a gesture that had cost her precious rationed ingredients. Even though they could have been severely sanctioned, the Hermann family entered the emptied Sommer apartment. They sat on the floor near the piano, one of the few items still on hand, while Alice played Chopin's *Nocturne in B-flat minor* and a movement from a Beethoven sonata. As a final parting gift, Mr. Hermann handed over the soccer ball that his son and Rafi had played with so often.

In the early morning hours of July 5, 1943, Alice, Leopold, and Rafi made their way toward the Exhibition Hall where deportees assembled. Once there, they donned cardboard signs tied with string around their necks indicating their deportation numbers—Leopold DE 162, Alice DE 163, and Rafi DE 164. What followed were two exhausting days of queuing up for hours in lines as the Sommer family worked their way through a series of five registration tables while SS guards scrutinized their every move. Leopold's foresight to pack a small folding chair proved invaluable as young Rafi could sit during their waiting when he grew too tired or fidgety to stand. At one table, Nazi officials forced them to relinquish their apartment keys and food ration cards. At another table, the Sommers turned over any cash they possessed and completed a lengthy questionnaire that declared all of their possessions. Finally, at the end of a trying first day, they eagerly stretched out on straw sacks intended to serve as mattresses. Lying down felt wonderful after being on their feet all day until, a few minutes later, they started to itch. Bed bugs and lice had infested the straw mattresses. Too exhausted to notice, Rafi spent the night in blissfully unaware sleep. Alice, however, endured a miserable night scratching and watching cockroaches and rats dart freely around them. The next morning, they resumed the interminable waiting in lines. The officials at the fourth table seized all valuable coins and jewelry, but fortunately, married couples could keep their simple wedding bands. The fifth and final table accomplished their complete separation from society as Nazi officials presented the Sommer family with documents that stripped them of their Czech citizenship and therefore all of their civil rights. Their passports now identified them as residents of the Ghetto. The next morning, following another uncomfortable night, the Sommers lined up for transport. Yet again, they stood waiting for hours, watching the frail and elderly collapse to the ground. Then, at last, they climbed aboard a train for the two and a half hour journey to Terezín.

Alice, Leopold, and Rafi arrived at Terezín on July 7, 1943, and proceeded through its rigorous induction protocol that included stripping for a health screening and receiving crudely administered inoculations for typhus and diphtheria, all accompanied by interminable periods of standing and waiting for further instructions. As part of the process, Alice and Leopold had to declare their professions on documents that would determine their labor assignments. The ever resourceful Leopold had anticipated this and had apprenticed to a locksmith in Prague so he could list a useful trade. Alice indicated her occupation as a pianist. After spending the night in a make-shift quarantine, the last night all three of them would ever sleep together, the Sommers stepped inside the heavily fortified gates of Terezín. Immediately, camp authorities separated Leopold from Alice and sent him to the men's barracks. At only 6 years old, Rafi remained with Alice, sharing a bunk in the women's barracks. She instructed him to always speak Czech and to pretend that he did not understand German. Determined to protect her sensitive child from the horrors of the ghetto, Alice surround him with as much laughter and optimism as possible. "I made up stories constantly. I was laughing. Never did I let my son see my fear or worry. And tears had no place in a concentration camp. Laughter was our only medicine."[14] Some 50 years after the war, Rafi would credit his mother with not only his physical survival, but his psychological safekeeping, which left him with almost no bad recollections of those times. "In the middle of hell, my mother created a Garden of Eden for me."[15]

As soon as she entered the ghetto, Alice launched a desperate but fruitless search for her mother. She later learned that the Nazis had shipped Sofie Herz to the extermination camp Treblinka on October 19, 1942, a mere three months after her arrival in Terezín. She did not survive Treblinka. Drawing strength from her music, Alice quickly joined the ranks of other gifted pianists in Terezín who presented solo recitals and participated in chamber music, including Edith Steiner-Kraus, whom Alice had met in 1937 and the two had become inseparable friends. Edith had been born in Vienna and recognized early on as a gifted child prodigy. Alma Mahler, the wife of Gustav Mahler, had heard Edith play as a small child and recommended her to famed teacher Artur Schnabel, who subsequently accepted her as the youngest student in his studio. Like Alice, Edith had enjoyed a successful performance career before circumstances sent her to the ghetto. Several times while in Terezín, Edith's name appeared on Auschwitz deportation rosters, but the popularity of her piano recitals miraculously resulted in her removal from the list every time.

True to his word, Otto Zucker approached Alice after only a few days in Terezín about creating a series of piano recitals. She eagerly drew up four different programs from her extensive repertoire of works by Beethoven, Bach, Brahms, Schumann, Chopin, and various Czech composers. For the pianists, they possessed the advantage of having so much material memorized from their pre-war careers that they were not as limited by the lack of sheet music as other musical endeavors. Alice's first recital in Terezín included Beethoven's *Appassionata Sonata*, a piece that audiences all over Europe had celebrated Alice's interpretation of, to the extent that it had become a signature piece. Also on the program, Alice played a Bach partita and a couple of the Chopin études that she had felt mysteriously compelled to prepare in the months leading up to her deportation. For Alice, Bach's music evoked a depth of spirituality that surpassed all others, and so her beloved Bach *Partita in B-flat Major* constituted an apt opening piece on this memorable recital. Not surprisingly, Alice's inaugural program elicited a lengthy and enthusiastic applause. Throughout their first year in the camp, Leopold and Rafi could be found on the front row at Alice's performances. Concerning the other concert goers, an impressive number of renowned artists and intellectuals, Alice often felt in an odd way that she was performing for the most distinguished audiences of her career, which included Sigmund Freud's sister Adolfine, Henry Kissinger's aunt Minna, and Franz Kafka's sister Ottla, to name only a few. Eventually, Alice would present over 100 piano recitals in Terezín, repeating those five programs up to 20 times each. On July 29, 1944, Alice's recital incredibly featured all 24 of Chopin's Op. 15 and Op. 25 études, a task rarely undertaken by great pianists even in the most ideal situations, earning a reputation as one of the most impressive creative feats at Terezín.

Accustomed to at least four hours of practice a day, Alice felt genuine loss at the mere one hour allotted to her each day, a paltry amount of time for someone of her background and usual practice regimen. But like the others in Terezín, she had to work, first in the laundry then later splitting mica chips to insulate electronics. From 9–10 a.m. each day, Alice practiced in a small room with a piano that sported sticking keys and a broken pedal. She refused, however, to allow these obstacles to lessen her devotion to music, later recalling, "Music was life. We did not, could not, would not give up."[16] One day soon after Alice's arrival, the door to her practice room opened and composer Hans Krása, whom Alice had known in Prague, entered and complimented her playing. It was a tearful reunion between colleagues. Krása then requested permission to just sit and listen to her practice, which she readily granted. Eventually, officials increased Alice's practice allowance to two hours a day because of the great demand for her recitals. Fortunately, a fellow prisoner trained as a piano tuner did his best to keep the pianos in Terezín tuned and in as good a repair as could be managed under the circumstances.

In addition to solo recitals, Alice participated in collaborative programs with other musicians. When Alice accompanied soloists, young Rafi assisted as her page turner. Before long, word spread about his skill, and other pianists frequently invited him to turn pages for them as well. The musicians at Terezín stubbornly fought against a descent into mediocrity, but instead committed themselves to attending to even the slightest details needed to create great music, believing that there was something deeper at stake than just playing notes. "As our situation became more difficult," explained Alice, "we tried even harder to reach for perfection, for the meaning in the music. Music was our way of remembering our inner selves, our values."[17] Nevertheless, Alice's pianist friend Edith Steiner-Kraus often expressed exasperation after the war when people would ask her about the quality of the musical performances in Terezín. According to her, they failed to grasp that the meaning of their music had little to do with the traditional ways of evaluating music in terms of technical proficiency and artistic interpretation. Edith responded to these inquiries saying, "You'll never understand, or get close, to what music truly meant to each of us as a sustaining power and as a way of using our skills to inspire, beyond criticism, beyond any superficial evaluation. We *were* music."[18]

In any spare time between work and concerts, Alice secretly taught piano lessons to some of the children as part of a collective effort to provide a varied education, especially in the liberal arts, to the large number of children in the ghetto. In order to usurp the Nazi restrictions that prohibited schools or classes in Terezín, teachers devised clever ways of delivering instruction, including the use of songs and games to teach history, language, literature, geography, and many other subjects. Arts activities also offered a means of occupying the children and bringing some order to their days, as well as reconnecting them to their pre-war lives and their heritage. Most importantly, art created opportunities for them to express their feelings and process their traumatic situation. As one child wrote in a poem,

> *Ah, home, home,*
> *Why did they tear me away?*
> *Here the weak die easy as a feather*
> *And when they die, they die forever.*[19]

Friedl Dicker-Brandeis, a Jewish artist from Vienna, had trained in art and design at the famed German Bauhaus art school where she studied printmaking, typography, and textile design. The Third Reich deported her, along with her husband Pavel, to Terezín in December 1942. While imprisoned there, she secretly taught 600 children to draw, sew, paint, and make puppets with art supplies she had smuggled into the camp. Although these art materials had taken up valuable weight in the 110 pound limit the Nazis imposed, Friedl considered them essential because she knew about the children there, and her experiences as an educator and art therapist had taught her the importance of providing children in trauma with expressive outlets. She allowed the students to depict whatever subjects or emotions they desired, and only imposed one rule—each must sign his or her name. She would not allow these children to be invisible or anonymous. Friedl became one of the many heroes of Terezín who faced great risk and personal sacrifice for these young people. But as one of her students later explained, "Heroism wasn't in the clandestineness but in the will to create, to paint, to write, to perform, and to compose in hell."[20]

Friedl lived in L410, the barracks that housed girls, and served as one of their around-the-clock caretakers. She even arranged a formal exhibition of the children's art work in the basement of her barracks. The Nazi command allowed prisoners at Terezín to receive parcels from outside the camp two or three times a year, and while most asked for food, medicine, or clothes, Friedl begged her friends to send art supplies for the children. Another of her students, Helga Pollak, could still vividly conjure, many years after the war, a vignette of these activities and their restorative impact.

> I can still see the table in the middle of the room with pencils on it, paintbrushes, colors, and paper. The paper was very poor quality, often waste paper or paper left over from some old package. Each child could draw freely according to his imagination and wishes. This was extraordinary. It gave us a different life, another atmosphere.... There was something about her way of teaching that made us, for the moment, feel free of care.[21]

When Friedl learned in the fall of 1944 that camp officials had added her name to the transport list for Auschwitz, she stuffed approximately 4,500 pieces of the children's art work into two suitcases and hid them in the attic of her barracks. She then boarded the train on October 6, 1944, along with 30 of her students. Neither she nor these children survived Auschwitz. But the precious art work in those suitcases did endure and can be viewed today in a permanent display at the Jewish Museum in Prague, a powerful testimony to the sacrifice of Friedl Dicker-Brandeis and to the power of art.

The young people of Terezín left a profound legacy in the form of their music, art pieces, diaries, and poetry. The most famous of these memorials remains a poem written by Pavel Friedmann on June 4, 1942, titled "The Butterfly," which since the war has served as the basis for many works of art that remember the lost children of the Holocaust, including a song cycle and a play. In his poem, Friedmann describes seeing a magnificently beautiful butterfly, but laments that now as a prisoner of Terezín, he only has the memory of that sight. The poem concludes with the moving lines,

> ...I never saw another butterfly.
> That butterfly was the last one.
> Butterflies don't live in here, in the ghetto.

Pavel Friedmann died at Auschwitz on September 29, 1944.

Educating and tending to the children of Terezín became a mission for numerous remarkable individuals, including Zeev Shek, who proved to be a caring and innovative teacher in the camp. A politically active Czech Zionist, Shek had been involved in the *Hechalutz* movement, a Zionist youth movement that rallied and educated Jewish young people, teaching them skills that would be useful in Palestine, such as farming and construction. Shek had also worked with Jewish children in an orphanage in Prague, where he earned a reputation for his effective teaching methods and expertise. Jakob Edelstein, the first head of Terezín's Jewish Council of Elders, contacted the 24-year-old Shek and boldly implored him to come voluntarily to Terezín to help the children there. Shek agreed, arriving in October 1943. Having always espoused a progressive view of education, Shek approached this

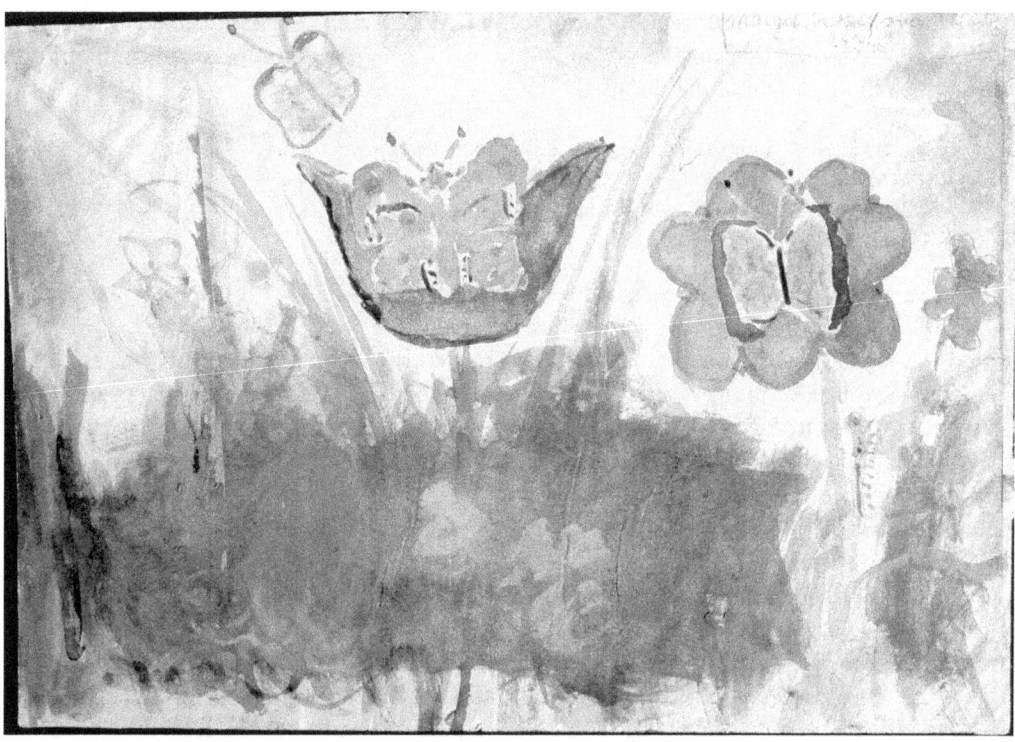

"Flowers and Butterfly," by Margit Koretzova (8/4/1933–4/10/1944), Czech Republic. A drawing by one of the 15,000 children who passed through Terezín concentration camp as preserved by their art teacher Friedl Dicker-Brandeis (Werner Forman Archive/State Jewish Museum, Prague; HIP / Art Resource, NY).

daunting mission with a renewed sense of purpose and a list of clearly defined outcomes. Shek later explained,

> ….we wanted to bring these children out of the ghetto spiritually, mentally sane, so that they would become quite normal people. I would call it 'positivistic approach to life,' this normalization under abnormal circumstances, giving all these people a kind of belief that under any circumstances you are a human being, and it is up to you to react as a human being. They can break your body; they can't break your spirit without your cooperation. This is what we used to tell them. After all, the logical way to fight death is to stay alive, isn't it?[22]

Although not a professional musician, Shek had studied voice in Prague. He considered music to be a vital part of any curriculum and also essential for instilling pride of heritage among the Jewish children in Terezín through Jewish patriotic songs. While in the camp, Shek became reacquainted with 17-year-old Alisa Ehrmann, whom he had known as part of the youth movement in Prague. They fell in love and married in secret six months after his arrival. But soon after, in October 1944, Shek volunteered again, this time for a transport to Auschwitz. His mother had been placed on the deportation list, and he refused to let her face that alone. Before Shek departed, he asked his wife to continue his work of documenting everything that happened in Terezín. He knew the import and urgency of having a testimony to the atrocities that could be revealed after the war in hopes that the world would not fail to believe or close its eyes to what had occurred. She immediately began keeping a detailed diary, with expertly rendered drawings.

One of the most heartbreaking accounts in Alisa Shek's diary described watching a train being loaded for Auschwitz, which would include a great number of children and the meager belongings of all of the doomed.

> Everyone had so little, and it seems even this little will be taken from them. ... I entered the room, small children aged 3 to 10, shouting. Everyone has a small backpack, eyes wide open, among them those with a scary expression of maturity and quiet. It seems they will cling on to their belongings, but never again to their childhood.[23]

Alisa Shek was still alive when the Soviets liberated Terezín in May 1945, and even more miraculously, her husband Zeev Shek survived Auschwitz. In 1946, they reunited in Prague. According to their son Daniel Shek, "An invisible hand granted both of them, each in their own way, a drop from the so small and so miserly cup of miraculous acts..."[24] Zeev Shek zealously continued to undertake important work, including an instrumental role in the founding of Israel's Foreign Ministry. Later, he served as the secretary to Israel's first prime minister, Moshe Sheratt, and then as the Israeli Ambassador to Italy. He died suddenly in Rome of a heart attack in 1978 at age 58. Alisa Shek continued to be an outspoken voice for the victims of the Holocaust until her death in 2007.

In addition to its use as a learning tool by Shek and others, music served as an effective means of distracting the children of Terezín from their hunger and fear, as well as providing them an outlet for expressing their feelings. They could sing in various ensembles, including a girls' chorus directed by Karel Berman and a children's chorus conducted by Rudi Freudenfeld. Talented young people could participate in additional musical study with Rafael Schächter and audition for the more advanced musical productions and performances. Children also took instrumental lessons from some of the expert players and teachers in the camp. Pianist Bernard Kaff established a make-shift conservatory in Terezín, and since his students had no money, they would clean for him in exchange for lessons. He even organized a small group of them to supervise and enforce the practice schedule for the limited pianos available. He cleverly called it the *Pianistenpolizei* (Pianists' police). In addition, musical leaders in Terezín staged two elaborate children's opera productions, Mozart's *Bastien and Bastienne* and *Brundibár* by the Jewish Czech composer Hans Krása. *Bastien and Bastienne* was performed 30 times with string quartet accompaniment under the baton of Hans Jochowitz and with sets designed by the architect and stage designer František Zelenka, who had worked for the National Theatre in Prague.

The production of Krása's *Brundibár* undoubtedly constituted the most impressive undertaking for the children at Terezín. Born in Prague in 1899, Krása showed an extraordinary talent for the piano at an early age. Wanting to champion his son's musical giftedness, Krása's father, a well-connected lawyer, bought him an extravagantly expensive Amati violin when Krása was only 10 years old and arranged for lessons. When Krása composed his first piece for orchestra at age 11, his father hired a spa orchestra from Salzburg to perform it. This would become the trend in the early years—Hans would write, and his father would arrange a performance. Krása later graduated from the German Music Academy and began working with the famed teacher and conductor Alexander Zemlinsky at the German Theater in Prague. Zemlinsky became his most important mentor, and when Zemlinsky took a job at the Berlin State Opera, his protégé followed him there.

But despite his talents, education, and opportunities, Hans Krása suffered from what some might call "plain laziness." He enjoyed a Bohemian lifestyle as a young man, visiting daily with friends and engaging in lively discussions with other intellectuals. He rarely sat down to compose, and thus his compositional output remained meager in the 1920s. In 1926, he did publish a set of songs titled *Five Songs for Voice and Piano*, but then waited six years before producing any new pieces. Such obvious lack of discipline could probably be blamed on his doting father, who had eagerly provided everything without requiring that the young boy put forth much effort. Krása's career also seemed affected by some apparent jealousy among the other Czech composers who refused to accept him into their inner circle. His ease of obtaining performances of his compositions, despite his lethargic work ethic, most likely contributed to his ostracism, especially since the performance opportunities had extended to the international stage. The Boston Symphony Orchestra, under the baton of Serge Koussevitzky, had performed one of Krása's symphonies in November 1926.

Shunned by his peers, Krása spent time instead with writers and artists involved in Czech avant-garde theater, including the playwright Adolf Hoffmeister, with whom he would collaborate multiple times. Krása did complete a couple of major works in the early 1930s—a cantata *Die Erde ist des Herrn* (The Earth is the Lord's) in 1932 and also that same year an opera *Verlobung im Traum* (Betrothal in a Dream). Garnering immediate acclaim, the opera received a production by the German Theater in May 1933 with George Szell conducting and earned the Czechoslovak State Prize for Composition that year.

When the Third Reich invaded Czechoslovakia, Krása appeared taken by surprise. Having made no provisions for an escape, he could only watch while family and friends, including Hoffmeister, departed. Nazi officials deported Krása to Terezín on April 10, 1942, where he became the head of the entire music division of the *Freizeitgestaltung*. He contributed musically to the camp as a pianist, accompanist, conductor, and composer. He wrote pieces of chamber music, including *Tanz* (Dance) for string trio in 1943, and reworked a former piece for string quartet called *Theme with Variations*, which the Terezín String Quartet performed several times. In August 1944, two months before his deportation to Auschwitz, he wrote his last piece, *Passacaglia and Fugue*, a challenging chamber work for baritone, clarinet, viola, and cello. Hans Krása died in the gas chamber at Auschwitz on October 17, 1944, alongside many of his colleagues from Terezín.

Of the numerous successes in symphonic, choral, and chamber music, Hans Krása inscribed his most lasting and poignant legacy in the form of a children's opera. He wrote *Brundibár* with his playwright friend Hoffmeister for a competition in 1938. The two had collaborated previously in 1935, with Krása composing the incidental music for one of Hoffmeister's plays. But in the end, the competition never took place because of the Nazi advance on Czechoslovakia. After the German occupation and enactment of strict censorship in the arts, Jewish musical performances could still occur in Jewish orphanages, even though the Nazis had banned them in public places. Nevertheless, audiences attending these performances had to come and go carefully in the dark because of laws forbidding the assembly of Jews and also due to curfew restrictions. Rudolf (Rudi) Freudenfeld oversaw the orphanage known as Hagibor in Prague. A great advocate of music, Freudenfeld had made friends with many of Prague's prominent musicians and composers, including Hans Krása, Gideon Klein, and Rafael Schächter. Alice Herz-Sommer performed several recitals there, as well, presenting music by Schubert, Mendelssohn, and Beethoven. Freudenfeld also asked her to give a few programs geared specifically toward the children, who had little to fill their time since their German occupiers had prohibited so many activities, including a formal education.

Over the years, Freudenfeld had mounted several children's operas at his facility. In July 1941, Rafael Schächter, aware that Krása's *Brundibár* had never been performed, suggested that they stage it there at the orphanage and began work on rehearsals and logistics right away. He unfortunately failed to see this project realized, due to his deportation to Terezín in November 1941, before the opera's scheduled premiere. With Schächter gone, Freudenfeld assumed the role of producer, while František Zelenka designed both the sets and directed the opera. Although originally scored for orchestra, their production had to settle for a trio of piano, violin, and percussion. Lacking separate printed parts, the violinist and percussionist were forced to play by reading over the pianist's shoulder from the one piano reduction.

Camp poster for the staging of the children's opera *Brundibár* by Hans Krása (Herrmann's Collection, Terezín Memorial, © Zuzana Dvořáková).

A moral fairy tale, *Brundibár*'s story unfolds through six casted roles (three humans and three animals) and a chorus of villagers. Two small children, Aninka and Pepíček, summon a doctor for their mother, who lies in bed gravely ill. The doctor informs them that she must have milk to get well. Distraught because they have no money to buy milk, the children decide to stand on the street corner and earn money by singing and dancing for the townspeople. But Brundibár, the cruel organ-grinder, refuses to share the spotlight and chases them away. Heartbroken, the children sit down on the sidewalk. Then miraculously, three kind animals—a cat, a dog, and a sparrow, come to their aid. With help from the animals and other children in the village, Aninka and Pepíček resume singing and collecting donations from passersby. Incensed at being outwitted, greedy Brundibár steals the money. But again, the animals and children intervene, chasing him and recovering the money. In the end, the good-hearted citizens banish the evil organ-grinder from their village.

The highly successful premiere of *Brundibár* at the orphanage took place in the winter of 1942 for a limited audience of 150 people, but neither Krása nor Zelenka witnessed it because by then they had joined Schächter in Terezín. Sadly, the opera experienced only one repeat performance as the Reich had even begun to deport orphans to the ghetto. By July 1943, Freudenfeld and all of the children had vanished. In time, all involved, including Krása, his collaborators, and the children, reunited in Terezín. Krása decided to mount a new production in the camp from that one piano score, the only remnant from the opera that he still possessed. He re-orchestrated it for a small chamber orchestra composed of flute, clarinet, guitar, accordion, trumpet, piano, four violins, cello, bass, and percussion. The numerous fine musicians in the camp eagerly filled the orchestra roster, with the only non-professional instrumentalist being a 10-year-old boy from Denmark who played the difficult trumpet part. Freudenfeld served as the musical director and Schächter as the conductor, although some sources have indicated that Freudenfeld conducted. Regardless, both Freudenfeld and Schächter played important roles in preparing the production. Rehearsals took place in the attic of the boys' barracks, also known as the boys' home L417. Despite the heat and dust, the children loved practicing, a welcome respite from focusing on their empty stomachs and the equally gnawing fear of transport to Auschwitz. According to Ela Stein, who was cast in the role of the cat, "When we were singing, we forgot all our troubles…. It was possible to have hope."[25] Alice Herz-Sommer's son, 6-year-old Rafi, became the youngest member of the cast as the sparrow.

Brundibár premiered in Terezín on September 23, 1943, with three dozen children singing to the accompaniment of the chamber orchestra. The overwhelming demand for the free, but required, tickets made them extremely difficult to obtain. In fact, the opera became so popular that they staged it every week for some 55 performances through September 1944, recasting as necessary due to transports. For those in the camp, the symbolism of this particular opera was multifaceted. It featured a cast of children who represented the possibility of a future for the Jewish people, and the narrative of the opera itself demonstrated that good would triumph over evil. There was no doubt for those watching the production, except for the oblivious Nazis, that the evil organ-grinder represented Hitler. The final few lines of the opera clearly declaimed the intent and spirit of the story as the children sang, "He who loves justice and will abide by it, and who is not afraid, is our friend and can play with us."[26]

Tragically, almost every performer and audience member would die in Auschwitz. Krása and most of the children who had performed in *Brundibár* boarded a train headed for Auschwitz in October 1944, where they died within a few days, except for Gideon Klein who survived until January 1945. Rudi Freudenfeld and Ela Stein were two of the few from the *Brundibár* production to survive. On May 6, 1946, they had a chance meeting in Prague as people took to the streets to celebrate the anniversary of the end of the war. They reminisced about the wonderful time they had performing the opera, and Freudenfeld concluded by saying, "*Brundibár* was our life. We will never forget it."[27]

Around the same time of the children's opera project, the musical community at Terezín undertook another impressive musical feat through the visionary leadership of Raphael Schächter—Giuseppe Verdi's *Requiem*. Schächter began plans to perform the dauntingly complex work sometime in the late spring or early summer of 1943, and by September, he had assembled a large chorus and secured four remarkable soloists, including bass Karel Berman. Schächter approached this production with an almost obsessive, fanatical fervor, as if "preparing a requiem for all the victims of Nazi crimes."[28] But not everyone thought that Schächter's intention to perform a Catholic liturgical piece in a Jewish concentration camp appropriate. Dr. H.G. Adler, in particular, criticized the choice after the war in his exhaustive book, *Theresienstadt 1941–45*. Others, however, have conceded that rather than a religious statement, Verdi himself had most likely intended this grand setting of the Requiem mass to be more operatic than liturgical, and so Schächter's love of opera probably accounted, at least in part, for his impetus to program the work.[29]

Undeterred by criticism or circumstance, Schächter assembled 150 prisoners in small rehearsal groups, due to the lack of space, and taught them Verdi's *Requiem* from hand-copied chorus parts or merely by rote from the one choral score that he had smuggled into Terezín. Rehearsals took place in the evenings after the hard labors of the day, accompanied by Gideon Klein on a harmonium, but the fairly decent piano located in the hall would be used for the performances. Although or perhaps because the singers had no guarantee that they or any of their fellow performers would still be in Terezín the next day or even alive, they defiantly sang of death and the future condemnation of their captors, proclaiming the message through the Latin text that the Nazis would be damned in the final judgment.

> *Day of wrath and doom impending…*
> *Oh, what fear man's bosom rendeth,*
> *When from heaven the Judge descendeth,*
> *On whose sentence all dependeth.*

The long-anticipated premiere occurred on September 6, 1943, and right after, camp officials shipped almost the entire choir to Auschwitz. Refusing to give up, Schächter assembled and rehearsed another chorus and presented a repeat performance on January 2, 1944. Again, he lost most of the singers to Auschwitz and stubbornly rebuilt the choir for a third performance. In the end, Schächter produced around 15 performances of the work in its entirety, with chorus members being lost to death camps after each. Terezín survivor, Joseph Bor, vividly remembered attending one of the performances, which he later captured in *Terezín Requiem*, a historical novel depicting the rehearsal and preparation processes as well as the remarkable performance. Although Bor took some dramatic liberties in his novelization of the event, such as having it accompanied by a full orchestra, the book's vital message of music's unassailable power to memorialize, empower, and uplift rang true. "We are remembering you now, our dear ones, an eternal memorial to you who have died for us. And you, prisoners in the concentration camps, be strong and courageous in invincible faith and hope."[30]

In addition to Verdi's *Requiem*, choirs in Terezín performed other large-scale sacred works in 1944, including Franz Joseph Haydn's *Die Schöpfung* (The Creation) in February 1944 and Felix Mendelssohn's *Elijah* during the summer of 1944, both accompanied by the piano and conducted by Karl Fischer. *Elijah* was scheduled for repeat performances into October 1944, but because of the large transports to Auschwitz that fall, the final performance may not have occurred. That the Nazi command would allow any performance of Mendelssohn's music, which had been banned since the 1930s because of his Jewish heritage, revealed another of Terezín's perplexing conundrums.

Besides these grandiose musical productions, the ghetto experienced other dramatic events in 1944. During the early summer, Terezín underwent a radical cosmetic transformation, a beautification process the Germans called *Verschönerung*, which included cleaning and making improvements throughout the camp. Camp officials ordered prisoners to scrub the sidewalks on their hands and knees with brushes, as well as to paint, landscape, hang curtains, remove the third tiers on the bunk beds, and stage end tables with books in the barracks to create a cozier atmosphere. Part of the "clean up" also included ridding Terezín of about 7,500 of the old and infirm, who went straight to the gas chambers at Auschwitz between May 16 and May 18, 1944. All of this was done in preparation for the arrival of three representatives of the International Red Cross—two from the Swiss Red Cross and one from the Danish Red Cross. This committee had requested permission to visit Terezín in light of persistent rumors of barbaric conditions and inhumane treatment of Jewish prisoners. The Third Reich agreed to the inspection only because the Nazi command felt that Terezín could play a pivotal role in their elaborate propaganda campaign to convince the world that the Jews were not only treated well, but living idyllic lives. To accomplish this, though, camp officials had to stage an elaborate farce, with the forced participation of many in the camp.

Part of the staging for the visit even included the construction of a phony bank and the distribution of "funny money," fake paper currency with a picture of Moses holding the Ten Commandments, all so that the Jewish prisoners appeared to possess money and the latitude to make purchases. Other structural additions included a bakery and a coffee shop, which showcased delicacies that the starving residents of Terezín were not allowed to eat. Camp officials completed the illusion by distributing nice clothing to the prisoners and setting up vignettes that depicted smiling children and contented adults.

The Nazi leadership considered music to be an important component in the subterfuge, so command performances of *Brundibár* and Verdi's *Requiem* became part of the inspectors' itinerary. In fact, the Nazis deemed *Brundibár* so vital to the masquerade that SS Hauptsturmführer Karl Rahm ordered the production moved from the small auditorium housed in the Magdeburg barracks to the gymnasium that had a large stage and orchestra pit. He also insisted that the sets, which he considered drab, be redesigned overnight to feature bright, vibrant colors. Again, the obtuse Nazis who championed this work as a convincing example for the Red Cross delegation failed to comprehend the message of the opera or care that the opera was being sung in Czech, even though they had ordered all operas in Terezín to be sung in German. Maybe they regarded a children's opera so insignificant as to not be bothered to know the translation.

The Nazi command tightly controlled and choreographed the one-day inspection on June 22, 1944, so that the visiting delegation, escorted by the SS at all times, saw only what they were intended to see and not allowed free reign of the camp or to speak with any prisoners. In the end, the charade did dupe the two Swiss representatives on the committee, but not the Danish official, who delivered a negative report of the farce he had witnessed. As a result, Christian X, the King of Denmark, demanded that the Nazi government return the 466 Danish Jews imprisoned at Terezín to Denmark. Fearing further exposure, the Nazis acquiesced and allowed ambulances to transport those prisoners out of Terezín.

In conjunction with the Red Cross visit, the Reich forced Kurt Gerron, a well-known German-Jewish actor and director imprisoned at Terezín, to make a propaganda documentary of life in the ghetto titled *Der Führer schenkt den Juden eine Stadt* (The Führer Gives the Jews a City). Gerron recoiled at the thought of aiding the Nazis in this deceitful enterprise, but had little choice. In return for his cooperation, camp officials promised Gerron that he and his wife Olga would be protected from deportation to the East. Gerron assumed creative control, writing the script and designing the storyboards for the film. He also insisted that a professional camera crew from Prague be brought in, and despite Nazi worries that this could expose the real situation at Terezín to these Czech civilians, they relented because of their desire for a high quality film. The filming took place between August 16 and September 11, 1944, with prisoners assisting in various assigned duties including makeup and hair. The SS forced others to act out contrived scenarios. The most tragic of these being that of a small Jewish boy made to run down the street chasing a ball, which a Nazi guard then caught and kindly returned to him with a pat on the head. Not included in the footage, of course, was their murder of the same child a few weeks later in Auschwitz.

The crew also filmed music performances, including excerpts of the children singing in Krása's *Brundibár*, along with a performance of Pavel Haas' *Study for Strings* by Karel Ančerl's string orchestra. Additional scenes showed people dancing in the café to the Ghetto Swingers. The camp leadership acquired concert attire for the performers, although with dress shoes harder to come by, sometimes clever arrangements of potted plants had to be used to hide their feet. Gerron hoped that those viewing the film would see beyond the obvious, into the deeper meaning of the images, especially through the eyes and faces of those depicted. The vacant stares and lifeless or terrified expressions that accompanied automaton-like movements told a different story than whatever costumes they had been made to wear. The film's soundtrack, the melancholy and achingly beautiful slow second movement of Mendelssohn's *Trio for Piano, Violin, and Cello in D Minor*, constituted another attempt by Gerron to provide unspoken commentary that illuminated the truth behind the images.

The camera crew completed the filming near the end of the war and sent the footage first to Prague for editing, and then on to Berlin for final editing and distribution. But the Third Reich never released the documentary as intended. They destroyed the only copy in Berlin before their surrender, although some fragments were discovered after the war in the editing room of the Czech production house. As with so many of the large-scale pursuits in Terezín, the film had precipitated more death. After its completion, the Nazi command ordered a mass deportation of 11 convoys loaded with 18,000 prisoners, including 47-year-old Gerron and his wife, despite prior assurances of protection. The Reich felt compelled to silence him immediately because his knowledge of the production of the pseudo-documentary posed too great a threat. The SS guards at Auschwitz summoned him by name from the cattle car and marched him directly to the gas chamber. Olga Gerron also died at Auschwitz. With a great loss of life, the farcical visit and the film had constructed a grandiose deception comparable to a "Potemkin Village," the fake villages that Grigory Aleksandrovich Potemkin built to convince the Russian empress Catherine the Great that the situation was far better than it actually was.[31]

This still from the propaganda film *The Führer Gives a City to the Jews* shows a concert in the Terezín concentration camp, August 1944 (bpk Bildagentur / Art Resource, NY).

But despite whatever illusion the Nazis projected to the world outside of the ghetto, the reality from its earliest days in 1941 was grounded in dread and fear of the trains that took people away from Terezín. The constant threat of deportation weighed heavily on every person and every activity at Terezín, as did the uncertain fates of those already gone. The Nazi command's official statements to the ghetto residents consistently maintained that these transports led to labor camps where the war effort needed a steady supply of workers. Without access to unbiased information, those living in Terezín could not know that extermination constituted the primary objective. On September 6, 1943, 5,007 Jews departed from Terezín for Auschwitz in the largest single group ever transported from there in one day. But oddly, the guards at Auschwitz did not subject these new arrivals to the harsh selection and quarantine procedures. They did not shave their heads nor confiscate their belongings and clothes. Even more surprisingly, none were gassed, despite the fact that camp officials sent all 695 Jews arriving from the Westerbork camp in Holland that same day to the gas chambers.

Instead of the standard protocol of separating the families, the SS housed the September 6 Terezín transport in a special section of Birkenau that they kept segregated from the rest of the camp, eventually becoming known as the *Theresienstadt Familienlager* (Terezín Family Camp). Although the men and women slept in different barracks, these Terezín families could at least live in the same camp. Here, the Nazi command even allowed the prisoners to create a school for the 285 children under the age of 14. Fredy Hirsch, a German-Jewish educator who had worked with the children in Terezín, took charge of the teaching. While possessing books remained forbidden in the rest of the Auschwitz complex, those in the *Familienlager* could read. Fredy placed a young girl named Dita Polach in charge of the children's books, which numbered approximately 18. She would later be known as "the librarian of Auschwitz."[32] Exempt from the typical work duties, these special prisoners were encouraged to continue the artistic activities and productions that they had in Terezín. In response, some of the musicians staged a small children's opera, really just a play with the addition of folk songs, based on the tale of Snow White. Without a piano, they relied on a harmonica for accompaniment. Their bizarre situation grew even more perplexing as various SS and Kapos from Auschwitz attended musical events in the family camp.

Rumors of this unusual subcamp circulated throughout Auschwitz and caught the interest of Alma Rosé, the niece of Gustav Mahler who had enjoyed a successful career as a violinist before being arrested and sent to Auschwitz, where the SS forced her to conduct an orchestra of female prisoners. Because of the time she had spent in Czechoslovakia during her marriage to Czech violinist Váša Příhoda, Alma wondered if there might be any musicians or intellectuals in that group that she knew. With the *Familienlager* set up just across the railroad tracks from the Music Block where her orchestra lived and rehearsed, Alma could stand outside her quarters and watch the comings and goings of those prisoners. She especially looked for her uncle Eduard Rosé, whom she thought might be there. Unbeknownst to Alma, he had died at Terezín on January 21, 1941.

Suspicious of their unprecedented status, residents of the family camp grew worried that their situation served as a masquerade for a malevolent Nazi scheme that would render them pawns in a rigged game. As a result, some rallied to form a resistance, albeit too late. On March 1, 1944, SS officials informed the prisoners from the September 1943 transport that they were being relocated to another camp, but in fact, the camp command had slated them for gassing. Guards moved them to the Quarantine Blocks in the men's camp at Birkenau on March 7. During the evening of March 8, the SS ordered the entire camp on lock down, with no one allowed outside their barracks, while these men, women, and children were murdered in the gas chambers. The SS only spared 13 doctors and nurses and 11 sets of twins for Dr. Mengele's experiments. Fredy Hirsch, who had not been fooled by the Nazi talk of relocation, swallowed poison rather than submit to their will. The poison did not kill him as intended, but he was unconscious when the guards carried him into the gas chamber.

Inexplicably, the mass execution on March 8 only affected the prisoners from that one specific transport. The 5,008 other men, women, and children from Terezín who had arrived in December 1943 or on one of the nine subsequent transports continued to live in the special family camp until July 1944 when the camp command officially closed it after another liquidation via the gas chamber. Large transports continued to come from Terezín in the fall of 1944, 12 between September 23 and October 28, 1944, totaling 23,500 people. These train cars, in particular, contained many of the prominent musicians of Terezín, including the Ghetto Swingers and most members of Ančerl's string orchestra, along with Ullmann, Berman, Schächter, Ledeč, Ančerl, and Krása. Dr. Mengele ordered the death of most upon arrival. Schächter lived for several months at Auschwitz before succumbing in 1945 on a death march. Only Ančerl and Berman of those six musical leaders survived the war. Ančerl became the conductor of the Czech Philharmonic and then later of the Toronto Symphony from 1969 until his death in 1973 at age 65. Berman returned to the Prague Conservatory and completed his degree in voice and stage direction. He performed in operas throughout Europe and worked with the National Theatre in Prague. He died on August 11, 1995, at age 76.

In the end, the Third Reich sent almost 90,000 prisoners from Terezín to Auschwitz, including 6,300 children. The Council of Elders at Terezín had successfully kept children age 11 or younger off the transport list until September 1943, when the Nazis even began to ship infants to their deaths in the East. Of the total Terezín prisoners sent to Auschwitz, only about 3,000 survived. As with so many of the Nazi actions that appear nonsensical upon initial glance, a closer inspection reveals a calculating intentionality endemic to their stratagems. This was true of the *Familienlager*. Similar to the "Potemkin Village" analogy, this contrived place in Auschwitz where select Jewish prisoners received special treatment had been designed with the same intention, a pseudo-touchstone that the Nazi command could point the world to as refutation for any negative claims. The Reich further cemented this particular hoax by having the Terezín deportees write letters upon their arrival to family and friends still in the ghetto that described their relocation to much better living conditions. This request or demand for letter writing continued through subsequent transports. For those entering in March 1944, the SS handed them a postcard with instructions to write a similar message, but date it three weeks in the future. The guards gassed the new arrivals immediately, and then three weeks later, mailed their postcards.

As Nazi leaders shipped Terezín residents to the East, the flow of new prisoners into the ghetto perpetuated a morbid cycle, leaving the long-term Terezín inhabitants, like Alisa Shek, exhausted and despondent. As the uninitiated poured through the gates with no idea about life in the ghetto, she expressed this frustrated weariness in her journal. "We are so tired of teaching our captivity to others."[33] The daily suffering also increased as troubling reports surfaced that the transports to the East were not intended as labor supply, but actually bound for extermination camps. As always, the Nazi ability to control information kept their captives at a disadvantage. The leader of the Council of Elders, Jakob Edelstein, inquired about the veracity of the rumors. Nazi officials assured him that they were untrue and then shipped him to Auschwitz.[34]

In the fall of 1944, ghetto officials again circulated information that the Reich desperately needed laborers, and they intended to relocate all of the young, strong men from Terezín to these work details. But the residents of Terezín harbored deep suspicions that, with the war continuing to shift in favor of the Allies, the Germans feared that these men would organize an uprising within the camp, which indeed some had been discussing. The rumors materialized into reality when approximately 5,000 able-bodied men under the age of 55, including Alice's husband Leopold Sommer, climbed aboard trains, destined not for labor projects, but Auschwitz.

After the substantial transports that fall, most of the artists left behind in Terezín were women such as Alice Herz-Sommer. In October 1944, the camp leadership assigned Alice a new job of splitting mica chips to insulate electronics that required a 45-minute march to the processing center. Alice and her fellow workers sat for hours in under-heated huts using treacherously sharp chisels to split mica, an especially dangerous task for the delicate hands of a pianist. They then tested the chips for strength, always struggling to meet their quota for each day. Three days a week, Alice worked the early shift from 6 a.m. to 2 p.m., and the other three days, from 2 p.m. to 10 p.m. Despite such exhausting work, Alice still made time for music. While large productions, such as operas and orchestral works, grew increasing difficult to mount due to the loss of so many musicians, recitals and chamber music still occurred frequently in Terezín. Pianist Edith Steiner-Kraus presented 10 performances of an all-Bach program, and as late as February 7, 1945, Alice Herz-Sommer gave an all-Chopin recital. Alice also continued to give Saturday concerts geared toward the children, which taught them about the composers as part of the performance.

On April 10, 1945, Alice performed a special recital featuring some of Beethoven's sonatas for piano and violin with her brother Paul Herz, who had smuggled in the scores to these favorite pieces of his and Alice's. Paul had arrived late to Terezín on February 11, 1945, because his marriage to a non–Jew had kept him from being deported until near the end. Initially, camp officials assigned Paul the grueling task as a human-mule harnessed to a cart that he had to pull around at a construction site, loaded down with timber and rubble. According to the Nazi command, this building project of a deep square recess was going to be an artificial lake and duck farm, but to the prisoners working, it seemed much more likely that they were digging a mass grave. Indeed, the Nazis had calculated that by forcing prisoners down into this large pit and then filling it with water, they could drown up to 15,000 at one time. Fortunately for Paul, whose health had declined rapidly after only four days, Arnošt Weiss, a friend he had played chamber music with before the war, recognized him. Weiss headed up the Works Department at Terezín and immediately arranged to have Paul transferred.

Also in February 1945, the SS introduced plans for the construction of several air-tight rooms at Terezín and a large fenced-in area near the perimeter wall. They ordered prisoners working in the relevant offices to begin on those projects. But after examining the blueprints, the workers became increasingly convinced, despite Nazi assurances to the contrary, that these were plans for gas chambers, and that the proposed outdoor enclosure was not intended to be a pen for chickens. They stirred up so much trouble that the Nazis abandoned both projects. After the war, a Nazi official on trial provided evidence of the Reich's desperation toward the end of the war to dispose of witnesses to their atrocities. He admitted that the rooms were indeed gas chambers and that the fenced area would have corralled prisoners while guards turned flame throwers on them.

Meanwhile, in those early months of 1945, the International Red Cross solicited the Third Reich for a second visit to Terezín. At first, the Nazi command felt great reluctance to expose the camp to another inspection, but Heinrich Himmler convinced them that it should be allowed. With the war going so poorly for the Germans, the eagerness with which Himmler appeared to acquiesce to the Red Cross might have stemmed from his hope for a deal at the end. Himmler directed Eichmann to survey the Terezín camp in March to ascertain its fitness for an April 6 inspection. Although Eichmann reported that all seemed ready, Himmler insisted on an additional round of beautifications, which included painting and cleaning. Aware that the musical offerings were now limited, the Nazis worried that they would have little to show the Red Cross or the world as an "alibi." So with the Red Cross visit looming, the camp commandant approached Hanuš Thein, a singer who had studied at the Prague Conservatory and worked as a director at the National Theatre in Prague, and ordered him to organize a children's opera production in the vein of *Brundibár*. Initially, Thein felt overwhelmed by such a daunting task, as the number of children and professional musicians had been severely reduced in the ghetto. Thein then remembered that a production based on the popular Czech children's book *Broučci* (Fireflies) had been staged earlier in Terezín by actor Vlasta Schönova. Written by a Czech minister named Jan Karafiát and first published in the late 19th century, the book told the charming fairytale of Brouček, a little firefly boy who discovered that the world was not always a friendly place, but that regardless, he must shine his light. Back in 1943, professional dancer Kamila Rosenbaum had read

Karafiát's book to some of the children in Terezín and helped them depict the story through dance. She then asked Schönova to collaborate with her in creating a dramatic production. She wrote the script, and Karel Švenk, a frequent participant in Terezín's cabarets, arranged Czech folk songs. Artist Friedl Dicker-Brandeis made their costumes. The combined effort of so many great artists yielded a successful production that enjoyed 28 performances.

By 1945, Kamila Rosenbaum, who had first choreographed the story, had been sent to Auschwitz. So, Thein approached Schönova about reprising *Fireflies*, but she declined at first, not wanting to be party to Nazi deceptions. But Thein appealed to her again and prevailed, having championed the Czech nationalism inherent in the story. The camp command ordered conductor Robert Brock to write music for the new production, allowing him only three days to complete the task. He worked feverishly day and night to arrange Czech folk songs for a 30-member orchestra, cleverly concealing the Czech national anthem within the overture for the work. As with *Brundibár*, Nazi officials allowed *Fireflies* to be performed in Czech. In the end, this production represented more of a triumph for Czech patriotism than a Nazi ploy. The symbolism of the children as fireflies illuminating hope for the future uplifted and strengthened the weary prisoners of Terezín.

The premiere of *Fireflies* took place on March 20, 1945, to a sold-out audience. The second performance also quickly sold all 700 tickets, with eager people trying to sneak in through windows. Then on April 6, Paul Dunant, the single Red Cross representative sent to inspect the camp, sat in the audience. But in fact, Dunant seemed to do little in the way of inspection and kept his visit short. Most likely he knew that the end of the war was quickly approaching and that the Red Cross would be moving into the camp soon. *Fireflies* experienced around 15 performances in March and April 1945, but the last one had to be cancelled because, on the afternoon of the intended performance, several "death transports" from various extermination camps, including Buchenwald and Auschwitz, arrived in Terezín with train cars full of the dead and the dying—12,000 souls in 10 days. The Nazi frenzy to evacuate the death camps as a desperate attempt to conceal war crimes had ironically circled back to Terezín. So, Hanuš Thein ended up unloading corpses instead of overseeing the scheduled production. With these new arrivals, the population in April 1945 rose to more than 17,500. Alice's son Rafi exhibited especially great compassion for these suffering people, probably realizing that his father could be in a similar condition, and together with Alice, Rafi helped to find water and food for them. It is unknown whether Rafi participated in the *Fireflies* production, but with his precocious musical talent, it would certainly have been possible.

Despite the dire situation at Terezín in the spring of 1945, Hanuš Thein became involved again in a large-scale musical production, what would be the last one. The Commandant ordered Thein, as he had with *Fireflies*, to stage Jacques Offenbach's opera *The Tales of Hoffmann*. The Commandant's insistence on that particular opera surprised Thein, not only because it was such a complicated opera, but even more baffling, because the Nazi government had banned all of that Jewish composer's music. The surrealness compounded for Thein when the Commandant handed him a full score for the opera that the National Theatre in Prague had been forced to relinquish to Terezín. Thein's mandate included two caveats: to produce the opera quickly and to shorten it from almost three hours to one. Although a daunting task, Thein embraced it enthusiastically. The opera premiered in April 1945, and following the performance, Thein hid the valuable full score. After the war, he told the librarian for the National Theatre that he had hidden it. Thein refused to enter Terezín again, so the librarian retrieved the score, still exactly where he had stashed it.

In addition to the opera production, other small-scale musical events continued that spring, but at a dwindling pace. Alice Herz-Sommer sat down at the piano on April 25, 1945, for what would be her final performance in the ghetto. Before the month of May could arrive, the music in Terezín fell forever silent. Knowing that they were about to finish on the losing side of the war, the SS began destroying evidence of the crimes and atrocities in Terezín by burning documents and even confiscating the urns of ashes that residents had kept of their loved ones, so as to leave no evidence of the extent of the mortality. In late April, a severe typhus epidemic broke out, and Paul Dunant returned with the International Red Cross on May 2 to deal with the highly contagious disease and the staggering population of now approximately 30,000. Three days later, on May 5, the SS abandoned the camp, and the dire situation deteriorated into complete chaos, with people attacking one another for food and behaving like animals. Finally, the Soviet liberators entered Terezín on May 9, but all those in the camp had to stay there in quarantine at least two weeks because of the typhus outbreak. As in the other camps, it was a slow and painful process to reintegrate these people into society, as many were without family or country. By the end of June, Terezín still housed 6,000 of its former prisoners, leaving its pre-war population to wait until August to return to what remained of their homes in the fortress town.

When forming a summative assessment of Terezín, it remains important to consider that the widespread and almost stereotypical tendency to depict it solely as a cultural Mecca where artists and intellectuals immersed themselves in their craft presents a one-sided and reductive picture of life there. Both joy and misery existed simultaneously. According to survivor Alfred Kantor, "Terezín was a unique place: a piano concerto in a rooftop one night, and a transport to death the next day."[35] Accounts from survivors that frame their time in the ghetto only in terms of its deprivation must be acknowledged as equally valid as those which celebrate the positive. Holocaust scholar Amy Lynn Wlodarski cautions that the need of some to focus only on finding "heroes" or evidence of spiritual resistance and redemptive narratives within Holocaust recollections can create an imbalance in the collective testimony of survivors, causing those victims who shared no stories of triumph to be marginalized.[36]

Concerning Terezín specifically, those who arrived prior to 1943 tended to speak more about the affirming presence of the arts in their daily lives, even to the extent of considering life in Terezín as a fundamental cultural education that they would not have received otherwise. Those who came later, after the mass deportations limited artistic activities, seemed to characterize little or none of Terezín as a "cultural oasis within the Holocaust."[37] Architect and painter Norbert Troller arrived at Terezín in 1942 and became one of the fortunate to survive. His description of life there reflected the paradoxical nature of that place. "Life pulsated with incredible optimism, fatalism, with life-affirming self-deception, with never-ending hope so inherent in Jewish people. It seemed at times almost normal, carefree, without much thought."[38] In the end, the recollections concerning the arts at Terezín certainly encompassed the full continuum of experience, and long after the war, left some harboring "guilt for having enjoyed Terezín's cultural events or for seeming to diminish Jewish suffering through their specific memories."[39]

Nevertheless, even after more than 70 years, the creative and artistic happenings at Terezín have not paled in their remarkable nature. Consummate artists, writers, and musicians produced high quality work. The motivations behind the unprecedented levels of creation in a concentration camp present as equally complex and multi-faceted as the memories of the survivors. For many, art provided an escape, a way to establish some sense of normalcy, a "rhetorical creation."[40] It also offered a means of spiritual resistance against their captors. At the same time, the creative process generated a sense of hope that there was a need to continue practicing one's craft, so that when the war ended, when freedom came, that they would be equipped to resume their former professional lives. This can be seen clearly in the case of Karel Frölich, the great violinist who actively participated in the musical life of Terezín. He assumed the post of concertmaster with the Grand Opera in Prague in May 1945, the same month of his liberation.

While some in Terezín drew motivation from their own self-interests, others derived a sense of purpose from how they could be of service to their fellow captives. In the trying situation that they found themselves, each artist probably experienced a composite of divergent feelings and motivations. Ultimately, that so many of them continued creating right up until their deaths stands as a testament to the courage and strength of character that they possessed. As Viktor Ullmann declared while in Terezín, "…by no means did we sit weeping on the banks of the waters of Babylon … our endeavor with respect to Arts was commensurate with our will to live."[41]

Through her great resolve and a miraculous intervention, Alice Herz-Sommer, along with her son Rafi, lived to see the liberation of Terezín. Rafi became one of the few children to survive Terezín and would make his life's work in music as well, as an accomplished cellist and conductor. In the end, it was Alice's music that saved both of their lives as she had so presciently felt before their deportation. A young Nazi soldier in Terezín, whose mother had been a gifted pianist, adored Alice's playing and listened at the window when she gave recitals. He secretly assumed the role of their protector, eventually confessing to Alice that he had made sure that she and her son never had their names entered on the transport list to the death camps.

In May 1945, right before the liberation, Rafi fell seriously ill with measles, and Alice cared for him day and night. When the Soviet liberators arrived on May 8, Rafi still felt too weak to walk, so Alice ran outside with him in her arms to get a glimpse of the tanks heading toward them, greeted by shouts from her fellow captives of "Freedom!" Afterwards, an official from the Jewish Agency arranged for Alice and Rafi to recuperate for a month on a farm outside of Prague. Throughout the summer, she searched daily for news of her husband Leopold, although she sensed in her heart that he had not survived. Alice eventually found his name on a list of the deceased. He had remained alive at Auschwitz, but after being sent to Dachau as the Allies approached, he died of typhus and starvation on March 28, 1945, one month before its liberation. After the war, a man who had been by Leopold's side when he died brought Alice the precious tin spoon that Leopold had packed in his rucksack in preparation for their deportation to Terezín. He had clung to it as a means of survival through the various camps. Except for her memories and a couple of photographs, this spoon was all Alice had left of her beloved husband.

Alice and Rafi returned to Prague in late July 1945, but the place of their birth did not embrace the reunion. Anti-Semitism still overshadowed the city, and those who had promised to safeguard their belongings had either disappeared or had no intentions of returning them. The strangers living in the Sommers' apartment, similarly, refused to vacate. Alice also found the Czech government unwilling to restore her citizenship despite her many visits to bureaucratic offices and their interminable questions and forms. The fate of Jews returning to Czechoslovakia seemed dependent on whether, before the war, they were considered more Czech—spoke Czech and read Czech newspapers, or whether they were predominately German in speech and culture. So for Jewish Czechs like Alice, who had been active in German circles, the government had little interest in welcoming them home.

Fortunately, Alice's brother Paul and his wife Mary offered them a place to stay until they could figure out other arrangements. Of Aryan descent, Mary had continued to live in their apartment during Paul's interment at Terezín. Paul and Alice had always shared a special bond, although Alice's other siblings felt less charitable toward Paul. They considered him a hopeless drunk and gambler, but Alice chose to focus on the warm heart she saw in her brother. To support herself and Rafi, Alice resumed teaching piano lessons, although she had to give the lessons in the students' homes until she could secure her own piano. She searched for her beloved Förster grand piano in a warehouse of Nazi-confiscated instruments, but could not locate it. With the assistance of Rafi's excellent ear, they selected instead, a Steinway grand with a bright, clear tone.

Intent on her son's musical education as well, Alice taught Rafi a piano lesson every morning before school. He had shown great interest in music from his earliest days, sitting as a toddler on his mother's lap while she practiced. By the time Rafi started kindergarten, his parents had discovered that he possessed perfect pitch. In Terezín, Rafi had participated in various musical activities, and now with the war behind them, he excelled at the piano. But despite his love and aptitude for the instrument, Rafi discovered his true passion in the cello. Meanwhile, Alice also focused on reviving her own career. She triumphantly performed over Czech radio her signature piece, Beethoven's *Appassionata Sonata*, declaring to the world that both she and her music had survived.

As Alice and Rafi worked to rebuild their lives, Czechoslovakia was rapidly succumbing to a new kind of tyranny imposed on it by the Potsdam Conference. In July 1945, Winston Churchill, Harry Truman, and Joseph Stalin met to craft the post-war organization of Europe. The resulting agreement granted Stalin control of Prague, and with that, the Soviet Red Army ushered in Communist control of the

Back home in Prague, Alice gives Rafi a piano lesson in 1945 (courtesy Reinhard Piechocki).

country. These Soviet soldiers ruthlessly hunted down Germans and German sympathizers, initiating their own ethnic cleansing campaign. President Edvard Beneš returned from exile in England and followed similar suit, ordering the expulsion of millions of Sudeten Germans. Soldiers loaded these people into cattle cars and dumped them on the German and Austrian borders, abandoning many there to die from lack of food and shelter. Beneš also ordered the massacre of thousands of non–Czech citizens. Alice was shocked and appalled by these actions. "Before the war, we—Czechs, Germans, Jews—were friends and neighbors. Most of us were bilingual. We had two mother tongues, Czech and German.... Before the war we lived all together as Czechoslovaks."[42]

The NKVD, the Soviet equivalent of the Gestapo, prowled the streets of Prague looking for any reason to detain someone. In May 1945, they arrested a Czech journalist named Michal Mareš. The Soviets threw Mareš into solitary confinement, although he held a membership in the Communist Party, and on three separate occasions hauled him outside blindfolded to be executed by a firing squad. But each time, the soldiers shot into the air, one of their particularly cruel forms of torture. The government eventually released Mareš, who then happened to hear Alice's performance on the radio broadcast. He had known her before the war and had been quite fond of her. Actually, Alice had suspected at the time that he was in love with her, despite being 20 years her senior. They reconnected, and Mareš soon took on the role of suitor to Alice and surrogate father to Rafi. Eventually, Mareš made his intentions known that he wanted to marry Alice and adopt 8-year-old Rafi.

As an educated and well-travelled man who loved classical music, Mareš represented an ideal match for Alice. But also as a dedicated journalist, he felt compelled to continue reporting on the atrocities being committed in Czechoslovakia against ethnic Germans and Jews, despite the dangers that such work presented. The Soviets arrested him several more times and expelled him from the Communist Party. In February 1948, another arrest and trial for treason left him sentenced to prison for seven years. Alice's family living in Palestine read the reports of the heinous acts in Prague and urged Alice to immigrate immediately with Rafi. At first, Alice held out in hope of Mareš' early release, but finally decided that she must get Rafi to safety and that Mareš could join them later.

Alice and Rafi immigrated to Israel in 1949, where both learned Hebrew. By the time they arrived, Palestine had officially become the State of Israel, a momentous achievement marked by a joyful ceremony presided over by Prime Minister David Ben-Gurion in Tel Aviv on May 14, 1948, with the nation's new anthem, "Hatikvah" (The Hope), being performed by the Palestine Orchestra. They lived with her sister Mizzi at first, before eventually securing their own apartment in Jerusalem. Alice joined the faculty at the Jewish Academy of Music, later renamed the Rubin Academy of Music. She made a conscious decision not to disclose to her students or their families that she was a Holocaust survivor. When asked about this choice later, Alice resolutely answered, "My students and their families did not need to be burdened with that part of my past."[43]

Alice never saw Michal Mareš again. After languishing for years in a harsh Soviet prison, Mareš suffered from poor health, plus the Communist government had instituted strict policies that prevented travel to anywhere outside of the Soviet bloc. Mareš died in 1971 and belatedly received full exoneration from the Czech government in 1991, 20 years after his death. Alice never remarried, despite a number of suitors in Israel.

Alice performed frequently in Israel, but only occasionally in Europe. Her plans to revive an international concert career yielded to her desire to provide stability and create a new life in Israel for herself and Rafi. Reminiscent of the house concerts from their life in Prague before Terezín, Alice instituted weekly musicales on Sunday afternoons in her Jerusalem apartment. These became extremely popular and much anticipated events, even to the extent that sometimes the apartment door had to be left open so that overflow crowds could listen from the hallway. In addition to Alice's family and newly made friends, fellow pianist and Terezín survivor Edith Steiner-Kraus frequently attended and performed. Golda Meir, who would become Israel's first female prime minister, came as well. She and Alice formed a deep friendship that lasted until Golda's death in 1978 from cancer. But regardless of the influential people who surrounded her, Alice always placed her son at the center of her life, and he reprised his accomplished role from Terezín as page turner for these musical afternoons.

While studying music and the cello at the Academy of Music where his mother taught, 17-year-old Rafi received the opportunity to play for the famed cellist Paul Tortelier, who had come to Israel for a year-long sabbatical. Impressed with the young man's abilities, Tortelier arranged for a scholarship to the Paris Conservatory, and Rafi studied there with him, graduating with the top prize. Rafi's career as a cellist continued to blossom as he performed on stages around the world, receiving numerous awards and accolades, including the Piatigorsky Artist Award in Boston and second place in the Munich International Cello Competition in 1963. He married Sylvie Ott and moved to London where he became the head of the cello department at the Royal Northern College of Music in Manchester in 1967, a post he kept for 22 years. He and Sylvie had two sons, David and Ariel. After divorcing in 1978, Rafi married a French cellist named Geneviève Teulières. Then in 1989, he accepted a teaching position at the Guildhall School of Music and Drama in London, while continuing to perform extensively. Also a talented conductor, Rafi conducted the First Chamber Orchestra at London's Royal College of Music.

Alice traveled frequently over the years to visit Rafi and her grandchildren. She and Rafi also performed many concerts together in Europe, South America, and the United States in the late 1960s and 1970s. Alice immigrated to England at age 83 to live near her son after he expressed repeated concerns about her traveling at an advanced age. At first, Alice was extremely reluctant to leave her adopted home in Israel, a country that had so fully welcomed her. Both she and Rafi shared an enduring love and affection for Israel. As a Holocaust survivor, Rafi had been exempt from the required two years of military service, but he had waived this right because he wanted to give himself fully to the country that meant so much to them. He had ended up playing cello in the army orchestra. But now after all of these years, Rafi lived abroad, and Alice's sisters had died. Alice finally agreed to the move since she enjoyed the musical life of London and time spent with her son and grandsons.

Alice insisted, however, that her relocation to London in no way signaled retirement because she remained in great health and loved teaching. Alice quickly adapted to life in her new city and established a routine that included swimming a mile every day and eating a healthy diet. She also acquired a group of eager students who came weekly to her small apartment. Life proceeded smoothly and joyously until 1986 when Alice received a diagnosis of breast cancer. The surgeon recommended that she forgo surgery, since at age 83, her tumor would be slow growing and that she would probably die naturally before the cancer could progress too far. Both Alice and Rafi vehemently rejected that prognosis. Determined to live for many more years, Alice opted for surgery. This turned out to be a wise choice. Alice resumed her active lifestyle. In addition to her musical activities, she enrolled in adult continuing education courses at the University of the Third Age, a school designed as part of Cambridge University for retired people. With Alice's mind still sharp and curious, she especially enjoyed a variety of philosophy classes and attended three times a week until age 104.

On November 13, 2001, Rafi and his Salomon Trio gave an evening performance in Israel as part of a concert tour. Afterwards, he told his friends that he felt unwell. At the hospital, doctors diagnosed Rafi with an aortic aneurysm and rushed him to surgery. Tragically, he never woke from the anesthesia. Rafi's shocking death at age 65 became the toughest struggle of Alice's life. They had shared a remarkably close relationship, and at 97 years of age, she now faced life without him. Alice's friends and neighbors grew increasingly worried as her music fell silent with grief. But as time passed, Alice found the strength to sit at the piano and play a few minutes of Bach before heartache forced her to close the keyboard cover. Gradually, music came back to her, and she again embraced her guiding principle of always finding the positive in any situation. Later, when discussing Rafi's death, Alice said, "I am thankful that he did not suffer. He had a beautiful last day. I am thankful that his last memories were of the music. I am thankful that he did not know that he was going to die so that he did not have to be afraid."[44] Indeed, regardless of the hardships she endured throughout her long life, Alice remained steadfastly committed to the beauty of life. "Every day is a miracle. No matter how bad my circumstances, I have the freedom to choose my attitude to life, even to find joy. Evil is not new. It is up to us how we deal with both good and bad. No one can take this power away from us."[45]

After Rafi's death, Alice reaffirmed her dedication to music. She practiced religiously two and three hours a day, playing Beethoven, Chopin, and Bach from memory, even as she crossed over the 100-year milestone. She freely admitted, "I am Jewish, but Beethoven is my religion."[46] As she had throughout her career, Alice always began her practice sessions with Bach, whose music she recognized as fundamental both for her technique and for her soul. "Bach is the philosopher of music.... For me he is the God of all of the Gods of Music."[47] She also frequently welcomed other musicians into her tiny apartment to play chamber music. Her enthusiasm for life attracted people to her, and her fluency in languages—German, English, Czech, and French, provided ease of communication with many. After immigrating to Israel, Alice never returned to the land of her birth, although Czechoslovakia became free and democratic again in 1989. While other former prisoners of Terezín attended reunions, Alice felt no interest. Her Czech citizenship had never been restored to her. She was an Israeli citizen, living in her newly adopted country of England. That was enough for her.

Alice attributed many factors to her long life, including her perpetual and unshakeable optimism, as well as a healthy lifestyle. While in London, she implemented a strict diet for both her well-being and practicality, eating the same meals every day. Toast and cheese for breakfast and chicken soup for lunch and supper, with the occasional fruit snack or sweets brought by a visitor. She continued to be self-sufficient in shopping and preparing her food until she turned 105, after which she agreed to receive a daily meals on wheels delivery at 1 p.m. While embracing the gift of life as fully as possible, Alice also affirmed the challenges of living past the century mark, when the number of friends and family that have been lost along the way presses heavily on the soul. "My life has been marked by its highs and lows like other people but to have a life that is longer than most people's is, I feel, both a test and a gift."[48] Upon her death on February 23, 2014, Alice Herz-Sommer was 110 years old, the oldest known Holocaust survivor. Her amazing life and journey had inspired numerous books and documentary films, including the Oscar-winning documentary short, *The Lady in Number 6*, an award received sadly one month after her passing.

Alice Herz-Sommer at her flat in Belsize Park, London in June 2010 (Sophia Evans /eyevine/ Redux).

Alice's influence can be seen throughout the world in the countless students she taught, some becoming well-known in the musical world, others passing their knowledge on to the next generation. Many legacies can be traced back, like a family tree, to the skillful and profoundly caring teaching of Alice Herz-Sommer, including that of internationally renowned violinist Gil Shaham, whose mother Meira Shaham had been one of Alice's students. Alice not only survived, but flourished personally and musically. She lived a life that spanned the entire 20th century and the first 14 years of the 21st century, facing whatever came with an optimistic spirit and a contagious, unapologetic laughter that could not be silenced by the Nazi atrocities that resulted in her and Rafi's imprisonment and the murder of her husband, mother, and countless friends. For Alice, above all else, she steadfastly proclaimed, "I am still grateful for Life. Life is a present."[49]

5

Władysław Szpilman and the Warsaw Ghetto

Whosoever saves a single life, saves an entire universe.
—The inscription on the "Righteous Among the Nations" medal awarded by the Yad Vashem for heroic acts in saving Jewish lives during the Holocaust. It is the highest honor the State of Israel can confer on a Gentile.

For September 23, 1939, the Polish State Radio had scheduled Władysław Szpilman to perform an all–Chopin recital for live broadcast. Szpilman had worked at the radio station as a pianist and composer ever since Adolf Hitler's rise to power drove him back home to Warsaw from Berlin. Born on December 5, 1911, in Sosnowiec, southern Poland, Szpilman discovered at an early age that music came naturally to him, most likely since he descended from generations of talented Polish-Jewish musicians. Szpilman supplemented his inherited abilities with an impressive pedagogical pedigree. At the Chopin School of Music in Warsaw, he studied piano under Aleksander Michalowski, a renowned interpreter of Chopin. Then in 1931, Szpilman enrolled at the Berlin Academy of Arts, where he took composition courses with Franz Schreker, who had been a violin pupil of Arnold Rosé at the Vienna Conservatory and then had embarked on a successful career as a conductor and a German opera composer. Also at the Berlin Academy, Szpilman studied piano with Artur Schnabel. Schnabel influenced Szpilman greatly because of his flair for performance. Schnabel maintained a busy international tour schedule as a solo pianist and as a collaborative pianist, performing chamber music with other leading musicians of his day, such as violinist Bronisław Huberman and cellist Pablo Casals. After school, Szpilman launched an active performing career that imitated that of his teacher—chamber music with renowned musicians, including violinist Bronisław Gimpel, as well as solo piano repertoire. Szpilman also loved composing in a wide variety of genres. In addition to a violin concerto and a suite for piano called *Zycie Maszyn* (The Life of Machines), he wrote scores for numerous films and many highly successful popular songs.

But despite the many talents that Szpilman possessed, on September 23, 1939, the main skill he needed involved how to make it to the radio studio alive. As German bombs and artillery shells rained down, Szpilman dodged in and out of buildings and other shelters, waiting for some semblance of safety between each onslaught before edging his way a little further. He finally arrived unscathed, and at the appointed time, Szpilman sat down at the piano for that familiar ritual of preparing his body, hands, and mind to enter that holy moment of making music. But this process was certainly not as easy or reassuring as it had been even a month earlier, before the Nazi invasion of Poland. Nevertheless, he readied himself to bring music to the people of Warsaw, who needed it now more than ever. Szpilman never wavered during that live recital even though explosions continued all around the outside of the building, making it difficult to even hear himself playing. After finishing his performance, which had included Chopin's beloved *Nocturne No. 20 in C-sharp minor*, Szpilman decided to wait around in hopes that the barrage would lessen, rendering his walk home a bit safer. He did not know it, but the recital he had just given would be the last live music broadcast from the Polish State Radio until 1945.

Celebrated as both the political and cultural capital of Poland, the city of Warsaw lies next to the Vistula, the largest river in Poland. Warsaw traces its roots back to medieval villages, from which it grew to become the capital city in the 17th century. During the 18th and 19th centuries, Warsaw strengthened into a major economic and industrial force and developed a rich cultural life in theater, literature, and the other arts. But Poland's prime geographic location in Eastern Europe rendered it of great strategic importance and therefore highly coveted by its neighbors. As a result, the capital city was no stranger to war and had to rebuild itself out of the ashes many times from conflicts with the Swedes, Prussians, and Russians before even the dawn of the 20th century. Warsaw's motto fittingly proclaims, "*Contemnit procellas*" ("It defies the storms").

Even with Europe's struggling economy in the interwar years, the Warsaw of the early 20th century expanded its industrial complex through aircraft manufacturing and its reputation in the music world through the founding of two prestigious musical competitions: the International Chopin Piano Competition in 1927 and the Henryk Wieniawski International Violin Competition in 1935. Warsaw had proven itself to be not only a progressive city economically and culturally, but also socially, with a long history of offering asylum to Jews who had fled anti–Semitic pogroms in Western Europe. Nevertheless, anti–Semitism smoldered underneath the city's surface during the early years of the 20th century. While some of the wealthier Jews resided in Warsaw's finer neighborhoods, most lived a semi-sequestered life in the Jewish Quarter, which allowed many to retain their traditions, language, and rich culture.

Władysław Szpilman in an undated publicity photo.

But regardless of their street address, the Jewish population as a whole constituted an integral part of the city. Warsaw published six daily newspapers in Yiddish, while only two dailies in Polish. The Jewish residents founded 100 modern Jewish schools for their children in Warsaw alone and supported a vibrant arts community. One of Warsaw's literary treasures in the early decades of the 20th century was Jewish writer and poet Rachel Auerbach, who worked as an art and literary critic and also focused on writing about the lives of women. Life felt so content in Warsaw that Auerbach, like so many others, refused to acknowledge the impending threat from Hitler. After the war, she freely admitted that "…we should have seen the worst coming. But we did not want to know the truth. We protected ourselves from the truth. We did not want to see it."[1]

The Poles and Germans certainly made no secret of the fact that they had been enemies since the Middle Ages. The Polish people had suffered greatly from numerous German occupations, even as recently as 1915–18, and for many in Poland, "…Slavs fighting Teutons had achieved the status of patriotic tradition."[2] But they never counted on Stalin forging an alliance with the Nazis. When Hitler signed a Nonaggression Pact with the Soviets in the summer of 1939, that treaty paved the way for the Germans to seize Poland without fear of retaliation from its Russian neighbor. At 4:45 a.m. on September 1, 1939, German planes entered Polish air space and unleashed the first flurry of bombs.

After the political maneuverings of the summer, the German invasion of Poland did not take the Szpilman family or the other Polish residents completely by surprise. They felt fairly confident that their own military forces, coupled with their British and French allies, would end the encroachment soon. Still, the falling bombs and shelling that shook the city sent panicked residents scrambling to shelters. Szpilman went to work that day at the radio station and found it chaotic, as they needed to interrupt scheduled programs to report the latest news. The information they broadcasted to the city via home radios and the outdoor speakers mounted on poles throughout Warsaw constituted the only real-time news source. Szpilman adapted fairly quickly to the pandemonium on that first day, but found his colleague, whom he referred to as "Dear old Professor Usztein,"[3] fretting about the uncertainties. Accompanying at the piano framed the only life Usztein knew and provided the mooring that gave structure not only to his days but to his life. Szpilman described it as, "Whereas other people measure out their lives by days and hours, his had been measured for decades by piano accompaniments. When the professor was trying to remember details of some past event, he would begin, 'Now let's see. I was accompanying so-and-so at the time…'"[4] So, Szpilman assured the distraught Professor Usztein that their music would still be needed, but just on a more erratic schedule than usual. This observation turned out to be correct, and Szpilman and Usztein both found themselves at the studio's piano that day and for the next few weeks.

But by September 20, Poland and its allies had yet to halt the German onslaught, and so the bombing and shelling continued unabated. Nevertheless, Szpilman was still determined to make the dangerous trek to the radio station every day, as shells whistled overhead and shrapnel rained down. He often had to plot a circuitous route that involved ducking and dodging incoming explosives. It would have looked like one of the great comedic scenes from a Charlie Chaplin film, had it not represented a somber reality. The honeymoon period for the Poles, if there had been one, was definitely over. They now watched with horror as their military and political leaders fled the capital, and the Germans advanced nearer each hour to their goal of conquering Poland.

Along with these stark realizations came a burgeoning sense of mistrust and paranoia as people clamored to identify who among their neighbors might be a German spy or collaborator. The Szpilman family had temporarily relocated to an apartment in another area of the city that they deemed safer. They learned that an elderly spinster, who was a music teacher, lived in one of the other apartments in that building. She subscribed to a strict daily routine and did not like to have it altered. This included her two hours of piano practice before lunch and the three times a day that she fed the birds she kept in a cage on her balcony. When the music teacher refused to interrupt her practicing by going down into the air raid shelter when the sirens sounded, several suspicious tenants decided that she must be working for the Nazis and sending coded messages through her piano music. Eventually, a group of women from the building tied up the poor woman and shut her in the cellar along with her birds. They had not caught a spy, but they did save the piano teacher's life, because several hours after the kidnapping, a shell completely destroyed her apartment.

Despite the Armageddon that Nazi Germany had unleashed on his beloved city, Szpilman demonstrated the staunch resolve of the Polish people by playing a live broadcast recital of Chopin's music on September 23. After his performance ended, the radio station switched to a recording of Rachmaninov's *Piano Concerto in C minor*. Toward the conclusion of its hauntingly beautiful second movement, a German bomb hit the station, and the Warsaw Radio fell silent.

Now without his job to provide distraction, Szpilman tried to occupy himself by working on a piece he was composing, a concertino for piano and orchestra, but found himself unable to concentrate. September 25 and 26 saw no letup in the onslaught, and more and more of the city crumbled into inhabitable ruins. Szpilman spent those two days standing up in a crowded bathroom with nine other people. When they emerged after two days, he could not imagine how they had managed to fit that many people in such a tiny bathroom nor how they had survived when everywhere he looked was rubble. On September 27, Warsaw fell.

With Warsaw surrendered to the Germans and the bombings ended, the Szpilman family returned to their home on Sienna Street. Miraculously, it remained intact, and so they attempted to resume their lives as best they could. Szpilman's father, in particular, wanted to pretend that nothing had happened and would shut himself away for hours with his violin, preferring music to any talk of the war or of their German overseers.

Within a few days of the occupation, the Germans began hanging posters throughout Warsaw that announced their pledge to take care of the Polish people and to make sure that they had food and work. These posters even assured the Jewish residents that they would retain all of their rights and property. There was, of course, no veracity in any of those promises for either the Poles or the Jews. But in the early days, the city of Warsaw seemed suspended in a strange purgatorial state in which its citizens burned angrier at their own politicians and military officials who had failed to protect them, than at their German occupiers. That would soon change as the Nazis revealed their true intentions.

Surprisingly, some of the early atrocities committed by the Germans were not leveled at the Jews. The Nazis hated all of the Poles, not just the Jewish ones. Instead of merely occupying Poland and governing its people, they wanted to take the land, the *Lebensraum* (living space), for the German people. They hoped that eliminating the brain trust of the country would make it much easier to accomplish this, so they rounded up and executed members of the Polish intelligentsia. They also instituted control over information and knowledge by banning the press and shutting down high schools and universities. Now that the real dangers to the Polish people had been revealed, the instinct for survival changed the dynamics.

In quick order, Warsaw evolved into "a city crowded with predators and prey of all sizes, including the decent and bribable, the indecently unbribable, a hard-core criminal, opportunistic denizens, people hobbled by fear, Nazi sympathizers, and risk-takers who juggled their own and other lives like lit torches."[5]

Meanwhile, the Nazis conspired to plunder any Polish assets and artifacts that might be of value or interest. While they certainly sought significant works of art and other prized treasures, the German leadership also coveted some less obvious items. The Nazi obsession with genetics extended to animals and so obtaining the purest breeds as specimens for German zoos became a priority. They decided to pillage them from wherever they could. Lutz Heck served as Hitler's chief zoologist and as director of the Berlin Zoo. Heck had also formed a close friendship with the powerful Nazi official Hermann Göring, as the two shared a love of hunting and ecology. So with the invasion of Poland and the support of Göring, Heck turned his attention to the animals at one of Europe's largest zoos—the Warsaw Zoo. Dr. Jan Zabiński, a noted biologist and author, served as the director of the Warsaw Zoo. He relied on assistance from his wife Antonina, who possessed an uncanny ability to communicate with animals, especially untamed or highly agitated ones. Those who had seen her at work knew her as an animal whisperer. Before the German invasion, Heck visited their zoo under the auspices of wanting to befriend the two zookeepers as colleagues and fellow animal lovers. But once the Germans seized control of the city, Heck's true motives became clear. He intended to commandeer all of their prized stock for shipment to his zoo in Berlin, and any animals left behind would then be shot for meat to feed the German soldiers.

As Polish assets accumulated in its war coffers, Germany began planning for the consolidation of Poland's large Jewish population. This would entail the massive effort of exporting Jews from rural regions and concentrating them into just a few major cities, all to allow for easier monitoring. In the meantime, punitive legislation that restricted Jewish movements and access throughout Poland placed an invisible cordon around them. Some of the provisions in these new laws included stripping Jews of their driver's licenses and forbidding their use of public buses or railways.

Music and other cultural activities that had enjoyed such vibrancy in Warsaw faced a crisis as well. As Nazi legislation shut down schools and limited Jewish access to places and activities, Poland's cultural organizations, which included music ensembles and theater troupes, suffered a similar fate. German officials relied on these disruptions to the lives of the Polish people as another effective means of achieving the Nazi agenda. But as had happened in other culturally rich cities such as Prague, the citizens of Warsaw refused to live without art, and so they drove these activities underground. Concerts and recitals moved to people's homes by private invitation. Musicians found each other and formed clandestine ensembles and staged performances in unconventional venues. But for all of these events, both audience members and performers maintained a vigilant eye because of the great risk. If German authorities discovered them, prison would be the least sentence incurred, but shipment to camps or even immediate execution seemed the more likely.

Meanwhile, the Jewish population of Poland remained a formidable obstacle for Germany. In the early years of the Nazi administration, officials had disagreed markedly about how best to deal with their Jewish problem. Some believed that the solution lay in the formation of ghettos, while others felt that segregating the Jews into one, crowded location would incite further difficulties, such as creating a breeding ground for epidemics that could then spread to the general population. The detractors also suggested that cloistering the Jewish residents into ghettos would fail to accomplish one of their main priorities—the total exclusion of Jews from the German economy.

In arriving at a final decision, the Nazi leadership found plenty of historical precedence to review. The Jewish people had endured a long history of being cordoned off from the rest of the population, usually out of fear or jealousy. The Venetians had originated the concept of Jewish ghettos in the 16th century, and the Catholic Church of that time had also fiercely supported the ghettoization of Jews so that they would not contaminate Christian converts. Even into modern times, it proved common in European cities such as Prague, Vienna, and Warsaw for the Jews to live in their own quarter, a term that could be considered a euphemism for the ghetto except that it did allow for a more voluntary and porous framework than a mandatory sequestration. So in the early 20th century, most Jews, out of the comfort and security that came from being surrounded by the familiar, chose to reside in these neighborhoods or quarters, where they found themselves densely packed into a limited geographic area, and thus perpetuated the age-old tradition of segregation.

So, the Nazi government merely looked to history to provide a solution for isolating the Jewish populations of certain cities. Within a few months of his rise to power, Hitler studied the past actions of the Catholic Church toward what they had also considered a Jewish pestilence. He then used the Church's centuries of animosity toward the Jews as justification for his own burgeoning policies and easily disregarded any inconsistencies, including that his motivation stemmed solely from racial hatred while the Church's had been fueled by religious intolerance. Other significant disparities also existed between the two comparisons. The Church had grudgingly allowed the Jews in ghettos to conduct their daily lives with a modicum of freedom and to govern themselves with their own laws, while also dangling the option for conversion to Christianity as a path out of the ghetto. While this segregated life often brought suffering, many of the Jewish ghettos from previous centuries had flourished. These ghettos bore little resemblance to what the Nazis envisioned, which would eventually play a crucial role in the planned extermination of a people. The Nuremberg Laws of 1935, which provided the framework for determining who constituted a member of the Jewish race, would become the cornerstone of ghettoization, and then genocide.

As the debates continued among German officials, Peter-Heinz Seraphim, a leading Nazi historian and sociologist, cautioned that he and other scholars believed that the concentration of Jews into restricted living spaces in the way of 16th century Rome and Venice had actually strengthened the population and cultivated unity, rather than crippling their influence, because the Jews had still been permitted freedom of movement and an active engagement in the city's economy. This arrangement had also served the Church well, as it wanted the estrangement but needed the support of Jewish commerce. Seraphim insisted that instituting a more complete quarantine from all aspects of German life presented the only way that a ghetto system for the Jews would accomplish the Nazi agenda. In the end, Hitler and his second-in-command Hermann Göring decided in favor of establishing ghettos, but not on German soil, as the presence of Jewish ghettos in German cities would not accomplish a *Judenfrei* (free of Jews) Reich.

Instead, the leadership of Nazi Germany concluded that creating Jewish ghettos in Eastern Europe would prove quite useful and expedient. Despite how inconvenient the Jews of Western Europe seemed to the Nazis, the *Ostjuden* (Eastern European Jewry) aroused their hatred above all others. Both Slavic and Jewish, these people would find no mercy from their Nazi occupiers. As isolation plans began to take shape for Poland, and then later for places in Hungary, Czechoslovakia, and Romania, "the Nazis' anti–Semitism transformed the ghetto into a means to accomplish economic enslavement, impoverishment, violence, fear, isolation, and overcrowding in the name of racial purity—all with no escape through conversion, and with unprecedented efficiency."[6] But despite the stark differences between the medieval incarnation of a ghetto and the Nazis' aberration, the world seemed oblivious. So either through an ignorance of history or just plain apathy, the international community allowed this new definition of a ghetto to slip into the vocabulary without much of a blink.

So with little fear of a global outcry, German officials ordered the construction of ghettos. The inexpensive cost and easy availability of barbed wire made the process happen quite efficiently and brought the added bonus to Hitler of giving the ghettos' inhabitants the look of caged animals on display. These Nazi ghettos were intended in their early days to serve as repositories of slave laborers and as holding cells until the Jews could be expelled. But in time, the horrible conditions in the ghettos would take their toll on the residents through filth and disease, making the Nazi leadership less inclined to use them as workers or facilitate their emigration to other countries. The Nazis would show photos from the ghettos to substantiate their claims that the Jewish race was sub-human, and that for the preservation and sanctity of the Aryan race, only complete extermination would suffice. And with that, the ghettos would fully transition to waiting areas for genocide.

Yet unaware of these developing plans for a ghetto, the city of Warsaw slipped toward its first winter of occupation. The Germans began another round of hanging posters, but these read quite differently from the placating ones during the early weeks of the occupation. Restrictive rules and regulations were plastered across these new posters, as well as warnings of the serious violations that carried the death penalty. But in time, some of these threats proved to be meaningless bravado. Instead, the Polish citizens learned "…that the real danger was what could happen to you totally unexpectedly, out of a blue sky—unannounced by any rules and regulations, however fictitious."[7] As November 1939 came and went, the German agenda for the Poles grew more apparent, and the tenor of the residents' feelings toward their occupiers certainly changed. "…a wall of hatred had been erected between Germans and Poles, and neither side could climb it thereafter…"[8]

But there seemed no reprieve from any of the regulations applied exclusively to the Jews, as the Nazis began to systematically strip them of their money, properties, businesses, and finally their lives. The abysmal treatment of the Jews did not just stem from some practical necessity stipulated in a ledger or on a map, but also from a wicked desire to degrade and dehumanize them. The German soldiers in the streets competed with one another about who could invent the best "games" for the Jews, such as making a group of Jewish women remove their underwear and use it to scrub floors and toilets, then put it back on wet. Intentional humiliations also served as the motivation for certain laws, including the decree that required all Jewish men to bow to every German soldier they encountered. For Szpilman, this particular legislation proved so denigrating and infuriating that he would walk through back streets and alleys, even though it made the trip much longer, just to avoid contact with any soldiers. Meanwhile, some Jews began trying to escape toward the East, where they hoped to find refuge from this awful treatment in Russia. Many of Szpilman's musical colleagues chose to flee, and most were successful. Some ended up back home, however, having been beaten and relieved of their possessions; and a few were murdered.

Szpilman's family decided to stay and hope for a swift defeat of Germany by the Allied Forces, even though it felt as if an invisible noose grew tighter around their necks each day. That winter, Szpilman observed a fracturing of the city and the society that he had known and loved.

Two lives began to go on side by side: an official, fictional life based on rules which forced people to work from dawn to dusk, almost without eating, and a second, unofficial life, full of fairy-tale opportunities to make a profit, with a flourishing trade in dollars, diamonds, flour, leather or even forged papers—a life lived under constant threat of the death penalty...[9]

While not tempted to engage in the black market, the Szpilman family found little legitimate options still available to them for earning a living. Szpilman's father, mother, and sister Halina gave music lessons to bring in some income. His sister Regina, who could no longer practice law, took up tutoring, and his brother Henryk taught English lessons. Meanwhile, the family gradually sold off possessions. Somehow only Szpilman, himself, languished without a means of revenue, and so tried to content himself with composing. Fortunately, his home always resounded with music, and sometimes a violinist friend would come over so they could play chamber music together. Revisiting a favorite Beethoven sonata seemed the most effective means of lifting his spirits and restoring some sense of normalcy.

With December 1939 came a new humiliation—a branding of the Polish Jews that required them to wear white armbands sewn with a blue Star of David. For these Jewish residents who had been so proud of their acceptance and assimilation into the culture of modern-day Poland, it felt like a slap in the face that propelled them back to the Middle Ages. Meanwhile, more Jewish refugees poured into Warsaw every day, but not of their own free will. The Germans had made good on their plans to consolidate all the Jews into major cities, leaving the beautiful countryside *Judenfrei*. Soldiers rounded them up in rural areas and threw them into the back of cattle trucks, where they stood for days without food or water as their homes receded farther and farther into the distance. The freezing temperatures in these trucks, along with the deprivations, meant that when the vehicles unloaded in Warsaw, many of those standing shoulder to shoulder in the group had become frozen corpses.

During the thaw of spring 1940, the Germans racked up new victories with the occupations of Holland and Belgium and the fall of Paris. It seemed that there would be no stopping the Nazi war machine. Then, in September 1940, the Germans began shipping Jews out of Warsaw to labor camps, where they worked in horrible conditions with little food. Their health deteriorated rapidly, and tuberculosis became a common affliction. The Germans forced all those left behind in the city to do at least six days of physical labor, as assigned, each month. This requirement especially troubled Szpilman, who could not risk injury to his hands that were his livelihood, and so he tried to find ways to shirk this mandate.

The Germans also launched a new propaganda campaign that autumn. Theaters throughout Poland began to show Nazi films that detailed the risks posed to Polish citizens by their Jewish neighbors who lacked basic hygiene and carried diseases, such as typhus. Officials also circulated thousands of posters and pamphlets that bore the slogan, "JEWS—LICE—TYPHUS."[10] The German government hoped that these measures would convince the Poles that the threat of Jewish-born disease made it essential to isolate these people into their own quarter where they could have the freedom to enjoy their cultural and religious practices, but while surrounded by a wall to prevent the spread of contagions. As long as the Poles accepted this narrative, then the Nazi government anticipated less resistance to their plan for ghettoization.

Having meticulously set the stage for a ghetto in Warsaw, the Nazi command issued the official decree in October 1940 that divided the city into three living areas: German, Polish, and Jewish. This new legislation also stipulated that all citizens must move to their assigned region by the end of the month. For the Jews, this meant the walled ghetto that was being constructed from brick and barbed wire in a part of the already existent Jewish Quarter. Any non–Jewish residents living in that area were evicted. This new home for the Jews would not include any parks or areas for recreation and relaxing, but would be near a railway station to facilitate future Nazi plans.

But despite all of the well-laid bureaucratic stratagems, the mass relocation of all of Warsaw's Jews presented a monumental challenge. At the time of the German invasion, the Jewish population of Warsaw numbered 350,000 or one-third of the entire city's population, ranking it the largest and most diverse group of Jews in the world. They had been assimilated and acculturated within the city at all levels of political, social, and cultural life and enjoyed freedom without restriction. Their customs and eccentricities seemed accepted by the Poles, who fostered their own share of peculiarities as one of the most superstitious cultures. Now, with the forced resettlement at hand, the Jewish population, which had absorbed refugees from the rural areas, strained at almost half a million. Nevertheless, Nazi officials prepared to squeeze them all into an area of less than 20 square blocks, which was smaller than New York City's Central Park and geographically occupied only 3 percent of the city of Warsaw. Later, one resident would aptly call the claustrophobic Warsaw Ghetto a *Todeskätschen* (a little death chest).[11]

So starting in October, the Jews of Warsaw consolidated behind the wall. Ironically, some of the Jews initially felt freer inside the ghetto because they no longer had to look over their shoulders for the Gestapo as they walked through the streets or worry about the ever-increasing list of anti–Semitic rules. But then on November 15, 1940, the Nazi government sealed the ghetto. Now with the Jews closed in a walled cordon, Warsaw fractured into two starkly contrasted cities—one with room to stroll freely through parks and enjoy a fill of food at outdoor cafés and another with scarcity and overcrowding, where six or seven people shared one room and where the cramped streets would eventually be lined with beggars and corpses. But in actuality, Warsaw harbored yet another city besides the two separated by a tangible wall. Historians estimate that at least 20,000 Jews went into hiding rather than be imprisoned in the Warsaw Ghetto, and so amid the "Aryan" sectors existed an "embedded city of fugitives."[12]

During the mass resettlements, the Szpilman family fared better than some because their apartment on Sienna Street already sat within the area selected for the ghetto, so all six of them could remain in their familiar home. They were almost penniless by November 1940, having sold anything of value many months before, including their most precious possession—the piano. Their area of the ghetto housed other members of the artistic and intellectual community whose financial situation mirrored that of the Szpilmans, but it contained some of the more prosperous families as well. The manner in which the Germans had chopped up the streets to create a walled border had resulted in this region of the ghetto being relatively small. But moving away from Sienna Street toward the north revealed a disparate scene—a much larger sector where poverty and the unrelenting assault of disease and vermin resided.

With the sealing of the ghetto, Szpilman experienced a sense of confinement that he described as almost worse than being in an actual prison. In the ghetto, people knew only the illusion of freedom as they walked through the streets and in and out of the buildings, but a whole world still existed outside the locked gate where they also used to walk and now could not.

> I think it would have been psychologically easier to bear if we had been more obviously imprisoned—locked in a cell, for instance. That kind of imprisonment clearly, indubitably, defines a human being's relationship to reality. There is no mistaking your situation: the cell is a world in itself, containing only your own imprisonment, never interlocking with the distant world of freedom.[13]

To combat his claustrophobia, Szpilman established a regular routine for himself in the mornings that constituted breakfast and then a long walk through the ghetto, during which he visited with people and sought out the latest news. He never made peace with the walls, though.

> They barred my way when I wanted to walk on and there was no logical reason to stop me. Then the part of the street on the other side of the wall would suddenly seem to be the place I loved and needed most in all the world, a place where things must be going on at this very moment that I would give anything to see—but it was no use. I would turn back, crushed, and I went on like this day after day, always with the same sense of despair.[14]

After spending all morning conducting his "rounds," Szpilman would stop by Nowolipki Street to assist his brother. Henryk had refused on principle to join the Jewish Police Force, even though it provided financial security and had become a popular choice among young intellectuals. He knew the organization was fraught with corruption and wanted no part in it. Instead, he sold and traded books on the street. When lunchtime arrived, Szpilman would help his brother carry the books home, and the entire family would sit down to a meal that his mother could magically pull together in an elegant way, although they had little resources and hardly ever any meat.

Henryk's small book business found a receptive audience in that part of the ghetto. The Jewish people's love of books, music, and the arts had accompanied them into their new cloistered environment. Drawing together a vast and diverse group from such an enlightened city as Warsaw, the ghetto naturally cultivated a robust cultural life. The preservation and dissemination of knowledge remained of great importance to the Jews, and so these "people of the book" wanted to surround themselves with the printed word. Because of the weight and bulk of books, however, those relocating to the ghetto were limited in how many they could bring. But in time, through pooling resources and some smuggling from the outside, the ghetto housed 18 bookstores and 24 lending libraries. The Judaic Library evolved into the intellectual center of the ghetto early on and served as an excellent venue for lectures and small artistic events. Almost immediately, a ghetto newspaper, *Gazeta Żydowska*, came into being and circulated important news around the ghetto, as well as advertisements from musicians who were available to perform in private homes for dinners, celebrations, or recitals. Actors also promoted themselves in the newspaper and prepared monologues and poems that they could be hired to deliver. Organizing house concerts came easily, as Warsaw's residents had already been forced to do that from the early days of the Nazi occupation. These worked especially well in the ghetto because of the strict curfew each evening. If an event was scheduled to last past 8 p.m., then the hosts understood that their guests would be spending the night.

Fearful of the strength that can arise from people uniting behind a common cause or even affinity, the Germans set limits on the types of organizations that could be established behind the wall, just as they had in the city of Warsaw. The *Judenrat* (Jewish Council) was the only governing body allowed to exist within the ghetto, a group the Nazis knew would do much of their "dirty work" for them. Many of the elite and powerful members of the Jewish Council did take advantage of the poor and disenfranchised, including allocating them less food and worse housing. The only other form of internal authority came from the Jewish Police Force, a group that often committed acts of brutality, cruelty, and theft, instead of assisting and keeping the peace among their own people. In the end, the Jewish Police would decide which names of their fellow ghetto residents would appear on deportation lists to the camps.

Nazi officials also allowed some social welfare organizations to exist, but did not officially authorize any cultural associations. So acting under the umbrella of the Jewish Society for Social Welfare, a group of residents came together to provide a vision and logistical support for the ghetto's cultural offerings in hopes of restoring some semblance of the normalcy and beauty of their previous lives. This Central Events Commission also functioned as a sort of union by representing performers to ensure their fair treatment and pay, especially in light of the differing status of those who had worked as professional musicians before the war and those considered merely amateur hobbyists. During the Commission's first year of operation, hundreds of musicians signed up on its roster. The group also worked to bring arts education to the youth and to showcase the ghetto's young talent as much as possible. Their results during that inaugural year seemed miraculous in such a sealed and uncertain environment, with over 1,800 performances, including eight orchestral concerts. While working to fulfill their mission to meet the needs of artists seeking employment and of citizens longing for solace and escape, the Central Events Commission embraced an even more profound calling. They believed that creating and sustaining a vibrant cultural life within the ghetto forged a promise that there would be life after this horrible war, and that until then, the Jewish people's rich artistic traditions would be held in trust for when that day dawned.

Beyond the nobleness and needfulness of its cause, the Central Events Commission actually owed a great deal of its success to the minimal interference of the Germans. Uncharacteristically, the Nazi command took a relaxed, almost lackadaisical, approach to regulating the cultural activities in the Warsaw Ghetto. In other occupied regions and camps, highly specific rules governed what music Jews could and could not perform, and those guidelines were strictly enforced and carried severe punishments if violated. Officially, the same requirements applied to the ghetto in Warsaw, except the German authorities proffered little interest or oversight in the artistic realm inside this particular wall. Maybe they hoped that the residents' immersion in cultural activities would serve as a deterrent to resistance and provide a false sense of autonomy and security. The Germans also might have been of the mindset that the Warsaw Ghetto existed only as a temporary holding pen for these people, who would be eliminated in due time, so why not let them "make hay while the sun shines."

The cultural life of the Warsaw Ghetto did indeed provide for both distraction and engagement. Even among the deprivation, energy could still be found for passionate debates about art and its relationship to the Jewish experience and identity. Some accused the fully assimilated artists of abandoning their roots and only contributing to the advance of Polish culture. These artists would then counter by citing the backwardness of traditional Jewish culture and declaring that artists solely striving within the Jewish tradition had failed to keep up with the times and had thus rendered themselves irrelevant. These same intractable debates had raged during the interwar years and now left an unnavigable interstice amid the artistic community of the ghetto. As a result, cultural programming and activities were often sharply divided by language and class.

Fortunately, for the diverse backgrounds and sensibilities of the ghetto's citizenry, theatrical productions offered a highly accessible art form that could accommodate, and sometimes even bridge, their divides. In fairly short order, professional theater venues began to appear and eventually totaled five: two in Yiddish and three in Polish. The first, named Eldorado, opened on December 6, 1940, less than a month after the sealing of the ghetto. The Eldorado became an extremely popular entertainment location and even featured its own in-house orchestra conducted by A. Walstein.[15] Comedies, musical revues, and variety shows constituted the standard and most favored offerings for all of the theaters. Satirical productions, in particular, had delighted Eastern European audiences during the interwar years, and so the spirit of that genre lived on in the Warsaw Ghetto. While a few serious plays did receive productions, it seemed that parody, comedy, and satire best met the needs of the ghetto's psyche. The preferred music in these theaters also resonated those same sentiments and usually consisted of familiar tunes from films, musicals, and cabarets.

In addition to the popular pre-war repertoire, some newly composed pieces gained a place on the stages of the Warsaw Ghetto. These usually took the form of songs with lyrics that recounted the challenges and absurdities of ghetto life and, as a result, found a receptive and sympathetic audience. Common topics included hunger, poverty, loss, and death, as well as outrage at those who oppressed them from both inside and outside the wall. Many of these songs centered on the plight of their children, who they viewed as the only hope against the extinction of the Jewish people, and so anger and sorrow over their children's begging, smuggling, and dying poured forth through singing. But not all songs focused on the miseries of the ghetto. The tradition of the medieval *chansons de geste* received a revival as songwriters chronicled the heroic deeds of those within the ghetto. The spiritual condition of the ghetto also made its way into the lyrics. A few of the new songs called the community to a renewed faith in God, while others expressed the opposite—laments whose words cried that despite the promises of Holy Scripture, their God had abandoned them.

Along with the rise of theaters at the end of 1940, the Warsaw Ghetto also formed a symphonic orchestra—the Jewish Symphony Orchestra. The orchestra received official approval from the Nazi command, as had the theaters, along with the stipulation that its concerts contain no music by Aryan composers. In reality, though, German officials ignored their own mandate, and the orchestra freely performed Bach, Mozart, Schubert, and Beethoven often. Two conductors who had maintained active careers in Warsaw, Marian Neuteich and Adam Furmanski, took on the job of finding musicians and directing the ensemble. Assembling a full symphonic orchestra in the ghetto proved much more difficult than establishing small chamber ensembles, jazz combos, singing groups, or theatrical troupes. The strong Jewish tradition of playing string instruments provided players to fill the string sections, but securing professional-level woodwind and brass players, who were also familiar with the classical repertoire, presented more of a challenge. Nevertheless, on November 25, 1940, only 10 days after the sealing of the ghetto, Neuteich conducted the orchestra's first concert. It took place in the Femina Theater, which could seat over 800, and featured two works by Beethoven—the *Coriolan Overture* and the *Piano Concerto in E-flat Major*. The group also performed Grieg's incidental music from *Peer Gynt*. Other concerts soon followed that also focused primarily on the standard Germanic repertoire, but included some Tchaikovsky.

Although grateful to attend orchestra concerts again, audience members did note that the daily realities of the ghetto presented numerous impediments to the production of truly polished performances. These included inadequate venues and unreliable electricity, which often resulted in uncomfortable temperatures, poor acoustics, and dim lighting.

Other detrimental factors came from the physical conditions of the musicians, where hunger and deprivation left many of them weak and lacking the stamina needed for practicing. Rehearsals were also curtailed by space limitations, as so many individuals and groups vied for the performance venues, and thereby money-making opportunities. So, the Jewish Symphony Orchestra struggled to have adequate rehearsal time, and when it did, the musicians frequently suffered through cold that stiffened their fingers and dimness that made it almost impossible to read the music. Still, they pressed on because they understood the importance and the power of music for them and their listeners.

In addition to the physical and environmental hardships, one of the biggest challenges for the orchestra and the other music ensembles remained the lack of printed music. Whatever pieces had been brought in, or could be smuggled in, limited the repertoire possibilities for a string quartet or an orchestra. Often, all the orchestra had available was the conductor's score, and so the musicians hand copied each of their parts from that one score. In 1941, a new conductor, Szymon Pullman, took over the Jewish Symphony Orchestra, and listeners noted that the ensemble expanded both in numbers and quality under Pullman's baton. The orchestra grew to nearly 80 members, many of whom had performed in prestigious Polish ensembles before the war, such as the Polish Radio Orchestra, the Warsaw Philharmonic, and the Warsaw Opera Orchestra. The orchestra's roster of performers also included three pianists who had been finalists in the prestigious International Chopin Piano Competition. Not satisfied with the group's limited repertoire, Pullman stretched the orchestra's programming to encompass a wider range of music, including the addition of masterworks by French composers.

Cafés also contributed to the variety of music available in the ghetto and provided another important performance venue for musicians to earn much needed income. As many as 60 cafés, bars, and coffee houses existed along the crowded streets, offering both indoor and outdoor spaces for dining and entertainment. With high prices, their clientele consisted of just the wealthy and elite of the Jewish community, who still retained enough money to spend on pastries and other delicacies, all eaten while enjoying an array of live music, comedy, and theatrical sketches. Some of the cafés offered such high quality food and entertainment that Polish and German officers also dined among the posh Jewish residents. The music for these venues usually featured soloists or small groups, but one of the larger ensembles also played in café gardens. This group of 40 musicians, known as the Order Service Orchestra, consisted of members of the Jewish Police Force and professional jazz musicians under the baton of Szymon Kataszek. The excellence of this band helped it gain quite a reputation in the ghetto and made it a favorite among those with the privilege of frequenting the cafés.

One of the most fashionable and sought-after of the cafés was Café Sztuka, located along Leszno, a thoroughfare nicknamed the "Broadway of the Jewish Quarter."[16] As the ghetto's largest café, Sztuka provided its patrons both indoor and outdoor dining and featured prominent musicians and celebrities from pre-war times as entertainment. It also developed a reputation for its comedy sketches, which as time went on, featured sharp and biting criticism of corrupt Jewish officials and members of the Jewish Police Force. Sometimes the subject matter also took the form of a dark, gallows humor, eliciting laughter from the audience over starvation and typhus epidemics. For some, finding the ability to laugh at themselves and their circumstances seemed a viable coping mechanism. Others regarded their laughter as a weapon against the Nazis, something that could not be taken away from them.

Besides the comedy, one of the biggest draws to Sztuka was singer Wiera Gran. Gran represented that completely assimilated class who had long ago put aside any thought or acknowledgment of being Jewish. Her husky crooner voice brought her audiences sentimental songs from the interwar years, including "Her First Ball" that Szpilman had written. Gran's music provided escape and allowed the listeners to float away to times and places not limited by a cordon topped with barbed wire. As with the laughter, some felt that the ability to enjoy music and to dance to its rhythms constituted a form of spiritual resistance, a means of showing the Nazis that they had not broken the spirit and the soul of the Jewish people.

But Café Sztuka also harbored some troubling undercurrents. The murkiest aspect of the café involved who actually owned it and pocketed the profits. The arrangement appeared to be some kind of perverted collaboration between the Gestapo and the Jewish Council since Gestapo members could be seen dining there with certain greedy Jewish powerbrokers. Known smugglers and collaborators also sat at Sztuka's tables, and in time, some ghetto residents concluded that this café's main attraction had shifted from entertainment to under the table deals. At the very least, the decadence of this handful of Jews, who pampered themselves while never or only rarely offering their money to assist the starving and dying around them, incited great animosity, and the dealings and people associated with the Sztuka certainly blurred the distinction between friends and foes.

Outside of the posh cafés and orchestra concerts, the musical life of the Warsaw Ghetto moved to a different cadence. The rich tradition of Yiddish folk songs encouraged singing, either alone or collectively, as an accompaniment to daily chores and routines. Street musicians had been common in European cities before the war, and their music had livened up the landscape for those walking to work or milling about in parks or open spaces, while providing a source of extra income for the performers. Within the ghetto, buskers also took to the street, even those musicians who would not have lowered themselves to perform for spare change before the German occupation. The air often reverberated with people singing and playing instruments, either by themselves or in small bands, all in hopes of enough coins to feed their stomachs. But on most days, there was little money to be made; and during bad weather, there was nothing.

So, a stroll from one length of the Warsaw Ghetto to the other revealed the complete spectrum of music making. As with other facets of life, the residents tended to cater toward whatever musical and artistic events coincided with their social standing, education, and experiences before the war. But these decisions sometimes communicated much more than just stylistic preferences or socio-economic status. Within the climate of the ghetto, a demarcation developed between cultural events deemed wholesome and socially acceptable, such as lectures and chamber recitals at the Judaic Library or concerts by the Jewish Symphony Orchestra, and the seedier, often vulgar entertainment at places like Café Sztuka. The practicing religious community especially condemned certain venues and activities as promoting hedonistic pleasures and contributing to the moral decline of the ghetto. One person even declared that the Warsaw Ghetto was turning into "Sodom and Gomorrah."[17]

Despite the overwhelming need for solidarity, all aspects of their existence, not just artistic expression, demonstrated that the stratification that had characterized Jewish life outside of the wall had fully reconstituted itself within the wall. Language proved a critical demarcator in the socio-economic divide. Polish emerged as the principal language of the ghetto and of its powerful decision makers. So, those who only spoke Yiddish suffered both political and cultural disadvantages. Even religion separated this Jewish population since the ghetto housed the orthodox, the nonobservant, and even some who had converted to Christianity. But other determining forces also contributed to a person or family's well-being and lifestyle in the ghetto, especially the circumstances surrounding their arrival there. Jews who had lived in Warsaw held an advantage over the refugees who entered with so few belongings. At least the city's own Jews retained much of their property that they could sell and barter for food and other necessities. Historians estimate that half of the residents, around 200,000, had been locked inside the ghetto with no means of supporting themselves. In time, of course, the assets of the more privileged would run out as well. Only a handful of the wealthiest would continue to live well and wield their money and influence.

The soup kitchens in the ghetto did try to serve as a kind of equalizer to bridge the gap between the two worlds, both in terms of meeting food needs and also in a cultural sense. They became places where important discussions could be conducted amid the bustle and smells of meal preparation and where information could be disseminated among those working for underground organizations. Rachel Auerbach oversaw one of the soup kitchens and easily transformed it into an intellectual, literary, and cultural hub. At times, meals at these feeding stations felt more like arts club meetings that would have happened in a pre-war coffee shop, rather than the true social welfare that they represented. Soup kitchens also provided ready-made spaces for musical performances. For those who could not afford to attend orchestra concerts or shows at the cafés, music came to them there, often by the same performers from the elite venues.

But no matter how tirelessly the soup kitchens worked, the need always exceeded their resources, and so music also provided the painful soundtrack for the begging that became such a common scene in the ghetto's streets. Sometimes the father, mother, and children would stand together, with the father playing an instrument and the children holding out a hat or cup to collect alms. Others sang, hoping that their songs would touch the heart of a passerby. The majority of begging, however, was done by children alone. Their dirty faces and ragamuffin appearance as they played the harmonica or sang remain one of the greatest tragedies of the Warsaw Ghetto.

Szpilman witnessed these heartbreaking scenes every day, which only increased the pressure he felt to earn money so that his family would not starve or be forced to beg in the streets. Of the various performance opportunities available, the café venues gave him the best chance at a steady income. He started out at Café Nowaczesna, one of the seamier locations in the ghetto, where he regularly observed corrupt Jewish leaders and Germans brokering deals on the backs of the ghetto's citizens. He also found Café Nowaczesna to be a truly mean-spirited place that employed a bouncer to stand outside swinging a cudgel to keep away beggars or less desirables. Szpilman denounced the decadence and callousness of the people who arrived there without thought for the poor and starving.

> Rickshaws often came long distances, and the men and women who lounged in them wore expensive wool in winter, costly straw hats and French silks in summer…. They gave no alms; in their view charity simply demoralized people. If you worked as hard as they did then you would earn as much too: it was open to everyone to do so, and if you didn't know how to get on in life that was your own fault.[18]

The clientele at Café Nowaczesna also showed no regard for Szpilman's reputation as a renowned pianist and composer and certainly cared nothing about the music that he played. Just a short time of working there left Szpilman disheartened and jaded. "I lost two illusions here: my beliefs in our general solidarity and in the musicality of the Jews."[19]

Szpilman left Café Nowaczesna after a few months for a job playing at a smaller café on Sienna Street frequented by artists and members of the intelligentsia. He found likeminded

Street scene in the Warsaw Ghetto—a young violin player hoping for alms, 1941 (bpk Bildagentur /Joe Heydecker, photographer / Art Resource, NY).

people there who appreciated his music and with whom he could have stimulating conversations about art, literature, and philosophy. He particularly enjoyed the company of two of the café's regulars: the painter Roman Kramsztyk and the writer Janusz Korczak. Then after four months, he landed a better paying and more prestigious job at Café Sztuka.

Café Sztuka prided itself on a high level of artistic excellence, and so it was there that Szpilman truly shined as a solo musician and in collaboration with the best singers and instrumentalists in the ghetto. Although aware of the less honorable side of the Sztuka, Szpilman chose to remain focused on his craft and on the fact that he could make almost enough money to feed the six of them. He would have actually enjoyed his afternoons and early evenings playing at this café if the awful dread of the journey home had not weighed on him. Each night followed the same routine. Once the customers had departed, Szpilman received his pay and prepared to leave the café. The Sztuka represented a sort of oasis from the ghetto's suffering because of its wonderful music and because its clientele still fared comfortably. But stepping outside, Szpilman encountered a totally different scene that made the past few hours feel more like a mirage than a reality. The clock always neared curfew when he started his walk home, signaling the time of the evening when the mentally ill roamed the streets and desperate children scurried out to beg one last time for a crust of bread. But most of all, Szpilman dreaded the corpses. The mortality rate from disease and starvation had climbed so high that no one could keep up with the burials. To avoid the dangers of leaving decomposing bodies inside, families wrapped the naked corpses in paper and laid them in the streets. Every few days, a team of workers would collect them on carts for the mass graves in the cemetery. So each night as Szpilman made his way home, he kept a flashlight trained in front of him to avoid stumbling over the bodies. The only accompaniment to his nightly walk came from the wind as it rustled the paper shrouds of the dead.

At the one year mark since the sealing of the Warsaw Ghetto, conditions had deteriorated to such an extent that some referred to it as a "field of ruins."[20] The death toll from starvation and diseases such as tuberculosis, dysentery, and typhus had reached approximately 80,000. Typhus was particularly rampant in the ghetto, spreading through lice infestations that could not be controlled in such overcrowded and unsanitary conditions. Everything, from clothing to newspapers, sheltered the vermin. Lice could be seen crawling on the stairways and on crusts of bread. Since the Nazis enjoyed characterizing the Jews as lice-ridden and claimed that getting rid of them was "delousing" Germany, this epidemic played right into their hands. The number of dead from typhus alone escalated to approximately 5,000 per month. According to Szpilman, typhus became the main topic of conversation among both the rich and the poor. "...the poor simply wondered when they would die of it, while the rich wondered how to get hold of Dr. Weigel's vaccine and protect themselves."[21] The Nazis had hired a brilliant bacteriologist named Dr. Rudolf Weigel. Despite the disease's virulent nature, Weigel had managed to develop a typhus vaccine. With its soldiers lice-ridden as well, the German army was desperate for his vaccine. So, for those in the ghetto who still had money to bribe guards and policemen, this precious vaccine could be acquired for themselves too.

Meanwhile, the Nazis shipped out thousands for forced labor, including those as young as 14 and as old as 60. For those left behind in the ghetto without any money, the meager rations of only 181 calories per day allotted by the Germans could not sustain life and so smuggling presented the only conduit for survival. Some German and Polish guards were open to accepting bribes, which certainly aided the Jewish community in securing supplies from the outside. But most of the time, residents had to devise clever tactics for sneaking out of the ghetto, which they accomplished through underground tunnels, sewers, and holes in houses that bordered the "Aryan" side. Children often served as the gophers since their small size made them less conspicuous and better able to move in and out of tiny openings. All those involved knew that if caught outside the wall, the penalty was either imprisonment or execution. The fact that they had witnessed German soldiers shooting children in the back over a pilfered potato or loaf of bread proved that there would be no mercy. But without those who took that great risk, the ghetto population would have perished within a short time. Nevertheless, the death toll continued to rise. The loss of life did not ease the overcrowding, however, because the Nazi command replaced those dead with more refugees each day. The new arrivals brought with them horrific stories of executions and unfathomable atrocities, and by 1942, newcomers also told of the death camps and mass extermination.

As he observed this relentless cycle of life and death within the wall, a historian named Dr. Emanuel Ringelblum became convinced that the Jewish people must record their own history in the Warsaw Ghetto rather than let their story be viewed by the world through a German lens. He organized a clandestine group of writers, scholars, and Jewish leaders to create a secret archive. They referred to their organization by the code name Oyneg Shabes (the joys of Shabat). Under Ringelblum's leadership, 60 people joined the archive staff, including poet Rachel Auerbach. They wrote daily diaries that detailed everything that happened; nothing was deemed too mundane to include. They also recorded the stories told to them by the refugees. In addition to these narratives, they collected artifacts. As with the diary entries, anything and everything warranted inclusion. The archive contained underground newspapers, Nazi announcement posters, drawings, photos, poems, and even food tin labels. It also stored important information about the cultural life of the ghetto, such as concert posters and reviews published in the *Gazeta Żydowska*. Ringelblum's project needed to serve as an exhaustive testimony that would tell the whole story and the unvarnished truth of their lives after they were gone.

The archive of the Oyneg Shabes not only detailed the struggles of Warsaw's Jewish population at the hands of their exterminators, but also the suffering created from the inside. Not all of the difficulties in the Warsaw Ghetto could be directly attributed to the Nazis. Some responsibility lay with their fellow Jews and with the way ghettos functioned differently than concentration camps. German bureaucracy and oversight managed the concentration camps meticulously from within. But the ghettos sealed all of the Jews in a vacuum from which they were expected to govern themselves. The resulting petri dish of scarcity, ineffective leadership, and greed eventually grew into a survival of the fittest contest with no rules of engagement. Ghetto resident Michel Mazor spared none of the horrific details in delivering his scathing indictment after the war.

> It was unbridled chaos, into whose whirlwinds victims were randomly tossed. This is why the most helpless among the ghetto inhabitants, those who died right out on the sidewalk, exposing their hunger-swollen legs to passersby, could feel, more than camp inmates could, that they were living at the furthest limits of decay and abandonment in the strange universe surrounding them.[22]

But during this time when so many inflicted intentional harm, much help also came to the Jews from their neighbors. Historians estimate that between 70,000 and 90,000 of Warsaw's citizens aided the Jewish population to escape or hide. Heartbroken at the loss of their beloved animals and their zoo, Jan and Antonina Żabiński decided to transform their home and zoo facilities into a waystation to shelter Jews and facilitate their escape outside of the city. Their commitment came, of course, with terrible risk, not unlike "sleeping with dynamite."[23] Jan also joined the Polish Underground and bore the code name "Francis," after Francis of Assisi, the patron saint of animals. An astute problem solver, Jan devised an ingenious plan to start a pig farm at the emptied zoo. He easily obtained Nazi approval because he told them that the pigs would be used to feed German soldiers. Jan also convinced them that to make the operation successful, he would need the scraps from the Warsaw Ghetto for pig food. So, right under the noses of Nazi soldiers, Jan made regular trips to the ghetto and smuggled people out buried in truckloads of slop. Meanwhile, Antonina managed all of the "guests" at their home and made sure that everyone stayed quiet and out of sight during the day. An accomplished pianist, Antonina would begin playing the piano at midnight to alert everyone that it was safe to emerge from hiding. She also used certain piano pieces as a warning signal if an unexpected visitor arrived at the house. If she could not get to the piano, Antonina would begin to sing loudly the chorus "Go, Go, Go, to Crete" from Offenbach's opera *La belle Hélène*. Magdalena Gross, an internationally renowned Polish sculptor and the first Jew to find refuge at the zoo, believed that song would forever quicken her pulse and trigger the urge to hide.

In time, another resident moved into the zoo who had performed as a professional pianist before the war. Along with a gray cat named Balbina and a few parakeets, Witold Wroblewski brought impromptu recitals of Rachmaninoff and Chopin, which added beauty to their days and a nostalgia for the lives they had enjoyed before 1939. Wroblewski's presence also provided them a bit of safety at times because he was a Pole, not a Jew in hiding. The Nazis had placed him at the zoo to start a fur farm. So, his day job involved raising foxes whose fur could be used for coats to keep German soldiers warm.

Jan worked tirelessly around the clock and tried not to let his mind dwell too long on the surreal nature of their lives or the atrocities he observed, but Antonina wrestled daily with the soulless acts being committed against an innocent people. Antonina's keen ability to calm even the wildest animal gave her particular pause when she witnessed the barbarity that human beings inflicted on each other. She often asked herself why it was that "animals can sometimes subdue their predatory ways in only a few months, while humans, despite centuries of refinement, can quickly grow more savage than any beast?"[24] No satisfactory answers could be found for such questions, and so putting energy toward saving as many lives as possible served as a response. Collectively, Jan and Antonina Żabiński helped over 300 Jews. Also among the hidden people lived a menagerie of animals that they were committed to rescuing. The odd assortment included birds, rabbits, baby foxes, a pig, a muskrat, and a badger. The Żabiński home at the Warsaw Zoo proved essential to the success of the underground network. Workers in the underground aptly referred to it as "The House Under a Crazy Star" because of the eccentric and chaotic comings and goings of the two-legged and the four-legged. At times, it resembled an "oversized curiosity cabinet" more than a villa.[25] But to their friends, the Żabiński home would affectionately be known as "Noah's Ark."[26]

Along with help from the Żabińskis, the ghetto's residents received lifesaving assistance from Irena Sendler, a 30-year-old Polish Catholic social worker employed at the Welfare Department in Warsaw. Her physician father had instilled in her a strong sense of social justice and sacrificial giving. As a young child, Irena had watched him treat Jews infected with typhus that other medical personnel would not touch. She also saw the cost of such compassion, as he succumbed to typhus in 1917. During the early months of the occupation, Irena continued to advocate for the poor and disenfranchised in Warsaw. But then in 1940 when the Germans sealed the Jews behind the wall, she temporarily lost any means to help them. Undeterred by circumstances or her small stature of less than five feet tall, Irena used her position in the Welfare Office to obtain a pass to enter the ghetto under the auspices of doing sanitary checks, using the Nazis' own fear of infectious diseases to her advantage. Once inside, she brought aid to the people and devised a plan to smuggle Jewish children out of the ghetto and into hiding places in the "Aryan" parts of the city. She found plenty of orphans to collect, but Irena also undertook the heart-wrenching task of persuading parents to let her carry away their children. Like Jan Żabiński, Irena invented clever methods for smuggling out the children, such as hiding them in garbage, toolboxes, and even in coffins. She also used the labyrinth of underground passageways and sewers as escape routes.

The magnitude of the work that needed to be done proved so great that Irena could not manage alone. She recruited a group of friends to assist her, and together they obtained forged papers for each child. These papers contained not only new names but Catholic birth certificates so that the children could be hidden at over 200 convents and Catholic orphanages throughout Warsaw and the surrounding countryside. This dangerous work was made even more difficult because of the young ages. Irena coached the children carefully so that their new names became commonplace to them. She taught them the prayers and catechisms that young Polish Catholic children should know in case any Germans questioned them. In addition to rescuing the children out of the ghetto, Irena insisted on being able to reunite them with their families after the war. So to this end, she kept meticulous records of each child's birth name, reassigned name, and placement location. She scribbled this information, in a code she invented just for this purpose, onto scraps of tissue paper used to roll cigarettes. Irena knew to take great precautions because the work required her to involve so many people, and she knew that someone could easily betray her to the Gestapo to curry favors for themselves.

Still, thousands of children remained stuck in the misery of the ghetto, and so other residents worked to make them as happy and distracted from fear and hunger as they could be. One group of actors reenacted Disney's animated film *Snow White and the Seven Dwarfs*, which had been released in Polish cinemas in 1938. Seeing scenes from the film along with hearing the wonderful songs certainly brought smiles to their faces. Artist Gela Sekstein, whose paintings had been displayed in numerous exhibitions in Warsaw before the war, taught art classes for the children. She also helped them create costumes for the children's theater presentations that some of the ghetto's actors organized.

Meanwhile, Szpilman and his family continued to exist hand to mouth, eating up his income from the café each day. But still, Szpilman knew that they were more fortunate than many because he did have a useful talent that could provide at least a modest income. He saw what happened to people without resources as they grew more desperate and had to risk their lives more frequently to smuggle food from the outside. One day while walking near the wall, Szpilman saw a child who had snuck out and was in the process of pushing the sacks of food back through the wall. What happened next would be a scene that he would never forget.

> His skinny little figure was already partly in view when he suddenly began screaming, and at the same time I heard the hoarse bellowing of a German on the other side of the wall. I ran to the child to help him squeeze through as quickly as possible, but in defiance of our efforts his hips stuck in the drain. I pulled at his little arms with all my might while his screams became increasingly desperate, and I could hear the heavy blows struck by the policeman on the other side of the wall. When I finally managed to pull the child through, he died. His spine had been shattered.[27]

As the situation within the wall deteriorated, the need for the arts grew even more acute. So during the summer of 1941, some in the ghetto who still had means came together to form a patronage committee to support chamber music and solo recitals. They scheduled these events in a variety of venues, including apartments, cafés, and the soup kitchens. Violin and piano recitals that featured members of the orchestra proved especially popular. Repertoire for most of the performances derived predominately from the Germanic tradition, as did the orchestra's concerts; so, the music of Beethoven, Schubert, Brahms, and Haydn graced these programs frequently. Audiences also enjoyed voice recitals. Many notable singers lived in the ghetto, but one young soprano, Marysia Ajzensztadt (Eisenstadt), stood out in particular. Her father had been a prominent musical figure in Warsaw and had encouraged his daughter's music education, which included piano studies at the Chopin High School in Warsaw. When the Nazis forced Marysia and her parents behind the wall, she had not launched her performing career yet, and so she made her debut in the ghetto. With her father accompanying at the piano, Marysia sang a diverse range of repertoire, spanning opera to Yiddish folk songs. Soon, she earned the moniker, "the nightingale of the Ghetto." Everyone who heard her knew that she would sing on the world's most prestigious stages as soon as the war ended. But in 1942, the Jewish Police rounded up Marysia and her parents for deportation to an extermination camp. While boarding the train, she became separated from her parents, and when she ran to jump into the same car as them, an SS officer shot her. Marysia Ajzensztadt had just turned 21 years old. Speaking about her after the war, Szpilman concurred, "She would have been a famous name to millions now for her wonderful voice, if the Germans had not murdered her."[28]

The inestimable loss of young talent also impacted the Feldschuh family. Reuven Feldschuh (Ben-Shem), a Zionist and Polish intellectual, lived in the ghetto with his wife and daughter. Like the Oyneg Shabes, he believed strongly in the need to document the true Jewish experience, so he started a diary. Reuven and his wife, a musicologist named Pnina, had a daughter who was a child prodigy. Eleven-year-old Josima had performed with the newly formed Jewish Symphony Orchestra on March 15, 1941. Concert posters hung throughout the ghetto displayed a pre-war photo of a smiling Josima seated at the piano, her ringletted hair tied with a bow. The orchestra's program for the evening proved quite ambitious, including the Overture to Mozart's *The Marriage of Figaro*, Mozart's *Symphony No. 40 in G minor*, and Schubert's *Unfinished Symphony*. The young piano virtuoso was featured as the soloist for Mozart's *Piano Concerto No. 9 in Eb Major*. In addition to performing, Josima also composed solo works for piano that she wrote out in a notebook. The following year, Josima contracted tuberculosis. Because of her illness, the Feldschuh family would risk an escape from the ghetto in February 1943 and go into hiding in Pustelnik, a small village about 25 miles east of Warsaw. The 14-year-old Josima tragically died only a few weeks later on April 21. Unable to bear the loss of her daughter, Pnina committed suicide shortly after. Only Reuven survived the war, and with him the diary, 800 pages of meticulous record-keeping on life in the ghetto, which would serve as one of the most important primary sources from that time. He had also safeguarded Josima's precious notebook of compositions. Many of her works, including *Mazurek No. VI, Op. 10*, *Sabbathiada No. 1, Op. 14*, and *Sonata, Op. 17*, continue to be performed today as a memorial to her and the other amazing musicians of the Holocaust who refused to abandon their passion for music despite their intractable circumstances.

In the early months of 1942, almost a year after Josima Feldschuh had performed with the Jewish Orchestra, Maestro Pullman brought in a young conductor named Israel Hamerman (Izrael Hammerman) to assist him with the orchestra. Together, they drafted exciting plans for more orchestral performances. But then without warning, the Nazi command, who had remained tolerant and even dismissive concerning the orchestra's programming, did an about-face on April 15, declaring a two-month ban on the orchestra due to violating the rules about Aryan composers. The orchestra, along with the many other ensembles and soloists, had never tried to conceal that their performances featured music of the great masters. Concert posters and the ghetto newspaper had openly advertised the repertoire, and so the sudden reversal baffled everyone. Because of what would transpire later that summer, this two-month injunction would turn into a permanent loss. The Jewish Symphony Orchestra of the Warsaw Ghetto never played again.

As seen with the sudden orchestra ban, the warming breeze in the spring of 1942 seemed to carry paradox with it. All would remain relatively calm in the ghetto for a time, and then for no apparent reason, the Gestapo would storm in during the early evening or the middle of the night, grab people from their homes, and shoot them in the streets. Then just as abruptly, they would drive away, their vehicles bumping over the dead bodies. Life in the ghetto would proceed the next morning as though nothing had happened. In May, the Nazi command announced that they would be rounding up a group of able-bodied men for a work detail outside of the camp. However the Germans never intended those men for a labor project, but instead used them as a test group to assess the new gas chambers and crematoria at Treblinka.

One evening in June, the Szpilman family had just finished dinner when they heard a commotion. They watched the SS storm into the building across the street and drag several men outside. The SS then entered a third floor apartment, exactly opposite from the Szpilman's dining room window, where a family sat eating at their table. When the SS stormed in, they ordered the family to stand, but the old man was crippled and could not. In a fit of rage, one officer picked up the man, chair and all, and pitched him out the third floor window. The Jewish men who had been rounded up were then made to run in front of the Nazis' vehicle, trained in the beam of light from the search lamp mounted on top. One by one, the soldiers picked them off with their guns. The next morning, except for needing to step around the dead bodies in the street, everyone pretended that the incident had never occurred.

Szpilman had certainly learned never to underestimate the barbarous cruelty of the German soldiers. He found that even the beauty of music could be twisted by them into a weapon to torment and humiliate the ghetto's residents for their own sadistic pleasure. On at least one occasion, Szpilman observed guards ordering musicians into the street to perform dance music and then forcing residents to dance. Intending to create a grotesque spectacle, the soldiers picked only those who would make the most "amusing" dance couples, such as the fat, the short, or the crippled. "The Germans stood around this 'dance floor,' roaring with laughter and shouting, 'Faster! Go on, faster! Everybody dance!'"[29]

Spring gave way to the heat of summer, and the calendar edged closer to the two-year anniversary of the Jewish sequestration behind the wall. On Saturday, July 18, Szpilman and another pianist named Andrzej Goldfeder played a benefit concert for Leon Boruński, a well-known musician and former finalist of the Chopin International Piano Competition. Boruński suffered from tuberculosis in the ghetto at Otwock, a small town outside of Warsaw noted before the war for its sanatoriums and mental hospital, which still continued to operate even since the Germans had reconfigured the area into a Jewish ghetto. This charity event took place at the Café Pod Fontanna for the remaining elite of the ghetto. According to Szpilman, it was a lovely evening. He and Goldfeder had established their piano duo a year earlier and really enjoyed performing together. As Szpilman lounged outside smoking at intermission, his painter friend Kramsztyk walked by with a serious expression. Despite Szpilman's encouragement, he refused to come inside or be cheered. Kramsztyk had heard from reliable sources that the Germans intended to resettle the residents of the Warsaw Ghetto. But these types of rumors and false alarms had circulated before and never panned out, so Szpilman chose to disregard the warning. Instead, his focus remained on the much anticipated concert that he and Goldfeder were giving in the garden of the Café Sztuka on the following Saturday to celebrate their one-year anniversary as a duo. The day after the benefit concert, Sunday, July 19, Szpilman played during the afternoon in the garden at a Nowolipki Street café. He noticed that, although the tables held their usual large crowd, the mood seemed more somber than jovial. Still, he walked home lost in his excited thoughts about the upcoming anniversary concert, unaware that he had just played his last performance in the ghetto.

The action began on Tuesday, July 21, when the Germans arrested some key Jewish officials and functionaries, a few of which they executed. By the afternoon of July 22, Nazi troops had entered the ghetto to coordinate large deportations to the extermination camp at Treblinka, which lay about 50 miles to the northeast of Warsaw. Posted notices informed the population that all Jews deemed fit to work would be transported to the East to work in German factories and live in barracks. The flyers also detailed that those departing could take luggage weighing up to 20 kilos plus a two-day food provision and that they should bring their jewelry. Noticeably absent from this posted decree was the signature of the Jewish Council's chairman, Adam Czerniaków, which always adorned this type of document. Czerniaków knew the truth about the destination of the trains and had been frantically trying to lobby for a different solution other than sending thousands to the gas. But he made little progress in saving his fellow citizens and so committed suicide by a cyanide tablet on July 23. All stores and shops remained closed as the Germans, aided by the Jewish Police Force, began a systematic sweep through the ghetto. They would stop in front of a building and blow a whistle, indicating that everyone in that building must immediately assemble in the street to be taken to the train station. During this period, known as the Great Deportation, the Jewish police officers received orders from the Nazi command to select 7,000 residents per day; and if they failed to meet the quota, they and their families would be sent to their deaths.

Within just a few days, the ghetto's residents grew even hungrier and more desperate with all of the shops closed and trade suspended. Nothing short of apocalyptic could describe their situation. The number of people working for the Oyneg Shabes had dwindled to half, and so the remaining members decided that the time had come to bury everything they had collected in their archive. They placed the artifacts and narratives, the unadulterated testimony of the Warsaw Ghetto, into metal boxes and buried them deep in the dirt of a cellar below one of the buildings. Rachel Auerbach also gave one of her personal notebooks to Jan Zabiński, who buried it in a glass jar on the grounds of the zoo.

Szpilman felt especially useless to his family during this time. Ever since the war began, he had believed that his reputation made him the most likely of the six to find a solution to whatever problem beset them. That pressure bore down upon him day and night. But with no financial resources and no ideas for saving his family, a defeated Szpilman just laid on the bed while his father sought refuge in his violin. In just a few days, however, Szpilman's musical connections did bring them a bit of a reprieve. His pianist friend Goldfeder worked at the ghetto's collection center, which now undertook the enormous task of sorting through all of the furniture and belongings of those who had already been deported. He got Szpilman and his brother and father jobs there, which included housing and food. Somehow, they managed to move his mother and sisters into the barracks as well, although they did not work. So each day, Szpilman made his rounds through the ghetto, hauling every abandoned item, from mirrors to underclothes, back to the storehouse. He found it difficult, of course, not to think about the fate of those who had once used or cherished these belongings. On August 2, the German command issued an order that all Jews living in the small ghetto area, which included Sienna Street, must vacate those quarters by 6 p.m. Fortunately, the bosses at the collection center allowed Szpilman to retrieve what items he could from their apartment. He grabbed his compositions along with some clothes and bedding. He also gathered his father's violin into his arms.

Despite the fear and misery that surrounded him, Szpilman could still find hope for humanity in the ghetto's courageous and compassionate souls, especially his friend Janusz Korczak, who had dedicated himself to caring for the children who lived there. A pediatrician by training, Henryk Goldszmit had also enjoyed literary acclaim under the pen name Janusz Korczak. In addition to novels, he wrote successful parenting guidebooks such as *How to Love a Child* and *The Child's Right to Respect*. In 1912, he put aside his successful medical practice to establish an orphanage in Warsaw founded on progressive ideologies and a humanistic, moral education. He committed every złoty and all of his time to the children. When the Nazis ordered the Jews into the ghetto, Korczak moved himself and the orphans into it, although his renown could have bought him a pass. He continued to devote himself to their emotional and physical well-being. He taught them, cared for them, and entertained them with his vivid imagination and flair for storytelling. He had grown into a man of many talents. He confessed one day to a friend, "I am a doctor by training, a pedagogue by chance, a writer by passion, and a psychologist by necessity."[30]

Korczak had many friends and followers on the outside who were prepared to assist him in escaping the ghetto, but he repeatedly refused their offers, saying that he could never abandon the children. Speaking about his friend Korczak after the war, Szpilman said, "Korczak's true value was not in *what* he wrote but in the fact that he lived *as* he wrote."[31] Korczak grieved at the suffering of the children around him and wanted to relieve it in any way he could. To focus their mind away from the pains of hunger and sickness, he wrote a simple prayer and taught them to recite it. "Thank you, Merciful Lord, for having arranged so wisely to provide flowers with fragrance, glowworms with the glow, and make the stars in the sky sparkle."[32]

When the officials selected his beloved orphans for deportation to Treblinka on August 6, 1942, Korczak voluntarily climbed into the train with them so that they would not be scared. His actions asserting his belief: "You do not leave a sick child in the night, and you do not leave children at a time like this."[33] A photograph exists from that day that shows Korczak surrounded by 192 children, several small hands in his, as they walked toward the train. Szpilman witnessed the tragic scene. He saw a German soldier order a young boy in the group who carried a violin under his arm to move to the front and play the violin to accompany the children's processional. Korczak had told the children to put on their best clothing in celebration of leaving the crowded, dirty ghetto and heading to the countryside where they could play. So, the children smiled and sang as they walked to the train. Joshua Perle, another eyewitness to the scene, recorded this sacred moment in his memoirs. "A miracle occurred, two hundred pure souls, condemned to death, did not weep. Not one of them ran away. None tried to hide. Like stricken swallows they clung to their teacher and mentor, to their father and brother, Janusz Korczak."[34]

For his willingness to board the train with full knowledge of what that meant and to enter the gas chamber clinging to the orphans of the Warsaw Ghetto, the Poles revere Korczak as a martyr. To the nation of Israel, he stands for much more. They consider Janusz Korczak to have been one of the legendary Thirty-Six Just Men, whose goodness in the face of a terribly wicked world constitutes the sole reason that the human race continues to be spared from total destruction. "The legend tells that they are ordinary people, not flawless or magical, and that most of them remain unrecognized throughout their lives, while they choose to perpetuate goodness, even in the midst of inferno."[35]

On August 16, ten days after Korczak's departure, Szpilman received the dreaded order for deportation, as did his mother, father, and sister Regina. For some reason, the German bureaucrats had decided to let Halina and Henryk stay behind and work at the collection center. Szpilman approached his impending death with resignation, knowing that he had truly done everything possible to protect his family. When they arrived at the *Umschlagplatz*, the designated place at the border of the ghetto where the railroad tracks lay, they joined the crowd already waiting for their Doomsday Clocks to signal the end. For some, it had already run out. Corpses littered the ground as the result of trigger-happy German soldiers who at the slightest provocation had shot those already condemned to die. Their cruelty also extended to turning off the water in this holding area so that none of the people forced to sit there all day in the suffocating heat could have a drink. The children and elderly, in particular, sagged under the heat and dehydration, already so weak from chronic malnutrition.

Later in the afternoon, Szpilman watched a new group arrive that included Halina and Henryk. They had chosen to volunteer for deportation rather than let the rest of their family go to their fate without them. By the time the train finally arrived at 6 p.m., thousands were crammed into the *Umschlagplatz*, with the armed Jewish police and German soldiers maintaining strict control to deter any hint of resistance. As the Szpilman family lumbered toward the train's cattle cars, the overwhelming smell of chlorine assaulted their noses, and they struggled to imagine why these compartments reeked so strongly of bleach. The whole scene invited sensory overload with the smells, the crowds, and the heat, all mixed with the fear of thousands who had lost any say-so in their lives. But before Szpilman could step into the train car with his family, an unknown hand grabbed him and pulled him away from the boarding lines. He looked around frantically, but never identified who had done this. Instead, he tried to make his way back inside the police cordon so he could board with his family, but the dense crowds blocked him. One Jewish police officer saw him and yelled, "What the hell do you think you're doing? Go on, save yourself!"[36] Rooted in place, Szpilman hopelessly watched his family climb into the train, and then his father, the last to board, turned toward his direction and their eyes met. Szpilman would always remember this last glimpse of his father. "He was pale, and his lips trembled nervously. He tried to smile, helplessly, painfully, raised his hand and waved goodbye, as if I were setting out into life and he was already greeting me from beyond the grave."[37]

As the train car doors slammed shut, Szpilman took off running blindly through the soldiers and police still milling about. He heard the train pulling away from the station and caught a Jewish police officer's comment to the SS at his side, "Well, off they go for meltdown!"[38] Any vague hope, however tenuous, that Szpilman had clung to about his family now evaporated. He scrambled through the streets and happened to run into a relative who had joined the Jewish Police Force. Although Szpilman thought little of this individual, he needed to survive and so accepted this man's offer to come to his home. After a lonely night without his family, Szpilman went to see someone he knew well from the cafés whose father had been appointed as the new chairman of the Jewish Council. Mieczysław Lichtenbaum arranged for Szpilman to be assigned to a demolition crew that was tearing down part of the ghetto wall so that the area could be reincorporated into the "Aryan" side of Warsaw.

And so, the following day, Szpilman stepped outside of the ghetto for the first time in almost two years. An outdoor market selling all types of produce and bread sat near the work site. Szpilman borrowed 50 złotys from a fellow worker and bought bread and potatoes. That night he was able to eat his fill and still have enough left to sell. With the gross inflation of the ghetto, he made a profit and thus embarked on the first commercial enterprise of his life.

Szpilman had somehow defied the odds stacked so heavily against him—something he would continue to do again and again. After six weeks of mass deportations, the Germans had transported Europe's largest Jewish population to Treblinka, and only 60,000 remained in the Warsaw Ghetto. By the end of 1942, the total number sent to the gas chambers of Treblinka would reach 312,000. With the exception of Auschwitz, Treblinka would murder more Jews than any other extermination camp, approximately 900,000, even though it operated for only a brief time from July 1942 through November 1943.

Szpilman continued to work on demolishing that section of the ghetto. He and the other men took the wall down as slowly as they could get by with so that the job could last longer. But before the project had concluded, the working conditions changed. The Germans had hired a group of Lithuanian thugs to help police the ghetto, and it became their job to guard the workers. Their new keepers would not let them buy food at the market and decided one day to do their own "thinning of the herd." They divided the men into two groups and motioned Szpilman to stand with those on the right side. They ordered everyone lined up on the left to lie down and then shot them all in the head. Szpilman had been granted another stay of execution, but found little consolation in this terrorizing game of Russian roulette.

After his crew completed the wall project, Szpilman moved around to different living quarters, following the various work assignments. Some of the tasks proved manageable, but others brought him near collapse. At one job, he was forced to carry loads of brick stacked on a board across his back. The German in charge tortured Szpilman by insisting that he run with the staggering weight. When he failed to keep up the pace or dropped any of the bricks, the overseer would beat him with a hide whip imbedded with lead balls. The intolerable working conditions no longer felt countered by the relief that came from proving useful to the Germans. As the mild weather of autumn gave way to winter's frostiness, even workers found no security. Selections for deportation continued, and Szpilman marveled at how the Germans could ship their skilled laborers, including carpenters and barbers, to their deaths. But of course, nothing ever trumped Nazi Germany's top priority—the eradication of the Jews.

Meanwhile, the ghetto's underground resistance movement prepared to fight. Although only about 60,000 remained of the almost half a million that had been sealed behind the wall in 1940, many believed that the Germans would never be content with even this remnant of Polish Jewry remaining alive. Szpilman and his work group used their daily forays outside of the ghetto as opportunities to liaise with the Polish underground and to smuggle in ammunition and grenades that they mixed in with the potatoes and beans they purchased. Sneaking in the various weapons carried enormous danger, but it seemed far riskier to leave themselves unarmed. The underground's members aimed some of their first reprisals at insiders, fellow Jews who operated as collaborators and spies and bargained away the lives of their neighbors. After resistance fighters murdered two of them, a wave of fear spread among the rest of their corrupt ilk.

The first few weeks of 1943 progressed in much the same way except that when the Germans rounded up more people to ship East, they encountered some armed resistance.

The ghetto felt poised to explode like a powder keg. In February, Szpilman decided to attempt an escape. Through an intermediary, he established contact with two of his friends, a singer named Janina Godlewska and her actor husband Andrzej Bogucki. They agreed to hide him, and so the three of them began to craft a plan. On Saturday, February 13, during the commotion caused by a scheduled inspection of the building where his crew worked, Szpilman pulled off his Star of David armband and simply walked away with the Aryan workers as they headed home. Andrzej met him nearby, and the two walked as fast as possible in the falling dusk. The terrifying journey through the streets seemed to take forever. Szpilman knew that his pronounced Jewish features would give him away if anyone stopped to take notice. Finally they reached the apartment building, and Janina took Szpilman to the fifth floor where he would hide in an art studio. His only worldly goods besides the clothes on his back were a fountain pen, a wristwatch, and his compositions.

He remained secreted away in the art studio for two weeks before receiving another offer of assistance through Edmund Rudnicki, his former music director at the Polish Radio Station. Edmund arranged for him to move into the home of a man who had worked as an engineer at the station. That night, Szpilman encountered a piano for the first time in seven months. The family encouraged him to play, but he felt extremely reluctant to make music after all that had transpired. He finally acquiesced out of a sense of obligation to these people who risked their lives to shelter him, but it was not a satisfying experience. Szpilman's grueling physical labors and lack of piano practice had left his fingers stiff and uncooperative. He also found no joy in hearing his own music again. Instead, he felt that "…the sound was irritatingly strange, grating on my nerves."[39]

Because of the dogged Jew-hunting that the Germans engaged in day after day, it remained too dangerous for Szpilman and his hosts if he stayed in any one place for long. The Germans had begun to conduct a complete census of the city of Warsaw, which meant that they went from door to door, counting and checking registrations in hopes of finding the many Jews they knew were being hidden. Another former colleague, conductor Czesław Lewicki, offered an unused apartment that he owned as a new location, so Szpilman moved in there on February 27. At that time, Czesław lived with a kind couple, Dr. and Mrs. Malczewski. She and Czesław shared the responsibility of making periodic visits to deliver food and supplies. Szpilman's only challenge was not making any noise that would alert residents in the neighboring apartments to his presence. He occupied his days with reading and enjoying the comfortable environment where he did not suffer from the terrible hunger. He felt so grateful to be away from the verbal and physical abuse at the hands of the Nazi soldiers. But, he also mourned what he knew to be the almost certain loss of his whole family.

In April 1943, Heinrich Himmler, one of Hitler's most loyal servants and sycophants, decided to give his Führer a special birthday present—the complete liquidation of the Warsaw Ghetto. Himmler chose April 19, 1943, the day before Hitler's birthday, for the planned offensive. This date felt especially satisfying to the Nazis' love of symbolism as it coincided with the first day of Passover, the sacred Jewish holiday that commemorates their great exodus from the bondage of Egypt. But when Himmler's squads arrived at the ghetto at 4 a.m., they did not encounter the sleeping, docile people they had anticipated. Instead, they found an armed Jewish resistance lying in wait. The frustrations over their powerlessness had finally reached a boiling point, and so they had vowed to take on their captors, no matter the cost. In addition to attacking the Germans with guns and other weapons that they had managed to smuggle into the ghetto, the resistance fighters lobbed Molotov cocktails. Built from enclosing a flammable liquid, such as gasoline, in a glass bottle stoppered with a burning rag, these homemade incendiary devices had been invented by Franco's Nationalists during the Spanish Civil War of 1936–39, and then adopted by the Finns during the Russian invasion of Finland, known as the Winter War, in November 1939. As a mocking jab at their enemies, the Finns had named their "bombs" after Russia's Foreign Minister Vyacheslav Molotov. Now, fast-forwarded to the spring of 1943, ironies abounded as these weapons, named after the man who had brokered the Nonaggression Pact between the Germans and the Russians back in 1939, hurled through the air toward Nazi soldiers from the hands of the Poles, who in two years would be liberated by the Russians.

Having retreated from the ambush on April 19, the Nazis regrouped and returned the next day armed with dogs and flamethrowers. But still, the guerrilla warfare of 1,500 desperate Jews presented a formidable force. The Warsaw Ghetto Uprising lasted for four weeks, a surprisingly long time given the resistance's limited numbers and arsenal. The Germans put a final stop to the rebellion by setting fire to the ghetto, which razed thousands of apartments and shops, and burned many of the residents alive. Some managed to escape and find shelter through underground organizations such as at the Zabińskis' zoo. Others chose to commit suicide rather than be captured by the Germans. In the end, 7,000 Jews lay dead compared to only 16 Germans. The ghetto residents left alive numbered around 22,000, and the Germans sent them all to the death camps of Majdanek and Treblinka. Fire as an act of immolation, a long-time Teutonic fantasy for destroying the Jews, had been made reality.

In May, Czesław brought the news of the Ghetto Uprising along with his delivery of provisions. As Szpilman processed this information, the flurry of conflicting emotions threatened to overwhelm him. He certainly felt pride in how heroically his people had held off the Germans despite the staggering odds. But he also grew sickened from the great loss of life and from the horrific stories of women who had jumped from buildings with babies in their arms rather than be captured by the Germans. The following month, Czesław arrived at the apartment in a panic, insisting that they both needed to flee because the Gestapo suspected him of hiding a Jew. But Szpilman decided that he did not have the strength to run. Instead, he thanked and embraced his friend, and then stayed behind to await his fate.

In solidarity with some of his fellow Jews from the Uprising, Szpilman resolved to commit suicide rather than be taken alive by the Germans. His initial plan involved jumping off the balcony of his apartment, but then he reconsidered and decided that hanging himself would be easier and less dramatic a gesture. He fashioned a noose from a cord he found, rigged it to a hook in the wall, and waited. Several days went by before the Gestapo arrived on his street with their trucks. After seeing them from his window, Szpilman quietly sat down in a chair under the noose and braced himself for the pounding at the door. Meanwhile, the Germans dragged people out of neighboring buildings and even from some of the lower floors of Szpilman's building, but they never came to his door.

A whole week went by, and still Szpilman remained safe, except for the dwindling food supplies. He rationed them as best as he could, but soon he was down to nothing. After two days of only water, he decided to risk going out to buy a loaf of bread rather than sit there and die of starvation. He lived for 10 days on that single loaf. Then in late July, someone did arrive at his apartment door, but it turned out to be Czesław's brother, not the Gestapo. He informed Szpilman that the Gestapo was still searching for his brother, and so a man named Szałas, who worked with the Polish underground, would be taking care of him. Szałas, however, proved unreliable. When he did bother to show up, he always came with a readied excuse about why he had been delayed in bringing the food and why in only such meager

As the days turned into weeks, whenever Szpilman grew despondent, he would reread the newspapers that the German officer had wrapped around the food. The stories of the Allied victories and the impending German defeat renewed his determination to survive. He remained perfectly quiet during the day as the soldiers worked in the building, then late in the night after they had gone, he would venture out to get water from the bathtubs. On December 12, Szpilman received a final visit from the officer, along with a large supply of food, a German military overcoat, and a down blanket. The German said that he was leaving Warsaw and again encouraged Szpilman to hang on, that the end was near. As he turned to go, Szpilman called out to him. "I never told you my name—you didn't ask me, but I want you to remember it. Who knows what may happen? You have a long way to go home. If I survive, I'll certainly be working for Polish Radio again ... if I can help you then in any way, remember my name: Szpilman, Polish Radio."[47]

Szpilman did hang on as Christmas and then New Year's Day came and went. Finally, on January 17, he heard the German soldiers fleeing from the building. The loudspeakers outside in the street crackled to life with messages in Polish that declared the liberation of Warsaw and the defeat of their German occupiers. Szpilman carefully ventured down the stairs, clad in the overcoat that the officer had given him to stay warm. He stepped outside into the cold air and saw two women in the street, one carrying a bundle and one a female Polish soldier. He called out to the civilian, who then shouted in alarm that there was a German at the entrance of the building. The Polish soldier turned and fired at Szpilman. Her shot missed, giving him time to scramble back upstairs to his attic. Meanwhile, the women summoned more Polish soldiers. After living in hell for six years, Szpilman could not believe that he was finally going to die at the hands of his own people because of a German coat. He began shouting in Polish for them not to shoot him, and eventually convinced them of his identity. They took him to their headquarters so he could eat and bathe. After a few weeks of recovery, Szpilman walked around Warsaw, aching at the destruction of such a grand and noble city. He had escaped the terrible war with his life, but so much of what mattered had been stolen from him. His parents and siblings would never even have a final resting place that he could visit, and his mourning for their loss joined the nationwide lament for three million murdered Poles.

Some of Warsaw, along with countless Polish lives, could have been spared if the Soviet Army had not continued to sit just miles outside of Warsaw from the summer of 1944 until they finally rolled into the city in January 1945. But despite their failure to intervene as the Germans made a final push to extinguish the city and its residents, the Polish people still cheered their arrival and greeted them as liberators. In time, the Poles would discover that they had just traded one oppressor for another. Polish partisans and those who had worked so bravely for the underground resistance would particularly find life difficult under Soviet control.

The Red Army's claim on Poland had not been won without its own cost in bloodshed, having lost over 120,000 soldiers on their advance. The capital city that they entered, one of their long-desired victor's spoils, no longer resembled the glorious Warsaw, but merely a lamentable shell of that city, with 85 percent of its buildings reduced to piles of rubble. All that the eye could see and that the nose could smell hailed of death and debris. With the destruction of the buildings and infrastructure of a given place, many accompanying parts of a culture perish alongside, including libraries. Poland had lost an incredible amount of stored knowledge, including 80 percent of all the country's books. Still, the Poles flooded back into their beloved Warsaw, despite the devastation and the lack of any modern comforts such as transportation and electricity. With so few habitable structures remaining, some continued to live in the underground cellars and crypts where they had hidden during the war.

But not all of Warsaw's ruins concealed merely rubbish waiting to be hauled away. Somewhere buried under those insurmountable piles of rubble was a cellar with a dirt floor that hid the Oyneg Shabes archive. Of the 60 Warsaw Ghetto residents who had worked to compile it, only three remained alive, one of those being Rachel Auerbach. Emanuel Ringelblum, whose vision had guided the project, had been executed along with his wife and young son in 1944. Excavation began after the war, and in September 1946, the workers found the archive intact. Its value cannot be overestimated as the most important source of information about the lives of Eastern European Jewry during the Holocaust. Items from the archive remain on display today at the ZIH Jewish Historical Institute in Warsaw. Along with the work of the Oyneg Shabes, Rachel Auerbach was also able to retrieve her personal notebook that Jan Żabiński had buried at the Warsaw Zoo.

These archival testimonies were not the only lost treasures of Warsaw to rise from the ashes. The Nazis had arrested Jan Żabiński in 1944 for his participation in the Warsaw Uprising and sent him to a German POW camp. He survived, but did not return home to reunite with his wife and two children until the spring of 1946. He immediately set about to repair and repopulate their zoo. On July 21, 1949, the Warsaw Zoo reopened, larger and more spectacular than its pre-war incarnation. In September 1965, the Yad Vashem bestowed on Antonina and Jan Żabiński the "Righteous Among the Nations" status for their heroic work in saving Jews during the Holocaust. It remains the highest honor the State of Israel can confer on a Gentile. For each recipient, the Yad Vashem plants a young tree along the Avenue of the Just, where it can be watered by the Jordan River. The "Righteous" also receive a medal inscribed with these words—"Whosoever saves a single life, saves an entire universe."

With the liberation of Warsaw, Irena Sendler also emerged from hiding. Irena and her colleagues had inherited a living legacy from the 2,500 Jewish children they had saved. Scholars estimate that for every child Irena rescued, ten other people had involvement in saving that child as well, and had therefore put themselves in grave danger. The Nazis practiced collective punishment, meaning that anyone violating the law by harboring a Jew would have seen their families executed as well as lost their own life. And so, during such perilous times, daily acts of salvation for the Jews did not come via the tactical maneuverings of armies, or from a miraculous parting of the Red Sea, or even from the magical clay golem of Jewish folklore. The selfless deeds of ordinary people, such as Oskar Schindler, Jan Żabiński, and Irena Sendler, saved their neighbors, one by one.

After the war, Irena Sendler dug up the glass jars that had protected the lists of the hidden children's names and locations and began the painstaking process of trying to reunite them with their parents. Tragically, she discovered that almost all of the parents had been murdered at Treblinka. Irena's sorrow for these orphans joined with the collective mourning for the 1.5 million Jewish children murdered during the Holocaust. Only 11 percent of Europe's Jewish children had survived the genocide. The Communist government that took over Poland following the war suppressed the story of Irena and her colleagues, branding them Fascists. It took many years for their triumphant story to become known to the world. In October 1965, Yad Vashem recognized Irena's heroic efforts to save Jewish lives by declaring her "Righteous Among the Nations." Irena Sendler passed away at age 98 in Warsaw on May 12, 2008. And as she took her final breath, Irena experienced the comforting presence of her dear friend Bieta, whom she had smuggled out of the Warsaw Ghetto as an infant, stuffed in a toolbox.

With the end of the war, more and more of the atrocities committed by the Nazis, especially those in Eastern Europe, came to light and left the world to wrestle with how something that depraved could have occurred and how it could be prevented in the future. In 1949, African American scholar Dr. W.E.B. Du Bois made a trip to Poland and witnessed first-hand the devastation of Warsaw. Du Bois had studied at the University of Berlin and traveled throughout the major cities of Europe at the end of the 19th century. During that time, he observed anti–Semitic attitudes and rhetoric and also took note of how Jews tended to live separately from society in their own quarters. As a philosopher and activist, Du Bois became curious about how the experiences of black citizens in the United States compared with those of Jews in Europe. In his writings from 1917, he drew a parallel between the prejudicial treatment and sequestration of the Jews in Europe and similar situations in his country that had led to the race riots in St. Louis. Although certain distinctions existed, Du Bois could easily see how the ramifications from the subjugation of a particular race by another race crossed national and cultural boundaries, and he eventually concluded that this level of discrimination did not stem solely from skin color and ethnicity, but from "…cultural patterns, perverted teaching and human hate and prejudice, which reached all sorts of people and caused endless evil to all men."[48]

Black servicemen during World War II who witnessed the liberation of Jewish concentration camps also felt a unique resonance with these unwanted people, and their experiences and reflections after the war further informed Du Bois' research. Then following his visit to Poland in 1949, Du Bois wrote his strongest words on the subject.

> I have seen something of human upheaval in this world. The scream and shots of a race riot in Atlanta; the marching of the Ku Klux Klan; the threat of courts and police; the neglect and destruction of human habitation; but nothing in my wildest imagination was equal to what I saw in Warsaw in 1949. I would have said before seeing it that it was impossible for a civilized nation with deep religious convictions and outstanding religious institutions; with literature and art; to treat fellow human beings as Warsaw had been treated. There had been complete, planned and utter destruction.[49]

In his book, *The Vanished City*, survivor Michel Mazor described the loss that occurred in Warsaw from a more personal and spiritual vantage.

> Everything around them disappeared—the milieu in which they had lived, their relatives, their friends, ordinary acquaintances, the people they kept company with for many years as well as those they knew only by sight or encountered through public or private dealings. Many families completely disappeared, without leaving behind even distant relatives as survivors, or so much as a family photo, or a single identifiable tomb…[50]

But Mazor trusted that Warsaw would rebuild itself in time, as it had done repeatedly. The number of statues and monuments that grace the city in memory of its many heroes demonstrates that Poland will always be "…a country half submerged in its heavily invaded past, fed by progress, but always partly in mourning."[51]

The resilience of the city of Warsaw reflected that very strength in the Polish people. After the war, Szpilman stepped right back into his life, making it mirror the one before 1939. He performed as a soloist and in chamber ensembles, while working again for the Polish Radio as the director of its Music Department from 1945 to 1963. Szpilman married a Catholic physician named Halina Grzecznarowski in 1950, and their son Christopher was born the following year. After 1963, Szpilman focused on touring. He gave thousands of recitals and concerts throughout the world, including with the Warsaw Piano Quintet that he and his violinist friend Gimpel had founded. Szpilman also continued to compose and retired from touring in 1986 to devote himself more fully to composition. His oeuvre eventually included almost 500 songs, many of which reached the top of the Polish pop charts and have remained staples in the Polish popular music genre. He wrote film scores and incidental music for radio broadcasts, along with symphonic works. His love and compassion for children manifested in his compositions as well, resulting in numerous children's songs and music for children's theater productions.

Szpilman had published *Death of a City* in 1946, a memoir in Polish about his years in the Warsaw Ghetto and his miraculous escape from the jaws of death. But his story and his compositions remained unknown to most of the world due to repression by Poland's Communist government. Finally, after 52 years, his memoir received a German translation and republication in 1998, then a release in English the following year. This rebirth of his amazing story catapulted him to international attention with the 2002 Academy Award Winning film, *The Pianist*, directed by Roman Polanski. Tragically, Szpilman did not live to watch his story depicted on the film screen by Adrien Brody. He passed away in his beloved Warsaw on July 6, 2000, at age 88.

Szpilman never reunited with that tall, elegant German officer who had saved his life near the end of the war. The Soviet Army had captured Captain Wilhelm Hosenfeld during January 1945 and held him in harsh conditions. About two weeks after Szpilman emerged from hiding, one of his colleagues from the Polish Radio, a violinist named Zygmunt Lednicki, was making his way back to Warsaw when he passed a group of German POWs in a temporary camp surrounded by barbed wire. Lednicki approached the fence and began shouting insults at the prisoners. He railed against them for the years of his life they had taken and for having stolen his violin. One of the Germans, a man in poor physical condition, came over to the fence and asked Lednicki if he knew a man named Szpilman. Lednicki replied that he did, and the German cried out, "Tell him I'm here. Ask him to get me out. I beg you…"[52] A Soviet guard pulled Hosenfeld away before Lednicki could get his name.

Szpilman did not learn his savior's name until 1950. At which point, he tried to intervene with the Polish government, but since Captain Hosenfeld was being held by the Soviets outside of Poland, nothing could be done. The full account of Hosenfeld's sacrificial acts would eventually come to light. Aggrieved and repulsed by his own government's treatment of Jews and Slavs, Hosenfeld had tried to help them. In the end, he saved not only Szpilman's life, but the lives of many other Jews as well. After being tortured by his captors and then suffering a series of strokes, Hosenfeld died in a Stalingrad POW camp in 1952. Szpilman deeply regretted not being able to help his rescuer, but did find some closure when he visited with the Captain's family in 1957 while on a concert tour in West Germany. In 1998, Szpilman applied for Hosenfeld to be recognized by the Yad Vashem. After an extensive documentation process, Captain Wilhelm Hosenfeld posthumously received "Righteous Among the Nations" status in 2008, another testament to "Whosoever saves a single life, saves an entire universe."

6

Olivier Messiaen: A Composer Confronts the End of Time

And the angel which I saw stand upon the sea and upon the earth lifted up his hand to heaven, And sware by him that liveth for ever and ever... that there should be time no longer.
—*King James Version*, Revelation 10:5–6

Following the immeasurable artistic triumphs of the 19th century, many composers struggled with feelings of disillusionment and disorientation as they encountered the truly terrible acts wrought by the 20th century before it had even reached its half century point. In referring to this troubled era of human history, acclaimed American composer and conductor Leonard Bernstein pronounced it "the century of death."[1] The difficult times propelled some composers toward experimentation and the subsequent creation of masterworks with dark and violent themes that they coupled with equally challenging musical elements. These works became what French composer Olivier Messiaen called "black masterpieces" and included *Salome* (1905) by Richard Strauss, *The Rite of Spring* (1913) by Igor Stravinsky, *Wozzeck* (1922) by Alban Berg, and Benjamin Britten's *Peter Grimes* (1945). But other artists, such as Maurice Ravel and Ralph Vaughan Williams, felt no obligation to match the tone of the century, and instead provided a counterpoint to it by infusing peace, light, and beauty into their compositions. Meanwhile, some of the same composers who had contributed the more disturbing pieces repented or at least sought balance through uplifting works, as seen with Stravinsky's *Symphony of Psalms* (1929) and Strauss' *Four Last Songs* (1948).

In addition to their artistic and existential battles, composers also faced the possibility of a literal battlefield. During World War II, the revered and renowned were not guaranteed a pass from military service so that they could continue to think and create in their ivory towers. The same had been true during the Great War, as Fritz Kreisler, one of the world's finest violinists, fought in the trenches.[2] Artists, actors, composers, and writers reported for duty alongside the average conscripted soldier and fell prey to the same horrors of war—watching their comrades die violent deaths, or being captured, or even sacrificing their lives. As in the wars before and after, some who returned never felt the same and wrestled, either successfully or unsuccessfully, with the atrocities they had engaged in or witnessed. Several noted composers also found themselves cogs in the machinery of war, including Olivier Messiaen. A devoutly religious French organist, Messiaen had earned a reputation in Paris and abroad for his prodigious talent and unorthodox musical ideas. But as the 1930s drew to a close, Messiaen, in the prime of his career, was forced to take a detour by a world that lay on the brink of apocalypse, and via this unintended path, he contributed in a significant way to the distinctive genre of works composed during captivity.

Olivier Messiaen was born in Avignon, France, on December 20, 1908. Messiaen's mother, the poet Cécile Sauvage, had written a set of 20 poems, *L'âme en bourgeon* (The Budding Soul), during her pregnancy that reflected on her experiences of domesticity and her pending motherhood. Later, her son related that these poems greatly influenced his development into an artist, almost as a self-fulfilling prophecy delivered through his mother. Soon after Messiaen's birth in Avignon, the family relocated to Ambert. Then in 1913, Messiaen's brother Alain was born. Their father Pierre could best be described as a man entranced by words. He taught English and translated Shakespeare into French. With the outbreak of World War I, the French government turned Pierre Messiaen into a soldier, and Messiaen's mother and her two sons went to live with her mother, Marie Sauvage, in Grenoble.

As a result of having a poet for a mother and a Shakespearean scholar for a father, the precocious Olivier Messiaen inhabited a world of words, gravitating especially toward poetry and fairytales. By age 8, he was reciting entire works of Shakespeare for his family. He particularly loved the plays that embodied an undercurrent of the supernatural, such as *A Midsummer Night's Dream* or *Macbeth*. Messiaen's enchantment with the dramatic arts led him to build a theater out of boxes and other materials he found around the house. He then positioned his creation to where light from a window could shine down and illuminate the stage, an early demonstration of what would become his lifelong fascination with light and color. Messiaen also began teaching himself the piano and composing canons. Although not musicians, his family recognized the child's unusual ability and arranged for his first formal lessons in 1917. That same year, Messiaen completed one of his earliest piano compositions, *La dame de Shalott* (The Lady of Shalott), based on a poem by Tennyson. Instead of the typical toys a boy might want for Christmas, young Messiaen requested vocal scores from great operas, including Mozart's *Die Zauberflöte*, Gluck's *Orfeo*, and Wagner's *Die Walküre*. With his early devotion to and remarkable understanding of opera, it seemed destined that his composition career would focus on that dramatic art form. But interestingly, Messiaen would only write one opera, and that would be toward the end of his life.

In 1918, after the war, Messiaen's father took the family to Nantes, where Messiaen studied piano with a variety of teachers and began harmony lessons with Jehan de Gibon. Right away, Gibon became an important figure in the young musician's life. He handed the 10-year-old boy his first score of Debussy's opera *Pelléas et Mélisande*, music that would profoundly impact the aspiring composer. Then in 1919, after only six months in Nantes, Messiaen's father accepted a job teaching in Paris at the Lycée Charlemagne, and the 11-year-old Messiaen gained entrance to the Paris Conservatory. But despite their abbreviated time together, he and Gibon had forged an indelible bond and would remain in contact until Gibon's death in 1952.

The years that Messiaen spent at the Paris Conservatory represented an iconic time for the city and offered a diverse cultural education for any developing artist. Paris of the 1920s was a vibrant locale where jazz and cabarets flourished, and Stravinsky and other artistic giants created masterpieces. Parisian audiences hungered for the latest international trend, whether it took the form of their passion for all things Russian or for the truly exotic that had been introduced to them in 1889 when the city hosted the World's Fair (*Exposition Universelle*). Paris' cosmopolitan arts scene also included the Brazilian composer Heitor Villa-Lobos, whose dazzling orchestrations would influence a generation of young composers, particularly Messiaen.

Somewhat paradoxically, the 1920s also showcased the revered tradition of French organ writing and playing. Messiaen could travel throughout the city hearing the great masters who sat ensconced on Paris' organ benches: Louis Vierne at the Notre Dame Cathedral, Charles Tournemire at Ste. Clotilde, and Charles-Marie Widor at St. Sulpice. Their virtuosic playing, mastery of improvisation, and grandiose compositions for organ had a considerable impact on the religiously seeking young man. With much of Paris ambivalent toward conventional religion, the world of the French organist-composer provided an acceptable outlet for composing sacred music. Since the organ was most typically found in churches, then it seemed natural, or even inevitable, that the subject matter of its repertoire would so often inhabit the spiritual realm.

Under the tutelage of the Conservatory's impressive faculty, Messiaen explored a comprehensive curriculum that included piano, harmony, music history, and even percussion. He took organ lessons from Marcel Dupré, whom Messiaen referred to as the "Liszt of the organ."[3] Dupré had studied with Vierne and Widor; and since Vierne had been a student of the great French organist and composer César Franck, he passed down the influence and expertise of two generations of French organists. Paul Dukas, the famed French composer whose 1897 symphonic poem *L'apprenti sorcier* (The Sorcerer's Apprentice) would find its unlikely way into a beloved Disney classic, taught composition to Messiaen. Dukas especially guided him in techniques to achieve orchestral brilliance and dramatic presentation. By the conclusion of his studies at the Conservatory, Messiaen had won five first prizes in a variety of musical disciplines, including piano accompaniment, counterpoint, history, organ, and composition.

As a student, Messiaen had already begun to distinguish himself as a composer in his own right and not merely as an apprentice. He left school with a diverse portfolio of completed repertoire, including songs, organ works, a piano prelude, and three orchestral pieces. Messiaen entered works in the coveted Prix de Rome competition in 1929 and 1930, but failed to win, joining the ranks of other distinguished composers, such as Stravinsky and Ravel, who were denied this prestigious honor.

By this time, Messiaen had also become a zealously devout Catholic. Messiaen's dedication to the Catholic faith, like his early self-directed exploration of music, had evolved on its own, as neither of his parents were religious. The mystical aura that attracted him to Shakespeare and opera also seemed to resonate with him through Christian liturgy and ritual, and this newfound devotion became deeply entwined with his calling to write music. Many centuries earlier, medieval composers had placed their focus on God, but then with the dawning of the Renaissance, the pendulum of intent had begun to swing from the divine toward the human. Messiaen would now emerge as the composer whose works represented spiritual themes and the quest for a connection with God more than any composer since the Renaissance. With this, Messiaen set himself on a challenging course to depict and illuminate through music the most profound events of the Judeo-Christian heritage, those which pointed most emphatically to the divinity of Christ, namely the Incarnation, Transfiguration, and Resurrection. Messiaen shied away from religious motifs that involved humanity's fall and the subsequent redemption that required the crucifixion and death of the Savior, topics which had been the more frequently used subject matter of sacred works, such as the Passions of J.S. Bach, Pergolesi's *Stabat Mater*, and Haydn's *The Seven Last Words of Our Savior on the Cross*.

Messiaen's Catholic faith formed the gateway through which he worked. Striving for piety was not completely foreign to the French musical world, as can certainly be seen in the works of Charles Gounod and Gabriel Fauré, but it did not proffer the easiest path toward public appreciation. Messiaen's resulting pieces often found Catholic audiences offended by the extravagance and opulence of the sound, which they thought gaudy and vulgar. While non–Catholics were equally put off, but for the opposite reason that his music carried too much "scent of incense."[4]

But regardless of whatever criticism or misunderstanding resulted from his unconventional ideas, Messiaen remained perpetually curious about the world around him, both natural and man-made, and he greeted each new discovery as a potential compositional device. Messiaen had been exposed to the gamelan music of Bali for the first time in 1931 at the *Exposition Coloniale* in Paris. That sound and musical concept planted a seed in him, which while not bearing fruit right away, can be seen in his works from the 1940s onward. Messiaen also found inspiration in the French artist Robert Delaunay, who represented an offshoot of Cubism, known as Orphism, which infused intensely bright colors within geometric abstractions. In time, Messiaen developed a truly unique composition style from the convergence of diverse but interconnected thematic and musical elements: religion, mysticism, ornithology, ancient Greek modes, medieval plainchant, nonwestern music systems, timbre, and the exploration of time.

Indeed, even as a young man, Messiaen donned many hats—performer, composer, religious pilgrim, and amateur ornithologist. He also invented for himself the moniker, "rhythmician," because of his almost obsessive need to dissemble the conventional sense of musical time in order to discover a novel way to envision the temporal element, the equivalent to reinventing how space could be configured and perceived in the visual arts.[5] In the traditional Western rhythmic system, beats are grouped into meters, establishing a pattern of accented and unaccented pulses. These metered groupings then propel the music forward through time, synchronized to a single clock. But Messiaen's interest lay in liberating music from what he viewed as the confines of meter so that each pulse carried an equal emphasis, which would then allow the music to be more oriented in the present moment, rather than engaged in the process of moving toward a time-based destination. Once achieved, there would no longer be a clear distinction between the past, future, and present, just a sense of being in the now, almost as multiple clocks or pendulum metronomes operating at different speeds simultaneously. As a result of these experiments, sometimes Messiaen's music moves at a quick, almost frantic tempo, racing in a circular stasis that serves as the harbinger of the late 20th century's great minimalist composers Philip Glass and Steve Reich. At other times, Messiaen's compositions unfold at a slow and deliberately prolonged pace as the space between each pulse comes to signify the infinite nature of Messiaen's most cherished temporal concept—eternal time.

The most conducive and accessible mode for Messiaen's experiments with time and also with tone color became the organ. The obvious contradiction with this, however, lay in the inherent conservative nature of the organ and the organ repertoire. Nevertheless, Messiaen boldly approached it in a way that no other composer had ever dared, bringing innovation to an instrument that most people thought of as residing in the musical ideas of the past. Music critic Paul Griffiths has compared Messiaen's re-conceptualization of the organ to the seminal advances that his American contemporary John Cage would create with prepared piano.

Messiaen published his first work for organ, *Le banquet céleste* (Heavenly Feast), in 1928 when he was only 19 years old. Its most striking characteristic remains the incredible slowness with which it proceeds, a veritable glacial pace that demonstrates, even in this early opus, Messiaen's preoccupation with infinity and the eternal. At a glance, *Heavenly Feast* appears to be a short work, consisting of only 25 bars of music. But in reality, if played at the tempo indicated by the composer, it lasts a full six minutes. The organ's ability to sustain indefinitely made it the perfect venue for expressing eternal time. In works with a sound medium that was incapable of that kind of sustain, such as the piano, Messiaen would instead employ harmonic stasis and circular rhythmic repetition to conjure a sense of the infinite.

In September 1931, at age 22, Messiaen received the appointment of titular or principal organist at La Trinité (Trinity) in Paris, becoming the youngest person to ever be named as a head organist in Paris. The grand organ at Trinity had been designed by master organ builder Aristide Cavaillé-Coll and provided Messiaen with a majestic instrument on which to perform and compose. His Sundays demanded an exceedingly busy playing schedule with three masses and a vesper service. Each required a different set of repertoire, which varied in style from simple plainsong, to pieces from the Western canon, and his own compositions. But despite the rigorous nature of the position, Messiaen adored Trinity and, except for a brief break during the war (1940–41), would remain in this post, keeping vigil on that mighty organ bench, for more than 60 years until his death in 1992.

Messiaen's rather prosaic job as organist at Trinity intrigued many composers, who either admired or at least acknowledged the significance of the avant-garde ideas that Messiaen had introduced to Western music. Curiosity led American composer Aaron Copland to visit Messiaen's church in 1949 to ascertain what type of music such an unconventional composer could possibly be playing for those congregants on any given Sunday. Copland's diary recorded the surreal experience: "Visited Messiaen in the organ loft at Trinité. Heard him improvise at noon. Everything from the 'devil' in the bass, to Radio City Music Hall harmonies in the treble. Why the Church allows it during service is a mystery."[6]

Indeed, throughout his lifetime, Messiaen remained a mysterious and somewhat elusive figure. A great admirer and interpreter of Messiaen's music, renowned Finnish conductor and composer Esa-Pekka Salonen visited the composer's apartment in the 18th arrondissement of Paris during the latter part of Messiaen's career. He found it surprisingly located in an old building, with only a modest décor that consisted mostly of plastic crucifixes. One of the conductor's main motivations for coming to Messiaen's home was to browse his bookshelves and record collections to discover what the mighty composer listened to and read. But Salonen came away disappointed, having seen only the Bible and recordings of Messiaen's own works.

But despite Messiaen's eccentricities, or maybe because of them, he always managed to acquire a gaggle of friends and followers. While still a student at the Paris Conservatory, Messiaen had met violinist and composer Claire Delbos, who also studied there, and they gave recitals together that featured some of the great works of the violin and piano repertoire. Soon, a romantic relationship developed, and they married in June 1932. His wedding present to her was a new piece, *Thème et variations* (Theme and Variations) for violin and piano, which became part of the recitals that the couple continued to perform during the early years of their marriage. Later, she composed some pieces for her husband as well, including works for organ and songs based on his mother's poems.

Throughout the 1930s, Messiaen eagerly explored novel musical and artistic ideas, including the newly developing field of electronic instruments that would become a groundbreaking medium for avant-garde composer Edgard Varèse. Messiaen also aligned himself with three likeminded composers: Andrè Jolivet, Jean-YvesDaniel-Lesur, and Yves Baudrier.

Collectively, they called themselves "La Jeune France" (Young France) and began to organize concerts to promote their own works. The group championed a musical style that scoffed at what they saw as frivolity and insincerity in the French neoclassical works and in the writings and philosophy of Jean Cocteau. As a playwright, novelist, filmmaker, and artist, Cocteau had become quite influential, advocating an aesthetic philosophy grounded in simplicity and clarity, although his involvement in Dadaism would also indicate a satirical view of society following World War I. Confident in the authenticity of their counter-message, "Young France" would continue to be active in the music world until the renewed animosity between France and Germany in 1939 forced them down divergent paths.

In 1936, Messiaen and his wife moved to a house by the water in Petichut, and he began teaching at Ecole Normale de Musique and the Schola Cantorum that same year. After a tragic series of miscarriages, they rejoiced at the birth of their son Pascal on July 14, 1937. But just as life seemed to be falling into place for the composer and his growing family, disaster loomed on the horizon. In the neighboring country of Germany, unrest had been steadily building throughout the 1930s, and soon that trouble would spill into the laps of the French as well.

In response to the growing fear of war with Germany, France initiated a buildup of its military forces. The French government drafted Messiaen on August 25, 1939, the same day he completed his large organ cycle, *Les corps glorieux* (The Glorified Bodies). After failing the eye exam, he was assigned to serve as a medical orderly instead of a combat soldier and stationed in Sarralbe in northeast France. Less than two weeks later, when the Nazi government invaded Poland on September 1, 1939, France and Britain declared war on Germany. For months, little came of the fact that France and Germany were officially at war. The French had suffered such heavy casualties in the Great War via their offensive maneuvers that they opted this time for a strategy based on defense of the Maginot Line, a series of fortifications they had constructed on the frontier-border with Germany, and would wait until later to mount a significant offensive if the situation warranted it. But in May 1940, the Germans launched a blitzkrieg assault on Belgium and Holland and then into France. In less than two months, France was forced to surrender.

Messiaen was stationed by this time in Verdun, where he met two fellow musicians—clarinetist Henri Akoka and cellist Etienne Pasquier. It would be through their relationship that Messiaen's future masterpiece, *Quatuor pour la fin du Temps* (Quartet for the End of Time), would experience its nascency. Messiaen's new comrade Etienne Pasquier had been born on May 10, 1905, in Tours. For his family, life revolved around music. Both of his parents taught and performed—his father on the violin and his mother on the piano. Soon after starting cello lessons at age 5 on a small cello about the size of a viola, their son Etienne displayed a prodigious talent. He entered the Paris Conservatory in 1918 at age 13, and in 1921, received a first prize there in cello. After school, he embarked on a professional career, becoming the youngest player in the Concerts Colonne orchestra. Etienne's two older brothers also played stringed instruments—Jean, the violin and Pierre, the viola. In 1927, the three brothers founded the Trio Pasquier. In time, their trio would become one of the most respected chamber groups in the world, performing with international celebrity musicians such as Jean-Pierre Rampal and receiving commissions from well-known composers, including Darius Milhaud and Bohuslav Martinů.

In 1929, at age 24, Etienne Pasquier married singer Suzanne Gouts and joined the prestigious Paris Opera Orchestra. As with Messiaen, the French government called up Pasquier for military service in 1939 and sent him to fight on the front lines in Lorraine.

6. Olivier Messiaen: A Composer Confronts the End of Time

After falling ill in 1940, he was transferred to Verdun, where one of the music-loving French generals had started a small orchestra. Pasquier's new assignment placed him in charge of four other musicians, one of whom happened to be Olivier Messiaen.[7] After developing an easy rapport, Messiaen introduced Pasquier to his interest in ornithology, and the two spent hours listening to and analyzing the chorus of birds at dawn. Their birdsong adventures soon led to a composition for solo clarinet called "The Abyss of the Birds," since by then, another musician, Henri Akoka, had entered their lives.

Henri Akoka had been born in Algeria on June 23, 1912. He came from a musical family, as well, but not at the professional level of Pasquier's. An amateur trumpet player, Akoka's father Abraham wanted his children to undertake serious music study that could lead to careers, so he relocated the family to Ponthierry, France. There, Henri studied clarinet, and his older brother played the tuba. Together with their father, they performed in a band. The 14-year-old Henri also played in the cinema for silent films. In time, Henri went to study at the Paris Conservatory and earned a first in clarinet in 1935. After his studies, Akoka began auditioning for a job in a professional French orchestra and eventually secured a position in the Orchestre National de la Radio in Paris. But the draft interrupted his career, and he was sent to play in the military orchestra at Verdun. After establishing a friendship with Messiaen and Pasquier, Akoka received a newly composed piece from Messiaen that had been inspired by birdsong and by Akoka's remarkable clarinet playing.

Meanwhile, the German incursions into France were yielding vast numbers of POWs, about two million from just the northern region. On June 20, 1940, enemy troops marched into Verdun and captured all three musicians along with thousands of other French soldiers. Two days later, the French signed an armistice with the Germans that would go into effect on June 25. It established a demarcation line to separate the German-occupied lands of northern and western France from the southern part of France, which was to remain a free zone with a capital in Vichy. But the Vichy government was not really free or autonomous. Instead, it fell subject to Nazi policies, including the deportation of Jews, and in the end, its officials would be branded Nazi collaborators.

The Germans marched their captives from Verdun on a 43-mile trek without food or water to an open field near Nancy. Pasquier felt particularly grateful to the younger and more robust Akoka, who provided both emotional and physical support to him on that grueling march. Upon arriving in Nancy, the POWs finally had access to water after days of debilitating thirst, and at once began to fight over getting to it first. But a parched and exhausted Messiaen sat down instead and began studying the score to Stravinsky's *Les Noces* that he had stuffed into his pocket. He noticed another man nearby reading a book, also not engaging in the demeaning water brawl, an Egyptologist named Guy-Bernard Delapierre. Recognizing each other as kindred spirits, the two men struck up a conversation and a friendship that would last beyond the war.

When taken prisoner, Akoka had not yet read through "The Abyss of the Birds" piece Messiaen had just written for him. But fortunately, during the whole ordeal, Akoka had managed to keep his beloved clarinet with him, and so in that field, he played the composition for the first time. According to Pasquier, who held up the music for him, Akoka's sight reading was accompanied by the occasional grunt of exasperation due to the work's difficult demands, which required a variety of extended techniques including squawks to imitate the birds.

After approximately three weeks in that field, the Germans moved the prisoners to Stalag VIII A. In addition to constructing ghettos and concentration camps to deal with their "Jewish problem," the German government also had to accommodate vast numbers of prisoners of war from invaded and conquered territories. By the end of the war, the Germans had built over 150 POW camps for the approximately 10 million soldiers that they captured. As with the concentration camps, these facilities were designed as a system of compounds that often contained a main camp with numerous subcamps spread out near important work sites. The German military organized the POW camps by rank into two main types: Oflags for officers and Stalags for non-commissioned officers and other rank soldiers. The camps required most to work at hard labor to benefit the German war effort, and the conditions usually failed to comply with the Geneva Convention, leaving the POWs malnourished and deprived of basic medical and hygiene care.

The main camp at Stalag VIII A sat on approximately 12 acres in Görlitz, Germany, with multiple annexes in the surrounding area. The inaugural group of prisoners, about 8,000 Poles, arrived on September 7, 1939. At this time, the construction of the camp had not been completed, so the guards forced the prisoners to build their own barracks, while living in crowded tents. As Germany continued to fare well in 1940 and 1941, Stalag VIII A evolved into a large compound that functioned as its own microcosm. The camp infrastructure expanded to over 50 barracks, in addition to a kitchen, latrines, showers, and two infirmaries. It also contained a chapel where services and prayer could take place. In time, the camp added facilities geared toward leisure and entertainment, such as an auditorium for concerts, plays, and lectures, as well as a camp library that grew to 10,000 volumes by 1943.

As the Germans conquered more territories, Stalag VIII A filled with a diverse contingency of prisoners, including French, Belgian, Russian, Italian, American, and British. By the time of its closure in 1945, Stalag VIII A had processed approximately 120,000 prisoners through its gates. In dealing with housing logistics of that magnitude, the camp command usually based barrack assignments on nationality, especially separating Western and Eastern Europeans, so that the deep hatred that the Germans harbored for the Poles and others of Eastern European descent could be paraded openly in most aspects of daily life, including their access to mail and leisure activities. But sometimes other homogenizing factors were taken into account. For example, all of the Catholic priests, regardless of their country of origin, lived together, as did all those who worked in the kitchen. But for all, the prisoner barracks offered no luxuries, just the typical three-tiered bunks and some wooden benches and tables. Most held between 175 and 200 prisoners and were heated by only a single stove, which proved wholly insufficient in the bitterly cold winters.

During that notorious summer of 1940 when Messiaen and his comrades arrived at Stalag VIII A, the camp housed some 30,000 captured personnel, most of them French. The German government had not really expected to conquer France so quickly and now had hordes of captured French soldiers to accommodate, without really having the physical structures or food supply to do so. As a result, brutal conditions prevailed, with the prisoners having almost nothing to eat. Some days, only one bowl of a watery soup provided the sole sustenance. Other days, a piece of black bread constituted the only ration except for the hot drink meant to pass for coffee. Eventually, the Red Cross did manage to get some food parcels into the camp, which helped a little. But still, the prisoners were losing weight quickly and their overall health was declining to the point that some lost teeth and hair. That winter, as the temperatures plummeted to 25 degrees below zero, the prisoners suffered from the bitter cold and its complications, such as frostbite and chilblains. Some died of malnutrition and exposure.

With the prestige and security of his organ bench at Trinity so far removed, Messiaen faced the harsh and demeaning intake procedures instituted by the Nazi guards, including being stripped naked. Undeterred by the loss of his clothes, he clutched his satchel tightly to his naked body, since it contained his most important belongings—musical scores. Inside the case lay a set of miniature scores to a wide range of works from Bach's *Brandenburg Concerti* to Berg's *Lyric Suite*. Messiaen had no intention of turning those over despite the insistence of a German guard armed with a submachine gun. Somehow, Messiaen's formidable will prevailed, and the guard relented. It would be the beginning of many special privileges that Messiaen would garner among the music-loving Germans. With Messiaen an internationally renowned composer, and not a Jew, he became a commodity to be protected and possibly exploited for propaganda. Other musicians in the camp received certain considerations as well, sometimes merely in the form of a bit of extra food or more wood to keep their barracks heated. The guards often gave them choicer and easier work assignments, such as in the kitchen or the laundry, instead of marching outside to do heavy labor in the elements. Messiaen's standing earned him an exemption from any work, and so he focused on composing and rehearsing, and then reading in his spare time. This situation was not unique to Stalag VIII A. Other German POW camps, such as Stalag IX A in Ziegenhain, provided their musician-prisoners with exceptional treatment that made life just a little bit less miserable. But again as with Terezín, the Nazis seemed to have an eye on the propaganda benefit that could be had from informing the Red Cross and the international community about the artistic activities that they allowed to flourish in their POW camps.

In many ways, Stalag VIII A resembled the Nazi ghetto Terezín, which housed large numbers of Jewish-Czech artists, musicians, actors, writers, and intelligentsia. The captives at Stalag VIII A attempted to make their lives as tolerable as possible by organizing cultural activities. Within their camp, gifted artist-soldiers, such as Messiaen, created a veritable center of artistic excellence through regularly scheduled chamber music recitals, art exhibits, plays, and variety shows that lifted the spirits of the prisoners and infused excitement into their monotonous and uncomfortable days. In time, the German command decided to convert Barrack 27 into an auditorium, consulting Messiaen and other musicians and actors to help with the designs for the space. As a result, workers transformed the laundry room into a makeshift stage and placed wooden benches to seat an audience of some 400 people. The first performance held in the new theater took place on November 24, 1940, and the venue quickly became the scene of numerous concerts, with music ranging from popular and folk songs to classical works. Eventually, music ensembles that had started as small ragtag groups expanded until the camp featured a jazz band and an orchestra of about 45 members conducted by a Belgian prisoner named Ferdinand Carrion.

The number of highly skilled musicians in Stalag VIII A certainly assisted people like Carrion in forming quality ensembles, and with the constant influx of prisoners into the camp, there was always the opportunity to "discover" new talent. One day a violinist of some renown from Vilna named Max Beker approached Carrion about auditioning for the orchestra. Beker's musical pedigree included a family of professional musicians. Most notably, his father had attended the St. Petersburg Conservatory and played the oboe with the Vilna Symphony Orchestra. After studying the violin at the Vilna Conservatory, Beker had performed professionally until being drafted into the Polish Army in March 1939. He was captured by the Germans in September 1941 and transferred in 1942 to Stalag VIII A. Beker had managed to acquire a violin from a kindly Austrian man he met during his work details, and so he eagerly auditioned for the orchestra's conductor. Upon hearing this talented violinist, Carrion wanted Beker as his concertmaster and appealed to the Commandant, who did grant permission for Beker to join. He became both the orchestra's sole Jewish member and sole Polish Army member.

Meanwhile, a theater troupe also formed, and the new facility showcased various dramatic presentations, ranging from comedies to more serious plays, and from classical works to modern. The seriousness of their endeavors can be seen in their successful petition to the camp command for the construction of a prop room where costumes and scenery could be created, maintained, and stored. Led by Albert Moira, the camp's visual artists contributed to the scenery for theatrical productions and also created a variety of artwork, from paintings to sculptures, which were displayed in exhibitions. But while the German officials did provide support for the artistic events, they also censored the musical and theatrical performances, especially banning anything nationalistic from their prisoners' respective homelands. The Nazi guards also relished the control they had to limit electricity and heating during the winter, which could make rehearsing almost impossible. Nevertheless, spirited and enjoyable performances and skits, including war satires, took place. But as the war dragged on, the Germans seemed less generous toward these activities at Stalag VIII A, so that in 1943, they only allowed six each month. By 1944, they permanently closed down the auditorium as punishment for an illegal radio station they discovered being operated from within the camp.

One of the great supporters of the arts at Stalag VIII A was a guard—Hauptmann Karl-Albert Brüll. While a dedicated German patriot, Brüll felt no alliance with Nazi doc-

Stalag VIII A Orchestra, with Max Beker as concertmaster and Ferdinand Carrion as conductor, c. 1942 (archive of Sonia P. Beker, author of *Symphony on Fire: A Story of Music and Spiritual Resistance During the Holocaust*).

Stalag VIII A Orchestra performing at the infirmary, c. 1942-1944 (archive of Sonia P. Beker, author of *Symphony on Fire: A Story of Music and Spiritual Resistance During the Holocaust*).

trines, especially concerning the Jews. He was an educated man, having been a lawyer before being called up for military service, and spoke fluent French because his Belgian mother insisted that he be bilingual. His language skills made him particularly valuable to the French prisoners who appreciated having a guard that they could speak to in their mother tongue. Brüll gained a reputation for being sympathetic toward any Jews in the camp, which there were since the French army did not institute a ban on Jewish participation until late 1940 after France's surrender to Germany. Brüll advised Jewish soldiers imprisoned at Stalag VIII A not to attempt an escape from the POW camp because they were actually safer there as captured soldiers than they would be on the streets as Jews. In time, however, the German command deported any Eastern European Jews from their POW camps to destinations unknown. Western European Jews in Stalag VIII A were allowed to remain there, which proved especially good news for Henri Akoka, the only Jewish member of Messiaen's trio of musician friends.

Brüll loved music and felt it almost an honor to have such a prestigious composer among them. According to several witnesses, he arranged for Messiaen to work in an empty barrack that was guarded, often by himself, so that the composer would not be disturbed. Messiaen's second wife Yvonne Loriod, however, disputed this account, claiming that the composer was locked into a disgusting latrine in order to have uninterrupted composition time. Regardless, Messiaen was provided with a special dispensation in the form of a private space to compose, but whether it took the form of a clean and quiet barrack with a guard outside or a less desirable venue can be debated. Brüll certainly supplied Messiaen with whatever materials he needed, including pencils and staff paper.

While officially housed in Barrack 19A with other French and Belgian prisoners, Messiaen often sought respite with the Catholic priests. He felt at ease among these likeminded men who shared his deep devotion to the Catholic faith, plus found their quarters quieter and therefore more conducive to reading and score study. On Sundays, Messiaen could always be found in the chapel praying. While Messiaen moved through his day with a modicum of freedom, Etienne Pasquier had been assigned an arduous and dangerous job in a granite mine about 60 miles from camp. One day, an actor friend of his named René Charles informed the German command about Pasquier's reputation as a celebrated cellist and insisted that this kind of work might injure his hands to where he could never play the cello again. Fortunately, Pasquier's name was familiar to some of the guards because of the success of the trio he had formed with his brothers. But if they needed any proof, Pasquier could produce the press releases that he had the vain habit of carrying with him. In the end, the Germans transferred Pasquier to cooking duty, an especially privileged position because it gave him access to extra food for himself and to smuggle out to his comrades. Because of his job in the kitchen, Pasquier bunked with the other cook staff-prisoners.

Not long after their internment at Stalag VIII A, the three friends met violinist Jean Le Boulaire, who arrived there later that same summer. Le Boulaire's life would be forever changed by the fate of his barrack's assignment, which placed him sharing a bunk with Henri Akoka. The discovery of another talented musician sent Akoka straight to Messiaen with the details. Born on August 2, 1913, Le Boulaire had grown up in Saint-Ouen-sur-Seine, France. At age 7, he began to study the violin and then enrolled at the Paris Conservatory when he was 14 years old. Although he and Messiaen studied there at the same time, they had not been acquainted. Le Boulaire had actually served two stints in the military. The first had been from 1934 to 1936. Then as France entered the war, the military reenlisted him in 1939. Le Boulaire's unit had fled from France to England following the Battle of Dunkirk in June 1940. When they reentered France on their way to Paris, the Germans captured them. Now, in this unlikely of places, he joined an unorthodox chamber group, the final complement to the quartet that Messiaen had been envisioning.

One night in the camp, Messiaen dreamed about the angel who would announce the end of time, as described in the Book of Revelation. "And the angel which I saw stand upon the sea and upon the earth lifted up his hand to heaven, And sware by him that liveth for ever and ever… that there should be time no longer."[8] After that dream, Messiaen began to envision a piece that could create a musical representation of the prophesized apocalypse, a work he would title *Quatuor pour la fin du Temps* (Quartet for the End of Time). Like *The Glorified Bodies*, Messiaen's organ composition from the previous autumn, *Quartet* would sprout from eschatological roots, as the composer remained fascinated with the final judgment of the human race and the destiny of the soul after the end of the world. Intent on establishing the connection, Messiaen inscribed at the top of his completed *Quartet* score a reference to those apocalyptic events recorded in the 10th chapter of Revelation: "In homage to the Angel of the Apocalypse, who lifts his hand toward heaven, saying, 'There shall be time no longer.'" A prophecy in its own right, Messiaen's new work truly became "…a quartet for all time, based on the Apocalypse and written in apocalyptic times, music for the future, defiant of the past, music for the moment, and for eternity."[9]

Following months of intense work, *Quartet for the End of Time* emerged as a uniquely complicated piece, comprising eight movements and lasting approximately 50 minutes.

    I. Liturgie de cristal (Crystal Liturgy)—quartet
   II. Vocalise, pour l'Ange qui annonce la fin du Temps (Vocalise, for the Angel Announcing the End of Time)—quartet
  III. Abime des oiseaux (The Abyss of the Birds)—clarinet alone

IV. Intermede (Interlude)—violin, clarinet, and cello
V. Louange a l'Eternite de Jesus (Praise to the Eternity of Jesus)—cello and piano
VI. Danse de la fureur, pour les sept trompettes (Dance of Wrath, for the Seven Trumpets)—quartet
VII. Fouillis d'arcs—en—ciel, pour l'Ange qui annonce la fin du Temps (Tangle of Rainbows, for the Angel Announcing the End of Time)—quartet
VIII. Louange a l'immortalite de Jesus (In Praise of the Immortality of Jesus)—violin and piano

The piece's difficulty manifested not only technically for the performers but also conceptually. Messiaen's lifelong devotion to theological exploration and spiritual profundities had coalesced into a work that embodied the essence of his personal religious journey. *Quartet* also provided a forum to display his equally zealous musical experiments with time, timbre, and harmony. Knowing that this composition would present challenges to even expert musicians, Messiaen wrote a detailed preface to explain its intricacies and complexities for the work's publication after the war. In this preface, he outlined the musical goal of the piece. "Its musical language is essentially ethereal, spiritual, Catholic. The modes, realizing melodically and harmonically a sort of tonal ubiquity, bring the listener closer to infinity, to eternity in space. The special rhythms, independent of the meter, powerfully contribute to the effect of banishing the temporal."[10]

But despite the unity present in the composition's thematic and musical inspirations, *Quartet* can also appear to be a disjointed work. Its apparent incongruity stems from several factors, including that not all of the movements use the entire quartet of players. But more significantly, a few of the movements, such as "The Abyss of the Birds," were written prior to Messiaen's dream and can therefore seem only retroactively aligned with the thesis of the work. Contradictions also confront the listener's ear. Juxtaposed with the quite modern, and at times almost harsh music of *Quartet,* lie two beautiful movements, the "Louanges" or hymns of praise. Both originate from previous works by Messiaen, again contributing to the debate about the coherency of the theme. The fifth movement, "Louange a l'Eternite de Jesus" (Praise to the Eternity of Jesus) for cello and piano, was based on a composition titled *Fête des belles eaux* (Festival of Beautiful Waters) that Messiaen wrote in 1936 for six ondes Martenot, an experimental electronic instrument similar to the theremin. It was commissioned to accompany the fountains at the Paris Exhibition in 1937, requiring an intricate musical choreography to align with the movement of the water show. "Louange a l'immortalite de Jesus" (In Praise of the Immortality of Jesus), the final movement for violin and piano, originated from an organ work written in 1930 called *Diptyque*. It remains unknown why Messiaen chose to use borrowed material for the fifth and eighth movements, although some historians have suggested that he might have felt pressure to complete the work. It does seem likely that he wanted to provide solo movements for the other two instruments since the clarinet had such a virtuosic showpiece, but this could have been accomplished through newly composed music and would not have been dependent on recycling past work.

In the end, through an intriguing process that involved writing, arranging, borrowing, and assembling, Messiaen arrived at eight movements. His post-war preface discussed this intentional choice, but as with many of Messiaen's "explanations," it can lead the reader deeper into the labyrinth. "This *Quartet* comprises eight movements. Why? Seven is the perfect number, the Creation in six days sanctified by the divine Sabbath; the seventh day of this repose extends into eternity and becomes the eighth day of eternal light, of unalterable peace."[11] But oddly, in the eight-movement design, only half involve all four players. The third movement calls for clarinet alone. Movement five requires only cello and piano, and a violin and piano duo perform the eighth. The fourth movement is scored for a trio of violin, clarinet, and cello. So, during the course of the almost hour-long work, each instrument falls silent for at least 10 minutes, and instead of the expected grand finale to complete such a lofty opus, the piece concludes with only the violin and piano, leaving the clarinet and cello in silence for the closing 10 minutes of the piece. This unorthodox structure for a chamber work that designates itself a quartet in its very title has led to questions about whether the composer's choices represented a fragmented or flawed conception of the piece or merely constituted another intentional means of challenging centuries-old rules and expectations.

But despite whatever debates surround the architecture of *Quartet*, it remains patently clear that the piece represents Messiaen's complete embrace of a concept of musical time that deviated from the traditional approaches to pulse and meter. Messiaen's early rhythmic explorations, especially in irregular meters and unsteady pulses, had been influenced by Stravinsky's ballet *The Rite of Spring* and by the rhythmic patterns, known as tala, in the classical music of India. Messiaen expanded these ideas by breaking down rhythm into just two basic lengths, long and short, and then reconfiguring them into unorthodox patterns. This became one of the many techniques that he employed in *Quartet*. Since the entire premise of *Quartet* rested on a passage that claimed "…there shall be time no longer," Messiaen's temporal experiments contributed to the piece's conceptual realization. Although he might not have intended to bring about a complete halt to time, Messiaen could at least "…hint that time is more unruly and uncomprehended than earlier music had assumed."[12]

While the musical mechanics remain puzzling and at times impenetrable, the fact that Messiaen chose an apocalyptic theme for this work has remained the easiest aspect of the composition to understand. The Book of Revelation, with its colorful and astounding imagery, was one of Messiaen's favorite books of the Bible. As a child, Messiaen had loved fantasy and fairy tales, and this seemed to be the most fantastical of all tales. By the end of his career, Messiaen had composed a total of eight pieces that were inspired directly by the Revelation to John. Only one of those preceded his composition of *Quartet*, so it appears that this work unleashed a great passion for that subject matter.

It certainly does not seem a stretch that the cataclysmic events described in the Book of Revelation would be brought to mind during the apocalyptic times of World War II, although Messiaen rejected any suggestion that the parallel served as an impetus for *Quartet*. Messiaen did admit that being in the camp renewed his interest in reading and studying that final book of the New Testament. Along with his beloved musical scores, Messiaen's satchel held a small volume that contained the Psalms, the Gospels, the Epistles, and the Book of Revelation. At first, being imprisoned in the POW camp had caused Messiaen to sink into great despair. He felt that he would never compose again because all of his musical knowledge had somehow deserted him. But as he read in his little book, especially about an angel with a rainbow over his head, Messiaen began to rediscover hope. During this same time, as a result of food deprivation, he experienced spectacularly colored dreams while he slept that reminded him of the vivid allusions in the apocalyptic story. The kaleidoscopic visions that appeared in the prophetic narrative melded in his mind with the stained glass images from church windows that had mesmerized him since childhood. Messiaen then translated it all into a corresponding palette of chords and melodies to render a musical painting of the end of time.

In addition to religious iconography, Messiaen's *Quartet* showcases his love of birdsong, a fascination that had begun as the composer explored the countryside in Aube at age 15. While a few earlier composers and works had incorporated avian sounds, such as

Vivaldi's *The Four Seasons* (1725), Beethoven's *Pastoral Symphony* (1808), and Respighi's *Pines of Rome* (1924), Messiaen became the first composer to employ birdsong as a defining musical device. But of course, the birdsong in *Quartet* also raised some questions after the war due to Messiaen's own account of its inception. The issue centered on whether the fourth movement, "The Abyss of the Birds," was truly composed with *Quartet* in mind or was retrofitted into the work. Messiaen certainly loved the sound of the clarinet, most likely because it could imitate the various chirps and tweets of his beloved birds. So the presence of both the clarinet and birdsong in *Quartet* would not be surprising. But the story of the clarinet solo movement being written in Verdun before Messiaen's capture lends credence against any theory that the theme and construct of the grand piece was formed prior to his incarceration in a POW camp. When considering the complexity of factors surrounding the composition, it seems quite reasonable to conclude that the actual vision for *Quartet* unfolded over time, in response to Messiaen's various experiences at Stalag VIII A, and that Messiaen labored as an architect to build a monumental artifact that could transcend the circumstances in which he found himself.

That such a complex and profound work as *Quartet* found its genesis in the miserable and dehumanizing environment of a POW camp certainly demonstrated not only Messiaen's genius but his resilient spirit. Fortunately, the blossoming artistic and cultural life that paradoxically existed at Stalag VIII A provided the composer with several key factors needed to bring his new work to fruition, including a performance space and an interested audience. But first, the group of musicians poised to learn *Quartet* had to solve their most pressing problem—that only Akoka had an instrument.

Unlike in the concentration camps, where storehouses overflowed with instruments confiscated from the Jews, Stalag VIII A only had whatever a few captured soldiers might have brought in, plus some supplied later by the Red Cross. As with most items, instruments could be obtained by the prisoners if they somehow managed to earn the necessary money. As to Messiaen's immediate need of a violin and cello, less than 10 of the 30,000 soldiers in the camp possessed a string instrument, so the prospect of sharing presented a substantial logistical problem. Instead, Messiaen again garnered another special dispensation due to his reputation and to the Germans' desire to appear as patrons of the arts. According to an account by Abbé Jean Brossard, a French priest interned at Stalag VIII A, the head of the camp, Commandant Alois Bielas, decided to facilitate the acquisition of the instruments required to rehearse and premiere *Quartet*. Soon, Le Boulaire did get a violin, but the specifics surrounding its procurement remain unknown. Accompanied by two guards, Pasquier was actually allowed to go to an instrument dealer in the town of Görlitz to select a cello. Fellow prisoners had donated money toward its purchase; so with the 65 marks in his pocket, Pasquier bought an instrument, bow, and rosin. After returning to the camp, he spent the evening serenading the men around him with unaccompanied Bach and the hauntingly beautiful "Swan" from Saint-Saëns' *Carnival of the Animals*. Hungry and despairing, these prisoners gratefully received the solace that came from such sublime and intimate music.

Now, the chamber ensemble possessed a clarinet, a violin, and a cello, but not yet a piano. So, they focused on rehearsing the only collaborative movement that did not need the piano—the fourth. For the other movements, each musician practiced their parts independently so that they would be prepared for the whole work when the piano arrived. Meanwhile, once the new auditorium was ready in November 1940, Messiaen appeared often on the stage there. Chamber music performances became regularly scheduled events at 6 p.m. every Saturday evening. After approximately an hour of music, variety shows would follow to be concluded by the 9 p.m. curfew. Attending the Saturday night program cost 20 pfennigs, but despite the admission charge, the audience seats were always full.

The renovated space also became a popular venue for a diverse array of lectures presented by the prisoners. Messiaen gave a particularly memorable talk, by request of a Catholic priest, on imagery in the Book of Revelation. Titled "Colors and Numbers in the Apocalypse," Messiaen's lecture received support from a substantial and attentive audience of Catholic priests, which in turn left the composer feeling encouraged and energized. Sometime in November after Messiaen's presentation, the camp authorities arranged for a piano to be placed in the theater. Although horribly out-of-tune, the piano added a much needed component to all of the various forms of entertainment and art that happened there. Messiaen, Akoka, and Pasquier used it to perform Beethoven's *Trio in B-flat Major, Op. 11* to an enthusiastic crowd of prisoners. But more importantly for them, this piano would now supply the missing instrument for the new work.

By this time, Messiaen's reputation as a brilliant thinker and musical genius had spread throughout the camp, and fellow prisoners clamored to meet with him to discuss art, religion, and philosophy. Others sought advice from him, almost like audiences with the Pope. His aura of mystery intrigued them, and they grew especially curious about the peaceful demeanor he maintained amid the dehumanizing conditions of the POW camp and the uncertainties of when and how the war would end. Similarly, some also wanted to understand his unwavering faith in God when their present world seemed abandoned to hell.

But after the piano arrived, Messiaen became singularly focused on rehearsing and revising *Quartet* in preparation for the upcoming premiere, leaving less time for his admirers. The camp commandant allotted Messiaen and his ensemble members four hours a day for practice, which included both independent and group rehearsals. On weekdays, because of work duties such as Pasquier's in the kitchen, they would rehearse in the evenings, then rely heavily on the free time on Saturday afternoons for additional practice. But there were certainly challenges, especially as they often had to deal with disruptions and conflicts due to the number of other people who wanted to be in the theater space. Following the rehearsals, anything that Messiaen decided to adjust in his composition, he did late in the evenings after everyone else had gone to bed.

The intensity of the rehearsal process served to give structure and purpose to their days, as well as to solidify them as a "band of brothers." Chamber music certainly affords a much different experience than playing in a large orchestra. It imbues intimacy to the players' communication and relationship, and as a result, musical conversations occur that allow personalities, temperaments, and ideologies to express and engage, affecting not only the learning process but the creative interpretation of the music. The fact that Messiaen's *Quartet* was a newly composed work, and therefore open to revisions as they worked through it, amplified the impact that the performers themselves had on the realization of its final version. Fortunately, all four men were extremely compatible, which proved to be of paramount importance in their current endeavor. Nevertheless, they did not share Messiaen's religiosity, which had formed the basis for the work. Le Boulaire and Pasquier had both been raised in the Catholic Church, but were not practicing—Pasquier claiming an agnostic stance, and Le Boulaire professing atheism. Of Jewish descent, Akoka was also not a practitioner of his religious roots. Instead, he aligned himself ideologically with the Communist theory of world revolution advocated by Leon Trotsky. Outspoken and unapologetically proselytizing, Akoka encouraged any who would listen to embrace the ideals of political revolution. His charisma easily engaged people in conversation, and as an extremely well-read person, Akoka could speak on a great many subjects.

But despite the comradery that existed among the quartet, the group could not be totally egalitarian. Messiaen was the leader, the authority figure; and his genius, coupled with the great admiration that the other musicians had for him, certainly placed him in that position without rancor. They relied on his brilliance from a musical standpoint, and they leaned on his faith and optimism. In their perilous situation, his assurance that God remained in control affected them, even though they did not directly share his convictions. Le Boulaire and Pasquier seemed particularly influenced by Messiaen's belief in divine providence, making them at least question their own resistance to it and wonder if maybe Messiaen had found the true path.

Akoka and Messiaen were more diametrically opposed in their ideologies. While Messiaen relied on God, Akoka placed his faith in humanity. He believed that surviving this camp and the war rested, not on divine intervention, but in the ability of human beings to design their own solutions. Fueled by this assertion and his revolutionary spirit, Akoka resolved, even from the earliest days of his imprisonment, that he must escape from the camp rather than sit passively, waiting for whatever might befall him. After months of planning and storing up provisions, Akoka attempted an escape with two other prisoners in September 1940. The day before, he urged Messiaen to go with him, but the composer refused, saying, "God has willed that I be here."[13] Undeterred, Akoka and his two comrades snuck out of the camp and made it 350 miles over the course of a week before being caught by German soldiers. During that perilous week, Akoka never lost his clarinet, and upon his return to Stalag VIII A, he played for the camp commandant, hoping to avoid a harsh punishment. Akoka's situation, as a Jew, was more precarious than that of the average POW, and he could have easily been executed or sent to a concentration camp. His music must have charmed the German, somehow. Akoka landed in solitary confinement for several weeks, but the cell was warm and had enough light to read. His friends brought him food, and he relished the solitude that left him alone with his books. Soon after his release back into the general population, Akoka became immersed in a new project, the realization of a piece of music that would leave an indelible mark on his life.

Akoka and his fellow musicians had to overcome many impediments in the POW camp to bring Messiaen's composition to life, but none of it compared to the truly daunting task of playing the difficult *Quartet*. Fortunately, the composer also served as their rehearsal coach, guiding them through his avant-garde ideas about time and timbre. Rhythmically, the music required exacting precision from all four players in order to stay together, while simultaneously demanding freedom from the traditional confines of beat and meter. Messiaen also specified a great range of dynamics, especially insisting on the softest possible sounds, which often conflicted with the actual capabilities of the instruments, particularly the clarinet. Pasquier struggled as well because some of what Messiaen was asking him to do had never been written for the cello, and so Pasquier had to invent the technique needed to execute the musical figures. He also argued with the composer over the impossibly slow tempo marking of the fifth movement for cello and piano. Messiaen wanted to recreate the musical effect of eternity that he had achieved so easily on the organ, but Pasquier contended that there were limits to the amount of sustain that a string player could achieve with a finite amount of bow to draw through a single note. In response, Messiaen merely offered words of encouragement to the cellist, insisting that he could do it. Le Boulaire had a similar problem and complaint with his solo movement. He understood that the composer sought to depict a serene and ethereal future, but the practical matter of executing the effect proved elusive. In fact, throughout *Quartet*, Messiaen gave little concern to writing idiomatically, which in turn, left the performers to wage war with their instruments. He instead trusted that this composition would transcend the mortal limitations of instruments and players.

During these rehearsals, as Messiaen's fellow musicians heard the piece unfold, they felt more than a little perplexed about how moments of intense dissonance could be interwoven with delicate consonance and how a lyrical tune could suddenly emerge from such stark discord. They also grew concerned about how an audience might possibly respond to such a work. So with his players worrying about both their own performances and the reactions from their unsuspecting listeners, Messiaen frequently had to ply them with words of reassurance, but all the while insisting that the work be played exactly as indicated, regardless of the challenges. For future performers and audiences, Messiaen's preface would have to serve not only as an explanation of the work's genesis, but also as a commentary and guide on meeting its musical and technical demands.

After several months of meticulous rehearsals, Messiaen scheduled the premiere of *Quartet* for 6 p.m. on January 15, 1941. Commandant Bielas seized on this as an opportunity to advance his own career by touting that a renowned composer had written and premiered a major work in his camp. Bielas ordered the printing of a program and insisted that it prominently feature the name of the camp—Stalag VIII A, alongside the usual information of date, composition title, and performers. Designed by a fellow prisoner named Henri Breton, this small, one-sided program also served as a poster and invitation; and as news of the impending concert spread, prisoners began clamoring to get tickets.

The total number of audience members present for the premiere has been the subject of much debate. After the war, Messiaen himself reported estimates of in the thousands, but contradictory research has led historians to consider this as either harmless or unintentional hyperbole that, in time, took on mythic status. The auditorium on that January 15 was indeed packed, but its limited size meant that probably no more than about 400 people could have fit; and since it occurred in the dead of winter, there would have been no possibility of its taking place outdoors. But regardless of the numbers, the audience certainly proved diverse. Messiaen's popularity among the Catholic priests meant that their contingent had a strong presence. Doctors, guards, and officers also attended, along with a motley crew of prisoners who hailed from all walks of life, from farm and factory workers to artists and members of the intelligentsia. Hospital staff even transported sick prisoners on stretchers and laid them on the floor in front of the first row. The internal and external conditions certainly appeared less than ideal for any type of performance. Bitterly cold temperatures outside, accompanied by heavy snowfall, left the theater inadequately heated in addition to its already dim lighting. The performers had no clothing suitable for this kind of event and had to borrow a mismatch of pieces from other prisoners. In the end, they looked more like hobos than professional musicians. On their feet, they wore wooden clogs for shoes. But in the dangerous cold and deep snow, wooden clogs were actually a luxury and a commodity greatly in demand in Stalag VIII A. So on this night, they kept the quartet's feet warm and dry, in a way that their other worn-out shoes would not have.

At the appointed time, the four musicians walked onto stage without receiving much notice because the hall buzzed with the noisiness of a large number of excited and rowdy audience members. Messiaen made several attempts to quiet the group; and when finally successful, he gave a brief introduction to the piece. He wanted to share about his inspiration from the apocalyptic angel in Revelation and to explain his conceptual depictions of time and eternity. He even detailed some of the specific musical elements, such as modes and harmonic devices. Very few people in the audience were able to grasp, at least fully, what Messiaen described, but the aura of mystique and genius that surrounded him kept them respectfully attentive during the pre-concert lecture. Then when the music commenced, the protracted and unorthodox nature of the work became somewhat "lost in translation" to the untrained ears of the listeners. But while not truly understanding the composition, they did treat it with a silent deference throughout the performance.

As the last note of the piece reverberated through the theater, the audience continued their hushed vigil for a moment longer, followed by tentative applause that slowly grew into a fuller demonstration of appreciation for what had certainly become one of the most unique premieres in history. The performance generated lengthy discussions among audience members as they filed out and returned to their quarters. They wanted to understand, both musically and philosophically, what they had heard. Most remained perplexed, except for the realization that they had witnessed something great, something transcendent. The music had transported the room collectively out of the dire circumstances of that miserable camp. In the ensuing years, as the audience members and the performers recounted the event, the single consistent observation to emerge was that during that hour of music, the listeners sat in reverent silence as in a church. They sensed that they were somehow on holy ground.

That one evening and that one piece of music also left a profound impact on the performers. For Akoka and Le Boulaire, this premiere would be their first and last experience with *Quartet*, as their lives would diverge down different paths from their counterparts. In a few months' time, Messiaen and Pasquier would both perform the Paris premiere of the work and also play on its first recording in 1956 at the Scola Cantorum in Paris, the only recording ever made of Messiaen performing his *Quartet*.

As both the composer and performer, Messiaen would naturally serve as the primary witness for the historical record concerning the creation and inaugural performance of *Quartet*. Right away, however, Messiaen proved to be a somewhat unreliable narrator. When recalling the premiere, he embellished the event, even beyond his exaggerated audience size. Messiaen reported that the piano had sticking keys and that Akoka's clarinet was melted on the side. But the most legendary part of Messiaen's tale became that poor Pasquier had to play on a cello with only three strings. Frustrated by the misrepresentation, Pasquier continually insisted to the world and to Messiaen's face that his instrument possessed all four strings and that it would have been impossible to play that piece with a missing string. But when he would confront Messiaen, the composer would merely chuckle and then continue to tell the story of the three-stringed cello.

In light of these apparent discrepancies, researchers have worked to sift fact from fiction and thereby construct an accurate account of this important event. As a result, the prevailing view certainly concedes that the performance took place in poor conditions and with a less than acceptable piano, but acknowledges that some of the composer's other contentions fail to be rooted in reality. There has, of course, been much speculation about why such an esteemed composer, a man so religiously devout, would deliberately circulate misinformation. Did it just amuse him or was he looking for greater admiration? Or perhaps he was frustrated by the early criticism the work received. Through an extensive analysis of the composer's life, music, and philosophy, Messiaen scholar Rebecca Rischin has suggested that it seems more likely that this complicated man was trying to emphasize the miraculous nature of composing and premiering such a work in the horrible conditions of a POW camp. *Quartet* had been inspired by the grand intervention of divinity described in the Book of Revelation, and Messiaen wanted to make it clear that this premiere, in this unlikely of places, had also been blessed by a divine touch.

> In perpetuating the legend of the three-stringed cello, Messiaen imbued his story with an even greater aura of the miraculous, with an image of birds flying over the abyss, a quartet of musicians rising above the Apocalypse, redeeming the earth through music. In tattered clothing, in bitter cold, and on broken instruments, and at a time in which a real-life Apocalypse must have seemed imminent to many, these four men sang of resurrection, leading their audience in a musical prayer.[14]

Today, there can be little doubt as to the sacredness that undergirds *Quartet for the End of Time* or that it stands as a sui generis work—unique conceptually, thematically, and musically. Many composers, from Arnold Schoenberg to Krzysztof Penderecki, have written music in response to World War II and the Holocaust, and works were also composed in the camps, particularly in the German concentration camp Terezín, where Czech composers such as Pavel Haas created new pieces. But Messiaen became the only major composer to be imprisoned during that war and to produce a masterpiece in captivity that would enter the celebrated Western musical canon. Messiaen's *Quartet* further deviates from many of the other wartime compositions due to its overtly religious theme, particularly since it imparts the point of view of affirming faith and devotion rather than providing an existential meditation about the seeming absence of the Divine in such unfathomably dark and evil times. But Rischin does caution that Messiaen's unfailing optimism must be considered in the context that he was not Jewish, and therefore not under threat of extinction.

In addition to the piece's significance within the larger scope of the Western oeuvre, *Quartet* also occupies a rather rare niche within Messiaen's own catalog of works since the composer hardly ever wrote chamber music. *Quartet* represents one of only five chamber compositions, with three of those stemming from his early career, prior to the war. Its instrumentation also qualifies as unusual since works for clarinet, violin, cello, and piano remain uncommon. Of course, Messiaen's decision must have been grounded at least somewhat in pragmatism. He used what was available, although the quartet configuration was certainly not his only option. Finally, in considering its influence on Messiaen's development as a composer, *Quartet* represents early and seminal inclusions of birdsong and temporal aberrations, and thus serves as a conduit for his lifelong musical explorations.

But for Messiaen and the other three musicians in 1941, thoughts regarding the future fate of *Quartet* probably did not venture beyond their immediate enthusiasm at having learned a unique and challenging work that they then shared on a snowy evening with their fellow captives. They actually had little time to contemplate such things or even consider a second performance, because in what could seem almost anti-climactic following the long-awaited *Quartet* premiere, Messiaen and Pasquier were released from Stalag VIII A less than a month later. As with so many aspects of this story, contradictory information abounds regarding the circumstances of that release. Suggested reasons range from the influence of Marcel Dupré, Messiaen's teacher at the Paris Conservatory, to negotiations by the Vichy government to secure the freedom of at least some of the intellectuals and artists who were part of the million plus French captured in 1940. Most likely, the truth lies in multiple forces and people.

Hauptmann Karl-Albert Brüll continued to be a supporter of Messiaen and enjoyed the thought of being friendly with a renowned composer. He informed Messiaen that some prisoners were to be released and that he wanted to help Messiaen be part of that group. At this time, the Germans appeared willing to release POWs who carried the military designation of "soldier-musicians," unarmed personnel whose conscription in the army had been solely to perform music. This was certainly the case for Akoka, but not true for Messiaen, Le Boulaire, or Pasquier. While many in the camp assumed them to be soldier-musicians, they had no papers that could impart that status. Fortunately, Pasquier learned that another classification of prisoner could also be freed—anyone who had been part of the unarmed medical personnel. But even though Messiaen had served as an orderly, for some reason, his papers must not have indicated that, and Pasquier did not qualify either. So under the supervision of Brüll, Pasquier forged his and Messiaen's papers, adding the designation of "orderly" to their rank.

In February 1941, Messiaen, Pasquier, and Akoka gathered with a group slated for release. But as Akoka was climbing aboard the transport, a German officer appeared and ordered him back down. Akoka protested, citing that he was a soldier-musician and therefore eligible for release. In response, the German just pointed and called him a Jew. So the devastated Akoka returned to Stalag VIII A, while Messiaen and Pasquier continued toward their freedom with a stop in Constance, Switzerland, and then on to a holding camp in Lyon, France. During their three-week stay at Lyon, Pasquier resumed his kitchen duties. Then, Messiaen and Pasquier boarded a train to Paris, where both spent several weeks recuperating with family. They needed food and rest to regain their strength so they could reclaim their lives. Messiaen longed to sit on the organ bench again at Trinity, and Pasquier was eager to rejoin the Paris Opera Orchestra.

By March, Messiaen had already resumed composing. In May, the Paris Conservatory appointed him to its faculty as the replacement for harmony professor André Bloch, who had been fired in 1940 as part of the anti–Semitic policies imposed by the German occupation. Messiaen had not yet recovered when he began teaching. A student in his first class, Yvonne Loriod, later recounted how taken aback she and her classmates were by Messiaen's physical appearance, a man painfully thin but with terribly swollen fingers caused by chilblains from the extreme cold of that camp. Malnutrition had also caused him to lose hair and teeth, and severe food rationing left him even in Paris without enough food, making rehabilitation a slow and difficult process. It also proved a challenging time for him emotionally. Messiaen's wife was unwell, and so he bore most of the responsibility to care for their son Pascal in addition to his jobs of organist, professor, and composer.

On May 17, 1941, Messiaen submitted his handwritten manuscript of *Quartet,* with all of the scribbled in revisions, to the French publisher Durand. As the one and only score that Messiaen had used in the camp, some of its pages absurdly bore a stamp indicating that it had been approved by the command at Stalag VIII A. Unfortunately, it would take Durand a year to publish the first edition, and then only in a limited run of 100 copies due to paper shortages. Undeterred by the delay, Messiaen scheduled the Paris premiere of the work for the following month on June 24, a Tuesday evening at 5 p.m., in the Théâtre de Mathurins. The concert organizers intended the event to be not just a showcase for this monumental composition, but a celebration of Messiaen's survival and reunion with his beloved Paris. The program featured many of Messiaen's other works, including a set of songs and the *Theme and Variations* for violin and piano that he had written in 1932 as a wedding gift for his wife. Messiaen played the piano part for his four songs performed by soprano Marcelle Bunlet, as well as for his *Quartet.* Messiaen's devoted new student Loriod turned his pages. Pasquier reprised his role as cellist in the quartet and brought along his brother Jean to play the violin part. Clarinetist André Vacellier was recruited from Paris' Opéra Comique to complete the ensemble. As in the camps, the audience and critics, although obviously more musically astute, struggled with the work's style and its religious implications. A few expressed actual anger by what they considered as its attempt at Christian apologetics.

Meanwhile, as Messiaen and Pasquier enjoyed their earliest days of freedom, Akoka and Le Boulaire were still imprisoned in the POW camp. Akoka ruminated day and night about how he could escape or secure a release. He discovered that the International Committee of the Red Cross (ICRC) had lodged a complaint that stated that any prisoners who had been born in the French colonies of Africa could not withstand the cold climate in Silesia and should be transferred to more suitable locations. Since Akoka had been born in Algeria, his dark skin finally proved advantageous for him. To pacify the ICRC, the Germans transferred Akoka in March 1941, along with a group of Arabs, to Dinan, France, from where they were supposed to be liberated. But something went awry with that plan, and the next month the Germans prepared to ship the whole lot back to Stalag VIII A. Fiercely determined not to go back there, Akoka concocted an escape plan. As the train passed through a French village named Saint-Julian-du-Sault, Akoka convinced his fellow passengers to help him climb through on opening in the roof of the car. So in the middle of the night and from the top of a moving train, he jumped, with his clarinet held tightly under his arm. He survived the fall, but lay unconscious at the side of a riverbank, with an injury to his hand. Two railroad workers found him and took him to a doctor, who at great risk decided not to turn Akoka over to the German authorities. Instead, he hid him in his home for a month while he recovered. Akoka then used his connections with a fellow student from his days at the Paris Conservatory to get a forged certificate of baptism that could help him escape to the Free Zone, which he did. By this time, the Orchestre National de la Radio had evacuated from Paris to Marseilles, and Akoka rejoined them there. Throughout it all, his clarinet had never left his side.

The war had certainly taken a toll on the Akoka family, as three of the four sons had ended up POWs. Their father, Abraham Akoka, who had served heroically in the French military during World War I, was then arrested on December 13, 1941, by French police on orders from the Vichy government. The initial reason for his arrest had nothing to do with his Jewish ancestry, but resulted from a roundup of anyone suspected of involvement with the French Resistance. Their real target had been his son Georges, an active member of the Resistance. But not being able to find him, the frustrated authorities retaliated by snatching his father. Abraham Akoka assumed that he would be released right away because of his status as a veteran. Instead, officials deported him to Auschwitz in September 1942, where the guards gassed him immediately upon arrival.

On November 11, 1942, the day the Germans seized control of all of France, Henri Akoka was living with his brother Pierre and sister Yvonne in Marseilles. Although food scarcity presented ongoing problems for them, the Akoka siblings worried very little about their Jewishness since they resided in the Free Zone. Now, with no such thing as a Free Zone, they procured false papers under assumed names, and when the Orchestre National de la Radio moved back to Paris, they used these forged documents to relocate with it. They managed to elude detection, and after the liberation of Paris on August 25, 1944, they reunited with their other siblings, all having miraculously survived. Now collectively, they could mourn their father's death and the subsequent passing of their brokenhearted mother in January 1943. Henri Akoka married pharmacist Jeanette Chevalier in 1947, and they had two children. Akoka continued a successful orchestral career, becoming the assistant principal clarinet for the Orchestre Philharmonique de Radio France in 1946. He was held in great esteem by his colleagues for his exceptional tone and technical facility. Some even christened him with the nickname, "the Kreisler of the clarinet."[15] He and Messiaen occasionally met up at various musical events, and their encounters remained warm, however infrequent. Akoka never played *Quartet for the End of Time* again. He retired as a professional orchestral musician in 1971 and died at age 63 on November 22, 1975. Messiaen sent a heartfelt condolence letter to Akoka's widow, in which he praised Akoka's artistry, intelligence, and charm. It was clear from the letter that Messiaen deeply felt the loss of Akoka, whose membership in the quartet at Stalag VIII A had forged an indelible bond between the two that transcended the earthly constraints of time and place.

For their compatriot Etienne Pasquier, life after his release from Stalag VIII A also ventured down a musical path. Following the Paris premiere of *Quartet* with Messiaen, Pasquier continued to perform during the war with the Paris Opera Orchestra and an occasional concert with his Trio Pasquier. But since travel remained impossible, the trio would have to wait to reclaim its pre-war stature until they could resume touring. After 1945, the Trio Pasquier did gain international recognition, performing approximately 3,000 concerts around the world. Pasquier also focused on reestablishing a life with his wife Suzanne Gouts, whom he had married in 1929; the two never had children. As with Akoka, Pasquier rarely saw Messiaen, but the two continued to consider each other fondly. After his retirement from playing, Pasquier was frequently called upon to speak about the premiere of *Quartet for the End of Time* in Stalag VIII A. Etienne Pasquier died on December 14, 1997, at the age of 92.

As Messiaen, Pasquier, and Akoka had restarted their lives in the early months of 1941, one member of their quartet had been left behind. After the departure of his three friends, Le Boulaire's life at Stalag VIII A seemed even more miserable. He decided to emulate his friend Akoka and attempt an escape in October 1941. The German guards caught him and two fellow prisoners after three days and sent them back to the camp. Toward the end of 1941, Messiaen's guardian angel Brüll again stepped in to help this last of the quartet's members. By this time, Brüll had become quite adept as a forger, somehow creating false stamps out of potatoes. He forged Le Boulaire's papers so that he was listed as an orderly and therefore eligible for release. Why Brüll had not done this back when he falsified documents for Messiaen and Pasquier remains unknown.

By early 1942, Le Boulaire had also returned to Paris, but spent his days feeling unhappy and unsettled. He had concluded that his career as a violinist was doomed because the interruption of the war had cost him those critical years that he had needed for studying and practicing. Concerned about Le Boulaire's depression, an actress friend suggested that he come read an audition with her at the Sarah-Bernhardt Theater. Surprisingly, the director Charles Dullin cast him for a minor role, but insisted that he change his last name to something shorter. So, Jean Le Boulaire forever became Jean Lanier. Next, he landed a substantial role in Shakespeare's *Richard III* and then was cast in the premiere of Jean-Paul Sartre's *Les mouches*. The theater stage provided a rebirth for Lanier that led to a prolific career in television and film and a dramatic personal life with several marriages and children. He died in Paris on April 9, 1999, at age 85.

While during their POW days, the four musicians' fates had been intertwined as they worked to prepare *Quartet*; after achieving their respective freedoms, each had to fashion his own destiny, including their leader. Despite his pre-war successes, Messiaen struggled to restart his career. He grew increasingly frustrated by the Vichy government's apparent ambivalence toward him, especially in failing to offer him a commission even though they were actively championing other French composers and artists. Messiaen's early days teaching at the Paris Conservatory similarly provided little satisfaction. Due to the school's conservative nature, Messiaen's appointment there had been off-putting to some of the faculty and government officials who feared the repercussions that his unorthodox approach to music might have. The Société des Concerts du Conservatoire even completely ignored Messiaen's *Quartet* when they sponsored a concert on January 11, 1942, featuring works written by "Composers in the Camp." The program included two pieces by composers Jean Martinon and Maurice Thiriet, both imprisoned in Stalag IX A. But to represent Messiaen, the concert organizers chose *Les offrandes outbliées*, a composition he had written in 1930. Some historians have suggested that the disregard for *Quartet* at that time had more to do with its religious subject matter and its lack of overt references to the POW experience than its unconventional musical style. Regardless, except for a few private performances, Messiaen would have to wait until after the war for his *Quartet* to receive its much due public hearing.

Messiaen's job at the Paris Conservatory also felt stilted because his teaching position had been limited to harmony courses only. Not being allowed to teach composition most likely stemmed from the Nazis' negative attitude toward modernists. They had labeled atonal and avant-garde works as part of their "degenerate" music list, along with jazz and pieces by Jewish composers. As a result, the Nazi government heavily censored performances of newly composed works by French composers. Nevertheless, Messiaen continued to compose prolifically on his own and without compromising his style, which did not reflect the stereotypical restrained music of the French masters, such as Gabriel Fauré and Erik Satie. Messiaen's harmonies often juxtaposed traditional chordal structures with experimental sounds, and his music oscillated back and forth freely between consonance and dissonance. Messiaen insisted "…that God was present everywhere and in all sound. Therefore, there was no need for the new to supersede the old…"[16] His openness to making room for all sounds within conventional Western music served as a role model for later composers, including John Cage. Indeed, Messiaen found inspiration sometimes in the most unlikely places. In his 1944 piano cycle, *Vingt Regards sur l'enfant-Jésus* (Twenty Contemplations on the Infant Jesus), even the influence of George Gershwin can be heard in the jazzy rhythms and the echoes of Gershwin's tuneful melodies.

Following some difficult months at the Conservatory, Messiaen enthusiastically accepted an invitation to teach informal composition courses out of the home of Guy-Bernard Delapierre, the Egyptologist that he had met during those early days of captivity when they had shared a moment of respite through reading while their peers fought over water. Messiaen attracted eager students, including Yvonne Loriod and Pierre Boulez, who became loyal followers. His disciples nicknamed themselves "les fléches" (the Arrows) and enjoyed invoking a pun on their teacher's name, referring to him as "Messiaenic." Of this group, Boulez, in particular, would become a shaping force in the avant-garde music of the second half of the century, alongside other visionary contemporaries such as John Cage, Luciano Berio, and Karlheinz Stockhausen.

Messiaen developed an especially close relationship with his protégé, the remarkable pianist Loriod. During this time, he composed two pieces dedicated to her, both of which she premiered—*Visions de l'Amen* (Visions of the Amen, 1943) and *Vingt regards sur l'-Enfant-Jésus* (Twenty Contemplations on the Infant Jesus, 1944). A strong and courageous woman, Loriod defied the Nazis by playing the works of Mendelssohn, a banned Jewish composer, for her recital encores. She also provided tremendous help and support to Messiaen throughout his wife's prolonged illness. Due to complications from a failed operation in 1949, Claire Delbos suffered cerebral atrophy leading to total amnesia and spent the remainder of her life in an institution. After her death in 1959, Messiaen and Loriod waited a respectful period before marrying in 1961. By this time, Loriod also taught at the Paris Conservatory and enjoyed an international career as a concert pianist, which included premiering many of Messiaen's works for the piano, as well as those of other composers such as Bela Bartók.

Despite Messiaen's rigorous wartime schedule, he embarked on an ambitious project to outline his compositional devices in a theoretical treatise, which was published in 1944 as *Technique de mon langage musical* (The Technique of My Musical Language). Never content with his own status quo, Messiaen began experiments in the late 1940s on a system that would expand the concept of serialism that Schoenberg had invented. In Messiaen's approach, later known as total serialism, music would be formed from patterns of not only pitches, as Schoenberg had done, but from predetermined sequences of other musical elements including rhythm and dynamics. Messiaen became the first composer to serialize three elements together in one composition, a piece for piano called *Mode de valeurs et d'intensités* (Scale of Durations and Dynamics, 1949). Later, Boulez would build on his teacher's method by adding articulation as another variable, thereby creating sets of ordered rhythm, pitch, volume, and articulation.

The post-war years presented challenges for many artists who struggled to create work that seemed relevant in this changed world, and Messiaen felt a bit lost as well, despite his forays into serialism. Then in the early 1950s, he embraced a new undertaking that would become his life's work—transcribing birdsong. Messiaen devoted much time and energy to organized birding trips, which allowed him to listen intently to their myriad of songs. He approached this endeavor, not as a hobbyist, but as a scientific researcher, carefully transcribing avian melodies into formal music notation. In time, he would

Olivier Messiaen with his wife Yvonne Loriod at the piano, c. 1971 (Nationaal Archief/Collectie Spaarnestad/Fotograaf onbekend).

travel all over the world carrying his bird identification manuals, binoculars, and a tape recorder. Messiaen's goal of creating a comprehensive musical catalog of birdsong was certainly not an easy venture, as the speed and high pitched nature of birdsong, plus unpitched sounds, proved difficult to confine to a traditional music staff. Messiaen had, of course, already experimented with incorporating bird sounds into his work, specifically a blackbird and a nightingale in his "The Abyss of the Birds" movement for *Quartet*. Now, birdsong melodies would become one of the dominant motifs in his instrumental works. His first piece to feature birdsong in this way was *Réveil des oiseaux* (Awakening of the Birds) for piano and chamber ensemble, which premiered in 1953. It displayed the songs of dozens of birds, and at one point, showcased 21 different bird species singing together at dawn. The use of this new device certainly represented a paradigm shift for the composer, as through it, Messiaen surrendered some of his compositional control to forces outside of himself, confessing that he was "anxious to disappear behind the birds."[17]

After having departed from sacred-themed works in the 1950s, Messiaen returned to those roots in the 1960s, completing a large-scale work for chorus, instrumental soloists, and orchestra in 1969 called *La Transfiguration de Notre Seigneur Jésus-Christ* (The Transfiguration of Our Lord Jesus Christ). Interestingly, Messiaen chose to incorporate Gregorian chant into this piece, heralding him back to the concept of medieval plainchant, which rejected any interest in the forward movement of time so as to search for the eternal and divine. This choice might also have served as his indicting response to The Second Vatican Council's decision just a few years earlier to shift the language of the Mass from Latin to the vernacular. But his return to the spiritual realm did not signal an abandonment of his birdsong. In fact, Messiaen grew more and more interested in the natural world and how it could be depicted in his compositions, eventually turning also to fauna and landscape elements.

In 1970, Alice Tully, the renowned New York arts patron, offered Messiaen a commission to write a piece for America's upcoming bicentennial celebration. Reluctant at first because of his dislike for New York, Messiaen finally acquiesced when Tully allowed that the theme could focus on another area of the United States. He researched the landscape of the U.S. in pursuit of an inspiring location, finally choosing the canyons of Utah. Messiaen timed a trip to view these canyons that coincided with a recording project in Washington State of his *La Transfiguration* and immediately fell in love with the vibrantly colored landscape. He could not help but also notate the songs of the birds he encountered there. Messiaen produced what would become possibly his greatest work, *From the Canyons to the Stars...* , a suite of 12 movements, lasting 100 minutes for solo piano and orchestra. In 1978, Utah returned the favor, renaming one of its mountains, Mount Messiaen.

By the early 1970s, a retrospective look at Messiaen's complete catalog of works clearly revealed a compositional design in which the perennial ideas that had grounded him from his earliest years allowed for interstices filled with his equally lifelong propensity for the unfamiliar. Yet, despite the love Messiaen had felt for opera since childhood, he arrived near the end of his career without ever having composed one. Then in 1975, Rolf Liebermann, the director of the Paris Opéra, asked Messiaen to write an opera for them. Messiaen declined at first, but eventually gave in to the extremely persuasive Liebermann. The resulting *Saint François d'Assise* (St. Francis of Assisi) became Messiaen's longest and grandest work. At over four hours, it ranked with the epic music dramas of Richard Wagner, and also like Wagner, Messiaen insisted on full control over all of the elements, which included writing his own libretto. He chose the subject of St. Francis because of how closely he considered the saint to resemble Christ and because of St. Francis' habit of conversing with birds. Messiaen began writing the libretto in the summer of 1975, but did not deliver the finished score to the Opéra until over eight years later in 1983. Musically, Messiaen's opera created a composite of his many compositional devices, combining elements from birdsong to unorthodox rhythmic structures, all shrouded within a theme of spiritual exaltation. In actuality, Messiaen had calibrated every aspect of his opera to a grand scale. The full score constituted 2,000 pages and called for a pit orchestra of 120 players that, in addition to extremely large brass and percussion sections, required three ondes Martenot, the electronic instruments that Messiaen had written for early in his career. Since the standard orchestra pit could not hold that many players, they spread out into the boxes of the audience and onto platforms added on each side of the stage. Messiaen had succeeded in literally juxtaposing the music and the drama, forcing the action to occur not above the orchestra, but within it.

By the time of the opera's premiere in November 1983, Messiaen had been gone from the Paris Conservatory for several years, having reached their mandatory retirement age in 1978. After a less than satisfying start at the Conservatory in 1941, Messiaen charted a path there that grew into a successful and fulfilling career. He stretched the curriculum and challenged his students to embrace not only contemporary classical works, but to explore nonwestern music. In 1966, after 25 years, he was finally allowed to teach actual composition courses. During this time, Messiaen evolved into an international celebrity, receiving commissions from all over the world and inspiring festivals devoted solely to his music.

In 1986, Messiaen received further proof of his adoration by the musical world and the French people when the government awarded him France's most prestigious medal, the Grand-Croix de la Légion d'honneur. Also as a testament to Messiaen's enduring legacy, *Quartet for the End of Time* had become one of the most widely acclaimed chamber pieces in the repertoire. It received a special 50th anniversary performance in Görlitz at St. Peter's Church on January 15, 1991, but Messiaen's declining health, plus the difficult memories associated with that place, prevented him from attending. Olivier Messiaen died the following year in Paris on April 28, 1992, at age 83. He had composed to the end, with his wife at his side to help him complete a last work, a piece for orchestra titled *Eclairs sur l'au-delà…* (Lightning over the Beyond…). It was finished only two weeks before his passing, surely a fitting theme for Messiaen's last days and possibly a harbinger that Messiaen's soul would soon ascend to the great beyond.

Along with an unfinished concerto for piano, cello, flute, and oboe, Messiaen left behind a monumental project, an intended seven-volume treatise that would encapsulate his entire creative process and product. Loriod labored with tireless devotion from 1992 to 2002 to finish her husband's magnum opus. On its completion, the seven-volume *Treatise on Rhythm, Color, and Ornithology* surpassed 2,100 pages. During those years, Loriod also became director of La Fondation Olivier Messiaen that had been established in 1994 to promote and preserve the composer's works. Part of the preservation charge involved the maintaining of Messiaen's beloved home and garden in Petichet, which had served as his retreat for over 50 years.

But while Loriod worked to bring closure to Messiaen's life, there remained an unresolved thread dating from his time in Stalag VIII A—Karl-Albert Brüll, the camp guard who had treated Messiaen so well during his captivity and had enabled his early release. After the war, Brüll remained in Görlitz, then part of East Germany, and resumed his work as a lawyer. He became involved in a failed political insurrection in 1948, resulting in a three-year sentence of hard labor. After being released from prison, he relocated to West

Germany. Brüll had never forgotten his fond association with Messiaen and wanted to visit the composer, but felt hesitant to approach him directly. Instead, in 1968, Brüll contacted another one of his former Stalag VIII A POWs, David Gorouben, a French Jew who had remained in touch with his erstwhile guard over the years. Brüll persuaded Gorouben to write a letter to Messiaen in an effort to reestablish their connection. The letter gently reminded the composer of Brüll's role in his liberation and requested a visit, but it does not appear that Messiaen responded. Gorouben then acquired Messiaen's home address and took Brüll there. But the concierge turned the two men away, saying that Messiaen refused to meet with them. The whole episode left Brüll terribly disappointed and hurt. According to Loriod, Messiaen later attempted to make contact with his former guard, but was unsuccessful.

In the years following Messiaen's death, researchers have continued to be drawn toward the fascinating life and work of this composer who stretched the musical language of Western music to unprecedented realms. But despite the many advances achieved by Messiaen, it truly remains his "…unswerving focus on God that gives his music its reason to be, and to be as it is."[18] "God spoke to Messiaen through sounding tones, whether the mighty roar of the orchestra or the church organ, the clattering of exotic percussion, or the songs of birds."[19] Messiaen certainly viewed the world and its natural elements through the lens of his spiritually attuned eyes. In an interview, he famously articulated his intersection of faith and music by saying, "My faith is the grand drama of my life. I'm a believer, so I sing words of God to those who have no faith. I give bird songs to those who dwell in cities and have never heard them, make rhythms for those who know only military marches or jazz, and paint colors for those who see none."[20]

Today, in Görlitz where Stalag VIII A once stood, there lies a memorial to all prisoners of war called the Place of National Memory. A veteran's organization known as the Society of Former War Prisoners of Oflags and Stalags of the Military District VIII had spearheaded the campaign for a memorial as there seemed a sense that the place and the suffering had been forgotten. The memorial was dedicated on July 22, 1976, and includes a plaque that bears this inscription: "A place sanctified by the blood and martyrdom of the prisoners of war of the anti–Hitler coalition during the Second World War, 22 July, 1976."[21]

Later, in 2004, plans were drafted to establish an international cultural and educational center on that site that would honor Messiaen's legacy and his universal philosophy of music. While serving as a reminder of the historical significance of what had happened there during World War II, the European Education and Culture Centre Zgorzelec-Görlitz would also invest in the future by training local students and offering a place where all people who shared the spirit of tolerance and openness could come to dialogue. After four years of planning, builders laid the foundation stone in 2008, and over the next seven years, the construction project developed into a large complex that housed a museum and state-of-the-art educational facilities. An association was formed specifically to support its mission called Meetingpoint Music Messiaen, and Messiaen's widow Yvonne Loriod became the main patron and visionary for the center, working tirelessly as an advocate until her death in 2010.[22] The Centre opened on January 15, 2015, 74 years to the day that Messiaen's *Quartet for the End of Time* premiered there in a POW camp.

7

Dmitri Shostakovich and the Musical Redemption of Leningrad

Music is life after all. What is life without music?
—Ksenia Matus, oboist in the premiere of the Seventh
Symphony in Leningrad, quoted in M. T. Anderson,
Symphony for the City of the Dead, 349

On the Eastern shore of the Baltic Sea stands one of the grandest symbols of the Russian people—the city of St. Petersburg. Founded in 1703[1] by Peter the Great as an homage to St. Peter, this new capital of Russia would provide the seat from which each Tsar ruled and held court for the next two centuries. Over time, St. Petersburg emerged as a progressive and forward-looking city and acquired the epithet, "Window to the West," as it most closely resembled its Western European counterparts in science, literature, and the arts. But with the dawn of the 20th century, that same enlightened region of Eastern Europe, while retaining the grandeur of its legacy for the wealthy, paradoxically still housed poor, undeveloped villages filled with hungry peasants. These citizens made up the majority of the Russia population, and due to an economy that had failed to industrialize and a social structure that had not evolved from medieval days, they lived not much differently from their ancestors. Russia's middle class citizens, in particular, could see how far their country lagged behind the modernization and prosperity of Western Europe and the United States. They knew that the sole way forward rested in bringing those ideas and structures to Russia, a move which could only happen by overthrowing the repressive rulers who held the country hostage to the status quo. As a first step, they tried to enact change by protests at the palace of Tsar Nicholas II, hoping that their pleas and petitions would move him to action. But at a march during the winter of 1905, the Tsar's forces turned on the protesters, slaughtering hundreds of them. This day, known as Bloody Sunday, would signal the beginning of the end for the 300-year Romanov dynasty.

Over the next 12 years, Russian citizens from all walks of life demanded change, protesting and challenging the poor living conditions as millions of their fellow residents starved to death. Some of these revolutionaries, however, crossed the line into violence, committing terrorist acts that resulted in thousands of fatalities. Still, the Tsar remained unmoved. While the majority of their people lived in desperate situations, the Tsar and his family resided in gilded palaces and enjoyed lavish dinners and parties, remaining ambivalent and out of touch with the people they were charged with protecting, even as a catastrophic war advanced to their doorstep.

With the start of World War I in 1914, the Russian Empire changed the name of its beloved city St. Petersburg to Petrograd, as a way to distance themselves from the language of their German enemies, since "burg" was the German word for fortress. Tsar Nicholas II, who had not been a particularly effective leader throughout failed military conflicts with Japan, proved equally inept during World War I. Instead of seeking counsel from the knowledgeable officials surrounding him, the Tsar relied on advice from a depraved dabbler in the occult and self-professed mystic and healer from Siberia named Grigori Rasputin.

As the Great War dragged on, the Russians suffered tremendous losses and came face to face with the reality that they no longer constituted the military might they had so prided themselves in being. As their economy and political problems found no reprieve, the unrest mounted. Revolutionaries murdered Rasputin in December 1916 in hopes of garnering the Tsar's attention, but again to no avail. Then on February 27, 1917, as a mob of protesters took to the streets once more, the tide finally shifted in favor of the revolutionaries. Instead of following the order given by the Tsar's police to quell the uprising with their sabers, the mighty Russian horsemen, known as the Cossacks, turned against the government and sided with the people. Chaos erupted in the streets as the police and the army battled each other and as emboldened workers accosted their oppressors, including cruel factory bosses. On March 2, Tsar Nicholas II abdicated, finally conceding that all was lost. The Russian leadership quickly established a Provisional Government and exiled the Tsar and his family to a place near the Ural Mountains. While this house arrest spared them for a time, the Tsar and his family would be executed the following year on July 16, 1918, because of fears that counterrevolutionary forces might free them.

During this tumultuous time, Dmitri Dmitriyevich Shostakovich, a young boy who would eventually rank as one of Russia's most influential composers, was coming into his own as a musician. Shostakovich had been born into a family who found their place among the intelligentsia and the revolutionaries, dating back to a great-grandfather who had been active in political uprisings in the 1830s and then a grandfather who had been exiled to Siberia for his involvement in a failed assassination attempt of Tsar Alexander II in 1866. Shostakovich also had an aunt who wrote pro–Communist documents, which she hid from the authorities in her stove. Another aunt had married a government insurgent and ended up spending time in prison.

The progressive spirit also resided as close as the young composer's home. Shostakovich's mother Sofia, an educated woman who had studied piano at the St. Petersburg Conservatory, helped Jews fleeing from the pogroms to find hiding places during times of intense anti–Semitism. Shostakovich's father, Dmitri Boleslavovich Shostakovich, had participated in the protest on Bloody Sunday in 1905. A graduate from St. Petersburg University, where he had studied mathematics and physics, he had remained in the city to work as an engineer at the Bureau for Weights and Measures. Known as a good-natured man with an excellent singing voice, Dmitri Boleslavovich Shostakovich also approached life as a perpetual optimist who loved to tinker with puzzles and gadgets. Shostakovich's parents had married in 1903 and welcomed a daughter they named Maria that same year. Dmitri, affectionately known by his family as Mitya, was born on September 25, 1906. A younger sister named Zoya would be added to the family in 1908. Like her brother, Maria would devote her life to music as a pianist, while their little sister Zoya would pursue veterinary medicine.

Shostakovich's parents surrounded their children with privilege, including not only a stellar education from tutors, but also material wealth in the form of servants and an automobile. They also provided them with a stimulating home environment that celebrated literature and music and regularly hosted a cadre of the cultural elite of the day. All three siblings received piano lessons and attended operas and concerts that exposed them to the music of the great Russian masters, such as Pyotr Ilyich Tchaikovsky. They also gained familiarity with the music of Mozart by listening to the cellist who lived in the apartment next door to them, whose practicing wafted through the walls. In fact, just walking through the magnificent city of St. Petersburg offered an education in itself, especially passing the many concert halls and locales associated with The Russian Five, also known as The Mighty Handful, an esteemed group of five 19th century Russian composers. The goal of this group, which included Alexander Borodin, Modest Mussorgsky, and Nikolai Rimsky-Korsakov, had been to create a truly nationalistic style of Russian art music, instead of mimicking the classical tradition from Western Europe. One of their inspirations had rested in the influential Russian writer Alexander Pushkin. Pushkin had brought legitimacy to the Russian language as a medium for literature, poetry, and song, much in the same way that Goethe had solidified the suitability of the German language for artistic expression. Since language constitutes such a fundamental element of nationalism in any given people, Pushkin certainly instilled pride among Russians with works such as his much celebrated novel *Eugene Onegin*, which later became the basis for an opera by Tchaikovsky. Another of Pushkin's creations, a poem, also inspired Rimsky-Korsakov's fairy tale opera, *The Tale of Tsar Saltan* (1900). Shostakovich's parents took the children to see a production of this opera. All three were thrilled by the many fantastical aspects of the story, especially by the prince who gets turned into a bumblebee and flies around accompanied by a mesmerizingly fast instrumental interlude. "Flight of the Bumblebee" would become not only the most enduring piece from the whole opera, but arguably one of the most recognizable pieces in the Western canon.

When not engaged with exciting operatic productions and other cultural events, the young Shostakovich appeared quiet, shy, and introspective, preferring to keep his own company on long walks. But paradoxically his family also knew him to be a prankster who took delight in small acts of mischief. Shostakovich approached music, however, with a seriousness and maturity way beyond his years. He had begun piano lessons in 1915 at age 9 with his mother and then later enrolled at a notable music school run by Ignatiy Gliasser. In just two years, Shostakovich had acquired an astounding proficiency throughout the piano repertoire, from the fugues of Bach to the sonatas of Beethoven and the polonaises of Chopin.

Meanwhile, the events of February 27, 1917, warranted great excitement in the Shostakovich house as the parents celebrated what certainly marked the end of the Tsar's reign and the dawn of the change for which they had been hoping and striving. The enthusiasm extended to their children as well, who tied on red arm bands and marched around the apartment. Then in March, during bitterly cold weather, millions of citizens of Petrograd, including the Shostakovich family, lined the streets to witness the funeral procession and then burial of the fallen heroes of the Revolution. On returning home, 10-year-old Shostakovich sought solace at the piano, composing a memorial piece he called, *Funeral March for the Victims of the Revolution*. It became a companion piece to an earlier composition, *Hymn of Freedom*, also in honor of the Revolution.

During March 1917, conflicting opinions arose among the Revolutionaries over what the best configuration of the government should be in terms of ruled by the workers, or a republic, or a Communist state. More and more factions sprang up with their own ideologies and agendas, and each littered the streets with propaganda flyers and posters. Even as supporters of the Revolution, the Shostakovich family, with their privileged life, found themselves targets in the fervent campaign against the bourgeoisie (middle class). One day, soldiers accosted them in the road as their driver drove them through town and ordered that they turn the vehicle over to the Revolution. They acquiesced, and in time, the Revolutionaries requisitioned most of the privately owned automobiles in Petrograd.

The following month, Vladimir Lenin, the founder and head of the Bolshevik Party (later known as the Communist Party), stepped onto the scene. Lenin had become a follower of the German philosopher Karl Marx in 1889. While Lenin was working in St. Petersburg as a lawyer, the government arrested him in 1895 for his Marxist views and sent him to Siberia for three years. He then moved to Western Europe and spent most of World War I in Germany and Switzerland. After years of estrangement from his motherland, Lenin returned to Russia in April 1917. By this time, the Provisional Government put in place following the abdication of the Tsar was transitioning the country from its long-held monarchy to a republic. Lenin wanted to overthrow the Provisional Government and have the country ruled by his party, the Bolsheviks, who advocated for a totalitarian Socialist agenda in which the government would own all industry and provide all services. In this system, the workers or proletariat, would assume control of the government and finally occupy their just position in society. Lenin and his followers called for the demise of capitalism and the end of private property. They denounced the privileges of the wealthy and the bourgeoisie and vowed to distribute goods and food equitably to all people. Revolutionary Leon Trotsky joined with Lenin and became his trusted advisor and an instrumental figure in the Bolshevik Revolution. Lenin would later reward him with the post of Foreign Commissar.

Lenin brought together workers, soldiers, and peasants to form his own military force known as the Red Guards. That October, they positioned *Aurora,* one of their battleships, to shoot blanks at the Winter Palace, where the Provisional Government had established its headquarters. Finding the Palace scantily defended, the Red Bolshevik Army stormed it, and the nascent government quickly surrendered. This bloodless coup, named the October Revolution, marked Russia as the first Communist state. But in reality, Lenin's supporters constituted only a small portion of the population, and his Party would never have won through an election. So while the people of Russia had rejoiced in the streets at the Tsar's fall back in March, the Bolsheviks' seizing of power was met with much less enthusiasm, even though the ideas espoused by Lenin and his Party were meant to resonate with the majority of Russians who had not enjoyed the quality of life that the wealthy and powerful had during the reign of the Tsars.

Following the October Revolution, as promised, the new Communist government launched their great utopian experiment by placing the workers in charge of the factories that the state now owned and by confiscating the vast farm lands from the estate owners on behalf of the serfs. The leadership also pledged equality for all Russia's citizens, regardless of gender, race, or background, along with assurances of an abundant food supply and the development of an industrialized economy and modernized infrastructure that could compete on a world stage. The state's renewed support for education, science, and the arts ushered in a new political and artistic era that pointed toward a triumphant Russian future that would be achieved through machines and technology and be depicted by artists and writers in a new Futurist style that embraced science fiction. But while being given this much needed support and experimental freedom, artists also fell subject to an equally adamant, and at times paradoxical, mandate to make their creations accessible and useful to the masses.

But in the end, the ascendency of the Bolsheviks following the October Revolution proved to be difficult to maintain because of the Party's many enemies, launching Russia into a long and bloody civil war that would last until 1920. Nevertheless, Lenin's government successfully negotiated, through Foreign Commissar Trotsky, a truce with the Central Powers in March 1918. The Treaty of Brest-Litovsk ended Russia's involvement in World War I, an unpopular war that had resulted in massive casualties for the Russians. But despite that diplomatic triumph, the Russian Civil War continued another two years, finally ending with Lenin and his Party still in control and their enemies put aside for good. Lenin's government moved forward with a restructuring of the country, dividing it into four distinct areas labeled republics and drawing power from the small but numerous workers' councils throughout Russia, known as soviets. Lenin designated Moscow as the new capital city for Soviet Russia because he wanted to distance himself and his Bolshevik Party from Western influences; and since St. Petersburg/Petrograd represented that "Window to the West," he thought it paramount to relocate his government's headquarters. Then in 1922, the country took on a new name to reflect its reorganization—Union of Soviet Socialists Republics (USSR). By the mid-century, as the Soviet Union created additional republics, including Estonia and Latvia, it would geographically become the world's largest country, occupying one-sixth of the Earth's landmass. Indeed, much about this state would rank on a grand scale, with 100 distinct nationalities within its borders that spanned 11 time zones, all framed by the world's longest coast lines and spanning the world's largest frontiers.

Throughout the early months of Bolshevik rule, the Shostakovich family maintained their prominent status in the city of Petrograd and continued to be engaged in the politics and art of the time. Although descriptions of the October Revolution usually label it as a bloodless coup, casualties did result—most notably two murdered members of the Provisional Government. The funeral for these men would usher in a lifelong pattern of contradiction for Dmitri Shostakovich. The young boy was asked to play the piano for the memorial service. He chose his *Funeral March for the Victims of the Revolution*, which he had played in early 1917. But now, the Revolutionaries memorialized in that piece had murdered these two people, so the definition of victim took on a strikingly different implication.

The Shostakovich family entertained frequently during the years of the Civil War, hobnobbing with many of the cultural elite of their city, including the poet Anna Akhmatova and the composer Alexander Glazunov. Their home would be overflowing with guests talking animatedly, and then there would, of course, be music and dancing. When it came time for the music, another of their precocious child's paradoxes would be on display. Dmitri Shostakovich would quietly enter the room, a bony child wearing glasses. But when he climbed onto the piano bench, a dramatic transformation took place. He would play like a man of great strength, pounding out lively and robust tunes. Then, upon sliding off the bench, he reverted instantly to that former shy and unassuming figure who vanished from the room.

One of the highlights of these soirees hosted by the Shostakovich family came from watching Glazunov, the esteemed head of the Petrograd Conservatory, play the piano. He refused to part with his cigar and so kept it between two of his fingers while he played, sending plumes of ash into the air and onto the keys. Taking advantage of their friendly relationship, Shostakovich's mother appealed to Glazunov during one of their parties. Even though her gifted son was only 13, she wanted him to study at the Conservatory. Glazunov did concede to let the boy take the entrance exams, which indeed proved him musically astute beyond his years. So in 1919, 13-year-old Dmitri Shostakovich entered the Petrograd Conservatory and began to study piano with Leonid Nikolayev and composition with

Glazunov. From this moment in his adolescence, Shostakovich accepted the calling for his life—a devotion to music that would never waver.

Shostakovich's dogged dedication to his studies and craft served him well since there was nothing easy about life at the Conservatory in 1919. In addition to the curricular rigors, the raging Civil War left the city with ever dwindling resources of food and fuel so that the students and their teachers suffered from both hunger and cold as they worked together. During the piano class, the students wore coats, hats, and gloves and would rotate their seating periodically so that each took a turn next to the little stove that they fed with whatever scraps of wood they had collected during their walk to school. But while whoever was scheduled to play next would do their best to warm their hands by that stove, in the end, it made little difference as the frigid ivory piano keys caused their fingers to sting on contact, then ache, and then fall numb.

While Shostakovich studied at the Conservatory, the Bolsheviks appointed a Commissar of Enlightenment, Anatolii Lunacharskii, to set up schools, music instruction, and concerts throughout the villages and near factories and farms as part of their agenda to bring education and the arts to all the Russian people. Commissar Lunacharskii's progressive initiatives to tackle illiteracy proved especially effective, and quality music that had once been inaccessible found its way to the masses. Trucks loaded with pianos and other instruments drove musicians to remote locations to present free concerts. Shostakovich and his fellow students participated in these programs and were especially grateful whenever an audience member handed them a chunk of bread or a cup of precious soup.

To accompany these cultural education initiatives, the new Communist government launched an unprecedented campaign of propaganda via art, conscripting visual artists, filmmakers, writers, actors, and dancers to promote the Bolsheviks' utopian ideals by bringing work into the streets for everyone to see. As a result, the streets often played host to dramas, concerts, and exhibitions that championed the Russian way of life and celebrated a new era in which art would rise from the proletariat and not the bourgeoisie. The 1920s ushered in a time of focusing on modernization and ingenuity, a looking toward technology, machines, and avant-garde experiments to symbolize a Russia moving forward to not only keep pace with the Western world, but to surpass it. Lenin particularly liked film, which he saw as the most effective tool for telling a memorable story and promoting a cause. As a result, science fiction became a preferred medium for filmmakers, as well as for playwrights and artists from a variety of disciplines. Gone were landscape paintings and portraits of the Russian bourgeoisie. Instead, budding Futurists painted fantastical portraits of machines and outer space, and designers focused on an array of flying apparatuses, from blimps to jet packs. Also looking to the future, poets and composers sought to capture the essence of modernity in words and music.

In addition to the work of the Futurists, another progressive artistic style, Constructivism, also gained ground during the 1920s. Constructivists embraced geometry, using shapes as the basis for their abstract creations, and launched a groundbreaking poster movement that had a large impact on the art world. Constructivism also found its way into the design of daily household items such as furniture and plates as a mean of making their work accessible to the average citizen, an important tenet of the Bolsheviks.

The concept of cutting-edge creation certainly appealed to the young Shostakovich. He found particular inspiration in the Futurist and outspoken radical Vladimir Mayakovsky, whom he observed speaking and performing around the city. Mayakovsky, along with like-minded artists, had published a manifesto titled *A Slap in the Face of Public Taste*, in which they sounded the death knell for the art of the past and declared the dawning of an artistic revolution dedicated to innovation. Mayakovsky's revolutionary zeal also extended beyond the arts. He had joined the armed Revolution at age 12 and found himself imprisoned for a time by the Tsar when he was 16.

So along with their fellow artists and writers, composers also embraced the zeitgeist of freedom and experimentation, with many of them producing music that sounded quite dissonant and unconventional. Their sonic innovations even included the creation of new sound media, such as the electronic instrument invented by Russian scientist and musician Leon Theremin that would bear his name. The sounds of factories and industry, with their machinery and whistles, also invaded the aural landscape of compositions in the 1920s, harbingers of what would come later with avant-garde American composer John Cage. These futuristic soundscapes included *The Leap of Steel* (1925) by Sergei Prokofiev and *Rails* (1926) by Vladimir Deshovov.

But the new modern palette from which artists could create did not prove to be a divining rod toward a triumphant motherland. The future they so optimistically and idealistically depicted did not capture, in fact, a representation of reality, but merely provided a panacea for the masses. For despite the hopes and plans of the Bolsheviks, Russia's industry and economy continued to decline. So, the free lease on modern art served to give the people hope of what was to come and probably as a distraction from the bleakness of their daily lives. Throughout the Civil War and then in the years after, unrest remained as workers and peasants realized that the Communist government had not delivered on its promises. The government, not the workers, controlled the industry, and the government, not the peasants, owned the food supply coming from the fields they labored to cultivate. As in the days of Tsar Nicholas II, Lenin's government responded swiftly and violently to quell any resistance. The Communist leadership then further alienated a large segment of Russia's population when they declared war on religion, tearing down places of worship, including churches, temples, and mosques, and desecrating holy relics and the bodies of saints. The government persecuted the faithful and drove out or even killed their spiritual leaders, all leading to distrust and a festering hostility from the fervently pious Russians.

Times proved hard even for families such as the Shostakoviches. Along with their neighbors, they began to sell or barter their belongings in order to buy food. Then, during the winter of 1922, Shostakovich's father fell ill. What began as a cold, quickly escalated into pneumonia. He succumbed on February 24, a devastating loss for the family. Shostakovich's grief found its way naturally into music. He composed a set of piano duets to play with his sister Maria, later published as *Suite for Two Pianos in F-sharp minor, Op. 6*. The composition's emotional underpinnings, as well as its musical content, demonstrated an exceptional level of maturity for a 15 year old. Shostakovich unified the various pieces within the *Suite* by a series of repeating tones that signified tolling funeral bells. These haunting and insistent notes open the work, and then periodically interrupt the music, injecting and coloring the musical moment with the reminder of loss and grief.

With the death of Shostakovich's father, the family lost its only source of income and faced destitution. Shostakovich's mother entered the workforce, taking on various clerical jobs that paid little and sometimes required 13 hour shifts. The family also opened its home to boarders, subdividing the apartment for the extra income. Apartment overcrowding from extended family or paid lodgers was becoming more and more common throughout Petrograd as the hard times pressed down on everyone and as more and more people flocked to the city from the countryside in hopes of acquiring factory jobs. But regardless of the dire circumstances, Shostakovich's mother remained determined that her son's future and continued study at the Conservatory must be made a priority above all else. She believed that a destiny of greatness lay within him.

In September 1922, six months after his father's death, Shostakovich turned 16. The young music student worked tirelessly in school, until the following year, when he fell ill with lymphatic tuberculosis. Even after undergoing an operation to remove the diseased gland, the tenacious Shostakovich continued to perform on recitals at the Conservatory with a bandaged neck. But despite the bravado, he remained unwell. His doctor sent him to a sanitarium at Gaspra in the Crimea because of its warm climate and ocean, hopeful that the frail young man could make a full recovery. The respite proved an incredibly happy time for Shostakovich. His sister Maria came with him, and their days filled with playing music and frolicking in the outdoors. This physical activity in the warm climate certainly strengthened him in body as well as in mind and soul. While there, Shostakovich fell in love with Tatiana Glivenko, who was visiting on holiday from Moscow. The two young people enjoyed a whirlwind romance throughout the summer, but then each went their separate way to their hometown cities. The feelings they had for each other, however, would not be so easily dispatched.

Not long after Shostakovich's return, his beloved city would again face another name change. When Vladimir Lenin died on January 21, 1924, following a series of strokes, the Communist leadership determined that there be no remaining allegiances to or nostalgia for the Judeo-Christian religion through the rock of the Church, Saint Peter, or to the hundreds of years of tsarist rule that included Peter the Great. Instead, Lenin would assume the status of revered icon. Just a few days after their leader's death, the city became Leningrad. This would remain its name for the next 67 years until June 1991, when the impending collapse of the Soviet Union allowed for the restoration of its name to St. Petersburg.

Also with Lenin's death, the Soviet government needed a new head of state. Joseph Stalin had fought during the Revolution and had shown ruthless determination for the cause during the ensuing years of the Civil War. This doggedness had promoted him up through the ranks and led to his appointment by Lenin as the General Secretary of the Party in 1922. But on his death bed, Lenin came to regret that decision as he no longer trusted this man on whom he had bestowed such power. After Lenin's passing, Stalin indeed seized control of the Soviet state, ushering in an era of iron rule.

Stalin assumed leadership with an ambitious goal in mind—to transform the entire country, from peasants to industrial workers, into a single, mechanized entity. The new government outlined strategies for accomplishing this in what was labeled the Five-Year Plan. The crux of their plan for industrializing the country depended on importing machinery from other more industrialized countries, which would be paid for by bartering grain. As a result, they needed millions of acres of farmland to produce this currency. Stalin dispatched his secret police into the countryside to force farmers to cede their land to collective farms and to join the labor there. Not surprisingly, many of these farmers resisted and suffered steep penalties for their lack of cooperation, which included having their houses burned, being sent to concentration camps, or even death. This heavy-handed approach also created a culture of tattletales, in which some tried to garner special favors by informing on their neighbors if they suspected them of holding back property from the government. The vitriol and fear of the government had metastasized throughout the citizens. In the end, so much grain would be exported that the Russian people, including those who labored to grow it, starved. Approximately six million died as a result of Stalin's Five-Year Plan.

7. Dmitri Shostakovich and the Musical Redemption of Leningrad

Similar atrocities happened in the factories as well. The government levied tremendous pressure on workers to meet unrealistic quotas, and the punishment for failure proved equally severe. Government overseers frequently accused workers of sabotage for poor output yields and had them sent away, including those with essential skills and expertise. But instead of ferreting out saboteurs, these purges resulted in a self-defeating policy since production yields only declined further as the most skilled laborers disappeared.

At first, people living in the large cities of Leningrad and Moscow, such as the Shostakovich family, remained unaware of the violence being perpetrated against their fellow citizens in the more rural areas or about the staggering number of people who were starving to death. The government controlled all information, including the newspapers. The official Party newspaper, *Pravda*, functioned solely as a propaganda rag that spouted obsequious praise for the government and spurred its readers toward even greater adherence to the Communist ideals. Its pages were filled with success stories of increased industrial production and access to education throughout the Soviet Union. *Pravda* also delivered news of a declining West that would soon be superseded by the great Soviet nation.

After his recuperation at the seaside during the summer of 1923, Shostakovich took a job playing piano to accompany the silent films at a cinema called the Bright Reel in his home city. Although it provided him with a much needed paycheck, the job required long hours that stole time from his composing and proved boring for a musician of Shostakovich's exceptional talent. The scarcity of time indeed haunted Shostakovich, whose impending graduation from the Conservatory was contingent on completing an entire symphony as his final project under the supervision of his composition teacher Maximilian Steinberg. Shostakovich also complicated his constrained schedule by repeated trips to Moscow as he and Tatiana were still in love. When not traveling, performing, or composing, Shostakovich indulged in his other great passion—soccer. Although he had never played the sport, he attended matches obsessively and religiously, cheering on the Leningrad team.

Toward the end of 1925, Shostakovich finally completed his large-scale graduation project. The finished work, his First Symphony, consisted of the traditional four movement structure, lasting almost 30 minutes. It expressed the variety of moods, from solemn to exuberant, that would be expected in a Russian symphony and coalesced Shostakovich's many diverse influences, including Gustav Mahler, Igor Stravinsky, the 19th century Russian masters, and his own teachers. The composition demonstrated a remarkable proficiency in symphonic writing and orchestration for a young man relatively new to writing for orchestra. Shostakovich dedicated the work to his dear friend Mikhail Kvadri. Later in 1929, when the Soviet government executed Kvadri as a counterrevolutionary during Stalin's crackdown, that dedication was also expunged.

Shostakovich's First Symphony was to be premiered by the Leningrad Philharmonic under the baton of Nicolai Malko on May 12, 1926. To lend support to its promising pupil, the Conservatory provided the necessary funds to have the orchestral parts hand-copied for the performance since Shostakovich himself had no money. The premiere proved a great success for the 19-year-old composer. His work was well received by the audience members, who applauded enthusiastically as Shostakovich took multiple curtain calls. The musicians who had just performed the work also voiced their approval. Soon, Shostakovich even began to receive congratulations from abroad, including a supportive letter from Alban Berg, the Austrian composer and protégé of Arnold Schoenberg. One year later, in May 1927, the celebrated German conductor Bruno Walter programmed the work on a concert by the Berlin Philharmonic, a monumental moment in Shostakovich's career, as his first major opus received a premiere in the West. Additional performances and accolades followed. The United States premiered the piece in November 1928, with the legendary Leopold Stokowski conducting the Philadelphia Orchestra.

The success of his First Symphony led to a commission in 1927 from the Department of Agitation and Propaganda for a piece to mark the 10th anniversary of the October Revolution. Shostakovich decided on a large-scale choral-orchestral work. He initially titled it *To October,* but then opted for that as a subtitle, choosing instead for this work to stand as his Second Symphony. A true musical revolutionary, Beethoven had broken ranks with the traditional structure of the symphony by adding choral parts to his final Ninth Symphony, and with that unconventional move, the symphonic genre would never again remain limited to only orchestra. A master of symphonic writing, Mahler certainly embraced the use of a chorus in three of his symphonies, so Shostakovich stood in good company with his decision. This latest work also exhibited Shostakovich's forays into the futuristic style of the time through his inclusion of the sounds of the factories and the songs of the workers who proclaim the glory of the Communist ideals. He even utilized the blowing of a real factory whistle to announce the symphony's finale performed by the chorus singing a rousing worker's hymn that recounts the great fortune brought to them by Lenin and the October Revolution. With all of these elements plus Shostakovich's written dedication that read, "Proletarians of the World, Unite!," the symphony certainly had the resounding ring of propaganda to it. Later, it would be one of many works that scholars would reflect upon as they sought to ascertain whether Shostakovich's musical declarations in support of the Communist government stemmed from sincerity, or satire, or appeasement, or possibly some combination.

That same year, Shostakovich competed in the International Chopin Competition in Warsaw, earning an honorable mention. But despite his virtuosity at the piano, Shostakovich saw his musical destiny as only being fulfilled through composing music. Also in 1927, Shostakovich received an offer from the acclaimed Russian stage director, Vsevolod Meyerhold, to come to Moscow and write music for some plays he planned to produce. Meyerhold had fully embraced the Futurist school of thought, with the sets of his recent plays featuring unconventional backdrops of valves and machinery. Meyerhold also possessed a knack for satire and parody that thrilled his audiences. Shostakovich eagerly accepted the invitation and traveled to Moscow in January 1928 to work with this director whom he so admired. He lived there for several months, lodging with Meyerhold and his family.

One of the most important opportunities for Shostakovich through his new friend Meyerhold involved the staging of the play, *The Bedbug,* by the Futurist writer Vladimir Mayakovsky, whom Shostakovich had admired as a child. The story centered on a young man who becomes frozen in a basement on his wedding day and remains in that state until he thaws in the future—1973 to be exact. By this year, all of the Communist ideals have been fulfilled, including the end of poverty. But as a result, the newly awakened man discovers that some of his favorite pastimes, such as smoking and drinking, have disappeared as well. The people of the future put him on display so that everyone can see a representation of the disreputable past. The man's only companion in this nightmare is a bedbug that had frozen with him in that basement and has also come back to life. Meyerhold had recommended Shostakovich for the score. But unfortunately, Shostakovich and Mayakovsky failed to hit it off right away and seemed at odds when it came to a musical vision for the work. Every day, Shostakovich liked his idol less and less and found him to be insincere and materialistic. Mayakovsky enjoyed a party lifestyle in Paris and seemed to have grown bored with the

Communist cause, which probably accounted for his envisioning of the future as he did in his play. In the end, the play flopped, and the Communist authorities did in fact feel disrespected by the plot. Some of the critics, as sort of a warning shot across the bow, suggested that maybe Shostakovich should focus on loftier projects and music. Mayakovsky quickly fell out of favor with the new Stalinist government, which seized his travel visa and ordered him to tone down his rhetoric that took such a satirical view of the Communist utopia that he had once so fervently championed. The following year, on April 14, 1930, instead of continuing to live under the new repressive government, Mayakovsky committed suicide with a bullet to the heart.

Meanwhile, amid *The Bedbug* disaster, Shostakovich procured the opportunity to write a score for the silent film *New Babylon*, which would be released in 1929. His music would provide a soundtrack for the story of the 10-day rule in 1871 of the government in France, known as the Paris Commune, following the Franco-Prussian War. The years that Shostakovich had spent as an accompanist for silent films greatly benefited him now that it came time to explore an even closer relationship between music and image. The resulting score was witty and clever, making musical allusions to the French national anthem and other well-known French tunes such as the "Can Can" from one of Jacques Offenbach's operetta. It would be the first of many film scores throughout his long career.

Shostakovich still hoped to continue writing for the stage and became interested in a work by the 19th century Russian writer Nikolai Gogol, a short story called "The Nose." The subject matter seemed perfect for the times as it told the absurd story of a nose, which having abandoned a man's face, went around the city trying to land a government job. Shostakovich decided that this was exactly the tale he needed for his first opera. So with the help of two friends, Shostakovich drafted a libretto and then set about composing the music. He proudly created a score befitting of such a wry narrative, complete with unconventional sounds and music to intensify and even exaggerate further the outrageous and nonsensical action on stage.

The first sign of trouble for Shostakovich came after the June 1929 premiere of his opera *The Nose*. Although the audiences loved it and hailed it a hysterical comedy, the critics felt otherwise as they already sensed the turning of the tide away from freedom of expression and experimentation. They branded Shostakovich's opera as "formalism," a new catchword for any artistic product that the government felt too closely aligned with modern Western aesthetics and thereby proved inaccessible to the common man and inconsistent with the Communist ideals. Its usage signaled a swift death to any project. As a result, the authorities cancelled all productions of *The Nose*. This opera would not be presented in Russia again until 1974.

Undeterred, Shostakovich composed another symphony the following month. Shostakovich's *Symphony No. 3* consisted of four continuous sections, rather than separate movements, and ended again with a choral finale. The inspiration for this composition also hailed from the realm of the revolutionary—this time in support of the May Day festivities, which the Soviet government had earmarked as a celebration of "International Workers' Day." Shostakovich again used a laudatory proletarian text, possibly as a reflexive response after the denouncement of his opera. The Leningrad Philharmonic premiered the work on January 21, 1930, the sixth anniversary of Lenin's death.

The Soviet artistic landscape had certainly experienced a dramatic shift in just the six years since Lenin's passing. Despite his promotion of the arts while in power, Lenin had lacked the musical interest or ambition that Stalin now had. Lenin had feared that music, for himself and his cause, could have too much of a softening effect, and therefore interfere with the requisite resolve to subdue counterrevolutionaries and meet any unrest, resistance, and criticism with crushing force. Lenin had chosen instead to support experimentation in music and the other arts that focused a visionary eye to the future of machines, space, and technology. But with Stalin's ascendency, this unabashed exploration came to an end. Stalin avowed that music should be "for the people" and accessible to the common man. He also decreed that the primacy of Soviet music should be to serve the State by upholding its interests, which included the elevation of the ordinary citizen. As a result, artistic expression succumbed to strict totalitarian control as a tool of propaganda and state politics. This censorship and manipulation coincided with the Fascist control of all media and the creation of a secret police to monitor its citizens' activities, including their musical preferences. Like Adolf Hitler, his counterpart in Germany, Stalin collected recordings and was quick to express his opinions on music. But unlike Nazi Germany, the Soviet Union's censorship of music would not stem from a genocidal intention, although it would result in many deaths, but would target modernism, which Stalin considered to be steeped in Western formalism.

So, with the 1930s, came a government-dictated reversal for artists. No more science fiction and Futurist themes—instead a form of realism that portrayed everyday people in their quotidian lives. But how truly realistic these works of art would be depended on interpretation because the mandate allowed for only optimistic depictions of Russian life, and not of the escalating violence toward dissidents or the growing mounds of bodies. To aid in implementing and overseeing this new musical vision, the government created a sort of steering committee in 1932 known as the Union of Soviet Composers.

Shostakovich had taken the chastisement over his opera seriously and shifted his focus in the early 1930s mainly toward ballet, theater, and film work that closely aligned with government sentiments. These creations struck a heroic and joyous tone that celebrated Russian life and its great successes in factories and farm collectives. These works included the ballet *The Bolt* (1931) that championed ridding the factories of saboteurs, the film score to *The Counterplan* (1932), and another ballet in 1935 titled *The Bright Stream*, a utopian depiction of agricultural collectives. He even wrote lighthearted jazz-based music and parodies of well-known tunes for a bizarre and risqué vaudeville show in 1931 called *Declared Dead,* the performance of which curiously coincided with a gas-attack training session that the government had arranged for Soviet youth. Such a demeaning project for a composer of Shostakovich's genius certainly showed the level of fear among artists and the extent to which they would go to appear not only compliant with their government, but useful as well. His apparent acquiescence, however, did not preclude Shostakovich from pushing back at times. The repression of his creative freedom exploded in November 1931 in the form of a manifesto he called the "Declaration of a Composer's Duties," in which he outlined the detrimental effects that limiting the acceptable aesthetics to the idealized folk styles of workers and peasants would have on Russian music.

The zeitgeist of 1930s Russia could not completely estrange Shostakovich from his love of opera. So despite the disastrous repercussions of his first opera, Shostakovich again launched another operatic project. This one would be based on the 1865 novella, *Lady Macbeth of the Mtsensk District,* by Russian writer Nikolai Leskov. Loosely crafted after Shakespeare's tale of love, murder, and intrigue, this story featured a bored Russian wife who takes a lover while her husband is away. When the two philanderers are discovered by her father-in-law, they kill him and then also murder her husband upon his return. The two lovers marry, but never enjoy their nuptials because the discovery of the husband's corpse in the cellar leads the authorities to arrest the couple and send them to Siberia.

Shostakovich worked on this project off and on over several years, and while doing so, dealt with his own tumultuous passions. He and Tatiana had continued to see each other as Shostakovich traveled back and forth to Moscow. Both engaged in other relationships on the side, but for Shostakovich, those meant nothing but companionship. He viewed only his relationship with Tatiana as of any permanent substance. Then during one visit, Tatiana confessed to him that she could no longer endure their long-distance relationship nor Shostakovich's own failure to offer any sign of lasting commitment to her. She had also grown weary of Shostakovich's over-bearing and controlling mother, who wanted him all to herself, and to that end, meddled in his relationships. Instead, Tatiana announced her intent to marry someone else the next day. A devastated Shostakovich returned home to Leningrad, but still held out hope that Tatiana would regret her decision and come back to him. He continued to pursue her until May 1932 when she had a child. He decided, then, that he must let her go. Two weeks later, he impulsively married a young physicist named Nina Varzar, whom he had been casually dating. Now, the Shostakovich home grew even more crowded with the addition of the newlyweds and the palpable angst of Shostakovich's mother over their elopement.

Also in 1932, the newly formed Union of Soviet Composers elected Shostakovich to its membership, a cautious alliance that would present both opportunities and frustrations for the young composer. In 1933, Shostakovich completed *24 Preludes for Piano* and *Concerto No. 1 in C minor for Piano, Strings and Trumpet,* followed by *Sonata in D minor for Cello and Piano* the following year. Shostakovich also continued to work on *Lady Macbeth*, finally securing a premiere for January 1934. Ever mindful of the need for government support, Shostakovich sought and received an advanced endorsement for the work from Anatolii Lunacharskii, the Commissar of Enlightenment, whom he had invited to attend a rehearsal. In the end, his highly anticipated opera actually enjoyed a dual premiere, two days apart, in Leningrad and Moscow. After the opening performances, audiences and critics in both locations praised the opera, declaring it a masterful triumph of Soviet music. Word of the opera's success quickly spread around the world, igniting a clamorous rush to stage *Lady Macbeth* on a global scale from South America to Sweden.

But the artistic victory of *Lady Macbeth* proved an incongruous soundtrack to the escalating horrors unleashed by the government in 1934 as a response to the assassination of Stalin's closest friend and advisor, Sergei Kirov. Following Kirov's death, Stalin ordered the severest measures for anyone suspected of a terrorist act against the Soviet government, including a trial that would take place no later than 10 days after the arrest. With hardly any time to prepare a defense, those found guilty also received no chance for an appeal, just a swift execution. Emissaries of the government launched a witch hunt for those that the Soviet state could declare enemies of the people and then banish to gulags and simply make disappear. By 1935, the accusations and executions had spread to even children as young as 12 years of age. The mid–1930s had ushered in what would later be known as the "Great Purge" or the "Great Terror."

While during the early 1930s, major Russian cities, such as Leningrad and Moscow, had been somewhat immune from the violence taking place out in the countryside. But now even the great metropolises cowered as the Soviet secret police eagerly trolled the streets for people to accuse and arrest. Day and the night, the government rounded up innocent citizens on bogus charges and then relocated them—some to faraway work camps and some to their graves. Leningrad found itself a particularly favored target as Stalin had always despised the city for its Western-like ways. That Stalin himself probably ordered the assassination of Kirov because of rumors that some Party members favored Kirov as a replacement for Stalin only further exemplifies the insidious nature of this enhanced terrorism.

With such intense scrutiny about the style and messaging of the arts during this time, Shostakovich and fellow artists came under attack from the government with accusations of creating "formalist" art that lacked accessibility by the average citizen. Composers labeled as too modern included Igor Stravinsky, Arnold Schoenberg, Paul Hindemith, and Sergei Prokofiev, among many others. Artists joined the great numbers of Russians who were being arrested and tortured, or shipped off to work camps in Siberia, or who simply disappeared as part of the Great Purge. Referring specifically to music, historian Alex Ross would later pronounce it "the most warped and tragic phase in twentieth-century music."[2] People like Leon Theremin, who had been celebrated for their innovation during the 1920s, now found themselves dangerously out of favor. Soviet officials sent Theremin to Siberia in 1938 and then later forced him to use his expertise to invent weapons and surveillance equipment for the Red Army and the KGB.

As the Shostakovich family watched thousands be arrested, they too feared the sound of a knock at the door. This ever-present dread along with the tension from an overcrowded apartment contributed to Shostakovich's failing marriage. After only a few short years, the two divorced, and Shostakovich began planning a permanent move to Moscow. But this never materialized because his ex-wife soon realized that she was pregnant, and the two remarried. Shostakovich then made an appeal to the government for a separate apartment for the newly expecting couple, knowing that their only chance of happiness rested on a private living arrangement. Fortunately, the government had reserved an apartment building just for composers and agreed in the fall of 1935 to allow Shostakovich and his wife to move in there.

Meanwhile, Shostakovich's *Lady Macbeth of the Mtsensk District* continued to enjoy a successful run. A frequent audience member for operas and ballets at Moscow's Bolshoi Theatre, Stalin decided to see this opera there on January 26, 1936. Shostakovich happened to be in Moscow at the time, and on receiving word of Stalin's intended presence, he made sure to be there for the performance as well. The now 29-year-old composer felt understandably apprehensive, knowing how much depended on the approval of the Communist leader. His worries proved justified because something about the production did not please Stalin, who left before its conclusion. Shostakovich, who had hoped to be congratulated afterwards, now felt both disappointment and dread. All of his emotions coalesced into fear when two days later an editorial titled "Muddle Instead of Music" appeared in the Communist Party newspaper *Pravda*. In this editorial, the writer denigrated Shostakovich's opera on both its musical merit and its morality. The review also contained a warning for the composer—if he continued on this same course, it would not end well.

Unfortunately, this would only be the first in a series of articles that condemned Shostakovich and put all other composers on notice. Even though *Lady Macbeth* had been well-received with over 200 performances during the past two years, the opera was quickly withdrawn. The Great Terror had now made a quite personal introduction to Shostakovich. The composer also discovered the fickleness of some of his colleagues. Fearing their own denouncement, many artists, writers, and composers hastily added their voices of condemnation for Shostakovich's "formalism" and avowed their whole-hearted agreement with the *Pravda* articles. The Composers' Union of Leningrad, of which Shostakovich counted as a prominent member, also turned against him, spouting that all of their previous support for his opera had been misguided and repenting for not realizing the error in their comrade's music sooner. His director friend Meyerhold, with whom he had collaborated in Moscow in the late 1920s, remained one of the few to stand by Shostakovich. Meyerhold bravely spoke out in support of freedom for the modern artist and for the work of his dear friend.

Along with the volley of criticism emerged a warped rubric that left Shostakovich unable to measure up to any approved standard. Paradox ruled as he received condemnation for writing overly complex and inaccessible music, while simultaneously being censured for writing too simply and idealistically. The target seemed to always be on the move, blown by the winds of exaggerations and lies. The Communist leadership now proclaimed Shostakovich as an elitist bourgeois, as "not for the people"—a dangerous moniker in 1930s Russia. Despite past accolades for his nationalistic Russian spirit, Shostakovich, along with his music, had now been declared an enemy of the people.

In desperation, Shostakovich appealed to the one confidante he had who was well placed in the government, a marshal in the Red Army named Mikhail Tukhachevsky. Also an amateur violinist, Tukhachevsky had been friends with Shostakovich for a long time, and the two enjoyed talking and playing music together. When Shostakovich visited his friend in Moscow to share the deeply troubling developments, Tukhachevsky agreed to intercede on his behalf with Stalin. Shostakovich departed feeling optimistic, thinking that the government would soon extend an olive branch to him. But nothing of the sort happened. Shostakovich eventually traveled back home to tend to his pregnant wife in Leningrad and to continue work on his Fourth Symphony. Unbeknownst to the two men during their meeting, Tukhachevsky's name had been added to Stalin's growing list of people he wanted to disappear, and so the appeals on behalf of Shostakovich fell on deaf ears. Later in 1937, the Soviets would enlist a double agent to broker a deal with the Nazis to create a false trail of evidence that indicted Tukhachevsky as a traitor and German spy. Stalin feared the influence that Tukhachevsky held with the Red Army, and the Germans feared the ways that Tukhachevsky sounded the alarm in the Soviet military about the future threat of Germany and the need for the Red Army to modernize with tanks and artillery instead of relying on the cavalry as they had in the First World War. So, in the end, it proved advantageous to the Germans to assist the Soviets in eliminating this particular problem. The unfounded conviction and subsequent execution of such a progressive thinking officer in the Red Army would be one of many strategic and tactical errors that Stalin would make in the coming years that would leave him and his country vulnerable and ultimately crippled before an invading German army.

Now that Shostakovich had been identified as a potential threat to the Communist state, the NKVD, Stalin's secret police and the precursor of the KGB, placed the composer under surveillance, following him and tapping his phones. Shostakovich fell into a deep despair over the maligning criticisms and the ongoing censorship of his music. His status as a musical pariah also meant a great reduction in income, since commissions had dried up along with performance royalties. Shostakovich had no escape route. The government prohibited even unrestricted travel from one city to another, and any Soviet citizen visiting another country must leave behind their family as hostages to insure their return. So if Shostakovich attempted to defect, his family would be severely punished. Those closest to the composer feared that his mounting depression would lead him to take his own life. The esteemed Russian poet Maxim Gorky even appealed to Stalin himself for a reprieve for

Shostakovich, citing that a suicide by such an internationally esteemed figure would reflect poorly on the country and the Communist Party. But as with Tukhachevsky, Gorky seemed to no longer hold much influence. A few months later, on June 14, 1936, the poet was assassinated by the head of the NKVD.

On May 30, 1936, Shostakovich's spirits did lift with the birth of his daughter Galina. That same month, the ever-determined composer also completed his Fourth Symphony. After the dire warnings about his music and with the unrelenting persecution of so many artists, Shostakovich would have been wise to compose a symphony that strictly adhered to the aesthetic and political criteria of the times. Instead, he insisted on continuing to be true to his own voice, which resulted in a not only unorthodox but bizarre symphonic work. It contained elements of the futuristic sounds and blaring dissonances from the 1920s, all coalesced into a style writer M.T. Anderson described as "a parade of grotesque portraits, some playful, some clumsy, and some malevolent"[3] and suggested might have been a sonic retaliation for the brutalization Shostakovich had undergone at the hands of the State and his colleagues. Nevertheless, the Leningrad Philharmonic and conductor Fritz Stiedry made arrangements to premiere the work in December of that year. But in the end, some of the musicians expressed reluctance since Shostakovich had been censured, and the premiere never took place. Shostakovich himself withdrew the piece during the rehearsal process, citing his own dissatisfaction with the work he had created. But in fact, pressure had been exerted from the authorities who refused to allow the piece to be performed. For the next 25 years, the many pages of music to Shostakovich's Fourth Symphony lay abandoned and forgotten in the library of the Leningrad Philharmonic. It finally received its long overdue premiere by the Moscow Philharmonic on December 30, 1961.

Meanwhile, the crazed fervor of mass detentions came close to home for Shostakovich as the secret police arrested both his sister Maria and her husband, sending Maria away into exile and her husband to a gulag where he died. The NKVD also sent Shostakovich's mother-in-law to a work camp and seized his uncle, who then disappeared without the family knowing what happened to him. The entire judicial system now emanated from the mind of a mad man, where even the meteorologists were charged with sabotage if a weather event ruined a crop. By 1937, Stalin instituted arrest quotas throughout the Soviet Union, with specific numbers indicated for executions and exile to gulags. Only the numbers mattered, not the reason nor the individual. Not even those who carried out these orders remained safe. Stalin also purged the NKVD, the government, and the Red Army as he grew paranoid about whether these individuals had accrued enough information, power, and influence to oust him.

Shostakovich could not help but think that he would be arrested any moment. He kept a packed suitcase by the door. At times, he even slept in the hallway outside his apartment so that when they came for him, that they would not enter the apartment where his wife and child laid. Nevertheless, he kept writing, beginning his Fifth Symphony after the arrest of his friend Tukhachevsky and during his wife's second pregnancy. Unlike the Fourth Symphony's thwarted premiere, the Fifth Symphony did receive an inaugural performance by the Leningrad Philharmonic in November 1937. It certainly proved to be a nerve-wracking concert for Shostakovich who knew what was at stake—no less than his life if this latest piece failed to mollify his accusers. But regardless, he had not played it totally safe. The composition still presented a powerful message, which many recognized as a response to the government's terrorizing of Soviet citizens, including the beautiful slow movement that seemed a requiem for all those who had died.

7. Dmitri Shostakovich and the Musical Redemption of Leningrad 201

But although many of the elements that had been objected to in the Fourth Symphony had just been repackaged in this latest piece, Shostakovich did present them a bit more judiciously and within a more traditional structure that appeared to be a somewhat repentant response to the criticism handed down to him by the government. The symphony concluded on a triumphal and optimistic tone, and as that final note sounded, the audience of approximately 2,500 rose to their feet in an exuberant ovation that lasted for 30 minutes. They had found a safe way to affirm and acknowledge this composer and his musical message, and similar standing ovations accompanied Shostakovich's Fifth Symphony in performances throughout the Soviet Union. Although a few critics made derogatory comments, it appeared that Shostakovich's voice had been deemed acceptable again.

A few months later, Shostakovich and his wife welcomed a son, Maxim, on May 10, 1938. Shostakovich enjoyed another time of elevated spirit over this latest family addition, which in turn buoyed him to write a String Quartet and then a Sixth Symphony. He had also accepted a teaching post at his alma mater, the Leningrad Conservatory, quickly becoming a favorite professor among the students. With his ever increasing personal and professional responsibilities, Shostakovich adopted a rigorous and disciplined schedule that included, regardless of the day, his dressing in a formal suit and sitting down to compose at 6 a.m. every morning. But while Shostakovich settled into a predictable routine with his family and students, the barbaric interrogations and torment continued all around him. In 1939, the State arrested Vsevolod Meyerhold, Shostakovich's friend and outspoken supporter following the *Lady Macbeth* incident. Government thugs subjected Meyerhold to the cruelest tortures for months until he finally agreed to sign a bizarrely worded confession of how he

Dmitri Shostakovich composing in the 1940s (Getty Images).

had conspired against the Soviet Union, which then resulted in his execution on February 2, 1940.

Meanwhile, Stalin had more to contend with than just the Soviet propaganda machine and his country's internal strife. He had not been the only determined and ruthless dictator to rise to great power during the 1930s. Both Adolf Hitler and Joseph Stalin maintained a keen awareness of the other's presence on the world stage; and although ideological enemies—Nazi Fascism leaning to the far right and Soviet Communism leaning to the far left, their respective quests for domination at all costs forged an unholy kinship. "In this way, Communism, moving to the left, and Fascism, on the other hand, moving to the right, met like fists behind the back and clutched each other there, where none could see."[4]

Nevertheless, Stalin also feared Hitler, whose massive armies snatched up sovereign nations rather effortlessly. The March 1939 invasion of Czechoslovakia had come right to Stalin's doorstep, intensifying the Soviet people's distrust of the Nazis. As he would discover much too late, Stalin was indeed justified in his wariness because Hitler secretly eyed the Soviet Union with a sinister strategy that anticipated many chess moves ahead to when the Third Reich would invade Russia and consume its land and resources. The Nazi creed declared Russians, as Slavs, to be subhuman, and would in time incite its followers to wage a war against the Russians that would not just conquer, but annihilate them as a people. Then the victors, the superior Aryan race, would expand into those vast, fertile lands that overflowed with natural resources. "Russia would become breadbasket, oil field, and Teutonic playground in the thrilling gymnastic future of the triumphant Nazi Reich."[5]

But before that could happen, some cunning initiatives and cloying deceptions would have to be put in place. Meanwhile, Stalin and his advisors deliberated about their own defense strategies should the Third Reich launch an invasion. The impoverished Russian economy, along with a decimated army, posed almost insurmountable challenges for the Soviet leadership. In the end, they decided to try to protect themselves through diplomacy. Their first hope rested in forming an alliance with England and France as a preemptive protection from Nazi incursions. But not surprisingly, the English and French were not particularly eager to form a coalition with Stalin's Communist government. After a series of delaying tactics, the English finally during the summer of 1939 dispatched a member of the Admiralty, a man who possessed no real authority, to meet with Soviet officials. Offended by such a weak gesture, the Soviets realized that the English possessed no true interest in being their ally. That only left them with a more terrifying option—forge a direct alliance with Nazi Germany. This proved to be exactly what the Reich needed for their future intentions. So in contrast to how unenthusiastically the English and French had responded to Stalin's overtures, Hitler courted Stalin by sending not merely an envoy or attaché but his Foreign Minister, Joachim von Ribbentrop, who arrived in style replete with 32 assistants and his own musical ensemble to play the Third Reich's national anthem, "Deutchland Über Alles."

An experienced negotiator, Ribbentrop had already assisted in building alliances between the Third Reich and other dictatorships—Japan in 1936 and Italy in 1938. This time, in August 1939, he met with Soviet officials, including the recently appointed Soviet Foreign Minister Vyacheslav Mikhaylovich Molotov. On August 23, 1939, the world stood by astounded while two enemies, the USSR and Nazi Germany, signed a nonaggression treaty and trade agreement known as the Molotov-Ribbentrop Pact. In addition to promises that neither country would invade the other, the accord stipulated that Germany would sell equipment that Russia desired, and Russia, in turn, would sell its natural resources such as oil, grain, nickel, and wood. Since both countries were getting what they needed, it seemed the perfect deal. But in actuality, the trade agreement had certainly duped the Soviets, who would uncomprehendingly provide Germany with the very resources it would require to invade them in the future. Plus the Nazi government could now focus on contending with the West without also fighting a war to the East. The German-Soviet Nonaggression Pact also outlined a secret protocol concerning the fate of the rest of Eastern Europe, which the two powers agreed to carve up and divide among themselves. As a result, less than two weeks later, on September 1, Germany invaded Poland without fear of Soviet reprisal. Since Britain and France had sworn to defend their ally Poland, both had no choice but to declare war on Germany. Thus, the dominos had begun to fall, launching another global war.

Back in the Soviet Union, the alliance with Germany had come as a tremendous shock to the citizens, who had watched so many of their comrades slaughtered under the suspicion of collaborating with the Nazis. Now, Stalin issued an about-face. Anyone caught criticizing or working against the Third Reich would be arrested. The absurdity of such a reversal clearly manifested in the situation surrounding the Soviet film, *Alexander Nevsky*, for which Prokofiev had composed the score. Set in the Middle Ages, the film depicted an epic struggle between a Russian hero and invading German hordes, ending, of course, in victory for the Russian. Produced with great extravagance and expense, *Alexander Nevsky* had been hailed as a masterpiece at its release in late 1938. But with the recent "friendship" between the Russians and Germans, Soviet officials ordered the film out of circulation.

Following the invasion of Poland, the Germans continued their aggressive campaign to conquer more lands, sweeping through the Low Countries to occupy Denmark, Holland, and Belgium. They also took on the French. Meanwhile, Stalin annexed the eastern part of Poland per the agreement and then made further incursions to force other countries into the USSR, namely Latvia, Lithuania, and Estonia. These actions left Soviet citizens confused because their country was not supposed to be at war—the Nonaggression Pact with Germany ensured their neutrality, or so they thought. Of course, the secret protocol between these two Axis nations that allowed for the gutting of Eastern Europe remained unknown to them. Stalin's ambition also inclined toward Finland, under the auspices of securing the city of Leningrad, which lay so close geographically. Known as the Winter War, the invasion of Finland resulted in terrible losses for a Soviet army that had already been depleted of key leaders and officers as a result of Stalin's purges. The cleansing of the Soviet military had especially targeted those who advocated for modernizing the army as preparation for a possible invasion by the Germans. But now, an extremely nervous Stalin realized that if the Red Army could not win battles against a small, primitive army on skis, as that of Finland, that it had little hope of withstanding a German blitzkrieg. Stalin's only consolation rested in what he perceived would be a long and drawn-out conflict between Germany and France, which would weaken the Reich and buy him more time to rebuild his military. But after less than two months of fighting, the French capitulated by signing an armistice agreement on June 22, 1940, an outcome that shocked the world and even the Germans.

Hitler enjoyed the symbolism of dates, and so exactly one year after the armistice with a defeated France, on June 22, 1941, he launched an invasion of Russia. Known as Operation Barbarossa, the incursion into Russia began at 4 a.m. on the longest day of the year, breaking their almost two-year nonaggression treaty. On the heels of so many easily won campaigns, Hitler and his advisors estimated that it would take a mere four months to accomplish the occupation of the Soviet Union. The Reich believed that the harsh Russian winters represented the only real threat to the German military, so officials specifically planned the invasion for the summer, confident of a victory before the snow started falling. Well-versed in the economic and military deficiencies of the Soviet Union, the Germans had relished building up their own reserves from the natural resources that the unsuspecting Soviets exported to them. As Hitler prepared to conquer another Slavic country and commandeer its land, he compared his intention to how the United States had snatched up the land it wanted from the Native Americans, a strategy he planned to emulate. To have enough living space and natural resources, the Reich determined that the Slavs could not just be conquered and sequestered, but must be annihilated, and to that end, the Nazi leadership estimated that it could kill about 30 million of them as part of the invasion.

With a German invasion underway in the dead of night, the Soviet military, caught unawares, stood by ill-prepared because Stalin had refused to admit in the preceding months that he had been duped. Hitler had played Stalin with a long con, starting with the trade agreement and then moving into a campaign of misinformation and false assurances in January 1941. The Nazi leader warned Stalin to pay no attention to any intelligence that pointed to an impending German invasion of the USSR, explaining it as an attempt by the British to undermine their strong partnership. Hitler also informed Stalin that he too had received reports that the Soviets planned to invade Germany. He pledged that he would ignore all that information if Stalin would do the same, cautioning that the volley of misleading intel would only increase in the next few months as the British war effort grew more desperate.

As Hitler predicted, the spies and assets Stalin had put in place began to report signs that a German invasion was imminent, as they not only heard rumors but saw German troops amassing on the borders and Nazi planes flying reconnaissance missions daily over Soviet military bases, bridges, and railways. One informant notified Stalin that it would happen in June, and then even updated the intelligence to the specific date of June 22. The British government also tried to warn Stalin by the intelligence it received. But an obstinate Stalin quickly dismissed all the warnings and reports, holding firm to his assurances from Hitler. Stalin's spies inside the Reich, known as the Red Orchestra, became so desperate to convince Stalin of the looming invasion that they even appealed to the United States, hoping that Stalin would believe it from the U.S. government. All fell on deaf ears.

The reasons for Stalin's refusal to heed so much corroborated information and from so many trustworthy sources proved multi-faceted. Pride certainly played a role, not wanting to admit that he could be manipulated or double-crossed. But Stalin had not been so delusional to think that Germany would never pose a threat to the Soviet Union; instead, he believed that, for now, the Germans were fighting on enough fronts that they dared not risk opening up to the East. Stalin hoped that the Red Army would be strong enough by 1943 to launch a preemptive attack against a preoccupied Germany. So in final analysis, it fell in line with Stalin's agenda to continue insisting that anything to the contrary constituted misinformation and misdirection. Meanwhile, the Nazi government laughed and planned. "As the writer Alexander Solzhenitsyn observed, 'Not to trust anybody was very typical of Josef Stalin. All the years of his life did he trust one man only, and that was Adolf Hitler'—the twentieth century's most notorious genocidal liar."[6]

As June arrived, two of Stalin's top advisors, Defense Minister Timoshenko and General Zhukov, tried anew to convince Stalin that the intelligence all pointed to an impending invasion. But still, Stalin refused to act. The Soviet leader paced the floor restlessly as the clock struck midnight, announcing the summer solstice, June 22. He stayed up until 3:30 a.m. and then retired to bed, feeling assured that there would indeed be no attack. Thirty minutes later, Axis armies, made up of German, Croatian, Romanian, and Finnish soldiers, advanced over Soviet borders, the largest incursion force in the history of Europe.

As the tanks and armored divisions crossed Soviet borders, German planes appeared in the skies as well. They unleashed a barrage of bombs on cities and air bases and dropped magnetic mines into the sea that would adhere to Russian ships and then explode. Having not been given authorization to engage, the Soviet military sat by impotently as the German planes enjoyed free rein on their country. It took only a few minutes for the Germans to destroy 738 Soviet aircraft left sitting unprotected on airfields. After only a few hours, that number soared close to 1,200. When faced with the senseless decimation wreaked on his Air Force by unopposed German planes, one Soviet commander shot himself in the head.

At the Kremlin headquarters, Defense Minister Timoshenko and General Zhukov received reports within minutes of the invasion about the encroaching troops and the massive bombings, but they possessed no authority to order Soviet troops to engage. That order could only be given by Stalin himself. They phoned his residence, but Stalin's assistant hesitated, not wanting to wake the leader who had just fallen asleep. Zhukov insisted, shouting that the country was under attack. When Stalin finally came to the phone, he again refused to acknowledge the reality of the situation. He instead ordered that troops should not engage, citing that this merely constituted a test by the Germans or the work of a saboteur bent on destroying the pact between the two allies. Later that morning, the German Ambassador himself showed up at Foreign Minister Molotov's office with the official message that Germany had declared war on the Soviet Union—only then did Stalin face the difficult reality. Nevertheless, by noon, confusion still prevailed within the Soviet government and military. Communication proved almost impossible because the Germans had secretly cut the lines a few hours before the start of the offensive. Those military leaders who did manage to get through encountered only uncertainty, shock, and pandemonium. Finally, after the onslaught had been underway for hours, the government broadcasted an announcement via loudspeakers throughout the country, informing the Soviet citizens that they were under attack by the Third Reich and proclaiming that they should all unite for a swift defeat of their enemies.

In the month preceding the invasion, Shostakovich had enjoyed a particularly pleasant time with his family as they vacationed at a cottage on the nearby Gulf of Finland, a welcome escape from the unrelenting heat of Leningrad. Back home in June, Shostakovich experienced the delight of that strange time, the "White Nights," when Leningrad's closeness to the Arctic Circle renders it about 80 days in which the sun hardly sets. With it still daylight at midnight, the residents celebrated the stark contrast with the dark, harsh winters they endured. Throughout this time, Shostakovich continued his work at the Conservatory, which neared the end of term. Conservatory faculty administered a round of final exams on the morning of June 22. Still a fanatical soccer fan, Shostakovich planned to attend a soccer match later that day. He and his close friend Isaak Glikman were actually en route to the stadium when the war broadcast erupted over the loudspeakers. This experience constituted the first of many poignant moments the two men would share during their four decades of friendship, much of it chronicled in hundreds of letters the two exchanged until Shostakovich's death.

Despite the terror and mistrust that had dominated Soviet lives for so many years, the threat from an outside enemy sparked a nationalist fervor, and thousands began to volunteer for military service. As in other cities, Leningrad's streets overflowed with people clamoring not only to answer the call to defend Mother Russia, but to stockpile food from the stores and withdraw their money from the bank. Shostakovich went to enlist along with Venjamin Fleishman, one of his students. Officials eagerly accepted Fleishman into the military, but rejected Shostakovich. The country had other plans for its talented composers and musicians. Soviet leaders understood the power of music, and they wanted to harness this power to spur their citizens toward greater patriotism. They also knew the importance of using their gifted artists and writers as part of the war effort to counteract the German assertion of the inferiority of the Slavic race and therefore its artistic creations.

Not surprisingly, the Red Army had little to offer in resistance to the German advance. What antiquated planes remained proved ineffective against the more modern planes of the Luftwaffe, and the same was true of the Soviet tanks. Stalin's government had committed a terrible misstep in not heeding the admonishments of its military officials about the need to modernize the army. The war turned into a massacre with no mercy shown to POWs or Soviet civilians since the Germans had declared the Slavic people as subhuman, as they had the Jews. A crushed Stalin scampered into hiding at his country house, abandoning his country to fend for itself. After several days, the beleaguered Kremlin leadership met to decide on a strategy. In the end, they drove to Stalin's home and persuaded the leader that he could defeat the Germans. Their motivational speech worked, and he returned with them to the Kremlin.

By June 27, city officials in Leningrad began calling on the residents to participate in the war effort for several hours a day through civil defense duties. Shostakovich found himself digging ditches in addition to his musical contributions as pushback against the Nazi debasement of Russian culture. He performed with and wrote music for a traveling performance troupe organized from Leningrad that eventually presented as many as 160 concerts per month. Despite all of the suffering that the government had unleashed on him during the 1930s, Shostakovich had never wavered in love for and dedication to his country.

On July 2, Shostakovich tried to volunteer for a more active role in defending his city, but officials again thwarted his desire to join the military. Instead, they assigned him to firefighter duty on the roof of the Leningrad Conservatory, where his job entailed watching for any incendiary Nazi bombs that might land on the roof and then extinguishing them. His look-out post comprised only one part of a massive undertaking where civilians perched on roofs throughout the city to prevent building fires. The city labored at a feverish pace to dig bomb shelters and to protect its structures and cherished artifacts. Priceless artwork came down from walls and off pedestals to be either hidden or shipped outside the city for safekeeping. Government leaders even ordered factories dismantled, and the equipment and skilled workers shipped out of the city to prevent it all from falling into German hands. Through excruciating work and in perilous conditions, laborers rebuilt 92 factories so that the critical defense manufacturing for the war effort could continue. Never one to be deterred, Shostakovich penned the beginning of a Seventh Symphony on July 19, not knowing that this work would become a musical chronicle of the war and a rallying cry for the Soviet people.

Meanwhile, the Germans captured one city after another, discovering along the way that not all of the Soviet citizens considered them an enemy. People in places so oppressed by Stalin, such as Ukraine, Latvia, and Estonia, viewed the approaching German troops as possible liberators who might restore their places of worship and break up the punishing collective farms. But soon, they realized that the Germans held no interest in living peacefully with a newly conquered people. They wanted these Slavs gone—either by death or by shipment to Germany as slave labor. And so, these people who had now suffered mightily

7. *Dmitri Shostakovich and the Musical Redemption of Leningrad* 207

Dmitri Shostakovich on firefighter duty during the Siege of Leningrad, July 1941. Found in the collection of the State Russian Film and Photo Archive, Krasnogorsk (HIP / Art Resource, NY).

from both sides launched their own formidable underground resistance groups to derail the invaders, and in the process revealed one of the many ironies of this war—that "if Germany had not worked so hard to make itself hated, it could perhaps have conquered whole Soviet territories without a fight."[7]

With each new village and city conquered, the Nazis crept ever closer to Leningrad, and so during July, residents began evacuating. Shostakovich, however, adamantly refused to leave the city of his birth, partly out of stubbornness but also because the writing on his new symphony was going so well that he did not want to disrupt his creative process. His wife and two children still remained at their vacation cottage near the Gulf of Finland. But with the Finnish army moving against the Russians, Shostakovich realized that he must relocate his family so he moved them to Vyritsa, a town south of Leningrad. With reliable news unavailable to him or any Soviet citizen, he had no way of knowing that Vyritsa lay directly in the path of the approaching German army.

Meanwhile, the officials of Leningrad maintained a positivity campaign, assuring their residents of a German defeat before they would ever reach their city. They also guaranteed Leningrad's citizens of adequate food supplies as they began issuing food ration cards on July 18. But despite the propaganda, Leningrad faced an imminent threat from Nazi ground forces, and so the Soviet government banded together groups of civilians, young and old, to start digging a massive ditch around the city that would stop the advancing German tank divisions. A colossal undertaking, the Luga Line of trench and barbed wire stretched almost 350 miles. Fortunately, it had the desired effect, and by mid–July, the Soviets had finally managed an initiative to stall the march on Leningrad. Helped along by heavy rains that grounded Nazi tanks in impenetrable mud, the Luga Line bought precious time for the city to prepare.

By August, Shostakovich's wife and children had been forced to return to Leningrad because of the German advancement, and yet, Shostakovich still resisted evacuating himself and his family. Instead, he bid frequent goodbyes to his friends and colleagues, which often included him playing snippets of his evolving symphony on the piano. Most of the faculty and students of the Leningrad Conservatory relocated to the town of Tashkent, but they did so without their esteemed Professor Shostakovich. Government officials also transported the Leningrad Philharmonic and its conductor Yevgeny Mravinsky to a town in Siberia called Novosibirsk.

But fleeing the city grew more dangerous by the day as the Germans and Finns had cut off most of the train lines in preparation for laying siege to Leningrad, and any trains still operating risked bombings from Nazi planes. Thousands of young children being evacuated by train to the countryside became the collateral damage of the war as they perished from the bombs or were mowed down by machine guns as they ran from the wreckage. In late August amid these terrors, Shostakovich's wife confronted him with the reality that he was risking his family's life for the sake of his work. Her angry pleas reached him, and Shostakovich finally relented, admitting that they should leave the city. He made plans for them to depart via train in two days. But, they had waited too long. On August 25, what would be the last train departing from Leningrad with evacuees had sped ahead feverishly as it saw German paratroopers descending from the sky. The Germans bombed and destroyed the last railway line that day. Two months into the conflict, only about 636,000 people had managed to evacuate. With the Germans also having conquered the Luga Line that had momentarily held them back, they surrounded the city of Leningrad, cutting it off from receiving supplies and troops. Thus began the siege of Leningrad, where 2.5 million people still remained. It would become the longest siege ever recorded—880 days, to be surpassed only between 1992 and 1996, during the 1,425-day siege on Sarajevo.

Shostakovich finished the draft of the first movement of his Seventh Symphony on September 3, sometimes working on the roof while attending to his firefighter duties. Later, he recalled that sense of urgency he felt by saying, "I couldn't not write it. War was all around. I had to be together with the people. I wanted to create the image of our embattled country, to engrave it in music."[8] Within a week, he had begun the second movement as heavy bombing and shelling tormented the city from morning until dark, and sometimes even late into the night. Massive formations of planes targeted important buildings and infrastructure, as well as caused widespread damage to homes, businesses, and the like. Raging fires throughout the city filled the air with thick, black smoke. Despite the previous assurances from Leningrad's officials, food had already grown scarce, requiring Leningrad citizen to scrounge throughout the city every day to find enough to feed themselves and their families.

The Soviet army assigned to defend Leningrad proved ill-equipped in every way. They even resorted to the construction of wooden tank decoys by artists from the Mariinsky Theater in hopes that a show of strength might deter the Germans. They must have been believable decoys because Nazi planes targeted them in several bombing raids. But in the end, this sleight of hand did nothing to prevent the German campaign for Leningrad. Instead of devising real military solutions and strategies, Stalin resorted to his usual foolish response when faced with bad news by accusing military leaders of incompetence and ordering their arrest or execution. This, of course, only further incapacitated the Soviet military and caused officers to withhold critical information because of the tendency to "shoot the messenger." The morale remained so poor among the Russian soldiers that protocols had to be put in place to shoot any soldier trying to desert or surrender to the German side. The policy also included executing the soldier's family as well. In the end, about 3,000 soldiers lost their lives at the hands of their own comrades.

For Hitler, all proceeded as planned. He had made clear his intentions to annihilate completely the residents of Leningrad. Wiping out significant portions of the Russian population proved essential in providing the *Lebensraum* (living space) that the Nazis desired. To accomplish this, Reich officials sought the advice of a nutritionist named Ernst Ziegelmeyer, who concluded that the food situation was so dire in Leningrad that there would be no need to invade the city with ground troops and risk German casualties—that soon the decimation of the 2.5 million residents would happen "naturally." This plan also carried the advantage of saved resources from not having to care for prisoners, as corpses were immeasurably cheaper to manage. So, Hitler accepted the recommendation to maintain the siege and let the unwanted people die of starvation. But Field Marshal Wilhelm Ritter von Leeb did express concern over one possible consequence of that strategy. He worried that as Leningrad's citizens grew more desperate for food that they would try to charge enemy lines to escape and that starving women and children would beg young, susceptible German soldiers for help. To eliminate this prospect, Leeb ordered that landmines be placed as an additional cordon around the perimeter of the city. He also directed that anyone who managed to escape past the minefield should be shot by long-range snipers.

By September, hunger and long food lines accompanied by the soundtrack of bombs constituted the daily routine. But determined to complete his Symphony, Shostakovich often continued to work during air raids, only reluctantly packing up his manuscript and carrying it with him down into the air raid shelter. On September 17, Soviet officials asked Shostakovich to speak about his Seventh Symphony at the Leningrad Radio House. Word had spread about this composition that would represent the trials of the Leningrad people and sound a triumphant defeat of the German *Wehrmacht* (war machine). On his way to the radio station, Shostakovich had to seek protection in a bomb shelter as air raid sirens blared. When the all-clear sounded, he barely had time to rush into the station to make his air-time appointment, thankfully still clutching the sheet of paper on which he had typed what he wanted to say. The esteemed composer communicated to those listening that he had completed two movements. He also praised their city and encouraged everyone to take heart and persist despite the perilous times. "I'm telling you this so that the people of Leningrad listening to me will know that life goes on in our city."[9]

Shostakovich began writing the third movement that night by candlelight since he no longer had electricity in his apartment. As food and electricity grew scarcer amid the incessant bombings, uplifting the spirit and morale of those left in the city became increasingly important, as evidenced by the many who clung to the inexplicable hope that Shostakovich's new Symphony provided. But while feeling a strong sense of duty to care for his comrades, Shostakovich also experienced overwhelming grief for the city of his birth. Despite the danger, he would often venture out for walks and take in with wide-eyed horror the destruction of so grand a city. "I looked at my beloved city with pain and pride. It stood singed in fires and tempered in battles. It had suffered the deepest anguish of the war..."[10] The grimmer the situation looked for the residents of Leningrad, the more determined Shostakovich became to finish this composition. "I kept working day and night. There were times when the anti-aircraft guns were in actions and bombs were falling, but I kept working."[11] On September 29, having just turned 35-years-old four days earlier, he completed the third movement, a slow dirge that expressed profound sorrow and longing, laying bare the soul of those under siege.

The following day, Shostakovich received notification that he and his family would be airlifted to Moscow the next day, but that unfortunately this transport could not include his mother, sister, or nephew. Shostakovich protested and was subsequently assured that they would be evacuated soon on another flight. So, the family prepared to depart, aware that they could take very little with them. For Shostakovich, leaving behind any of his precious music scores seemed unimaginable, but he only took three pieces of music: his in-progress Seventh Symphony, his opera *Lady Macbeth*, and his much beloved score to Stravinsky's *Symphony of Psalms*. Miraculously, after all of the chaos and destruction that would befall the city, Shostakovich would eventually return and find that all of his scores had been saved and stored by the Leningrad Philharmonic.

After a harrowing flight over enemy lines in which the plane was fired upon but remained unscathed, the Shostakovich family landed outside of Moscow, where a car waited to convey them to the city. They arrived in Moscow only to discover that the Reich had launched a major campaign against the capital that very day, known as Operation Typhoon. By this point, the Soviet casualties could only be described as devastating—approximately 45,000 per day for a total of 3 million soldiers, in addition to huge aircraft losses and about 20,000 tanks destroyed. While the Red Army had dwindled to only a little over 2 million soldiers, the Germans controlled 45 percent of the Soviet population. For two weeks, the Shostakovich family lived in Moscow's Moskva Hotel and hurried down to the hotel's damp basement for the frequent air raids. Party leaders made as much use of Shostakovich as they could for propaganda. "His made a compelling story, that of a courageous young composer resisting evacuation to defend his native city not only by physical deeds but also through one of the most venerated of human endeavors—one inherently antithetical to the destructive impulse of war—the creation of art."[12]

At the end of two weeks, Moscow proved too vulnerable, and the government evacuated the Shostakovich family again, this time by train toward the east. As they made their way to the train station, Shostakovich witnessed a city in chaos, devolving into violence and rampant looting. As people grew desperate to escape, but had no means, they descended upon the wealthy and well connected as they left via cars and trucks, blocking the roads and even pulling some from their vehicles. The grisly scene unfolded through a haze of thick smoke, partially due to the bombings, but also because Kremlin employees frantically burned documents lest they fall into the hands of the Nazis.

The Shostakovich family managed to make it safely aboard a train bound for some unknown destination, although not all of their luggage got loaded. Far from the luxuries of a journey on the *Orient Express*, the poor conditions on this train included over-crowding and food shortages. The Shostakoviches shared Railway Car No. 7 with other artists, writers, musicians, and even dancers from the Bolshoi Theatre, all crammed in at more than twice the intended capacity. At one point, Shostakovich's precious score for the Seventh Symphony, which had been wrapped in a blanket for safe-keeping, disappeared amid the chaos. It was not located until the fourth day of the journey, covered in urine on the floor of the bathroom. Somehow the blanket had protected the irreplaceable score so that it suffered little damage from its unfortunate ordeal.

On October 22, after a miserable week on the train, Shostakovich and his family disembarked at the town of Kuibyshev. As on the train, their new home overflowed with artists, dancers, and fellow composers. The city also housed the Soviet government, which had fled Moscow along with the relocated defense factories. The transformation of this rural town, where horse-drawn carts on dirt roads constituted the main form of transportation, into a bustling headquarters must have been quite a shock for its long-time residents. Workers had converted a school into housing for the evacuees, and the Shostakoviches shared a small classroom with another family before eventually acquiring their own private room. It certainly seemed an odd juxtaposition to see some of Russia's most renowned artists, musicians, and writers congregated in such a place and under such circumstances. Still, they had shelter and food, and most continued to find solace and escape in their art.

But Shostakovich had not fared well since the relocation. All of the stress of the evacuation and the harrowing train ride, plus the chaos of the resettlement, left Shostakovich unable to write. He worried constantly about his beloved Leningrad and about the family he had left behind, who had not been evacuated despite the promises. Once so determined to complete the Seventh Symphony, Shostakovich seemed devoid of his muse. To a friend he wrote, "You know, as soon as I got on that train something snapped inside of me.... I can't compose just now, knowing how many people are losing their lives."[13] So for now, the fourth movement, the finale of his great masterpiece, would have to wait.

Meanwhile, as Shostakovich struggled to acclimate to his new living situation, winter arrived in Leningrad. With temperatures plummeting below zero, residents scrambled to keep warm without coal, firewood, or electricity. Most lacked windows and walls as well, stranded in a city completely cut off, with no means of importing any of the necessities for a desperate population. Faulty planning, poor choices, and blatant denial among city officials had left Leningrad vulnerable. Back in the summer, city leaders had actually turned away a convoy bringing Leningrad an extra stockpile of food stores for the winter because they thought accepting those supplies would undermine the message of prosperity and confidence that they touted. The tragic results of this one misstep cannot be overemphasized. These same officials had also unwisely stored all of the city's food reserves in 38 warehouses clustered at one location. Inside, these dilapidated buildings contained the essentials of cooking oil, sugar, and wheat—the difference between life and death. The stupidity of that decision became all too clear in the early weeks of September. Upon learning of this concentration of supplies, the Nazis bombed those structures, destroying everything.

So in addition to freezing to death, Leningrad's citizens were dying of starvation. The desperation drove people to scrape off wallpaper for any nutrients from the paste and to bake bread from sawdust for the cellulose. People dismantled furniture to get at any glue that could be consumed. Mad with hunger, they experimented with anything and everything, even devouring lipstick. The Germans accented the misery with a campaign designed solely to taunt and dehumanize the starving residents. Leaflets fluttered down from the sky and covered city streets, all bearing the same message—"Finish your bread; you'll soon be dead."[14]

As dead bodies piled up around the city, the frozen corpses would sometimes be missing a limb, as the extreme hunger had driven some to cannibalism. Bodies and body parts also disappeared from morgues or anywhere the dead lay. The corpse-eating form of cannibalism proved the more common, but not exclusive, as hunger-induced desperation and insanity caused residents to kill even their own family members for food. By the end of the siege, the government had arrested over 2,000 people for cannibalism, but only those who had actually killed received the maximum punishment—execution.

But stories of kindness and generosity of spirit abounded throughout Leningrad as well. Many citizens formed collective groups to live and work together, which provided much needed physical and emotional support. Sometimes these people belonged to the same family, but often they just created their own kinship. One group of teachers made it their mission to search throughout the city, building by building, for abandoned and orphaned children, of which there were many. Overall, people sought solace however they could, and one of their favorite refuges became the public library, which refused to close despite the terrible siege. The library provided a kind of sacred space for Leningraders to congregate among their beloved books. Interestingly, its collection actually grew during this time as librarians purchased books from those who needed money to buy food and also scrounged the city for abandoned books to rescue.

After months of crushing defeats, the tide of the war finally began to shift in favor of the Soviets during December 1941 as German forces, who had expected victory before the brutal Russian winter set in, now found themselves ill prepared. With temperatures dipping to minus 40 degrees, the Nazi military struggled with inadequate clothing and rations in addition to troop exhaustion and equipment failures from the cold. The Red Army seized this advantage, countering the German advance and pushing them back from their intended occupation of Moscow, where Stalin had stubbornly stayed put, refusing to evacuate with other government officials to Kuibyshev. Germany's unsuccessful bid to capture Moscow proved costly, losing them about 500 tanks and 24,000 soldiers. The Japanese bombing of Pearl Harbor on December 7 also benefited the Soviets, since it forced the United States to enter the war. The U.S. now found itself a reluctant ally of the Soviets, as various treaties and pacts forced Great Britain, the United States, and the Soviet Union into an alliance against the Axis powers in Germany, Italy, and Japan.

With news of some Soviet victories and the anticipation of help from the United States, Shostakovich once again resumed work on his Symphony, after a month and a half absence from composing. He began sketching out the fourth and final movement, which would emerge as a celebratory ode to Mother Russia's victorious triumph over her enemies. The composer stated his inspiration for the ending as simply, "I want to describe a beautiful future time when the enemy will have been defeated."[15] Officials had relocated Shostakovich and his family to a two-room apartment and provided him with a piano. Sitting at that piano, he had made many attempts to regain a desire to compose, but had previously been unsuccessful, to the great distress of those around him. But now, the muse had anointed Shostakovich again, and so he worked, finishing his Seventh Symphony, the Leningrad Symphony, on December 27.

As Shostakovich began to play excerpts of the finished work on the piano for his friends and neighbors, they asked him questions about the true meaning of the work. They wanted to know what each movement symbolized and how closely the various motives functioned as leitmotifs for the current war. Shostakovich carefully answered all of their queries, concluding with an overarching explanation that the work represented the physical and psychological battles of the Soviet people to overcome the scourge of Fascism. But he also reminded them that Fascism could take on many forms, not just what the Nazis embodied, and that "…this music is about all forms of terror, slavery, the bondage of the spirit."[16] After the war, this statement would lead noted musicologists to regard the Seventh Symphony as not merely an indictment against Hitler and his campaign to destroy Leningrad, but also against Stalin himself, who had wreaked so much damage on the city and the entire nation.

Now that Shostakovich had completed the work, the government pressed to have it premiered as quickly as possible, wielding it as a cultural and emotional weapon against their enemies. While also eager for a first performance, Shostakovich remained distracted with worry about his family in Leningrad. He heard from them infrequently, and the news that he did receive spoke of malnourishment and desperation. Getting letters and money to them proved almost impossible. So with great persistence, he lobbied to secure their evacuation. But, at least for now, Leningrad remained inaccessible.

The season of the year had arrived when Leningrad experienced about 18 hours of darkness per day. Residents at that time described the city as shrouded in an eerie silence. The Germans had suspended their bombing campaigns, seeing no use in wasting ammunition on a people who were dying at a rate of 10,000 or more a day. Not even the barking of a dog could be heard—they had all been eaten. With the ground frozen to impenetrability, the living heaped corpses onto ever-growing stacks. At times the dead just lay wherever they had collapsed, the brutal temperatures enveloping them in a burial cloth of ice, in an almost state of petrification. "Gradually, like the immigration of an insidious, phantom population, Leningrad belonged more to the dead than to the living. The dead watched over streets and sat in snow-swamped buses. Whole apartment buildings were tenanted by them, where in broken rooms, dead families sat waiting at tables. Their dominion spread room by room, like lights going out in evening."[17]

Those still alive in Leningrad found themselves facing the greatest moral challenge of their life. Some rose above, while others succumbed to theft and murder. All bore the mark of their dire circumstances. As a result of the prolonged malnourishment, the population developed dystrophy, an atrophying of the body that caused them to move and speak haltingly, like malfunctioning automatons. Even though factory workers received a bit of extra rations, the meager supplement was not enough to ward off this condition, and so they now operated equipment with slow, mechanized movements. For many of the other residents, the dystrophy rendered them incapable of any movement, and so they just sat and waited for death.

In the early months of 1942, despite the deprivation and death in Leningrad, the radio station continued to broadcast, airing poetry readings and pre-recorded music in addition to political speeches. Any time the defiant people of Leningrad could still read, write, perform, and create, they waged a psychological battle against an enemy who had condemned them to extinction. All of these activities boosted morale, helping people to survive against all odds. But because of the extreme situation, the radio station could not broadcast continually; so during inactive times, it would leave a metronome going, whose steady tick tock filled the silent airways. For some, it must have seemed like the ticking of a countdown clock to their own demise. One of the Leningrad residents, a young nurse named Elena Martilla, compared it in her diary to "…a simple distant and weak but living pulsation … the pulse of a fatally ill patient in the silence of a ward."[18]

Leningrad longed to premiere Shostakovich's new Symphony since the city's plight had inspired the work. But so many of Leningrad's musicians had either evacuated or died, that it proved impossible. Instead, the world premiere of Shostakovich's Seventh Symphony would have to take place in Kuibyshev, with its cadre of talented musicians and its distance from the battlefront. After much discussion, officials scheduled the concert for March 5, 1942, to be performed by the Bolshoi Theater Orchestra and conducted by Samuil Samosud. Shostakovich was well acquainted with this popular Russian conductor, who had conducted some of his other premieres, including *The Nose* in 1929 and *Lady Macbeth of the Mtsensk District* in 1934. After working at various theaters in Leningrad, Samosud had moved to

Moscow in 1936 to accept the position of chief conductor at the Bolshoi Opera. But while Samosud had earned Shostakovich's admiration for his interpretation of operatic and theatrical works, the composer felt less sure of Samosud's ability in regards to his Leningrad Symphony, as the work called for an unusually large orchestra, which in the end totaled 109 players.

But once the rehearsals began, Shostakovich felt greatly reassured as to his own sound writing and to the skills of Samosud and the orchestra. For months, the hype and publicity over this new work that would be the very embodiment of Russian nationalism had certainly put high expectations on any composer and premiere. In addition to articles published in Party newspapers, reporters from around the world had shown interest as well, including *New York Times* reporter Ralph Parker who interviewed Shostakovich in Kuibyshev. The resulting article, "Shostakovich, Composer, Explains His Symphony of Plain Man in War," had presented an image of the Soviet composer and his noble cause that could be easily related to by readers in the United States.

After weeks of intensive rehearsals, the day for the premiere finally arrived. Despite his tremendous nerves, Shostakovich gave an introduction at the opening of the concert. He declared, "Music is my weapon. We are struggling for the highest human ideals in history. We are battling for our culture, for science, for art, for everything we have created and built…. I dedicate my Seventh Symphony to our struggle with fascism, to our coming victory over the enemy, and to my native city, Leningrad."[19]

Fortunately for Shostakovich, the Soviet authorities in attendance, as well as the orchestra musicians and the audience, received the Leningrad Symphony with much enthusiasm. The premiere had also been broadcast throughout the country via radio. So in addition to the average Russian citizen who had tuned in, Shostakovich's Conservatory colleagues in Tashkent had also listened with great anticipation, as did other celebrated musicians such as violinist David Oistrakh, who had sat by his radio in Moscow. The consensus came without hesitation that this work represented both a musical and spiritual triumph. "The resonance of its reception and the immediacy and universality of its morale-boosting effect turned it almost overnight into a potent national—even international—symbol of just cause and steely resolve in the war against fascism. It anchored itself in the popular consciousness as an instantaneous cultural icon, something totally unprecedented for a serious symphonic work."[20]

The resounding success of the premiere just added to Shostakovich's already bolstered spirit. In the weeks leading up to the performance, he had received the miraculous news that the government finally planned to evacuate his mother, sister, and nephew. The frigid winter temperatures had caused Lake Ladoga, which formed the eastern border of Leningrad, to freeze solid enough that transports back and forth across the ice became possible. Supplies started to arrive, and evacuees to depart. But it proved a risky endeavor, because the Germans had full view of the convoys and regularly fired upon them. As a result, large craters opened up in the ice. The drivers of the trucks could not always see those breaches, and many plunged everyone aboard to a watery grave. The brutal temperatures also caused numerous deaths in those weakened souls who huddled in the backs of the unheated trucks as they slowly traversed that frozen evacuation route known as the Road of Life. In the end, thousands perished on this highway, yet it saved even more through successful evacuations and food supply deliveries.

This Road of Life also made possible the arrival of Shostakovich's family in Kuibyshev on March 19. With them, they brought harrowing stories of a city devastated and overrun with the agony of the dead and the dying. Shostakovich learned that many of his friends and colleagues had perished, including his dear student, Venjamin Fleishman, the one who had walked that first day with Shostakovich to volunteer for the military. Before the start of the war, Shostakovich had been supervising Fleishman's composition project, an opera based on a Chekhov short story. But Fleishman had put this project on hold to fight in the People's Volunteer Guard and had been killed a few months later on September 14, 1941. As a tribute to his fallen student, Shostakovich would later complete the opera, titled *Rothschild's Violin*, and arrange for its staging at the Leningrad Conservatory in 1968.

On March 20, the Soviet government flew Shostakovich, Samosud, and members of the Bolshoi Orchestra to Moscow to prepare for the capital's premiere of the Leningrad Symphony. The work had to be rehearsed and readied for a March 29 performance, with the combined forces of the Bolshoi Orchestra and Moscow's All-Union Radio Orchestra. The venue for this important event was none other than the Hall of Columns, which resided in the House of Unions. This building's palatial ballrooms had housed many elite concerts and events since the 18th century and had been referenced in famous works of Russian literature such as Tolstoy's *War and Peace*. The House of Unions had provided performance space for many of Russia's finest composers, including Tchaikovsky and Rimsky-Korsakov, and had also hosted other great foreign musicians such as the Hungarian piano virtuoso Franz Liszt. Again, the audience and the government greeted Shostakovich's Seventh Symphony with tremendous applause and enthusiasm. The following month on April 11, Soviet officials awarded it the Stalin Prize, the highest honor a work could receive.

The success of the Leningrad Symphony premieres certainly paved a successful future career path for Maestro Samosud. In 1943, he would return to Moscow as the director of the Stanislavsky Opera and Ballet Theatre, and then in 1951, the 67-year-old conductor would found a new orchestra devoted to performing operatic music for radio broadcasts. But the ensemble would quickly surpass that limited role and officially change its name to the Moscow Philharmonic Orchestra in 1953. Samosud would remain in his post as conductor there for several years, passing away in Moscow in 1964 at age 80.

Meanwhile, as other Russian cities and countries enjoyed performances of Shostakovich's Seventh Symphony, Leningrad, the city for which it had been written, still saw no hope of a premiere. Back in early 1941, Leningrad had overflowed with musicians, including the faculty and students at the Conservatory, but by the end of that year, fewer and fewer remained, either as the result of evacuation or death. Of the multiple orchestras that had supported the city, only a remnant of players from one orchestra lingered—the Leningrad Radio Orchestra. They, along with other musicians, theater and dance troupes, and artists, endeavored to maintain the active and rich artistic life of the city despite the daily worsening circumstances. Concerts and recitals took place under miserable conditions, and yet, audience members still showed up to listen in the dark and the cold. Organizers planned a large event at Philharmonia Hall for November 22 that would feature music, drama, and dance. The sheer determination of Leningrad's artistic community can be seen in the ballet dancers, who continued to push themselves despite their starvation and dystrophy, dancing in layers of clothing to combat the cold. One of the city's most talented pianists, Vladmir Sofronitsky, who also happened to be the son-in-law of the famous Russian composer Alexander Scriabin, performed a recital in the Pushkin Theatre. He played the program wearing gloves with the fingers cut out, the only option for battling such extreme temperatures. But reflecting back on the performance many years later, Sofronitsky related how both his experience as a performer and the audience's reaction had been heightened because of their souls' desperate need for this musical nourishment, especially since attending any event during this time required stepping around and over the corpses that lay everywhere.

Along with these planned events throughout the city, the Leningrad Radio continued to broadcast music live, as well as poetry readings and dramatic presentations, all of which reached not only the residents but the fighting soldiers as well. But in time, the various performers grew too weak to continue despite the government having allotted many of them extra rations so they could continue to boost morale for the Soviet war cause. The Leningrad Radio Orchestra played its last live radio performance on January 1, 1942, which featured excerpts from Rimsky-Korsakov's opera *The Snow Maiden*. Wracked by sickness, hunger, and death, the orchestra then disbanded. The tenor who had sung on that broadcast died later the same night from starvation. While a smattering of small musical performances still happened throughout the city during those winter months, music on any grand scale ground to a halt.

In March 1942, government officials in Leningrad ordered a renewed effort to bring music back to the ravaged city. Karl Eliasberg, the Radio Orchestra's conductor and the only prominent conductor left, ventured throughout the city trying to locate his musicians. A poster campaign, as well as announcements via the loudspeakers, called for all musicians to report in and register at the House of Radio. In turn, orchestra members would qualify for extra rations, as Eliasberg had negotiated for them to join other influential artists from the city at a government feeding station set up in the Bolshoi Theatre. As in the Nazi concentration camps where musicians who could provide entertainment and utilitarian music often stood a greater chance of survival, the musicians of Leningrad who could prove useful to the Soviet war machinery were now being given, albeit too late for many, a possible reprieve from the shadow of death.

In addition to the push to restart the Radio Orchestra, other groups of musicians, artists, dancers, and actors also came together to present events for the city. The grand Philharmonia Hall remained miraculously intact and able to serve as a venue. The building had lost electricity during the heavy bombing, but officials had restored its power as part of the effort to make these crucial gatherings possible. But even as some progress took place among the artistic community, the losses of giants in the field continued to accumulate. On March 8, Igor Mikhlachevsky, the director of Capella, the oldest choir in Russia, died. The conductor of the Radio Choir, V. Maratov, succumbed the next day. The toll of the deprivation appeared to be no respecter of persons and fell on the young and old, the educated and the uneducated alike. According to 18-year-old nurse and aspiring set designer, Elena Martilla, the residents of Leningrad resembled walking skeletons, with even the young appearing to be in their late years. She walked now with a cane and had been mistakenly addressed as "grandmother." As she slowly made her way through the city to the School of Arts, she recorded in her diary, "...I met more dead than living—ten dead for every five alive..."[21] In response, she clung to her art, and the more she painted, the more resolute and defiant she became. "I realized that I will not die—this I felt with every cell of my dystrophic organism and it infused me with strength. Now I had caught my second wind, no, my tenth. I even became happy..."[22]

Meanwhile, Maestro Eliasberg scheduled the first rehearsal of the reconstituted orchestra for March 30. But when the day arrived, only 15 players, all extremely weak from hunger and exposure, showed up to practice in the freezing room. The 35-year-old Eliasberg was not in good shape either. He could barely lift his arms to conduct even though the government had been housing him at the Astoria Hotel, which included a feeding station for the elite citizens of Leningrad. Too frail to even walk to the rehearsal location, Eliasberg had to be pulled on a sled, as did one of the cellists, Nikolay Kramov, who sat cradling his cello as the sled hauled him through the desolate streets. This first practice, intended for three hours, lasted only 15 minutes. The players simply lacked the stamina to continue longer, despite Eliasberg's attempts to spur them on, saying, "Dear friends, we are weak but we must force ourselves to start work."[23]

Regardless of the disastrous first rehearsal, Eliasberg refused to forsake his charge. The conductor saved many lives by getting musicians to the rehearsals and to feeding stations. One day, he even discovered percussionist Dzhaudat Iaydarov lying in a pile of corpses on the street, having apparently died on his way to rehearsal. But on closer examination, Eliasberg detected a slight movement from Iaydarov's fingers and quickly summoned help to carry the poor man inside and to find some rations. But Eliasberg's interventions did not always prove successful. Some players were just too far gone by the time the government proffered an intervention. N. Trakan, one of the orchestra's double bass players, died while at the feeding station.

As the orchestra continued to rehearse, Eliasberg realized that the group was not yet ready to tackle large works, so instead he scheduled a concert of short, familiar pieces for April 5 at the Pushkin Theatre. The program certainly put on a nationalistic display with excerpts from Tchaikovsky's *Swan Lake*, Glazunov's *Ouverture solenelle*, and Glinka's overture to *Ruslan and Ludmilla*. Mezzo-soprano Nadezhda Velter and bass Vladimri Kastorksy also sang arias from operas by Tchaikovsky and Glinka. But despite the iconic setting and the beloved repertoire, the reality persisted that the auditorium, so cold that the players and the audience could see their breath, held a group of people almost unrecognizable to what they had been a year earlier. Their oboist, Ksenia Matus, described it as a gathering where "…there were only the ghosts of listeners, and on the stage the ghosts of performers."[24] Nevertheless, the audience applauded enthusiastically, although it created little noise due to their mitten-encased hands. These people had traded priceless food rations for a ticket—the power of music so dramatically on display.

A week later on April 12, the orchestra miraculously put on another concert of all new repertoire at Philharmonia Hall. They again played music by Tchaikovsky, from *Eugene Onegin* and *The Nutcracker*, as well as aria excerpts from *The Golden Cockerel* by Rimsky-Korsakov and Alexander Serov's *Rogneda*. The program also featured non–Russian works, including Liszt's *Hungarian Rhapsody No. 14*, Rossini's overture from *William Tell*, and the overture to Gounod's *Faust*. The orchestra continued throughout April and into the summer to present concert after concert of challenging works, some for radio broadcast and some in various performance venues throughout the city. In light of the rigorous schedule from those months, it would appear that the musicians must have dramatically recovered their full health. But nothing could have been further from the truth. They continued to struggle to find the strength to play, and they continued to die. Bassoonist Grigorii Zakharovich Yeryomkin described the experience with heartbreaking clarity. "We had to overcome the pain of sitting on our bones, because our muscles had wasted away. We tried putting soft things under us, but the pain did not go away."[25]

As spring arrived in the city, the warm rays of the sun infused the starving citizens with renewed energy. But these welcomed temperatures also brought the thawing, and with it, the hideous revealing of the corpses all over town that had lain hidden underneath mounds of snow and ice. So, the residents of Leningrad, forever proud of their city, took to the streets to clean up the death and detritus of war. Determined to defy the Nazi plan to exterminate them, they planted gardens with seeds that had managed to arrive via the Road of Life. The warm air, and the sense of hope that blew in with it, led people out into the sunshine to sit on a bench and read. These beleaguered people, having survived the worst winter of their lives, longed for anything that could approach normalcy and for any grasp at the simple pleasures of life so easily taken for granted.

While his beloved city experienced this moment of renewal, Shostakovich longed for a performance of the Seventh Symphony by his beloved Leningrad Conservatory Orchestra, which remained in Tashkent. The orchestra's director, Pavel Serebryakov, also wanted to schedule a premiere by his ensemble and sent word to the composer about getting a copy of the score. Shostakovich replied that he wanted his friend and colleague Isaak Glikman, who had fled to Tashkent along with the other Conservatory faculty, to come to Kuibyshev to collect the music. So in the role of a musical ambassador, Glikman embarked via train in April, on what would certainly not be an easy or relaxing journey in the midst of war. He had needed to provide his own food for the trip, so the Conservatory, after much debate, arrived at the number of 20 meat pies for the 10-day train ride. Once underway, Glikman discovered that the pies were rock-hard; and when he finally managed to break one apart, he saw black dots about the size of poppy seeds moving about in it. Tashkent ants had infested the whole lot. But with no other food available, Glikman had little choice but to eat those pies, ants and all.

When the train pulled into the station at Kuibyshev on April 15, Glikman and Shostakovich felt tremendous joy at being reunited. As the two friends caught up on essential news, Shostakovich warned Glikman of a typhoid epidemic in the city and that he should take care to stay away from crowds and public transportation. The composer's apartment in Kuibyshev was already overcrowded with extended family, so Glikman would sleep on the sofa in Shostakovich's study for the extent of his stay. After a month-long visit, Glikman returned to Tashkent with a score and parts in hand. One of Russia's most respected conductors, Ilya Musin, directed the Leningrad Conservatory's performance of the Seventh. Now, almost every Soviet city that could generate enough skilled players to perform the work scrambled to schedule their own "premiere" of the Leningrad Symphony.

But the primary objective remained to stage a performance of Shostakovich's Seventh in the city for which it had been written. The residents of Leningrad had heard about the popularity of their Symphony from a broadcasted radio lecture, "The Symphony of a Heroic Fight for Victory," which had aired during April as the excitement over the work reached international proportions. But the musical successes of Shostakovich's Seventh could not remedy how poorly the war was going for the Allies. The spring thaw had reenergized the Germans in their quest to conquer Slavic lands, and news from the Pacific had proved equally grim following the American surrender of the Philippines on April 9. So, the timing finally seemed right for bringing the hope of this masterwork to Leningrad. City officials again sought musicians from throughout the city and ordered those away on military duty sent back to supplement the current Radio Orchestra. While the necessary personnel arrangements were made, a Soviet pilot secretly flew a copy of the Leningrad Symphony score into the city, a great risk since he would be easily in the enemy's sights. The government conscripted residents for the painstaking task of copying out all of the necessary parts by hand with rulers to draw the staves. Producing that many pages of legible music severely taxed the already malnourished and weak in Leningrad.

Meanwhile, the reputation of the Seventh Symphony continued to spark a demand for the score so great that around 700 copies had to be printed despite the shortage of paper.

For ease of shipping to far away destinations, workers photographed the parts and score then reduced them onto microfilm strips. The Soviet Union especially focused on securing performances in London and in the United States, which they believed would vastly boost Russia's standing in the war. They achieved this goal by the summer, when the first performance in the West took place on June 22, 1942, as a live broadcast from a BBC radio studio with Sir Henry Wood conducting the London Philharmonic. The choice of date proved significant indeed, as it marked the one year anniversary of the Nazi invasion of Russia. Wood and his orchestra presented a concert performance the following week to a sold-out audience at the Royal Albert Hall on June 29.

A month earlier, on May 30, 1942, a mysterious diplomatic pouch carrying a wooden box of microfilm arrived at the U.S. State Department in Washington, D.C., where officials then passed it on to the Soviet Embassy. On June 2, a representative from the Am-Rus Music Corporation, an organization the Soviets had contracted to promote Russian music, assumed the task of getting this score into the hands of American conductors, in hopes of forging a better relationship with the United States, but also out of sheer desperation because the war was going so poorly for the Allies. By this time, the Nazis had consumed most of Europe and proved equally adept at devouring Russian land. This box of microfilm had certainly traveled an arduous and circuitous route of 10,000 miles via a U.S. Air Transport Command plane. Travel during the war, when air, land, and sea all ran the risks of an encounter with the enemy, had presented an almost intractable challenge for getting this item from Russia to the United States. In the end, the precious cargo had flown via the Middle East to North Africa then to Brazil, including stops in Tehran and Cairo. When it finally touched down in Washington, D.C., an American agent almost lost the package when he foolishly left it unguarded on his restaurant table while he went to the restroom and returned to find his table completely cleared. Fortunately, after just a few panicked moments, he saw a busboy with a tray of trash and noticed the wooden box among the detritus.

On June 3 in New York City, experts unrolled the over 100-foot strip of microfilm that contained the score and parts to Shostakovich's Seventh Symphony, a total of 2,750 pages of music. As they began to stretch it across a light table and examine it with their magnifying glasses, the poignant inscription, "Dedicated to the City of Leningrad," appeared first. After the viability of the microfilm had been verified, the Am-Rus Music Corporation put its agent Eugene Weintraub in charge of promoting the piece in the United States and securing a premiere. Weintraub received overwhelming interest as there had never been such a competition among famous conductors to be given the opportunity to perform a premiere. Among those vying for the honor were Artur Rodzinski with the Cleveland Orchestra, Serge Koussevitzky at the Boston Symphony, and the Hollywood maestro Leopold Stokowski. Stokowski, in particular, seemed a strong contender as his credentials included high-profile premieres, such as the U.S. premiere of Mahler's Eighth Symphony in 1916 with the Philadelphia Orchestra, and he had also garnered considerable attention on the world stage for conducting the score to Disney's *Fantasia* in 1940.

But in the end, Weintraub and his team chose Arturo Toscanini and the NBC Radio Orchestra in New York to give the U.S. premiere of the Seventh, via live broadcast from Studio 8-H on July 19, 1942. It certainly seemed an odd choice since Toscanini had never been known as a champion of Russian music and had passed when offered the opportunity to conduct the U.S. premiere of Shostakovich's Fifth Symphony. In comparison, Koussevitzky and Stokowski were much better suited to the task and both voiced their objections vehemently. Nevertheless, the clout and influence of NBC had won the "bid." Out on summer break, the NBC musicians had to be recalled and additional musicians hired for such a large orchestra. Meanwhile, a team of photographers worked around the clock to prepare the necessary copies of the conductor's score and instrument parts from the microfilm, a monumental task that required enlarging all of the pages to normal size and making over 2,000 individual prints in the dark room.

Toscanini also began the process of preparing. His incredible mind was adept and disciplined to commit scores completely to memory, and so the conductor took the 252-page score with him for a three-day retreat and emerged with it securely memorized. With only four rehearsals to master the immense work, Toscanini and the orchestra worked as quickly and efficiently as possible. When the broadcast time finally arrived, 4:15 p.m. EST, all of the arduous weeks and tedious logistics felt justified as one of the most significant compositions of the era reached a broadcast audience of millions throughout the U.S. The decision to open the program with "The Star-Spangled Banner" then proceed with Shostakovich's Leningrad Symphony created a meaningful juxtaposition that would have seemed untenable a year earlier, but even then echoed of a strange, if not ironic, incongruity. The following month on August 14, Koussevitzky did have the privilege of conducting the first concert performance in the United States at the Berkshire Symphonic Festival with an audience of 5,000. Within six months, Shostakovich's Seventh Symphony had been performed some 62 times in the U.S. alone. But rather than being thrilled by the acclaim, Shostakovich grew wary of all the attention, knowing Stalin's extremely jealous nature and how easily fame and recognition could turn against a Soviet composer and end in his banishment or even death.

But fortunately for Shostakovich's welfare, the Soviets wanted his Seventh Symphony to gain as much notoriety as possible in the United States, as they desperately needed the country's aid in the form of military equipment and food shipments. President Roosevelt readily grasped the importance of equipping the Russians to hold off the advancing Germans, especially since the U.S. continued to fare poorly in the war in the Pacific and certainly, at least at this time, could not engage the Germans directly. But not all Americans had been as eager to lend support to the Soviets, whom many still distrusted since they had been their enemy until only quite recently. But now, the Soviet strategy of using Shostakovich and his Leningrad Symphony to win over the American populist had gained traction despite the great political and cultural divide between the two nations. Over the summer of 1942, great enthusiasm developed among Americans for this brave composer and his besieged city, especially after *Time* magazine placed Shostakovich on the cover of the July issue that released the week before the U.S. premiere—the first time any composer had ever graced its cover. The sympathetic article inside appeared tailor-written to present this Russian composer as not so different from them and to make supporting him and his beleaguered comrades seem an extension of American patriotism. In the end, the Soviets did receive those much needed supplies, both military and humanitarian, and war relief drives throughout the U.S. also contributed funds to the struggling nation. Stalin failed, however, to secure the commitment of a land force that would counter the Nazi encroachment on the USSR. That Second Front would not come until 1944.

During the same month as the first performance of the Seventh in the United States, rehearsals finally began in Leningrad for its premiere on August 9. But despite the importance of performing this composition as the city lay under siege, preparing the Seventh constituted only one of many responsibilities heaped upon those musicians as they continued to give concerts of other repertoire and as those "on loan" from the military or other essential duties had to complete that work in addition to practicing. Unsurprisingly, the orchestra members struggled with the length and difficulty of Shostakovich's Seventh, lacking the physical stamina and the emotional strength to embrace such a daunting piece. Players sometimes fainted during rehearsals because of their weakened conditions, and some died before the Leningrad premiere could take place. Nevertheless, the orchestra persevered despite the odds. The percussionist Dzhaudat Iaydarov, whom Maestro Eliasberg had literally scooped up from a pile of corpses in the street, remained present in the orchestra and determined to do his part to make this performance a reality. The encouraging presence of their conductor certainly played a crucial role in motivating the musicians, as did the not-too-veiled threats issued from government officials "reminding" them of the urgency for a successful premiere. The Soviet leadership needed its citizens to maintain their nationalistic resolve and for that united spirited to be on display for the whole world to see. Stalin also wanted another high-profile artistic success to camouflage the police state that still existed in the Soviet Union, where beatings, interrogations, executions, and disappearances continued unabated under the cover of war.

Along with the push to master Shostakovich's Seventh Symphony, July also brought a renewed Nazi offensive against Leningrad—Operation Nordlicht (Northern Light). The fall of Leningrad, as predicted by Hitler's advisors, lagged way behind schedule, causing Hitler to grow impatient with the siege. He remained eager for the complete annihilation of the population of Leningrad, and for any Russian left alive to be driven to Siberia. To hasten his agenda, Hitler ordered another direct onslaught of shelling and bombings on the city. So as a result of the prolonged siege coupled with the new assault, another 15,716 people in Leningrad died in the month of July. Now, those still alive in the city constituted only one for every four people who had been registered as residing there in the 1939 census.

Despite the fresh horrors unleashed during July, the plans for the Shostakovich premiere remained resolute. The date for the fateful concert, August 9, had been carefully chosen. At the start of the siege a year earlier, Hitler had bragged that on that date he would be feasting and celebrating in Leningrad's Astoria Hotel. Now, not only had Hitler's timeline been thwarted, but the hotel no longer offered a luxurious destination, only a hospital for the starving and dying. As the city moved forward with the concert, many logistical considerations needed attending to besides just the preparation of the musicians. One of the critical components was the use of loudspeakers to broadcast the concert to all corners of the city. The military also served an imperative function in the success of the evening due to fears that the Germans would launch a bombing attack on Philharmonia Hall, which would present an especially visible target on that evening since it would be lit up with electric lights for the concert. To counteract the threat, the Red Army devised Operation Squall, a decoy attack on German lines on the opposite side of Leningrad. This military diversion would prove successful, allowing the concert to proceed uninterrupted by shelling, although neither the performers nor the audience knew the reason.

On August 9, the 335th day of the insidious siege, Leningrad's population awoke miraculously energized at the promise of this concert. Not only would the cultured citizens who had attended similar events prior to the war be present in the audience, but also surviving residents from all walks of life, many of whom had given up food in order to purchase a ticket. Regardless of their respective backgrounds, all strived to don their "finest" clothes over their thin frames and to be as well groomed as could be done under the circumstances. As the audience members filed into the Hall, some found themselves squinting because their eyes were so unaccustomed to the electric light emitted by the chandeliers. The auditorium lacked enough seats for the overflowing crowd so many remained standing, pressed tightly together. Among them stood an 11-year-old boy named Yuri Ahronovitch, who would one day become a great conductor and have the privilege of conducting Shostakovich's Seventh for himself.

Meanwhile, the musicians prepared for the start of the concert by bundling up in multiple layers of clothes despite the summer heat because their emaciated bodies struggled to regulate temperature. They had needed to rehearse the large work in small sections, allowing time to rest. They had succeeded in playing straight through the work only three days before the premiere. Now, they summoned all of their reserves to bring this meaningful work, this historic concert, to their people. As the orchestra members made their way to the Hall, they could not help but think of the colleagues they had lost in the process. A total of 27 musicians who had begun the rehearsal cycle would be absent from the stage that night—two soldier-musicians had been killed and 25 others had died of starvation.

At 6 p.m., Karl Eliasberg strode onto the stage to enthusiastic applause and spoke the following words as an introduction to the work. "Comrades, this is a great event in the cultural life of our city. It is the first time you will hear, in a few moments, the Seventh Symphony of our compatriot Dmitri Shostakovich. His symphony calls for strength in combat and belief in victory. The performance of the Seventh in the besieged city itself is the result of the unconquerable patriotic spirit of Leningraders. Their strength, their belief in victory, their willingness to fight to the last drop of blood and to achieve victory over their enemies. Listen, Comrades."[26]

As the triumphant final notes of the Seventh Symphony still hung in the air of Philharmonia Hall, the audience wept, cathartic streams of tears that cleansed their ravaged souls. This music, written just for them, seemed all the more meaningful because of the minute by minute uncertainty of their lives. For some, this might be the last music they ever hear. The supervisor in the radio booth that evening, N. Belyaev, would hear countless performances of Shostakovich's Seventh throughout his career. But thinking back on that night, Belyaev maintained, "I have never again experienced the incomparable impression left by the performance on 9 August 1942, with Eliasberg at the conductor's stand and performed by the starving people who were my comrades at work, and with whom I kept vigil during the shellings and bombings that engulfed our dear city."[27]

This music also imbued the people of Leningrad with a renewed sense of pride and with the undying belief that they would prevail and that their ideas, stories, music, and works of art would not only survive, but stand triumphant in the face of time and their enemies. According to an audience member, "One cannot speak of an impression made by the symphony.... It was not an impression, but a staggering experience. This was felt not only by the listeners but also by the performers who read the music sheets as if they were reading a living chronicle about themselves."[28] Certainly for the musicians who had struggled to make the impossible possible, the memory of that night would remain vividly with them for the rest of their lives. Many years after the war, Viktor Koslov, who had played clarinet, said in an interview, "...the concert itself—it was our answer to the suffering. I have seen it in my sleep many times, and still hear the thunder of applause from the audience. That will be the last image before my eyes when I die."[29]

In addition to its effect on the performers and audience that evening, Shostakovich's Seventh Symphony impacted a third group of people in Leningrad—the German soldiers. The notes of the orchestra reverberated through the loudspeakers and drifted across the enemy lines to where those tasked with the destruction of the city and its people sat with their weapons. At that moment, music assumed the role of a psychological weapon waged

7. Dmitri Shostakovich and the Musical Redemption of Leningrad 223

by one nation against its foe. The spirit of fortitude proclaimed through the piece led some of the enemy soldiers to conclude that night that they would never conquer Leningrad and that "…there was something stronger than starvation, fear and death—the will to stay human."[30]

The battle for Leningrad continued for another year and a half after the concert, but with a different feeling in the air, one of hope and impending triumph. When reflecting on that night, Maestro Eliasberg described the genesis of this reversal of fortune. "People just stood and cried. They knew that this was not a passing episode but the beginning of something. We heard it in the music. The concert hall, the people in their apartments, the soldiers on the front—the whole city had found its humanity. And in that moment, we triumphed over the soulless Nazi war machine."[31] The tide of the war had indeed begun to shift toward an Allied victory. The Soviets made progress on their front against the Germans and managed to get food and oil supplies into Leningrad. On January 18, 1943, they broke through the enemy blockade that had encircled the city for so long, allowing more access in and out of the city until the siege finally ended a year later on January 27, 1944. The dead in Leningrad numbered around 1.5 million.

Regrettably, the dangerous conditions had prevented Shostakovich from being present in his beloved Leningrad for the premiere of his Seventh Symphony. Then soon after, Shostakovich contracted typhoid fever and spent three weeks in a sanitarium. Once recovered, the ever industrious Shostakovich traveled back and forth from Kuibyshev to Moscow, working on a variety of projects that included an opera, a piano sonata, and chamber music. In March 1943, Shostakovich and his family relocated permanently to Moscow, where he began teaching at the Conservatory there. During that summer, he worked on an Eighth Symphony, while also continuing to compose music for the government to entertain troops and boost the morale of citizens. The international success of the Leningrad Symphony once more allowed Shostakovich to ascend to the rank of "the premier Soviet composer" in Stalin's mind. As a result, the composer received several honorifics during 1943, including the prestigious Order of Lenin. Alexander Fadeyev, an influential member of the Union of Soviet Writers, also endorsed the supremacy of Shostakovich's work, pronouncing that Shostakovich's Seventh should be the touchstone for all Soviet creations. Speaking of the Seventh, he declared, "Let us try to create now, during the war, works that are real, serious, big, but ones that can be used right now as weapons, not set aside for later.… Make it, for now, like the Seventh Symphony."[32]

But the spirit of camaraderie espoused by artists such as Fadeyev contrasted sharply to the mindset and activities of the Red Army. The influence of decades of Lenin's and then Stalin's climate of retaliation and murder surfaced in the cruel and barbaric ways in which the Soviet soldiers dealt with the enemy and their own people. The years of purges and terror had hardened them so that to take a life seemed of no greater consequence than a menial daily task. As the war drew to a close, the Red Army even turned on its own soldiers who had been captured by the Germans. Instead of hailing them as heroes, the Soviet military branded them as traitors, resulting in either their execution or exile to Siberia.

In the end, the divisive struggles and reckless self-sabotage within their military and government did not prevent the Soviets from landing on the winning side, but certainly set the tone for the ensuing years. With the German surrender on May 8, 1945, the victory for the Soviet Union felt somewhat tainted as that nation's casualty numbers exceeded more than all of the other countries combined, around 27 million or over 13 percent of the population. According to Field Marshall Alan Brooke of the British Army, "It was the Russians who provided the oceans of blood necessary to defeat Germany."[33] This staggering death toll further sobered the Soviet citizens as it proved startling close to the number of 30 million that Hitler had pledged to annihilate. So with the Soviet Union emerging from the war with devastation not only in lives lost, but in its economy and infrastructure, it would soon turn on its Allies, including the United States that it had so eagerly courted just a few years earlier. This post-war Soviet mindset would usher in decades of tension and mistrust between the two countries.

The fickleness of the Soviet government would soon turn against Shostakovich as well, in the form of renewed allegations of formalism. Despite his international popularity and the accolades he had received from the government for his Leningrad Symphony and other contributions during the war, Shostakovich enjoyed little security. As feared, Stalin felt threatened by anyone who had risen as a hero of the war and especially related to the siege of Leningrad. He tried to restore balance through fabricating charges of traitorous behavior by leaders or of bourgeois leanings by the intellectuals. As a result, life only got worse for Soviet composers in the late '40s and '50s.

The first formal denouncements of Shostakovich's work appeared in 1948. In February, the Central Commission issued a pronouncement, later called the "Historic Decree," that resulted in the banning of numerous works by composers now labeled as formalists. These prohibited pieces included Shostakovich's Sixth, Eighth, and Ninth Symphonies, along with works by Prokofiev and many other Soviet composers. The government, however, did not dare to disavow Shostakovich's Seventh Symphony directly. Instead, they relied on implied accusations, citing that the Seventh possessed a victorious tone even though their country was losing the war, but that the Eighth Symphony, when the tide of the war had reversed, proved gloomy and despairing. Party officials hoped that planting the suspicion that Shostakovich's music contained a coded message supporting the downfall of the Soviet Union would taint the composer's reputation as a great Russian patriot.

Life for Shostakovich continued in a downward spiral throughout 1948. Thugs vandalized his home, and the Moscow Conservatory dismissed him from his teaching position. He and his family now faced a dire financial crisis. In turn, many who had been devoted friends and colleagues betrayed him by siding with the government for the sake of their own careers and safety, including his long-time friend Tikhon Khrennikov, the new head of the Composers' Union.

And so the dance of in and out of favor that had defined Shostakovich's life swayed on to the beat of an erratic drummer. After Stalin's death in March 1953, the reign of terror appeared to have reached its end. Prisoners in the work camps were released and made their way back home. A new climate of openness even prevailed for a time that acknowledged the atrocities committed by Stalin and his purges. Nikita Khrushchev assumed the leadership of the Soviet Union; and even though he denounced Stalin's ways, Khrushchev maintained the country as a police state and ushered it into the intense era of the Cold War and the Iron Curtain.

The new government did lift the ban on Shostakovich's work, and the composer was again allowed to travel outside of the country to speak and give performances. But ever fearful that Shostakovich would defect, officials never let his family travel with him and insisted that he always be accompanied by KGB officers. During one of his visits to the United States, crowds gathered outside Shostakovich's hotel window with signs encouraging him to escape out the window and seek political asylum. But Shostakovich would never have entertained such an idea. He remained utterly devoted to his wife and family.

7. Dmitri Shostakovich and the Musical Redemption of Leningrad

Shostakovich continued to be active in the musical life of his homeland as much as possible, astutely able to stick his finger into the air to see which way the political winds blew on any given day. He produced a prolific oeuvre that included 15 symphonies and 15 string quartets in addition to ballets, operas, sonatas, choral works, and many more. His music chronicled the history of not only his life, but that of his country's, as it embraced the Futurists of the 1920s, then fell into the terrors of the 30s, and then continued to twist and turn on the global stage. Of a generous nature, Shostakovich provided financial support to his friends and their families who had suffered under denouncement and attempted to use whatever influence he could muster to rehabilitate reputations and clear the names of the innocent. He continued to mourn the loss of so many friends and great Soviet artists. He especially grieved over those who had disappeared and had no proper burial place at which to rest and receive tribute.

In hindsight, Shostakovich could see that the tightrope that Stalinist Russia had forced him and his fellow artists to walk had offered no truly secure path. They had faced the difficult choice of whether to use their art to challenge Fascist ideologies and risk their careers or even their lives, or to feign allegiance to the Party platform through insincere creations. In the beginning, some had even wholeheartedly saluted the Communist agenda toward the arts, believing that the State's newfound interest in the arts would benefit them. They hoped that the Russian government would become the patron they had needed for so long, ever since diminishing support from the Church and the wealthy during the early years of the 20th century had left them struggling. Still, others embraced Communism as the way to defeat the bourgeoisie, whom they blamed for the decline of artistic support and taste.

These complicated and circuitous rationales and motivations have fostered many debates in the ensuing years about Shostakovich's true feelings and role under Stalin. Was he committed to the regime and eager to support it through his music or was he anti–Communist and using his music to convey, in coded-form, his secret convictions? Because words needed to be so carefully measured and contradictions appeared throughout Shostakovich's lifetime and writings, it remains difficult for scholars to know the answers to those fundamental questions. Even many of the details about Shostakovich's life remain dubious due to conflicting biographies and memoirs. The oppression and censorship that the composer and his family endured made it often unsafe to provide accurate accounts of events or truthful testimony. "In a regime where words are watched, lies are rewarded, and silence is survival, there is no truth."[34] Similar questions have been raised about the great German composer and conductor Richard Strauss and his relationship to the Nazi Party. But in regard to those who navigated such treacherous times, it has proven too reductionist to relegate them to black and white categories. Human beings, more often than not, abide in a gray area, particularly in such untenable circumstances. Music historian Alex Ross provides the apt verdict that "these composers were neither saints nor devils; they were flawed actors on a tilted stage."[35]

Dmitri Shostakovich passed away at age 68 on August 9, 1975—33 years to the day that his Seventh Symphony premiered in Leningrad during the siege. His beloved city again became known as St. Petersburg in 1991 following the collapse of the Soviet Union. Leningrad had survived "the twin monsters of the century"[36]—first Stalin's great hatred carried out through mass purges and then Hitler's blind and insidious plot to destroy it. The Leningrad Orchestra presented a reunion concert of the Seventh in 1992 on the 50th anniversary of the premiere. Only 14 of the original musicians were still living. That night, oboist Ksenia Matus shared his recollections from that fateful performance. "So many years have passed since that day and memory is a funny thing, like drying paint. It changes color as it dries. But that symphony has stayed with me the way it was that night. Afterwards, it was still a city under siege, but I knew it would live. Music is life after all. What is life without music? This was the music that proved our city had come back to life after death."[37]

8

The Vocal Orchestra: Female POWs on Sumatra

I go my way singing What ere fate be bringing.... No trouble I'll borrow, A fig for the morrow. I'll sing to the end.
—Margery Jennings, one of the many nurses imprisoned by the Japanese as they overran the Dutch and English colonies of the Pacific. See Ian MacLeod, *I Will Sing to the End,* 153

On December 7, 1941, a bomber adorned with the blazing red Rising Sun symbol of Japan dropped out of the clouds at 7:55 a.m. over the U.S. Naval Base at Oahu, Hawaii. Immediately, hundreds of additional Japanese planes materialized, and the attack on Pearl Harbor commenced. In a matter of minutes, two-thirds of the United States' aircraft in the Pacific had been destroyed along with eight battleships. Over the next 24 hours, a simultaneously coordinated assault would also be underway in Hong Kong, Singapore, and Malaya. Although the specific strike at Pearl Harbor took the United States by surprise, some show of aggression from the Japanese was not unexpected. Relations between the two countries had been declining over Japan's incursions into China, and the subsequent U.S. retaliations of freezing Japanese assets and instituting an oil embargo. Japan had actually been spreading its imperialist wings for more than a half century, causing conflict with Russia and China. Starting in the late 19th century, both Japan and Russia set their hegemonic sights on the Manchurian region of China in order to control the Liaodong Peninsula, an important trade route, and to build connecting railways to benefit them militarily and economically. Tensions ran especially high between Japan and China, as Japan also vied for dominance in Korea because of its rich coal and iron resources. This contention led to the first Sino-Japanese War that lasted from 1894 to 1895. Japan prevailed in this campaign, revealing China as too militarily weak to compete on the world stage. As a result, Japan demanded the ceding of the Liaodong Peninsula as their victor's spoil, but Russia intervened and convinced them to drop that claim. Then in 1898, Russia struck a private deal with the Chinese for a 25-year lease on the Liaodong Peninsula, which included permission to construct a series of interconnected railways. Naturally, the Japanese were incensed by Russia's cunning advancement into the very territories they coveted, eventually leading to a brief Russo-Japanese War in 1904–1905. When Japan emerged the victor again, Russia surrendered all of its interests in that region to the Japanese.

Japan continued to make its imperialist ambitions felt by the Chinese throughout the early decades of the 20th century, culminating in a 1931 Japanese military campaign, which after only a few months earned them complete command of Manchuria. Japan worked tenaciously to build on that region's natural resources and transform it into the most industrially developed part of China, which could then function as a support base for their future plans of Asian dominance. Japan announced later in 1934 that it desired nothing less than control of all of China, not just the area north of the Great Wall. The Chinese countered with a show of resistance, but it did little to whittle away at the mighty Japanese army. Their conflict escalated to an official war in 1941, the Second Sino-Japanese War. But as Japan refocused its energies on advancing through the rest of Asia toward occupied colonies such as Hong Kong and Sumatra, the fight with China reached a stalemate. Hoping that the resolution lay in diplomacy, Britain and the United States convened negotiations with the Japanese in an attempt to curb their absolutist agenda. As a precaution, however, the British and American governments recommended that their citizens living in Japanese-occupied regions of China evacuate. Diplomatic talks were still ongoing when the Japanese launched their December 7 campaign.

Japan's primary objective entailed sweeping through what was known as the Orient and "liberating" it from the white colonialists, so that this part of Asia, with its rich culture and natural resources, could be just for Asians—a plan they codified as the Greater Eastern Co-Prosperity Sphere. In order to accomplish this, Japanese leaders devised a military strategy to push rapidly down the Malay Peninsula and commandeer island after island and the resulting wealth of oil, tin, and rubber resources. This ingenious and unexpected maneuver took the armies of first the British and then the Dutch colonies by storm and surprise.

At the time of the Japanese invasion, the Indies, consisting of 13,000 islands spanning five million square kilometers, belonged to the Netherlands. They had officially become a Dutch colony in the early 19th century, after having enjoyed a 200-year trading history, particularly in spices. The Dutch had benefited from a monopoly on that trade, and then later established prosperous commercial enterprises there in tea, coffee, rubber, and eventually oil. Queen Wilhelmina had served as the reigning monarch of the Kingdom of the Netherlands since 1890, but the Nazi invasion and occupation of the Netherlands in 1940 had forced her into exile in London.

The British also had a lengthy and advantageous colonial relationship with areas in the China Sea, including Malaya. Prior to the Japanese incursion, Malaya represented a place of comfort and luxury, especially for colonial women. It offered a warm climate and a native population eager to be employed to perform the menial tasks of life, such as landscaping, cooking, cleaning, and child tending. The wives enjoyed an affluent lifestyle provided for them by their husbands, who were either entrepreneurs overseeing mines and plantations or civil employees who ran the government and supervised the maintaining of order that supported the lifestyle of the Empire. Part of colonial life on Malaya involved sending the children back and forth to Europe for their education. To facilitate this, the Peninsular and Oriental Steamship Company, known as the P & O, oversaw the transportation logistics, and with such a large number of families, banked a hefty profit. In addition to the wives of the colonial scions, European colonies also needed professional women who contributed to a successful society as teachers, nurses, and secretaries. Women also participated in life there as representatives of religious institutions, including Catholic nuns and Protestant missionaries.

The population of Malaya was diverse, consisting of about two million Chinese, 700,000 Indians, and a large contingency of Eurasians, a multiracial people of European and Asian ancestry. These groups co-existed with the approximately two million native Malays. Not only ethnically diverse, the Malayan residents spoke numerous languages and dialects. The polyglot community shared Malay as their common language, and so the colonists used it to communicate with them as well. But although the colonial women and the various local populations lived in relatively close proximity, a distinct demarcation was maintained. The British upper class kept themselves segregated into their own communities and insisted that it was just "not done" to venture into the parts of their town where other ethnicities, such as the Chinese, lived and shopped. The British felt proud of what they had accomplished on the Malay Peninsula—"turning an untamed, jungle country not only into a beautiful playground but a place of profit."[1] They had created a paradise replete with their social values and their pleasures, and had not found it necessary to be bothered about any inconvenience this might have caused for those living there before them. Both the British and the native population accepted that the current social order and caste system would endure indefinitely. But ironically, the rigid social order and division of labor that stood as such a hallmark of colonial society also contributed to how quickly it collapsed in the wake of the swift and decisive Japanese onslaught. "An unshakeable edifice to all outward appearances, calm and unchanging with its hierarchies settled and its racial boundaries finally drawn, it was not equipped for the sudden arrival of interlopers who not only disregarded its principles but were bent on casting them out altogether."[2]

For the comfortable colonists in Malaya or Singapore, the year 1941 still marked a time of prosperity and easy living. War-torn Europe had little direct impact on them and could be easily out-of-mind. Even as they watched British military forces building up around them that year, few seemed troubled that this composed the prelude to war for them as well. The soldiers and the various accompanying personnel, including the military nurses from the Queen Alexandra's Imperial Military Nursing Service (the QAs), just blended into life there, especially the nightlife of dining, drinking, and dancing. In addition to the British army, Singapore's martial presence contained an essential contingent of Australian forces, since having military strength in such a strategic geographic location to Australia constituted a vital component of their state security.

Japan's invasion of Malaya commenced at 1:15 a.m. on December 8, 1941, as rubber assault-crafts filled with Japanese soldiers landed on the beaches of the Malay Peninsula. In much the same way that the American colonists had employed stealth fighting tactics that baffled and out-maneuvered the British soldiers during the American Revolution, the Japanese had towns surrounded and cut off before the residents were even alerted to their presence. They rolled in like a menacing fog that came on suddenly and enveloped completely. Unprepared for this type of warfare, the British military quickly ceded land to the Japanese and retreated with the evacuating civilians down the peninsula.

With each of Japan's conquests, the spoils of war would not only comprise the natural resources they coveted, but all of the luxury of living that the Dutch and British colonists had amassed. The lavish homes and venues of entertainment, not to mention extravagant possessions, must have seemed a "garden of earthly delights" to the average Japanese soldier. The British had controlled Malaya for over a hundred years and, in that time, had built a paradise for themselves. Now, an unlikely enemy sat poised to take it all.

Also on December 8, Japan launched a second offensive against a British crown colony—Hong Kong. The enemy again quickly gained the upper hand, and on Christmas Day, the British surrendered. In addition to forcing the forfeiture of a colony, the campaign in

Hong Kong unearthed the brutal nature of the Japanese soldiers. They had perpetrated a barbaric assault on a Red Cross hospital there, viciously stabbing their bayonets into the doctors and the wounded servicemen lying in hospital beds. They raped the nurses repeatedly, and murdered some as well. The threat from the enemy now proved even more perilous than the loss of pride and property.

But as the Japanese bested the numerically superior forces of the British Empire down the Malay Peninsula, government officials offered a slow and somewhat tepid response, a denial of reality, which then informed the mindset of the civilian population. This false sense of security prevailed even as the invasion forced the colonists to abandon their homes and flee further south. They clung to what they considered a fail-safe contingency plan—refuge in Singapore, a British stronghold deemed impregnable. As Malaya lost more and more ground to the Japanese, Singapore did receive its evacuees, to the point of overflowing. Still, there remained a naïve resolve that no further escape would be necessary. Later, when they finally shed the cloak of their self-delusion, it would be too late.

As the Japanese made landfall on the Malay Peninsula and bombarded Hong Kong on December 8, they also initiated an air-raid campaign on their ultimate prize—Singapore, who had left the lights burning brightly for the enemy, as no blackout orders had been issued. Six days earlier, on December 2, the *Repulse* and the *Prince of Wales*, two battleships belonging to the British Royal Navy, had arrived in Singapore to provide support to the fleet in the event of Japanese aggression. But instead of keeping their presence a secret, announcers advertised it over the radio, supposedly in an attempt to make the residents feel more secure. In less than a week, Japanese bombers had interred both ships in the bottom of the sea, certainly a portent of what was to become a humiliating defeat in that region for the British and her Allies.

It took just a few weeks for Japan's Imperial Army to assume control of the entire Malay Peninsula. The Japanese also conquered the Dutch colonies of the East Indies with a decisive victory. Although the Dutch and British had substantial military resources, the stealth and agility of the Japanese military campaign overtook them so quickly that they could not react in time or with any effectiveness. "A small, compact, highly mobile force took on an army of vastly greater size and turned its strength into a weakness so that the giant blundered about, hampered by its own weight and entangled by its own limbs."[3] Meanwhile, both the military and civilian populations continued their sense of denial and sangfroid until the very end. They could not fathom that these "little yellow men" could overpower them, and as a result, not only suffered a swift military defeat, but delayed the evacuation of women and children until the enemy had infested the islands and the waters, so that there was no longer a safe escape route.

The intense bombing of Singapore, sometimes a simultaneous release from as many as 81 aircraft, continued all through the month of January, as more refugees poured into the city along with wounded and retreating military personnel. Commerce, however, continued in the city, with some stores experiencing record sales as the people who had fled with only the clothes on their backs needed all sorts of supplies. Despite the bombardment, no real shortages of food or alcohol existed yet, so many still sought out the evening pleasures of dining and dancing. The cinema also maintained its popularity. Stubbornly, the European civilians stayed, refusing to give up what they had created and determined to display their "stiff upper lips" to the native population and to each other. As a result, a ship that departed for England from the Singapore harbor in mid–January sailed only half-filled.

Toward the end of January, a speech by Winston Churchill to the House of Commons aired over the radio, and in it, the Prime Minister acknowledged the dire situation in the Far East and warned that more bad news from that front should be expected. With Churchill's admission, those in denial finally conceded that the fall of Singapore was imminent. In response, the government issued evacuation orders for the women and children of European descent. The native populations, who had played such an integral role in the lives of the colonists, would be surreptitiously abandoned. British officials relegated the burden of organizing the evacuation to the P & O Steamship Company, who mired and delayed the process by requiring that evacuees officially register for passage, when it would have been quicker to fill boats to their capacity from the docks. The bureaucratic process forced women and children to stand for hours in indeterminable lines that stretched outside and down street, where the merciless tropical sun beat down upon them and where Japanese aircraft flying overhead could threaten them. Whenever a plane would appear, those waiting would throw themselves into ditches, then have to organize back in a line again. The P & O hastily assembled an evacuation flotilla totaling 44 vessels. But with the Japanese in command of the air and sea around the islands, only a few would elude capture or a watery grave.

By early February, the signs of the fall of Singapore could not only be seen, but heard and smelled. In an effort to leave little that could aid the enemy, the banks burned money, producing a strange odor that wafted through the city. They also packed valuables into crates and dumped them into the sea alongside fleets of new vehicles. Hotels and restaurants smashed bottles of wine and liquor, as the inclination for savagery was greatly compounded when the Japanese soldiers were drunk. Singapore's basic utilities and water works began to fail as the bombing took its toll on the infrastructure. Looting by some of the native population became a common problem, and at one point, stores began just to give away their merchandise rather than have it still sitting on shelves or hanging on racks when the Japanese marched down the street.

Now with the impending evacuation of women, children, and nonessential male civilians from Singapore, the P & O scrambled ineffectually to equip its armada of mismatched vessels with some type of defensive fire power. The *Mata Hari*, one of P & O's 1,000-ton steamships, had been converted to a "warship" by attaching only two guns to her, one at the stern and one on the upper deck. A cargo ship, the *Vyner Brooke*, had been outfitted so scantily to defend itself that it seemed that officials thought that merely adding the initials HMS to her name would suffice. Nevertheless, on February 12, 1942, 47 crew members and 181 evacuees boarded the *Vyner Brooke*, a ship designed for only 12 passengers.

One of the evacuees aboard the *Vyner Brooke* was Betty Jeffrey, a member of the Australian Army Nursing Service (later called the Royal Australian Army Nursing Corps). Betty had served alongside her fellow nursing sisters in Malaya starting in 1941, attached to the 8th Division A.I.F. After the Japanese invasion, they had evacuated to Singapore and cared for the sick and wounded there. Now, Australian military officials ordered the evacuation of the nurses, which would be accomplished in two groups. The first left on February 11, 1942. Although the menacing presence of Japanese ships and bombers made it treacherous to be on the sea, this group managed to make it home safely to Australia. Betty Jeffrey boarded the *Vyner Brooke* on February 12, 1942, as part of the second group of 65 nurses, for a voyage that would not reach its intended destination. The ship's atmosphere bordered on chaos due to overcrowding and to the frantic nature of some of the passengers. As many of the women seemed frazzled at being on their own for the first time, the nurses took charge.

Their training and experience had equipped and required them to be self-sufficient and to administer any situation effectively and efficiently.

The *Vyner Brooke's* passenger manifest also included Shelagh Brown. Shelagh's father, E.A. Brown, had been the choirmaster for 40 years at St. Andrew's Cathedral in Singapore, a church with the typical high Anglican structure and ethos. His charisma and his passion for music had earned him the moniker "the man who put the Sing in Singapore."[4] He had passed on his love of music to his daughter. When she and her mother loaded onto the ship, Shelagh insisted on taking her beloved viola with her. Tragically, it would soon sink down into the water of the Bangka Strait with the belongings of the other passengers, as well as some of their lives. In addition to all the miseries that Shelagh would endure in a Japanese internment camp, she would perpetually mourn her lost instrument. Deciding what to do with precious possessions, whether they had monetary or purely sentimental value, proved extremely difficult for the evacuating women. Many had no choice but to leave them behind or destroy them to prevent their falling into the plundering hands of the Japanese. Others tried to hide them, such as one woman who stuffed a bundle of photographs behind the organ pipes in St. Andrew's Cathedral. After the war, she reached her hand behind the pipes and joyfully discovered them still there.

A friend of the Brown family, Dorothy MacLeod, joined them on the *Vyner Brooke*. Dorothy had been born in Singapore to English parents and received the typical education in Europe. She spoke fluent French and was gifted in many areas, including as a seamstress and singer. During the 1920s, her beautiful contralto voice had earned her leading roles in productions of Gilbert and Sullivan operettas, such as *Mikado* in 1927 and *HMS Pinafore* in 1929, often starring opposite of E.A. Brown. Her husband Donald was an accomplished piper, and together in the late 1930s, they broadcast radio programs to Australia. Dorothy also entertained the Australian and British troops stationed in Singapore in 1941 and early 1942. Music constituted an integral part of her life, and her son Ian later recalled the pleasant childhood memory of falling asleep at night to the sounds of his mother singing and playing the piano.

Norah Chambers, a gifted violinist, also boarded the doomed *Vyner Brooke*, completely unaware that, in due time, she would create a profound and life-changing expression of the power of music. Norah had been born in Singapore in 1905. Her father, John Hope, worked as a mechanical engineer there. After attending boarding school in England, Norah entered the Royal Academy of Music in London, where she studied piano, violin, and chamber music. There, she also played in the orchestra under the legendary conductor Sir Henry Wood. After completing her education, Norah settled, along with her mother and two sisters, in Malaya with her father in 1927. With this move, the three women became accustomed to a life of leisure, with Chinese servants to take care of the tedious domestic chores and daily drudgeries. Norah married a civil engineer named John Chambers in Malaya on March 1, 1930, and their only child, a daughter named Sally, was born there in 1933. Norah had always been an intelligent, energetic, and driven woman, and now she found herself somewhat bored. So, in looking for some fulfilling activities to structure her day, she naturally reached for her violin and began to give lessons to the children in her community. Sir Henry Wood had made quite an impression on Norah as a student, and through his influence, she had also learned how to conduct. But she had not planned for a career in an orchestra, either as a violinist or conductor, because at that time, professional orchestras only hired men, with the exception of harpists. Later, after the war, Norah reflected wryly that it took a prison camp to give her the opportunity to lead an orchestra.

8. The Vocal Orchestra: Female POWs on Sumatra

Norah Chambers as a student at the Royal Academy of Music in London in the 1920s (courtesy the Helen Colijn Archives).

The town of Kuala Trengannu, where the Chambers lived, became an early target of the Japanese. Although initially uncertain if there was any need for alarm, Norah arranged for their 5-year-old daughter to be transported to the south to Kuala Lumpur. Soon after, news of numerous Japanese landings reached them. Fearing that they would be surrounded with their escape routes cut off, the civilians in Kuala Trengannu evacuated under strict orders to abandon all belongings. They were now fleeing for their lives, with no safe refuges except the remote jungles, since the Japanese had made landfall in the northern and southern parts of the peninsula and had infested the water to the east. That these civilians hiked into rugged and untamed territory that would have challenged even the most seasoned explorer attested to the severity of their plight. They combatted intractable vines and undergrowth, meager food supplies, and persistent leeches. They also battled their imaginations, which in that dark, overgrown world conjured up the enemy hiding and watching them from every bush and shadow.

After five days of those conditions, the evacuees stumbled onto a train track and miraculously caught a train to Kuala Lumpur. From there, Norah and her family eventually made their way to Singapore, where both her sisters and their husbands and children lived. Once there, Norah delayed escaping to England for numerous reasons, including that both her father and husband had taken ill and been hospitalized. Her father suffered from a serious liver condition, and her husband John had contracted typhus from a rat bite during their perilous journey through the jungles of Malaya. She spent long nights at the hospital, as bombs rained around them. She watched nurses position patients under their beds to provide some shelter. Norah covered her husband and father with pillows, poor protection, but all that could be done as they were both too ill to move. Some of the nurses placed metal hats on their patients' heads, and when those ran out, they improvised with bed pans. As conditions in Singapore deteriorated, Norah's sister Barbara made the decision to evacuate to England with her sons. Norah now faced the tough dilemma of whether to leave her sick father and husband and flee with Sally on that ship or send Sally with her sister and join them later. She decided to let her daughter sail with Barbara, and several weeks later, on February 12, Norah, along with her husband John and sister Ena, boarded the *Vyner Brooke*.

As Norah prepared to set sail, Margaret Dryburgh, who would later partner with her in the most important musical endeavor of their lives, was also loading onto an evacuation ship. Margaret had been born in 1890 in the northern England coastal town of Sunderland, the daughter of William Dryburgh, a Presbyterian minister. Having been an inquisitive and musically precocious child, Margaret attended Newcastle College, part of Durham University, where she studied music and education. She graduated with a B.A. in 1911 and accepted a position teaching Latin and history at Ryhope Grammar Girls' School, where she also led the school choir. But Margaret's real passion and calling had always been to serve as a missionary to China, which became reality when the Presbyterian Church posted her there in 1919. Margaret worked in Swatow, South China for the Presbyterian Women's Missionary Association from 1919 to 1925.

Margaret Dryburgh at her graduation in 1911 (courtesy the Helen Colijn Archives).

In 1925, because of intense persecution by the Chinese government, Margaret was reassigned to Singapore. A considerable Chinese population lived in Malaya and Singapore, having immigrated there in pursuit of better economic opportunities. For missionaries seeking to evangelize the Chinese, these locations proved easier to access, and so along with entrepreneurial colonists who had established communities there for civil administration and resource development, Protestant and Catholic missions flourished as well, creating schools, building hospitals, and meeting a variety of humanitarian needs.

The Presbytery asked Margaret to take over as the principal of the Choon Goan School in the Katong region of Singapore. The school had been in operation for 10 years, but had been plagued by mounting problems. Margaret's leadership quickly transformed it into an efficient and successful educational institution. The Presbytery then expanded the opportunities in the region by establishing an English girls' school called Kuo Chuan School on Bishon Street. Margaret became the principal there and also served as the organist at the Presbyterian Church located on Orchard Road, a prominent boulevard frequented by the English for shopping and entertainment. Orchard Road, in that one street, represented the ideal life the British colonists had shaped for themselves. When the war broke out in 1941, Margaret and five other Presbyterian missionaries remained in Singapore, ministering to the Christian Chinese communities and doing what they could to calm fears and provide encouragement. Eventually, with four of the six missionaries being female, mission officials decided that they should evacuate with the other women on February 12.

As the ships departed Singapore that fateful February day, the crews knew that they were taking a great risk in entering the open waters, with the treacherous minefields laid by the Japanese and the relentless bombers in the sky. The evacuation ships headed for the Bangka Strait, a narrow waterway to the south that now bore the nickname "Bomb Alley." But what they did not know was that the Imperial Japanese Navy lay in wait. A fleet consisting of an aircraft carrier, three destroyers, and two cruisers had been positioned by Admiral Ozawa in that area to intercept any ships escaping from the region. Because of their vantage point in the East Indies, the Dutch learned of this Japanese trap and frantically began relaying coded messages to the Singapore station to warn them not to set their evacuation ships on that course. The arrival of these warnings coincided almost exactly with when the ships were setting sail, but in another inexcusable breakdown of the British military, those who received the messages could not decode them because the official in charge of the code books had already fled and taken them with him out of fear that they would fall into the hands of the Japanese. This tragic misstep would cause untold suffering and loss of life.

Two days into the voyage, on February 14 at 2 p.m., six Japanese bombers attacked the *Vyner Brooke*. She managed to zigzag in the water enough to dodge 26 bombs, but then the 27th struck her solidly. The terrible damage to her keel caused the ship to list immediately. The bombers executed another pass, damaging many of the lifeboats, as they aimed their machine guns toward the passengers on the deck. The captain gave the order to abandon ship. With only three of the lifeboats still seaworthy, most escaped the ship by sliding down ropes, which left their hands burned and the skin hanging in strips. Those in the water were 10 miles from the closest shore, in a waterway known for its cruel currents. They were also saturated with oil from the damaged ship. The blackness of the oil quickly covered those in the water, making it difficult to hold on to rafts or floating debris and searing their skin in the blazing tropical sun.

Gradually, survivors of the *Vyner Brooke* floated like flotsam onto Bangka Island, near the town of Muntok. Some had been in the water for eight hours, and others more than 60 hours. A small island in the South China Sea, Bangka had been of little importance in the region until the evacuation of Singapore. It sat along that ill-chosen escape route via the Bangka Strait, which British officials had erroneously thought offered the safety of the Dutch East Indies. Instead, the Japanese warships lay in wait, mercilessly attacking ship after ship and leaving all manner of people, including women and children, in the waters to drown or wash up on the shores of Bangka Island. But sometimes, help could be found. One cluster of survivors struggling to swim through the last difficult current near the shore sought assistance from a Malay fisherman in a canoe. He paddled to shore with the refugees clinging to the sides. As a reward, one of the women handed him two dollars.

One of the first large groups from the *Vyner Brooke* to make landfall contained a few servicemen, 22 Australian nurses, and some other women. They spent a day and a night on the beach without any sign of other inhabitants or the Japanese. Because some were wounded, a naval officer decided to walk to Muntok and present himself and his fellow survivors to the Japanese. He hoped that they would deal less harshly with them because of the women and wounded. Before the officer returned, however, the civilian women decided to make their own way toward Muntok, leaving the nurses behind to care for the wounded. He did eventually return to the beach with a Japanese officer and 10 of his soldiers, who ordered the survivors to form two lines by gender. The Japanese soldiers marched the men at gunpoint a little ways away and shot or bayoneted them all. They then forced the 22 nurses to enter the sea, where they shot them from behind with machine guns. The wounded had been left lying in the sand on their makeshift stretchers, and the Japanese finished them off before abandoning the carnage they had created, unaware that two had survived the massacre. A bullet had gone straight through the side of Vivien Bullwinkel, one of the nurses, and wisdom told her to lie in the water as if dead. One of the bayoneted men was also alive, and she cared for him for 10 days before he died. As other shipwreck survivors drifted to the apparent safety of the shore, they had no idea of the new potential danger they faced. In fact, Vivien Bullwinkel kept this atrocity a secret, as she feared for her life as the only living witness. In 1946, she would finally tell her story in Tokyo at the War Crimes Trial.

Shelagh Brown and her mother had managed to stay afloat and together by clinging to the side of a raft with a few other people. After a considerable time bobbing in the currents, they sensed vibrations from the propeller of a ship, but could not be sure from which direction because of how pitch black the night became in the middle of the sea. Regardless, this development brought such relief as they assumed that a rescue was at hand. But unfortunately, the propeller belonged to an enemy ship in the process of deploying Japanese soldiers in armed landing crafts for an invasion of Sumatra, one of the four largest islands in that region. Sumatra presented many geographical challenges for this group of marauders—swampy coastlines on its east coast, dense jungles along its west coast, and high mountain ranges running the entire length of the island. The soldiers did take notice of the people in the water, but continued toward their mission without intervention. Several hours went by as the water-logged survivors clung precariously to the raft, watching the Japanese ferry supplies and personnel from the main ship to the beach and worrying about the danger that the constant flurry of the propellers posed to their submerged legs and torsos. The next morning, after having been ignored all night, the women were finally lifted out of the water and taken on board a Japanese barge that then deposited them on the shore of Bangka Island. Once they reached land, a Japanese soldier grabbed for a long sword. The women assumed that they were about to be run through, but instead, he used it to cut open a coconut and give them the milk to drink. Even drinking proved difficult, however, because all of the swimming in the salt water had made their mouths unbearably sore. Nevertheless, it was a gracious gesture that these soon-to-be prisoners would only occasionally witness during their captivity, as cruelty and disdain predominated. "In the years to come the women were to become used to the existence of this polarity, without ever coming to understand it very much better, and as an unstated threat to add to the more obviously apparent sources of fear and insecurity it retained its effectiveness to the end."[5]

Norah Chambers and her husband John had ended up on a raft with Norah's sister Ena. Although it kept them out of the water, a raft had almost no chance of being propelled from the open sea to land. They were fortunate to be spotted by a launch carrying two RAF soldiers, who came alongside and hauled them aboard. These two soldiers courageously brought them all the way to the long pier at Muntok, which jutted out about a quarter of a mile into the water. As the evacuees climbed onto the pier, the Japanese took notice and began firing on the launch. Miraculously, the rescued all made it safely to shore, and the launch with the two RAF soldiers sped away without being hit. An additional group from the *Vyner Brooke* managed to swim to the pier with a woman in the late term of her pregnancy. But the harrowing time in the water had been too much physically, and the woman miscarried there on the pier.

Meanwhile, the evacuation voyage of the *Mata Hari* faced the same difficulties and thwarted journey as the *Vyner Brooke*. Departing also on February 12, she managed to maneuver successfully through the Japanese minefields. Then, in the early morning hours of February 14, the crew noticed six people in the water, survivors from a ship sunk earlier by one of the Japanese destroyers positioned in the Bangka Strait. Armed with this vital information, Captain Carston changed course and decided to weave in and out of the small islands, sailing only at night, and then taking shelter during the day. But despite the attempts at concealment, a squadron of Japanese bombers spotted them and unleashed a barrage of firepower before flying off, thinking they had irreparably damaged the ship. But miraculously, she emerged unharmed, although with one human casualty. So the *Mata Hari* continued on, resuming her evasive strategy, while those on board tried to distract themselves with singing, card games, and pantomime skits.

The following night, they sailed directly into a fleet of enemy ships, who fixed the *Mata Hari* in their searchlights. Captain Carston now faced a difficult decision. If his ship had been populated exclusively by military personnel, his training and obligation would have led him to engage the enemy, even though severely outnumbered. But with a substantial number of non-combatants on board, Carston felt that surrender remained the only appropriate course of action. He ordered Lieutenant Cleveley to send a Morse code message to inform them that the ship carried women and children. When the message received no reply, the Captain reluctantly moved the women to the deck so that they could be visible to the enemy. In response, the Japanese switched off the search lights, and they were enveloped in darkness yet again. Believing that she had been set free, the *Mata Hari* continued her course for the next two hours, before being unexpectedly lit up again by Japanese search lights. The cat and mouse game had come to an end, and the process for an official surrender commenced. It was February 15, the same day that Singapore proved lost as well.

The fall of Singapore hammered a significant nail into the coffin that represented the decline of the great British Empire, which had famously been described as so vast that "the sun never set upon it." At one time, the British Empire had spread to encompass 57 colonies and territories and to control about 20 percent of the entire world's population. Along with its colonial rule of India, Britain amassed a significant asset for the Crown with its colonization of Singapore and Malaya. The Japanese occupation and crushing defeat of British forces in this region, culminating in the fall of Singapore on February 15, 1942, certainly rocked the Empire, and then the independence of India in 1947 delivered the end of an era.

Accompanied by Singapore's death knell, the evacuees from the surrendered *Mata Hari* arrived at the Muntok pier via Japanese launches, and after having been stripped of their watches and jewelry, remained there under guard without food or water. In time, the Japanese corralled all of the various people who had landed on Bangka Island into the center of town in a building that used to be a cinema. The room included captured military men, medical personnel, missionaries, and an assortment of civilians, representing British,

Australian, and Dutch nationalities. The doctors and nurses among them tended to the ill and wounded as best they could with what limited supplies they had. Sickness, both acute and chronic, would present constant problems for these prisoners. Some suffered from pre-existing ailments that had received treatment at home, but now there was little to remedy them or the newly infirm.

The Japanese soon moved the women and children to some nearby barracks designed to house native workers, known as coolies. Forced to sleep on sloping cement slabs, this would be their temporary home for two weeks. It was in this location that Margaret Dryburgh made her first overtures as a spiritual guide to this motley group. Because she had not spent time in the water, Margaret had retained her Bible, and another woman there possessed a prayer book. So Margaret announced that she would be engaged in prayers and Bible readings each morning and evening and welcomed any who would care to join her.

On March 2, 1942, the Japanese reported that they would be instituting a more permanent housing solution for the various prisoners. The women and children would be leaving the coolie barracks and, along with the men, would be heading for the island of Sumatra and a town called Palembang. As they waited at the Muntok pier for the four decrepit freighters that would transport them the 55-mile journey via the Musi River, the color of the early morning sky began to shift as through a slowly revolving kaleidoscope. In time, the heavens revealed a breathtakingly beautiful sunrise, framed by a perfect rainbow. This moment held great symbolic meaning for Margaret Dryburgh. Over the next three years, she would often remind the women around her to "look up" as a source of hope and encouragement, that the splendor of God's creation represented freedom, for the sky contained no barbed wire. As was her custom, Margaret preserved this occasion in a poem.

> We captives left the pier before dawn
> To meet a future dark with threatening fear.
> 'What lies ahead.' Our anxious spirits sighed.
> A wondrous rainbow arch with vivid glow
> Proclaimed the answer. 'Hope on, hope on' it cried.
> 'Hope on,' reflected colours echoed low.[6]

After docking on the Sumatran mainland and waiting hours for trucks, the captives found themselves the main attraction in a bizarre, parade-like spectacle in which natives lined the roads into Palembang, waving Japanese flags and cheering for their own occupier's conquests. It certainly pointed to a cultural reversal, as the locals, who had long labored as servants to many of these women, now stood unencumbered, watching their former employers ride by weary, filthy, and defeated. Japanese photographers were on hand, as well, to document the spoils of their great army.

Sumatra had been a Dutch colony for over 200 years, and its southern capital, the city of Palembang, had provided a comfortable way of life for the Dutch in the same way as Singapore had for the British. But now "under new management,"[7] all that the colonists had built and acquired belonged to the Japanese. In early March 1942, the Japanese had not yet rounded up all of the Dutch residents on Sumatra. The process by which they interned European civilians living in the East Indies, mostly Dutch nationals, depended on a variety of factors, such as whether certain individuals were deemed necessary in helping the Japanese restore or maintain manufacturing or other essentials to the economy and public works. In the end, the Dutch internees numbered approximately 100,000. This included a substantial population of women and children confined in more than 18 internment camps in the East Indies, spread throughout the four largest islands—Sumatra, Java, Borneo, and Celebes.

Some historians suggest that Japan's choice to enact a large-scale internment system might have been a reprisal for the United States' internment of Japanese-Americans; although President Roosevelt did not issue that Executive order until February 19, 1942, and by then, the Japanese had already started confining European nationals in the Indies.

On March 6, a few days after the internees had been paraded through the streets of Palembang, a young Dutch woman on Java named Helen Colijn boarded the *Poelau Bras* with her family in an attempt to flee the Japanese. Helen's father, Dr. Anton Colijn, was a Dutch oil executive on the small island of Tarakan, then a part of the East Indies, where he helped run Bataafsche Petroleum Maatschappij (BPM), a subsidiary of Shell. His wife Zus lived there with him, and they had raised three daughters. The Colijns were a well-to-do family, and their daughters had been brought up with a myriad of opportunities and luxuries from coastal horseback rides to ski trips in the Alps. Helen and her sister Antoinette had attended boarding school in the Netherlands. While home for a holiday visit in 1939, the two girls found themselves unable to return to school due to the outbreak of World War II. Instead, they moved to the island of Java where their younger sister Alette lived with another Dutch family so she could study at the high school in Bandung.

In 1941, while Helen visited again on Tarakan, her father shared his mounting concern that Japan would enter the war and come straight for this island with its rich oil reserves, oil so pure that it did not even have to be refined, going straight from the earth into the ship. In that eventuality, his company was prepared to set fire to the oil fields and wells to deny the Japanese the fuel they so needed, a common military strategy known as the "scorched earth policy," which prevented an invading enemy from commandeering any resources that would be valuable to them. In the wake of such a substantial threat, Helen tried to convince

Antoinette, Helen, and Alette Colijn at their parents' home two years before the Japanese attack on the Netherlands East Indies, c. 1940 (courtesy the Helen Colijn Archives).

her mother to come stay with them on Java, but her mother had trained to be a Red Cross nurse and refused to leave.

The Japanese did indeed come for Tarakan in January 1942, one month after the bombing of Pearl Harbor. When they found the oil on fire and useless, the irate military officials imprisoned some of the Dutch nationals, including Helen's mother and father. Remarkably, Helen's father managed to escape, but could do nothing to help his wife, and so he joined his three daughters on Java. Island by island, the Japanese, with their substantial manpower and machinery of war, defeated the smaller Royal Netherlands East Indies Army and the ineffective Allied forces there. After the Japanese landed on Java on February 28, 1942, Anton Colijn used his connections to secure passage on a ship bound for Australia. Regrettably, the girls would have to leave their mother behind, but hoped that once they arrived in Australia, that their father could secure her release through the International Red Cross, since the imprisonment of Red Cross nurses violated all international conventions. Interestingly, this was not the first time their mother had been a prisoner of war. As a 9-year-old child, she, along with her mother and four siblings, had been imprisoned in a concentration camp by the British during the Boer War in South Africa. Later, amid her own internment, Helen would remark, "Don't you think it's ironic that the idea of a concentration camp for women and children was first dreamt up by the English Lord Kitchener.... Now the Japanese are putting English women and children in a Kitchener-style camp."[8]

On March 6, 1942, 21-year-old Helen and her sisters Antoinette and Alette, aged 20 and 16 respectively, climbed aboard a Dutch freighter ship with their father. The *Poelau Bras* had a large crew of 80, and although the exact number of fleeing passengers is unknown, a rough estimate places it between 170 and 250 people. The ship's evacuation strategy depended on getting to the middle of the Indian Ocean as quickly as possible, where it would be out of the range of Japanese bombers stationed on the islands. But unbeknownst to the captain, a Japanese aircraft carrier had been positioned out in that ocean, and so their distance from land would not shield them. At 11:02 a.m. on March 7, 1942, passengers on deck observed three specks in the sky heading toward them, eventually revealed to be Japanese planes with the dreaded red disk of the Rising Sun emblazoned on them. They unleashed a torrent of bombs, making direct after direct hit. Passengers at first hid below deck, then as the ship began to take on water, they scrambled to the lifeboats. Only three lifeboats managed to get into the water.

Doggedly, the aircraft continued to attack the ship and now the lifeboats. Unmoved by the passengers waving white flags in surrender, the Japanese peppered them with machine gun fire, a scene that would haunt Helen. "I watched the people waving the white sheet, but it would be many years before I could cry for them—over my typewriter—finally feeling the agony of begging for mercy while the planes went right on machine-gunning."[9] The *Poelau Bras* disappeared from view at 11:36 a.m. It had taken only 34 minutes for the enemy to sink her. This ship became one of 40 Dutch military or merchant vessels sunk either by bombers or submarine torpedoes during the three-month campaign to capture and occupy the Dutch East Indies. The loss of life from the shipping attacks alone totaled approximately 3,000 people.

Helen and her family managed to make it into a lifeboat, but then a bomb hit the water and capsized it. They stayed afloat because of their lifebelts, but slowly drifted apart, eventually losing sight of one another. After some time, Helen encountered another lifeboat, and even though it was full, the passengers pulled her aboard. She discovered with great relief that her father was in the boat. Unfortunately, her sisters were not. The vessel had been supplied with two emergency water tanks, but gun fire had punctured one and the precious water was lost. Now, the 25 people in the boat, plus a dog named Whiskey, would have to share the meager supply. The skipper informed them that they should reach land in just a couple days. The lifeboat came equipped with six oars, although after a day or two of hard rowing in the stifling heat with little water, they suspended that effort. Instead, they raised the sails at night when a gentle breeze blew across the ocean, while in the day, the absence of any wind left the passengers feeling like meat dried in the sun.

Due to overcrowding, they had to take turns lying down in the bottom of the boat, one at a time for two-hour intervals. To pass the long nights as the temperature became mild, they sometimes sang old American folk songs that they knew, such as "Home, Home on the Range," as well as various Dutch songs. They also sang hymns, which Helen found to be a particularly meaningful experience that stayed with her long after the war. In her memoirs, she confessed, "Even now, I can never hear 'A Mighty Fortress Is Our God' without thinking of our puny lifeboat sailing over an immense ocean along a shimmering path of moonlight, and a group of tattered, shipwrecked souls pouring out their hopes in Luther's powerful hymn."[10] But on the nights when the wind blew hard, the salt water sprayed up, drenching the passengers and leaving them to shiver uncontrollably in the cold night air. The next day, the sun and heat would dry and then burn them. They had exchanged one misery for another. During the times of extreme cold or heat, there was no singing, only silence.

A couple of days turned into three and then five. Finally, after seven wretched days in the lifeboat, suffering from desperate thirst, they glimpsed land. At first, they wondered if what they saw was a mirage, because they had already experienced a few of those. Thankfully, it proved to be the edge of the coast of Tabuan Island in southern Sumatra. On Friday, March 13, 1942, the weary passengers climbed over the side of the boat and waded onto dry land. Quickly, one of the passengers, a native Javanese, scaled a coconut tree and tossed down coconuts. They found a sharp stone to puncture the shells so they could drink their fill of the precious milk.

After some reconnaissance, Anton Colijn encountered a native man. He spoke to him in Malay, the lingua franca of the various Dutch colonies both for communication among islanders who spoke a variety of languages and between the local populations and the Dutch settlers. Although poor, the man ordered a small boy to bring a pot of rice from the village, their first food in a week. Helen's father questioned the man about the location of the Japanese on the island and then crafted a plan. He knew about a lighthouse on Sumatra where he believed they could make contact with some Dutch citizens and hopefully find his other two daughters. He realized that they could not stay exposed where they were and that such a poor village could not feed 25 extra mouths, plus face harsh reprisals from the Japanese for helping them.

Not everyone wanted to go with Anton Colijn's plan, so a few people came along with Helen and her father, while the others pursued different courses of action. After a short boat ride, they walked toward the lighthouse, which proved further than they had hoped. Altogether, it took about 20 hours of arduous hiking, with most of them barefoot, having lost their shoes in the water. Helen marveled that her father, the oldest of the group at 47, remained so physically strong after the harrowing ordeal of the lifeboat. But he was a robust man, having always ascribed to a strict regimen of exercise and physical fitness. As an avid mountain climber, Anton Colijn had undertaken numerous expeditions. At this perilous moment, he also drew strength from a deep, abiding faith in God.

Heading for that lighthouse turned out to be the right course. There, they met some

Dutch associated with the BPM oil company and discovered that Antoinette and Alette had miraculously made it safely there two days earlier in the second lifeboat, although Antoinette had a deep laceration on her arm from the bombing. It was now infected and oozing pus, but they had no way of treating it other than keeping it covered with bandages. The generous Dutch people living in the region had been caring for the two girls and now welcomed Helen and her father. Soon the news of their presence reached the Japanese, and three soldiers came to see them and record their names. One of the Japanese soldiers showed genuine concern about Antoinette's arm and ordered another to fetch a medical kit. He then gently unwrapped her bandage and applied a white powder, presumably a sulfa antibiotic, and then rewrapped it. This gesture of kindness greatly surprised Helen and her family, who had heard the stories of Japanese brutality. The official then ordered them to report to the town of Krui the next day. Anton protested that they could not make it that quickly. They had just hiked barefooted for days and had painful sores on their feet, which made walking impossible. They would have to travel by the slower method of an ox cart, to which the soldiers acquiesced. At one point on the journey, they passed a village and saw a woman setting out bowls of rice and fish on mats. She called to them, saying that the Japanese had ordered her to feed them as they went by—another strange and unexpected turn of events.

When questioned by the soldiers, Anton had wisely stated his occupation as a geologist, which it had been in his early career, because he feared reprisals for the destruction of the oil wells. Anton was also the son of the former Dutch Prime Minister Hendrikus Colijn and had served in the military, information he hoped to keep secret as well. The Colijn family eventually met up with other Dutch citizens being taken into custody, and they collectively speculated about what the Japanese master plan could possibly be. The islands in the East Indies were home to over 100,000 European nationals, and it seemed unfathomable that Japan intended to incarcerate them all in camps. During the next few years of internment, there would be ongoing bafflement over Japanese actions and motivations, which often seemed nonsensical or contradictory. Helen noted later that one of the only consistencies she could find in the Japanese was that if an order was given, pretty soon the next person to show up would issue an opposite order. This became apparent for the first time as the soldiers separated the women and men into their respective trucks for transportation to join the other internees in Palembang, a fiasco that turned into "a haphazard and lengthy procedure involving orders and counter-orders."[11]

The new prisoners also learned right away during the assembling of the convoy that one of the favorite words of the Japanese guards was *lekas*, meaning quick. It seemed that everything had to be done quickly, even if there appeared to be no necessity for a rush, and the soldiers often relied on the bayonets fastened to the ends of their rifles to encourage the speedy execution of their orders. The trucks finally departed, taking them to a train station where they boarded cattle cars with another group of captives so that their 20 now numbered about 60. The train ride then gave way to a ferry on this convoluted trek. Once on land, the soldiers again segregated the men from the women and children. The men would be heading to the Palembang jail, where the Japanese held the male POWs, and the women and children would be taken to another camp. Helen now understood that she would have to survive without her father's guidance and advocacy for however long it took to sort this out, hopefully only a few days or weeks. Loading the trucks bound for the women's camp, the soldiers ordered the female internees to sort themselves into groups of 20. Unsure with whom to stand, the Colijn sisters noticed a group of Catholic nuns and decided to partner with them. Helen realized in that moment that she had "never talked to a Catholic before, let alone a nun."[12] Later, when reflecting on this decision, she gratefully revealed that "…this war-imposed meeting in the Palembang street was the beginning of life-long friendships."[13]

The women's camp at Palembang actually consisted of a series of 14 small houses lining both sides of a street named Irenelaan in a Dutch suburb that had been built and inhabited by European citizens, who had either fled as the Japanese approached or been forcibly evicted. Now empty, these homes contained no furniture, no electricity, and no running water. The women and children now numbered approximately 400, and somehow their captors expected them to fit into 14 small bungalows, each designed to house only four comfortably. As a result, the garages attached to each bungalow became a separate "house" as well. Everyone slept on the cold, hard tile floor or whatever they had in their possession to cushion themselves, such as empty rice sacks stuffed with grass. They were starting from scratch with no beds, no food, no wood, and no stoves.

It was into this precarious living arrangement that the latest gathering of women and children entered, which included the Colijn sisters and 25 nuns from the Dutch Order of St. Borromeus under Mother Superior Laurentia. Having arrived in Sumatra from Holland four years prior, the nuns had done remarkable work in setting up a convent and a boarding school. But now, they were captives as well. Both their Mother Superior and Sister Catharinia would become significant figures in the life of this diverse assembly, which now featured more than 25 nationalities, including English, Irish, Scottish, American, Dutch, Canadian, South African, French, Russian, German, Icelandic, Chinese, Balinese, and various interracial combinations in the Eurasian population.

When Helen arrived, she immediately noted that the camp was occupied by an odd assortment of women, some appearing to be in their late twenties and some with white hair. She observed also a variety of attire, from men's army shirts to sarongs. Many were barefooted, and some had their hands bandaged. The housing assignments separated the women into specific groups, usually by nationality, called *kongsis* (Chinese for partnerships). This partnering most likely resulted not from any sense of racism or overt nationalism, but just out of a natural inclination that being with your own people, those who share your cultural experiences, would be easier and more comforting in such a stressful time. Since the small houses were already overcrowded, there was a scramble about where the new arrivals would bunk. The contingency of Australian nurses quickly chimed in that they could make room for Helen and her sisters, since they and the Colijns had no belongings to take up space.

A woman with a Cockney accent eagerly supplied the missing information to Helen and her sisters. She told them that about 140 of those in the camp had been escaping from Singapore aboard three different ships, the *Vyner Brooke, Giang Bee*, and *Kuala*, which had all been sunk by Japanese bombers, and that a fourth ship, the *Mata Hari*, had been captured. She had been aboard the *Vyner Brooke* and explained that many of them had been forced to slide down the ropes on the side of the ship, shearing the skin off their hands, which is why they remained bandaged. Helen also discovered that there were already four other survivors from the *Poelau Bras* present, so with their arrival, a total of seven. As Helen heard the various stories of shipwreck, deprivation, and separation, she was overcome by profound grief. Remembering that moment, she later wrote, "For the first time, the enormity of suffering that this war was causing overwhelmed me."[14] While the war had been confined to the European continent, it had seemed so distant and abstract to Helen, but not anymore. After the terrifying bombing of her ship, a desperate week in a lifeboat, and then the trek through the jungle, it felt all too real.

There continued to be much speculation in the early days about why the Japanese would imprison women and children who had no ties to the government or military, who posed absolutely no threat to them. The nurses in the camp also emphasized, as Helen had about her mother, that the Japanese were violating all international conventions by incarcerating them and the nuns. Sister Catharinia had heard a rumor that the Japanese were trying to protect them from the native population, an unlikely scenario that the women dismissed outright. But, in reality, not every civilian of European descent made the Japanese roster of internees. Any Swiss Nationals were immediately released since Switzerland remained a neutral country. Similarly, the Japanese did not detain German citizens due to Japan's alliance with Hitler's regime. The status of the Eurasians proved a more complex issue. The Japanese government gave women who were part-Asian a choice whether to stay or be released. Surprisingly, some of the Eurasians decided to remain in the internment camp as they had nowhere else to go during the current occupation and had no way of providing for themselves. Ironically, some also feared being "unprotected" outside of the camp because of stories about the soldiers raping women.

This whole situation of so many female prisoners presented a significant and somewhat unexpected repercussion for the Japanese. In their military plan, they had accounted for the male POWs that would be customary for any war. But what they had not calculated on was that their method of conquering the islands and assuming complete control would mean that they also had other human resource problems. "Together with the prizes and trinkets of victory came what must have seemed to the Japanese literally a monstrous regiment of women."[15] This eventuality was further complicated by rigid Japanese ideologies. Japan had never ratified the Geneva Convention, which outlined international law for the treatment of prisoners and civilians during a military conflict, because it did not align with their philosophical views about capture and collateral damage. Their attitude of disdain and dishonor for anyone captured came from the ancient Samurai teachings, known collectively as the Bushido Code. Not merely a set of suggested guidelines, The Code was revered with a religious fervor. For Japanese men, defeat in battle was a "terminal condition."[16]

But regardless of their cultural tenets and mores, the Japanese now had to contend with a large population of POWs, which they did by instituting their quintessential sense of order and discipline. As with the Nazi guards in German concentration camps, the Japanese command became obsessed with counting the prisoners, a procedure known as *tenko*. A guard would blow a loud, shrill whistle to summon the internees outside, regardless of the weather, to be counted and to bow deeply to their captors as a symbolic bow to Hirohito, Emperor of the Land of the Rising Sun. The guards of the women's camp seemed especially fond of waiting to have *tenko* until the sun had risen to its highest, leaving the women and children to stand unprotected in the merciless tropical heat. The entire daily ritual was well choreographed. After the whistle sounded, the women lined up quickly for the counting, and then as a guard yelled, "*Keirei!*," they would all simultaneously make a deep, ceremonial bow. Any act deemed disrespectful, such as smirking or bowing at a skewed angle, would result in punishing face slaps or shin kicks. Sometimes the reprisal for one person's offense would be levied on the whole camp by making them stand for hours in the sun. This imposed rite represented a continual source of frustration for the women. Some found a way to accept it through imagining that they bowed in respect to God or to another person they loved or admired. One of the women, a great lover of classical music, chose different composers to rest her mind on during the bows. She insisted, "No Japanese can control our minds."[17] According to Helen, "At first, I found it difficult to distance myself from the real situation. The guard and his hateful whistle were a constant reminder of captivity. But I, too, learned to bow to the emperor without giving *him* a thought."[18]

Rather than ruminating on ceremonial absurdities, the minds and energies of the captives needed to focus on surviving in less than ideal circumstances. Conditions in the houses remained primitive, especially concerning waste disposal. The drains were little more than cutouts in the ground, through which septic waste should flow. But without water, it did not flow. Instead, the waste frequently backed up, and the Japanese forced the women to clean out the drains. With so little water and in the tropical heat at the Equator, the task was odious and unsafe. In addition to dealing with public works problems, the women struggled to feed themselves and their children. The food, both quantity and quality, varied from week to week, but regardless, it was usually past the ripe stage and never enough. Often the bags of dry rice contained weevils, stones, and broken glass, so it had to be picked through one grain at a time. A local man came periodically to camp with a cartload of fruit, sugar, tea, and various vegetables that could be purchased by the women who had money.

While many of the women who had carried belongings into the camp had money, most of the women who arrived via a shipwreck did not. Their money had ended up with all of their other possessions in a watery grave. As a result, they tried to come up with jobs around the camp that could earn them money from their "wealthier" peers. At one point, a debate began about pooling all of the money into one collective pot and then buying what the camp needed from that, a tactic used successfully in other POW camps. But in the end, most declined to support the proposal. The mothers especially felt reticent to turn over any of the money that they had been given by their husbands for the care of the children.

While their community functioned relatively well in solving minor internal disputes or in devising ingenious solutions to their practical problems, they did not yet have a successful system by which they could request what they needed from the Japanese. If an individual woman walked up to a guard and asked for something, it normally fell on deaf ears. In time, the guards, already weary of what they saw as a constant barrage of appeals, demanded that the women name official representatives who would serve as liaisons. As a result, the camp elected two such spokeswomen. The Dutch selected the Reverend Mother Laurentia and the English appointed Dr. Jean McDowell, a well-respected doctor whom many had known in Singapore. While some of the Dutch Protestants initially balked at being represented by a Catholic, they could not deny that she exuded an impressive amalgam of decorum and tenacity. So, together Mother Laurentia and Dr. McDowell served as a collective interlocutor, presenting themselves to the guards with needs on behalf of the entire camp. The two walking together toward the guard house must have been quite the picture. The nun wore a blue habit that one of her fellow sisters had recently made for her. The garment was more loose-fitting and therefore more suitable for the heat and work of the camp. Dr. McDowell owned the only stethoscope in the camp, and she made sure to wear it around her neck when she approached the Japanese because she felt that her status as a physician would hold more sway for requests, especially those about medical supplies and food. The official language of these negotiations was a stilted Malay, but since their captors denied almost all petitions, any language barriers seemed a moot point.

So with almost no help from their jailers, the women resorted to making what little they did have count for as many uses as possible, however unlikely. But miraculously, they did possess one item of luxury among the barrenness and poverty. House Number 7, inhabited by the Australian nurses, strangely had a piano. Although it served as a bed at night for one of the nurses, the piano became a draw during other times, as the captives longed for music and entertainment, and anything that resembled their former lives. Their piano conjured music's inherent power to build community no matter the circumstance. "Music seems to survive, and even flourish, amidst the most terrible privations. In Palembang, it marked a distinct turning point in the dissonance which existed between the women as they struggled to come to terms with each other and with their new environment … it was the catalyst that made all kinds of blendings possible."[19] And so, music became a part of the prisoner life in Palembang, with impromptu concerts every Saturday evening by the various women singing in English or Dutch, with that blessed, battered piano providing the accompaniment.

The joy brought by the music inspired other forms of entertainment that served both to amuse and distract. One of the most popular pastimes became skits that parodied camp life, such as "Ration Parade."[20] But any silly topic could become the subject of one of their sketches. In "Melbourne Cup," the women acted out a derby—playing the parts of the horses, jockeys, and announcers.[21] The laughter left everyone pleasantly exhausted when they finally bedded down at night.

At the center of organizing the entertainment was Margaret Dryburgh, the Presbyterian missionary who had already provided spiritual nourishment for the captives. An accomplished musician, Margaret played the piano for some of the camp's more talented singers, including Norah Chambers and Dorothy MacLeod. Margaret's outward appearance belied the true spirit within her that proved vivacious, intelligent, warm, and creative. She had the stereotypical school-teacher/missionary look, with a short and stocky build, thick glasses, and dull brown hair in a bun at the back of her neck. She wore a rather plain, shapeless dress, complemented by sensible Mary Jane–style shoes.

While using her creative energies to foster merrymaking, Margaret never neglected her primary calling. She organized church services for Sundays in the garage where she lived at House Number 9 and invited anyone who desired to come by each night for evening devotions, which would include scripture, prayers, and song. Some in the camp had attended Margaret's church on Orchard Road in Singapore and remembered fondly her excellent organ playing and how she had given piano lessons to the children there. In July 1942, after about five months in captivity, Margaret wrote a hymn, which would endure as her greatest legacy. It was a profound and moving song of prayer, praise, and encouragement for these women. She called her five-stanza hymn, "The Captives' Hymn."

Father, in captivity,
We would lift our prayers to Thee.
Keep us ever in Thy love,
Grant that daily we may prove
Those who place their trust in Thee
More than conquerors may be.

Give us patience to endure,
Keep our hearts serene and pure,
Grant us courage, charity,
Greater faith, humility,
Readiness to own Thy will,
Be we free, or captive still.

For our country we would pray,
In this hour be Thou her stay.
Pride and sinfulness forgive,
Teach her by Thy laws to live.

*By Thy grace may all men see
That true greatness comes from Thee.*

*For our loved ones we would pray,
Be their Guardian night and day,
From all danger keep them free,
Banish all anxiety.
May they trust us to Thy care,
Know that Thou our pains dost share.*

*May the day of freedom dawn.
Peace and Justice be reborn.
Grant that nations, loving Thee,
O'er the world may brothers be,
Cleansed by suffering, know rebirth,
See Thy kingdom come on earth.*[22]

"The Captives' Hymn" received its premiere on Sunday, July 5, 1942, in the garage church with three women—Shelagh Brown, Dorothy MacLeod, and Margaret Dryburgh, singing it a cappella. From that Sunday on, this hymn would be sung every week until the end of the war by the entire congregation who showed up for Sunday worship. Later, one of the women admitted that the hymn was difficult to sing, not musically, but emotionally, because of the heartrending message in the words. Betty Jeffrey later shared about the indelible impact that this hymn had on her life. "To hear people of all colours and creeds singing this each Sunday, is one of the things I shall never forget."[23] The hymn also said much about its author, about her generous and forgiving spirit. Reflecting on this hymn and its writer, Helen Colijn wrote, "She showed no bitterness or anger, only courage and hope that o'er the world nations may brothers be.....Margaret Dryburgh's 'Captives' Hymn' as an instrument of peace."[24]

Margaret had not only written the words, but the melody and harmony as well. Much later after the war, a musicologist from Indiana University, Dr. K. Marie Stolba, was asked to analyze the melody of "The Captives' Hymn." She concluded that it appeared to be derived from fragments of various hymn tunes that Margaret would have known and creatively knitted together to provide a tuneful and singable melody for those under her spiritual care. This hymn signaled the true beginning of Margaret Dryburgh as the spiritual leader and resident patron saint of the internment camp. Through Margaret's encouragement, many of the women learned to deal with the frustrations of their captivity by focusing on a higher power. But Margaret's influence did not occur via overt proselytizing, but through leading by example and allowing the women to connect with God in their own way and in their own time. She believed that this internment had blessed her with yet another opportunity to spread the love of God.

As well as the spiritual still point, Margaret's garage housed the educational center of the camp. With the internees, especially the Dutch, came an abundance of children, at one time numbering as many as 92, ranging from infants to school-aged. Drawing on her experience as an educator and school administrator, Margaret organized teachers and classes. Some of the women also invented competitions, games, and other fun activities for the young people. Sister Paulie, a Dutch nun, offered drawing and painting lessons to them and some of the adults, with the art supplies she had managed to bring with her.

But despite the various activities now available, music remained the most popular and significant, especially corporate singing that buoyed the spirits of everyone. Mother Laurentia organized and led two choirs for the Dutch, one for the children and one for the adults. The British and Australians participated in a glee club, which they eventually renamed the Camp Choral Society, and a church choir, both conducted by Margaret Dryburgh, whose remarkable musicianship included perfect pitch. Her genius made possible "a positive explosion of musical talent that immeasurably leavened the dark, empty evenings in the camp."[25] Norah Chambers, who had the most prestigious musical training of anyone in the camp, also helped out with the English singing groups. The biggest challenge for these various choral groups was the lack of sheet music. A single copy of the *Presbyterian Church Hymnary* was one of the few song books in the camp. Instead, the women relied on their memories for most everything they sang, and individual choir members scribbled out copies of the words, if needed, on whatever paper they could find.

The derelict piano from House Number 7 was used to accompany the choirs as needed. A woman who had been a member of the Dutch Salvation Army had somehow managed to bring a small harmonium to the camp, which became a crucial component of the Dutch church services. But when it also started being part of the evening entertainment, several of the strict church members objected, saying that the harmonium should remain pure and unadulterated by the secular music. They especially resisted its role in accompanying dancing, an activity they frowned upon. The heated debate volleyed back and forth for a while, which although childish, generated some much needed distraction in their humdrum camp lives. In the end, the owner of the instrument declared that if the fighting did not stop, she would put the instrument away and no one could use it. And so with that, the matter was settled as if dealing with a bunch of pre-school children.

On the evenings when no special activities were planned, the women strolled up and down the street. During these walks, the rumor mill worked overtime, spreading whatever one person might have heard, often something about the Allies being close or that the Red Cross was coming to the camp. Most knew not to put much stock in the veracity of these tales, but just thinking that they could be true did instill a sense of hope, however fleeting. The captives struggled to receive any accurate information about the war or their own status. Yet, stories always circulated that they were being moved somewhere, including even to a lunatic asylum. Anything seemed possible, except that the Japanese would let them go home.

As the months dragged on, the women came to recognize even more fully the valuable asset they had in Margaret Dryburgh, including the knowledge she possessed from having spent considerable time in the Far East. In addition to organizing choirs, spiritual gatherings, and educational activities, she wrote songs, poems, and prose that delighted her fellow internees. Margaret was such a kind and generous person that, even in the deprivation of the camp, she loved to give gifts, especially on birthdays. Her presents almost always took the form of an expertly rendered drawing or a cleverly written poem or song. One of these was sung to the tune of the old English nursery rhyme, "Who Killed Cock Robin?," but with wry, new words by Margaret.

> *All the folk in the camp stopped a-fretting and a-grieving*
> *When they thought that Palembang they'd soon be leaving.*
>
> *Who made the camp? We, said the Japs,*
> *We're altering the maps, we made the camp.*
>
> *Who lives in the camp? We, said internees,*
> *Not long, if you please, we live in camp.*
>
> *Who keeps them in? I, said the sentry,*
> *I stand at the entry, I keep them in.*

> *Who brings the food? I, said the lorry,*
> *It's little, I'm sorry, I bring the food.*
>
> *Who feeds the camp? I, said the rice,*
> *Each day twice or thrice, I feed the camp.*
>
> *Who makes rice nice? We, said the beans,*
> *With eggs, yams and greens, we make rice nice.*
>
> *Who cooks the food? I, said the fire,*
> *A fan makes me higher, I cook the food.*
>
> *Who brings the shop? I, said the bullock,*
> *I climb up the hillock, I bring the shop.*
>
> *Who chops the wood? I, said the axe,*
> *I hurt many backs, I chop the wood.*
>
> *Who digs the holes? I, said the chungkal,*
> *I work in the jungle, I dig the holes.*
>
> *Who heals the sick? The doctor said, I,*
> *I've no great supply, I heal the sick.*
>
> *Who helps the people? We, said the committee,*
> *We need all your pity, we help the people.*[26]

In the late summer, Margaret helped start and produce a monthly camp publication, with the assistance of a "staff" of six to write the articles. It included a column on cooking, a section designed specifically for the children, and even a crossword puzzle. Information about the various church services and Bible studies fell under "Church Notices." There was also a medical advice column that offered ideas from pounding egg shells into a powder as a calcium supplement to making sure to cover any scratches as they could soon turn into serious tropical ulcers in that climate and without antibiotic treatment. The newsletter was typed on a dilapidated typewriter, with great care taken about its layout and design, including the creation of a symbolic emblem, described in detail in Helen Colijn's diary. "It is representing the British and The Netherlands flags. The cross formed between the flagstaffs symbolizes the cross we have to bear in common. The sparkling diamond in the intersection represents the noble effort of the internees of both nationalities to beautify their lives."[27]

The first issue of the camp newsletter came out on August 16, 1942, in both a Dutch and English edition. The inaugural editorial read as follows,

> We have the pleasure in starting a new periodical on its career and trust it will receive a welcome. Although we are not a large community, it is surprising how little we know about each other, and we hope that by sharing a common news bulletin we may help to strengthen the bonds between us by getting to know each other. 'United we stand, divided we fall' is a saying that has proved true only too frequently of late. We trust that we shall learn to weld ourselves into a common loyalty and aim, sharing each other's joys and troubles and working for a common purpose.... So this little paper joins the ranks of the newly born in the camp. May its career be successful, though none of us wishes it will be long.[28]

But despite the numerous distractions that the women had invented for themselves, the reality remained that their lives were not their own and that each day presented additional worries and challenges concerning food, water, and illness. Fortunately, during that first year in the house camp, the Japanese allowed the Charitas hospital in Palembang to stay open, with healthcare provided by the Dutch Franciscan nuns and several physicians, including a Dutchman named Dr. Peter Tekelenburg. These Catholic nuns belonged to the Charitas order and had come to Palembang in 1926 to start a mission, which included a hospital. After many years of work in less than adequate facilities, the sisters had overseen the construction of a new, well-equipped hospital in 1940. But the Japanese occupiers immediately seized it for their own military hospital and forced them back to their former building, which had already been stripped of its medical equipment and converted to a school. The savvy nuns, however, had prepared for this eventuality by hiding equipment, medicine, and other supplies as the Japanese army advanced toward the city. They had also managed to conceal their wiliness with straight faces as they exited their new hospital for the last time, walking by the Japanese soldiers with bundles of medical supplies hidden among their voluminous and inviolable habits. They would remain a courageous and steadfast force to be reckoned with in the coming years.

The guards allowed anyone who became ill in the women's camp to go to the Charitas hospital for treatment. An old, decrepit ambulance would arrive once a week to pick up patients that Dr. McDowell had put on the list. The women who had been pregnant at the time of their detainment also delivered their babies there. A total of six babies were born during those first few months in camp. But pregnancy ceased to be a concern after a while, as malnutrition had stopped menstruation. It was not uncommon for severe emotional or physical distress to halt the menstrual cycle, which would normally resume on its own in a few months after circumstances returned to normal. For the women in this internment camp, it took up to three years after the war ended for their cycles to return and regulate. Reflecting on it later, Helen Colijn drolly insisted that "its absence was one of the best things that happened to us in the camp."[29]

The Charitas hospital also cared for the male prisoners housed at the Palembang jail and the local population. Although they had limited access to equipment and medications, the healthcare staff was able to make a difference for the patients sent to them. Prisoners with only minor needs could be treated and sent home the same day. For those requiring longer hospitalization, the Japanese insisted that the wards be strictly segregated to prevent interaction among the male and female inmates. This did not deter them, however, from smuggling notes back and forth or from orchestrating the occasional clandestine visit. Women waiting to be transported to the hospital sometimes sewed notes in their clothing to be passed to the men's camp. The hospital superintendent, Mother Alacoque, greatly assisted in shuttling correspondence between the two wards.

Except for the rare trip to the hospital, the women had no break from their dismal surroundings, and so they attempted to do what they could to bring beauty to themselves and their living spaces. If a bush beyond the fence was flowering, they would snag a bloom to put on their table. They also tried to maintain social rituals, such as afternoon tea. With no actual tea to be had, they concocted a poor substitute from rice and sipped it from chipped cups or halved coconut shells. They lacked the necessary ingredients to make real cookies and experimented with baking tiny rice patties instead. Their spoons for these tea parties varied from a silver spoon brought in with someone's belongings to even a shoe horn. When reflecting on these afternoons after the war, Helen shared, "In the camp I thought those make-believe teas silly. Now I realize that the structure and etiquette those meetings imposed helped to make an untenable living situation more tenable."[30]

To occupy their time during the day, the women played cards or arranged language lessons from one another. They also organized lectures and discussion groups on literature and a variety of subjects—anything to keep their minds working. Some of the titles of these talks included "Working in a Cotton Mill," "Life of Rudyard Kipling," "Life of a London Mannequin," and "Life of Chopin."[31] A few built mah-jongg sets, a time-consuming process that involved chiseling wood out of the rafters in their houses and then meticulously carving and decorating the 144 tiles needed for the game. They then sold them to earn money. These chosen pastimes, from the lectures to the tea parties, revealed that most had come from middle and upper class society, where participating in leisure activities constituted a substantial part of their daily lives.

Regardless of social status, the women spent time sewing. Not strictly just a chore or a hobby, the use of needle and thread met essential needs in the camp, especially for clothing. Needlework, which had been so closely tied to the work of women since ancient times, would not only serve a critical function in their lives as prisoners, but would also take on historical significance in the aftermath of the internment. In the historicity of POWs, the written word in the form of diaries or letters has constituted the most valuable of the primary sources concerning prisoner experiences. But for these women interned in the Far East, their needlework should be considered another compelling primary source, as many female prisoners documented their experiences through textile art. With paper scarce, they did not always have the opportunity to keep journals, and even if paper was available, they feared the Japanese, who had forbidden them to write. But these encumbrances did not preclude them from making a record. With needle and thread, the women could embroider names, places, and events; and these creations read just as powerfully as written diaries because they were also conceived in the moment, capturing what happened in real-time. One important example of this came from Dr. Marjorie Lyon, an Australian surgeon serving in the Malayan Medical Service. She and her colleague Dr. Elsie Crowe stayed in Singapore to treat the wounded until February 13, 1942, when they evacuated. Their ship, the *Kuala*, became another casualty of the Japanese bombers, and the two doctors ended up in the Sumatran internment camp. Dr. Lyon and the other medical personnel worked tirelessly to keep the women and children alive. She also kept a record of names, dates, and locations, not on paper, but embroidered on a silk panel. She survived the war and so did this silk panel, which provided valuable documentation on the plight of the female internees.

The daily regimens that the women had adopted out of necessity for survival and sanity experienced an exciting up-ending one day after about seven months in the camp as someone shouted that they saw the men walking by. The women scrambled onto the rooftops or any place they could get an aerial view. Sure enough, in the distance, they could see the male prisoners in formation, walking two abreast, with the Japanese guards flanking the rows. They yelled and waved clothing or towels, and the men responded with their waves. The women soon discovered that the Japanese were having the male internees build themselves a new camp because the Palembang jail was needed to house locals who had violated Japanese policies. The daily procession to and from their work detail became a highlight for the women, especially the mothers, who would line up the children for their fathers to see. As the end of December approached, they decided to give the men a special gift. On Christmas Day, instead of shouting their usual greetings, the camp choral society, led by Mother Laurentia, serenaded them with carols—first, "O Come All Ye Faithful" and then, "Silent Night." In that moment, all movement ceased, as the men and women stood transfixed with tears in their eyes. William McDougall, an American war correspondent who had been aboard the shipwrecked *Poelau Bras* and subsequently taken prisoner, remembered vividly, even 40 years later, hearing those carols. "We stood there with the guards around us. The guards—they were entranced too. It really was so moving, we wept. Even now I think how wonderful that was, to give us life."[32] After the war, William McDougall would decide that he no longer held a passion for reporting the news. He was ordained a Catholic priest in 1952, a calling certainly influenced by moments such as these.

On that Christmas, in addition to having sung to the men, the women tried to make the most of what they could scrounge together for a meal and as little gifts for each other and the children. In the evening, the children processed around the camp holding lit candles and then forming a circle to sing carols, which created a tableau both meaningful to the captives and incongruous to their surroundings. The day after Christmas, what they would have celebrated as Boxing Day under normal circumstances, became mostly life back to normal as they vied for food and water. But one more holiday treat awaited them that evening, a concert by a joint Dutch and British choir that Mother Laurentia had organized and rehearsed for weeks. They performed a musical setting of the Magnificat, the song of Mary recorded in the Gospel of Luke as she reflected on the reality of being the intended mother of the Christ child. It begins with the familiar words, "My soul doth magnify the Lord." Always appropriate to the season, the Magnificat seemed especially significant and relevant as it highlighted a woman's response to unexpected circumstances, which certainly resonated with these women who were responding to an unheralded disruption in their way of life.

As the new year of 1943 rolled around, the women no longer got to see the men traveling to the construction site. Their camp had been completed, and they had taken up residence in it. Despondency rained down on the female captives who had been so energized and encouraged by these daily encounters. Their depression soon turned to dismay and fear when they received word that the Japanese intended to move the men to Bangka Island, and that the women and children would be relocated as well.

In March 1943, while the women waited to see if the rumors would become reality, they decided to compile a community lending library so that the limited books in the camp could circulate more freely. They collected books that the prisoners had brought, as well as any abandoned in the homes by the previous occupants. Surprisingly, the book repository amounted to about one book for every three people and featured books in Dutch, English, and French, including *Gone with the Wind* by Margaret Mitchell and Victor Hugo's *Les Misérables*. They resided in a large box labeled simply, "Camp Library," to be overseen by Helen Colijn, self-appointed camp librarian. She felt particularly relieved that the books had been gathered and set aside before the paper ended up as kindling for the stove fires.

On April 26, 1943, they still remained in the house camp, and the choral society gave a concert that afternoon of Irish, Scottish, and English songs, followed by the whole camp singing the traditional English hymn, "Jerusalem." Despite the many deprivations they endured, the women were grateful that the Japanese allowed them to participate in skits and choirs, which was not true in some of the other camps where music and acting were forbidden. Still, the pressure to stay out of trouble with their captors always weighed heavily on them, especially as the rules and personnel seemed to be in constant flux.

Their camp overseers proved an interesting assortment of people. There were the well-dressed Japanese officers, who held themselves with great decorum and dignity, but did not actively participate in the daily life of the camp. Sometimes the head official, the camp commandant, would not be seen for weeks. The women wondered what this man had done to deserve such an inglorious position at a remote women's camp on the island of Sumatra. The lower-ranking Japanese guards that they interacted with on a quotidian basis were in general uneducated and unkempt. Their manner of dealing with the women usually fluctuated between only two responses—to ignore or to lash out. Concerning the latter, the violence certainly escalated when the guards had imbibed too much rice wine. Enraged at the minutest action they deemed an offense, they would tear through the houses, upending belongings as they rummaged for contraband or hidden diaries.

The cruelty of the guards became something to never underestimate, especially after they caught a Chinese man throwing a loaf of bread over the fence to the women as part of the black market. The guards tied him to a pole in the camp with his arms above his head and the rope fastened around his neck in such a way that if he lowered his arms he would be strangled. After hours of the women and children witnessing this man's agony, Mother Laurentia pleaded with the guards to let him go, but they refused. The man suffered for three days before finally dying. This traumatic event stayed with them long after. Theo Rottier, who had been one of those children, still suffered from post-traumatic stress as an adult and could not bear to see any kind of violence depicted on television. He confessed that the man's cruel, slow death had haunted him to such an extent that he went back to the house camp in 1973 and stood on the very spot of the horrific incident, hoping that seeing it again would bring respite and closure.

Shortly after the murder of the Chinese local, the guards shouted an order that all boys in the camp aged 11 and 12 be brought forward. They forced them to strip and then, based on physical development, decided which would no longer be considered children. Despite the desperate begging of the mothers, the Japanese moved most of them to the men's camp. Recent events caused this separation to be even more agonizing as they feared that the soldiers' tempers had grown more volatile. Indeed, the brutality of the Japanese guards continued to manifest, particularly in the barbaric way they treated animals. Any dog or cat that had the misfortune to wander into the women's camp, and especially if it befriended the women and children, was destined for the sadistic attentions of the Japanese. A particular black cat that the children had named Hitam was singled out one day by a guard who kicked him to death in front of the children.

Due to the unpredictable nature of the guards, one day aggressive then the next passive, the captives chose to tread carefully, and sometimes gave up altogether in trying to discern motives and forecast outcomes. Helen Colijn summarized it simply as, "Throughout our internment, the Japanese remained impossible to fathom or understand."[33] In commenting on the sometimes erratic and bumbling behavior of the guards, Shelagh Brown recorded in her diary, "It is really just like a comic opera to see these men in action!"[34] Helen wondered later, after the war, how much the language and cultural barriers between the women and the guards exacerbated their difficulties. The Japanese culture of that time valued the submissiveness of women and considered any of their own captured soldiers to be so dishonored that only suicide could restore their honor. The Japanese code of conduct also called for a stoic resolve that prohibited complaining of discomfort or need. So since these prisoners were both women and captives, who regularly voiced their dissatisfaction, they garnered little respect from their captors.

But no matter the level of intimidation and debasement levied by their guards, the real danger lay outside of the camp and had been lurking undetected in Palembang since 1942. The Japanese secret police, the Kempeitai, served a role similar to their Nazi counterparts, the ruthless and dogged Gestapo. But the Kempeitai were known for their even more barbaric bent. They tortured information from people through all kinds of means, including pulling off fingernails and waterboarding, all expressly sanctioned by their government. Tojo, the Japanese Prime Minister, had been a member of the secret police, so with guidance from the highest levels and a detailed military training handbook that outlined methodologies, the Kempeitai operated with unchallenged authority and skill. Their most pressing directive starting in 1942 was to ferret out what they believed to be an underground Dutch resistance, which by the middle of 1943 they concluded was being operated out of Charitas hospital. As a result, they arrested and tortured some of the doctors and Mother Alacoque, the hospital superintendent. The Japanese government sentenced Dr. Ziesel, one of the senior medical staff, to death and beheaded him in November 1943. After being tortured and held for several months in solitary confinement, Mother Alacoque spent the next seven years in prison.

Although the guards had not inflicted some of their most depraved methods of torture on the women in the camp, they did employ strategies to subjugate prisoners as outlined in the handbook, including a myriad of physical deprivations compounded by the emotional anguish of not being allowed to write and receive letters. Gaining access to the handbook after the war finally provided some clarity to what had often seemed random and nonsensical behavior on the part of their captors. But the particularly keen intellect of Margaret Dryburgh, coupled with her equally acute observance of human behavior, led her to deduce the ways and means of the Japanese without needing the benefit of hindsight and reflection. She chose to share her enlightenment in her usual way, through words. She crafted her own version of Lewis Carroll's famed tale, *Alice's Adventures in Wonderland,* which she called "Alice in Internment Land." Her droll literary adaptation of their circumstances hit spot on, and as always, her wry prose found an enthusiastic audience among the women.

After about a year into the internment, the Japanese high command decided to share the burden of guarding the women's camp with the local Javanese police. It seemed that Japan now felt confident enough in their control of Sumatra and its surrounding geographic areas to move some of their military personnel to other locations in the South-East. Known by the derogatory term *Hei Hoes,* the Javanese guards were less strict and less intimidating, armed with only revolvers instead of the menacing rifles with bayonets affixed. Lacking in discipline, they could often be found sleeping while on duty, and if discovered, would incur the wrath of the Japanese soldiers who still maintained ultimate control of the camp.

Eventually, after several months, Japanese threats to relocate the prisoners became reality. When the men received the definitive word that they would be moved to Bangka Island, they guessed that their current, newly constructed camp was going to be used as barracks for the Japanese military. So based on that assumption, they determined to render it as inhospitable as possible. They transformed the wells, their main source of water, into landfills, dumping all of their rubbish into them. They stripped the camp of any usable items and made sure that it looked like a pig sty. They felt some sense of justice in all this as they loaded onto a ship to sail down the Moesi River to Bangka Island and whatever nightmare might await them there. Tragically, these men could not have known that instead of housing soldiers in their abandoned camp, the Japanese had decided to transfer the women and children there.

The women walked the one mile to their "new" camp in September 1943, just as Mother Nature unleashed torrents of rain, turning the whole low-lying area into a pond. Right away, they realized that what they had considered horrible in their previous camp was a picnic compared to what life would be like here, just down the road. The entire rectangular compound occupied about the size of a football field. The barracks building appeared crudely constructed with palm fronds for a roof and contained one communal kitchen and two bathrooms. A guard house sat in the middle of the compound, which also included space designated for an infirmary, since by this time, the Charitas hospital had been closed. The women were expected to sleep in long rows, on bamboo platforms called *balai-balai*, with only about 20 inches of personal space. Storage came at a premium too. Any personal belongings had to fit into the approximately 24 inches allotted on the shelf that ran the length of the barrack wall. The camp ended up more overcrowded than it might have been because women and children from another camp were added, plus the nuns that had worked at the Charitas mission.

In addition to its cramped quarters, this camp sat atop a swamp, where the swarms of mosquitos made it a breeding ground for malaria. The rats and mud contributed to the unhygienic conditions as well. But still, the hardest reality for the new residents to adapt to was the total lack of privacy. Their internment now represented communal living to the extreme—sleeping together, bathing together, eating together. Even the latrines could not provide a moment of privacy, as the half doors on each cubicle shielded nothing. The latrines themselves were so filthy and primitive that, on seeing them for the first time, one Scottish woman exclaimed, "I wouldn't put my cows in here."[35] For bathing, the women had to use a communal basin in the bathroom. They would stand around it and take the equivalent of bird baths because of the water scarcity, usually allotted only what would fit in a five pound butter container. The women had gotten used to cooking independently in their own *kongsi*. Food preparation now proceeded predominately on a large-scale for the whole camp, with no room for personal decisions.

Of all of the assaults on space and identity, the most aggrieved stemmed from no alone time. The only respite came from walking around the compound, but since other women did the same, it lacked any true solitariness. But the walking did serve at least one valuable purpose—it helped distract them from the itching. Soon after arrival in this camp, a new affliction had entered their lives. Despite the absence of a rash or any visible irritation, their skin itched so mercilessly that they wanted to claw it, but scratching would only open the skin and risk it developing into a tropical sore.

Because their challenges and burdens had multiplied in this camp, the women gave up most of their leisure activities, such as glee clubs, lessons, skits, and lectures. They had been forced to abandon their library at the former camp, as well, since it proved too difficult to carry. All they seemed to have energy for now was getting through the daily work it took just to stay alive. The requisite tasks functioned in a community-based labor scheme. People were needed to cut vegetables, haul water, bring in wood, and clean the rice, which still arrived contaminated with rocks and broken glass. Then, they faced the miseries of cooking in the tropical heat. Norah Chambers and a Dutch women named Saartje Tops volunteered to be in charge of the kitchen, which meant that they had to be up no later than 5 a.m. to get the fires started so that breakfast could be made. But none of the meal preparation could happen without wood, which constituted another struggle. A local worker brought wood deliveries periodically and just dumped them outside the gate of the camp. Women assigned to wood-collection duty hung a basket on a long pole, which they then carried filled with wood by positioning the pole across the shoulders of two people. To keep everything balanced, it worked best if the women were the same height and if they trotted more than walked. While wood-related chores happened sporadically, finding enough water was a daily problem. They only had water in the wells when it rained, and without any properly sealed buckets to haul it up, what collected there offered little use. A single tap with running water had to serve the whole of the camp, and women lined up by the hundreds for the chance of some water from it. Sometimes out of sheer meanness, the Japanese would turn off the water to that one spigot. The perennial shortage made tasks even more miserable for the cleaning squads, particularly related to scooping out the latrine, which was as dangerous a job as it was disgusting.

While most of the women in the house camp had willingly pitched in to accomplish the work that needed doing, some had refused to help. Instead, they constantly complained, especially of having to take care of their children, since in their former lives, they had procured nannies to do all that. In this communal camp, it became even more critical that everyone contribute, particularly as more and more fell ill or lost so much weight and strength that they were unable to work. But there still remained women who shirked their duties. Discussions ensued to determine if there was any way to force them to work or even levy a punishment such as a fine. Someone suggested withholding their food if they refused to participate, but Mother Laurentia immediately countered that, saying, "It would be a sin to deprive anyone of food in our miserable conditions."[36] So, they chose to rely on the small perks that went along with each job as incentives, such as wood haulers could keep wood slivers to use for various personal needs. Those who emptied the latrines could wash up in a bit of heated water from the kitchen. These seemingly insignificant "gifts" made a marked difference in the endless days of monotony and deprivation.

In addition to a more strenuous daily work schedule, life had become emotionally harder for the women since they had not had any communication with their men and young sons on Bangka Island. Finally, a guard walked in one day carrying a bag filled with letters from the men. Receiving news that they were still alive thrilled the women and children. But the bag also contained another message—a list of the deceased. For the women who faced this devastating news, there was little to offer as comfort, not even a private space in which to mourn. Among those not directly affected by the deaths, there still emerged a palpable sense of alarm that the camp on Bangka Island must be even worse than their own situation if it was claiming the lives of its prisoners.

Amid the setbacks and exhaustion, some continued to yearn for enjoyable activities that could distract and so decided to pass the time by "collecting" recipes. Each would write down her favorite recipes on scraps of paper. They would then discuss these mouth-watering dishes and at meal times even pretend to eat them, instead of rice and rotten vegetables, claiming that this made them feel more satisfied. Another more tangible diversion came into their lives after three months in this camp when the Japanese built a multi-purpose structure in the middle of the camp. Called a *pendopo*, this pavilion-like construction common to the islands would house church services on Sundays and serve as a school for the children during the week. In due time, this unlikely space would also miraculously transform into a concert hall.

As 1943 neared its close, the women, many of whom would soon reach their two-year anniversary as prisoners, grew even more disheartened. They longed to feel comfortable and safe. They wanted to go home. So in the midst of this incredible suffering, Norah Chambers and Margaret Dryburgh stepped in with an idea. The church choir that Margaret had formed back in Garage Number 9 had continued to sing. But when Margaret suffered a particularly bad bout of dengue fever, the loss of her leadership and of the choir's music was sorely felt in the camp, which in turn prompted Norah to envision an unconventional choral ensemble—a vocal orchestra. This unique group would perform classics from the orchestral and piano repertoire, and they would do it without instruments or words, just vocalises. As described by Norah, "We hummed to get sounds and used consonants to get rhythms and light and colour from the voices."[37] By performing the instrumental music of the great composers with their voices on oohs and ahhs, they would become a vocal orchestra.

8. The Vocal Orchestra: Female POWs on Sumatra

The success of this endeavor would ultimately rest on their cherished Miss Dryburgh. Margaret had relied on music throughout all of her many postings as a missionary, believing fervently in its transformative power, and had carried that same conviction with her to internment life. Back during the better days in the house camp, she had written a poem, "In Foreign Land We Live Interned," that made clear her faith not only in music, but in the remarkable ability of the human mind to summon musical memories.

> *A sudden thought the mind did cheer*
> *Much music that Thou once did hear*
> *Is stored in memory*
> *It lives forever. Bring it forth*
> *Use our own instrument of work*
> *Sing. Thou wilt happier be.*[38]

Margaret had encouraged the women in the house camp to remember the songs of their youth, which she then transcribed to paper. But now, with the prisoners' memories exhausted of songs, Margaret realized that Norah's novel idea to sing instrumental music meant that no words were necessary, which also provided a practical solution to the language barriers. Plus, without text to dictate the meaning, all who listened could have a uniquely personal experience and let the music speak what they needed it to say.

So with her extraordinary musical recall, Margaret began transcribing beloved classics from the orchestral and piano repertoire onto scraps of paper, with no sheet music to reference or no piano to sound it out on first. After the war, when asked if Margaret had possessed some type of eidetic memory for music, Norah dismissed the suggestion, explaining instead, "Margaret carried the sounds of the music in her head, not a picture of the printed scores."[39] She also praised Margaret's gifted ear by saying, "You could go to her, hum a tune and straight away she could write it down and harmonize it."[40]

Margaret's arrangements for the vocal orchestra also demonstrated her ability to create stand-alone miniatures from complex symphonic works, intuitively knowing just how to condense and arrange them. Fortunately, Norah and Margaret got along quite well, and the two worked together to fill in the harmonies and adapt the transcriptions for four voice parts—1st and 2nd soprano, and 1st and 2nd alto. Although Margaret certainly came from a different background and was 20 years Norah's senior, the universality of the music they loved bridged those divides. Margaret's training and experience, plus her deeply held convictions about the intersection of faith and music, made it seem providential that she was here, at this time and in this place, to bring a life-changing musical idea to fruition.

Norah and Margaret successfully recruited singers from throughout the camp, including Dutch, British, and Australian. Helen Colijn's sisters Antoinette and Alette quickly signed up as they had loved being part of Margaret's groups in the other camp. Sadly, Helen herself had never been musically gifted so she chose to be a spectator instead. Many of the talented singers who had entertained the women in the house camp, including Norah's sister Ena Murray, joined as well. But the group welcomed anyone who wanted to belong, even if they could not read music. So, the roster of singers included some who had formal choral experience and some who did not. The two leaders decided that the first piece to teach the vocal orchestra should be Tchaikovsky's "Andante Cantabile," which they viewed as simple and straight forward enough to make a good training piece. As the conductor of the ensemble, Norah exhibited a patient but exacting teaching style as they rehearsed at night to the light of a single bulb in the kitchen.

In speaking after the war about Norah and these make-shift rehearsals, Antoinette

Colijn said, "She never let a false note or a muddled phrasing go by. She made us go back again and again, until we got the music just right…. But to sing measure 32 and 33 correctly became very important and took your mind off whether you were hungry, or thirsty, or feeling sick, or just plain down in the dumps."[41] Norah shared a similar sentiment, "We clean forgot where we were during those rehearsals, and, you see, that was so important."[42] The vocal orchestra became a true community effort. The stronger singers sat with the weaker and helped them learn and stay on their parts. They shared a common love of music, which they now focused toward an ambitious goal—an inaugural concert scheduled for December 27, 1943.

On the day of the performance, the residents of the camp still did not know what pieces were on the program. The singers had kept a veil of secrecy over the details of the concert to make it all the more thrilling, and indeed excitement built all day for that 4:30 p.m. event. Helen's sisters had recruited her to walk around the compound beating a wooden spoon on a tin butter container and reminding everyone of the concert. No one needed the reminder, of course, since it had been all anyone could talk about for weeks, but Helen's enthusiastic town-crier routine certainly added to the overall anticipation. Mothers especially looked forward to this special event for their children, who had so little to occupy their time and who had missed out on so many normal opportunities. The mothers tried to tidy their children, running a wet comb through their sons' hair and retrieving a hair ribbon stowed away from better times for their daughters. The women did their best to spruce themselves up as well, such as sharing a rare tube of lipstick. Some even decided to put on their "liberation dresses," special dresses they had sewn in the early days of the house camp to wear when they walked out victoriously to freedom, which they thought would not be that long.

Sadly, some of the women and children who wanted to attend were too sick with dysentery or malaria. Only a few in the camp refused to take an interest in the concert. They thought that the Japanese would not take too kindly to this assembly, since they had forbidden organized groups, and so considered it reckless to risk retaliation for a silly music event. One even remarked, "It's absurd to waste precious energy singing. The singers should be using their energy for just staying alive!"[43]

The afternoon concert would take place in the new *pendopo* at the center of camp, although it would not be large enough to accommodate everyone. Most of the audience would be standing outside the *pendopo* or sitting on its railings, with the children seated on the dirt floor in the front row. The altered schedule for the day included an early dinner so that the concert could start at 4:30 p.m. and be concluded before dark, which in the tropics, came on suddenly and completely. Few watches still functioned, making exact times often difficult to pinpoint. But a couple of the Australian nurses involved in the vocal orchestra had working time pieces, and Norah would consult them for an accurate start time.

Norah and Margaret had worked tirelessly to organize a performance event that would be meaningful to the singers and to the listeners, and feel as much like a traditional concert as possible. The format consisted of two sections, separated by a 20-minute intermission to allow the performers time to rest. For the audience, refreshments and what passed for coffee in their camp would be served during the break. The program featured an impressive repertoire, both in quantity and diversity, including Dvořák's "Largo" from the *New World Symphony*; "Shepherd's Complaint" from Mendelssohn's *Songs without Words*; "Andante Cantabile" from Tchaikovsky's *String Quartet No. 1*; Chopin's *Raindrop Prelude*; Beethoven's *Minuet in G*; Debussy's *Rêverie*; the Irish Folk Song "Londonderry Air"; and MacDowell's "To a Wild Rose." Known for her stunning soprano voice, Ena Murray would sing the "Faery Song" aria from Rutland Boughton's opera *The Immortal Hour*, to the vocal orchestra's accompaniment. This and future concerts would also include at least one solo by Dorothy MacLeod, known affectionately as "Mac," whose charming voice had been a fixture in the operetta world of Singapore. Because of the time of year, the vocal orchestra added some Christmas-themed pieces at the end, starting with the "Pastorale" from Handel's *Messiah* and then a few carols, but without words. These would be followed by an invitation for all to sing along to "Auld Lang Syne."

Indeed, at 4:30 p.m. sharp, Norah Chambers and the women's vocal orchestra, 30 members strong, processed into the *pendopo* from behind the kitchen area. They carried stools for themselves and their own hand-copied sheet music. Norah had employed several music scribes, including Antoinette Colijn, to write out the parts on whatever paper scraps could be found. No one had a ruler, so the lines of the staves had to be painstakingly drawn. Unlike the audience, the performers had not dressed up for the concert. Not all of the members had dresses or anything special they could don, so collectively they chose to just wear their normal daily clothes, which for most meant shorts and tank tops. Margaret Dryburgh wore the same dress that the women had first seen her in, although it appeared much more faded and worn than it had been then, and strings now held together her sensible shoes. Norah conducted the concert in a pair of beige slacks and a blouse, both graciously given to her by a fellow prisoner, since she had lost everything with the sinking of the *Vyner Brooke*. Most of the singers had bare feet, with a few wearing *terompahs*, the wooden sandals with rubber straps that had been common household shoes for upper-class women in the tropics. The singers' attire also included the now familiar bandages on arms and legs that covered tropical sores.

After the orchestra members had taken their seats, Norah stepped forward and read a prepared introduction written by Margaret Dryburgh.

> This evening we are asking you to listen to something quite new, we are sure: a choir of women's voices trying to reproduce some of the well-known music usually given by an orchestra or a pianist. The idea of making ourselves into a vocal orchestra came to us when songs were difficult to remember, and we longed to hear again some of the wonderful melodies and harmonies that uplifted our souls in days gone by. So we make our humble attempt to let you hear some of the masterpieces of the musical world as well as we can remember them…. We do not profess to reproduce the effects or quality of stringed or reed instruments. But as the lovely melodies and harmonies of the Great Masters greet your ears, may you imagine you hear them. The choir will remain sitting, as does an orchestra, to conserve their energies…. So close your eyes, and try to imagine you are in a concert hall hearing Toscanini or Sir Thomas Beecham conduct his world-famous orchestra.[44]

Handwritten copy of Dvořák's "Largo" used by the vocal orchestra in its concerts (courtesy Stanford University Libraries).

After her opening speech, Norah turned toward the choir and lifted her arms, just as Margaret hummed the starting pitch. The first notes to materialize into the air formed the haunting opening to Dvořák's "Largo." Then, where the iconic English horn solo would enter, there was instead that melody produced in Margaret's rich alto voice. It remains unknown how many of the singers or audience members understood that the palpable longing expressed in this second movement from Dvořák's *New World Symphony* represented his incredible homesickness while living in the United States from 1892 to 1895, away from his beloved Czech homeland. Dvořák had also drawn inspiration for the work from the plight of the Native Americans and black Americans. Their music and story became central to this symphonic composition, which the New York Philharmonic premiered on December 16, 1893. Several years after the composer's death, William Arms Fisher, one of Dvořák's American students, took his teacher's haunting "Largo" melody and added words, resulting in the song "Goin' Home" (sometimes known as "Going Home"). First published in 1922, Fisher's song was later mislabeled as a Negro Spiritual, depriving its writer of the credit. It went on to achieve great popularity as a Gospel song and then a jazz standard. Whether anyone in this Japanese internment camp knew of Fisher's version is also unknown. But if they had, what apt opening words it expressed for them in their present circumstance.

> Goin' home, goin' home, I'm a goin' home;
> Quiet like, some still day, I'm jes' goin' home.
> It's not far, jes' close by, through an open door...

As the "Largo" soared through its first big crescendo, Helen Colijn experienced the music as a physical sensation. "I felt a shiver go down my back. I thought I had never heard anything so beautiful before. The music didn't sound like a women's chorus singing songs. It didn't sound precisely like an orchestra either, although it was close. I could imagine I heard violins and an English horn. The music sounded ethereal, totally unreal in our sordid surroundings."[45] But as the "Largo" continued, a discordant sound joined it—the angry grunts of a Japanese guard pushing his way through the crowd of listeners, bayonet firmly affixed to his rifle. He marched all the way up to the railing of the *pendopo*, but then froze. He stood silent and transfixed, making no further encroachment toward the singers. He maintained this post for the remainder of the concert's first half.

The audience had been asked to hold their applause until after the last piece before intermission. When the clapping did begin, it sounded thin and tentative, as they were unsure how the Japanese would react to an enthusiastic expression. But, almost immediately, they abandoned their fears and clapped boldly, accompanied by shouts of "Bravo!" The singers did not bow as would be customary in a concert, most likely due to the camp *tenko* ritual. Not familiar with Western culture, the Japanese guards might have mistaken the performers' bows as some kind of insult or even as a gesture of honor toward Emperor Hirohito.

While the choir rested in the kitchen, the Australians poured hot beverages for the audience members, and the Dutch served little cookies they had made out of rice flour, water, and a tiny ration of sugar. Helen noticed with curiosity that one of the servers offered a cookie to the guard who had become an audience member. After a moment's pause, he accepted and even voiced a thank you. Watching this scene unfold, Helen succumbed to a moment of compassion for her captor. She could imagine that he probably hated this war too and missed his homeland and his family. In a way, Helen concluded that he was as "caught up in the idiocies of war"[46] as they were.

The unequivocal success of the concert for the singers and the listeners could be seen on their faces and heard through their enthusiastic words. Betty Jeffrey wrote, "This music is quite the most wonderful thing that has happened in this camp so far. None of us have ever heard women's voices anywhere better than this orchestra."[47] The performance inspired her to join the ensemble and declare, "It is absolutely marvelous, the most fascinating thing I have ever done."[48] Through the music, many reconnected with their inner strength and with the Divine, reigniting a spiritual resistance against their captors. Helen remarked, "The music renewed our sense of human dignity. We had to live under bestial conditions but, by Jove, we could rise above them!"[49]

Right away, people clamored to know when the next concert would be, not even caring if it just reprised the same pieces. Never one to back down from a challenge, Margaret Dryburgh set out to "remember" more pieces and capture them on paper for the vocal orchestra. In addition to what had been learned for the first concert, the choir eventually augmented their repertoire with the following pieces:

Bach	Jesu, Joy of Man's Desiring
Barratt	Coronach (A Highland Lament)
Beethoven	First Movement (from *Moonlight Sonata*)
Brahms	Waltz No. 15
Chaminade	Aubade
Chopin	Prelude No. 6 and Prelude No. 20
Dvořák	Humoresque
Grieg	Morning (from *Peer Gynt* Suite)
German	Shepherd's Dance (from *Henry VIII Suite*)
Godard	Berceuse (from *Jocelyn*)
Grainger	Country Gardens
MacDowell	Sea Song
Mendelssohn	Venetian Gondola Song No. 3
Mozart	Allegro (from *Sonata in C*)
Paderewski	Menuet a l'Antique
Ravel	Bolero
Schubert	First Movement (from *Unfinished Symphony*)
Schumann	Dreaming (from *Scenes of Childhood*)

In the end, the vocal orchestra amassed a repertoire of approximately 30 pieces and presented three or four additional concerts, performing until their membership had dwindled so significantly from illness and death that it was no longer feasible. Surprisingly, the Japanese never attempted to forbid the concerts or interrupt them during a performance, although they did push back with petty harassment. On one occasion, a guard demanded that Norah include a Japanese song on the concert. When she refused, he made her stand outside, unprotected for hours in the blazing sun. Later, an especially harsh camp commandant named Captain Siki reprimanded the women for what he viewed as the shameful act of singing while a war raged. Nevertheless, Japanese officers sometimes attended the performances, strolling in as if they had received special VIP invitations. After one concert, they even gave the vocal orchestra five cans of SPAM as a gesture of appreciation.

But as the vocal orchestra offered much needed psychological and emotional respite during the early months of 1944, camp conditions deteriorated in terms of food scarcity and disease to the extent that women and children began to die. One of the early casualties was a young Sacred Heart nun, who had taught the children in the house camp. Now, her emaciated body lay, shrouded by a white sheet, in the *pendopo*. The remaining nuns kept vigil with prayers and liturgical rites, but the other internees avoided the area. It represented a too-painful reminder of their perilous situation. The needlessness of the death weighed heavily on them, knowing that this woman would have lived with only a nominal increase of food and access to basic medications.

The sparse quantity at meal times was only part of the problem with their food supply. The lack of nutrition in their diet created an array of difficulties, including beriberi, which was rampant around the camp, along with malaria and dysentery. Resulting from a thiamine vitamin deficiency, beriberi disease caused fluid to form beneath the skin, leading to swelling in the legs and arms to such an extent that they could not bend. It also made the skin so "wet" from underneath that it would sluff off at the slightest touch. In time, the fluid retention in the extremities would fatally spread to the organs and heart.

Now that death had set up residence in the camp, the prisoners faced it as bravely and practically as they could. Often women who were dying, or who just knew that it grew closer every day, would scribble out a will on a scrap of paper. All belongings, whether it be a pair of sandals or a mosquito net or a few quinine pills, were of priceless value; and unless they specified who among their fellow captives to bequeath each to, they feared that the Japanese would pilfer it for their own coffers.

The receipt of these parting gifts and anything extra that the women might earn could mean the difference in life or death. In addition to the various money-making enterprises of cooking, sewing, or haircutting, some would offer up a possession in a raffle. Raffle tickets would be available for purchase, and then the winner of the drawing would receive the "prize." Even women who might not need that particular item sometimes bought a raffle ticket for the chance to resell it at a later date. During these contests, Helen Colijn, known for her devout faith, wanted to believe that she bought these raffle tickets predominately out of a sense of benevolence, of contributing to the collective good. Never truly convinced of her own motives, Helen did conclude, "Generosity became a more and more precious quality in the fight for survival and the choice between 'good for others' and 'good for ourselves' was the subject of much debate between my sisters and me."[50]

As evidenced throughout 1944, the resourcefulness and fortitude of the female collective had grown exponentially during their years of captivity. Some of the women, the "helping" population of nuns, missionaries, and nurses, had arrived more accustomed to a disciplined and maybe even ascetic lifestyle. For those who had lived a rather leisurely way of life, the transition proved more difficult. In general, the colonial women initially seemed ill-equipped to cope in a situation without the social boundaries and conventions that had given structure to their days and lives. "Even the immutable rules of caste and class, immovable pillars of colonial society, were stripped of their comforting solidarity as the whole framework of their existence was tested brutally by the enforced egalitarianism of total poverty."[51] The women of privilege also lost the patriarchy that had grounded them. Whether among fathers, brothers, or husbands, these women were acculturated to a social order where the men in their lives made the major decisions, and this had hindered them in many ways from developing problem-solving and decision-making skills.

In fact, for all the female internees, there was at least some sense that they had always been subjugated because of their gender, and as a result, adjusting to the present dynamic with their captors might not have been as much of a stretch for them. But for the men accustomed to being the "kings of their domain," this captivity became an even more bitter pill to swallow. In considering the practical aspects of survival, the men did maintain the advantages of their physical strength and ability to build and bring about capital improvements to their camps, although this probably failed to measure up to the women's domestic skills that were so invaluable to daily survival. But in the end, it was truly the female population who underwent a radical and empowering transformation that surpassed any individual or collective weaknesses and deficiencies.

When the Japanese chose to deal with the unanticipated hordes of women by imprisoning them together in an isolated environment, instead of further suppressing them, it triggered the ironic rise of a kind of feminine power and self-determination that most of these women had never known. One survivor after the war reflected, "Because we had no men to help us it was only our strength and nobody else's. I learnt that women can be very brave, very tenacious. If it had not been for that we would not be here now."[52] Another shared a similar realization. "I grew up in those camps. I came out of myself and realized my strengths. I shall always be grateful for those years. It was the best school there could have been."[53] This collective experience had all of the makings of a social science experiment, a case study "long before it became fashionable to examine women for their strengths rather than their weaknesses, to ask what they are able to accomplish rather than underlining what they cannot…"[54] It revealed that the most important resource these women possessed was their community, which enabled them to find the inner strength to adapt to and persist within their circumstances. They cultivated their skills and their minds, and learned to trust and rely on each other. Within their cloistered walls, they developed a matriarchy—a society for women, by women.

Not surprisingly within this long and all-female sequestration, whispered gossip periodically surfaced about women who might have been inclined toward or participating in homosexual relationships, such as two women sharing the same *balai* and mosquito net. At the time, with the subject of homosexuality still taboo and many of the women extremely naïve, it was not discussed openly in the camp, but merely alluded to with slight innuendos or eye winks. Whether the witnessed incidents constituted a purely platonic need for comfort and the practicality of not having enough supplies or whether there truly was a sexual component continued to be a subject of debate. But certainly as their situation deteriorated, a few of the women chose to use their sexuality to garner favors. These women "visited" with various Japanese men and returned with food and sundry items. At first, the other female internees condemned them and spoke harshly of their behavior. These remonstrations were not so much a moral judgment, but an indictment of what they considered the betrayal of making "friendly" overtures toward the enemy. Sometimes, the women shared what they had been given, and the criticisms softened into gratitude. For those unwilling to feed themselves through that means, they had to obtain the necessary extras through the local black market, which was secretly and cautiously conducted through a small opening in the bamboo wall of the camp. The women often relied on the Eurasians with their fluent Malay to conduct the negotiations. Regardless, the price was always exorbitant and the whole transaction risky, as no one had forgotten about the execution of the Chinese man.

Then, in the spring of 1944, the camp administration went through a similar shift to what had happened in 1943, only in reverse. The Japanese military once again assumed complete control over the camp and relieved the Javanese police from any involvement.

With the change, a new camp commandant, Captain Siki, arrived with a ferocity and doggedness that left the women in little doubt about what was in store for them. He was accompanied by a second-in-command, so overweight and porcine, that the women immediately dubbed him—"Ah Fat." The duo now in charge of their camp looked like a caricature lifted straight from the pages of a comic book.

Despite the subhuman conditions of the camp, Japanese officials still insisted on absurd displays of pageantry and protocol. So on April Fool's Day, an irony not lost on the women, the new commandant sat regally at a table in the *pendopo* to survey his captives, ordering "Ah Fat" to present each one to him formally with a bow. But "Ah Fat" had failed to notice the patch of slippery mud in the area where the women were to bow, and so the decorum the Japanese so desired was repeatedly thwarted as the women slipped and fell into the mud. The spectacle infuriated the Japanese, but greatly amused their prisoners. Betty Jeffrey wryly recorded in her diary, "Poor old Tojo, nothing ever comes off with dignity and something always goes wrong."[55]

Under Captain Siki's new regime, the women were to be weighed once a month and given vaccinations against typhoid and cholera, measures that seemed to indicate more concern for their health. But the guards did not increase the paltry rations, and as the women continued to wane, the mandatory monthly weighings stopped. Some wondered if the vaccinations, instead of for their welfare, had been a precaution for the health of the guards, to minimize their risk from an epidemic. The Japanese did seem perpetually fearful of germs, which the women cleverly used to their advantage. Faking a tubercular coughing spell never failed to send the guards scurrying.

By May 1944, the prisoners had gone 12 months without any protein, and many weighed less than 90 pounds. Then unexpectedly, the guards brought them a bit of fresh fish, followed by a few chickens a couple of days later. A new pattern had emerged from their captors—some days almost nothing to eat and then the random "gift" of something actually nutritious to fill their empty stomachs. As they waged the battle against starvation, the women continued to be plagued by lack of hygiene. They had not seen even a sliver of soap in a long time and, with water so scarce, could only try to stand under the leaking roof when it rained to clean themselves. Disease had also become a constant companion since moving into this camp. Fortunately for the sick, there were four women doctor-prisoners in the camp, plus the many nurses, all of whom sacrificed their health by working around the clock to tend to the infirm and dying, with almost no supplies. If the Japanese had only supplied them with quinine for malaria and something for dysentery, the medical personnel would have been able to save lives and greatly reduce suffering.

The one commodity that the women could continue to count on from the Japanese was their changeability. During the spring of 1944, Captain Siki received orders to cut prisoner rations and to institute a policy of "no work, no food" for those under his command. When the Japanese announced that the women would be required to plant gardens of cassava in their camp, a collective cry of protest went up, not only because of the work required, of which no one felt able, but also the loss of precious space for walking. So in a scene worthy of the "theatre of the absurd," the women began tilling the ground for planting during the heat of the day and with inadequate equipment. The tool provided, a *chungkal*, had a wooden handle and a heavy iron head that weighed over 20 pounds. Although the women could barely lift it in their weakened conditions, the soldiers insisted that the women raise and strike in unison as in a chain gang and stood ready with their rifles to confront anyone they saw out of rhythm. One of the particularly nasty guards examined the women's hands for blisters. If he did not see any, he concluded that they had not worked hard enough and kept them digging until blisters appeared.

After the planting, with almost no water in the camp, the Japanese forced the women to march with buckets a half-mile down the road to retrieve water and then throw it on the cassava patches, even though they so desperately needed the water for drinking, cooking, and hygiene. As most of them had not had shoes in years, all of this was undertaken with bare feet. When there happened to be some water in the camp well, the Japanese refused to let them use that dirty water for the plants. One day, a woman could not resist smuggling the clean water inside for herself, and a guard beat her bloody for the offense. The Japanese also insisted that the women "fertilize" the cassava by scooping out the contents of the septic tank and dumping it on the garden. The heat and sun quickly dried the waste into dust, which then blew all over the residents of the camp and everything in it, creating not only filth, but a breeding ground for disease. Betty recorded, "I feel I will never be clean again."[56] As a result, typhoid joined the list of ailments. But through it all, many remarkably managed to keep their sense of humor intact, evidenced by another entry in Betty's diary. "Next war we have all decided to set off at once for the South Pole with plenty of clothes and some sugar!"[57]

As the length of the internment dragged on, accumulating more and more unconscionable behavior by their captors, the women often revisited the single question that they wanted answered—why? To offer only one explanation for such deplorable treatment would certainly be reductive in such a complex and multi-faceted situation, but the convergence of two fundamental factors lends at least some understanding to the more existential inquiry. The first was that the Japanese Imperial Army consisted mostly of peasant soldiers who had been conscripted for military service, and not educated, cultured men. Secondly, these men had been heavily indoctrinated about traditional gender roles. The 17th century Japanese venerable tome *Onna Daigaku* (Greater Learning of Women) relied on Confucian philosophy to outline the importance of a social hierarchy dictated by gender and age, and served as an instructional manual for how women should function within Japanese society. The book criticized what it defined as inherent flaws in the female sex, such as silliness and jealousy. As a result, the concept that women should work particularly hard in domestic duties and in the soil became widely accepted. The primitive tools that the guards provided for the interned women, such as the *chungkal* for gardening and a mattock for grave digging, all incompatible with the tasks at hand, were the same implements used by the peasant women of Japan.

But despite the daily mistreatment of their female prisoners, the guards insistently referred to themselves as their "protectors."[58] Unsurprisingly, the women certainly rejected this notion. One of Betty's entries summed up the general feeling. "They are not human, they are just beasts."[59] Their hatred toward the Japanese compounded as the women discovered more about the mean-spirited withholding of items that would provide them physical and emotional succor, including Red Cross aid packages filled with food, medicine, mosquito netting, and letters from their families. Betty Jeffrey did not receive her first letter from home until August 1944, by which point she had had no word from her family for three years. The women heard a rumor from a reliable Japanese source that the guards had failed to hand over about 300 letters addressed to the internees. The women were not even sure if anyone knew about them or where they were until they saw a parcel arrive on July 11 marked American Red Cross. Then, they watched with great bitterness as the soldiers helped themselves to most of the contents without a modicum of remorse.

That same day, Betty documented an incident involving a Scottish woman whom the guard summoned to stand before him and receive punishment, although for what, no one knew. As he raised his hand to slap her, she yelled for him to stop, which surprisingly he did. She then took out her denture and removed her glasses. That accomplished, she faced him as if to say that he could proceed. "He was puzzled for a moment, then threw back his head and laughed and walked away. It was priceless to watch."[60] It also represented another snapshot of the incongruity of Japanese behavior on any given day and of the challenges in maintaining their sanity among such dissonance. As Betty continued that day, "We live from day to day, nobody bothers about what will happen next week. Why worry? We can't do anything about it."[61]

Exactly one month later, on August 11, 1944, a piercing air raid siren split through the sky, followed by the sound of anti-aircraft fire and then the boom of exploding bombs. The women could see fires in the distance where the Allies had targeted the town of Pladju, which housed a large oil refinery. The Dutch had disabled the facility in anticipation of the Japanese invasion, but it had since been made re-operational. The prisoners greeted these sights and sounds with unveiled enthusiasm and as a possible sign that the war was finally ending with a Japanese defeat. One woman declared that the roar of these falling bombs was "like the voices of angels."[62] A few days later, the Allies unleashed a similar campaign on Pladju—followed only by silence. The momentary hope of liberation again succumbed to the depression of captivity.

The announcement of another pending relocation came not long after these two bombing raids. The women and children would be uprooted from Sumatra and carted back to Muntok on Bangka Island, where many of them had washed ashore over two years earlier. The thought of moving weighed heavily since they never knew what lay in store, only that their most recent transfer had certainly brought a downgrade in conditions. Those still able to "look on the bright side" dwelled on the fact that they would be on the same island as the men, and so there might be an opportunity to see them or at least attempt some form of communication. As always, conjecture about Japanese motives ran the gamut, but the favorite theory claimed that this change of venue signaled that Allied forces would soon liberate Sumatra. It certainly seemed a viable explanation, and the Nazi regime would employ a similar strategy of shuffling concentration camp prisoners from camp to camp as the Allies drew near. The Japanese had, in fact, evacuated a small camp in Benkulen about 280 miles to the east and crowded those 100 women and children into the Palembang camp. With their number at approximately 700 now, they would be hauled to Bangka Island in three groups. After a typical false start that had internees packing then unpacking, the first group departed in October 1944.

The passage to the next camp for the second group proved a particularly wretched experience aboard a ramshackle boat in miserable weather, with many of the prisoners sick or even dying. As the storm raged around them, a guard shouted in Malay, "Don't move about…. The ship is old!"[63] But this warning seemed hardly necessary since everyone in the overcrowded vessel felt so weak that their only movement was to pass a tin dish back and forth to vomit in. At one point, a soldier handed them an empty helmet to use as a chamber pot. This small kindness amid an intractable situation caused Helen Colijn again to pause. "Once in awhile, with a single such gesture, a Japanese would emerge from the great mass of 'the enemy' and plant himself in my memory as an actual human being."[64]

If it had not been for the sacrificial work of the nuns and nurses, there would probably have been few survivors from the internment. They labored tirelessly in whatever camp or vessel that they found themselves. On this particular storm-tossed journey, whenever a wave was poised to crest over the boat and onto the sick who lay on its deck, one of the Charitas sisters would cry, "'Here she comes.' Then the nuns would stretch their bodies over the poor souls to shield them as best they could. When the water receded, the nuns' white habits clung to their bodies and revealed their bony hips and flat bosoms."[65] But despite these heroic interventions, some did not survive the trip.

Arriving at their latest camp, the internees were relieved to find recently constructed barracks that were clean and allowed more sleeping and living space than at the former camp. Trees and an abundance of green foliage surrounded them, making the air feel fresher. The nurses quickly set up a hospital, as the number of ill continued to mount. But as ever, the Japanese provided almost no supplies, giving them 100 quinine pills every six weeks, which for 700 people living in these conditions proved useless. An additional health threat developed right away—a mysterious sickness with a high fever that they labeled "Bangka fever." They would later learn that it was an especially virulent strain of malaria. As its victims lay suffering in the night, unsure of whether they would survive to see the dawn, a jungle bird could be heard singing a beautiful song, a bird that the native population ominously referred to as the Death Bird. For many, the high fever never broke, causing its victims to slip into unconsciousness and then death.

Sometimes the women who died left behind one or more children. Again, the nuns stepped forward and enfolded these camp orphans into their care. By the end of the war, 26 of the Dutch children had watched their mothers die and been "adopted" by the Sisters of Carolus Borromeus. One young child, Isidore Warman, had arrived at that first house camp already an orphan. He had been aboard the *Vyner Brooke* with his parents, and they had not survived the shipwreck. Margaret Dryburgh had assumed care for him. He would survive to see the liberation, and after over three years in captivity, the 6 year old was finally reunited with relatives.

With the death total rising almost every day now, the women worked in pairs on grave duty. Having to dig the graves proved nearly impossible as the women hardly had enough strength to walk to the site, much less pick up the heavy mattocks given for the job. Their pleas for shovels were ignored. Helen Colijn often helped prepare the burial plots. Unwell, she sometimes had to pause, hoping the guard would not notice, because her heart raced or because she almost blacked out. Once the pair of diggers reached a certain depth, one of them had to climb into the grave to scoop out dirt, an experience that felt too ominous to contemplate. Betty Jeffrey's diary continued to document the hard work and resilience she witnessed in the exhausted and emaciated women around her, saying, "….it is extraordinary how a person can have malaria and a temperature of over 104° every week or so and yet be able to work in between bouts of it."[66] As it seemed to her that these women had nine lives, she concluded, "There is no doubt about it, women *are* cats."[67]

When one of the women or children died, a nun or missionary would say a few words at the burial. Then someone would lay wild flowers on the grave and mark it by a small wooden cross. Norah Chambers and a woman named Mrs. Owen had learned how to use hot nails to burn inscriptions of the names into the wood, which they would do for each deceased. Not surprisingly, their spiritual shepherd Margaret Dryburgh often presided over the funerals. She would recite from one of her favorite psalms, usually Psalm 121, and lead the mourners in a few verses of the hymn "Just as I Am." She would also read a passage from the Book of Revelation and conclude with this evening prayer from the Book of Common Prayer.

Lord, support us all the day long, until the shadows lengthen and the evening comes, and the busy world is hushed, and the fever of life is over, and our work is done. Then in thy mercy grant us a safe lodging, and a holy rest, and peace at the last. Amen.[68]

Toward the end of 1944 and the long months of early 1945, the women faced almost unbearable circumstances, as they lost the battle to malnutrition and disease one by one. But despite the likelihood of death and "faced with the removal of nearly everything that they would once have considered made living worthwhile,"[69] the women remained courageously determined to live, with only two instances of suicide known out of the hundreds imprisoned throughout the multi-year internment. Many managed an almost Zen-like mindfulness. Reflecting about her internment, a woman named Elizabeth Simons wrote, "We lived in the present, having learned that the past could not help us and that there might not be another day."[70]

They also learned to treasure the small joys. Helen often volunteered for the onerous job of emptying the latrine because it allowed her to go, unaccompanied by guards, outside of the camp. There, she could savor a stolen moment of freedom, later recalling, "Once I saw a hibiscus in bloom and picked one of the fiery red blossoms to put behind my ear. What I liked most of all was seeing the colorful butterflies. We never saw them inside the camp."[71] Her longing to behold beauty, especially that of a butterfly, shared a similar sentiment with that of a young man in the Nazi ghetto Terezín, whose famous 1942 poem included the lament, "I never saw another butterfly..."

For the women who had held out hope of seeing their male family members on Bangka Island, their faith in that reunion began to waver. Even though they now resided close to the men's camp, they had no communication or sightings. All they received were the occasional death lists, a particularly cruel gesture by the Japanese who could have easily allowed a letter or note to be exchanged. Mother Laurentia received the deceased notices and then went about the painful process of informing any of the affected women. Those with loved ones in the men's camp held their breath as she walked back and forth, afraid that her next stop would be them. In addition to Mother Laurentia as comforter, the women could always turn to Sister Catharinia, known for her strength and compassion, "a specialist in giving succor amid awfulness."[72] She had also never shied away from tackling the practical and had proved herself particularly skillful at mending roofs. The women would never forget the sight of Sister Catharinia hitching up her habit and climbing up onto a leaking roof.

In an attempt to bolster their spirits, Margaret and Norah rallied the remaining members of the vocal orchestra to perform music in the hospital barrack in December 1944. But soon after, more singers died, and the vocal orchestra fell forever silent. As the death totals continued to rise, Betty commented in her diary on January 23, 1945, "...there are no old people left in camp now."[73] That the deaths were completely avoidable filled the women with rage at their captors who stubbornly withheld food and medicine. Betty remarked that anger over their senseless brutality hit her sometimes when she saw their flag waving above the camp. "How we hate that infernal red blob!"[74] By March 20, 1945, the years of deprivation and the further declining conditions left Betty at her lowest so far. She wrote, "Find it very hard to write these days as there is nothing pleasant to write about. Camp life is just an existence now. No more concerts or charades or sing-songs; when the day's work is done people go off to their beds and lie there until morning."[75]

On Easter Sunday, April 1, 1945, their beloved Dorothy "Mac" MacLeod, whose music had brought such joy to them all, perished. Like so many others, she had endured with remarkable fortitude for three years, but her body could no longer withstand the abuse. Margaret Dryburgh presided over her funeral, commenting on the gift of her beautiful voice, and then reciting the words of Psalm 121 as encouragement to the living.

> I will lift up mine eyes unto the hills from whence cometh my help. My help cometh from the LORD, which made heaven and earth. He will not suffer thy foot to be moved: he that keepeth thee will not slumber. Behold, he that keepeth Israel shall neither slumber nor sleep. The LORD is thy keeper: the LORD is thy shade upon thy right hand. The sun shall not smite thee by day, nor the moon by night. The LORD shall preserve thee from all evil: he shall preserve thy soul. The LORD shall preserve thy going out and thy coming in from this time forth, and even for evermore.[76]

That same month, the Japanese once again transferred the prisoners. Another arduous journey, by sea, by train, and then by truck, would return them to Sumatra. As usual, they did not know if this seemingly nonsensical relocation had been founded in a proper rationale coordinated from Tokyo. All they knew for certain was that each move proved harder, requiring them to leave behind precious belongings and their dead. They would be forced to walk for miles and then be transported in uncomfortable boats or trucks, even though they hardly had the strength to carry their meager possessions—all to end up in likely worse conditions. Bitterly, they abandoned all of the cassava that they had labored over, without even tasting one bite.

This time, the guards crammed the women and children into airless ships, where the heat bore down like a furnace. Most suffered from dysentery, and the nurses felt a sense of duty to care for the ill as best as they could, despite being unwell themselves. Betty Jeffrey often tended the sick throughout her long internment beside her good friend and fellow Australian nursing sister Iole Harper. She wrote in her diary describing Iole's heroic efforts on this last relocation.

> As long as I live, I will never forget Iole emptying and dragging bedpans in the sea. The Dutch nuns managed to get some bedpans with handles on board. We hadn't seen them before. Iole would tie a piece of rope through the handle, then she would get out on the six-inch ledge that ran around the *outside* of the ship. Pat and I would hold her hand and arm while she tossed the bedpan in the sea, and the drag every time nearly pulled her into the water. I can't remember how often the girl did that, but she must have done it fifty times. If ever anyone deserved a Victoria Cross she did.[77]

Some died during the voyage and were buried at sea. Those who managed to make it to land climbed into filthy train cars, the sick lying on stretchers. Everyone rode in the pitch dark with no air. Having lost six more on the train, they finally arrived in the small town of Loebok Linggau[78] in southern Sumatra. After the three-day journey, most were nearly dead from hunger, thirst, and exposure. The Japanese loaded them into the back of trucks, which drove at break-neck speed to an abandoned Dutch rubber plantation named Belalau, the largest rubber plantation on Sumatra. The Dutch had destroyed its manufacturing equipment as part of the scorched earth policy, and now, it would house their new prison.

With great relief, one of the first things the women noticed was a fresh creek running right through the property. The plantation also provided a pleasant place to walk around, especially among the blooming allamanda bushes. Betty recorded that, for the whole first day she was there, she found herself singing the great Anglican hymn "All Things Bright and Beautiful."[79] But despite its homage to nature's magnificence, Belalau harbored an eerie sense of isolation, as it sat in the middle of a dense jungle about 250 miles from the familiar city of Palembang. Being sequestered so far into the jungle interior made the women worry whether any eventual Allied liberators would be able to find them.

Soon after arriving at the rubber plantation, on April 21, 1945, the remarkable Margaret Dryburgh died. She had fallen desperately ill during the transportation to this camp and never recovered. A woman of letters, she had been keeping a secret diary that included poems and sketches, in addition to an account of camp life. Her last entry described the "ghastly journey" in which "I had to be transferred to the stretcher."[80] Norah sat at Margaret's side in the camp hospital near the end. She later recounted those final moments in a private publication of Margaret's diary.

> When I went to see her she was semi-conscious. She recognized me and tried to speak. After a struggle, I found that she was trying to say her favorite psalm, the 23rd. I stumbled through it, to the best of my ability. Then there was silence. Suddenly, in a strong voice, and with a smile, she said, 'That's what I wanted.' She passed away shortly afterwards. I helped to bury her and before the coffin was closed put a bunch of flowers in her hands. She looked so peaceful and content, for she had done her job and done it well. Her grave was marked by a simple wooden cross. We planted some flowers and a big alamanda at her head, as she always loved flowers so much.[81]

Now, with so many weak and dying, funerals were rarely attended by anyone other than the people who carried the coffin. But this was not the case for Margaret's funeral. All of the remaining vocal orchestra members stood by her grave, along with many others whose lives she had touched in countless ways. She had entreated them to "look up" for strength and encouragement, and she had brought them together in community. Speaking of Margaret, Betty wrote, "What a wonderful person she was, and how hard she worked to give the people in the camp such pleasure!…Miss Dryburgh's death has caused much sadness throughout the whole camp."[82]

Margaret's internment had never dimmed her creative spirit, but had instead become her collective magnum opus. In addition to composing the arrangements for the vocal orchestra, Margaret had written both the words and music for songs that the glee club sang, as well as anthems to be performed on Sundays by the church choir. Never far from pencil and paper, she even completed two books of poetry while imprisoned. Now, the entire ethos of the camp suffered from the loss of such an irreplaceable figure. Her grave would soon be overtaken by the greedy jungle, but her impact on these women would never be erased.

Just a few days after Margaret's funeral, Mother Laurentia walked toward Helen Colijn with the dreaded news that her beloved father had passed on March 11. His daughters learned later, from a man who had been interned with him, that Anton Colijn had died peacefully, confident that he was going to live and be reunited with his family. His unflinching optimism led him to turn aside his friend's suggestion to write a final note to his family. Indeed, mental and emotional strength, coupled with faith, did make a difference in how people endured and even died in such horrific situations. This man commented after the war, "Thanks to his deep faith and enormous optimism, he did not suffer as much as many others."[83]

In early May 1945, the Japanese delivered a large collection of mail to the internees, dating from 1942 and 1943. Some people got as many as 20 letters that had remained undelivered for two or three years. But the "honeymoon" of the new camp with its lush greenery and fresh water had ended as food supplies dwindled to only rice and rotten sweet potatoes. The sweet potatoes actually arrived in good condition, but the guards cruelly let them lay in water and sun for three or four days before allowing the prisoners to have them. By then, they were barely edible, although starving people had no choice but to eat them. Then one day, the Japanese surprised the prisoners with a delivery of five pounds of meat, but since it had to be shared among the entire camp population, it served little use. By this time, the women had become desperate enough to eat anything they could get their hands on, including a half-starved goat and a small monkey that they turned into monkey stew for 600 people. Life at this point, what one described as a zombie-like existence, revolved solely around scrounging for food and medicine. Since they were equally plagued by starvation and disease, it was hard for them to choose whether to barter food for medicine or vice versa.

On May 15, 1945, to the astonishment and wry amusement of the women, the camp command announced that a Japanese Military Band would be coming to entertain them the following day. Betty surmised that such a ridiculous idea must be just another form of torture, right up there with starving the prisoners and withholding Red Cross parcels. She supposed that it must be "…the last item on their list of 'How to Treat Prisoners.'"[84] When the band arrived, not a single prisoner climbed the hill to hear them, which infuriated the Japanese, who sent a stick-wielding guard to force them hurriedly to the concert spot. But to their great surprise, the music sounded really wonderful, especially the German overtures and waltzes. They sat down under the shady rubber trees and enjoyed the instruments that they had not heard for years. According to Betty, "Most of us wanted to howl when the music started; I know I had a terrible struggle for the first 10 minutes. For two hours we all forgot we were prisoners."[85]

The summer months brought no change to their daily trio—disease, deprivation, and death. Then on August 25, 1945, the camp commander Captain Siki summoned the women and children to the guardhouse. He stood on a table so he could be heard and, speaking in Malay, announced "*Perang habis*" ("The war is over"). He did not provide any details, such as that it had ended nine days earlier or even who had won. It was as impossible as ever to discern what the Japanese were thinking, especially Captain Siki, who would eventually receive 15 years in prison for his role in the mistreatment of POWs.

Some of the expressions of joy from the now "former captives" came quite naturally and spontaneously in the form of music, as the British and Australians sang "God Save the King" and the Dutch, "The Wilhelmus." No longer needing to keep her diary a secret, Betty wrote, "The war is over. Who will be first here to take us home? *We are free women!!!*"[86] Many grabbed whatever food they had been hoarding and ate it. After a three-year wait, it only took three days for the Japanese to hand over the stockpiles of food, medicine, and other items that they had withheld. The treasure trove included sugar, meat, butter, bananas, and pineapples, along with various medicines that had been so desperately needed. But the severely malnourished people had to be careful about consuming large amounts of food. One woman did die from too much sugar.

The freed male and female internees quickly learned that the vast rubber plantation had been housing both of their camps since the move from Bangka Island, a simultaneously frustrating and marvelous reality. It seemed like a dream as the women looked up to see the men and boys walking into their camp, and then enfolding them in emotional embraces. Some of the reunions proved awkward, especially for the children who did not recognize these bearded, disheveled men as their fathers. For Norah, who lay in bed unwell, the sight of her husband John coming toward her seemed nothing short of miraculous. Although as bone thin as she was, he had survived an ordeal where the death rate for the men hovered around 55 percent. Helen was also quite ill in the hospital barrack. At six feet tall, she weighed less than 90 pounds. The man who had been her father's friend visited her, carrying a much worn Bible filled with her father's penciled annotations. Somehow her father had managed to keep it with him the whole time and had used it to give sermons at camp church services on Sundays.

The days following the announcement conjured a strange, "through the looking-glass" sensation. The flag of Japan still flew over the camp because no Allies had made it there yet for the Japanese to surrender to. The British had been assigned to accept the surrender of the 80,000 Japanese soldiers on Sumatra, but were still in India. Despite how it might have felt to the former prisoners, the Allies had not forgotten or abandoned them. Their situation and eventual liberation had actually been given considerable attention during the final stages of military planning.

As the United States made preparations to end the war via two atomic bombs, the fate of the large numbers of Allied POWs weighed on their minds. The brutal behavior of the Japanese army toward civilian and military prisoners was well documented, as was their refusal to accept the Geneva Convention's guidelines. The Allies feared that the time it would take to secure the vast Japanese-occupied territories, following the surrender in Tokyo, would allow the camp commanders to take out their frustrations on the captives. In addition to the threat posed by the Japanese, the Allies also voiced concern over the newly emboldened nationalist groups. As the Japanese spread their creed of returning Asian lands to Asians, that rally cry had radicalized certain nationalistic sects among the various islands, who were prepared to take matters into their own hands if the Allies prevailed, lest the status quo of European rule be reestablished in their homelands. The Allies' unease was indeed founded. Immediately after Japan's capitulation, a group of Indonesian nationals slaughtered 26 Swiss men, women, and children, living in a community outside of the city of Medan in northern Sumatra.

To further compound the precarious POW situation, the Allies could not even be certain where the prison camps were located, especially on Sumatra. So, they devised a two-stage reconnaissance and rescue mission in July 1945. Major Gideon Jacobs, a 23-year-old South African who served in the Royal Marines, would lead this clandestine assignment. Sent from the South East Asia Command headquarters in Ceylon (present day Sri Lanka), Jacobs parachuted into Sumatra along with four other men—a Dutchman, a Chinese who had lived in Java, and two Australian wireless operators. Their orders were to wait for the signal, a password over the wireless that would confirm Japan's surrender. They would then immediately liaison with the Japanese military to ascertain the locations of the camps and to secure the prisoners before any reprisals could take place.

After receiving the awaited signal, Jacobs and his team made their presence known to the Japanese High Command in Medan. Getting the information they needed proved difficult, especially with 80,000 Japanese soldiers on Sumatra and the nearest Allied troops in Burma. Major Jacobs' skills of diplomacy prevailed, however, and a Japanese escort flew him around the island in a Japanese military aircraft to visit and map the camps. For the POWs he encountered, Jacobs regrettably had to relay the message that, for now, they would have to remain in the camps under Japanese supervision until the Allied forces could physically reach them.

But despite the apparent cooperation from the Japanese, Major Jacobs was not informed about the men and women imprisoned on the rubber plantation. He stumbled upon this information through a clever stroke of detective work that began when he learned about the massacre of the nurses and servicemen on Bangka Island in 1942. Although Vivien Bullwinkel had thought herself the only survivor, two of the men had lived also. One of them, Ernest Lloyd of the Royal Navy, informed Major Jacobs about the incident, which led Jacobs to the conclusion that more women must have washed ashore on Bangka Island. So working from that assumption, he sat out to learn of their fate. The first Allied soldiers walked into the women's camp on the afternoon of September 7, 1945. Major Jacobs discovered the worst conditions he had yet witnessed, including the appalling sight of emaciated women and children. He immediately radioed for air support in the form of food and medical supply drops. A Dutch Navy plane dropped large food containers into the area, which included bread that had been baked that morning on the Cocos Islands and then flown five hours to the rubber plantation.

In addition to food and supplies, the Allied soldiers brought all of the news of the war, including of the atomic bombs whose catastrophic destruction had forced the capitulation of Japan. Their reports also included rumors that the Japanese had intended to kill the prisoners in many of their camps and that the scheduled date for the Belalau camp had been August 31, the birthday of Queen Wilhelmina. After the nuclear strikes on August 6 and 9, the plans for camp exterminations were supposedly abandoned. It is unknown whether this slaughter of the women and children would have been carried out; but at the rate that the captives were dying from starvation and disease, if the war had continued much longer, very few would have been left. Now, for those who had survived, all they wanted was to go home. But the evacuations of the prisoners from the numerous camps proved a painfully slow process, with many having to languish in squalid conditions for months. A total of approximately 130,000 Allied civilians had been interned by the Japanese in the Far East, with camp locations scattered throughout Hong Kong, Java, Singapore, Sumatra, and the Philippines. About 41,000 of them were women.

One of the first groups to depart from Belalau were the Australian nurses. When they had boarded the *Vyner Brooke* on February 12, 1942, there had been 65 of them. Twelve had died in the bombing of the ship or soon after in the water. Of the 53 who made it to shore, only 24 now boarded the Australian Air Force flight to Singapore, where they would be transported to the new Australian hospital there. These nurses received an enthusiastic welcome and the much needed care of food, hot showers, and clothes. They recuperated for a couple of weeks before sailing for Australia. Betty Jeffrey arrived in Melbourne on October 24, 1945, finally home at age 37. She enjoyed one day there, before being sent to the hospital, where doctors diagnosed her with tuberculosis. She had to spend most of the next two years in the hospital, a particularly cruel fate for someone who had just survived three and a half years in a POW camp. In time, Betty recovered and partnered with Vivian Bullwinkel to advocate for the building of a memorial museum in Melbourne for their heroic contingent of nurses. They prevailed, and the Melbourne Nurses Memorial Centre opened in 1949, with Betty serving as its first director. In 1987, she was awarded the Order of Australia for her service. Lieutenant Agnes Betty Jeffrey died on September 13, 2000, at 92 years of age. Lieutenant Colonel Vivian Bullwinkel received numerous awards, including the Florence Nightingale Medal. She never forgot her fallen sisters and returned to Bangka Island in 1992 to dedicate a memorial to them. She died at age 84 on July 3, 2000.

The same plane that had evacuated the Australian nurses returned for a second run to transport more hospital patients, followed by additional flights to airlift the remaining Dutch and British citizens to Singapore. For those leaving Sumatra via air, a special sight awaited them below, in the water where many of them almost drowned in 1942. No longer controlled by enemy vessels, the ocean was now teeming with Allied ships, a visible assurance of their safety and proof that the war had indeed come to an end.

As Helen Colijn and her two sisters boarded one of the evacuation flights, they felt so grateful that all three of them had survived, while still grieving the loss of their father. A few weeks after their release, they received the long-awaited news about their mother, whom they had last seen in 1941. Zus Colijn was alive, having endured a series of internment camps as her daughters had. After the war, Helen moved to California, as did her mother and sisters, and became a language teacher. While the details remained fresh in her mind, she wrote down her memories of the evacuation attempt, the shipwreck, and then her years of internment, which would later form the basis of a documentary and book, both titled *Song of Survival*. She published two additional books about Holland and worked as an editor for *Sunset* magazine. Helen died on April 26, 2006, at age 85.

As Norah Chambers walked to board the final evacuation vehicle, she heard something behind her that sounded like the rhythmic ostinato from Ravel's *Bolero*, a complicated piece that she had so meticulously taught her vocal orchestra. She turned and saw those precious Dutch nuns, complete with Mother Laurentia and Sister Catharinia, serenading her departure, a moving tribute to the life-affirming work she had accomplished through music. At the sight of these nuns singing, Norah later recalled, "I unashamedly wept."[87]

But not all of the former prisoners would be departing by air and sea. Some who had lived in Sumatra before the war boarded trains bound for Palembang. Among this group were the Dutch Carolus Borromeus Sisters, who would remain behind to resume their ministry, which now included the camp orphans under their care. They worked diligently to locate relatives who could receive the children. Although the camp at Belalau had been completely emptied by the end of October, it took a full year before the last child waved goodbye to the nuns. In 1948, Sumatra, along with the rest of the former Dutch East Indies, became an independent republic known as Indonesia.

Once the women left the camp, the joy of their freedom soon collided with the difficulty of assimilating into a world that now seemed foreign to them. After having had their physical needs met, the women found little available to assist them in the re-acclimation process. They would have to rely on time. For those who had a calling, like the nuns, or a profession, like the nurses, it proved an easier transition because there was a particular niche for them to fit back into, as well as work to be done that had defined their identity before the war and now helped redefine it after those long years. Nevertheless, for better or worse, these women would never be the same people that they were before 1942.

After the war, some of the women reflected specifically about how their time of internment had challenged and changed them in unexpected ways. Their diaries, memoirs, and testimonies provided a necessary means by which they could be seen for their own lives and experiences, and not through the lens of the men in their lives. One woman remarked, "Looking back I still feel the warmth of those women I had the privilege to live with for nearly four years. In that sense I left the camps with regret. We hated saying goodbye to each other. It was a terrible break. We had all been together in the struggle to survive and we knew each other so well."[88] Another woman related, "Funnily enough, camp life was an extremely rich period. Yesterday had happened, tomorrow might never come, so you lived for the day and the people who were there. There were no other encumbrances whatsoever."[89] "You could be eccentric if you wanted to be and nobody commented. A lot of us did what I suppose would now be called off-beat things," recounted another survivor. "You were free to indulge in whatever it was that you wanted to pursue that in some way expressed yourself. Not before or since have I lived a life as rich. You could be exactly who you were—find yourself, I would say. Once we came out we were less free."[90]

The complex adjustment process manifested not only on an individual level with each returning POW, but in a collective, national sense as well. As they began to repatriate, the women soon discovered that some governments and societies adapted more easily and more charitably than others. Many of the British women had accepted the offer of free passage to England, only to be disheartened when their homecoming did not warrant a national celebration, as it had with the Australian survivors. For some unknown reason, government officials had actually ordered the downplaying of their arrival, requesting no press coverage and that no friends or relatives be there to greet them. Instead, the women were just quietly routed by train to their respective towns, slipping almost unnoticed into the bustling post-war country, and with little or no financial assistance. The ravaged British economy needed time to recover from the wartime austerity, and rationing continued to pose a major problem. A few extra clothing coupons were distributed to the survivors, but then one woman was berated by a shop keeper over the unfairness of her receiving those extra rations. Reclaiming the societal norms and niceties in which they had been raised, these women mounted little fuss over their unjust treatment. Instead, they exhibited great determination to move forward with their lives and not be forever imprisoned by what had happened to them.

After her unceremonious arrival, Norah Chambers experienced a tearful but awkward reunion with her daughter Sally, who had spent the almost four years safely in England thanks to the early evacuation with her aunt. In time, their mother-daughter bond reconnected. Not surprisingly, it was music that first bridged the divide. Norah had sung often to the young child, and Sally had not forgotten those songs. In 1952, the Chambers family settled in Jersey, the largest of the Channel Islands between England and France, along with Norah's sister Ena and her husband. Norah became the choir director at St. Mark's Church in the town of St. Helier, where she continued to live until her death on June 18, 1989, at age 84.

At times, the joy of their liberation and return home was tempered by thoughts of family and friends left behind in shallow graves outside of the various island prison camps. There seemed no justice and no closure for those fallen. For the few who had been married to British military officers, the government exhumed their bodies immediately after the war and gave them a proper burial in a military cemetery on Java. The remains of the other women and children, they left abandoned for the jungle to overtake. Because of the difficulties of retrieving bodies in such remote and inhospitable locations, some countries constructed perpetual memorials to honor the dead and commemorate the struggle and sacrifice of their interned citizens. The British government's failure to formally acknowledge the suffering and loss of its female civilians remains a source of frustration among many families of the survivors and the dead. Still today, no national memorial stands dedicated to these British citizens. The only official record of their passing can be viewed in Westminster Abbey, where seven volumes called the *Roll of Honour of Civilian War Dead, 1935–1945*, lists their names under a section labeled "Deaths at Sea and Abroad." But regardless, they have not been forgotten by those whose lives connected with them during that tragic time. In St. Mark's Church, there stands a simple wooden cross made from a 100-year-old piece of oak by the husband of Audrey Owen, a dear friend of Norah's during the captivity and one of the surviving members of the vocal orchestra. It bears the poignant inscription, "In the memory of those women who died in prison camps in Sumatra whose graves will never be found."[91]

For the women healing from the camps and the war, the memories of the vocal orchestra, whose music had helped them bear the burdens of those trying days, continued to bring solace. Norah Chambers reminisced that while singing, "In spite of all the smells and muck and goodness knows what, we literally forgot where we were."[92] Similarly, Betty

Jeffrey shared, "When I sang that vocal orchestra music, I forgot I was in the camp. I felt free."[93] Sister Catharinia expressed her thoughts in a more philosophical manner. "It was something that lived between us, and it made us more near together, that was the wonder of the music."[94] Helen Colijn acknowledged the difficulty of forgiving and letting go of bitterness. Her mother had shared after the war that the last words Helen's father had spoken to her before the Japanese led him away were, "Whatever happens to you don't feel bitter about it, because bitterness will destroy you."[95] In respect to the pursuit of grace and mercy, Helen realized that,

> Survivors of the South Sumatra camp find the task is made easier by the knowledge that out of our ugly place came beautiful music that now brings joy and solace to other singers and listeners around the world.... In the camp we saw the vocal orchestra music as yet another way of making something out of nothing, of making do with what we had, not as the amazing feat that people saw it for in later years, nor as material that would become the subject of articles and books.[96]

In May 1983, the Peninsula Women's Chorus, under the direction of Patricia Hennings, performed the arrangements sung by the vocal orchestra in a concert called "Song of Survival," at St. Bede's Church in Menlo Park, California. Having flown in from all over the world, nine former vocal orchestra members attended, including Sister Catharinia and Norah Chambers. Helen Colijn gave the introduction to the concert. During the performance, Helen took special notice of Norah. "At times, her face crumpled and tears came to her eyes. Later she told me she was seeing her battered singers in the camp, about half of whom died before release."[97] The final song on the program was "The Captives' Hymn." When the choir began to sing it, the survivors rose to their feet in a synchronous, automatic gesture that showed their reverence for the hymn's powerful message and for the memory of its beloved writer. The other audience members hesitated at first and then joined in solidarity with them. This concert would be only one of many tributes to the vocal orchestra in the coming years, including the 1986 documentary *Song of Survival*. Dutch composer Dirk Jan Warnaar composed an oratorio titled *Margaret,* based on Margaret Dryburgh's poems and writings from the prison camp. Dedicated to Norah Chambers, the oratorio premiered in Holland on May 4, 1990. Later, Australian playwright Mary Morris wrote the play *Voices* about these women's experiences, which was first performed in May 1997. That same year, Twentieth Century Fox released the feature film *Paradise Road*, with Glenn Close starring in the role of Norah Chambers and Pauline Collins playing Margaret Dryburgh.

Through the numerous published memoirs, musical tributes, and other media, the story of these remarkable women and their unique expression of music's redemptive power has forged an indelible legacy. But the fundamental truth of their experience was probably best captured in the simple poem "Philosophy," written in the camp by Margery Jennings, one of the imprisoned nurses, who tragically never made it home.

> *I go my way singing*
> *What ere fate be bringing*
> *I go my way singing.*
> *The world's my friend*
> *O life's not for sorrow.*
> *No trouble I'll borrow,*
> *A fig for the morrow.*
> *I'll sing to the end.*[98]

Epilogue: Out of the Ashes—The Israel Philharmonic and Violins of Hope

Wherever there were violins, there was hope.
—Amnon Weinstein, Israeli luthier, quoted
in James A. Grymes, *Violins of Hope*, 13

The vital connection between music and the Jewish people can be traced all the way back to ancient times. In the books of the law revealed to Moses, known as the Torah, the creation story unfolds, and with it, music. The Book of Genesis lists the descendants of Adam and Eve, and through this genealogy appears the only mention in the historical record of a man named Jubal, whom the writer importantly identifies as "the father of all who play string instruments and pipes."[1] Throughout Holy Scripture and the epic story of the Jewish people, music has remained interwoven with their lives and worship, while also adapting to changing cultural landscapes. String instruments have always constituted a favored medium for expression, and the lyre in particular held a cherished position for millennia. But then with the emergence of the violin during the Renaissance period, the Jews embraced a more modern and versatile instrument. The violin's appeal lay in its capacity to imitate the human voice and to convey a range of emotions that mirrored the very narrative of their existence, from singing for joy or weeping in lament. The violin also proved convenient because of its portability. It could easily be tucked under an arm or shoved into a handcart as the Jews moved or fled from place to place.

To maintain music's prominence in their communities, Jewish parents insisted that their children learn to sing and play instruments, particularly the violin. While the degree of aptitude varied among those who attempted to learn the violin, most could acquire a sufficient enough level of proficiency to contribute to the musical happenings of their village. But then on the rare occasion, the violin would fall into the hands of someone endowed with an extraordinary gift, such as the young Polish boy named Bronisław Huberman. Born on December 19, 1882, in Częstochowa, Poland, Huberman received a violin at an early age and soon demonstrated such prodigious talent that, as a 6 year old, he began studying with a teacher at the Warsaw Conservatory. Sensing that their child was destined for musical greatness, Huberman's parents later decided that they must get him to Germany. They saved money for a year and sold many of their belongings to scrape together the money needed to take their son to Berlin where he could study with a master teacher. Joseph Joachim, the renowned Hungarian violinist and pedagogue, taught at and served as the director for the Hochschule für Musik in Berlin. A protégé of Felix Mendelssohn, Joachim had also developed friendships with Robert Schumann and Johannes Brahms, both of whom had written works for him. So, when the great Joachim accepted the 10-year-old Huberman as a student, the family's sacrifice certainly seemed worthwhile.

Bronisław Huberman adored his new teacher and made considerable progress under his guidance. But Huberman's ambitious father, not unlike Mozart's father a century earlier, grew impatient to showcase his son's talent by touring him around the world. So, he yanked the 12 year old from his studies with Joachim and denied him any further education. Although Huberman hated to leave his beloved teacher, as a young boy, he had no choice but adopt the traveling superstar persona that his father desired. Huberman's father never failed to remind him of how his family's sacrifice had enabled him to study in Berlin, and instead of nurturing his sensitive son, he exerted extreme pressure on him to establish a financially sound future for his impoverished family. As a result, Huberman endured an abnormal and difficult childhood, the ramifications of which would plague him for the rest of his life.

On January 29, 1896, at age 13, Huberman played his first truly grand performance, a concert that would set the course of his career. The Vienna Philharmonic had invited Huberman, the acclaimed wunderkind, to perform the Brahms *Violin Concerto* with them at Vienna's Musikverein Hall. In addition to its prestigious nature, this opportunity also came with tremendous difficulty because of the repertoire. Brahms had written this concerto for his dear friend Joseph Joachim, who premiered it in 1879 with Brahms conducting on the podium in Leipzig. Unfortunately, reviews of the new composition proved tepid. Clara Schumann, for whom Brahms and Joachim had previewed the work, seemed one of the few at the time to realize its brilliance and to appreciate the unprecedented virtuosity required. But even though this technically demanding concerto had earned a reputation as "unplayable," the young Huberman eagerly tackled this piece so connected to his former teacher. As with Joachim, Huberman would forever be associated with the Brahms *Violin Concerto* and would perform and record it frequently for the next 50 years, famously declaring, "It is a concerto for violin *against* the orchestra—and the violin wins."[2]

Anticipation for the 1896 performance by the teenage Hu-

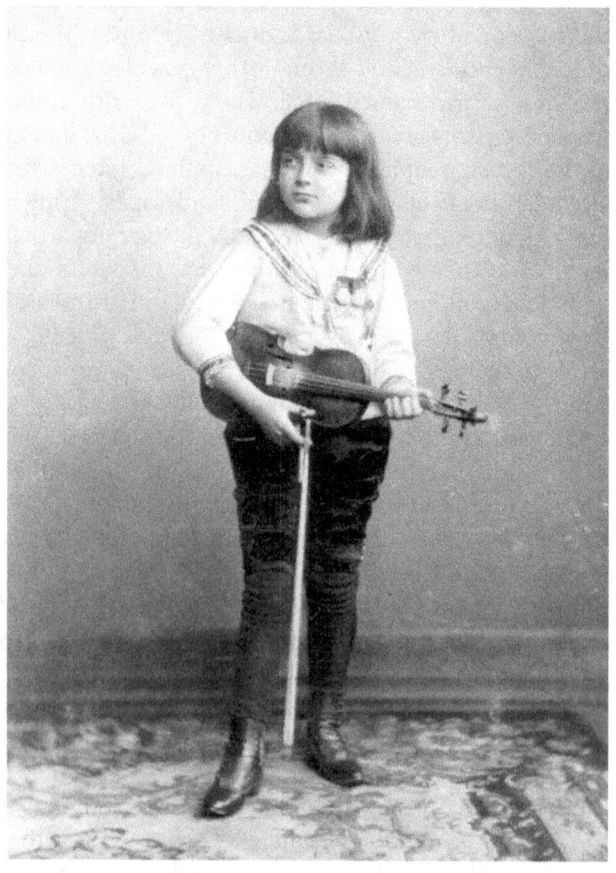

Early publicity photograph of Bronisław Huberman, c. 1889 (unknown photographer / courtesy of the Murray S. Katz Photo Archives of the IPO).

berman buzzed throughout Vienna, and curiosity over this rising superstar caused members of Vienna's elite musical scene to flock to the event, including Gustav Mahler, Anton Bruckner, and Johann Strauss. But that evening, the most daunting aspect for Huberman remained that Brahms himself sat in the audience. He had only agreed to attend grudgingly. The perpetually cynical Brahms had little tolerance for child prodigies and had set low expectations for what this young violinist might do with his concerto. Then Huberman played. It only took a few minutes before the composer began to change his mind, as he could not deny that a truly great artist lay inside this adolescent boy. After the concert, Brahms went backstage to meet Huberman. He congratulated him in an uncharacteristically profuse way and then, as he turned to go, slipped a note card into the youth's hand. Later, when Huberman examined it, he saw that Brahms had sketched out the opening bars of the concerto on the card, in addition to a complimentary note about his performance. Huberman kept that cherished memento for the rest of his life. In 2005, his granddaughter Joan auctioned it through Sotheby's in London, where it sold for over $17,000.

Huberman's triumph with the Brahms concerto led to performance opportunities throughout Europe and Russia, as well as the United States, where he debuted at Carnegie Hall in 1896. His father remained his constant companion as they traveled and also served as a fierce manager of his son's career and personal life. Practicing, performing, traveling, and making money were the sole activities during Huberman's formative years. In time, this intense focus and hard work would establish Huberman as one of the greatest violinists of the 20th century. He would be the first of that century's many legendary Jewish violinists, whose names would include Jascha Heifetz, Isaac Stern, and Itzhak Perlman.

During the year that Huberman turned 20, his father died unexpectedly, which rudely catapulted him out of the insular life that he had led. He soon discovered that the enormous amounts of money that he had been earning from years of relentless concert touring had been deposited in the bank under his father's name. As a result, he had no claim to his own hard-earned income, except what fell to him in the equal dividing up of the estate with his mother and siblings. Nevertheless, Huberman continued to devote himself religiously to his career, which necessitated his continuing to tour. Free from his father's constant pressure and nagging criticisms, Huberman found some relief in the control that he could now exact over his own schedule and performance choices. He determined, however, that he still could not spare time for a personal life or for participation in any recreational activities. The grueling pace that he had maintained for so many years certainly began to take a toll, and the young Huberman's appearance and demeanor worried his friends. The once energetic violinist now appeared pale and lifeless, leaving audiences to speculate about the exhausted figure who struggled to even walk out onto the stage.

Then in 1909, while giving a concert in Vienna, Huberman met a German actress of some renown named Elsa Galafrés. Although neither was particularly impressed with the other at this first introduction, they encountered each other again a few weeks later as they were both taking rest from their hectic performance schedules at a sanatorium in Dresden. They became lovers, and Huberman invited her to move into his villa in Vienna. Upon learning of these new living arrangements, Galafrés' parents protested because of Huberman's Jewishness. But their daughter assured them that neither she nor Huberman possessed any interest in marriage. Then the following year, Elsa discovered that she was pregnant and so the two grudgingly decided to marry since Huberman feared that a scandal could derail his career. They named their son Johannes, after the composer who had so encouraged the young Huberman. But marriage and fatherhood did not satisfy. Huberman's restless spirit could only be satiated through the concert spotlight, and his music would never take a backseat to anything or anyone. After a few years, a neglected Elsa left him for the Hungarian composer Ernő Dohnányi, whom she had a son with and then eventually married once a reluctant Huberman granted her a divorce. With Huberman showing little interest in his son, Dohnányi adopted Johannes.

Even with the start of World War I, Huberman continued to concertize and push himself to exhaustion. In 1916, he checked into a Viennese clinic to rest and restore his health. It was there that he met and fell in love with a nurse named Ida Ibbeken. She returned his feelings and became greatly devoted to him even though she realized from the beginning that his music would always take precedence. She somehow made peace with that reality, and although the two never married, Ida Ibbeken remained his lifelong companion, as well as his personal assistant.

Witnessing the horrors of the Great War profoundly impacted Huberman. He decided that he must acquire a better education, as his had been truncated at such an early age. Recent events had led him to believe that there was much that he needed to know about politics and the nature of the human condition. So in 1920, he put his music career on hold to enroll for two years at the Sorbonne in Paris. After completing his studies, he returned to the concert stage, but with an altered perspective especially attuned toward social issues. Huberman's emerging political conscience drew him to join with other intellectuals, such as Albert Einstein and Sigmund Freud, in advocating for a unified Europe that would prevent another war of global scale, a proposition known as the Pan-Europa movement. Concerning his own career, Huberman responded with the conviction that music should not be reserved for only the elite and privileged, but should be available to all. To that end, he began to perform free concerts for the poor. In a short period of time, Bronisław Huberman had acquired a greatly transformed worldview, and this new enlightenment would prepare him to undertake what would be the most significant accomplishment of his life.

While ultimately Huberman's dream of lasting peace in Europe through the Pan-Europa movement did not materialize, he found another path toward building a more hopeful world, which began through his bold stance against Fascism and the rise of Nazi Germany. Huberman received an invitation from conductor Wilhelm Furtwängler to perform as a soloist with the Berlin Philharmonic for its opening concert of the 1934 season. Even though Jews had been banned from performing in Germany by this time, Furtwängler held sway with the Nazi powerbrokers because of his internationally renowned reputation and their desire to keep him on the podium of Germany's finest orchestra. This enabled Furtwängler to successfully walk a tightrope with the Nazis during the 1930s and early 40s, but after the war, his acquiescence to the Nazi regime would stigmatize him for the rest of his career. Related to his orchestra's concerts for 1934, Furtwängler received special permission from Propaganda Minister Joseph Goebbels for the overture to Huberman by citing that the optics of featuring this world-class Jewish performer would look good internationally.

While Furtwängler's invitation was certainly lucrative, Huberman not only declined, but did so in a strongly worded letter, dated July 10, 1933, that he later released to *The New York Times* on September 14. In his response, Huberman sought to explain his position, both in terms of honored traditions and the unity of humankind. He pleaded for a reversal of Nazi policies based on shared humanity and culture.

> In reality it is not a question of violin concertos nor even merely of the Jews; the issue is the retention of those things that our fathers achieved by blood and sacrifice, of the elementary preconditions of our

European culture, the freedom of personality and its unconditional self-responsibility unhampered by fetters of caste or race.[3]

Huberman ended the letter by declaring his sorrow at being estranged from the musicians of Germany and from Furtwängler, whom he considered a friend, while reiterating that he could not in good conscience set foot inside Nazi Germany.

> I cannot close this letter without expressing to you my deep regret at the conditions that have resulted in my being separated for the moment from Germany. I am especially grieved and pained in my relationship of a friend of my German friends and as an interpreter of German music who very much misses the echo awakened in his German hearers. And nothing could make me happier than to observe a change also outside the realm of concert life which would liberate me from the compulsing of conscience, striking at my very heartstrings, to renounce Germany.[4]

As time went on, Huberman grew even more incensed and outspoken about the atrocities being committed against his people and also by what he viewed as the culpability of the educated German population. He denounced them for standing by mutely and indicted them as complicit in all that occurred.

Back in 1929, Huberman had given a series of concerts in Palestine that left him with a special affection for Tel Aviv and the Jewish community there. By his third visit in 1934, Huberman sold out 12 performances, so his sentiments of devotion certainly seemed to be reciprocated. Huberman also enjoyed working with conductor Michael Taube. Taube led the fledgling orchestra in Tel Aviv, which included some accomplished players who had been early refugees from Hitler's Third Reich. Although Huberman had never personally embraced Zionism, he began to change his mind in light of his visits to Tel Aviv and the escalating brutalities of the Nazi regime. As a result, Huberman contacted Tel Aviv's mayor Meir Dizengoff, who also served as president of the organization that sponsored the small orchestra. In his letter to the mayor, Huberman proposed expanding the orchestra in Tel Aviv by arranging immigration for some of Germany's displaced musicians, particularly wind players, and then securing well-known guest conductors from around the world to elevate the orchestra's status. He included a comprehensive plan that not only outlined how to strengthen the present orchestra, but proposed the establishment of music schools, whose students could eventually supply the talent needed to sustain the ensemble in the future. But despite the wisdom of Huberman's plan, it failed to receive the full endorsement from Dizengoff, and so Huberman decided to pursue an even more ambitious plan that he would organize and oversee—the creation of a new professional orchestra, whose entire membership would be Jewish musicians. He would personally bring the out-of-work musicians that the Nazis had dismissed to Palestine, and they would provide the talent needed for a first-class orchestra—the Palestine Symphony Orchestra.

Huberman felt that there was no better way to counter the hateful and destructive anti–Semitism of the Nazi agenda than to showcase the artistry of the Jewish people through the formation of an orchestra that would undeniably demonstrate their triumphant resistance to the international community. In his written proposal, Huberman declared, "To beat the world campaign of anti–Semitism it is not enough to create material and idealistic prosperity in Palestine, we must create there new gospels and carry them throughout the world. And the symphony orchestra, as I visualize it, would be perhaps the first and easiest step toward that highest aim of Jewish humanity."[5]

Huberman again turned to *The New York Times* as an ally. On February 9, 1936, he published an article titled "Orchestra of Exiles," which detailed his plan to create a world-class orchestra in Palestine. The orchestra's first concert would take place later that year in Tel Aviv on October 24. Then, over the next eight months, the orchestra would perform 60 more concerts in Jerusalem and Haifa, as well as Tel Aviv and some of the more rural towns. Huberman stated that he would use his contacts in the music world to secure well-known soloists and conductors. Another central element of his plan would involve bringing this glorious music to all people, not just the wealthy and elite. During his visit to Tel Aviv in December 1935, Huberman had performed two identical recitals—one for the more privileged citizens who were accustomed to attending programs such as that, and a separate one for the city's workers. He was astounded when the enthusiasm and respect shown by the latter audience equaled that of the more educated listeners. This experience had a tremendous effect on Huberman, and he vowed that the Palestine Orchestra's performances in the larger cities would be divided just as his recital had been so that everyone gained access. To accomplish this, ticket prices would be adjusted for the workers' concerts, but with no lessening of the orchestra's musical standards.

Two weeks later, *The New York Times* shared another exciting piece of news regarding Huberman's orchestra. He had secured Arturo Toscanini, the most celebrated conductor in the world, to conduct the first performance. In addition to his musical reputation, Toscanini had received special notoriety for his adamant stand against Fascism by boycotting both his Italian homeland and Nazi Germany. As the director of the New York Philharmonic, he had continued to be a particularly outspoken opponent of the Nazi agenda against the Jews. So, Toscanini's agreeing to work with this new orchestra of Jewish refugees provided another way for the conductor to honor his conscience and help a tormented people.

In his planning, Huberman also suggested some parameters for the repertoire that the Palestine Orchestra would perform that inaugural season. He hoped that the various guest conductors would program music by Jewish composers, and to that end, Huberman was delighted when Toscanini chose to include the incidental music to *A Midsummer Night's Dream* by Mendelssohn, a Jewish composer once celebrated by the German people, but now banned by the Nazis. Huberman's guidelines also stipulated that he wanted the orchestra to avoid music by any composers specifically associated with the Nazi government. This included Richard Strauss, who had been engaged in an ambivalent dance with the Third Reich since 1933. On this particular composer, Huberman declared, "We cannot hold a place for a man who, on the one hand has a Jewish daughter-in-law and a Jewish librettist, but on the other hand for materialistic reasons served as president of the Nazis' Reich Chamber of Music until the moment they kicked him out."[6]

Huberman's next step involved capitalizing on his celebrity status and the enthusiastic media coverage he had received in *The New York Times* to raise funds to support his project. During the early months of 1936, Huberman traveled throughout the United States giving benefit concerts in major cities, such as Los Angeles and Seattle. He played 42 benefit concerts in 60 days. For any of his performance tours, Huberman always traveled with two violins tucked into a double case. One was a 1731 Guarneri del Gesù that he had acquired in 1931, and the other was a 1713 Stradivari that had been gifted to him as a child in 1895 by Franz Joseph, the Emperor of Austria.[7] On February 28, 1936, during the fundraising tour, Huberman's cherished Strad was stolen from his dressing room at Carnegie Hall, while he performed on stage with the other violin. It would never be returned to him.

Refusing to let the loss of his beloved instrument derail his mission, Huberman pressed on to make the Palestine Orchestra a reality. A tremendous step forward occurred when he garnered the support of an important international figure and now ally—the

Jewish physicist Albert Einstein. Einstein, who had made his home in the United States in 1933 as a result of Nazi tyranny, became the head of the American Friends of the Palestine Orchestra. Through his influence, Einstein greatly assisted Huberman in securing funds for the orchestra, including organizing a large fundraising dinner at the Waldorf Astoria on March 30, 1936. By April, Huberman had raised over $15,000 and collected another $7,000 in pledges.

Huberman and his friend Albert Einstein at the physicist's home in Princeton, New Jersey, in April 1936 (courtesy the Murray S. Katz Photo Archives of the IPO).

Meanwhile, Huberman also worked to recruit Europe's finest Jewish musicians. Because he intended to create a world-class orchestra that could play even the most complex repertoire, he needed a large roster of around 75 players, which would require holding auditions in the major cities of Europe. Since Huberman had vowed not to enter Nazi Germany, he sent a proxy, Hans Wilhelm Steinberg, who had conducted the Jewish Culture League orchestras in Berlin and Frankfurt. Steinberg possessed the necessary contacts to move around the Jewish communities in Germany, especially among the musicians who had joined the various culture leagues, in order to identify those who might want to immigrate to Palestine as part of this exciting new orchestra. In time, the directors of these culture leagues, including their founder Kurt Singer, became angry with Huberman and Steinberg for poaching all of their good musicians. But as history would show, those who left for Palestine lived, while many of those who remained behind in the culture leagues did not.

Huberman conducted his own scouting in Austria since it had not yet been absorbed into the Third Reich. He also wanted to secure some talented musicians from the Warsaw Philharmonic, so he enlisted one of its violinists, Jacob Surowicz, to make arrangements for him to hear any who expressed interest. But because Huberman knew so many of these Polish musicians, he decided to hold blind auditions so that his personal relationships would not affect his choices. Surowicz himself, along with six of his colleagues, joined the growing roster of the Palestine Orchestra. In addition to those from specially chosen cities, Jewish musicians from all over the world approached Huberman for a chance at a new life. But no matter where Huberman traveled for the auditions, it weighed heavily on him that he could not accept everyone, since he believed that he was sentencing those he rejected to possible death. In the end, his 75 orchestra members hailed from more than 13 countries, ranging from Argentina to the Netherlands, and most had been members of major orchestras, such as the Leipzig Gewandhaus Orchestra and the Budapest Philharmonic.

But Huberman soon discovered that recruiting the musicians satisfied only part of the requirement to fill the seats of his orchestra. Acquiring immigration visas for the musicians and their families developed into such a major obstacle that it almost derailed his entire plan. The area known as Palestine, although small at only 2,400 square miles, carried a long and complex history dating back to ancient times. The region had been ruled by a variety of masters, including the Egyptians and the Persians, before coming under the control of the Ottoman Empire in the 16th century. But with the end of World War I, Great Britain now governed Palestine. The British had declared their support for establishing Palestine as a home for the Jewish people in November 1917 with a document known as the Balfour Declaration. The Allies supported the concept, and eventually in 1922, the League of Nations made it official by issuing the Mandate of Palestine, which entrusted the British government with the responsibility of creating a Jewish national homeland in Palestine. During most of the 1920s, the British placed no limitations on the number of immigration visas for any of the Zionists who wanted to resettle in Palestine and established the Jewish Agency to serve as the bureaucratic center for the immigration process. Those who migrated there brought their love of the arts and literature with them, in addition to their idealistic views of the future for the Jewish people. Their small community attracted renowned Jewish artists who brought music to them, and prior to Huberman's first visit in 1929, the great violinist Jascha Heifetz performed there in 1926.

But by 1929, the influx of Jews had led to escalating tensions among them and the Arab population, causing the British government to enact restrictions on Jewish immigration starting in 1930. The Jewish Agency now imposed strict guidelines for issuing visas. For wealthy Jews who could demonstrate a particular level of assets, these visas proved easy to obtain. But the musicians and their families that Huberman wanted to bring to Palestine did not even come close to meeting the financial threshold. After months of political maneuvering, Huberman finally scrounged up enough visas to move the musicians, their spouses and children, along with their parents and siblings, to Palestine, for a total of almost 1,000 people. Huberman's labor of love constituted an incredible act of salvation, as without these visas, most would have perished during the ensuing years.

The struggle to acquire the immigration documents, along with the frequent outbreaks of violence between the Arabs and Jews that threatened to erupt into a civil war, forced Huberman to adjust his timeline. The inaugural concert would be rescheduled from October 24 to December 26, and instead of starting rehearsals in September, the orchestra would convene for the first time in November. Even this slight delay caused untold hardships on the musicians who had already made the necessary departure arrangements based on the earlier schedule. But eventually, all of the promised musicians arrived in Palestine and began the process of coalescing into an orchestra. Their early rehearsals were split by sections—strings, winds, brass, so that the orchestra members could first establish a unified sound within their own instrument families before trying to create a blended and cohesive sonority across the entire orchestra. Even though all of the musicians possessed great technical skills and artistry, they were also diverse in terms of their training and performance experiences, which meant that this group needed to work especially hard to achieve the uniformity of style that distinguishes first-class orchestras.

Along with these musical pressures, the new arrivals also experienced the stress of having uprooted their lives to come to a place so geographically and culturally foreign to them. Most had exchanged major, bustling cities for this primitive desert, with its sweltering temperatures and swirling sand, where camels lumbered up and down the streets. Nevertheless, only two players, German violist Dora Loeb and Polish violinist Raphael Broches, chose to return to Europe after their first season with the Palestine Orchestra. Both perished in the Holocaust.

Meanwhile, Huberman worked to overcome the final obstacle that hindered his project's success—building a performance venue that could accommodate a professional orchestra. Tel Aviv's concert hall, where Huberman himself had performed so often, only seated 1,500 people. Huberman knew that the Palestine Orchestra with Toscanini on the podium would attract large audiences, so he arranged for renovations that would expand it into a grander hall with a broad stage and seating for 2,500. With the construction barely finishing on time, the orchestra did not get to practice in the new hall until December 4, less than a month before the inaugural concert. Fortunately, the skilled conductor Wilhelm Steinberg had thoroughly prepared the orchestra during the many rehearsals throughout the month of November and now planned to push for even greater refinement in anticipation of Maestro Toscanini's arrival one week prior to the concert.

Legendary for his musical prowess, Toscanini had also earned quite a reputation for his fiery personality, which could explode into fierce tirades during a rehearsal. So, the Palestine Orchestra awaited his arrival with an equal measure of anxiety and excitement. Finally, on December 20, Toscanini's plane touched down in Palestine, and the welcoming party drove the conductor directly to the concert hall. Not one for small talk, Toscanini unceremoniously strode onto the stage and announced that they would now rehearse the Second Symphony of Brahms. During the opening minutes of the piece, Toscanini approached the group as a patient teacher, gently and expertly molding the players into a sensitive en-

The Palestine Symphony with Maestro Toscanini, December 1936 (photograph by Rudi Weissenstein, The PhotoHouse).

semble. Then, he grew more demanding about meticulous details, before finally spurring them on with his characteristic flair as he shouted for them to match his passion for this glorious music. Toscanini's strategy worked, and in just one rehearsal, the Palestine Orchestra emerged with a dynamic new sound and a charismatic *esprit de corps*.

In the months leading up to the December 26 performance, many of Tel Aviv's residents had been skeptical about whether this new orchestra could really pull off a concert and about whether Toscanini would indeed follow through on his commitment to conduct it. But as news spread about the spectacular first rehearsal, concert goers overran the box office trying to acquire tickets. The whole scene resonated with chaotic madness and almost turned into a riot. Because the demand for tickets exceeded the number of seats available and in light of Huberman's democratic insistence that music be brought to all of the people of Palestine, the orchestra opened its last two rehearsals before the premiere to workers, teachers, writers, and other everyday citizens.

When the inaugural evening of December 26 arrived, the auditorium buzzed with a palpable excitement. No empty seats remained at the sold-out concert, and so hundreds of people stood outside in the rain in hopes of catching a few notes that might waft out into the streets. Toscanini had programmed an ambitious concert for the Palestine Orchestra's first performance, and as the start time approached, the musicians battled their nerves, knowing how much was at stake. Then, the great conductor strode onto the stage, and the audience collectively jumped to its feet to applaud him. The concert opened with Rossini's Overture to *The Silk Ladder*, followed by Brahms' *Symphony No. 2*. After intermission, the second half began with the *Unfinished Symphony* by Schubert. Next came two movements of Mendelssohn's music for *A Midsummer Night's Dream*, which ignited considerable enthusiasm among the Jewish audience. The concert concluded triumphantly with the Overture to Weber's opera *Oberon*.

The enthusiastic applause that erupted throughout the auditorium stemmed not just from the musical excellence of the performance, but also from the realization of the miraculous nature of this accomplishment. Defying all the odds, they had been given a world-class orchestra of their own people in Palestine. For the musicians, this triumph, in the face of all they had suffered and feared from the anti–Semitic assaults in their homelands, also constituted more than just an artistic success. They had received a priceless gift—the opportunity to save themselves and their families through music and the visionary spirit of Bronisław Huberman.

Within a span of only two weeks following Toscanini's arrival, over 15,000 people heard concerts and rehearsals in Tel Aviv, Jerusalem, and Haifa, with workers receiving tickets for one-fifth of the regular price. Toscanini left Palestine after the last performance on January 5, 1937, but would return in 1938 to conduct more concerts, with Huberman as the featured soloist. In the meantime, when the orchestra members were not performing or rehearsing, Huberman insisted that all of them teach to perpetuate the musical culture of the Jewish people and that region. Even with the onset of World War II, the Palestine Orchestra never faltered. Instead, it toured throughout the Middle East and performed 168 concerts for the Allied troops.

Meanwhile, as the Palestine Orchestra found its footing, another orchestra, also of an unprecedented nature, was forming—the St. Ottilien Jewish Orchestra. With the end of the war came vast numbers of people who had no family, no possessions, and no country in which to return. This was especially true for 200,000 Jews, most of them concentration camp survivors. In response to this humanitarian crisis, the United Nations Relief and

Rehabilitation Administration established displaced persons (DP) camps. With almost all of the DP camps located within Germany, the U.S. military faced the difficult task of managing these traumatized individuals. Caring for the Jewish DPs proved particularly challenging for a variety of reasons, including that many suffered from such poor health due to years of starvation and deprivation. In addition, they were often still targets of anti–Semitism, and so could not be mixed with other DP populations. The U.S. military brought in Rabbi Abraham Klausner to assist with this overwhelming situation. He decided to convert a Benedictine monastery named St. Ottilien into a DP camp just for Jewish survivors. Less than 35 miles from Munich, this monastery had functioned as a Nazi military hospital during the war and was currently treating over 400 Dachau survivors. The physician in charge, Dr. Zalman Grinberg, had been an inmate at Dachau himself. When the Nazis had abandoned all of Dachau's prisoners in the wake of the approaching Allies, Grinberg had led the group of 800 nearly dead people on a search for help, finally reaching the doors of St. Ottilien.

Among those who arrived at St. Ottilien were accomplished musicians who had created music, either freely or forcibly, in POW and concentration camps. Jewish violinist Max Beker had been a POW in Stalag VIII A, where the French composer Olivier Messiaen had been imprisoned. Beker came from a family of professional musicians and had studied violin at the Vilna Conservatory. In March 1939, while working as a professional musician in Vilna, he received a draft notice from the Polish Army. Less than six months later, he was captured by the Germans. Beker served as the concertmaster of the POW orchestra at Stalag VIII A, under the direction of the Belgian musician Ferdinand Carrion, for two and a half years until German officials evacuated the camp and sent Carrion home along with all the French and Belgian POWs. Nazi guards marched Max Beker and the other remaining prisoners for weeks, forcing them to sleep in stables or open fields, where they had to scrounge for every morsel of food they ate. American troops eventually discovered and liberated the group.

Also among the talented musicians seeking refuge at St. Ottilien were two sisters—Fania and Henia Durmashkin. Like Max Beker, the Durmashkin sisters had grown up in Vilna, Lithuania, within a family of devout and observant Jews. Their father, Akiva Durmashkin, was a well-respected musician and conductor who had studied at the Odessa Conservatory. Their brother Wolf had demonstrated exceptional musical talents from a young age and had later attended both the Vilna and Warsaw Conservatories. A brilliant pianist and conductor, Wolf Durmashkin had been appointed as the conductor of the Vilna Symphony Orchestra. Keeping with the family's tradition of musical excellence, both sisters studied at the Vilna Conservatory—Fania, the piano; and Henia, voice. But after the German invasion of Vilna on June 21, 1941, the Nazis forced the Durmashkins into the Vilna Ghetto.

Right away, the Vilna Symphony Orchestra launched an urgent appeal with the Nazi command, pleading that Wolf Durmashkin be allowed a special pass from the ghetto so that he could continue to conduct them, as he was essential to their continued success. Surprisingly, the Germans agreed to the request, and so Maestro Durmashkin traveled out of the ghetto for rehearsals and performances. But he also brought music into the Vilna Ghetto. Wolf Durmashkin smuggled in instruments that he had taken apart, so that the pieces could be easily concealed, then reassembled them once inside the ghetto. A piano materialized this same way. It had been found in a deserted home outside the ghetto by Jews sent on work details. They disassembled the piano and over a period of time carried it back to the ghetto bit by bit, hidden in their clothing. Eventually rebuilt, the piano added to the cultural life and provided Fania Durmashkin and the other pianists with a much needed instrument. Maestro Durmashkin also organized a 100-voice choir and an orchestra from those trapped behind the ghetto's walls. His groups exhibited an astonishing level of musicality and professionalism given their deprivations. The orchestra gave over 35 concerts, the first on March 15, 1942, and tackled an impressive level of repertoire, including Dvořák's *New World Symphony*, Tchaikovsky's *Fifth Symphony*, Beethoven's *Ninth Symphony*, Mozart's Overture to *The Marriage of Figaro*, and Chopin's *Piano Concerto in E minor*. The orchestra's final concert took place on August 29, 1943, less than a month before the liquidation of the Vilna Ghetto.

After the destruction of the ghetto, the Nazis sent Fania and Henia Durmashkin to various labor camps, then to Dachau. Camp officials assigned Fania to work each day in a doctor's house. This doctor treated her kindly and provided food and clothes that helped her and Henia survive. When advancing Allied troops neared Dachau, the guards sent the Durmashkin sisters on a death march, alongside the other remaining prisoners. The Nazis then deserted them in the mountains, where American troops eventually discovered the group and took them to St. Ottilien. Fania and Henia would learn later that the Nazis had murdered their beloved brother Wolf in September 1944.

On May 27, 1945, just 20 days after Nazi Germany's surrender, some of the musicians in the St. Ottilien DP camp organized what they called a liberation concert for their fellow survivors, some of whom were too weak to even sit up. After the success of this concert, the performers founded the St. Ottilien Jewish Orchestra, with Max Beker playing violin and another violinist named Michael Hofmekler conducting. Fania and Henia Durmashkin also joined the ensemble. The orchestra gave regular performances not only for the patients and displaced persons, but for American troops. With the use of a bus, the orchestra began to tour, clad in striped uniforms that symbolized the concentration camps. It performed at other DP camps and in numerous cities, including at the Nuremberg Opera House for those associated with the International Military Tribunal that had been convened for Nazi war crime trials.

After a year, the orchestra changed its name to the Ex-Concentration Camp Orchestra and relocated their base of operation to Fürstenfeldbruck. As a cultural ambassador, American conductor Leonard Bernstein traveled to Germany in 1948 to conduct the Munich Symphony Orchestra, and during this visit, he asked if there were any musicians nearby who had survived the camps. When the 29-year-old Bernstein learned about the Ex-Concentration Camp Orchestra, he signed up to conduct two concerts with them, one of which included Gershwin's *Rhapsody in Blue* with Bernstein at the piano.

Never intended as a long-term organization, the orchestra disbanded in 1949, as the displaced musicians found permanent homes. It had fulfilled the wonderful purpose of bringing together Jewish performers so they could not only minister to their fellow survivors through music, but also declare to the world that the Nazis had failed in silencing them and their culture. Although the ensemble no longer remained together, some of the bonds forged could not be separated so easily. Max Beker and Fania Durmashkin had fallen in love during their time in the orchestra. He planned to immigrate to the United States where some family lived, but Fania and Henia were set on going to Israel. Unable to resolve the apparent divide, Max Beker left for the United States. But love prevailed, and the two sisters soon followed. Max and Fania married and established a beautiful family. They remained in the United States, their adopted home, for the rest of their lives.

Meanwhile, Huberman's Palestine Orchestra had assumed an important role in the

Ex-Concentration Camp Orchestra in 1946 (archive of Sonia P. Beker, author of *Symphony on Fire: A Story of Music and Spiritual Resistance During the Holocaust*).

momentous, post-war era for the Jewish people and for Palestine. On May 14, 1948, during the ceremony that declared the establishment of the State of Israel, the orchestra performed the beloved Zionist hymn, "Hatikvah" (The Hope), a piece that embodied the enduring hope of a Jewish homeland and that would aptly become the national anthem of Israel. In resonance with its home's new designation, the Palestine Symphony Orchestra changed its name to the Israel Philharmonic Orchestra that same year. It remains one of the finest orchestras in the world, as well as a cultural treasure of the Jewish people. The Israel Philharmonic maintains an unbreakable legacy with those courageous men and women who played on its first concert, as many of their children joined its ranks and now their grandchildren feature among the present-day members.

During his 1948 tour that had included concerts with the Ex-Concentration Camp Orchestra, the young Leonard Bernstein had also conducted the Israel Philharmonic. For those living in that region, life had become extremely difficult due to the Arab-Israeli War, a vicious conflict that had sparked over the creation of Israel. But just as music had sustained people in concentration camps and ghettos, or throughout the devastating siege of Leningrad, the Israel Philharmonic offered the gift of music to uplift the spirit of the Jewish community, even amid the fear of violence and the severe deprivations of food and water. Over the next 20 years, Bernstein would be a frequent conductor on the podium of the IPO, traveling all over the world with this ensemble. His superb musicianship and passionate heart would help elevate its status as a truly great orchestra and shape its mission as a cultural ambassador.

After having set his new orchestra in motion, Bronisław Huberman had resumed his international touring career and established a home in Switzerland right before the annexation of Austria. In 1938, an airplane crash near Palembang, Sumatra broke multiple bones, including Huberman's left arm, and damaged several fingers on his right hand. He recovered through a long and painful rehabilitation and eventually began to concertize again. His philanthropic spirit compelled him to continue performing benefit concerts for those he saw in need from war and natural disaster. He became a U.S. citizen in 1941 and gave a concert at New York City's Lewisohn Stadium in 1942 for 7,000 people. But Huberman's health remained fragile from the accident and from the relentless schedule that he had demanded of himself over the years. Tragically, Huberman did not live to see the 1948 declaration of a state for the Jewish people or for his orchestra's transformation alongside. He died at his home in Switzerland on June 16, 1947, at age 64. Ida Ibbeken, the nurse he had met in 1916, had remained by his side. After his death, she moved to Israel and spent the remainder of her life honoring his legacy through translating his many speeches and correspondence, as well as compiling and maintaining his archives.

Bronisław Huberman has been called music's Oskar Schindler. He stood up to tyranny, intolerance, and racism, refusing to allow Nazi hatred to destroy the magnificent cultural heritage of the Jewish people. Huberman's action saved lives and also preserved the artistic tradition that these musicians represented. So despite the violinist's remarkable talent and storied career, his work in establishing the orchestra in Palestine would remain his most important and enduring legacy.

Violinists often live on not only through their recordings, but through the instruments they play, which carry as detailed a provenance as any great work of art. The Stradivari violin that was stolen from Huberman in 1936 at Carnegie Hall became the centerpiece of a story to rival any fictional thriller. In 1985, Julian Altman, a violinist who had played with the National Symphony Orchestra in Washington, D.C., confessed on his deathbed that the violin he had been playing for over 50 years was the stolen Huberman Strad. He made this admission to his wife Marcelle Hall, telling her that he had bought it from the thief for $100 back in 1936. After her husband's death, Hall revealed the secret and entered into negotiations with Lloyd's of London to turn the violin over to them. Despite the fact that she possessed stolen property and the mounting suspicions that Altman had been the actual thief, Lloyd's paid her a little over a quarter of a million dollars as a finder's fee and took possession of the instrument in February 1988. They subsequently sold it at auction for $1.2 million. This violin has continued to enjoy a vibrant life making music around the world. It currently resides in the hands of the acclaimed violinist Joshua Bell, who purchased it for almost $4 million in 2001.

As seen with the Huberman Strad, violins can take on their own story and legacy through the people who have touched them and the places where their music has been heard. Many of the players who immigrated to Palestine to play in Huberman's orchestra possessed very fine German-made violins. But then after the terrible atrocities committed by Nazi Germany, some of these Jewish musicians felt that their German violins had become tainted and refused to play them any longer. A few harbored such hate for anything associated with Germany that they actually destroyed their instruments. Others sold them to a violin repairman in Israel named Moshe Weinstein. Moshe had studied violin at the Vilna Conservatory, where he met his future wife, a piano student named Golda. He performed and taught in Lithuania, but as an ardent Zionist, wanted to move to Palestine. Moshe prepared for his immigration by apprenticing with a Jewish luthier in Warsaw because he had surmised that being able to repair violins in Palestine would be a steadier job than performing. He knew that wherever there were Jews, there would be violins. He and his wife immigrated to Palestine in 1938, and he set up his shop in Tel Aviv in 1939, the same year that his son Amnon was born. Five years later, they welcomed a daughter named Esther. In the end, those four were the only survivors. The entire rest of their extended family, over 400 people, who had remained behind were murdered in the Holocaust.

The first of the German instruments that Moshe Weinstein bought had been made by Benedict Wagner, an 18th century violinmaker. Although this Wagner had no connection with the notorious anti–Semitic composer, Richard Wagner, the violinist who owned this instrument wanted no part of it. Over time, Moshe collected 80 of these German violins, violas, and cellos, which he never sold, but just held on to in his workshop. Wanting to follow in his father's footsteps, Amnon Weinstein studied in the shop with his father and then spent additional time in Cremona, Italy, learning the craft. When Amnon took over the business following his father's death in 1986, he discovered the unsold German instruments and grew curious about their origin. His research on these instruments, especially the violins' connections to the Holocaust, planted the seeds for the Violins of Hope project.

Amnon had always been haunted by the loss of his parents' family in the Holocaust and by the emaciated survivors that, as a kid, he had seen arriving in Israel after the war. One day, in the late 1980s, an elderly man entered the shop carrying a violin. He explained that he had been forced to play it in Auschwitz, and even though he had never been able to play the violin again because of that association, he wanted to get it restored as a gift for his grandson. The violin had sustained considerable damage because of having been played outdoors at the camp and needed to have the top removed in order to allow a quality restoration. Amnon would never forget the moment when he opened up that violin and discovered that the hollow inside was filled with the ash that had rained down from the crematoria at Auschwitz. These various experiences inspired Amnon to seek out more instruments that had been played in the camps and ghettos. With the discovery of their stories, he came to real-

Amnon Weinstein, Israeli luthier and founder of the Violins of Hope Project, date unknown (courtesy Avshalom Weinstein / Photographer: Miki Koren).

ize that music had remained a powerful force throughout the Holocaust. More importantly, Amnon recognized, "Wherever there were violins, there was hope."[8]

The violins that Amnon collects as part of his Violins of Hope project range from very fine concert violins to the more folk-like instruments adorned on the back with a Star of David, indicating that they had been used in the performance of Klezmer music. Some of the violins are so well made and distinctive that their provenance can be traced, but others will remain forever unidentified. Regardless, Amnon has lovingly restored each one so that the beautiful voices of these instruments can be heard again. But it has not been an easy journey for him, as he must confront the dark histories of these violins that intersect with his own family's terrible losses. It takes great courage and generosity for him to place his hands on these instruments and coax them back to life. In 1998, Amnon's son Avshalom began to train as the third generation of luthier. Today, he continues to work alongside his father in the shop and also coordinates the Violins of Hope project, which now features over 50 restored instruments that travel around the world for exhibitions, educational programs, and concerts.

Despite the unspeakable acts of violence and the loss of millions of precious lives, beauty and music found a way to survive and even flourish after the Holocaust and World War II. As a Phoenix rising from the ashes, hope and love gave birth to the Israel Philharmonic, whose impact in the hearts and lives of the Jewish people and the world remains immeasurable. Similarly, the Weinstein family's Violins of Hope project provides a means of reconciliation and celebration through instruments that proclaim truth and peace on behalf of those who can no longer speak. As music continues to be heard through Jewish musicians and Jewish violins, these people claim a spiritual and cultural victory over those who had vowed to destroy them, and they offer a reminder to humanity of the imperative each faces to not only remember, but to ensure—Never Again.

Chapter Notes

Introduction

1. Victor Hugo, *William Shakespeare*, Translated by A. Baillot (Jazzybee Verlag, 2018), 43.
2. Aldous Huxley, "The Rest is Silence," *Music at Night and Other Essays* (Chatto & Windus, 1931), 19.
3. Julian Young, *Friedrich Nietzsche: A Philosophical Biography* (Cambridge University Press, 2010), 37.
4. Oliver Sacks, *Musicophilia: Tales of Music and the Brain* (Vintage Books, 2008), 329.
5. Lily E. Hirsch, *A Jewish Orchestra in Nazi Germany: Musical Politics and the Berlin Jewish Culture League* (University of Michigan Press, 2012), 5.

Chapter 1

1. Richard Wagner, *Richard Wagner's Prose Works, Volume 6*, Translated by William Ashton Ellis (Kegan Paul, Trench, Trübner & Co, 1897), 274.
2. See Timothy W. Ryback, *Hitler's Private Library: The Books that Shaped His Life* (Vintage Books, 2010).
3. Diane Ackerman, *The Zookeeper's Wife: A War Story* (W. W. Norton Company, 2007), 92.
4. Hannah Arendt, *The Origins of Totalitarianism* (Harcourt, 1994), 474.
5. Alan E. Steinweis, "Hans Hinkel and German Jewry, 1933–1941," *Theatrical Performance during the Holocaust: Texts, Documents, Memoirs*, edited by Rebecca Rovit and Alvin Goldfarb (Johns Hopkins University Press, 1999), 23.
6. See Paul Celan, *Selected Prose and Poems of Paul Celan*, Translated by John Felstiner (W. W. Norton & Company, 2001).
7. Alex Ross, *The Rest Is Noise: Listening to the Twentieth Century* (Farrar, Straus and Giroux, 2007), 335.
8. Ibid., 334.

Chapter 2

1. Eric Weiner, *The Geography of Genius: A Search for the World's Most Creative Places, from Ancient Athens to Silicon Valley* (Simon & Schuster, 2016), 263.
2. Ibid., 218.
3. Richard Newman and Karen Kirtley, *Alma Rosé: Vienna to Auschwitz* (Amadeus Press, 2000),

74. Many of the details about the Rosé family, both personally and professionally, come from the excellent research of Richard Newman, who was friends with Alfred Rosé after World War II. Newman's considerable work has ensured that the legacy of the Rosé family, and particularly of Alma Rosé, will not be forgotten.
4. Ibid., 101.
5. Gerda Weissmann Klein, *All But My Life* (Hill and Wang, 1996), 9.
6. Anne Frank, *The Diary of a Young Girl* (Wilco Publishing House, 2006), 212.
7. See Corrie Ten Boom, *The Hiding Place* (Chosen Books, 2006).
8. Since 2010, a sculpture of the upside down B, titled "To B remembered," has been used by the International Auschwitz Committee as an award to individuals who have worked to make sure that the atrocities of the Holocaust never occur again.
9. Newman and Kirtley, 268.
10. Robert Jay Lifton, *The Nazi Doctors: Medical Killing and the Psychology of Genocide* (Basic Books, 2017), 147.
11. See Shirli Gilbert, *Music in the Holocaust: Confronting Life in the Nazi Ghettos and Camps* (Oxford University Press, 2005). The excellent research of Shirli Gilbert, especially through her important volume on music during the Holocaust, has greatly contributed to the scholarly literature on the subject and has been a significant resource for this book.
12. See Primo Levi, *The Drowned and the Saved* (Simon & Schuster, 1988).
13. See Gilbert, *Music in the Holocaust*.
14. Klein, *All But My Life*, 89.
15. Michael Haas, *Forbidden Music: The Jewish Composers Banned by the Nazis* (Yale University Press, 2013), 273.
16. Primo Levi, *Survival in Auschwitz* (Touchstone, 1996), 51.
17. Gabriele Knapp, "Music as a Means of Survival: The Women's Orchestra in Auschwitz," *Feministische Studien*, Translated by Katherine Deeg, Anette Bauer, and Liane Curtis, vol. 1, 1996, 1.
18. Helena Dunicz Niwińska, *One of the Girls in the Band: The Memoirs of a Violinist from Birkenau*, Translated by William Brand (Auschwitz-Birkenau State Museum, 2017), 62.
19. Ibid., 88.
20. Pascal Quignard, *The Hatred of Music*, Trans-

lated by Matthew Amos and Fredrik Rönnbäck (Yale University Press, 2016), 129.
 21. Syzmon Laks, *Music of Another World*, Translated by Chester A. Kisiel (Northwestern University Press, 2000), 31.
 22. *Ibid.*, 55.
 23. *Ibid.*, 7.
 24. *Ibid.*, 99.
 25. *Ibid.*, 5.
 26. *Ibid.*
 27. *Ibid.*, 70.
 28. *Ibid.*, 48.
 29. *Ibid.*, 91.
 30. *Ibid.*, 101.
 31. Newman and Kirtley, 257.
 32. *Ibid.*, 268.
 33. Fania Fénelon and Marcelle Routier, *The Musicians of Auschwitz*, Translated by Judith Landry (Michael Joseph, 1977), 27.
 34. *Ibid.*, 93.
 35. *Ibid.*, 47.
 36. Anita Lasker-Wallfisch, *Inherit the Truth: A Memoir of Survival and the Holocaust* (St. Martin's Press, 2000), 18. Although several of the survivors from the Women's Orchestra published memoirs, Anita Lasker-Wallfisch's is particularly significant in not only the amount of information it provides about their time in Auschwitz, but also about the months spent at Bergen-Belsen following the evacuation of Auschwitz, as well as her time in a DP camp.
 37. *Ibid.*
 38. *Ibid.*, 72.
 39. Niwińska, *One of the Girls in the Band*, 102.
 40. *Ibid.*, 99.
 41. *Ibid.*, 101.
 42. Lasker-Wallfisch, *Inherit the Truth*, 84.
 43. *Ibid.*, 78.
 44. *Ibid.*
 45. *Ibid.*, 76.
 46. Niwińska, 113.
 47. Lasker-Wallfisch, 77.
 48. *Ibid.*, 91.
 49. Susan Eischeid, *The Truth about Fania Fénelon and the Women's Orchestra of Auschwitz-Birkenau* (Palgrave Macmillan, 2016), 1.
 50. Lasker-Wallfisch, 16.
 51. *Ibid.*, 144.
 52. *Ibid.*, 15.
 53. Elie Wiesel, *Night*, Translated by Marion Wiesel (Hill and Wang, 2006), 34.
 54. Newman and Kirtley, 18.
 55. *Ibid.*, 10.
 56. *Ibid.*

Chapter 3

 1. Paul Cummins, *Dachau Song: The Twentieth Century Odyssey of Herbert Zipper* (Peter Lang Publishing, 2001), 12. Paul Cummins became a friend of Herbert Zipper's near the end of the great conductor's life as the result of frequent meetings so that Cummins could collect research for his book on Dr. Zipper's life. To date, Cummins' book remains the only comprehensive biographical sketch of this great educator and humanitarian. His research and friendship with Dr. Zipper has contributed important information to the scholarly literature on Holocaust music and has provided much of the biographical information on Herbert Zipper and his family for this book.
 2. Susan Orlean, *The Library Book* (Simon & Schuster, 2018), 98.
 3. George E. Berkley, *Vienna and Its Jews: The Tragedy of Success 1880s-1980s* (Abt Books, 1988), 367.
 4. For the lyrics to "Dachau Song," see Cummins, *Dachau Song*, 89–90.
 5. See Frank Ephraim, *Escape to Manila: From Nazi Tyranny to Japanese Terror* (University of Illinois Press, 2003).
 6. Cummins, 133.
 7. Dorothy L. Crawford, *A Windfall of Musicians: Hitler's Émigrés and Exiles in Southern California* (Yale University Press, 2009), 99.
 8. Cummins, xiii.

Chapter 4

 1. At birth, their son was actually named Stephan after Alice's beloved piano teacher, Václav Štěpán. But as a young man he changed his named to Raphael and was affectionately known by his family and friends as Rafi. Since that is the name he was known by professionally, most sources use that name for him throughout the biographical record.
 2. Joža Karas, *Music in Terezín 1941–1945* (Beaufort Books, 1985), 7.
 3. Stoessinger, *A Century of Wisdom*, 118.
 4. This is a story told by American writer Anne Lamott. It does not appear in a printed article or book, but she has granted permission for it to be used and attributed to her in this book.
 5. Samuel M. Edelman, "Singing in the Face of Death: A Study of Jewish Cabaret and Opera during the Holocaust," *Theatrical Performance during the Holocaust: Texts, Documents, Memoirs*, edited by Rebecca Rovit and Alvin Goldfarb (Johns Hopkins University Press, 1999), 130.
 6. Karas, *Music in Terezín*, 85.
 7. Melissa Müller and Reinhard Piechocki, *Alice's Piano: The Life of Alice Herz-Sommer* (Macmillan, 2012), 166.
 8. Zdenka Ehrlich-Fantlová, "The Czech Theater in Terezín," *Theatrical Performance during the Holocaust: Texts, Documents, Memoirs*, edited by Rebecca Rovit and Alvin Goldfarb (Johns Hopkins Press, 1999), 235.
 9. Mirko Tuma, "Memories of Theresienstadt," *Theatrical Performance during the Holocaust: Texts, Documents, Memoirs*, edited by Rebecca Rovit and Alvin Goldfarb (Johns Hopkins University Press, 1999), 267.
 10. Karas, 79.
 11. *Ibid.*, 81.
 12. See Joshua Jacobson, "Music in the Holocaust," *Choral Journal*, vol. 36, no. 5, Dec. 1995, 9–21.

13. Karas, 197.
14. Stoessinger, 142.
15. *Ibid.*, xiii.
16. *Ibid.*, 108.
17. *Ibid.*, 97.
18. *Ibid.*, 98.
19. Susan Goldman Rubin, *Fireflies in the Dark: The Story of Friedl Dicker-Brandeis and the Children of Terezín* (Holiday House, 2000), 18.
20. Tuma, "Memories of Theresienstadt," 268.
21. Ruth Thomson, *Terezín: Voices from the Holocaust* (Candlewick Press, 2011), 41.
22. Karas, 88.
23. Ofer Aderet, "The Teenage Girl Who Documented the Last Days of Theresienstadt," *Haaretz*, July 19, 2016, http://www.haaretz.com/israel-news/.premium-1.731810, Accessed 22 July 2017.
24. *Ibid.*
25. Susan Goldman Rubin and Ela Weissberger, *The Cat with the Yellow Star: Coming of Age in Terezín* (Holiday House, 2006), 23.
26. Karas, 102.
27. Rubin and Weissberger, *The Cat with the Yellow Star*, 30.
28. Müller and Piechocki, *Alice's Piano*, 226.
29. Karas, 139.
30. Josef Bor, *The Terezín Requiem*, Translated by Edith Pargeter (The Aislaby Press, 1995), 124.
31. Karas, 155.
32. After her marriage, Dita Polach went by Dita Kraus. Holocaust memoirs and documents that refer to her even before her marriage use her married name of Kraus. Interestingly, she also sang in Terezín's production of *Brundibár*. See Antonio Iturbe, *The Librarian of Auschwitz*, Translated by Lilit Thwaites (Henry Holt and Company, 2017).
33. Alexandra Zaprude, editor, *Salvaged Pages: Young Writers' Diaries of the Holocaust* (University Press, 2015), 408.
34. There is some discrepancy in the record about the death of Jakob Edelstein. According to Melissa Müller's *Alice's Piano*, the SS shot him at Terezín after he was accused of falsifying prisoner counts in official reports.
35. Rubin, *Fireflies in the Dark*, 29.
36. See Amy Lynn Wlodarski, "Musical Memories of Terezín in Transnational Perspective," *Dislocated Memories: Jews, Music, and Postwar German Culture*, edited by Tina Frühauf and Lily E. Hirsch (Oxford University Press, 2014).
37. Wlodarski, "Musical Memories," 64.
38. Nobert Troller, *Theresienstadt: Hitler's Gift to the Jews*, Translated by Susan E. Cernyak-Spatz (The University of North Carolina Press, 1991), 35.
39. Wlodarski, 66.
40. Edelman, "Singing in the Face of Death," 131.
41. Karas, 197.
42. Stoessinger, 58.
43. *Ibid.*, 161.
44. *Ibid.*, 151.
45. *Ibid.*, 211.
46. *Ibid.*, 40.
47. *Ibid.*, 166.
48. *Ibid.*, xi.
49. *Ibid.*, xiii.

Chapter 5

1. *Who Will Write Our History*, Directed by Roberta Grossman (Katahdin Productions, 2019).
2. Diane Ackerman, *The Zookeeper's Wife: A War Story* (W. W. Norton Company, 2007), 38.
3. Władysław Szpilman, *The Pianist: The Extraordinary True Story of One Man's Survival in Warsaw, 1939–1945*, Translated by Anthea Bell (Picador, 1999), 26.
4. *Ibid.*, 26.
5. Ackerman, *The Zookeeper's Wife*, 240.
6. Mitchell Duneier, *Ghetto: The Invention of a Place, the History of an Idea* (Farrar, Straus and Giroux, 2016), 22.
7. Szpilman, *The Pianist*, 45.
8. *Ibid.*, 44.
9. *Ibid.*, 48.
10. Ackerman, *The Zookeeper's Wife*, 155.
11. Michel Mazor, *The Vanished City: Everyday Life in the Warsaw Ghetto*, Translated by David Jacobson (Marsilio Publishers, 1993), 19.
12. Ackerman, *The Zookeeper's Wife*, 173.
13. Szpilman, 62.
14. *Ibid.*, 63.
15. Many of the specific details in this book concerning the musical life in the Warsaw Ghetto result from the excellent research of Shirli Gilbert, whose book on music during the Holocaust has greatly contributed to the scholarly literature on the subject. See Shirli Gilbert, *Music in the Holocaust: Confronting Life in the Nazi Ghettos and Camps* (Oxford University Press, 2005).
16. Katarzyna Person, *Assimilated Jews in the Warsaw Ghetto, 1940–1943* (Syracuse University Press, 2014), 121.
17. *Ibid.*, 127.
18. Szpilman, 13–14.
19. *Ibid.*, 13.
20. Duneier, *Ghetto*, 20.
21. Szpilman, 17.
22. Mazor, *The Vanished City*, 20–21.
23. Ackerman, 226.
24. *Ibid.*, 239.
25. *Ibid.*, 119.
26. *Ibid.*, 310.
27. Szpilman, 12–13.
28. *Ibid.*, 16.
29. *Ibid.*, 67.
30. Ackerman, 183.
31. Szpilman, 15.
32. Janusz Korczak, *Ghetto Diary* (Yale University Press, 2003), 8.
33. Ackerman, 185.
34. *Ibid.*, 185–186.
35. *Ibid.*, 186.
36. Szpilman, 106.
37. *Ibid.*
38. *Ibid.*, 107.

39. *Ibid.*, 134.
40. *Ibid.*, 167.
41. *Ibid.*
42. *Ibid.*, 169.
43. *Ibid.*, 177.
44. *Ibid.*
45. *Ibid.*
46. *Ibid.*, 180.
47. *Ibid.*, 181.
48. W.E.B. Du Bois, "The Negro and the Warsaw Ghetto," *The Social Theory of W.E.B. Du Bois*, edited by Phil Zuckerman (Pine Forge Press, 2004), 45.
49. *Ibid.*
50. Mazor, 11.
51. Ackerman, 322.
52. Szpilman, 188.

Chapter 6

1. Leonard Bernstein, *The Unanswered Question: Six Talks at Harvard* (Harvard University Press, 1976), 313.
2. See Fritz Kreisler, *Four Weeks in the Trenches* (Trieste Publishing, 2017).
3. Paul Griffiths, *Olivier Messiaen and the Music of Time* (Faber and Faber, 2008), 26.
4. *Ibid.*, 17.
5. *Ibid.*, 243.
6. Alex Ross, *The Rest Is Noise: Listening to the Twentieth Century* (Farrar, Straus and Giroux, 2007), 486.
7. Almost all of the information known about the other members of Messiaen's quartet comes from the excellent research and scholarly work of Rebecca Rischin, whose book on the subject has dramatically changed the academic discourse surrounding *Quartet for the End of Time*. See Rebecca Rischin, *For the End of Time: The Story of the Messiaen Quartet* (Cornell University Press, 2006).
8. *King James Version,* Revelation 10:5–6.
9. Rischin, *For the End of Time*, 2.
10. *Ibid.*, 129.
11. *Ibid.*
12. Griffiths, *Olivier Messiaen and the Music of Time*, 106.
13. Rischin, 45.
14. *Ibid.*, 66.
15. *Ibid.*, 96.
16. Ross, *The Rest Is Noise*, 488.
17. *Ibid.*, 492.
18. Griffiths, 17.
19. Ross, 486.
20. B. V. Lawson, *Dies Irae* (Crimetime Press, 2015), 189.
21. Joanna Lusek, "Coincidentia Oppositorum, or Music as a Key to Memory: The Meetingpoint Music Messiaen as a Site of War Memory in Europe," *Mnemosyne and Mars: Artistic and Cultural Representations of Twentieth-Century Europe at War*, edited by Bragança, Manuel, et al. (Cambridge Scholars Publishing, 2013), 302.
22. *Ibid.*, 303.

Chapter 7

1. Prior to 1918, Russian dates were derived from the Julian calendar, now known as the "old style." Starting in 1918, Russia converted to the Gregorian calendar or "new style." This chapter's dates represent the "new style" as often as can be determined.
2. Alex Ross, *The Rest Is Noise: Listening to the Twentieth Century* (Farrar, Straus and Giroux, 2007), 237.
3. Anderson, *Symphony for the City of the Dead*, 105.
4. *Ibid.*, 152.
5. *Ibid.*, 4.
6. *Ibid.*, 163.
7. *Ibid.*, 240.
8. Laurel Fay, *Shostakovich: A Life* (Oxford University Press, 2000), 124.
9. Anderson, 232.
10. *Ibid.*, 243.
11. *Ibid.*, 245.
12. Fay, *Shostakovich,* 126.
13. Anderson, 264.
14. *Ibid.*, 266.
15. *Ibid.*, 278.
16. *Ibid.*, 279.
17. *Ibid.*, 287.
18. Brian Moynahan, *Leningrad: Siege and Symphony* (Atlantic Monthly Press, 2013), 307.
19. Anderson, 309.
20. Fay, 131.
21. Moynahan, *Leningrad*, 374.
22. *Ibid.*
23. Anderson, 336.
24. Moynahan, 394.
25. *Ibid.*, 422.
26. *Ibid.*, 483.
27. *Ibid.*, 484.
28. Anderson, 344–45.
29. *Ibid.*, 348.
30. *Ibid.*, 345.
31. *Ibid.*, 349.
32. *Ibid.*, 355.
33. *Ibid.*, 363.
34. *Ibid.*, 140.
35. Ross, *The Rest Is Noise*, 238.
36. Moynahan, 10.
37. Anderson, 349.

Chapter 8

1. Lavinia Warner and John Sandilands, *Women Beyond the Wire* (Arrow Books, 1997), 22.
2. *Ibid.*, 13.
3. *Ibid.*, 11.
4. *Ibid.*, 35.
5. *Ibid.*, 62.
6. *Ibid.*, 85.
7. *Ibid.*, 87.
8. Helen Colijn, *Song of Survival* (Headline Book Publishing, 1995), 116.
9. *Ibid.*, 26.
10. *Ibid.*, 37.

11. *Ibid.*, 94.
12. *Ibid.*, 101.
13. *Ibid.*
14. *Ibid.*, 103.
15. Warner and Sandilands, *Women Beyond the Wire,* 12.
16. *Ibid.*
17. *Ibid.*, 115.
18. *Ibid.*
19. Warner and Sandilands, 117–18.
20. Betty Jeffrey, *White Coolies* (Lewis Reprints Limited, 1973), 45.
21. *Ibid.*, 45.
22. *Ibid.*, 47–48.
23. *Ibid.*, 48.
24. Colijn, *Song of Survival,* 141.
25. Warner and Sandilands, 138.
26. Jeffrey, *White Coolies,* 45–46.
27. Colijn, 134.
28. *Ibid.*, 133–34.
29. *Ibid.*, 267.
30. *Ibid.*, 135.
31. Jeffrey, 75.
32. Colijn, 153–54. Note that some discrepancy exists among memoirs about whether this event occurred on Christmas Eve or Christmas Day.
33. *Ibid.*, 130.
34. Warner and Sandilands, 175.
35. Jeffrey, 85.
36. Colijn, 162.
37. Warner and Sandilands, 188.
38. Colijn, 183.
39. *Ibid.*, 257.
40. Warner and Sandilands, 138.
41. Colijn, 186–87.
42. Warner and Sandilands, 189.
43. Colijn, 169.
44. Colijn,174–75. These introductory remarks were written by Margaret Dryburgh, and the handwritten original, which contains the complete transcript, resides in the Department of Special Collections and University Archives at Stanford University.
45. *Ibid.*, 175–76.
46. *Ibid.*, 178.
47. Jeffrey, 87.
48. Jeffrey, 86.
49. Colijn, 186.
50. *Ibid.*, 191–92.
51. Warner and Sandilands, 14.
52. *Ibid.*, 5.
53. *Ibid.*, 4.
54. *Ibid.*, 15.
55. Jeffrey, 93–94.
56. *Ibid.*, 112.
57. *Ibid.*, 106.
58. *Ibid.*, 113.
59. *Ibid.*, 92.
60. *Ibid.*, 107.
61. *Ibid.*
62. Colijn, 203.
63. *Ibid.*, 205.
64. *Ibid.*, 206.
65. *Ibid.*
66. Jeffrey, 147.
67. *Ibid.*, 142.
68. The Book of Common Prayer (1928), 594–595.
69. Warner and Sandilands, 205.
70. *Ibid.*
71. Colijn, 217.
72. Warner and Sandilands, 8.
73. Jeffrey, 148.
74. *Ibid.*, 146.
75. *Ibid.*, 151.
76. *King James Version*, Psalm 121:1–8.
77. Jeffrey, 157.
78. It is also sometimes spelled as Lubuklinggau.
79. Jeffrey, 161.
80. Colijn, 224.
81. *Ibid.*, 224–25.
82. Jeffrey, 162.
83. Colijn, 226.
84. Jeffrey, 165.
85. *Ibid.*
86. *Ibid.*, 183.
87. Warner and Sandilands, 262.
88. *Ibid.*, 4.
89. *Ibid.*, 5.
90. *Ibid.*
91. *Ibid.*, 271.
92. Colijn, the photo caption of Norah Chambers.
93. Jeffrey, 187.
94. Colijn, the photo caption of Sister Catharinia.
95. *Ibid.*, 251.
96. *Ibid.*, 251, 253.
97. *Ibid.*, 247.
98. MacLeod, *I Will Sing to the End*, 153.

Epilogue

1. *New International Version,* Genesis 4:21.
2. No specific source can be identified, but this quote is famously attributed to Huberman and appears in program notes for some of the most prestigious orchestras.
3. Frederick T. Birchall, "Hubermann Bars German Concerts," *The New York Times* (14 Sept. 1933), 11.
4. *Ibid.*
5. Ida Ibbeken, *An Orchestra Is Born* (Yachdav, 1969), 17.
6. Grymes, *Violins of Hope,* 36.
7. There is some discrepancy in the record about this violin. One source says that it was given to Huberman in 1911 by another patron and another says he bought it that year. I have chosen to rely on the most recent research and scholarship of Josh Aronson and his excellent book on the subject. See Josh Aronson and Denise George, *Orchestra of Exiles: The Story of Bronsilaw Huberman, the Israel Philharmonic, and the One Thousand Jews He Saved from Nazi Horrors* (Berkley Books, 2016).
8. Grymes, 13.

Bibliography

Ackerman, Diane. *The Zookeeper's Wife: A War Story*. W. W. Norton Company, 2007.

Aderet, Ofer. "The Teenage Girl Who Documented the Last Days of Theresienstadt." *Haaretz*, July 19, 2016, http://www.haaretz.com/israel-news/.premium-1.731810. Accessed 22 July 2017.

Adler, H. G. *Theresienstadt 1941–1945: The Face of a Coerced Community*. Translated by Belinda Cooper. Cambridge University Press, 2017.

Anderson, M. T. *Symphony for the City of the Dead: Dmitri Shostakovich and the Siege of Leningrad*. Candlewick Press, 2015.

Archer, Bernice, and Alan Jeffreys. "The Women's Embroideries of Internment in the Far East 1942–1945." *Cultural Heritage and Prisoners of War: Creativity Behind Barbed Wire*, edited by Gilly Carr and Harold Mytum, Routledge, 2012.

Arendt, Hannah. *The Origins of Totalitarianism*. Harcourt, 1994.

Aronson, Josh, and Denise George. *Orchestra of Exiles: The Story of Bronsilaw Huberman, the Israel Philharmonic, and the One Thousand Jews He Saved from Nazi Horrors*. Berkley Books, 2016.

Bach in Auschwitz. Directed by Michel Daëron, Fox Lorber Centrestage, 2000.

Band, Edward. *Working His Purpose Out: The History of the English Presbyterian Mission, 1847–1947*. Ch'eng Wen Publishing, 1972.

Beker, Sonia Pauline. *Symphony on Fire: A Story of Music and Spiritual Resistance During the Holocaust*. The Wordsmithy, 2007.

Berkley, George E. *Vienna and Its Jews: The Tragedy of Success 1880s-1980s*. Abt Books, 1988.

Berkman, Franya J. *Monument Eternal: The Music of Alice Coltrane*. Wesleyan University Press, 2010.

Bernstein, Leonard. *The Unanswered Question: Six Talks at Harvard*. Harvard University Press, 1976.

Birchall, Frederick T. "Hubermann Bars German Concerts." *The New York Times* [New York City], 14 Sept. 1933, p. 11.

Bor, Josef. *The Terezín Requiem*. Translated by Edith Pargeter. The Aislaby Press, 1995.

Braun, Shony Alex, and Emily Cavins. *My Heart Is a Violin*. 1st Books Library, 2002.

Brown, Brené. *The Gifts of Imperfection: Let Go of Who You Think You're Supposed to Be and Embrace Who You Are*. Hazelden Publishing, 2010.

Brown, Steven, and Ulrik Volgsten, editors. *Music and Manipulation: On the Social Uses and Social Control of Music*. Berghahn Books, 2006.

Celan, Paul. *Selected Prose and Poems of Paul Celan*. Translated by John Felstiner. W. W. Norton & Company, 2001.

Center for American Music Preservation. "New England Song Series No. 2: The True Story of *Goin' Home* from Bohemia to Boston." *American Music Preservation*, http://www.americanmusicpreservation.com/GoinHome.htm. Accessed 10 March 2018.

Colijn, Helen. *Song of Survival*. Headline Book Publishing, 1995.

Crawford, Dorothy L. *A Windfall of Musicians: Hitler's Émigrés and Exiles in Southern California*. Yale University Press, 2009.

Creating Harmony: The Displaced Persons' Orchestra from St. Ottilien. Directed by John J. Michalczyk, Etoile Productions, 2007.

Cummins, Paul. *Dachau Song: The Twentieth Century Odyssey of Herbert Zipper*. 3rd ed., Peter Lang Publishing, 2001.

Dawson, Greg. *Hiding in the Spotlight: A Musical Prodigy's Story of Survival 1941–1946*. Pegasus, 2009.

DeLorenzo, Lisa C. *Giving Voice to Democracy in Music Education: Diversity and Social Justice*. Routledge, 2016.

Du Bois, W.E.B. "The Negro and the Warsaw Ghetto." *The Social Theory of W.E.B. Du Bois*, edited by Phil Zuckerman, Pine Forge Press, 2004, pp. 44–45.

Duneier, Mitchell. *Ghetto: The Invention of a Place, the History of an Idea*. Farrar, Straus and Giroux, 2016.

Edelman, Samuel M. "Singing in the Face of Death: A Study of Jewish Cabaret and Opera during the Holocaust." *Theatrical Performance during the Holocaust: Texts, Documents, Memoirs*, edited by Rebecca Rovit and Alvin Goldfarb, Johns Hopkins University Press, 1999, pp. 125–32.

Ehrlich-Fantlová, Zdenka. "The Czech Theater in Terezín." *Theatrical Performance during the Holocaust: Texts, Documents, Memoirs*, edited by Rebecca Rovit and Alvin Goldfarb, Johns Hopkins Press, 1999, pp. 231–49.

Eischeid, Susan. *The Truth about Fania Fénelon and the Women's Orchestra of Auschwitz-Birkenau*. Palgrave Macmillan, 2016.

Ephraim, Frank. *Escape to Manila: From Nazi Tyr-

anny to Japanese Terror. University of Illinois Press, 2003.

Everything Is a Present: The Wonder & Grace of Alice Sommer Herz. Directed by Christopher Nupen, Allegro Films, 2010.

Fay, Laurel. *Shostakovich: A Life.* Oxford University Press, 2000.

Fénelon, Fania, and Marcelle Routier. *The Musicians of Auschwitz.* Translated by Judith Landry. Michael Joseph, 1977.

Frank, Anne. *The Diary of a Young Girl.* Wilco Publishing House, 2006.

Gilbert, Shirli. *Music in the Holocaust: Confronting Life in the Nazi Ghettos and Camps.* Oxford University Press, 2005.

Goldfarb, Alvin. "Theatrical Activities in the Nazi Concentration Camps." *Theatrical Performance during the Holocaust: Texts, Documents, Memoirs,* edited by Rebecca Rovit and Alvin Goldfarb, Johns Hopkins University Press, 1999, pp. 117–24.

Goodall, Howard. *The Story of Music from Babylon to the Beatles: How Music Has Shaped Civilization.* Pegasus Books, 2013.

Greenberg, Robert. *How to Listen to Great Music.* Plume, 2011.

Griffiths, Paul. *Olivier Messiaen and the Music of Time.* Faber & Faber, 2008.

Grymes, James A. *Violins of Hope: Violins of the Holocaust—Instruments of Hope and Liberation in Mankind's Darkest Hour.* HarperCollins, 2014.

Haas, Michael. *Forbidden Music: The Jewish Composers Banned by the Nazis.* Yale University Press, 2013.

Hirsch, Lily E. *A Jewish Orchestra in Nazi Germany: Musical Politics and the Berlin Jewish Culture League.* University of Michigan Press, 2012.

Hugo, Victor. *William Shakespeare.* Translated by A. Baillot. Jazzybee Verlag, 2018.

Huxley, Aldous. "The Rest is Silence." *Music at Night and Other Essays,* Chatto & Windus, 1931.

Ibbeken, Ida. *An Orchestra Is Born.* Yachdav, 1969.

Iturbe, Antonio. *The Librarian of Auschwitz.* Translated by Lilit Thwaites. Henry Holt and Company, 2017.

Jacobs, G. F. *Prelude to the Monsoon: Assignment in Sumatra.* University of Pennsylvania Press, 1982.

Jacobson, Joshua. "Music in the Holocaust." *Choral Journal,* vol. 36, no. 5, Dec. 1995, pp. 9–21.

Jeffrey, Betty. *White Coolies.* Lewis Reprints Limited, 1973.

Johnson, Bruce, and Martin Cloonan. *Dark Side of the Tune: Popular Music and Violence.* Routledge, 2009.

Karas, Joža. *Music in Terezín 1941-1945.* Beaufort Books, 1985.

———. "Opera Performances in Terezín: Krása's Brundibár." *Theatrical Performance during the Holocaust: Texts, Documents, Memoirs,* edited by Rebecca Rovit and Alvin Goldfarb, Johns Hopkins University Press, 1999, pp. 190–200.

Klein, Gerda Weissmann. *All But My Life.* Hill and Wang, 1996.

Knapp, Gabriele. "Music as a Means of Survival: The Women's Orchestra in Auschwitz." *Feministische Studien,* Translated by Katherine Deeg, Anette Bauer, and Liane Curtis, vol. 14, no. 1, May 1996, pp. 26–34.

Korczak, Janusz. *Ghetto Diary.* Yale University Press, 2003.

Kramer, Aaron. "Creation in a Death Camp." *Theatrical Performance during the Holocaust: Texts, Documents, Memoirs,* edited by Rebecca Rovit and Alvin Goldfarb, Johns Hopkins University Press, 1999, pp. 179–89.

Kreisler, Fritz. *Four Weeks in the Trenches.* Trieste Publishing, 2017.

Kundera, Milan. *The Book of Laughter and Forgetting.* Translated by Aaron Asher. Harper Perennial, 1999.

The Lady in Number 6: Music Saved My Life. Directed by Malcolm Clarke, Reed Entertainment, 2013.

Lagerwey, Mary D. *Reading Auschwitz.* AltaMira Press, 1998.

Laks, Syzmon. *Music of Another World.* Translated by Chester A. Kisiel. Northwestern University Press, 2000.

Lasker-Wallfisch, Anita. *Inherit the Truth: A Memoir of Survival and the Holocaust.* St. Martin's Press, 2000.

Lawson, B. V. *Dies Irae.* Crimetime Press, 2015.

Levi, Erik. *Mozart and the Nazis: How the Third Reich Abused a Cultural Icon.* Yale University Press, 2010.

Levi, Primo. *The Drowned and the Saved.* Simon & Schuster, 1988.

———. *Survival in Auschwitz.* Touchstone, 1996.

Lifton, Robert Jay. *The Nazi Doctors: Medical Killing and the Psychology of Genocide.* Basic Books, 2017.

Lusek, Joanna. "Coincidentia Oppositorum, or Music as a Key to Memory: The Meetingpoint Music Messiaen as a Site of War Memory in Europe." *Mnemosyne and Mars: Artistic and Cultural Representations of Twentieth-Century Europe at War,* edited by Bragança, Manuel, et al. Cambridge Scholars Publishing, 2013, pp. 292–309.

MacLeod, Ian. *I Will Sing to the End.* Coco's Publications, 2005.

Manning, Molly Guptill. *When Books Went to War: The Stories That Helped Us Win World War II.* Houghton Mifflin Harcourt, 2014.

Mazor, Michel. *The Vanished City: Everyday Life in the Warsaw Ghetto.* Translated by David Jacobson. Marsilio Publishers, 1993.

Mazzeo, Tilar J. *Irena's Children: A True Story of Courage.* Gallery Books, 2016.

McDougall, William H., Jr. *Six Bells Off Java.* Sam Weller, 1955.

Moynahan, Brian. *Leningrad: Siege and Symphony.* Atlantic Monthly Press, 2013.

Müller, Melissa, and Reinhard Piechocki. *Alice's Piano: The Life of Alice Herz-Sommer.* Macmillan, 2012.

Newman, Richard, and Karen Kirtley. *Alma Rosé: Vienna to Auschwitz.* Amadeus Press, 2000.

Niewyk, Donald, and Francis Nicosia. *The Columbia Reference Guide to The Holocaust.* Columbia University Press, 2000.

Niwińska, Helena Dunicz. *One of the Girls in the Band: The Memoirs of a Violinist from Birkenau.*

Translated by William Brand. Auschwitz-Birkenau State Museum, 2017.

Orlean, Susan. *The Library Book*. Simon & Schuster, 2018.

Person, Katarzyna. *Assimilated Jews in the Warsaw Ghetto, 1940-1943*. Syracuse University Press, 2014.

Quignard, Pascal. *The Hatred of Music*. Translated by Matthew Amos and Fredrik Rönnbäck. Yale University Press, 2016.

Rischin, Rebecca. *For the End of Time: The Story of the Messiaen Quartet*. Cornell University Press, 2006.

Ross, Alex. *The Rest Is Noise: Listening to the Twentieth Century*. Farrar, Straus and Giroux, 2007.

Rovit, Rebecca. "Theresienstadt." *Theatrical Performance during the Holocaust: Texts, Documents, Memoirs,* edited by Rebecca Rovit and Alvin Goldfarb, Johns Hopkins University Press, 1999, pp. 169-75.

Roy, Jennifer. *Jars of Hope: How One Woman Helped Save 2,500 Children During the Holocaust*. Capstone Press, 2016.

Rubin, Susan Goldman. *Fireflies in the Dark: The Story of Friedl Dicker-Brandeis and the Children of Terezín*. Holiday House, 2000.

Rubin, Susan Goldman, and Ela Weissberger. *The Cat with the Yellow Star: Coming of Age in Terezín*. Holiday House, 2006.

Ryback, Timothy W. *Hitler's Private Library: The Books that Shaped His Life*. Vintage Books, 2010.

Sacks, Oliver. *Musicophilia: Tales of Music and the Brain*. Revised and expanded ed., Vintage Books, 2008.

Schumann, Coco, et al. *The Ghetto Swinger: A Berlin-Jazz-Legend Remembers*. Translated by John Howard. Doppel House Press, 1997.

Silverman, Jerry. *The Undying Flame: Ballads and Songs of the Holocaust*. Syracuse University Press, 2002.

Starns, Peggy. *Surviving Tenko: The Story of Margot Turner*. The History Press, 2013.

Steinweis, Alan E. "Hans Hinkel and German Jewry, 1933-1941." *Theatrical Performance during the Holocaust: Texts, Documents, Memoirs,* edited by Rebecca Rovit and Alvin Goldfarb, Johns Hopkins University Press, 1999, pp. 15-27.

Stoessinger, Caroline. *A Century of Wisdom: Lessons from the Life of Alice Herz-Sommer, the World's Oldest Living Holocaust Survivor*. Spiegel & Grau, 2012.

Szpilman, Władysław. *The Pianist: The Extraordinary True Story of One Man's Survival in Warsaw, 1939-1945*. Translated by Anthea Bell. Picador, 1999.

Ten Boom, Corrie, et al. *The Hiding Place*. Chosen Books, 2006.

Thomson, Ruth. *Terezín: Voices from the Holocaust*. Candlewick Press, 2011.

Troller, Nobert. *Theresienstadt: Hitler's Gift to the Jews*. Translated by Susan E. Cernyak-Spatz. The University of North Carolina Press, 1991.

Tuma, Mirko. "Memories of Theresienstadt." *Theatrical Performance during the Holocaust: Texts, Documents, Memoirs,* edited by Rebecca Rovit and Alvin Goldfarb, Johns Hopkins University Press, 1999, pp. 265-73.

Volavková, Hana, editor. *I Never Saw Another Butterfly: Children's Drawings and Poems from Terezín Concentration Camp 1942-1944*. Expanded 2nd ed., Schocken Books, 1993.

Vries, Willem de. *Sonderstab Musik: Music Confiscations by the Einsatzstab Reichsleiter Rosenberg under the Nazi Occupation of Western Europe*. Amsterdam University Press, 1996.

Wagner, Richard. *Richard Wagner's Prose Works, Volume 6*. Translated by William Ashton Ellis, Kegan Paul, Trench, Trübner & Co, 1897.

Warner, Lavinia, and John Sandilands. *Women Beyond the Wire*. Arrow Books, 1997.

Weiner, Eric. *The Geography of Genius: A Search for the World's Most Creative Places, from Ancient Athens to Silicon Valley*. Simon & Schuster, 2016.

Who Will Write Our History. Directed by Roberta Grossman, Katahdin Productions, 2019.

Wiesel, Elie. *Night*. Translated by Marion Wiesel. Hill and Wang, 2006.

Wlodarski, Amy Lynn. "Musical Memories of Terezín in Transnational Perspective." *Dislocated Memories: Jews, Music, and Postwar German Culture,* edited by Tina Frühauf and Lily E. Hirsch, Oxford University Press, 2014.

"Women POWs of Sumatra (1942-1945)." *Women in World History: A Biographical Encyclopedia*. https://www.encyclopedia.com/women/encyclopedias-almanacs-transcripts-and-maps/women-pows-sumatra-1942-1945. Accessed 16 March 2018.

Wynberg, Simon. "Music, Conscience, Accountability and the Third Reich." *The Orel Foundation*, Dec. 2011, http://orelfoundation.org/index.php/journal/journalArticle/music_conscience_accountability_and_the_third_reich/. Accessed 22 Jan. 2017.

Young, Julian. *Friedrich Nietzsche: A Philosophical Biography*. Cambridge University Press, 2010.

Zapruder, Alexandra, editor. *Salvaged Pages: Young Writers' Diaries of the Holocaust*. 2nd ed., Yale University Press, 2015.

Zipper, Trudl Dubsky. *Manila 1944-1945 As Trudl Saw It: Watercolors of Trudl Dubsky Zipper*. Crossroads School, 1994.

Index

Adler, Hans Günther 96, 106
Adler, Kurt 25
Ahronovitch, Yuri 222
Ajzensztadt, Marysia 141
Akhmatova, Anna 189
Akoka, Abraham 163, 178
Akoka, Henri 162, 163, 167, 168, 171, 172–173, 175, 177, 178–179
Alexander II (Tsar of Russia) 186
Alexander, Hans 58
All-Union Radio Orchestra 215
Altman, Julian 291
Am-Rus Music Corporation 219
Amsterdam 32, 33
Ančerl, Karel 94, 95, 110
Andis, Helly 71
Anschluss 23, 29, 67, 82
Ansorge, Conrad 81
Arab-Israeli War 290
Archduke Franz Ferdinand 22, 85
Arendt, Hannah 14
Assael, Yvette 47
Auerbach, Rachel 123, 135, 138, 143, 154
Auschwitz concentration camp 1–2, 15, 32, 34–37, 38, 40, 41–56, *57*, 58, 59–60, 61, 85, 86, 87, 89, 91, 92, 95, 96, 98, 100, 101, 102, 103, 105–106, 107, 108, 109–111, 113, 115, 146, 178, 292, 295*ch*2*n*8
Australian Army Nursing Service 229, 231–232, 236, 238, 243, 244, 245–246, 258, 262, 264, 266, 267, 269, 272, 273, 274, 276

Babi Yar 39
Bach, Johann Sebastian 9, 11, 17, 23, 25, 40, 58, 71, 79, 98, 112, 119, 132, 159, 171, 187, 261
Balfour Declaration 284
Barratt, Edgar 261
Bartók, Béla 20, 181
Battle of Dunkirk 168
Baudrier, Yves 161
Baumann, Kurt 16–17
Beecham, Sir Thomas 64, 259
Beethoven, Ludwig van 9, 17, 19, 20, 22, 23, 25, 28, 58, 63, 68, 73, 75–76, 79, 81, 97, 98, 103, 112, 116, 119, 128, 132, 141, 171, 172, 187, 194, 258, 261, 289

Beker, Max 165–166, *167*, 288, 289, ***290***
Belgium 31, 33, 55, 58, 84, 128, 162, 164, 165, 167, 203, 288
Bell, Joshua 291
Belyaev, N. 222
Belzec concentration camp 39, 40
Beneš, Edvard 82, 117
Ben-Gurion, David 117
Berg, Alban 18, 24, 157, 165, 193
Bergen-Belsen concentration camp 32, 55–58
Berio, Luciano 180
Berlin 11, 12, 13, 16, 17, 19, 51, 56, 73, 86, 87, 91, 93, 102, 108, 121, 125, 155, 193, 277, 278, 280, 284
Berlin Philharmonic Orchestra 12, 16, 193, 280
Berlin Symphony Orchestra 12
Berlin Zoo 13, 125
Berman, Karel 92–93, 102, 106, 110–111
Bernstein, Leonard 157, 289, 290
Bettauer, Hugo 22
Bielas, Alois 165, 171, 172, 173, 174
birdsong 163, 168, 169, 170–171, 176, 181–182, 183, 184
Bizet, Georges 94
Bloch, André 177
Bloorman, Leon 41
Boccherini, Luigi 52
Boer War 240
Bogucki, Andrzej 147
Bolshevik Party 188–189, 190–191
Bolshevik Revolution 66, 187–189, 192, 194
Bolshoi Theater Orchestra 210, 213, 215
book burning 65
Bor, Joseph 106
Borge, Victor 16
Borodin, Alexander 187
Boruński, Leon 142
Boston Symphony Orchestra 103, 219
Boughton, Rutland 259
Boulez, Pierre 180, 181
Boult, Sir Adrian 27, 30
Brahms, Johannes 19, 23, 46, 81, 91, 92, 98, 141, 261, 278–279, 285, 287
Brandeis, Pavel 99

Braun, Shony Alex 40
Brecht, Bertolt 65
Brenn-Kommandos 65
Breton, Henri 174
Britten, Benjamin 58, 157
Broches, Raphael 285
Brock, Robert 113
Brody, Adrien 156
Brooke, Alan 223–224
Brossard, Abbé Jean 171
Broučci (Fireflies) 112–113
Brown, E.A. 232
Brown, Shelagh 232, 236, 247, 253
Bruckner, Anton 19, 279
Brüll, Karl-Albert 166–167, 176–177, 179, 183–184
Brundibár 102, 103–106, 107, 108, 112, 113
Brunner, Alois 34
Buber, Martin 67
Buchenwald concentration camp 69–71, 72, 113
Budapest Philharmonic Orchestra 284
Bullwinkel, Vivien 236, 272, 273
Bunlet, Marcelle 177
Busch, Adolf 25
Bushido Code 244, 253
butterflies 100, ***101***, 268
Buxbaum, Friedrich 30

Cage, John 160, 180, 191
cannibalism 55, 211
Carnegie Hall 279, 282, 291
Carrion, Ferdinand 165–166, 288
Casals, Pablo 63, 121
Catherine the Great (Russian Empress) 108
Catholic Church 11, 14, 24, 27, 49, 62, 106, 126, 139, 140, 155, 159–160, 164, 167–168, 169, 171, 172, 174, 228, 234, 242–243, 245, 247, 249–250, 252, 262, 267, 288
Cavaillé-Coll, Aristide 161
Celan, Paul 18
censorship 2, 6, 10, 15, 16, 18, 19–20, 28, 66, 82, 91, 103, 107, 113, 141, 166, 180, 196, 199, 200, 224, 225, 280, 282
Chambers, John 232, 233, 234, 236, 271
Chambers, Norah Hope 232–234,

236, 246, 248, 255, 256–261, 267, 268, 270, 271, 274, 275, 276
Chambers, Sally 232, 234, 275
Chaminade, Cécile 261
Charitas Sisters (Catholic Order) 249–250, 254, 255, 267
Charles, René 168
Chekhov, Anton 215
Chopin, Frédéric 79, 81, 84, 98, 112, 119, 121, 122, 133, 139, 141, 142, 187, 194, 250, 261
Christian Social Party 22
Christian X (King of Denmark) 108
Churchill, Winston 116, 230–231
Cleveland Orchestra 219
Close, Glenn 276
Cocteau, Jean 162
Colijn, Alette 239, 240, 242, 257
Colijn, Antoinette 239, 242, 257–258, 259
Colijn, Anton 239–242, 270, 271
Colijn, Helen 239–247, 249, 250, 252, 253, 257, 260, 261, 262, 266, 267, 268, 270, 271, 273–274
Colijn, Hendrikus 242
Colijn, Zus 239, 240, 244, 273–274
Collins, Pauline 276
communism 6, 14, 61, 66, 116–117, 154, 156, 172–173, 186–226
constructivism 190
Coolidge, Elizabeth Sprague 30
Copland, Aaron 161
Crowe, Dr. Elsie 251
cubism 160
Czajkowska, Zofia 44, 45, 54
Czerniaków, Adam 143

Dachau concentration camp 2, 40, 43, 61–62, 67–70, 72, 76, **77**, 115, 288, 289
Dachau Song (Dachau Lied) 69, 72, 76, **77**
dadaism 162
Daniel-Lesur, Jean-Yves 161
Da Ponte, Lorenzo 19
"Death Fugue" 18
death march 55, 110, 288, 289
Debussy, Claude 158, 258
Delapierre, Guy-Bernard 163, 180
Delaunay, Robert 160
Delbos, Claire 161, 162, 177, 181
Denmark 31, 105, 107, 108, 203
Deshovov, Vladimir 191
Dicker-Brandeis, Friedl 99–100, **101**, 113
Diefenbach, Lorenz 34
Dijon 33–34
Disney 140, 159, 219
displaced persons (DP) camps 57, 288–289, 296n36
Dizengoff, Meir 281
Dohnányi, Ernő 280
Dohnányi, Johannes Huberman 279–280
Dollfuss, Engelbert 66
Drancy internment camp 34, 49
Dryburgh, Margaret 234–235, 238, 246–247, 248–249, 254, 256–260, 267–268, 270, 276, 299n44
Dryburgh, William 234
Du Bois, W.E.B. 155
Dukas, Paul 159
Dullin, Charles 179
Dunant, Paul 113, 114
du Pré, Jacqueline 59
Dupré, Marcel 159, 176
Durmashkin, Akiva 288
Durmashkin, Fania 288–289
Durmashkin, Henia 288–289
Durmashkin, Wolf 288–289
Düsseldorf 19, 64–65
Dutch Resistance 33, 254
Dvořak, Antonin 27, 75, 92, 94, 258, **259**, 260, 261, 289

East Indies 230, 235, 238–239, 240, 242, 274
Edelstein, Jakob 86, 100, 111, 297ch4n34
Ehrlich-Fantlová, Zdenka 90
Eichmann, Adolf 29, 33, 34, 85, 91, 112
Einsatzgruppen 14, 39
Einstein, Albert 65, 280, 283
Eliasberg, Karl 216–217, 221–223
English Chamber Orchestra 59
Ephraim, Frank 73, 77
Eppstein, Paul 93
Esso, Ima van 37
Ex-Concentration Camp Orchestra 289–290
Exposition Universelle (1889 World's Fair) 158
Eyle, Felix 59

Fadeyev, Alexander 223
Fauré, Gabriel 160, 180
Feldschuh, Josima 141
Feldschuh, Pnina 141
Feldschuh, Reuven 141
Fénelon, Fania 49–50, 52, 56
film music 42, 59, 76, 92, 108, 121, 132, 140, 156, 159, 163, 193, 195, 196, 203, 219
Finland 18, 148, 161, 203, 205, 207, 208
Fischer, Karl 107
Fisher, William Arms 260
Five-Year Plan 192
Fleischmann, Minna 98
Fleishman, Venjamin 206, 215
Flesch, Carl 30
formalism 195, 196, 198, 224
Foss, Lukas 16
Franck, César 159
Franco-Prussian War 195
Frank, Anne 32
Frank, Otto 32
Frankfurt 17, 19, 284
Franz Joseph I (Emperor of Austria) 21
Free Zone (France) 163, 178
French Resistance 49, 178
Freud, Adolfine 98
Freud, Sigmund 10, 22, 65, 67, 280

Freudenfeld, Rudolf "Rudi" 102, 103–106
Friedmann, Pavel 100
Frölich, Karel 95, 115
The Führer Gives the Jews a City (film) 108, **109**
Furmanski, Adam 18, 132
Fürstengrube (subcamp of Auschwitz) 92
Furtwängler, Wilhelm 15, 280–281
futurists 188, 190, 194, 196

Galafrés, Elsa 279–280
gamelan music 160
Geneva Convention 164, 240, 244
German, Edward 261
German Workers' Party 12
Gerron, Kurt 108
Gerron, Olga 108
Gershwin, George 180, 289
Ghetto Swingers 90–91, 108, 110
Giang Bee 243
Gibon, Jehan de 158
Gilbert and Sullivan 232
Gimpel, Bronisław 121, 155
Glass, Philip 160
Glazunov, Alexander 189–190, 217
Gliasser, Ignatiy 187
Glikman, Isaak 205, 218
Glinka, Mikhail 217
Glivenko, Tatiana 192, 193, 197
Gluck, Christoph Willibald 158
Gobineau, Arthur de 9, 13
Godard, Benjamin 261
Godlewska, Janina 147
Goebbels, Joseph 6, 15, 20, 65, 280
Goethe, Johann Wolfgang von 68, 187
Gogol, Nikolai 195
Gold, Arthur 40
Goldfeder, Andrzej 142, 143
golem 154
Göring, Hermann 125, 126
Gorky, Maxim 199–200
Görlitz 164, 171, 183, 184
Gorouben, David 184
Gounod, Charles 160, 217
Gouts, Suzanne 162, 179
Grab-Kernmayr, Hedda 89, 90, 93
Grabowska, Janka 149
Grainger, Percy 261
Gran, Wiera 134
"Great Terror" (Great Purge) 197, 198
Greater Eastern Co-Prosperity Sphere 228
Grieg, Edvard 132, 261
Grinberg, Dr. Zalman 288
Gross, Magdalena 139
Grynszpan, Herschel 70
Grzecznarowski, Halina 155
Guadagnini, Giovanni Battista 33, 59
Guarneri del Gesù, Giuseppe 282

Haas, Hugo 92
Haas, Pavel 91, 92, 94, 108, 176
Hácha, Emil 82

Index

Hall, Marcelle 291
Hamerman, Israel 141
Handel, George Frideric 94, 259
Harper, Iole 269
Haydn, Franz Joseph 22, 107, 141, 159
Hechalutz Movement 100
Heck, Lutz 13, 125
Heifetz, Jascha 279, 284
Heine, Heinrich 61, 65
Hellinger, Magda 37
Hennings, Patricia 276
Hermann, Johann 84, 97
Herz, Friedrich 79, 81
Herz, Georg 79
Herz, Irma 79, 80, 82, 118
Herz, Marianne "Mizzi" 79, 80, 82, 117, 118
Herz, Mary 116
Herz, Paul 79, 80, 112, 116
Herz, Sofie 79, 80, 81, 82, 84, 98, 120
Herz-Sommer, Alice 2, 79–85, 96–99, 103, 105, 111–112, 113, 114, 115–120
Heydrich, Reinhard 85
Hildegard of Bingen 9
Himmler, Heinrich 14, 34, 40, 61, 68, 112, 147, 150
Hindemith, Paul 64, 198
Hindenburg, Paul von 12
Hinkel, Hans 17
Hirohito (Emperor of Japan) 244, 260
Hirsch, Fredy 109–110
Hitler, Adolf 6, 9, 12–13, 15, 16, 18, 20, 22–23, 27, 28, 29–30, 31, 32, 34, 48, 49, 57, 61, 64, 65, 66, 67, 73, 76, 82, 83, 88–89, 96, 105, 108, 121, 123, 125, 126–127, 147, 150, 184, 196, 202–204, 209, 212, 221, 224, 225, 244, 281
Hoffmeister, Adolf 103
Hofmekler, Michael 289
Holland 28, 29, 31–33, 34, 41, 59, 65, 69, 109, 128, 162, 203, 243, 274, 276; *see also* East Indies; the Netherlands
homosexuality 13, 43, 61, 69, 263
Hope, John 232, 233, 234
Hosenfeld, Captain Wilhelm 152–153, 156
Höss, Rudolf 36
Huberman, Bronisław 121, 277–287, 290–291, 299n7
Huberman, Joan 279
Hugo, Victor 5, 252
Hutter, Trude 81
Huxley, Aldous 5

Iaydarov, Dzhaudat 217, 221
Ibbeken, Ida 280, 291
Israel 10, 58, 117–118, 119, 121, 144, 154, 269, 289, 290, 291–293; *see also* Palestine
Israel Philharmonic Orchestra 290, 293

Jacobs, Major Gideon 272–273
Jacquet, Violette 45
Janáček, Leoš 91, 92
Java 238, 239–240, 272, 273, 275
jazz 19, 40, 90–91, 96, 132, 133, 158, 165, 180, 184, 196, 260
Jeffrey, Betty 231, 247, 261, 264, 265, 266, 267, 268, 269, 270, 271, 273, 275–276
Jehovah's Witnesses 14, 61
Jennings, Margery 227, 276
Jewish Symphony Orchestra 132–133, 134, 141–142
Joachim, Joseph 277–278
Jochowitz, Hans 102
Jolivet, Andrè 161
Jongkees, Leonard 32
Joseph II (Emperor of the Holy Roman Empire) 85
Jüdischer Kulturbund (Jewish Culture League) 17, 284

Kaff, Bernard 102
Kafka, Franz 79, 80, 98
Kafka, Ottilie "Ottla" 98
Kantor, Alfred 114
Karafiát, Jan 112–113
Karajan, Herbert von 15–16
Karin, Michal 26
Kaspar, Emma 62, 63
Kastorksy, Vladmiri 217
Kataszek, Szymon 133
Kaufering (subcamp of Dachau) 43
Kempeitai 253–254
KGB 198, 199, 224
Khrennikov, Tikhon 224
Khrushchev, Nikita 224
Kien, Peter 92, 95
Kirov, Sergei 197–198
Klausner, Rabbi Abraham 288
Klein, Gerda Weissmann 31, 38–39
Klein, Gideon 91, 92, 93, 103, 105–106
Klemperer, Otto 16, 67
Kling, Paul 94
Kokoschka, Oskar 64
Korczak, Janusz 136, 144–145
Koretzova, Margit **101**
Korngold, Erich 16, 76
Koslov, Viktor 222
Koussevitzky, Serge 103, 219, 220
Krakow 27, 34
Kramov, Nikolay 217
Kramsztyk, Roman 136, 142
Krása, Hans 91, 99, 102–103, **104**, 105, 110
Kreisler, Fritz 27, 157, 179
Kuala 243, 251
Kuibyshev 211–212, 213–214, 218, 223
Kvadri, Mikhail 193

Laks, Szymon 42–44, 45, 46, 49, 50
Lanier, Jean 179; *see also* Le Boulaire, Jean
Lasker, Alfons 50, 51

Lasker, Edith 50, 51
Lasker, Edward 58
Lasker, Marianne 50, 51, 57, 58
Lasker, Renate 50, 51, 52, 56, 57–58
Lasker-Wallfisch, Anita 2, 50–53, 54, 55, 56–59
Latvia 15, 189, 203, 206
League of Nations 284
Le Boulaire, Jean 168, 171, 172, 173–174, 175, 177, 178, 179
Lecomte du Noüy, Pierre 13
Ledeč, Egon 110
Lednicki, Zygmunt 156
Leeb, Wilhelm Ritter von 209
Leeuwen Boomkamp, Constant van 33
Leipzig Gewandhaus Orchestra 284
Leipzig Radio Orchestra 65
Legarda, Benito 74
Legarda, Trinidad 72, 75
Lenin, Vladimir 188–189, 190, 192, 194, 195–196, 223
Leningrad 2, 185, 192, 193, 195, 197–201, 203, 205–206, 208–210, 211–212, 213, 214–218, 220–223, 224, 225–226, 290; *see also* Petrograd; St. Petersburg
Leningrad Conservatory Orchestra 218
Leningrad Philharmonic Orchestra 193, 195, 200, 208, 210
Leningrad Radio Orchestra 215, 216–217, 218, 220–222, 225–226
Leopold I (Emperor of the Holy Roman Empire) 21
Leskov, Nikolai 196
Levi, Primo 38, 39
Lewicka, Helena 149
Lewicki, Czesław 147
Lewin, Dasha 88
Lewin, Heinz 47
libraries 34, 65, 74, 110, 113, 130, 134, 153, 164, 200, 212, 252, 255
Lichtenbaum, Mieczysław 145
Liebermann, Rolf 182
Lippay, Alexander 72
Liszt, Franz 81, 159, 215, 217
Liwacz, Jan 34
Lloyd, Ernest 272
Lloyd's of London 291
Loeb, Dora 285
London 30–31, 58–59, 64, 118–120, 149, 219, 228, 232, **233**, 250, 279, 291
London Philharmonic Orchestra 219
Loos, Adolf 22
Lorenz, Konrad 13
Loriod, Yvonne 167, 177, 180–181, 183, 184
Lueger, Karl 22
Luga Line 207–208
Lunacharskii, Anatolii 190, 197
Lüneberg Trial 58
luthier 277, 291–293
Lyon, Dr. Marjorie 251

MacArthur, General Douglas 73, 75
MacArthur, Jean 75
MacDowell, Edward 258, 261
MacLeod, Donald 232
MacLeod, Dorothy 232, 246, 247, 259, 268–269
MacLeod, Ian 227, 232
Maginot Line 162
Mahler, Alma Schindler 24, 98
Mahler, Anna Justine 11
Mahler, Gustav 1, 10, 11, 16, 23–25, 30, 46, 60, 79, 80, 98, 110, 193, 194, 279
Mahler, Maria Anna 24
Majdanek concentration camp 148
Malko, Nicolai 193
Mandel, Maria 37, 44–45, 49, 52, 53
Mandl, Thomas 89
Manila 66–67, 71, 72–76, 77, 78
Manila Symphony Orchestra 72–76
Mann, Thomas 79
Maratov, V. 216
Mareš, Michal 117
Maria Theresa (Empress of the Holy Roman Empire) 85
Martilla, Elena 213, 216
Martinon, Jean 180
Martinů, Bohuslav 162
Marx, Karl 188
Mata Hari 231, 237, 243
Matus, Ksenia 185, 217, 225–226
Mayakovsky, Vladimir 190–191, 194–195
Mazor, Michel 138, 155
McDougall, William 251–252
McDowell, Dr. Jean 245, 250
Meir, Golda 118
Melbourne Nurses Memorial Centre 273
Mendelssohn, Felix 20, 42, 58, 103, 180, 261, 277, 282
Mengele, Dr. Josef 37, 40, 54, 91, 110
Menuhin, Yehudi 58
Messiaen, Alain 158
Messiaen, Olivier 2, 157–184, 288
Messiaen, Pascal 162, 177
Messiaen, Pierre 158
Metropolitan Opera Orchestra 59
Meyerbeer, Giacomo 10
Meyerhold, Vsevolod 194, 199, 201–202
Michalowski, Aleksander 121
Mikhlachevsky, Igor 216
Milhaud, Darius 64, 162
Moira, Albert 166
Molotov, Vyacheslav 147–148, 202
Molotov-Ribbentrop Nonaggression Pact 48, 123, 148, 202–203
Morris, Mary 276
Morse code 20, 237
Moscow 189, 192, 193, 194, 197, 198, 199, 200, 210, 211, 212, 214, 215, 223, 224
Moscow Philharmonic Orchestra 200, 215

Mother Alacoque 250, 254
Mother Laurentia 243, 245, 247, 251, 252, 253, 256, 268, 270, 274
Mozart, Wolfgang Amadeus 9, 17, 19, 22, 24, 40, 46, 63, 73, 74, 79–80, 93, 94, 95, 102, 132, 141, 158, 187, 261, 278, 289
Mravinsky, Yevgeny 208
Munich 15, 19, 27, 61, 67, 94, 118, 288, 289
Munich Agreement 82
Murray, Ena 234, 236–237, 257, 258–259, 275
Musin, Ilya 218
Mussorgsky, Modest 187

National Symphony Orchestra 291
NBC Symphony Orchestra 51, 219–220
neoclassical 162
the Netherlands 32, 46, 228, 239–240, 249, 284; *see also* East Indies; *see also* Holland
Neumann, Paula 15
Neurath, Konstantin von 85
Neuteich, Marian 18, 132
New York Philharmonic Orchestra 260, 282
Nicholas II (Tsar of Russia) 185–186, 191
Nietzsche, Friedrich 5
Nikolayev, Leonid 189
Niwińska, Helena Dunicz 41, 48–49, 52, 53, 56
NKVD 117, 199, 200
Nuremberg Race Laws 13, 27, 28, 91, 126

Offenbach, Jacques 10, 113, 139, 195
Oistrakh, David 214
Olewski, Rachela Zelmanowicz 56
Operation Barbarossa 73, 203–205
Operation Nordlicht 221
Operation Squall 221
Operation Typhoon 210
Orchestre National de la Radio 178
Orchestre Philharmonique de Radio France 178
Order of St. Borromeus 243, 267, 274; *see also* Catholic Church
Order Service Orchestra 133
Orient Express 210
ornithology 160, 163, 183
orphanages 51, 100, 103, 140
Ott, Sylvie 118
Otwock Ghetto 142
Owen, Audrey 267, 275
Oyneg Shabes 138, 141, 143, 154

Paderewski, Ignacy Jan 261
Palestine 51, 58, 82, 92, 100, 117, 281–287, 289–290, 291–292; *see also* Israel; Zionism
Palestine Symphony Orchestra 117, 281–287, 289–290
Pan-Europa movement 280
Paris 10, 11, 16, 22, 34, 42, 43, 49, 51, 56, 67, 70, 71, 72, 73, 118, 128, 157, 158–161, 162, 163, 168, 169, 175, 176, 177–183, 194, 195, 280
Paris Opera Orchestra 162, 177, 179
Pasquier, Etienne 162–163, 168, 171, 172, 173, 175, 176, 177, 178, 179
Pasquier, Jean 162, 177
Pasquier, Pierre 162
Pearl Harbor 32, 73, 212, 227, 240
Penderecki, Krzysztof 176
Pergolesi, Giovanni Battista 93, 96, 159
Perlman, Itzhak 279
Petrograd 186–189, 191; *see also* Leningrad; St. Petersburg
Philadelphia Orchestra 194, 219
Piatigorsky, Gregor 16, 118
Pleeth, William 58–59
Poelau Bras 239, 240, 243, 251
Polach, Dita 110, 297ch4n32
Polish Radio Orchestra 133
Pollak, Helga 100
Potasinski, Mila 37
Potemkin, Grigory Aleksandrovich 108, 111
Potsdam Conference 116
Prague 25, 54, 79–86, 90, 91, 92, 93, 94, 95, 96, 97, 99, 100, 101, 102, 103, 106, 108, 110–111, 112, 113, 115–117, 118, 125, 126
Pravda 193, 198
Příhoda, Váša 25–26, 27–28, 37, 110
Princip, Gavrilo 22, 85
Prokofiev, Sergei 191, 198, 203, 224
Puccini, Giacomo 46, 49, 94
Pullman, Szymon 18, 133, 141
Pushkin, Alexander 187

Rachmaninoff, Sergei 63, 139
Rahm, Karl 107
Rampal, Jean-Pierre 162
Rasputin, Grigori 186
Rath, Ernst vom 70
Ravel, Maurice 63, 157, 159, 261, 274
Ravensbrück concentration camp 33
Red Cross 32, 35, 55, 57, 107–108, 112, 113, 114, 164, 165, 171, 178, 230, 240, 248, 265, 271
Red Orchestra 204
Reich, Steve 160
Reichskulturkammer (Reich Culture Chamber) 15, 17
Reichsmusikkammer (Reich Music Chamber) 15, 19, 282
Respighi, Ottorino 171
Ribbentrop, Joachim von 202
"Righteous Among the Nations" 121, 154, 156
Rilke, Rainer Maria 79
Rimsky-Korsakov, Nikolai 187, 215, 217
Ringelblum, Emanuel 138, 154
Rodan, Mendi 10
Rodzinski, Artur 219
Roma (Gypsies) 13, 14, 15, 35, 69, 88

Roosevelt, Franklin Delano 15, 220, 239
Rosé, Alfred 24, 25, 26–30, 32, 59–60
Rosé, Alma 1–2, 21, 24–34, 36–37, 44–54, 59–60, 63, 110
Rosé, Arnold 23–25, 26, 28–31, 33, 53, 59–60, 121
Rosé, Eduard 23, 110
Rosé, Justine Mahler 23–24, 25, 27, 29, 60
Rosé, Maria Schmutzer 27, 29, 30, 60
Rosé String Quartet 23, 30, 31
Rosenbaum, Kamila 112–113
Rosenthal, Felix 63
Rossini, Gioachino 46, 217, 287
Rostal, Leo 51
Rothstock, Otto 22
Rottier, Theo 253
Rudnicki, Edmund 147
Russian Civil War (1917–1920) 189–192
Russo-Japanese War (1904–905) 227
Rutherston, Jeanette 64

Sacks, Dr. Oliver 5
St. Ottilien 288–289
St. Ottilien Jewish Orchestra 287, 289
St. Petersburg 165, 185–186, 187, 188, 189, 192, 225; *see also* Leningrad; Petrograd
Saint-Saëns, Camille 171
Salomon Trio 119
Salonen, Esa-Pekka 161
Salzburg 18, 29, 102
Salzer, Heinrich "Heini" 28, 29, 30–31, 32
Samosud, Samuil 213–214, 215
Sarajevo 22, 85, 208
Sarasate, Pablo de 27
Sartre, Jean-Paul 179
Satie, Erik 180
Sauvage, Cécile 158, 161, 162
Sauvage, Marie 158
Sayre, Francis 73, 74
Schächter, Raphael 92, 93–94, 96, 102, 103–106, 110
Schindler, Oskar 154, 291
Schmidt, Else 53–54
Schnabel, Artur 98, 121
Schoenberg, Arnold 16, 18, 19, 22, 23, 67, 76, 85, 91, 95, 176, 181, 193, 198
Schönova, Vlasta 112–113
Schopenhauer, Arthur 6
Schreker, Franz 16, 121
Schubert, Franz 46, 63, 92, 103, 132, 141, 261, 287
Schulz, Fanny 80
Schumann, Clara Wieck 278
Schumann, Heinz Jakob "Coco" 91
Schumann, Robert 19, 46, 80, 98, 261, 278
Schuschnigg, Kurt von 22–23
Schwarzhuber, Johann 41, 43

Schweitzer, Dr. Albert 64
Scriabin, Alexander 215
Seidls, Siegfried 85
Sekstein, Gela 140
Selmi, Giuseppe 58
Sendler, Irena 139–140, 149, 154
Seraphim, Peter-Heinz 126
Serebryakov, Pavel 218
serialism 16, 181
Serov, Alexander 217
Ševčik, Otakar 25
Shaham, Gil 120
Shaham, Meira 120
Shakespeare 158, 159, 179, 196
Shek, Alisa Ehrmann 101–102, 111
Shek, Daniel 102
Shek, Zeev 100–102
Sheratt, Moshe 102
Shostakovich, Dmitri 2, 186–201, 205–215, 218–226
Shostakovich, Dmitri Boleslavovich 186, 191
Shostakovich, Galina 200
Shostakovich, Maria 186, 191, 192, 200
Shostakovich, Maxim 201
Shostakovich, Sofia 186, 187, 189, 191–192, 197, 210, 214
Shostakovich, Zoya 186
Sibelius, Jean 18
Siberia 66, 186, 188, 197, 198, 208, 221, 223
Siege of Leningrad 2, **207**, 208–210, 211–212, 213, 214–218, 220–223, 224, 225–226, 290
Siki, Captain 261, 264, 271
Simon, Eric 72
Simons, Elizabeth 268
Singapore 227, 229, 230–235, 237, 238, 243, 245, 246, 251, 259, 273
Singer, Kurt 17, 284
Sino-Japanese War, First (1894–95) 227
Sino-Japanese War, Second (1937–1945) 228
Sister Catharinia 243, 244, 268, 274, 276
Sister Paulie 247
Smetana, Bedřich 92, 93, 95
socialism 65, 66, 188
Sofronitsky, Vladmir 215
Solzhenitsyn, Alexander 204
Sommer, Ariel 118
Sommer, David 118
Sommer, Leopold 81, 84–85, 96–98, 111, 113, 115, 120
Sommer, Raphael "Rafi" 81, **83**, 84–85, 96–99, 105, 113, 115–119, 296ch4n1
Sonderkommando 35
Sonderstab Musik 44
Sotheby's 279
Soyfer, Jura 66, 69–72
Spanish-American War 73
Spanish Civil War 148
Spitzer, Helen "Zippy" 36, 37, 44, 46

Die Stadt Ohne Juden (The City Without Jews) 22
Staercke, Marye 34, 59
Staercke, Paul 34, 59
Stalag VIII A 2, 163–179, 183–184, 288
Stalag IX A 165, 180
Stalin, Joseph 6, 18, 48, 66, 73, 116, 123, 150, 192, 195–209, 212, 220, 221, 224–225
Steinberg, Hans Wilhelm 284, 285
Steinberg, Maximilian 193
Steiner-Kraus, Edith 98, 99, 111–112, 118
Štěphan, Vaclav 81
Stern, Isaac 279
Stiedry, Fritz 200
Stockhausen, Karlheinz 180
Stokowski, Leopold 194, 219
Stolba, K. Marie 247
Stradivari, Antonio 31, 59, 282, 291
Strass, František 87
Strauss, Johann, II 27, 94, 279
Strauss, Richard 1, 15, 16, 19–20, 24, 25, 27, 29, 46, 63, 157, 225, 282
Stravinsky, Igor 19, 27, 64, 157, 158, 159, 163, 170, 193, 198, 210
Sudetenland 29–30, 82
Suk, Josef 92
Sumatra 2, 228, 236, 238–239, 241–266, 269–274, 275–276
Suppé, Franz von 46
Surowicz, Jacob 284
Švalbová, Manca "Dr. Mancy" 53–54
Švenk, Karel 93, 113
Switzerland 33–34, 69, 87, 107, 177, 188, 244, 272, 290, 291
Szell, George 16, 103
Szpilman, Christopher 155
Szpilman, Halina 128, 145
Szpilman, Henryk 128, 130, 145
Szpilman, Regina 128, 145
Szpilman, Władysław 2, 121–124, 127–130, 134, 135–137, 140–153, 155–156

Taube, Michael 281
Tchaikovsky, Pyotr Ilyich 25, 28, 44, 72, 132, 187, 215, 217, 257, 258, 289
Tekelenburg, Dr. Peter 249
Tellegen, Marie Anne 33, 59
Ten Boom, Corrie 33
Tennyson, Alfred Lord 158
Terezín (Theresienstadt) 2, 15, 79, 84–116, 118, 119, 165, 176, 268
Teulières, Geneviève 118
Thein, Hanuš 112–113
theremin 169
Theremin, Leon 191, 198
Thilo, Heinz 36
Thiriet, Maurice 180
Thoene, Bodie 1
Timoshenko, Semyon 204, 205
Tōjō Hideki (Prime Minister of Japan) 253, 264

Tolstoy, Leo 215
Tonneyck-Muller, Ingeborg 27
Tops, Saartje 255
Tortelier, Paul 118
Toscanini, Arturo 24, 29, 219–220, 259, 282, 285–287
Tournemire, Charles 159
Trakan, N. 217
Treaty of Brest-Litovsk 189
Treaty of Paris 73
Treaty of Versailles 29, 82
Treblinka concentration camp 40, 98, 142, 143, 144, 146, 148, 154
Trio Pasquier 162, 179
Troller, Norbert 114
Trotsky, Leon 172, 188, 189
Truman, Harry 116
Tukhachevsky, Mikhail 199, 200
Tully, Alice 182
Tuma, Mirko 90

Ullmann, Annie 96
Ullmann, Elisabeth 95
Ullmann, Felicia 95
Ullmann, Johannes 95
Ullmann, Max 96
Ullmann, Viktor 85, 91, 94, 95–96, 110, 115
Union of Soviet Composers 196, 197
United Nations 287–288
United States Holocaust Memorial Museum vi, 77
Utitz, Emil 96

Vacellier, André 177
Vallejo, Ernesto 75
Varèse, Edgard 161
Varzar, Nina 197, 198, 199, 200, 201, 207, 208, 224
Vaughan Williams, Ralph 157
Velter, Nadezhda 217
Venice 14, 126
Verdi, Giuseppe 46, 94, 106, 107
Verdun 162, 163, 171
Vichy 163, 176, 178, 179
Vienna 1, 11, 12, 15, 21–31, 42, 59, 60, 62–64, 65–67, 69, 71, 72, 77, 78, 80, 94, 95, 98, 99, 121, 126, 278, 279
Vienna Philharmonic Orchestra 23, 28, 59, 60, 94, 278

Vienna State Opera 11, 23, 24, 27, 28
Vierne, Louis 159
Villa-Lobos, Heitor 158
Vilna 42, 165, 288, 291
Vilna Ghetto 288–289
Vilna Symphony Orchestra 165, 288
Violins of Hope 277, 292–293
Vivaldi, Antonio 171
Vogel, Erich 91
Vyner Brooke 231–232, 234, 235–237, 243, 259, 267, 273

Wagner, Benedict 292
Wagner, Richard 9–10, 11, 19, 62, 158, 182, 292
Wallerstein, Konrad 95
Wallfisch, Benjamin 59
Wallfisch, Peter 59
Wallfisch, Raphael 59
Walter, Bruno 16, 24, 30, 31, 60, 193
Walton, William 64
Warman, Isidore 267
Warnaar, Dirk Jan 276
Warsaw 2, 16, 27, 40, 42, 121–156, 194, 277, 284, 288, 291
Warsaw Ghetto 2, 127–148, 149, 154
Warsaw Ghetto Uprising 147–148
Warsaw Opera Orchestra 133
Warsaw Philharmonic Orchestra 133, 284
Warsaw Piano Quintet 155
Warsaw Uprising 149–150, 152, 154
Warsaw Zoo 125, 138–139, 143, 148, 149, 150, 154
Weber, Carl Maria von 287
Webern, Anton 18, 24
Weigel, Dr. Rudolf 137
Weill, Kurt 16, 19, 64, 96
Weimar Republic 11–12
Weinstein, Amnon 277, 292–293
Weinstein, Avshalom 293
Weinstein, Esther 292
Weinstein, Golda 291–292
Weinstein, Moshe 291–292
Weintraub, Eugene 219
Weisbach, Hans 64–65

Weiss, Arnošt 112
Weissberger, Ela Stein 105, 106
Westerbork transit camp 32, 33, 109
Westreich, Emanuel 63
Widor, Charles-Marie 159
Wiegel, Hans 72
Wieniawski, Henryk 27, 122
Wiesel, Elie 59
Wilhelmina (Queen of the Netherlands) 228, 273
Williams, Pharrell 59
Winogradowa, Sonia 54
Winter War 148, 203
Wood, Sir Henry 219, 232
World War I 11–12, 25, 29, 31, 61, 62, 63, 81, 82, 85, 88, 95, 157, 158, 162, 178, 186, 188, 189, 280, 284
Wroblewski, Witold 139

Yad Vashem 121, 154, 156
Yeryomkin, Grigorii 217

Zabiński, Antonina 125, 138–139, 154
Zabiński, Jan 125, 138–139, 140, 143, 150, 154
Zaborski, Jan 42–43
Zelenka, František 102, 104, 105
Zemlinsky, Alexander 81, 95, 102
Zhukov, Georgy 204, 205
Ziegelmeyer, Ernst 209
Ziegler, Hans Severus 19
Zimche, Hilde Grünbaum 45, *57*
Zimmer, Hans 59
Zionism 23, 51, 100, 141, 281, 290, 291
Zipper, Emil 62, 63, 67, 71, 72, 73, 76
Zipper, Hedy 62, 72, 73, 76
Zipper, Herbert 2, 62–78, 296ch3n1
Zipper, Otto 62, 67, 72, 73, 76
Zipper, Regina "Rosie" Westreich 62, 63, 71, 72, 73, 76
Zipper, Trudl Dubsky 64, 65, 66–67, 71, 72, 73, 74–75, 76
Zipper, Walter 62, 67, 69, 71, 72
Zucker, Otto 96, 98
Zweig, Stefan 15

www.ingramcontent.com/pod-product-compliance
Lightning Source LLC
Chambersburg PA
CBHW080759300426
44114CB00020B/2761